DATA BASE
MANAGEMENT
SYSTEMS

SECOND EDITION

DATA BASE

MANAGEMENT

SYSTEMS

ALFONSO F. CARDENAS

Professor
Computer Science Department
University of California, Los Angeles

Consultant

ɰcb
Wm. C. Brown Publishers
Dubuque, Iowa

Copyright © 1985, 1979 by Allyn and Bacon, Inc.

Copyright © 1989 by Wm. C. Brown Publishers. All rights reserved

Library of Congress Catalog Card Number: 84–2811

ISBN 0–697–06948–6

Printed in the United States of America by Wm. C. Brown Publishers
2460 Kerper Boulevard, Dubuque, IA 52001

10 9 8 7 6 5 4 3 2

TO SANDY

CONTENTS

vii

3

DATA BASE CONCEPTS AND ARCHITECTURE   73

PREFACE

In the last few years a diverse and diffused body of technology, that is, knowledge, tools, practices, folklore, and commercial software systems, has emerged for designing large integrated data bases and data base-oriented information systems. This is a result of the recognized importance, need, impact, and economic justification of such systems in today's modern organizations. The inevitable emergence of computer applications and information systems as data base centered rather than traditional file-oriented (with its traditional drawbacks) is of major significance. It has precipitated extensive and much needed efforts and advances on data base design, implementation, and application.

This text constitutes a coherent presentation and appraisal of the fundamental technology and practice of data base and data management systems design, implementation, and application. High-level file organization, data base architecture and management, and commercially available generalized data base management systems (GDBMS) are examined. The important alternatives and issues are explored, as are various new approaches. The emphasis is on fundamental, practical, and generally applicable matters. The thrust of this text is illustrative and critical, and quantitative where possible, rather than qualitative and folkloric.

This book is intended to be a source of self-study for practitioners or students on the theory and practice of data base organization and systems. Most of the material was originally prepared for and is being used in two courses on data management systems offered at the University of California, Los Angeles, and in short courses on the subject conducted by the author for industry and government in the United States and abroad. The background required for an understanding and appreciation of the contents is the maturity of an advanced undergraduate student and basic knowledge of a computer system and of computer programming. Some knowledge of a high-level programming language (COBOL, PL/1, FORTRAN, etc.) is advised. The text is intended for information system specialists, computer scientists, systems analysts, application programmers, managers, and other professionals interested in this emerging, fast growing, and exciting field.

Chapter 1 traces the scenario and relates functionally the available data management technologies. The objectives of data base technology are outlined briefly. The architecture and realms of data base management are introduced. The subject matter is unfortunately fragmented and scattered; the jargon involved is often confusing and inconsistent. Needed definitions and the framework of the text are set forth.

Chapter 2 focuses on the data organization techniques that have been conceived to achieve more cost-effective access and management of data than can be provided by the basic file management of existing operating systems and associated programming languages (PL/1, COBOL, etc.). These data organizations, generally called secondary indexing methods or higher level file organizations, have been widely implemented in software and used to provide faster and more cost-effective access to data. List, multilist, partially inverted, fully inverted, ringed, and chained tree organizations are presented using examples. These canonical organizations are compared. Single-file examples are primarily used to illustrate the concepts without undue complexity.

After covering the fundamental data storage and organization technology in Chapter 2 and Appendix A, Chapter 3 presents the basic concepts and architectural framework of Generalized Data Base Management Systems, GDBMS. The functional relationship of generalized file management systems, GDBMS, data communication systems, operating systems, and application programs is traced. The objectives and associated concepts of data base technology are discussed. Data description, data manipulation, and query languages are introduced. The alternative approaches to logical organization of data are briefly introduced; hierarchical or tree, network, and relational models. The constituents of GDBMS are outlined. The realms and issues involved are indicated using the level by level framework of the Data Independent Accessing Model (DIAM). The Entity-Relationship-Attribute (ERA) model for conceptual data base modeling is introduced.

There are about a dozen major GDBMS in the marketplace comprising the bulk of installed robust GDBMS, still under 10,000 but growing fast in numbers. There are at least an equal number of additional systems claiming the characteristics of a GDBMS. In addition, starting in the early 1980s, there are tens of thousands of micro-GDBMS (as opposed to robust GDBMS) installed in the vast and growing micro/personal computer marketplace. All GDBMS feature either the hierarchic, network, or inverted hierarchic model of a data base. Chapter 4 presents a brief survey of the commercial marketplace. Names of GDBMS, vendors, prices, hardware configurations, and functional features are summarized with the aid of tables. Although it is not a complete survey, the systems covered represent the major portion of the installed GDBMS.

Chapter 5 is devoted to the network approach of the milestone CODASYL 1971 DBTG (Data Base Task Group) and 1978 Reports. There are many commercial GDBMS and new ones appearing following the DBTG architecture. The DBTG standard is used as the basis for this chapter. Low-level and physical organization strategies are covered.

Chapter 6 is devoted to CINCOM's TOTAL, one of the main two GDBMS in terms of number installed. It supports the network data base model and is conceptually, although not syntactically, DBTG-oriented. This chapter is an abridged presentation of the TOTAL approach.

Chapter 7 is devoted to IBM's IMS (Information Management System) which portrays the hierarchic approach. It was one of the earliest GDBMS and today is one of the main two products in terms of number installed. This chapter includes a presentation of the wide variety of physical data organizations and corresponding access methods of IMS.

Chapter 8 is devoted to INTEL's SYSTEM 2000, one of the main inverted hierarchic GDBMS. Basic knowledge of the inverted approach and strategy introduced in Chapter 2 is helpful to understand this chapter.

The relational model of data is a very attractive and promising new approach originating in the 1970s. It is being considered, developed, and initially used. Commercial fully relational GDBMS started appearing in the early 1980s. Chapter 9 presents the relational data base approach, avoiding the mathematical flavor of initial relational proposals and any specific commercial implementation.

Chapters 10 and 11 (new chapters) are devoted to the two major types of relational systems commercially available and represented by SQL/DS and Query-by-Example (QBE). Chapter 10 presents SQL/DS, introduced by IBM and followed by several vendors. Chapter 11 presents IBM's QBE. The attractiveness of the relational approach and the absence of a standard have resulted in a growing number of variations of these systems.

The architecture, data definition facilities for the global data base and for the user views of it, and the data manipulation facilities are introduced for each of the six systems in Chapters 5–11. The same data base and data accessing examples are carried throughout to illustrate the similarities, differences, advantages, and disadvantages of the approaches and the particular GDBMS—a major aim of this text not achieved in other references. Many examples are provided, as are exercises at the end of each chapter and selected solutions at the end of the text.

It is unfortunate that the terminology commonly used in the data management world is quite varied, and at times confusing and inconsistent. Each of the above preceding data base approaches and particularly each GDBMS carries a number of terms particular to it. We follow the terms used in practice by each, but we frequently equate them to equivalent terms of other systems as we compare the approaches.

Chapter 12 is devoted to the subject of normalization of data bases; it deals with important issues of logical data base design and semantics, particularly functional dependencies. This subject has emerged formally toward sound data base design along with the relational approach; however, the principles apply to both relational as well as to nonrelational data bases.

The design and development of data base-oriented application systems bring on a number of data base design and administration issues and trade-offs, as well as a number of other considerations with strong economic and human-behavioral overtones, often disregarded by the more technically oriented individuals. Chapter 13 discusses the data base design process. Alternatives, costs, and performance are reviewed. Quantitative performance aids and technology for designing data bases are overviewed using examples from existing systems. The issues and technology for security, integrity, data sharing and locking, and recovery of data bases are discussed and illustrated with examples from the GDBMS presented in previous chapters; the goal of this technology is to assist in preserving the accuracy and quality of the data base. The emerging functions of the data base administrator are reviewed.

Chapter 14 (a new chapter) introduces data dictionary/directory (DD/D) systems. The DD/D is a specialized data base containing descriptions of data base resources and other elements that are of concern to data base administration. The role of the DD/D in enhancing data base productivity and control is illustrated.

Chapter 15 (a new chapter) is devoted to data base machines. As a result of demanding environments with large data bases and very large data base transaction rates and of the evolution of GDBMS into maturity, data base machines are currently being investigated and debated and are emerging commercially. Data base machines perform a number of data storage, access, and manipulation tasks by more direct hardware approaches and tailored operating systems.

Chapter 16 (a new chapter) outlines the goals and characteristics envisioned and being investigated and developed in the 1980s for distributed data base management in a homogeneous and in a heterogeneous network of GDBMS. The spectrum of alternatives starting from a traditional centralized processing and data base toward a highly distributed processing and distributed data base approach is presented. Research challenges are indicated.

The data base approaches and specific systems that we address will carry through the late 1980s and into the 1990s. This technology is serving and will continue serving admirably an increasing number of users and applications.

I wish to express my gratitude to a number of people for their valuable criticisms and suggestions. For their detailed comments, I am grateful to E. Z. Nahouraii, Dr. M. E. Senko (who suffered such a premature death in 1978), L. O. Brooks, and W. Lockhart, IBM Corporation; Dr. E. I. Lowenthal and R. G. Parsons, INTEL Corporation; J. Lennon, Systems Engineering Laboratories; Dr. E. Sibley, University of Maryland; and four excellent reviewers who unfortunately shall remain anonymous. I thank also for their comments the many UCLA students and individuals from industry and government who participated in courses and seminars that I led on the subject. I thank also in relation to the second edition of this text: Dr. D. K. Hsiao, Naval Postgraduate School; Dr. D. S. Parker, UCLA; and several professors widely using this text in instruction. I acknowledge the valuable insights that I gained while on various consulting assignments for both users of data base technology and for developers of future data base management technology. Thanks are due to Ms. E. Joseph for the many arduous hours of typing this manuscript. Finally, I am grateful to my wife Sandy for enduring the endless hours over the years that I spent in producing the first edition and then the second edition of this book, hours that I took away from family life.

SECOND EDITION VERSUS FIRST EDITION

Since the writing of the first edition, data base technology and practice evolved significantly in various arenas. The second edition reflects this through the addition of five new chapters and a number of additions and revisions throughout the text. Of major importance is the evolution and commercial emergence in the 1980s of relational data base management systems, robust data dictionary/directory systems, data base machines, and the beginnings of distributed data base management. The new chapters are devoted to these major developments.

A. F. C.

DATA BASE MANAGEMENT SYSTEMS

1

INTRODUCTION

1.1 INTRODUCTION

We are in an age of information generation, collection, and processing. The volume of information generation, collection, and processing that we are witnessing today is unprecedented in history. Furthermore, this volume is increasing at a staggering rate and will continue exploding for many years to come. Electronic computing technology has already made its mark on our world, in our society, and its advances will continue widening the mark.

Private and public organizations as well as individual citizens in many nations are being increasingly affected and benefited by computerized data storage, management, and processing technology. People are seeing each day more and more directly the benefits of such technology. The large majority of collected information is not computerized yet. The cost of hardware and software for information storage and retrieval is decreasing at a very fast pace as the amount of information stored and managed via computers, from personal computers to gigantic computers, mushrooms. It is already foreseeable that a vast portion of our data needs will be stored more economically on computer files and data banks than on paper. Not only printed or tabular information is being stored; line drawings, photographs, voice records, and other types of information are being handled increasingly by advancing technology.

Two major areas of computing technology are the cornerstone of the information-explosion age: **data base management technology** and **telecommunications technology**. This book presents the fundamentals of data organization and data base management.

Since the late 1960s many organizations, governmental, industrial, and educational, have been developing large information systems (accounts management systems, parts management systems, marketing information systems, and so forth). More recently, organizations have begun integrating various computerized application systems and their associated data files into more powerful and beneficial data base centered information systems for the growing and maturing user community. The need to integrate scattered files and data into a more cost-effective data base for a variety of users with different data needs, interests, and priorities has brought on many challenges. These include the need for: more powerful data structures and file organization capabilities than provided in standard computing systems via languages such as COBOL, FORTRAN, PL/1, PASCAL, and RPG; data independence between application programs and particular structures of the data base; ability to share data among users; nonredundancy of information; high performance and efficiency; security; and integrity.

In the past few years a diverse and diffused body of technology, that is, knowledge, tools, practices, and commercial software systems, has emerged for structuring integrated data bases and data base oriented systems. The 1970s and 1980s have witnessed a number of milestones in data management technology. A number of generalized file and data base management systems have been developed to meet the challenges and needs of our time. A growing number of users are now exploiting the benefits of the available and fast-growing data base technology and know-how.

The objective of this text is to present a coherent introduction and examination of the fundamental technology and practice of data base and data management systems design, implementation, application, and management.

Hardware Technology

Computing technology has provided two basic types of technology for storage of data: main memory, in which relatively small amounts of data (usually on the order of millions of bits of data) can be cost-effectively stored temporarily for data processing purposes; and external storage devices such as tapes, disks, drums, mass storage systems, and so forth, in which much larger amounts of data can be stored on a permanent basis, at reasonable cost. Main memory provides access to data with microsecond speeds, whereas external storage, being largely electromechanical, provides access at speeds several orders of magnitude slower, in the millisecond range. External storage is several orders of magnitude less expensive than main storage.

The ideal partner of a Central Processing Unit (CPU) would be a system providing unlimited storage, any part of which could be made available without delay to the program or user requesting it. With today's technology this ideal is most closely approached only by main memory, but its cost limits it to a relatively small size and it provides microsecond and nanosecond speeds. Our growing data files, a number of them already containing a trillion bits of information (1,000,000,000,000 bits), can be stored cost-effectively only in external storage devices. Such devices are significantly slower than main memory (on the order of 1/1000) but significantly less expensive.

Direct access external storage devices (DASD) and on-line data bases are at the heart of the data base centered information systems. The growth of on-line applications and data stored is increasing dramatically.

The capabilities and limitations of the mass storage technology available shape the nature and form of data management technology and facilities provided to users. An understanding of storage technology is essential toward understanding, appreciating, and designing data management systems. To this end, Appendix A surveys the hardware storage technology available. It is expected that today's storage technology will be significantly improved in terms of higher recording densities, faster access times, and less cost per bit. However, it is unlikely that radical improvements or changes will take place in the near future. The gap between CPU-main memory speeds and external storage device speeds will remain. The nature and form of today's data management software technology will not be affected radically by foreseeable hardware advances. Thus, the data management fundamentals and technology that are addressed and foreseen in this text will be with us for many years to come.

Many tasks that are once well understood and performed via software may be feasibly and most cost-effectively performed in the long run by hardware-based implementations. Thus, we can expect that a number of data storage, access, and manipulation tasks performed today by software may eventually be performed by more direct hardware approaches. A number of research and development efforts point in this direction, for example, increasing associative memory efforts and back-end or dedicated data base processors, addressed in Chapter 15.

Basic Terms and Concepts

What is **data management**? It is a very general and catchall term that refers to the computer technology necessary for data collection, organization, storage, retrieval, and manipulation. The smallest unit of data usually considered is the **data item**, also called **field** or **attribute**; for example, employee number. A collection of data items constitutes a **logical record** or **entity**. A logical record **type** is a record with a particular data item makeup; for example, an employee record made up of employee number, name, and address. A **file** is a collection of occurrences of the same record type; for example, a file of employee records.

A **data base** is a collection of occurrences of a number of record types, where the record types and their occurrences are interrelated by means of specific **relationships**. The term **data bank** is a synonym of data base. A data base with a single record type is the traditional file. The term data base is in vogue and, thus, a number of individuals now refer to a large single file as a data base also. A data base is typically stored on direct access external storage devices.

So why is there a need for a data base? A data base is typified by a number of desired characteristics outlined in Section 1.3 and explored in more detail there. Among its most attractive features is that it is a collection of integrated, shareable, and nonredundant data. An integrated data base brings together a variety of data and interrelates it for a variety of users, not just for one user or for a limited few as in conventional files. Any one user or application program will hence be concerned only with a small subset of the data base. Subsets of different users may overlap, that is, portions of the subsets may be in common, as shown in Figure 1.1. The ability to share or use this data permits limiting the amount of redundant storage to a minimum.

A **data base management system (DBMS)** in its most general form is a software system capable of supporting and managing an integrated data base as

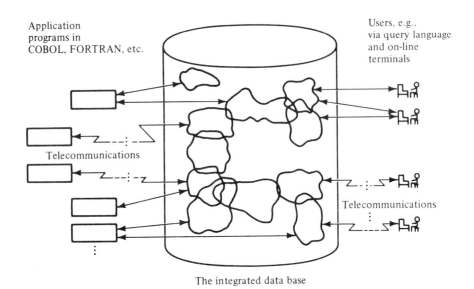

Application
programs in
COBOL, FORTRAN, etc.

Users, e.g.,
via query language
and on-line
terminals

Telecommunications

Telecommunications

The integrated data base

Figure 1.1.   *Schematic of an integrated data base system*

depicted schematically in Figure 1.1. Application programs written in conventional procedural programming languages such as COBOL, PL/1, FORTRAN,
and so forth, may access specified subsets of the data base. Individual users
may access on-line specified subsets via a nonprocedural query language, if one
is available. A subset could be one similar to a conventional single file, or one
which is made up of various record types and relationships, which by itself is
like a data base. Some of the application programs and users could be communicating via a telecommunications system from remote locations. Access to the
data base may be for the purpose of retrieving, adding, deleting, and updating
data.

1.2   HISTORICAL DEVELOPMENT AND
RELATIONSHIP OF DATA MANAGEMENT
TECHNOLOGIES

The main milestone of early data management software technology was
the development of COBOL by CODASYL (Conference on Data Systems
and Languages) in 1960. The COBOL report served admirably as the basis for
COBOL implementation by vendors. On the hardware technology side the
milestones were of course the development of tape devices along with early
computer systems in the 1950s, and subsequently the emergence of direct
access storage devices. The COBOL implementations of the early sixties, while

serving admirably, were found to need a number of additions beyond those in the COBOL report. The primary needs were powerful SORT utilities or packages and report writers. A **report writer** is a program that provides many facilities for editing, tallying, and formatting data, and performing other related tasks for generating more complex reports; these facilities go beyond the primitive ones as defined as part of the standard of programming languages.

Sort packages and report writers started to be developed as an addition to a standard programming language. RPG (Report Program Generator), which includes primitive facilities of COBOL and report writers plus some attractive facilities for file retrieval and updating not available in COBOL, was also developed particularly for smaller computer systems. RPG is still significantly used.

The late 1960s and early 1970s witnessed a number of milestones in software data management technology, as the growing number of computer applications demanded and afforded more encompassing, powerful, and efficient data management systems. Higher-level file organizations emerged to alleviate the mismatch between the increasingly complex multikey information retrieval demands of users and the single-key file facilities provided by the so-called **basic access methods** in an operating system, namely, sequential, direct, and indexed sequential access methods. Many large information systems (parts management systems, accounts management systems, and so forth) were developed. Organizations began both computerizing and integrating a number of application systems and their associated large files, and making them available to a growing and maturing user community. The concepts of modern integrated data bases began to evolve.

Enterprising user companies, mainframe vendors, software houses, and university groups, became aware of the critical need and payoff of bringing together and interrelating various data into an integrated and efficient data base. These groups started identifying and facing the challenge of data independence or immunity of an application program or user to changes in related applications, storage structures, and access strategies; flexibility in relating record types; nonredundancy of data; performance and efficiency; and security. Generalized file management systems (GFMS) and then generalized data base managment systems (GDBMS) and generalized data base/data communications systems (DB/DC) systems evolved. CODASYL presented its Data Base Task Group (DBTG) Report in 1971 as the basis for subsequent systems. Let us outline the chronological development and functional relationship of these data management technologies, shown schematically in Figure 1.2.

In the late 1960s and early 1970s GFMS were developed. A GFMS is a self-contained system integrating: all the facilities of report writers, report program generators, and sort packages; various facilities of COBOL; and a number of other useful file handling (not data base) facilities. Functionally,

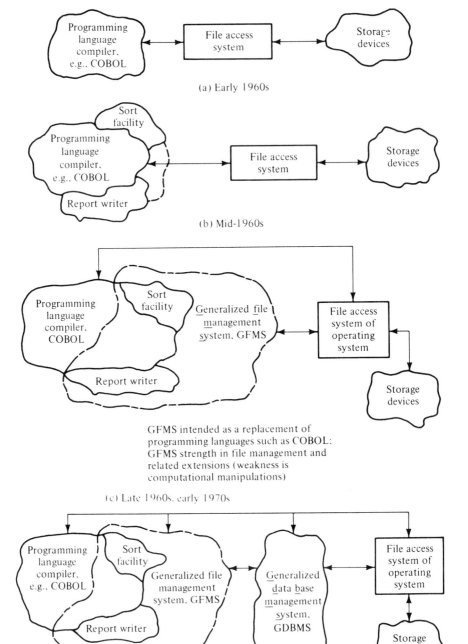

Figure 1.2. Chronological developmental and functional relationship of data management technology

8

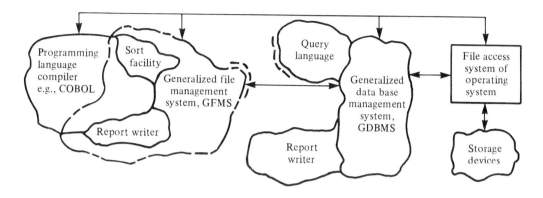

(e) Early 1980s on

Figure 1.2. continued

as shown in Figure 1.2, a GFMS can perform a great portion of what COBOL can do plus a lot more in areas where COBOL is weakest, namely, storage/retrieval and report writing. (When we refer to COBOL in our discussions we also mean any other programming language with similar record handling means.) Their intent is to replace COBOL and any other COBOL-like programming language in storage/retrieval-bound applications and communicate directly with and make use of the basic access methods of a host operating system for file definition, creation, retrieval, updating, manipulation, maintenance, and report writing. The common user language of most GFMS is a high-level, forms-oriented programming language with powerful operators for performing these functions easily without incurring the burden of programming in conventional programming languages. A hierarchical order would place GFMS at the top, then COBOL, and then assembly language. Most GFMS now provide interfacing points to programs written in programming languages for more complex CPU-bound data manipulation.

Reported productivity gains (in terms of programming manpower to implement and maintain application systems and produce reports) using GFMS instead of COBOL, FORTRAN, and PL/1 in I/O-oriented applications are in the order of from 4 to 1 to as much as 15 to 1 depending on the application; ratios of about 7 to 1 are most often cited by typical users. It is estimated that by the early 1980s there were at least 4000 GFMS installed, most of them provided by the top five vendors (most of whom, interestingly, are software houses). As shown in Figure 1.2, GFMS do not do everything that a programming language can do; the best GFMS claim to cover is anywhere from 60 to 80 percent of complex file management needs of commercial data processing. Thus GFMS are not intended to be a total replacement for programming languages. Whether or not a GFMS is significantly better than a COBOL-like language depends on the type of application and how much the bread-and-butter facilities of the

GFMS are needed. We shall not address commercially available GFMS in this text. However, they are a significant part of available data management technology.

In the late 1960s the need for integrating large files into a data base and the need for many users and/or application programs to effectively and efficiently access it led to the early data base management efforts. Conventional file structures, with their single-key or sequential single record-type limitation, were inadequate for such demanding environments and resulted in excessive processing times and external storage requirements. GFMS, limited by the underlying basic access methods of their host operating system, were also inadequate. **Higher-level data and file organizations**, frequently called **secondary file organizations**, emerged as an essential ingredient toward cost/effective data base management. They include multilist, ringed, chained-tree, and inverted data organizations. Figure 1.3 outlines the hierarchy of data management facilities.

In the 1960s a number of large organizations developed in-house specialized data base oriented systems using higher-level file organizations and interconnecting and interrelating files in various ways to form the data base. Mainframe vendors and software houses started on the road toward today's GDBMS. The early designs of the so-called hierarchic, network, and inverted-tree data base management systems appeared in the late 1960s. Designs of data base/data communications systems in which the data base and the data communication (or teleprocessing) facilities are highly developed in an integrated basis over and above those of a host operating system also emerged. Figure 1.2(d) and (e) summarizes the main functional relationships of today's data management systems:

1. Application programs in a conventional procedural programming language, or in a report writer language, communicate with the access methods of the host operating system for file accessing via the standard input/output statements of the language.

2. Application programs in a conventional procedural programming language, or in a report writer language, communicate with the GDBMS for data base access via an appropriate language interface provided by the GDBMS.

3. A very high-level query language particular to each GDBMS may be available for fast, usually on-line, low-volume data base accessing.

4. Application programs in a high-level GFMS language communicate with the access methods of the host operating system for file accessing via input/output statements of the GFMS language.

5. Application programs in a high-level GFMS language communicate with the GDBMS for data base accessing via an appropriate language interface usually available from the GFMS vendor.

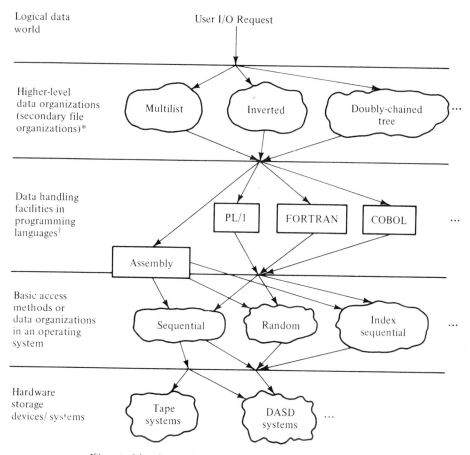

*Elements of these data organization approaches may be used in implementations of basic access methods and storage mechanisms.

†Higher level programming languages (COBOL, PL/I, etc.) are also commonly used to interface with data management systems (which use higher level data organizations) for all I/O of data in external storage; the programming languages are then used for all data manipulation in main-storage.

Figure 1.3. *Hierarchy of data management facilities*

6. Application programs in a high-level GFMS language communicate with an application program in a procedural programming language for computational-bound operations via an appropriate interface usually provided with the GFMS.

Figure 1.2(e) implies an increasing trend in the 1980s to integrate more the availability and use of the underlying technology of query languages, report writers/GFMS and GDBMS, which were originally rather separately developed by vendors. Such integrated software is referred to as **fourth-generation software** by some authors.

The last option (6) is not too widely exercised. The use of programs written in conventional programming languages to access files via the conventional file access system of the operating system is the traditional mode, is still the predominant one, and will predominate for the immediate future. The basic access methods or file management facilities of today's operating systems will be essentially the same in new operating systems and will continue at the root of all data management technology (see Figure 1.3). Familiarity with basic access methods is recommended for those being introduced to data management. Realize that there are probably over 150,000 computer installations worldwide using basic file management (in most cases still mostly tape management), while the rapidly growing number of GDBMS installations is still under 10,000 as of the early 1980s. This excludes the vast number of personal computers and "micro (or infant) GDBMS." The principles of modern GDBMS and their use via conventional programming languages and via on-line query languages are the central subject of this text.

1.3 WHY DATA BASE TECHNOLOGY: OBJECTIVES

The main objectives of data base technology are listed in Figure 1.4. GDBMS achieving such objectives are an invaluable and essential asset toward developing and supporting modern integrated information systems.

- Data independence
- Data shareability
- Non-redundancy of data stored
- Relatability
- Integrity
- Access flexibility
- Security
- Performance and efficiency
- Administration and control

Figure 1.4. *Main objectives of data base technology*

Data Independence

The concept of **data independence** is central to the data base approach. It denotes independence or insulation of application programs or users from a wide variety of changes in the specific logical organization, physical organization, and storage considerations of the computerized data base. **Physical data independence** is the ability to insulate applications from changes in the physical organization of the data used; for example, changes in the location of data (device x vs. device y), internal data links, internal sort strategies, access paths available (basic access method key, keys inverted, and so forth) and layout of data on the storage devices. **Logical data independence** is the ability to insulate applications from changes in the logical organization of the data base used.

File management facilities available via programming languages in conventional operating systems (sequential, random, indexed sequential) have suffered from the inability to provide data independence. For example, a change in the logical record description of a file involves reloading the whole file and modifying and recompiling every program using that file (even if the change is simply a rearrangement of the fields in the record description); addition or deletion of a field in the record description causes that much havoc. A change in the access key-name in I/O statements in the application program referring to random or indexed sequential access files requires either reloading the file to have the new access key-name or changing the logic or access strategy of the application program. Changing various physical structure aspects of a file may cause similar problems; for example, changing to a new storage device, or changing from fixed-length physical records to variable-length.

The seriousness of these problems becomes intolerable when interconnected multifile information systems are involved. In fact, the problems hinder or prohibit the interconnection of files and application programs, and hence the development of information systems.

Note that the lack of data independence arises due to *change*. The kinds of change cited, and many other kinds that the reader may visualize, occur often in actual practice due to unforeseen future requirements or due to plain changes of mind. They are a fact of life, be it business or scientific environments.

Data base technology strives to provide as much data independence as possible. There are many degrees of data independence. There is no industry-wide standard to measure or scale the degree of data independence. It should be stressed that there is no complete data independence since an application program cannot be shielded from all possible changes.

Since the 1960s the largest portion of the EDP budget of a typical installation goes to software and related aspects, not to hardware directly. A larger and larger portion is unfortunately being spent on application program maintenance and modification, much of it precipitated by changes of the type previously cited. Hence we see the significance of achieving a high degree of data independence. Different GDBMS provide different degrees of data independence.

Data Shareability and Nonredundancy of Data Stored

The goal is to enable applications to share an integrated data base containing all the data needed by the applications and thus eliminate as much as possible the need to store data redundantly. Applications require the ability to operate unaware of each other's existence. Concurrent views of the same data, control over access, control over intereffects among the independent programs, efficient access to different subsets of the data, and a host of other related needs must be provided.

The removal of redundancy is a road toward shareability. However, as we shall see, some data redundancy may be necessary for enhancing data base performance in terms of access time or for the convenience of the logical view of the user.

Relatability

Relatability is the ability of defining relationships between records or entities at the logical level just as conveniently as defining the records themselves. Relationships are as important and identifiable as any record and data attribute, and they must be definable and unambiguously managed by the data base system. Consider the data base shown in Figure 1.5 showing four interconnected files, each containing information on a given type of entity. For example, a given PURCHASE ORDER record is associated or connected with the corresponding VENDOR record (containing information on the vendor or supplier to whom the purchase order is sent) and with corresponding RAW MATERIAL INVENTORY records (containing in-house inventory information on the items ordered in the purchase order). The relationships linking

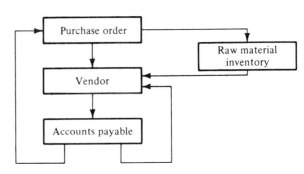

Figure 1.5.   A data base example

these entities are represented as connecting arrows in the schematic diagram outlining the data base.

Integrity

The term **integrity** refers to a variety of tasks, the main ones being: the coordination of data accessing by different applications; propagation of update of values to other copies and dependent values; and the preservation of a high degree of consistency and correctness of data. With many different users sharing various portions of the data base, it is impossible for each user to be responsible for the consistency of the values in the data base and for maintaining the relationships of the user data items to all other data items, some of which may be unknown to the user or prohibited for the user to access. A major goal of a data base system is to maintain control over and preserve the integrity of the data base.

Access Flexibility

Access flexibility is the ability to access any part of the data base on the basis of any access key(s) and logical qualification, via a high-level nonprocedural query language for browsing through the data base, or via input/output statements issued from the programs written in conventional procedural programming languages. The desired accessing flexibility is far beyond the limited accessing facilities provided by programming languages using the basic access methods (file management) of conventional operating systems.

Security

There must be proper mechanisms to assign, control, and remove the rights of access (read, insert, delete, change) of any users to any data items or defined subset of the data base. As the amount of data shared and the number of users increase, the task of the GDBMS to insure such security increases. A data item must be fully protected from unauthorized intrusion, be it accidental or malicious.

Performance and Efficiency

In view of the large size of data bases, and of demanding data base accessing needs, good performance and efficiency are major requirements. The greater the data base and the number of users, the greater the likelihood that a smaller percentage of the whole data base is of concern to any one user. Classical, inefficient, and exhaustive searching using only conventional file management facilities of operating systems is intolerable. The viability of an integrated data base is highly dependent on good performance and efficiency.

Administration and Control

A crucial ingredient to the introduction of data base concepts and soft-ware in any enterprise is the function of data base design, administration, and control. Responsibility for the description and control of data must not be diffused among the many users and analysts. It must be centralized and reside in the **data base administrator (DBA)**. The DBA is an experienced and highly qualified individual (or group of individuals) charged with such responsibility and other responsibilities that must be lifted away from any one user for the overall good. Overall data base design, data definitions, and the road map for users to access the data base must be accomplished by the DBA using special-ized data description and control languages and other facilities. The DBA also determines performance and efficiency levels while taking into account the overall good.

1.4   ARCHITECTURE OF A DATA BASE MANAGEMENT SYSTEM

Figure 1.6 shows the realms of data base organization. At the top level is the conceptual model of the data base as visualized by an individual. At the next level is an equivalent model of the user view of data, but organized in permissible logical structures and regulations of a particular data base system model. The third and lower level is the physical data base structure realm, representing all data definition directories, access paths, secondary data orga-nizations, basic access methods, storage layouts, and the actual data stored in mass storage devices.

There are three main types of data base models, and four types of GDBMS, in which records or entities and their relationships, i.e., logical data base structures, may be defined:

1. The **hierarchic model**, in **hierarchic GDBMS** and **inverted hierarchic-oriented GDBMS**.
2. The **network** model, in **network GDBMS** and **inverted network-oriented GDBMS**.
3. The **relational model**, in **relational GDBMS**.

These models are alternative approaches to viewing and manipulating data at the logical level, irrespective of any underlying and supporting physical data structures. The hierarchic, network, and relational models are available in today's commercial GDBMS. Some combination of models is a promising approach currently being considered and investigated for some GDBMS. Any logical data base structure can be defined in any of the models.

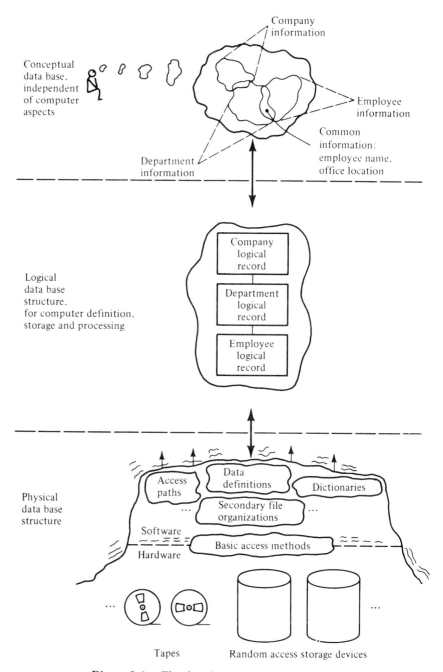

Conceptual
data base,
independent
of computer
aspects

Company
information

Employee
information

Common
information:
employee name,
office location

Department
information

Logical
data base
structure,
for computer definition,
storage and processing

Company
logical
record

Department
logical
record

Employee
logical
record

Physical
data base
structure

Access
paths

Data
definitions

Dictionaries

Secondary file
organizations

Software

Basic access methods

Hardware

Tapes

Random access storage devices

Figure 1.6. *The data base organization realms*

Figure 1.7 outlines the architecture of a data base management system.
Fundamental and common to all data base systems is the ability to:

1. Define the logical structure of the entities and relationships making up
    the data base. This logical structure is called the **schema** or **logical data
    base structure** and is defined by a data base designer or administrator
    (DBA) via a special **schema data description language (DDL)**.
    Several independent data bases may be defined.
2. Define and control access to any subset of the data base. The logical

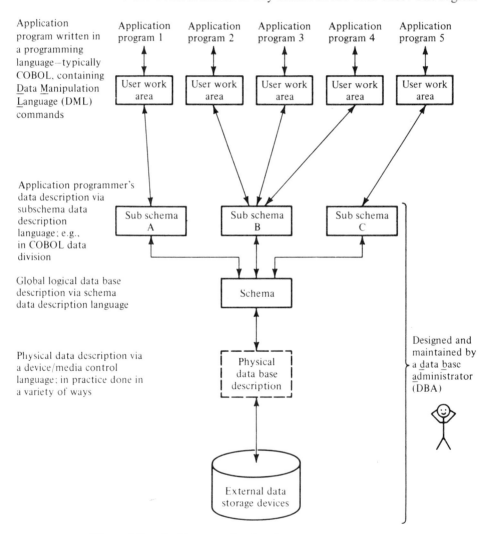

Figure 1.7.   *Architecture of a data base management system*

structure of this subset is commonly called a **subschema** and is defined by the DBA via a **subschema data description language**. It is an application or user's view of the logical description of the file(s) or data base, while in reality it is a subset of the global schema shared by a number of programs. Any number of subschemas may be defined on a schema (a subschema can be the whole schema). Any number of

	Single Data Item	Data Aggregate	Record	Subschema	Schema or Data base
Conventional COBOL & PL/1	Field, Elementary Data Item	Group Item	Record	File	File
CODASYL DBTG	Field, Elementary Data Item	Group Item	Record	Subschema	Schema
IBM's IMS	Field	Segment	Segment	Sensitive Segments; Program Communication Block	Data Base (Physical, Logical)
Cincom's TOTAL	Data Item, Field	Data Element	Record	Data Base	Data Base
Informatics' MARK IV (Generalized File Management System)	Field	Segment	Segment	File(s)	Master File(s)
Honeywell's IDS	Data Field	Group Item	Record	Subschema	Schema
Software AG's ADABAS	Field	Group of Fields	Record	File or Files of Program	Coupled Files or Data Base
INTEL's SYSTEM 2000	Element	Repeating Group	Record	Application Program Data Base; Subschema	Data Base or Schema
In Use by Various Individuals	Attribute	Attribute Group	Entity	Entity Set	(Whole) Entity Set
Relational Data Base Systems	Domain, Column	Relation or Table	Relation or Table	User Data Base, Data Submodel, View	Data Base, Data Model

Figure 1.8. *Common terms and equivalencies in the data management world*

programs can share a subschema; and different subschemas can overlap. The DBA defines a subschema first so that a user may then use it.
In personal data base cases the DBA and user are usually one and the
same person.

3. Access the data base, as per the subschemas defined, by a special **data
   manipulation language (DML)** or by a nonprocedural **query language**. The DML is generally used to access the data base from an
   application program written in a programming language, such as
   COBOL or PL/1. A user work area is a part of main memory for
   user/GDBMS communication in which a small portion of data being
   accessed or stored may reside temporarily.

4. Define the physical structure, organization, and storage layout of the
   actual data base. This definition is the responsibility of the DBA and
   in actual practice is done in a variety of ways, reflecting the different
   approaches and conventions required by each particular GDBMS.

There are about a dozen major GDBMS in the marketplace comprising
the bulk of installed GDBMS. There are many additional systems claiming the
characteristics of a GDBMS. They usually represent some form either of the
hierarchic, network, or relational model.

It is unfortunate that the terminology commonly used in the data management world is quite varied, and at times confusing and inconsistent. Each of
the preceding data base approaches, and particularly each GDBMS, carries a
number of terms peculiar to it. Figure 1.8 summarizes the main common terms
and equivalents; although only a representative sample of available GDBMS is
included, the bulk of the terminology involved is portrayed.

1.5   THE FILE AND DATA BASE DESIGN PROCESS

Figure 1.9 summarizes the file and data base design process. It is the
process of synthesizing the collection and associations of data to satisfy the
information storage, retrieval, and reporting requirements of users cost-
effectively, while meeting a number of constraints (not always mutually compatible) such as access time, flexibility of use, storage, security, auditing, and
recovery. The data base design process is in practice usually an iterative
process, just like the information system design process. Three major stages
are involved: logical data base design, physical data base design, and data base
operation followed perhaps by data base reorganization or redesign (due to
changes in requirements, transaction characteristics, and so forth). The separation is not always clear-cut between various steps comprising each of the major
steps. It is the DBA who is responsible for leading or carrying out this process.

The starting point of the data base design process is the identification of
information needs via systems analysis, leading to the identification of informa-

Phase 1 Logical Data Base Design			Phase 2 Physical Data Base Design			Phase 3 Data Base Operation and Reorganization	
Statement of requirements (information flows, data transformation, reports— queries, performance criteria)	Logical or conceptual data base structure in a given information model	a) Data base schema definition via the schema data description language. b) Subschema definition via the subschema data description language	Access path determination (e.g., secondary indexing)	Mapping and representation of logical data on physical data structures (e.g., DBTG areas)	Physical layout of data on storage devices available and determination of low level data management parameters (e.g., buffers, blocking, device areas)	Actual data base loading and installation	Tuning and retuning or redesign due to changing requirements

Note: There is a definite separation between logical and physical data base design. The separation is not always clear between various steps comprising physical data base design.

The data base design process, like the information system design process, tends to be an iterative process.

File and data base design is the process of synthesizing the collection and associations of data to satisfy the information storage, retrieval and reporting requirements of users cost-effectively, while meeting a number of constraints (not always mutually compatible) such as: access time, flexibility, recovery, storage, security, auditing, etc.

Figure 1.9. *The file and data base design process*

tion flows, reports, and queries that must be satisfied; of entities and relationships forming the conceptual data base in user terms (top of Figure 1.6); and of
performance criteria. The focus of this text is on the whole data base design
process outlined in Figure 1.9 after this most important initial step of systems
analysis has been accomplished. A major objective is to illustrate in detail the
fundamentals involved in this whole process, the alternatives and decisions
faced, trade-offs, state of the art, and trends foreseen.

1.6   IMAGE, TEXT, AND VOICE DATA MANAGEMENT

Today's GDBMS emerged and evolved to satisfy the specific needs of
management of record-type (COBOL-like) data. More recently, the need has
emerged to also manage growing volumes of image, text, and voice data, while
obtaining many of the benefits of commercial GDBMS (data independence,
security, nonredundancy and shareability, query languages, etc.). Image data
includes pictures, maps, drawings, and sketches. These types of data involve
orders of magnitude larger volumes of data than record-type data. For example, a single digitized picture may involve a 1000 by 1000 grid, with each grid
cell or pixel taking 8 bits to represent the level of each color. Also, the
operations to be performed on pictures and voice records are not necessarily
the same as for record-type data.

The evolution of various existing specialized and incompatible image and
voice data management systems into generalized data management systems is
being actively investigated, along with the possible extension/adaptation of
today's commercial GDBMS for such types of data. The integration of record-
type, image, text, and voice data management is a major need identified in the
1980s and being pursued. We shall address the results in the future as they
occur.

2
HIGHER-LEVEL ORGANIZATION AND MANAGEMENT

2.1   INTRODUCTION

The effective and efficient storage and retrieval of data items and records is the primary task of data management. The ability to locate records in a file cost-effectively given any field(s) or key(s) is essential to the effective operation of today's computer-based information systems. The basic file organizations, also called basic access methods or primary indexing methods, available in present-day computing systems via high-level (e.g., COBOL, PL/1) and assembly languages are the well-known sequential, random, and indexed sequential file organizations. Although the details of how these work may vary at the lower levels of the specific programming language, operating system, and machine (particularly for random and indexed organizations), they provide this limited entry capability to the stored data space: direct access to records on the basis of the field selected as the one and only access key when the file is initially created. This is a minimal facility, since in most actual environments it is essential to be able to access data on the basis of *any* one single key (each elementary data item or field is a candidate key) or combination of keys.

Consider the query or transaction "LIST ALL CLIENTS WHOSE BALANCE DUE IS GREATER THAN 1000, AND WHOSE INSURANCE COMPANY IS XXXXXX" coming from an on-line console or from a batch program. If neither of the query access keys k_1 and k_2, say BALANCE and INSURANCE_COMPANY, coincides with the system access key k_0, say CLIENT_NUMBER, then each of the N records in the file must be examined by the application program or the user to identify those that satisfy the query. If either k_1 or k_2 is in fact the system key k_0, then there are two possibilities:

1. If the query involves the logical conjunction k_1 AND k_2, then only a subset of the N records is actually retrieved and the program or user then examines this subset for those satisfying the other key.
2. If the query involves the logical disjunction k_1 OR k_2, then each of the N records must be retrieved and examined.

In any case, the fact is that many records that do not meet the query criteria are retrieved.

The complexity of retrieval increases with the number of logical operators AND and OR, and comparison operators $<, >, =, \neq$ involved in the query. See Appendix B for a method to characterize queries and their complexity. A query or I/O transaction request has the form: ⟨operation part⟩⟨qualification part⟩. For example:

LIST NAME, DEPARTMENT AND SALARY

Operation Part

$$\underbrace{\text{WHERE BALANCE} > 1000 \text{ AND INSURANCE\_CO} = \text{XXXXXX}}_{\text{Qualification Part}}$$

A number of important physically oriented data or file organization concepts and schemes globally termed **secondary file organizations** or **higher-level file organizations** have emerged through the years in order to alleviate the mismatch between the complex multikey information retrieval demands of users and the single-key basic facilities provided by operating systems. The use of the term "secondary" is unfortunate since such organizations are of primary importance in the management of data. The main ones are:

1. List and multilist organizations;
2. Partially inverted and fully inverted organizations; and
3. Ring and chained-tree organizations.

These are presented in the following sections.

Variations, extensions, and combinations of the basic schemes outlined in this chapter have been used. To complicate matters, there is a serious lack of consistent and coherent terminology among the many professionals involved in the data management area, e.g., computer scientists, data processing specialists, library scientists, and linguists. Furthermore, many of the techniques have evolved in a rather ad hoc, disjointed, and undocumented manner. Some techniques and concepts are referred to by several different terms, and sometimes a term is used by different practitioners in different ways. This chapter provides a road map through the main jargon and principles involved in practice. Table 2.1 lists the main terms and often heard synonyms.

Figure 2.1 summarizes the hierarchy of data management facilities (a repeat of Figure 1.3 for convenience). The higher-level file organizations have been invariably implemented in software. They generally utilize the underlying primary accessing mechanisms of the particular operating system, although in a few cases special basic access methods have been designed. Some implementations of the organizations have been written in languages such as PL/1 and FORTRAN, and others in assembly language. The term **data management system** is used to refer to a particular software package which uses a high-level file organization to support the capability of storing and retrieving (READ, INSERT, DELETE, UPDATE) data on the basis of more than just the primary access key of the underlying physical structures.

Let us identify in Figure 2.1 the nature of a possible inverted data management system. Going down in the hierarchy of Figure 2.1, it could be an inverted system written in PL/1, using a random access basic method and using a direct access storage (DASD). The particular random access facility used could be PL/1 REGIONAL (1).

The sophistication of the data management system determines, of course,

TABLE 2.1 File Organization Terms and Synonyms

Common Term Used Primarily in This Text	Synonym of Common Term
File organization	Data structures Data organization
Basic file organization	Basic data organization Primary index method Basic access method
Higher-level file organization	Secondary file organization Secondary data organization Higher-level data organization Secondary index structure Secondary index method
List	Chain
Multilist	List Threaded list Knotted list Linked list
Inverted organization	Indexed organization
Cellular multilist	Inverted-multilist
Ring	Chain Closed list Circular linked list
Ringed organization	Chained organization Hierarchical organization
Doubly-chained tree	Ringed tree Triply-linked tree Multiple attribute tree

Note: Various terms are (confusingly) used with more than one denotation, and the specific meaning is determined by the context involved. For example: "file organization" for either "logical file organization" or "physical file organization;" "key" or "index" for "key-value" or "key-name." The terms "file organization" and "data organization" are also used interchangeably, as are "file" and "data base" (when the data base is made up of only one file).

the complexity and effectiveness of information retrieval provided to users. The range of data management systems implemented is very wide, extending all the way from simple extensions of the basic access methods to truly generalized data base management systems.

Various combinations and variations of the organizations presented have been implemented and programmed by many practitioners through the years. Sometimes these designers have later realized that their designs are very much

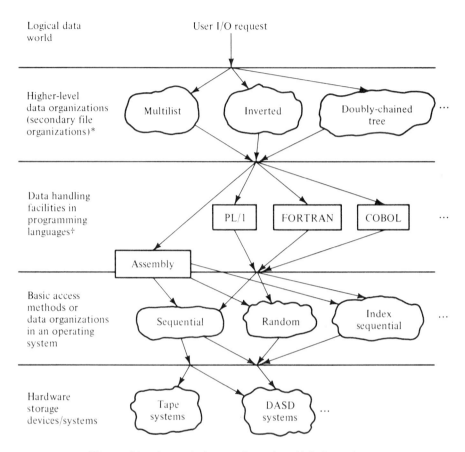

Figure 2.1. Hierarchy of data management facilities

like or essentially the canonical approaches outlined herein. When one looks at the complicated programs implementing such techniques, it is often difficult to visualize the data organization strategy used.

The data organizations presented in this chapter have been widely used in the form indicated or with extensions and hybrids by many practitioners in tasks other than the management of COBOL-like records. For example, many of the earliest reports in the literature on ringed structures stemmed largely from graphics systems architects. However, it should not be inferred that a given data organization is equally applicable or crucial to all data handling applications. A number of data organizations have been conceived for a limited variety of applications or different types of data. Some are more suitable and convenient, and essentially only applicable, to particular applications, such as object storage and retrieval via computer graphics[13,14,26,27,28] and pictorial/image data management.[36,37]

2.2   POINTERS

A **pointer** is simply an indicator which leads to a given data item or record from another point in the data space. A pointer can be:

1. The **machine address** of the record indicated.
2. The numeric **relative address** of the record indicated. Records could be sequentially numbered so that the pointer to a record would be its relative sequential number in the file. For example, the pointer pointing to a record in the PL/1 REGIONAL(1) organization and in most other primary random access organizations available is a relative sequential number. The correspondence between this relative sequential number and the real machine address is accomplished internally by the random access module of the operating system and transparent to the user of the pointer.
3. The **logical identifier** of the record indicated. A pointer whose value is a logical identifier, not an address, is called a symbolic pointer. It could be a numeric or nonnumeric data item uniquely identifying each record in the file. Note that an identification number such as a social security number can be considered a symbolic pointer as long as it does not entail relative address notions. The identifier is converted to the real record address by some transformation, such as a simple table look-up or other key-transformation scheme, internally in the machine and transparent to the user.

Table 2.2 summarizes the relative comparison of the three types of pointers, in order of increasing significance, with respect to: pointer storage, speed of traversal to the pointed record, and the degree of machine independence of data management software using the pointer type.

The machine address pointer is the most machine efficient with respect to storage and speed, but its sole use in implementing data management systems forces device and machine dependence. This may be intolerable because logical aspects are tied to physical aspects of the particular hardware.

The relative address pointer is perhaps the most popular. This can be readily used to point to records in the random access files set up via practically all high-level languages on computing systems. The machine independency is

TABLE 2.2   Comparison of Types of Pointers

Pointer Type	Pointer Storage	Speed of Traversal to Pointed Record	Machine Independency of Data Management Software Using the Pointer Type
Machine address	Lowest	Fastest	None
Relative address	Low	Fast	Moderate
Symbolic or Logical Identifier	High	Slow	High

high since no specific machine-dependent addresses are involved. Relative address pointers are particularly attractive when paging is used, i.e., when pages are moved from one level of storage hierarchy to another. A relative address could then have two entries: one for the relative page number and one for the relative position of the record within that page.

The symbolic pointer makes all concepts of physical location or sequencing transparent to whoever uses the pointer. It thus provides the highest level of independence, but it is the most expensive relative to storage and speed. An ISAM file is pointed to by symbolic pointers, and each identifier (the value of the pointer) is converted to the real machine address by the ISAM internal mechanisms (which in turn use their particular pointer types) transparent to the programmer. Records in PL/1 REGIONAL (2) and REGIONAL (3) files are pointed to by means of mixed symbolic-relative pointers, but the key transformation therein falls largely on the shoulder of the PL/1 file designer who sets up the file structure initially.

The speed of any pointer type depends directly on the physical position or distance between the source of the pointer and the data item pointed to. A pointer pointing to a record in the same cylinder is much faster than if it points to a record in another device, no matter what type of pointer is used. The speed gained by going from a slow pointer type to a faster one may not be sufficient to offset speed differences caused by physical organization and placement considerations. Physical storage and management of data organizations are thus very important and are addressed in Section 2.11.

The size of pointers can be reduced by encoding/decoding schemes, but this consumes time. So there is a trade-off. The size of a relative address pointer can be a byte or fraction of a byte, whereas a symbolic pointer generally entails one or several bytes once all related storage aspects are really accounted for. Data compression schemes and trade-offs apply equally to pointer data as to all other types of data. Pointer space has been reported to be a significant cost factor in some large data base cases. However, pointer speed is generally more of a problem than pointer space.

   A pointer to a record may be embedded in a record, or it may be placed in a directory. Remember that a pointer is basically like any data item. The implications of the alternatives are significantly different, as will be seen in the following sections.

2.3   LIST AND MULTILIST ORGANIZATIONS

   A **simple list** structure is a sequence of data elements or records linked by pointers. By including a pointer in each record to point to the next record that logically follows, the logical and physical organization can be completely different. Figure 2.2 shows a series of personnel records in noncontiguous

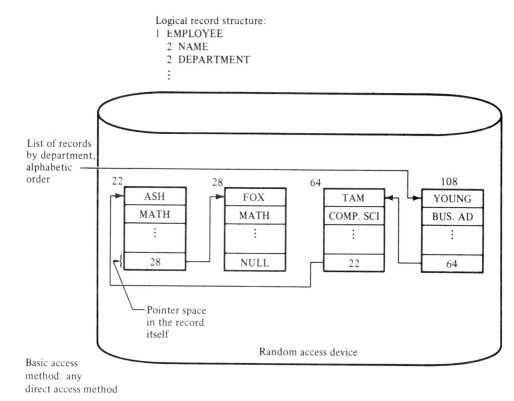

Figure 2.2.   *A series of records in noncontiguous physical positions linked logically by a single list*

physical positions linked logically by a single list, on the basis of department in alphabetical order. The **list length** is defined as the number of entries linked by the list. Note that a list costs one pointer space per record linked.

All list structures and all secondary indexing schemes necessitate the use of random access devices; they preclude tape implementation in almost all circumstances. A tape file could be viewed as a sequence of records in which the pointer is implemented by physical contiguity, i.e., physical and logical contiguity coincides. Records in the prime area of an indexed sequential file are physically ordered according to the logical sequence of the key chosen (thus no pointers are needed), whereas in the overflow areas their logical and physical position does not coincide and logical sequence is maintained via pointers.

Multilist Organization

Practically an infinite number of lists can be passed through a set of N records. A **multilist** organization is simply one which involves several lists. Figure 2.3 shows the basic multilist file organization. Each node represents a record. Records are shown placed in storage blocks or pages or in storage units

Basic multilist organization

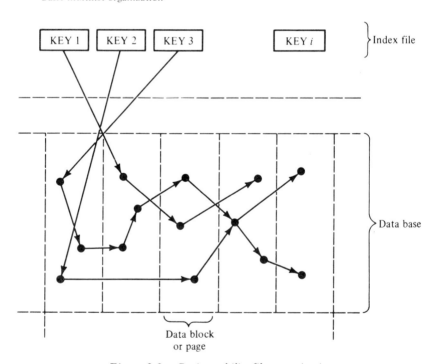

Figure 2.3.   Basic multilist file organization

of I/O from an external storage device. Figure 2.4 shows the personnel records threaded by two lists, one ordering all records by last name, and one linking records within a given age bracket. The use of the term "threaded" has led to the use of "threaded organization" as a synonym of multilist organization at times.

Quantization involves indexing on the basis of a range of key-values; its effect is to reduce the number of possible lists for a given key-name and to increase list length at the sacrifice of access speed to an individual record. Notice that by quantizing AGE values the list length of AGE is lengthened; in order to locate records of a specific age, let us say those whose AGE $=$ 30, the

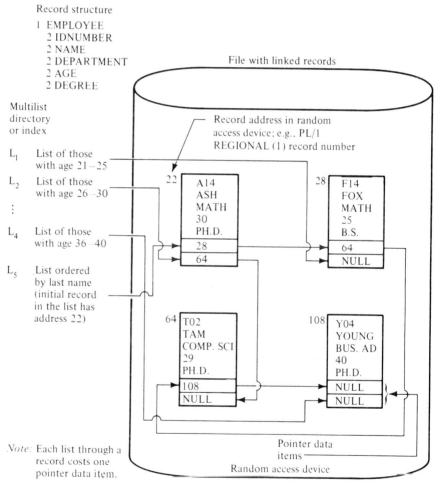

Figure 2.4.   *Multilist file organization example*

user or application program must search for them in the list linking those in the 26–30 AGE range.

The time required to access records is a function of the available access paths with respect to the access keys appearing in the query. For example, in Figure 2.4 if access is requested on the basis of DEGREE = PH.D., then all the records have to be accessed since there is no list on the basis of DEGREE. If access involves either or both of the list keys in a conjunct form, then the access will be very fast. For example, "LIST EMPLOYEES WITH AGE = 21–30 AND LAST NAME = CARDENAS" can be efficiently answered by retrieving the three lists L_1, L_2, and L_5 and detecting which records have in common the thread of L_5 and either L_1 or L_2; in this case no records satisfy this query.

Design and Trade-Offs

One of the tasks of the data base designer is to establish the best match between access paths and transaction requirements. However, the task is more complex when insertions, deletions, and updates (changing a record already in storage) are involved. Three facts permeate almost all data organizations:

1. The search and maintenance mechanisms for insert, delete, and update are actually more intricate and expensive than for record retrieval, frequently at least twice as expensive in processing speed;
2. As record retrieval time is optimized, the time taken to account for the other operations increases; and
3. Usually the optimization of storage is at the expense of execution time and vice versa.

For the multilist example in Figure 2.4, if FOX's age is to be changed to 26, then FOX will have to be taken off L_1 and added to L_2. In addition to the search for FOX via L_5 both L_1 and L_2 lists must be entered to update the pointers. If a record is to be inserted, then all the lists to which it belongs must be updated. If a record is to be deleted, e.g., delete FOX, then in addition to the search for it, all links through it must be updated. An alternative to avoid costly dynamic updating of pointers would be to flag the record as deleted (meaning that some bits will have to be carried in each record for this purpose) to provide virtual deletion and postpone physical deletion to some special maintenance program activated at a later time. However, virtual deletion may be unacceptable due to security or to storage cost considerations.

Pointer crawling operations require very exact software so that a link may not be lost in the process. A lost link may cause a disastrous effect. Stories of costly broken links abound in data management work. Intricate list structures complicate the task of data recovery and integrity.

2.4 INVERTED ORGANIZATION

A serious drawback of multilist organizations, as well as of variations of them, such as various ring structures discussed in Section 2.6, is that the search of a list involves actual retrieval of records in the list, examining each one for its pointer(s) and hopping to the next record. Thus, in Figure 2.4 the query "IS THERE ANYBODY WITH NAME = YOUNG?" can be answered only after every single record is retrieved. This entails access time in the milli-seconds-to-seconds range. The best performance of a list with N records is when its key-value is either unique for each record or the records are ordered and grouped by key-value if not unique; then on the average $(N + 1)/2$ records will have to be retrieved to find the desired one(s).

A better alternative is the so-called **inverted organization**, through which access time via the fields selected to be "inverted" can be significantly curtailed by several orders of magnitude over the multilist approach. Its basic structure involves:

1. The original records without any embedded pointers; and
2. The **inverted dictionary** or **directory** or **index** that contains certain field-values followed by the list of pointers to the records character-ized by such field-values.

The fields placed in the directory in order to provide fast access to records are called **inverted keys**, **indexed keys**, **access keys**, or plain **keys**.

Figure 2.5 shows the basic layout of the inverted file structure. Figure 2.6 is an inverted file structure for the records used in Figure 2.4. The pointers to records are record addresses or identifiers; a unique identifier must be assigned to each record, of course. The list of pointers, or pointer list, is often called an **accession list**.

Note that it is desirable that the pointers in the inverted directory, or the link pointers stored in the records in multilist organizations, be relative ad-dresses or identifiers rather than actual physical addresses. This permits changes in the physical location of the records pointed to without necessitating changes in the inverted directory, or link pointers; of course, the internal mechanisms or tables will have to reflect the correspondence between relative addresses or identifiers and the new physical locations. This independence is one of the goals of modern data management systems.

The **degree of inversion** refers to the extent to which field-values and pointers to corresponding records are placed in the directory; in other words, the extent to which access paths are established. The higher the degree of inversion, the larger the number of field-values inverted. Zero percent inver-sion is simply the underlying plain random or indexed sequential basic access method possessing one access key only. One hundred percent inversion means

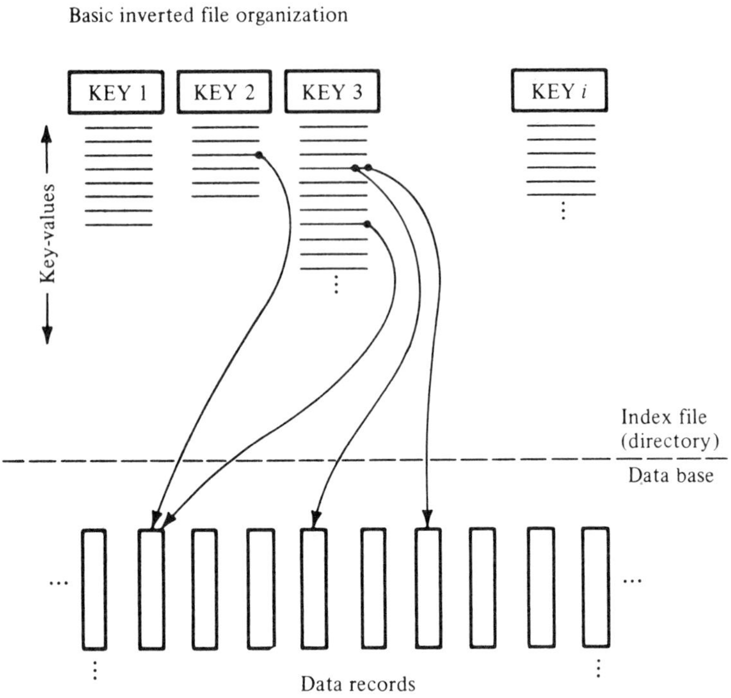

Basic inverted file organization

Figure 2.5. *Basic inverted file organization*

that every field-value of every field-name has been inverted, thus providing very fast access via any user access key(s).

The inverted organization is the fundamental structure for many systems. System Development Corporation's TDMS (<u>T</u>ime-Shared <u>D</u>ata <u>M</u>anagement <u>S</u>ystem)[3] was the earliest commercial generalized <u>d</u>ata <u>b</u>ase <u>m</u>anagement <u>s</u>ystem (GDBMS) that publicized formally the use of the inverted structure in the late 1960s. A number of successful GDBMS are inverted structure systems: INTEL's SYSTEM 2000[4] (which stemmed from the original TDMS), Software AG's ADABAS,[5] Computer Corporation of America's Model 204,[6] and Applied Data Research's DATACOM/DB.[7] The attention devoted to the inverted structure in this text is a reflection of its importance in the field. The following paragraphs provide the basics of such structure. In Chapter 8 the SYSTEM 2000 inverted approach is outlined. Although the basics are the same across commercial inverted systems, there are various differences at the lower-level programming depths proprietary to each vendor.

One of the great advantages of inverted organizations over other organizations is the ability to answer various types of queries involving the inverted field-values without retrieving the records themselves. Queries of the type

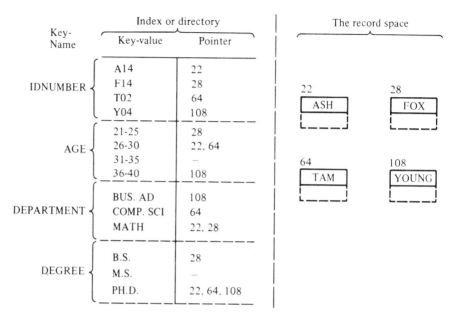

Figure 2.6. *Inverted file organization example*

"*Are there* any records that meet the following criteria?" and "*How many*
records are there that meet the following criteria?" can be quickly answered by
a search of only the inverted directory and ANDing and/or ORing the lists of
pointers corresponding to the access keys in the query.

In the example of Figure 2.6 the query "ARE THERE ANY PERSONS
IN DEPARTMENT = COMP.SCI AND WITH DEGREE = PH.D.?" is
answered by searching the DEPARTMENT and DEGREE sections of the
directory for COMP.SCI and PH.D., and retrieving the two pointer lists: "64"
and "22,64,108." The ANDing of the lists indicates that the record whose
identifier or location is 64 satisfies the query.

The inverted process of searching the directory and manipulating the
pointer list is obviously a more efficient search mechanism than the multilist
process of searching the directory, retrieving the first record in the list, and
examining its contents for pointer and common list information, retrieving the
next record and examining its content, and so on. Recall that the space taken
up by a pointer is only a few bits, much smaller than key-values. The effort in
initially setting up multilist and inverted structures is not too different.

Record insertion, deletion, and update are more costly than retrieval in any primary or secondary indexing organization. The following descriptions refer specifically to the inverted organization using the example in Figure 2.6.

1. Insertion—The record is stored and then every field-value of the new record corresponding to an inverted field must be taken into account in the directory. If the field-value already exists as an inverted value, then the identifier (a) could be added to the end of the pointer list, or (b) if pointers are in sequence in order to optimize conjuncting and disjuncting pointer lists, it could be inserted in its proper place after a binary search of the list (recall that each record has a unique identifier). If the field-value is not already in the directory, it is added and its list initiated.

2. Deletion—The record to be deleted must be first located as per whatever search criteria was specified, e.g., "DELETE ALL PERSONS WITH DEGREE = B.S." Then every pointer to this record must be also deleted. This necessitates going through the directory again and searching the lists in which the record identifier or address appears so as to delete it. If the record was only flagged as deleted, the directory would contain pointers to a logically deleted record and erroneous answers would ensue for questions normally answered by looking at the directory alone.

3. Update (change in place)—The record to be updated must be first accessed as per the search criteria, e.g., "UPDATE DEPARTMENT = COMP.SCI WHERE DEGREE = PH.D. AND AGE $\geq$ 36" would apply when all persons holding a Ph.D. and older than 35 years were transferred to the computer science department. Each record satisfying the search criteria (record 108 in this example) must be examined for the value in its DEPARTMENT field, so as to then delete its identifier from the pointer list of this value and add the identifier to the list of COMP.SCI. The status of the directory in Figure 2.6 after servicing this query would be (only affected portions shown):

DIRECTORY AFTER UPDATING

KEY-VALUE	POINTER
$\vdots$	$\vdots$
BUS.AD	—
COMP.SCI	64,108
$\vdots$	$\vdots$

The operators $>$, $\geq$, $<$, and $\neq$ appearing between field-names and field-values in the qualification part of queries, e.g., $A > 10$, involve more complicated and time-consuming searching mechanisms.

Notice in Figures 2.5 and 2.6 that every inverted value could be deleted from the original record without a real information loss. Thus, for a fully inverted file the result could be a very large directory which in itself is a huge file, plus a record space minus the inverted values which in itself is just a series of record addresses with zero information content. However, this storage saving possibility in the record space is usually not advisable because of:

1. The programming problems of handling records of varying size depending on the degree of inversion; and

2. The need for data independence of application programs, specifically "indexing independence" and "access data independence"; if key-values are removed from records a data administrator may no longer be free to add and remove inversion over time if various programs are sensitive to the particular field make-up of the records in the record space; and

3. Degradation in response time if the records have to be reconstructed (through the series of links that would have to be provided) to answer the query; access time might be severe and unacceptable if application programs, e.g., batch-oriented programs, involving retrieval of all or of a large percentage of the records are also involved, besides low-volume (typically on-line) queries.

By now the reader may have some ideas of where various other types of search optimizations may be worthwhile. What strategies to take and how to implement them are of importance. The ANDing and ORing of lists of pointers is certainly important. In large data bases (tens of thousands of records and more) a complex query will entail the manipulation of many lists with thousands of entries. Ordering, updating, reordering, conjuncting, disjuncting, and other operations present interesting optimization challenges. Optimization of manipulation of lists of pointers has been researched by a few authors,[8] and also by a number of architects implementing inverted strategies.

Index selection and management are the most crucial factors in the performance of inverted structures. They are the focus of the next paragraphs.

Multilevel Indexing

With high levels of inversion the directory is a large file posing the same search problem as the original set of records. So why not invert the index itself, resulting in a second index; and invert the second index resulting in a third index; and so on if possible? In other words, the strategy is a **multilevel index organization** exemplified in Figure 2.7 using the same file as before. Most implementations of indexed sequential (ISAM) files use internally a similar multilevel index organization; in ISAM the multilevel indexing is used to

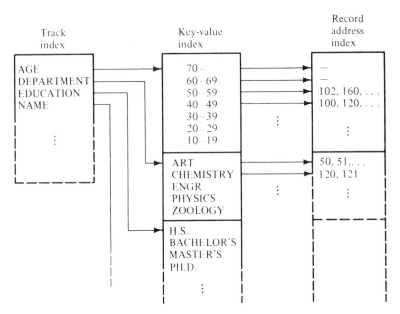

Figure 2.7. Sample three-level index of the inverted file organization

significantly enhance speed for the access key (the access key-name is that selected a priori when the file is created). ISAM can be viewed as a system with one-key inversion.

Inverted Index Selection

The basic question of what fields to invert is a crucial and difficult subject among practitioners. One major flaw in TDMS[3] was that all data bases were fully inverted and no partial inversion was allowed. All subsequent commercial inverted GDBMS (SYSTEM 2000[4], ADABAS[5], etc.) permit users to specify any desired level of inversion. This flexibility is a must in actual practice. The more access paths that are established to optimize retrieval, generally the more costly it is to update, insert, and delete. Thus, fields seldom used as retrieval keys should not be indexed. In current practice initial inversion selection is rudimentary at best; the selection of the inverted fields is improved only after costly trial-and-error approaches at run time. Changing the degree of inversion may be very expensive; in fact, in many commercial systems it may be done only by a costly reload of the whole data base. Few authors have suggested practical and specific guidelines for selecting the optimal, or close to optimal, inversion fields.

A first-order easy to use approach is described in Section 2.10 and the reader is referred to more refined but very complex approaches necessitating knowledge of detailed timing parameters and other implementation-dependent intricacies.[9,10,29]

The question of whether a file should be organized and searched as a plain sequential file or as an inverted file is a fundamental question, as well as when considering any other secondary indexing organization versus sequential organization. A useful design rule of thumb is that the average number of records qualified by an average query must be less than about 10 percent of the total number of records in the data base in order to justify the use of any secondary index organization in place of just plain sequential organization on tape. This is justified in Section 2.10. In the classical EDP application environment operating in the one-program, one-unintegrated file mode, sequential data organization is actually still the best in many cases. But as necessity and cost effectiveness force the integrated data base approach with many different programs operating on it, then the percentage of the total number of records or data items needed by any one program is lowered, thus making obsolete sequential organizations.

Multiattribute Indexing

Multiattribute indexing refers to indexing on several fields combined, thus providing higher-resolution access paths. Various confusing terms are often heard in reference to this practice. To illustrate multiattribute indexing, consider queries using access keys K_1, K_2, K_3. In some specific cases access may be faster by inverting on all three keys combined (e.g., a single list pointing to records with all three K_1, K_2, K_3 attributes), whereas in other cases speed may be increased by inverting on each of the three keys individually, i.e., have three lists. Matters become complex when updating comes into the picture. Lum[11] and Stonebraker[12] have addressed multiattribute indexing. Note that multiattribute considerations apply to any list-based or inverted structure.

The use of multiattribute indexing is not very frequent in actual practice. The reason is, in summary, that the time performance is very sensitive to changes in the contents of the data base and in the type and logical complexity of the queries. Multiattribute systems can be highly tuned, but only for very static environments. Even in manual and/or automated library retrieval systems, which are relatively very static (since the data base, i.e., the documents, and the indexing terms selected to reference the documents do not change with time), multiattribute indexing has not been used much; entry via the classical card catalog or index is single-key entry, by author or by document title.

2.5   HYBRID MULTILIST—INVERTED ORGANIZATION

Consider the basic multilist organization in Figure 2.3. One way of reducing the problem of having to search long lists unnecessarily is to limit list length. External storage devices and system software are bucket- or page-oriented, so that it is usually less costly to search a list confined to one page or cell (which can perhaps be retrieved in one I/O operation) than one list just as long but spanning across several pages. This leads to the often-called **cellular multilist** or **multilist-inverted structure** shown in Figure 2.8. Now the directory

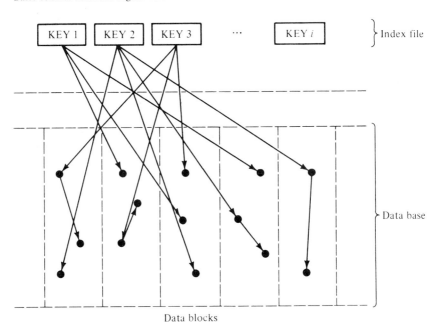

Basic cellular multilist organization

Figure 2.8.   Basic cellular multilist organization

has an entry, a pointer to the first record of every sublist, where each sublist is confined to a page or cell. Pointers still exist within records except for the last one in the sublist. If the length of each sublist is further limited to one record, then the inverted file organization results, as in Figure 2.5. The cellular multilist is a hybrid multilist-inverted approach.

2.6   RING AND CHAINED-TREE DATA ORGANIZATIONS

A **ring** data organization is simply a list organization in which the last record points back to the first record in the list, as shown in Figure 2.9. In a **multiring organization**, also called just plain **ringed-organization**, multiple rings pass through the records. Pointers are embedded in each record. As an example, visualize Figure 2.3 with the null pointer of every last record now pointing back to the head of the list. The head of each ring is the entry key into the data stored. Each ring is an access path.

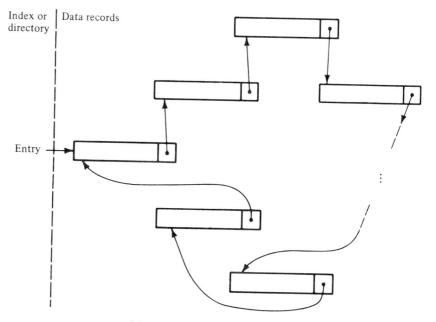

Figure 2.9.   *Ring organization*

Backward rings or lists may be also used in conjunction with forward rings as shown in Figure 2.10. One of the justifications for this extra storage expense is to save access time. If backward pointers are provided, then preceding records may be easily found; but if only forward pointers are provided then the rest of the ring may have to be traversed forward all the way to the preceding records from the original position. Pointers could also be stored in each record, or every so many records, to point to the start of the ring, thus enhancing the ability to navigate through the record space. This navigation and the software to support it become more intricate with the number of rings or access paths.

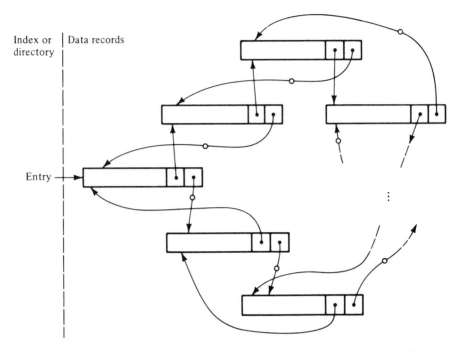

Figure 2.10. *Multiring organization with forward and backward pointers*

Designers of graphics systems were among the first to publicize ringed structures, as they used them for graphical representation of objects requiring very flexible manipulation. Among the earliest structures were CORAL's[13] and SKETCHPAD's,[14] in the early 1960s. Many ringed structures have been proposed and used in practice. The multilist and multiring organizations are the fundamental data organizations for the majority of today's GDBMS, as we shall see in Chapter 4–7.

The basic **doubly-chained tree** data organization is illustrated in Figure 2.11. Sussenguth[15] presented some of the basic aspects in 1963 and various other synonyms have been used for it, such as "threaded tree (with and without the dashed pointers)" and "triply-linked tree."[16] More recent work[17,24,30] presents the following specifications. In Figure 2.11 each level represents a key-name and each node represents a key-value. The leaves of the tree are the data records.

Three pointers are usually associated with each node. The *F* pointer (F-PTR) points to a set of key-values on the next lower level which are in those records having the key-value denoted by the node. This set of key-values is usually called a *filial set*. The *C* pointer (C-PTR) points horizontally to the next key-value in the filial set. It can also be used to traverse horizontally to the next

Basic doubly-chained tree file organization

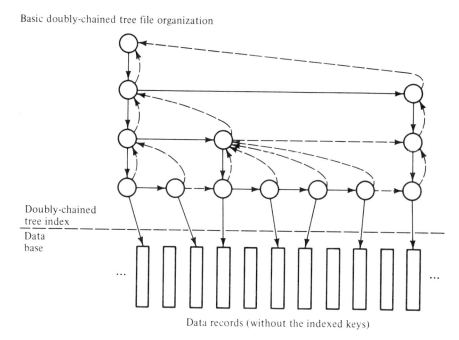

Figure 2.11.   Basic doubly-chained tree file organization

key-value in the filial set. It can also be used to traverse horizontally from filial set to filial set in the special case that it is in the last node of a filial set. The P pointer (P-PTR) points to the key value on the level above which is the parent of the filial set of which the node is a member.

Physically, the organization contains two types of blocks: (1) index blocks, containing key-values and associated pointers, and (2) data blocks, containing the records without these key-values. The index blocks contain the key-values and pointers selected to enhance the accessing of records. Only those keys which appear often as access keys in the queries are the ones that should be indexed or doubly-chained. Doubly-chained keys are analogous to inverted keys in inverted file organizations. For full double-chaining, all key values are placed in the index and hence every record becomes just an address. Sufficient pointers are supplied in the doubly-chained directory for reconstructing the original record from any point in the directory. Although tree representations of data have been used for a long time in numerous applications, the doubly-chained approach as a high-level file organization in a manner analogous to inversion has not been so clearly envisioned or exercised. The determination of the optimum degree of doubly-chaining is a subject of current research.

The illustrative example in Figure 2.12 shows in part (a) the actual data

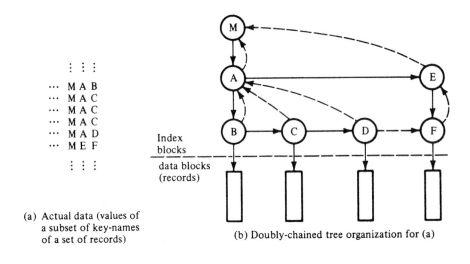

(a) Actual data (values of a subset of key-names of a set of records)

(b) Doubly-chained tree organization for (a)

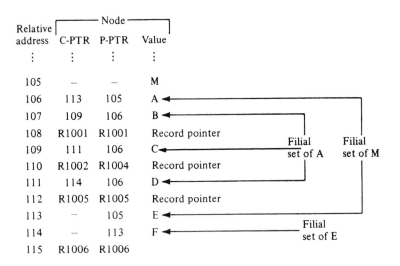

(c) Actual physical structure of (b)

Figure 2.12. *Example of the structure of the doubly-chained tree organization (a) actual data; (b) doubly-chained tree organization; (c) actual physical structure*

values of a subset of (1) key-names of a set of records, or (2) domains of tuples of a relation; in part (b) its doubly-chained tree organization; and in part (c) its actual physical structure. Figure 2.12(c) is one possible physical layout on today's one-dimensional storage devices. Note that the *F* pointer [down pointers in Figure 2.12(b)] is realized by physical contiguity.

Fully Ringed or Hierarchical Organization

If a set of records is fragmented such that it has all of its elementary data elements standing by themselves but connected to other items by a large number of rings, then a multiring or **fully-ringed structure** results. The name hierarchical organization has been also used for it at times.[1] The term hierarchic organization is also commonly used to denote the logical records defined in programming languages, as well as logical structures in GDBMS, particularly IMS. Thus the term hierarchical organization in reference to multirings adds to the confusing jargon. The best illustration of such a structure is an example. Figure 2.13 shows the structure for the example used throughout this chapter.

The reader should pace up and down the "hierarchy" in Figure 2.13 and realize how to search the structure. Notice how the multirings have really preserved the logical content of each record, although it may not seem so initially. The entry points to the structure are the initial pointers of the IDNUMBER, LASTNAME, DEPARTMENT and DEGREE rings. Entry points should be established according to the access requirements of queries. Assume that it is required to "LIST ALL EMPLOYEE INFORMATION ON THOSE WHERE DEGREE = B.S." The process of answering the query should be:

1. Enter the DEGREE ring and stop at B.S.
2. Go to the AGE hierarchy; it says AGE = 25.
3. Go to the LASTNAME hierarchy; it says LASTNAME = FOX
4. Go to the DEPARTMENT hierarchy; it says DEPARTMENT = MATH
5. Go the IDNUMBER hierarchy; it says IDNUMBER = F14
6. Finished!

Thus the answer to the query is that there is only one person who qualifies:

F14
FOX
MATH
25
B.S.

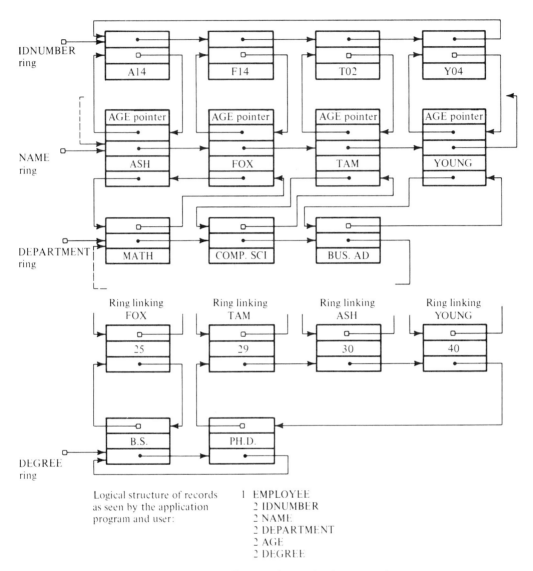

Figure 2.13. *Fully-ringed organization example*

The multiring structure is not the same as the doubly-chained structure. They both use one level of the hierarchy or tree for a given key-name and forward and next level pointers. This makes them appear rather similar. Note that at a given level a key-value may be repeated in the doubly-chained tree, but not in the ringed structure. Another distinction is that the multiring organization involves rings in the record space, whereas the doubly-chained tree organization involves chains (ring-like) in the index. The multiring structure is a more complicated structure and its programming does pose a pointer management workload, particularly for updates, inserts, and deletes. As an exercise, perform the command "UPDATE DEPARTMENT = COMP.SCI WHERE DEGREE = PH.D. AND AGE ≥ 36" which was exemplified for the inverted organization in Section 2.4, and then compare the work involved.

2.7   COMPARISON OF DATA ORGANIZATIONS

It is important to realize at the outset two factors. First, while it is acknowledged that low-level implementation-dependent factors (e.g., how data items and pointers are really mapped onto storage and how overflows are handled by each specific computing system) may have underestimated effects on the overall performance of any high-level file organization, it would be very difficult to account for microscopic and operating system dependencies in modeling and deriving the access time and storage requirement performance. However, it is possible and very necessary to conceive first-order quantitative relative comparisons. Second, no one high-level file organization is superior in all respects under all circumstances. There are situations in which a file structure represents significant advantages over the others.[17] The following observations and relative comparisons of multilist, and particularly of doubly-chained tree and inverted structures can be made, leading to useful design guidelines. These are derived from detailed analysis presented elsewhere.[24,25] The reader may refer to it for the details and justifications of the conclusions that follow.

Multilist Organization

The multilist organization usually compares very unfavorably to the inverted file and doubly-chained structure with respect to efficiency and cost-effectiveness of information retrieval. It takes as much storage as an inverted file and more than the doubly-chained organization. Its access time is generally much slower than that of any others because every record in the list usually has to be retrieved to obtain the one(s) desired.

Advantages of the Doubly-Chained Tree Versus the Inverted File Structure

The doubly-chained tree performs consistently better, relative to storage, than inverted file structures for most realistic files. The inversion of any field signifies additional storage for the field and its pointer space. This field would not be normally removed from the record so as to be able to answer queries requiring the information in the complete records (as opposed to queries asking only for existence and number of records). Thus the additional storage S_{IA} due to *record* space will be approximately:

S_{IA} = NKEY*NREC Words   NKEY $\equiv$ number of inverted field-names
                                 NREC $\equiv$ number of records in the file

assuming pessimistically one storage word for each field-value.

In contrast, double chaining involves pruning the records off the doubly-chained keys; the associated pointers enable reconstruction of any records. It is important to note that the doubly-chained tree organization may perhaps require even less space than the original sequence of records. This is illustrated by the seven-node representation in Figure 2.12(b) of the original 18 entries in Figure 2.12(a). Although storage for the pointers is an added expense, the net saving increases with the number of key-names (each key-name, or domain of a relation, corresponds to a level in the tree) and with the repetition of values for the same key-name. Thus, if the subset of data in Figure 2.12(a) were the same in every row, the tree would contain only three nodes. In the extreme case where no repetition of values occurs between rows, the tree would contain at worst as many nodes as there are values, plus pointer space, and thus no storage saving would accrue. However, the latter worst-case extreme will seldom happen in a real data file, since records naturally have some key values in common, e.g., a number of employee records have an attribute age equal to 25.

The *index* storage saved by the tree organization S_s *is approximately*

$$S_s = NREC*NKEY = \sum_{I=1}^{NKEY} NVAL(I) - 3*TNODES \text{ Words}$$

NVAL(I) = number of distinct key-values for the Ith key-name

if we pessimistically assume that the size of the pointer is one whole word, as is the node (key-value) itself. NREC*NKEY is the number of pointers in the inverted index. TNODES is the total number of nodes in the tree and is

$$TNODES \geq \sum_{I=1}^{NKEY} NVAL(I)$$

The storage savings of doubly-chained versus inverted structures is thus S_{IA} + S_s. S_s depends very much on the characteristics of the contents of the data file and on the selection and ordering of the key-names in the directory. The ordering is important, as can be seen by considering that if the order of the keys in Figure 2.12(a) were reversed, then the tree structure would increase to 12 nodes plus their pointers, as shown in Figure 2.14. Thus the total number of nodes is usually minimized when the key-names are arranged in the directory in increasing order of their different key-values.[18]

A second important advantage of doubly-chained trees is that when inserting, deleting, updating, or protecting a key, only one place is of concern, whereas in inverted structures such transactions have to be reflected in both the corresponding record and in the index.

A third advantage that may be often realized is in access time to answer a query. If there is a high relative frequency of occurrence in queries of K key-names out of NKEY indexed keys, then access time can be improved significantly by arranging the tree such that the first K levels correspond to these K keys. The case of K key-names corresponding to the first K key levels is a realistic case in which the data base administrator must provide fast access for $K + N$ keys, i.e., NKEY, where N is the set of keys that are used less frequently than the K keys, but also needs to give users of such N keys "fast" access (faster than having to search the data base extensively or exhaustively).

It is reported elsewhere that in some cases the doubly-chained structure may perform better, while in others it performs worse.[17] However, the comparison made there is for the worst case for the tree structure in which K access keys are used in a query, where the K keys do not correspond to the first K levels in the tree of NKEY levels.

Average access time is optimized by putting on the top levels of the tree the keys most frequently used in read commands and placing in the lower levels

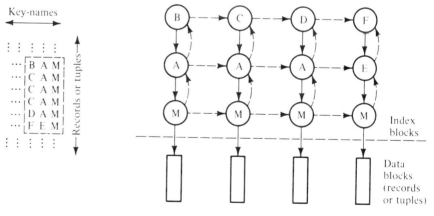

(a) Sample data values
(same as in Figure 2.12(a))

(b) Doubly-chained tree organization for the data in (a)

Figure 2.14.   *Example of the doubly-chained tree organization consuming maximum storage [compared to Figures 2.12(a) and (b)]*

the keys most frequently updated. Obviously, those keys not used as access keys and updated frequently should not be doubly-chained (indexed) at all. Thus, during system analysis it is important to identify the relative frequency of use of each key in read, update, insert, and delete commands.

Advantages of the Inverted File Structure

Queries of the type "Are there any XXXX which have attribute 1 and attribute 2?" or "How many XXXX are there which have attribute 1, attribute 2, . . .?" will tend to be more quickly answered by a search of only the inverted directory than by a search of the doubly-chained tree directory, particularly when attribute 1, attribute 2, and so on, do not correspond to the first K levels. A search through the tree directory automatically involves "reconstruction" of the pertinent records, even though the query does not ask for them (only for their existence and/or number).

A second advantage of the inverted structure is with respect to record insertion, deletion, and update. It is well-known that these operations cause havoc in just about any primary index organization (indexed, sequential, direct) and secondary organization. However, such operations result in more work and overhead time in double-chaining than in inversion due to the fact that (1) many pointers have to be updated in the surrounding (logical surroundings of the nodes in question), and (2) search of the node space is needed to locate the points of insertion. In inverted files such operations do not appear so difficult. For record insertion, all that is needed is to add the pointer at the end of each directory list corresponding to the key-values of the record already in the directory, and to add to the directory any of the new key-values (and their pointers) not already in the index. Record deletion involves just deletion of the pointers to the record, whereas in the tree structure it involves resetting the pointers in the surrounding space.

Programming Complexity

See Section 2.11.

Conclusions

In most practical applications, significant storage space savings may be realized by double-chaining in comparison with inversion; inversion entails additional storage. If the nature of the queries is such that a subset of the "inverted" access keys is most frequently used, then the access time performance of the doubly-chained structure stands out by arranging the tree such that the top levels correspond to this subset. If any subset of the keys is equally likely to be used, then this advantage does not predominate in as many circumstances, and file inversion may prove significantly better in some cases.

If the frequency of record insertion, deletion, and updating predominates over record retrieval, then the doubly-chained tree structure tends to be at a disadvantage due to the need also to update a number of pointers in the surrounding space. Queries asking only for the existence or the number of records satisfying various indexed attributes will be answered more quickly via the inverted directory.

2.8   DATA ORGANIZATIONS FOR MULTIFILE DATA BASES

An integrated data base is a conglomeration of interrelated files, segments, or relations. Data organization principles previously discussed are fundamental in organizing multifile associations.

Data Base Files and Relationships or Linkages

Figure 2.15 shows a typical large data base and its interfile *relationships* or *linkages* for a real-life industrial environment. Each file has its own record structure. Any subset of the 14 files shown can in itself be called a data base.

Figure 2.16 shows the subschema or logical structure made up of the Purchase Order (P.O.), Vendor, Accounts Payable (A.P.), and Raw Material Inventory (R.M.) files. Figure 2.17 shows the record detail and the interconnecting linkages. Only one sample record in each file is shown for illustration. Note that each record in the Accounts Payable file has only one real data value, Vendor #, and two pointers, the P.O. and Vendor links. These two pointers lead to the physical location of the associated P.O. and Vendor data.

The linkages in the example in Figure 2.17 are embedded in the records as elementary data items. Thus, in order to go from one record in one file to its related record in another, the source record must be retrieved into core so as to determine the pointer value. The files are organized like PL/1 REGIONAL(1) files and thus the pointer value is shown to be a relative disk address. Suppose symbolic pointers are desired instead; that is, each record as seen by the programmer should be identified uniquely and pointed to by an identifier, numeric or nonnumeric, which has no physical address connotations. Figure 2.18 shows a symbolic pointer version. This could be accomplished by implementing the files as ISAM or PL/1 REGIONAL(2) or (3) files, which transform internally and transparently to the user the symbolic pointers to real disk addresses.

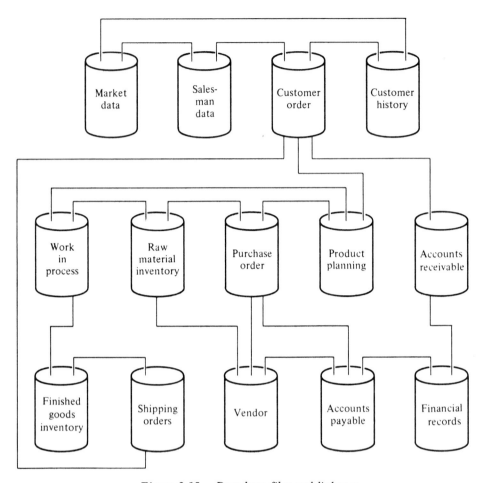

Figure 2.15. *Data base files and linkages*

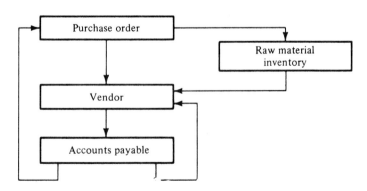

Figure 2.16. *A subschema of Figure 2.15*

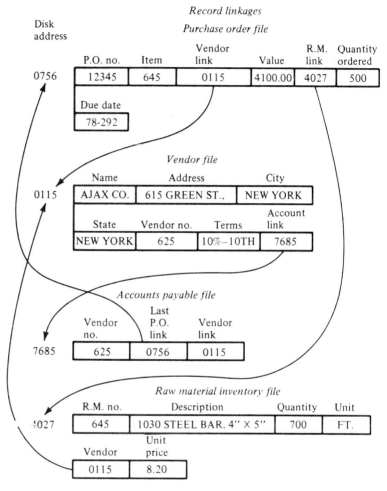

Figure 2.17.   *Record linkages (relative address pointers) of Figure 2.16*

Multikey Queries on Multiple Files

Suppose that a multikey query is made on a multifile data base and that the query keys are data items not all of which are in a single file. This poses many more problems and alternatives than for single files. For example, "LIST ALL VENDORS WITH PURCHASE-ORDER-VALUE > 600 AND ITEM DESCRIPTION = STEEL-BAR" in reference to Figures 2.16 and 2.17. The two main ways of searching for the answer are:

1. Serially-exhaustively using the linkages shown in Figure 2.17; and

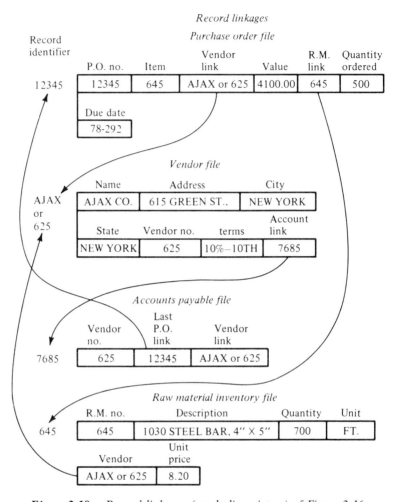

Figure 2.18. *Record linkages (symbolic pointers) of Figure 2.16*

2. Via secondary indexing that would have to be created as shown in Figure 2.19.

Let us look first at the serial-exhaustive approach. The best way is to first examine each record of the Purchase Order file and identify those with VALUE > 600. For each of these follow its RM link and see if its DESCRIPTION = STEEL BAR. If so, then follow the Vendor pointer and print out the corresponding VENDOR information. In Figure 2.17 the Ajax Co. record satisfies the query.

A more time-consuming way of answering the query is first to search the

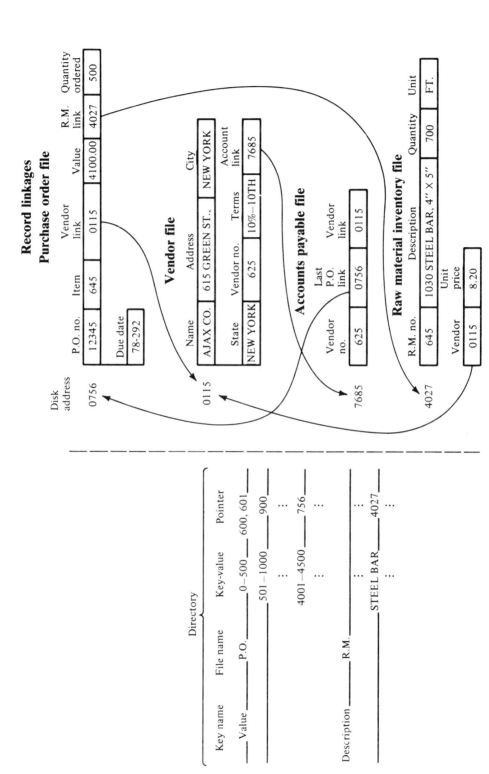

Figure 2.19. *Inverted multifile example (Figure 2.17 with partial inversion)*

57

Raw Material Inventory file and identify records with STEEL BAR. Unfortunately, there is no pointer from the R.M. file directly back to the P.O. file, and so three links have to be followed to find the corresponding Purchase Order: the Vendor link (115), the Account link (7685), and the Last P.O. link (756). The answer is the same, but the processing time is longer.

What has been illustrated is that even though the access paths are the same, just the way in which these paths are used has a marked effect on performance. Thus either the programmer or an intelligent programmed module in the system must choose judiciously what available access paths to follow for best performance. Navigation through the data base can be costly if not properly done.

Secondary indexing schemes can be applied to multiple files to provide much more cost-effective access than serial-exhaustive searches. Figure 2.19 shows the example in Figure 2.17 with VALUE and DESCRIPTION inverted. Since several files are inverted, in addition to the relative address there must be an indication of the file to which it refers. This indication could be carried in various ways. One of the easiest ones is to carry it in the directory along with the data name as shown. Now, in order to answer the query "LIST ALL VENDORS WITH PURCHASE-ORDER-VALUE > 600 AND ITEM-DESCRIPTION = STEEL BAR," do the following:

1. Search the directory for the desired qualification and obtain the corresponding pointers. They are P.O. 756 and R.M. 4027.

2. Retrieve these two records so as to follow their links to the Vendor file. The vendor pointed to by *both* links is a vendor meeting the criteria. A vendor pointed to by only one link does not satisfy the query.

Note that in the multifile case directory, pointer lists cannot always be just conjuncted and/or disjuncted to obtain an answer. Records must be fetched to obtain needed pointers. However, the answer to the query "ARE THERE ANY or HOW MANY VENDORS ARE THERE WITH PURCHASE ORDER-VALUE > 600 AND ITEM-DESCRIPTION = STEEL BAR" can be conveniently obtained without retrieving any of the records in the Vendor file. It is sufficient to just AND (AND in capitals will be used throughout the text to mean logical AND) the list of pointers obtained from the P.O. file (4027 in this example) and that from the R.M. file entry in the directory (ANDing the list of pointers in the directory does not provide the answer).

Without inversion, the amount of retrieval of unnecessary records is very high. If the P.O. file is chosen as the entry point, every record in it has to be retrieved, as well as every R.M. record corresponding to the case VALUE > 600. If the R.M. file is chosen as the entry point, every record in it has to be retrieved. Worse still, since there is no link directly from the R.M. to the P.O. file, records in the vendor and A.P. files have to be retrieved to reach the P.O. file. For every record for which DESCRIPTION = STEEL BAR, the corresponding Vendor, A.P., and P.O. records must be retrieved.

The determination of the optimum degree of indexing for multifile situations is obviously more complex. This is the subject of current research. In commercial GDBMS that have indexing facilities, such as inverted and relational systems, it is still largely a trial-and-error tuning process at run time.

2.9   INDEX ORGANIZATION AND OTHER DATA ORGANIZATIONS

The directory or index of a data base is itself a large file and may be as large as the original data base for very high degrees of indexing. But fortunately it is highly structured and a number of optimization approaches can be used. An entry in the index usually consists of a key-value followed by one or more pointers (see Figures 2.6 and 2.8). Thus, each entry is like a variable length record:

    1 INDEXKEY
        2 KEYVALUE
        2 POINTERS(N)

where N is the number of pointers for the particular key-value. It is very inefficient to search sequentially the large index file arising with high degrees of indexing. Any of the file organization techniques discussed thus far, or combinations of them, can be applied to the index no matter what data structure is involved by the index and the original records. Thus there is a very large number of combinations of techniques that can be used in a data management system. Two very attractive index organizations have been introduced already (1) multilevel inverted indexing (Figure 2.7) in Section 2.4: and (2) doubly-chained trees (Figure 2.11) in Section 2.6.

Several authors have shown that the combination of two different indexing techniques can perform better than a single indexing technique. This has been shown for multilist/inverted[31] and inverted/doubly-chained-like[32] combinations; the optimum mix of the two indexing methods has been reported.

Combined hashing and indexing approaches have been reported in the literature. Rothnie and Lozano[21] describe a combination of hashing and inversion and show that in some cases it can be better than inversion alone by factors of two to three; however, it is an untested heuristic approach, not simple. Pure hashing cannot be practically used when multikey queries are involved.

The B-tree (for Bayer-tree),[23] a single-key basic file organization widely extended and used as IBM's VSAM (an attractive alternative to ISAM),[38] has been extended also for multikey query servicing. Extended B-tree approaches and inverted approaches predominate in relational GDBMS.

Efficient directory or index management is the subject of current research. Refinements and extensions of the organizations presented in this chapter are being pursued, as are other different organizations.[35] Important unresolved issues include questions of centralized directories versus distributed directories in multifile and heterogeneous computer network environments, efficient index management in relational data base systems and in pictorial/image data management, and so forth.

2.10   TO INDEX OR NOT TO INDEX AND SELECTION OF INDEXES

The question of whether to organize and search a data file either 1) sequentially or 2) randomly with some secondary indexing superimposed is crucial. With a knowledge of the following measures which can be obtained at systems analysis time, a first-order determination can be made:

1. The **hit ratio** R, defined as the ratio of the number of records in the file or data base that satisfy the average query (be it a single or multikey query) to the total number of records NREC in the file or data base;

2. The average time T_r to access randomly the next record in the random access devices considered;

3. The average time T_x spent in going through the index (excluding data record retrieval time T_r); and

4. The average time T_s to access sequentially the next record in the tape or random access devices considered for the file sequentially organized.

The analysis proceeds as follows. If there are NREC in the file and R fraction of them are really qualified by the query, then the total access time is:

1. On tape or disk with the file sequentially organized: NREC $\times T_s$ msec since the entire file must be accessed. The access time can be (NREC/2) $\times T_s$ only in the very unlikely case that there is only one key in the query and that every record has either a unique value for that key or, if not, the records are ordered on the basis of that key so that all records with the same key-value are physically contiguous.

2. On disk: $R \times$ NREC $\times (T_x + T_r)$.

In general, the break-even point R_0 is:

$$\text{NREC} \times T_s = R_0 \times \text{NREC} \times (T_x + T_r)$$

$$R_0 = \frac{\text{NREC} \times T_s}{NREC(T_x + T_r)} = \frac{T_s}{T_x + T_r} \tag{1}$$

R_0 is the fraction of the file retrieved beyond which a sequential organization and search is the most cost-effective. Notice that R_0 is independent of the size of the data file.

Consider a particular example, assuming that T_x is ideally negligible. In a multiprogramming environment there is a high probability that in a single-head device the read head has been moved between input/output requests. Thus the average access time T_r may be the time to move across several cylinders, let us say 50 msec (typical for most DASD, including rotational delay and data transfer). Assume that the average time to retrieve consecutive records on tape is 5 msec (for the particular blocking factor chosen). Consequently,

$$R_0 = \frac{5}{50} = \frac{1}{10}$$

It has just been shown that no matter what secondary indexing is used and no matter how many records exist in the file, by determining the fraction R of records qualified by the average transaction load or query, one can determine quickly whether or not to index. R is crucial and can be approached as follows.

Records Qualified by a Query

The fraction or number of records qualified by a query is determined by:

1. The specific keys and logical complexity of the query. Appendix B defines how query complexity is characterized in this text.
2. The statistics of the contents of the data file, particularly the number of different key-values for each of the access keys.

The method for determining R will be illustrated for the case of two keys only. A specific example avoids long and intricate explanations.

Suppose that the application programs or queries access the file on the basis of two keys, k_1 and k_2; for example, one may need to obtain records of EMPLOYEES whose DEPT = SALES and HOBBY = GIRL-WATCHING. Assume: k_1 and k_2 have 12 and 9 different values, respectively, and are uniformly distributed, that is, every key-value of each key-name k_1 and k_2 characterizes the same number of records in the file (the list length for each key-value of a given key-name is the same); $T_s = 5$ msec, $T_r = 50$ msec, and T_x is much smaller. The break-even point $R_0 = 1/10$, as before. The analysis must consider the two query possibilities: (1)k_1 = key-value AND

k_2 = key-value; (2) k_1 = key-value OR k_2 = key-value. These two cases will be denoted as the k_1 AND k_2, and k_1 OR k_2 cases for simplicity.

k_1 = key-Value AND k_2 = Key-Value Case. R can range from 1/12 to 1/(12 × 9) to 0:

1. R = 1/12 for the case that all salespersons are girl watchers;
2. R = 0 for the case that no salespersons are girl watchers; and
3. R = 1/(12 × 9) for the average situation.

Thus the random approach is best since $R < R_0$ in all cases. As T_x comes into the picture due to indexing, R_0 decreases and may fall in the range of R. If uniform distribution of k_1 and k_2 is assumed (no clustering), then R averages most likely to around 1/(12 × 9). It is very unlikely in practice that T_x would be large enough to make R_0 be so small. From equation (1), T_x would have to be 980 msec for R = 1/(12 × 9). Thus secondary indexing is the best.

k_1 = Key-Value OR k_2 = Key-Value Case. R can range from 1/9 + 1/12 to 1/9:

1. R = 1/9 = .11 for the case that all salespersons are girl watchers
2. R = 1/9 + 1/12 = .19 for the case that no salespersons are girl watchers
3. Probably $R \approx \dfrac{.19 + .11}{2}$ = .15 on the average

Thus for k_1 OR k_2, sequential search is the best since $R > R_0$. As T_x comes into the picture R becomes much greater than R_0.

In summary, the relative frequency of k_1 AND k_2 versus k_1 OR k_2 will determine whether sequential search or indexing should be used. But the preceding analysis shows that the ratio of the OR to AND cases will have to be very large in order to justify sequential approaches, since with indexing the loss incurred for the OR case is much smaller than the very large gain for the AND case.

If now k_1 and k_2 both had three different key-values each (uniformly distributed), would indexing be justified? The answer is no. For the k_1 AND k_2 case, R ranges from 1/3 to 1/3 × 1/3 to 0. Most likely the query qualifies an average of 1/3 × 1/3 of the records which is greater than R_0 and hence sequential processing is the best. As T_x is taken into account this becomes even more convincing. For the k_1 OR k_2 case, R ranges from 1/3 + 1/3 to 1/3; hence sequential processing is always best.

As the complexity of the transaction load or query involved increases, the determination of R becomes more complex. The previous approach can still be used for higher complexities, although the difficulty of the combinatoric and mathematical analysis grows.

2.11   PHYSICAL STORAGE, IMPLEMENTATION, AND PERFORMANCE OF FILE ORGANIZATION

Once the *logical* structure of a file or data base has been determined, the important design task is to determine what is the optimum or at least "best" or appropriate physical structures (including physical access paths, storage mappings and so forth) for the situation(s) at hand while meeting a number of constraints. This can be effectively achieved only if the designer understands what the critical measures and parameters are that can be examined and controlled to optimize the performance of the alternative physical structures. In a nutshell, this is the problem, whether the designer has as a choice (1) the wide range of structures (organizations) described in previous sections or (2) the more limited range of structure options or variations offered in an already implemented system with a basic structure already chosen.

The best structure is one that minimizes the following cost function while satisfying various design constraints:

$$
\begin{aligned}
\text{Cost/unit period} = \ & [(\text{cost per track/unit period}) \\
& \times (\text{total storage required in tracks})] \\
& + [(\text{cost/second}) \\
& \times (\text{access time in seconds per average query}) \\
& \times (\text{number of queries, per unit period})] \\
& + [\text{an update cost function}] \\
& + [\text{other highly unquantifiable cost functions}]
\end{aligned}
$$

$$(6)$$

where unit period could be a day, week, or month. Design constraints such as "query response time must not be more than three seconds for most queries" only add complications to determining what is the best data base organization.

Total storage costs and average time to answer an average query in the preceding expression can be quantified. The update cost function is more difficult to define and quantify. When updating a data base(s) many side effects that are difficult to quantify at this state of the art are incurred. An example follows. When records are added to a data base structure, such as an inverted organization, based on underlying indexed sequential methods, these new records (or original records forced to be shifted by the insertion of the new records) are placed on so-called overflow areas. Records in overflow areas take longer to access than records in the original prime area. When records are deleted, the space freed is actually not necessarily made available for other new records, nor are other records shifted into the freed space. The result is that file performance can be so degraded that the whole data base has to be "purged," that is, dumped out, and then read-in again so that it occupies only prime area. In a highly dynamic data base environment, these may be frequently recurring expenses, very difficult to measure, which exist in addition to the more measurable update cost estimates.

The fourth element in Equation (6) termed "other highly unquantifiable cost functions" includes costs of initial programming, of reprogramming, of software maintenance, of documentation, and various others. These costs have been unfortunately highly elusive in the profession. There is a whole history of cost overruns in the development of just about every type of software system. Obviously, this fourth element applies when developing a data management system from scratch but not when utilizing an already existing and modern commercial system.

In relation to programming complexity, it is interesting to note that the large majority of over 200 UCLA graduate students given an assignment to program a small read-only data management system have chosen to implement the inverted organization rather than the doubly-chained tree organization. The frequently cited reasons for preferring inverted approaches are: easier to program and debug, and fewer pointer paths to follow and manage. A large number of pointer paths certainly complicate matters, since the developer has to keep tedious accounting of a large number of pointers. Even use of the high-level PL/1 pointer facilities does not avoid such drawbacks. The problem of lost and dangling pointers is well known.

Storage requirements and access time alone provide an important basis for comparing and evaluating alternative structures. The access time and storage requirements are a complicated function of:

1. Characteristics of the data contents of the data base, e.g., the number of distinct key-values of each field (key) of a record, distribution of key-values, etc;

2. User requirements, particularly the logical complexity of the queries or transactions, relative frequency of retrieval versus update, etc;

3. Storage device specifications, e.g., the average time to access a track on a disk, blocking factor, etc;

4. The particular structure chosen and the general programming and storage layouts or approaches used to implement it; and

5. The detailed programming aspects and the actual encoding and mapping of data items, indexes, etc., onto storage.

The basic methodology to compare and select an appropriate data base structure is the following: obtain measures of the relevant characteristics of the actual data base or of a representative sample of it and of the query requirements of the user; take into account device-related factors (e.g., timings, blockings); and then estimate storage requirements and the average access time to answer an average query for the various alternative file structures. On the basis of these two measures, an appropriate organization is chosen. Of course, the decision should be made taking into account also other highly unquantifiable cost factors which include relative costs of programming, reprogramming, maintenance, and documentation, for the case involving design and programming of the data base structuring system.

Unfortunately, in actual practice well-proven and specific guidelines are lacking yet as to what and how file and data base characteristics and user requirements affect performance and what the critical measures and parameters are that can be isolated and controlled to optimize performance. It is an elusive and complex task, particularly in commercial data base management systems involving a multitude of parameters and trade-offs, often conflicting. Yet, the data base designer or administrator must face this challenge. Section 13.3 gives an overview of quantitative performance aids and technology for file and data base design available in the marketplace. References 10, 17, 20, 23, 24, 25, 30, 32, and 33 provide fundamental insights by analyzing and modeling inverted and doubly-chained structures considering implementation-oriented aspects and deriving formulations for average access time and storage required. Observations and design guidelines stemming from this analysis were summarized in Section 2.7.

Implementation-dependent aspects have a large effect on data base performance—a fact often underestimated by those who have not really implemented and carried to completion data management systems and by those who have not used them extensively. Particular implementation approaches, programming languages and tricks, and actual mapping of data and indexes on storage all may have a significant effect on the feasibility and relative performance. Also, the relative importance and sensitivity of some of the elements are a function of the type and version of the file structure, and, to some extent, actual implementation details. To illustrate this, consider the effects of basic access methods underlying a data management system (refer to Figure 2.1). For example, there are three versions of the random access file organization supported in PL/1: Regional (1), Regional (2), and Regional (3). Each version uses different methods to manage storage and access records, although from the point of view of the PL/1 user these differences are essentially transparent. A specific case is the following difference between Regional (3) and the other two versions as implemented by IBM OS. When a record is deleted from Regional (3) files, the space vacated is not made available for future use (the complications to avoid this waste are such that the designers of the method chose to incur it), whereas in the others it is. So in Regional (3) the user is still paying storage for "deleted" records.

Perhaps the most important factor affecting total file structure performance is the manner in which the indexes or dictionaries and lists are managed and placed in storage. In highly inverted files with many different key-values, the directory becomes another file problem in itself, possibly of the same magnitude as the data base itself. When the lists are long, it will matter just where and how the pointers are managed. When a field value of a record is inverted, is the key in the record deleted in order to conserve total storage requirements? Or is the key left in the record to avoid programming problems of compacting records at the expense of storage? How physically close in actual storage space should records be to reduce the time taken in following pointers? Should the index be placed in a fixed-head area of the disk? More cases of this nature could be cited to point out their effect on file structure performance, aside from the effects of storage device specifications (e.g., time to position disk arm and access the desired address) and of data base and query characteristics. The file and data base designer must deal with a number of physical placement and storage mapping alternatives and parameters offered in commercial file management and data base management systems.

2.12 SUMMARY

Higher-level file organizations, also called secondary file organizations, have emerged in order to alleviate the mismatch between the complex multikey information retrieval demands of users and the single-key basic file organization facilities provided by operating systems and in order to separate logical organization from physical organization and storage of records. The random and indexed sequential basic access methods provide only limited access to the file by data content: fast access to a given record on the basis of the single access key or identifier selected when the file is first created. This is a minimal facility, since in a growing number of environments it is essential to be able to access data on the basis of the content of any single field of the record or logical combination of fields, while minimizing access time. Exhaustive searching and processing of all records in the file (this is the mode of operation of conventional report writing oriented systems and generalized file management systems) in order to locate the records that satisfy the complex demands may be avoided by proper use of higher-level organizations.

Higher-level file organizations clearly illustrate the possible separation between the logical and physical data organization realms: at the logical level the file appears as a set of records capable of being accessed by the data content of a variety of fields or combination of fields; at the physical level the file appears as the set of records properly transformed, perhaps dissected and invariably interconnected by various pointer mechanisms.

These techniques have been fundamental to the implementation and application of data base technology. Some of them have been developed in the past in software and applied also in operating systems, compilers, data processing application programs, and so forth. The main classes are: list and multilist, inverted, and ring and chained-tree organizations. Sections 2.1–2.6 presented them. Combinations and extensions of these organizations have been also implemented.

In order to benefit from the use of any higher-level file organization it is necessary to know a priori the type of file access needs in order to properly organize the file. The storage and access time performance may be very sensitive to certain design choices of the file designer, for example, the specific fields to be inverted. Unfortunately, no file organization nor set of associated parameters is the best for all situations, although inverted and chained-tree organizations tend to stand out. Section 2.7 compared their performance. Two facts seem to hold in most cases: access time is reduced at the expense of higher storage costs, and the time for read-access is reduced at the expense of higher time for insertions, deletions, and updates. Thus the file designer faces complex decisions which cannot be properly resolved without analyzing file contents, access requirements (e.g., logical complexity of queries), parameters of the particular higher-level file organization, and timing and storage characteristics of the software and hardware of the computer system used. Section 2.10 addressed the task of index selection. Section 2.11 reviewed the issues of performance.

The preceding data organizations are widely used in implementing and applying data bases made up of several interconnected files. Section 2.8 addressed the interconnection and accessing of related files.

REFERENCES

1. Dodd, G. D., "Elements of Data Management Systems," *Computing Surveys*, June 1969, pp. 117–133.
2. Lefkovitz, D., *File Structures for On-Line Systems*, Spartan Books, New York, 1969.
3. Bleir, R. F., "Treating Hierarchical Files in the SDC Time-Shared Data Management System TDMS," *Proceedings ACM National Conference*, 1967, pp. 41–49.
4. "SYSTEM 2000 Reference Manual," Intel Corp., Austin, Texas.
5. "ADABAS Reference Manual," Software AG, Reston, Virginia.
6. "Model 204 Reference Manual," Computer Corporation of America, Cambridge, Mass.
7. "DATACOM/DB Reference Manual," Applied Data Research Corporation, Princeton, N.J.
8. Anderson, H. D., "Optimal Selection of Secondary Indexes in Data Base Management Systems," Ph.D. Dissertation, SIS Department, Syracuse University, August 1973.
9. Lum, V. Y., and H. Ling, "An Optimization Problem on the Selection of Secondary Keys," *Proceedings, ACM National Conference*, 1971, pp. 349–356.
10. King, W. F., "On the Selection of Indices for a File," IBM Research Report, RJ1341, January 25, 1974, San Jose, Calif.

11. Lum, V. Y., "Multi-attribute Retrieval with Combined Indexes," *Communications of the ACM*, Vol. 13, No. 11, November 1970, pp. 660−665.

12. Stonebraker, M., "Retrieval Efficiency Using Combined Indexes," *Proceedings 1972 ACM SIGFIDET Workshop*, pp. 243−256.

13. Roberts, L. G., "Graphical Communication and Control Languages," in *Second Congress on Information System Sciences*, Spartan Books, Washington, D.C., 1964.

14. Sutherland, I. E., "Sketchpad: A Man-Machine Graphical Communication System," *Proceedings, Spring Joint Computer Conference*, 1963, Spartan Books, New York, pp. 329−345.

15. Sussenguth, E. H., "The Use of Tree Structures for Processing Files," *Communications of the ACM*, Vol. 6, No. 5, pp. 272−279.

16. Knuth, D. E., *The Art of Computer Programming*, Vol. 1, Addison-Wesley, Reading, Mass., 1969.

17. Cardenas, A. F., "Evaluation and Selection of File Organization—A Model and System," *Communications of the ACM*, Vol. 16, No. 9, September 1973, pp. 540−548.

18. Rotwitt, T., and P. A. D. deMaine, "Storage Optimization of Tree Structured Files Representing Descriptor Sets," *Proceedings, 1971 ACM SIGFIDET Workshop*, San Diego, Calif., November 11−12, 1971.

19. "Information Management System Virtual Storage (IMS/VS) Conversion Planning Guide," IBM Reference Manual, Form GH20-9034.

20. Lum, V. Y., "On the Selection of Secondary Indexes," *Proceedings 1974 ACM Conference*, San Diego, Calif., November 11−13, 1974.

21. Rothnie, J. B., and T. Lozano, "Attribute Based File Organization in a Paged Memory Environment," *Communications of the ACM*, Vol. 17, No. 2, February 1974, pp. 63−69.

22. Stanfel, L. E., "Tree Structures for Optimal Searching," *Journal of the ACM*, July 1970, Vol. 17, No. 3, pp. 508−517.

23. Bayer, R., and E. McCreight, "Organization and Maintenance of Large Ordered Indexes," *Acta Informatica*, Vol. 1, 1972, pp. 173−189.

24. Cardenas, A. F., and J. P. Sagamang, "Doubly-Chained Tree Data Base Organization—Analysis and Design Strategies," *The Computer Journal*, Great Britain, Vol. 20, No. 1, 1977, pp. 15−26.

25. Cardenas, A. F., "Analysis and Performance of Inverted Data Base Structures," *Communications of the ACM*, Vol. 18, No. 5, May 1975, pp. 253−263.

26. Williams, R., "A Survey of Data Structures for Computer Graphics Systems," *Computing Surveys*, March 1971, Vol. 3, No. 1, pp. 1−21.

27. *Proceedings ACM SIGGRAPH Workshop on Data Bases for Interactive Design*, Waterloo, Canada, September 15−17, 1975.

28. Cardenas, A. F., and R. W. Seeley, "A Simple Data Structure for Interactive Design/Drafting," *The Computer Journal*, Vol. 18, No. 1, 1975, pp. 30−33.

29. Schkolnick, M., "The Optimal Selection of Secondary Indices for Files," *Information Systems*, Vol. 1, 1975, pp. 141−146.

30. Kashyap, R. L., S. K. C. Subas, and S. B. Yao, "Analysis of the Multiple-Attribute Tree Data Base Organization," *IEEE Transactions on Software Engineering*, Vol. SE-3, No. 6, November 1977, pp. 451–467.

31. Yang, C. S., "A Class of Hybrid List File Organizations," *Information Systems*, Vol. 3, No. 1, 1978, pp. 49–58.

32. Liu, J. H., and S. B. Yao, "Multidimensional Clustering for Data Base Organizations," *Information Systems*, Vol. 2, No. 4, 1979, pp. 187–198.

33. Gopalakrishna, V., and C. E. Veni-Madharan, "Performance Evaluation of Attribute Based Tree Organization," *ACM Transactions on Database Systems*, Vol. 5, No. 1, March 1980, pp. 69–87.

34. Jakobsson, M., "Reducing Block Accesses in Inverted Files by Partial Clustering," *Information Systems*, Vol. 5, No. 1, 1980, pp. 1–5.

35. Pfaltz, J. L., W. J. Berman, and E. M. Cagley, "Partial Match Retrieval Using Indexed Descriptor Files," *Communications of the ACM*, Vol. 23, No. 9, September 1980, pp. 522–528.

36. Nagy, G., and S. Wagle, "Geographic Data Processing," *Computing Surveys*, Vol. 11, No. 2, June 1979, pp. 139–181.

37. Chock, M., A. F. Cardenas, and A. Klinger, "Manipulating Data Structures in Pictorial Information Systems," *Computer*, Vol. 14, No. 1, IEEE Computer Society, November 1981, pp. 43–50.

38. Comer, D., "The Ubiquitous B-tree," *Computing Surveys*, Vol. 11, No. 2, June 1979, pp. 121–137.

EXERCISES

1. Compare the multilist file organization with the inverted file organization with respect to the ease with which queries of the following types can be answered:

   (a) Are there any records in the file, where ⟨qualification part⟩?

   (b) How many records are there in the file, where ⟨qualification part⟩?

   Which of these file organizations would you choose for these types of queries? Why?

2. Suppose that the usage statistics of a file show that two fields, A and B, are by far the most frequently used as a basis for logically qualifying the desired records. Field A can have only one of three values, a_1, a_2, a_3, and field B can have only one of three values, b_1, b_2, and b_3 in a given record. Field A is seldom updated, whereas field B is updated very frequently by about half of the queries in which the field is involved. Would you invert on field A? On field B? Justify and explain your reasoning carefully.

3. Organize the following data records as a fully ringed structure (as in Figure 2.13).

NAME	OFFICE	DISCIPLINE	AGE
Baker	New York	Audit	29
Jones	New York	Audit	40
Stanley	Chicago	O.R.	23
Zook	Chicago	O.R.	36

4. Examine the fully ringed organization in Figure 2.13. Indicate carefully the steps that would be best to take in order to service the following requests:

   (a) For every department obtain a list of the names of its employees.

   (b) Obtain a list of the names of the employees who are between 25 and 30 years old and who hold Ph.D. degrees.

   (c) Delete all the information about the employee ASH.

   (d) How many employees are there who are in the MATH department and who are under 30 years old?

5. Consider the following data values in a subset of records in a file. Draw up the corresponding doubly-chained tree structure for (a) minimum storage space and for (b) maximum storage space. Show all links between the tree nodes.

Field Names

A	N	R
A	N	S
B	N	S
B	N	R
B	M	T
C	M	W
D	M	Z

Records

6. Consider the following statement: "Doubly-chained structured representation of a set of records always occupies more storage than the original set of records consecutively (physically) organized." Is this statement true? Always? Is it false? Always? Does it make any difference how you structure the index? Explain clearly, illustrating with carefully selected examples. For examples use the following file:

Field names

...A	N	R
...A	N	S
...B	N	S
...B	N	R
...B	M	T
...C	M	W
...D	M	Z

Records

7. Fill in the blanks (with *more*, *less*, *the same*, *does not change*) as is appropriate (assume the same list length or uniform distributions):
   (a) In the doubly-chained structure, queries referring to keys near the top of the index structure tend to take _____ average access time, compared to those involving keys near the bottom. Update type of queries involving updating of keys near the top of the index structure tend to take _____ average access time compared to those involving keys near the bottom.
   (b) In the inverted file structure, queries referring to subset X of the inverted keys result in _____ average access time compared to those referring to subset Y. (Keys X plus Y make up the whole index.) Assume the inverted structure discussed.

8. Examine the data base in Figure 2.18 and the record linkage or access paths available. For each of the following queries indicate the best access paths to follow in order to answer the query. Justify your choice.
   (a) Obtain the names of the VENDOR companies that are located in NEW YORK and supply STEEL BARS 4″ × 5″.
   (b) Obtain a list of the PURCHASE ORDER records that involve STEEL BARS 4″ × 5″.
   (c) Obtain the names of the VENDOR companies from which STEEL BARS 4″ × 5″ have been ordered with QTY-ORDERED (in the PURCHASE ORDER file) ⩾ 500.

9. What potential performance advantages or disadvantages does the cellular multilist organization provide with respect to the multilist and ring organizations? Also consider the possibility of using multiple CPUs or microprocessors to enhance high performance (access-time wise); how would multiple CPUs help, if at all?

10. Consider the possibility of inverting on combined key-values. As an example, for three inverted fields one would invert on all three key-values combined, that is, a single list pointing to records with all three key-values. This is in contrast to inverting each of the three fields individually, that is, having three lists, one for each individual key. What are the advantages and disadvantages of inverting on combined key-values? Explain. Overall, is it worth it?

3

DATA BASE CONCEPTS AND ARCHITECTURE

3.1   INTRODUCTION

The late 1960s and early 1970s witnessed a number of milestones in data management technology, as the growing number of computer users demanded and could afford more encompassing, powerful, and efficient data management systems. Many large information systems (e.g., parts management systems, accounts management systems) were developed. Organizations began the road toward computerizing *and* integrating a number of application systems and their associated large files, and making them available to a growing and maturing user community. Enterprising user companies, mainframe vendors, software houses, and university groups started identifying and facing the challenge of data independence between application programs and stored data, data shareability among many users, nonredundancy of information, relatability of data, performance and efficiency, security, integrity, and so forth. Generalized File Management Systems (GFMS) and then Generalized Data Base Management Systems (GDBMS) and Generalized Data Base/Data Communications (DB/DC) Systems came into being. CODASYL presented its Data Base Task Group (DBTG) Report in 1971 as the basis for subsequent systems.

The purpose of this chapter is to:

1. Trace the milestones and development of data management technology.

2. Show the functional relationship of basic file management, report writers, GFMS, GDBMS, generalized DB/DC systems, operating systems, and application programs and users.

3. Present the main goals and concepts of data base technology, namely: data independence, data shareability, nonredundancy of information, relatability, integrity, security, performance and efficiency, and administration and control.

4. Outline data description, data manipulation, and query language principles.

5. Introduce alternative logical data base models: hierarchic, network, and relational.

6. Outline the constituents of data management systems, their architectural levels using the formal framework of DIAM (Data Independent Accessing Model), and discuss the realms and issues involved.

7   Outline the entity-relationship-attribute (ERA) data base model.

In order to derive an appreciation and better understanding of the data base concepts to be introduced now, the reader should have an understanding of (1) the basic file management technology commonly available in operating systems via programming language (COBOL, FORTRAN IV, etc.), and (2) the technology presented in the previous chapter. However, this chapter, with the exception of the deeper discussion of the architectural levels of data management systems using the DIAM framework, will not presume microscopic knowledge of the many specific details involved.

3.2 CHRONOLOGY AND FUNCTIONAL RELATIONSHIP OF DATA MANAGEMENT SYSTEMS

The main milestone of early data management technology was the development of COBOL by CODASYL around 1960. Among its main benefits, and there are many that the reader realizes, was the identification and separation of (1) data manipulation and (2) data and file description at the program level. **Data manipulation** facilities are those used to process data in core. OPEN, CLOSE, READ, WRITE, and any other statements for I/O of data between main storage and external storage sometimes are usually included in this category, although not always. In a growing number of cases, due to CODASYL's 1971 DBTG report, the data manipulation language is considered to be made up of only I/O statements (Confusing, is it not?) **Data description** facilities are all those for describing the in-core data structures, external data structures and their aggregations as external files. The development of higher-level languages, especially COBOL for data management, is indeed one of the most significant developments in the history of computing technology.

The COBOL implementations of the early sixties were found to need a number of additions beyond those in the COBOL report which served as the basis for COBOL implementations. The primary ones were SORT packages and report writers. A **SORT package** is a very specialized module implementing some algorithm for sorting the records of a large file, and perhaps sorting and merging together multiples files.

A **report writer** is a program or utility that provides many facilities for editing output, tallying, formatting, and other related tasks needed to generate more complex reports; these facilities go beyond the primitive ones defined as part of the standard of a language. Some vendors have marketed SORT packages and report writers as attachments to various language implementations. Packages of the attachment type are often called **utilities**. See Figure 3.1. In the mid-1960s CODASYL revised COBOL and included SORT as a new verb in standard COBOL.

A number of so-called **report program generators** were actually developed before and during the COBOL beginnings. Today, the primary one is

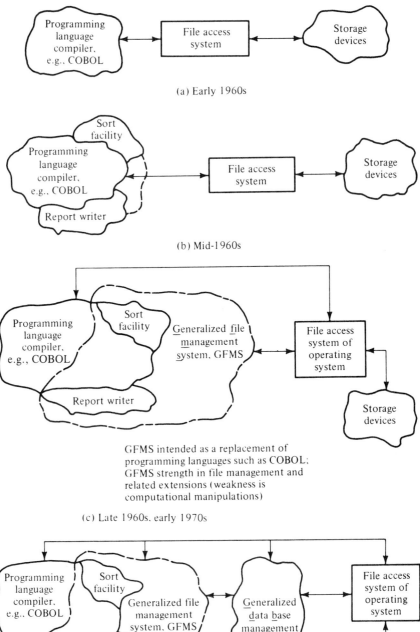

(a) Early 1960s

(b) Mid-1960s

GFMS intended as a replacement of
programming languages such as COBOL;
GFMS strength in file management and
related extensions (weakness is
computational manipulations)

(c) Late 1960s, early 1970s

(d) Early 1970s on

Figure 3.1. *Chronological development of data management technology*

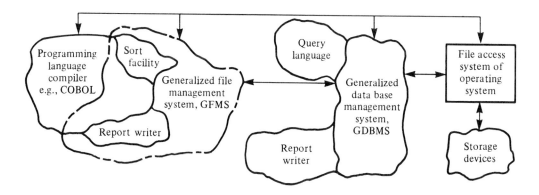

(e) Early 1980s on

Figure 3.1. continued

RPG (Report Program Generator) which includes primitive facilities of both COBOL and report writers plus some attractive facilities for file retrieval and updating not available in COBOL. RPG was and is used significantly in smaller computing systems for less complex file-oriented applications. For example, RPG II was practically the only programming language in the highly successful System/3 of IBM in the 1970s.

In the late 1960s and early 1970s, **generalized file management systems** were developed. These systems integrate various facilities of programming languages, report writers, report program generators, and SORT packages with a number of other useful data management facilities into a self-contained system. Functionally, as outlined in Figure 3.1, they can perform most of what COBOL can do plus a lot more in areas where COBOL is weakest, namely, I/O and report writing. Their intent is to replace COBOL and any other COBOL-like programming language in I/O-bound applications and commu nicate directly with the basic file management facilities of a host operating system for:

1. File and record definition;
2. File creation;
3. File retrieval;
4. File updating;
5. File manipulation;
6. File maintenance;
7. Sorting/merging, and
8. Report writing.

The language of most GFMS is a high-level forms-oriented programming language with powerful operators to perform these functions easily without incurring the burden of programming in conventional languages. A hierarchical order would place GFMS at the top, then COBOL-like programming languages, and then assembly language.

Informatics Inc. introduced the first successful and lasting full-fledged system in the late 1960s. Its current system, Mark IV,[2,3] is used in over one thousand installations. Applications Software Inc's ASI-ST[4] is another GFMS introduced in the late 1960s, and currently it is second to Mark IV in number of users. These and other GFMS usually come in three versions: one which is only a powerful report writer, an intermediate system, and the full-fledged system. Other popular GFMS are Data Analyzer[1] and EASYTRIEVE.

GFMS generally operate like an application program (many are written in FORTRAN, or FORTRAN and assembly language) on a host programming and operating system, and use the available access methods. Through GFMS languages, the programmer and also the nonprogramming-oriented user (who cannot deal with COBOL or FORTRAN-like languages) can specify, for example, retrieval of records on the basis of almost any logical expression using any data items of the record structure, without the limitations, burden, and concern of its particular sequencing (if records are stored as sequential tape files) or particular single access key (if records are stored in random or in indexed sequential files on direct access devices). Some of the techniques in Chapter 2 are used in very limited degree in implementing GFMS; the files are organized as per the basic file options of the operating system and are usually searched exhaustively to produce any report.

Reported productivity gains (in terms of programming manpower to implement and maintain application systems and produce reports) using GFMS instead of COBOL, FORTRAN, and PL/1 in I/O-oriented applications are typically in the order of from 4 to 1 to as much as 15 to 1 depending on the application;[4] ratios from about 6 to 1 and 8 to 1 are most often cited. As shown in Figure 3.1 functionally, GFMS do not do everything that COBOL-like languages do. The best GFMS include from roughly 60 to 80 percent of COBOL's facilities and exclude number-crunching commands. GFMS are designed to cover roughly 60 to 90 percent of complex file management needs of commercial data processing.Thus GFMS are not intended to be a total replacement for higher-level languages. GFMS are strongest where COBOL and others are weakest, namely, file management, and weakest where COBOL and others are strongest, namely, complex arithmetic and in-core record processing.

Most GFMS provide interface points to programs written in programming languages for more complex manipulations. For example, ASI-ST has an "own code module" that permits up to 25 exits to programs written in COBOL, PL/1, FORTRAN, or IBM assembler language.[4] Today's top GFMS are very efficient and in many cases may take even less machine time than an equivalent program in a conventional language.

In the late 1960s the need for integration of large files into a data base and the need for many users and/or application programs to access it effectively and efficiently led to the early data base management systems efforts. Conventional file structures were inadequate for such demanding environments and resulted in burdens in processing time as well as excessive auxiliary storage requirements. GFMS, limited by the conventional single-file structures of their host operating systems, were also inadequate. Various large organizations developed in-house systems using file structures of the type described in Chapter 2 and interconnecting such files to form data bases. Mainframe vendors and software houses started on the road toward today's generalized systems. The pioneering concepts and facilities were introduced by General Electric's IDS (Integrated Data Store) System[5] in the mid-1960s. It extended COBOL to permit definition of interconnected or chained aggregations of data and files. It was the first network model of data. System Development Corporation's fully inverted system TDMS (Time-shared Data Management System)[6] was another pioneer in the mid-1960s toward today's inverted hierarchic GDBMS.

IBM and North American Aviation (now Rockwell International), faced with the problem of managing the vast information related to the Apollo moon program in the late 1960s, started the project toward what would become in the 1970s IBM's IMS (Information Management System)[7] and also the first large-scale and generalized Data Base/Data Communications (DB/DC) System IMS DB/DC. A *DB/DC* system is one in which the data base and the data communication (or teleprocessing) facilities have been highly developed in an integrated basis over and above those of a host operating system. Other DB/DC systems followed in the 1970s, notably Cincom's TOTAL (the GDBMS) plus ENVIRON/1 (the generalized DC system).

In the late 1960s, a dedicated group of voluntary representatives from computer and software manufacturers, users in U.S. government and industry, and university researchers embarked in producing the milestone 1971 DBTG (Data Base Task Group) Report published in early 1971.[8] This proposed standard for GDBMS has become the basis for a growing number of systems. The DBTG system is the prime exponent of the network architecture, pioneered by IDS. Details of the historical evolution of GDBMS appear in reference 18.

Figure 3.1(d) summarizes the main functional relationships of data management systems in the 1970s and 1980s:

1. Application programs in a conventional procedural programming language communicate with the GDBMS or DB/DC system via an appropriate language interface provided by the system.

2. Application programs in a high-level GFMS language communicate

with the GDBMS via an appropriate interface usually provided with the GFMS.

3. A very high-level query language particular to each GDBMS or DB/DC system is generally available for fast, low-volume data accessing.

In addition, the functional relationships outlined earlier [portrayed in Figures 3.1(a), (b), and (c)] continue to hold. Thus, as an example of the advanced state of flexibility, an ASI-ST application program can communicate via ASI-ST interfaces with: (1) an applicaton program in COBOL, FORTRAN, PL/1, or BAL; (2) the conventional file management methods of the host operating system (IBM 360/370, 30XX and 4XXX systems); and (3) TOTAL or IMS.

GDBMS and DB/DC systems generally rely on an external conventional language, or on a GFMS language, to perform data manipulation in core. However, systems that have been extended from COBOL (like IDS and the DBTG proposals) could be considered to have their own data manipulation facilities. Almost all GDBMS and DB/DC do have some in-core data manipulation capability, however minor it might be. For example, a number of functions or processing modules are included in many GDBMS to compute, for example, maximum, minimum, average, or standard deviation of the desired records.

A GDBMS or DB/DC system permits the use of *transaction*-oriented languages, as well as of a nonprocedural English-flavored query language of its own. See Figure 3.2. The **language interface** function supports communication

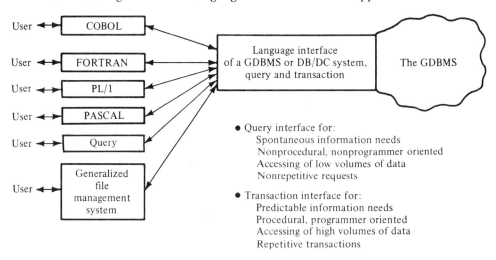

Figure 3.2.   *The language interface of a generalized data base management system*

of the GDBMS or DB/DC system with conventional programming languages, perhaps GFMS languages, and with its own query language. The **query interface** and its associated query language are designed to:

1. Handle spontaneous on-line information retrieval;
2. Provide a convenient nonprocedural, English-flavored, and non-programmer-oriented means to use the system;
3. Handle low volumes of data;
4. Access subsets of the data base satisfying a set of data content qualifications specified by the user; and
5. Service nonrepetitive and unrelated I/O requests

The **transaction interface** is designed to permit using a conventional programming language to:

1. Handle predictable information retrieval;
2. Support procedural, programmer-oriented requests;
3. Handle large volumes of data I/O; and
4. Service repetitive and related I/O requests, e.g., batch them.

3.3 CONCEPTS AND OBJECTIVES OF DATA BASE TECHNOLOGY

We will now introduce the main concepts and objectives of data base management systems. These objectives reflect the pressing needs of the modern data processing community (be it business or nonbusiness applications):

1. Data independence,
2. Data shareability,
3. Nonredundancy,
4. Relatability,
5. Integrity,
6. Access flexibility,
7. Security,
8. Performance and efficiency, and
9. Administration and control.

There are various tones and shades to a number of these objectives. They have been studied and debated a great deal by a growing number of people. Data base systems available achieve these objectives in various degrees and forms. There are no industry-wide standards, although CODASYL's DBTG

1971 report[8] has succeeded as the standard for many commercial data base systems. The 1971 DBTG report[8] and the 1971 GUIDE/SHARE report[9] on data base requirements (both written by committees of devoted individuals) are the documented milestones of concepts and proposals for modern data base technology.

GFMS and basic report writers do not achieve most of these objectives. As they evolve, some GFMS tend to offer some of these objectives to a limited degree, e.g., file security.

Data Independence

The concept of **data independence** is central to the data base approach. It denotes independence or insulation of an application program from the specific logical organization or physical organization and storage considerations of the data structures and files which it uses. Any changes in logical or physical organization or physical access paths should neither require changes in the application programs nor have a disastrous impact on them. Conversely, changes in the application program should not affect file structures.

Data independence encompasses the insensitivity of an application program to *changes* in:

1. The location of data (e.g., track x versus track y);
2. Physical representation (how data is actually represented in storage devices);
3. Physical data organization (e.g., inverted organization versus doubly-chained tree);
4. Access paths available (e.g., particular fields inverted);
5. Particular storage devices used (e.g., disk type A versus disk type B); and
6. Other independent programs sharing any of the program's data files.

Programs should not be subject to the impact of influences external to them. The ability to change the physical data organization without making obsolete the application programs is termed **physical data independence**. The ability of an application program to continue executing correctly using its own view of the data base in spite of changes to other parts of the whole logical data base is called **logical data independence**. The term data independence thus refers generally to both logical and physical data independence. Still, there are many degrees of data independence. There is no industry-wide standard to measure or scale the degree of data independence.

File management available in conventional operating systems via programming languages (sequential, ISAM, random) has suffered from the inability to provide data independence. Specifically, the following serious drawbacks may be cited. This is not an exhaustive list by any means and the reader may have experiences to add to it.

1. Modification or rearrangement of record levels in any of the files used by an application program necessitates both reloading of the file and modification and recompilation of the program and of any others using the file. For example, this is the case even if just the position of the fields AGE and DEGREE in the EMPLOYEE record description of Figure 2.4 are exchanged. This could be considered a rearrangement in the logical structure but not in logical content of the record.

2. Modification of the name, data type, or length of any of the elementary data items of records in a file requires reloading as well as modifying the record descriptions in every program using the file.

3. The "one-file one-program" tendency. A change in the logical record description of a file involves reloading the whole file and modifying and recompiling every program using that file. Conversely, a change in the record description at the program level requires changing and reloading the file involved. For example, a new application program needing to see and access only a subset of elementary data items in the file must conform to the one and only record description established by the program that loaded the file. All application programs must have exactly the same view of the file even if some of them do not need or should not have access to all fields.

4. Additions of more than one instance of an elementary data item or substructure in a record requires reloading the file and modifying and recompiling all programs using the file. This is the case if it is desired to store more than one DEGREE for employees in the EMPLOYEE file of Figure 2.4.

5. Extending the maximum permitted number of instances of an array of items or of a repeating group, beyond the number indicated when the file was loaded, may require that the file be reloaded and all related programs modified and recompiled. This may be the case, for example, if the number of occurrences of a repeating group needs to be increased.

6. Addition of a new data element to records necessitates reloading the file and modifying and recompiling all application programs using that file.

7. Change in the access key-name in I/O statements in the application program referring to ISAM or random access files requires either reloading the file to have the new access key-name or changing the logic or access strategy of the application program.

Note that many of these drawbacks are the result of *change*. These kinds of changes occur often in actual practice due to unforeseen requirements or just changes of mind. They always will occur occasionally, if not often. Note that these changes occur completely independent of any machine or efficiency considerations.

A large number of changes in the physical structure of a file could also be contemplated for efficiency considerations and for integrating other programs with the program using the file. For example, changing the blocking factor, changing a field representation from a decimal number to a binary number, or changing the fixed-length physical records to variable length. These generally require changing the file and/or record description in the application program and recompiling. Changing the sort key of the file or the access key in ISAM or other direct organization disrupts the associated application programs much more.

The seriousness of all these problems becomes intolerable when inter-connected multifile information systems are involved. For example, consider these problems in the realm of the four interconnected files in Figures 2.16 and 2.18.

A further complication that has been experienced and is being lived at many places is that application and systems programmers have not shielded sufficiently the logic and workings of application programs from physical structuring, access path considerations, and storage structures. Thus in many application systems a change in the existence of a pointer at the data structure level, for example, deleting the pointer from ACCOUNTS PAYABLE to VENDOR in Figures 2.16 and 2.18, will put out of order programs making explicit use of this pointer field in the ACCOUNTS PAYABLE file.

Data base technology strives to provide as much data independence as possible. There are various degrees of data independence provided by GDBMS. We shall explore this in more detail in later chapters and will show that many powerful data base systems still do open the door for application programmers to tie down the working of a program to the data base structures supported by the system. It should be stressed that there is no complete data independence since an application program cannot be shielded from *all* possible changes. The data management specialist must be aware of how data-independent a particular data management system is. What possible changes in physical file organization or location affect application programs? What changes in the data formats, record structures, relationships or access paths, and basic access methods necessitate application program modification? What kind and how extensive a modification?

Some may ask what is so bad about having to modify data declarations and processing commands dependent on them in an application program and/or data declarations in a file load program. Plenty. The costs of initial program development are high enough. Worse yet is reprogramming: it involves understanding in detail the program to be modified; a change in a small portion of the program may involve changes in other unsuspecting portions; the programmer making the modification may not be the original programmer and thus may have the added burden of a different programming approach than his or her own; documentation of the program has to be changed; and so forth. Maintenance costs are staggering in terms of direct manpower dollars, delays, disruption of other processes that depend on what is being reprogrammed, and opportunity losses (inability to derive benefits from new applications that would be implemented if reprogramming of old ones were not being incurred). The largest portion of the EDP budget of a typical installation goes to software and related aspects, not to hardware directly. Since the 1960s, a larger and larger portion is unfortunately being spent on program maintenance at the expense of added capabilities to existing application systems or developing new systems. Thus, the significance of achieving a high degree of data independence is evident. Data independence is a key ingredient to the modular and fast evolution of modern information systems and applications.

Data Shareability

The concept of **data shareability** goes back in the literature for many years. The idea is to be able to have different application programs share independently an integrated data base. Some applications may not be planned until after the completion and installation of other applications operating upon common data. Such programs require the ability to operate unaware of each other's existence. Provision of multiple concurrent views of the same data, control over access, control over intereffects among independent programs, efficient access mechanisms to different subsets of the files and fields, and a host of other related needs must be provided.

A great deal of the lack of efficient data sharing in classical file management is caused by the data dependence drawbacks outlined previously, for example, the inability of a program to see and share only a subset of data elements in a file used by another program. As a data base grows and as the number of users of it increases, it becomes more imperative to access efficiently only those subsets of interest to a particular program.

Nonredundancy

The traditional way of doing things, namely, collecting and coding data for specific programs and thereby "gluing" data more or less permanently and exclusively to those programs, has resulted in costly redundancy of records and files across the application systems involved (e.g., an accounts receivable system, a raw material inventory system). This traditional "one-file one program" evil has been the result of a number of technological drawbacks, especially, lack of data independence.

Let us trace the typical scenario which leads to costly data redundancy. A company develops a single application system, let us say, an accounts payable system AP. It uses three data files: F1 containing data elements a, b, and c; F2 containing d, e, and f; and F3 containing g, h, i, and j. Refer to Figure 3.3. Now the company wishes to develop a second system, let us say, a purchase order control system PO. It uses two files, F1 containing data elements a, b, and c and F4 containing e, f, i, and k. The developers of PO negotiate the use of file F1 with those in charge of the AP system who own the F1 file. Note that F4 is to include elements e and f already carried in file F2 and element i carried in F3. The possibility of forming a new file FN containing all of F2 and F3 plus k to be shared by AP and PO does not materialize because of a number of headaches. First, if FN is formed, then the application program(s) AP has to be modified to reflect the whole structure of the new file FN. Second, AP's staff does not want to keep track of any extraneous data such as k which is the direct concern of those in charge of PO. Third, the cycle of use of file F4 is different from that of F2 and F3, and some conflicts arise with respect to coordination of use of FN by the two applications, responsibility of control of integrity and security of data, and so forth. The headaches are just too many, so PO's staff develops file F4 all for itself and thus data elements, e, f, and i are now carried in two different places. Soon thereafter at any point in time, the values of e, f, and i may not be the same in both places due to differences in use by AP and PO, differences in updating cycle, or in interest in their accuracy.

A third application, let us say, a reporting and control system of raw material inventory RMI, is then developed. Similar situations arise as before and the end result might be a new file F5 with elements a, b, l, and m, thus duplicating a and b appearing in the file F1. See Figure 3.3. Other applications may be developed leading to the same problem.

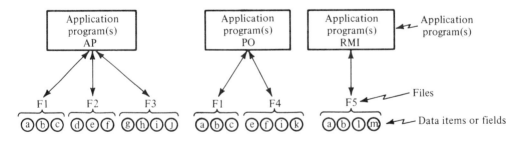

Redundancies: a, b, e, f, i twice

Figure 3.3. *The traditional approach to programs and data leading to redundancy of data stored*

After a few applications have been computerized in conventional practice, experience shows that there is a tremendous problem of redundancy which invariably causes inconsistency of data accuracy, format, and naming. Even if all administrative and cooperation problems that may have hindered the initial efforts to integrate the systems are eliminated, the problems of application reprogramming and redocumentation and of programming to control and coordinate the use of a shared data bank by many demanding programs (and others expected to join in) are gigantic.

Redundancy tends to grow. Its expense is very high for any sizable company. The worst feature is that the longer a company follows the traditional pattern and keeps adding new programs and redundant files of data, structured specifically and solely for those programs, the greater the task it must face when it finally assembles most or all its data in a single data base management system. Inconsistency of data is a major plague in large companies.

The goal of data base systems to permit and foster centralization and integration of all data of a set of applications into a data bank; that is, turn the situation in Figure 3.3 into that of Figure 3.4 showing the removal of redundancy. All data elements used by a group of programs and/or people should be centralized and shareable with proper control.

The removal of redundancy is a road leading to shareability. When two different applications need the same data item and they do not share it, redundancy results. However, some redundancy may be necessary in a data base environment irrespective of shareability problems. Some redundancy of data items inverted may be necessary to avoid excessive access time to records. True, redundancies entail the maintenance problems of ensuring that redundant information is consistent. The point that is being made here is that the intent of data base thinking is to eliminate redundancy as much as possible, and where it is convenient to incur redundancy for efficiency or internal GDBMS

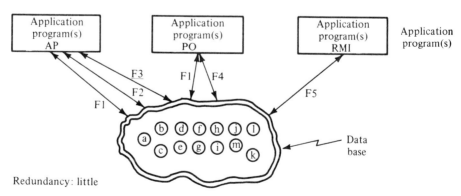

Figure 3.4.   *The data base approach to programs and data avoiding much redundancy of data stored*

reasons, then the application programmers and users are shielded from knowing and worrying about it. In the case of recovery/backup, the application
programmer must deal with a redundant image of all transactions from a
certain point in time onward, as well as with a copy of the entire data space at
that point, in order to be able to back up and recover the data, should there be a
problem.

Data Relatability

Data relatability is a term often used, but, unfortunately, not with the
same meaning by all concerned. However, in the large majority of cases it is
used to denote the property of the existence of relationships among different
logical records. A record represents a real-world concept about which information is recorded,* and has a number of attributes, e.g., name, address, department, and salary for an employee record. **Relationships** exist among records;
for example, children of a parent, degrees of an alumnus, skills of an employee.
Relationships are as important and as identifiable as any record and data
attribute, and must be definable and unambiguously managed by a data base
system such that other associations may be derived, for example, employees
with a given skill. Figure 3.5 shows by means of the pointed arrows the

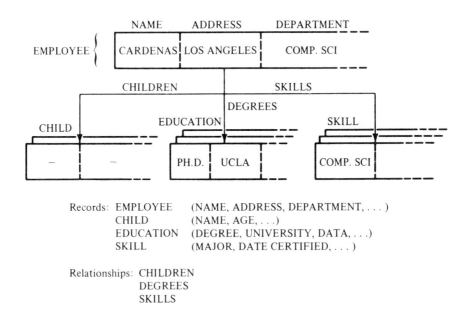

```
Records: EMPLOYEE    (NAME, ADDRESS, DEPARTMENT, . . . )
         CHILD       (NAME, AGE, . . .)
         EDUCATION   (DEGREE, UNIVERSITY, DATA, . . .)
         SKILL       (MAJOR, DATE CERTIFIED, . . . )

Relationships: CHILDREN
               DEGREES
               SKILLS
```

Figure 3.5. *Data relatability (relationships) in a data base*

*The term **entity** is frequently used in place of the conventional term "record" in reference
to this definition. We will address "entity" terminology in Sections 3.8 and 3.9.

relationships that may exist in an employee data base containing four record types.

The ability of defining relationships between records at the logical level just as conveniently as defining records is a major objective of data base technology. We will subsequently discuss various types of relationships and ways of representing them at the logical and physical levels.

Integrity

With many different users sharing the same data and now with all the relationships involved, it is impossible for each user to be responsible for the consistency of the values in the data base and for maintaining the relationships of the data items that users see to all other data items, some of which may be unknown to them or prohibited for them to access. A major task of a data base system it to maintain control over and preserve the integrity of the data base. The term **integrity** has evolved to refer to the coordination of data accessing by different programs, propagation of update of values to other copies and dependent values, and ensuring the validity of data (such as consistency checks and input and output editing).

Preservation of integrity includes also maintaining an **audit trail**, i.e., a log or record of all accesses and changes to every data item at every point in time in which an access or change takes place and of the interaction of programs and data, so that integrity may be *recovered* if an error is later detected. Integrity controls include **recovery controls**.

Access Flexibility

Access flexibility refers to the property of being able to access data easily and efficiently in a variety of ways. It is a loose term that includes: the ability to access data on the basis of any access keys and logical qualification (instead of being restricted to easy access only via the single sort or access key of basic access methods); the ability to use a query language that is nonprogrammer-oriented and English-flavored to efficiently browse through the data base in an immediate access mode; the ability for a program in a conventional programming language to use the data base and efficiently access any subset of the data; and the ability to use a number of mechanisms for much needed access control and data base administration.

Security

A data base management system must have the proper mechanisms to assign, control, and remove the rights of access (read, change, insert, delete) of any users to any data items. The system must ensure the security of data. Certain items, combinations of items, or selection of items may be sensitive and require high levels of authorization to access. Different persons may be constrained to see different selections of the data; for example, personnel data except medical or salary fields. Access control on the basis of data content may be necessary at times; for example, read-only permission for user X for only those records where salary ≤$30,000.

As the amount of data shared in the data base and the number of user programs increase, the task of the system to ensure security increases. A data item must be fully protected from unauthorized intrusion, be it accidental or malicious, by any user or application program. The data base administrator must have facilities to assign and control access privileges of users.

There may be an arbitrary and nebulous dividing line in some cases between integrity and security. For example, the protection of data against accidental, rather than malicious, changes may fall under either integrity or security. Security is concerned with malicious and unauthorized actions on a data base.

Performance and Efficiency

Good performance and efficiency of a data base system are major requirements in view of the large size of data bases. Every facility that must be implemented to support the objectives that have been stated is an additional burden to data base management system design, organization, implementation, *and* performance. The attractiveness and viability of a feature for a user are highly dependent on the performance and efficiency (cost) involved.

The need for sophisticated and efficient physical organization and management of data is magnified by the increase of data placed in the data base, relationships, number of application programs, query requests, and other demands. Note that the greater the data base and the number of users (individuals in on-line consoles using a query language, as well as transaction programs), the greater the likelihood that a smaller percentage of the whole data base is of concern to any one user. Thus classical inefficient and exhaustive searching using conventional data management facilities of operating systems is intolerable.

The higher-level data organization technology outlined in Chapter 2 has been an important development for implementing efficient physical organizations to support the logical requirements. At the same time, sequential processing of selected subsets of the data base must be possible with efficiency comparable to that if the subset were just a stand-alone sequential file. Figure 2.1 shows the hierarchy of data management facilities. Inverted organizations are highly oriented for efficiency of data accessing and are the basic structure of a number of commercial GDBMS.

A data base also magnifies the performance problems of change. Changes in the data base contents and transaction load are a fact of life. Access time, storage space, and throughput in general suffer with change in a much more complex and more difficult way to understand than when a simple file is involved. In the discussion of data independence we mentioned various degrees of independence or insulation of a program from the data stored. If due to a change only in the nature of the transactions (e.g., accessing records using different keys but involving no change in either application programs, fields used by the program, or stored data) access time performance becomes intolerable (and it does happen in GDBMS), is this a violation of data independence? The application program will still work but the access time to data is intolerably costly. Many say that this is not a violation of data independence; others say that it is.

A data base system ideally should have the ability to *tune*, *reorganize*, or *reinitialize* a portion of the data base or the whole data base so as to maintain an acceptable level of performance and efficiency under current priorities and demands. The 1971 GUIDE/SHARE report and other more recent writings state that a data base system must be able to measure itself as time goes by and reorganize itself so as to maintain an optimum level of performance for each user. This automation is an ideal goal, but unfortunately unattainable for several years to come. There are a large number of performance parameters and interrelationships involved that need to be understood first by designers of GDBMS. Furthermore, many users have different requirements over the same data, which cause performance conflicts (e.g., a group of users may need read-only access to some data, while another group needs to update it mostly). Thus, only the overall good could be optimized. Some applications might suffer in performance for the good of others.

Administration and Control

A crucial ingredient to the introduction of data base concepts and software in any enterprise is data base administration and control. Responsibility for the control and description of data must not be diffused among the many application programmers and analysts. It must be centralized on a **Data Base Administrator**, **DBA**, which could be one or several individuals. Descriptions and control of data stored must be factored out from the application programs (a basic notion of data independence), and must be declared in a manner common or compatible to all application systems and common programming languages. Overall data base design, data declarations, and the road map for users to use data are now the responsibility of the data base design−administration function using specialized data description, data control languages, and other needed facilities. Determination of performance and efficiency levels must take into account the overall good and thus resides in the data base administration function.

We will defer to Chapter 13 a summary of many of the responsibilities often attributed to the growing and maturing function of data base design—administration. These responsibilities will be pointed out throughout the following sections and chapters.

Dollars and Cents Benefit of Achieving Data Base Objectives

As we now delve into details in the following sections and chapters, let us make sure that we do not lose track of the benefit that all the previous objectives of data base technology seek in the overall sense: more productivity and more benefit per dollar invested. The development, integration, and maintenance of application systems (e.g., an order entry system, an inventory control system) are enhanced, tremendously in many cases. Many information systems could not exist today at all were it not for GDBMS. The return on the investment is much higher when data base technology is judiciously used. The total DP expenditures may not be lower after data base technology is used, since typically what happens is that the rate at which new application systems are developed increases. Another truth is that data base technology may mean the difference between being able and not being able to develop sophisticated and integrated application systems. Much of the emergence of the **management information system function** in modern organizations is due to the ability of developing data bases and integrated information systems.

3.4 SCHEMA, SUBSCHEMAS, AND RELATIONSHIPS

Fundamental and common to all data base systems is the ability to:

1. Define the logical structure of every instance of data that makes up the data base. This logical structure is called the **schema** or **logical data base description** (we will use these two terms interchangeably throughout the text, as is done in practice) and is defined via a special schema definition language by a data base designer or administrator. Several independent data bases may be defined.

2. Define and control access to any logical subset of the data base. The logical structure or description of this subset is commonly called a **subschema** or **view**. It is an application program or programmer's view of the logical description of his or her file(s) or data base, while in reality it is a subset of the global schema shared by a number of programs. Any number of subschemas can be defined on a schema; any number of programs can share a subschema; and different subschemas can overlap.

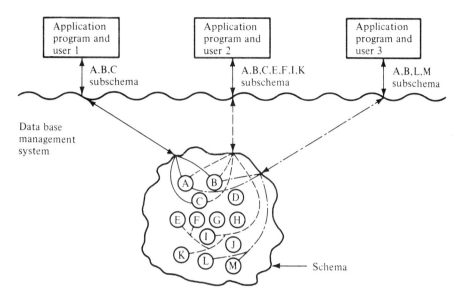

Fields or elementary items: A,B,C, . . .
Schema: the set of all A,B,C. . . . fields and their relationships
Subschema: a subset of A,B,C. . . . and their relationships
Physical data base: the set of all instances
   of A,B,C. . . . physically stored.

Figure 3.6. *Schema and subschemas*

Figure 3.6 shows this conceptually. The terms schema and subschema were originally introduced by CODASYL in the 1971 DBTG report.[8] A few practitioners and vendors use different terms for similar concepts. For example, IBM's IMS term for the schema is **physical data base description**; a subschema is termed the **sensitivity** of a particular application program or programmer. The terms logical data base description and schema predominate in actual practice. We use either term in this text.

Let us illustrate a schema, subschemas, and other important concepts with a specific example. Figure 3.7 shows as a schema a set of records of different structure shown interconnected by solid lines. This type of diagram is commonly used to denote schemas and subschemas. Of course, this has to be mapped by an individual into the equivalent formal definition in the data description language. Each record type is also called an **entity**. Each entity contains an arbitrary number of data items or fields, also called **attributes**. A solid line represents the relationship between one record and another. As stated earlier, a **relationship** is an indication of how a record is related to another. The relationship is as important and as definable as any attribute or record. In the CODASYL DBTG terminology a relationship is called a **set**.

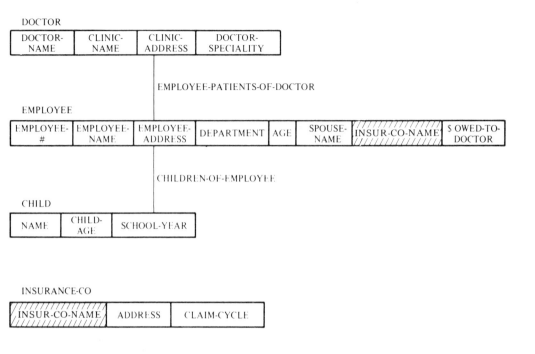

Schema contains: Four records—DOCTOR, EMPLOYEE, CHILD, INSURANCE-CO
Two explicit relationships— EMPLOYEE-PATIENTS-OF-DOCTOR
and CHILDREN-OF-EMPLOYEE
One implicit relationship— between EMPLOYEE and
INSURANCE-CO since INSUR-CO-NAME
appears in both records

Figure 3.7. *Example of a schema*

The DOCTOR record is connected to the record EMPLOYEE via the relationship EMPLOYEE_PATIENTS_OF_DOCTOR. The EMPLOYEE record is in turn connected to its CHILD(ren) via the CHILDREN_OF _EMPLOYEE relationship. Note that the record INSURANCE_CO is all by itself without an explicit solid line connection to other records. However, the EMPLOYEE record is definitely related to it, implicitly, via the attribute INSUR_CO_NAME carried within the record.

By carrying the identifier(s) of a record X or, in general, any attribute(s) of X also as attribute(s) of a record Y a relationship is effectively established between X and Y. One can thus represent the relationship between any two records in two ways as exemplified in Figures 3.7 and 3.8: *explicitly* and *implicitly*. This example shows the difference in viewing relationships between

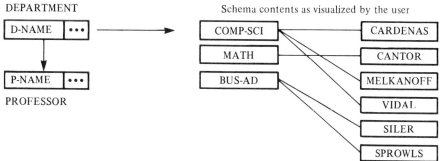

(a) Conventional schema

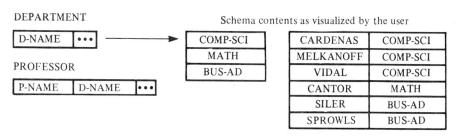

(b) Tabular, relational or flat schema

Figure 3.8.   *Equivalent ways of viewing the relationship between two entities or records: (a) conventional, and (b) tabular, relational, or flat*

the conventional *nonrelational systems* (explicit relationships) and the *tabular* or *relational systems* (implicit relationships) more recently advocated. Figure 3.8(b) shows the relational equivalent of the nonrelational schema in Figure 3.8(a). Explicit relationships are uniquely *named* in some systems and not in others, as we shall see.

Figure 3.9 shows two of the many possible subschemas from the schema in Figure 3.7. Again each subschema represents the particular schema of a given application program or user. Note that the following can be done in arriving at the subschemas:

1. Omit one or more records or entities from the schema;
2. Omit one or more relationships from the schema;
3. Omit one or more data items from a record or entity; or
4. Rearrange the relative order of data items within their containing record and introduce additional structure within the record.

Beyond these subsetting steps, not all data base systems or proposals permit exactly the same kind of subsetting. For example, only some systems, particu-

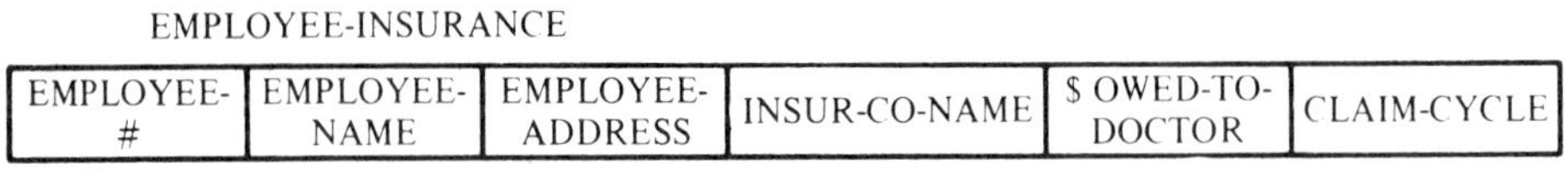

EMPLOYEE-INSURANCE

EMPLOYEE-#	EMPLOYEE-NAME	EMPLOYEE-ADDRESS	INSUR-CO-NAME	$ OWED-TO-DOCTOR	CLAIM-CYCLE

(a) Subschema as seen by the user or application program A

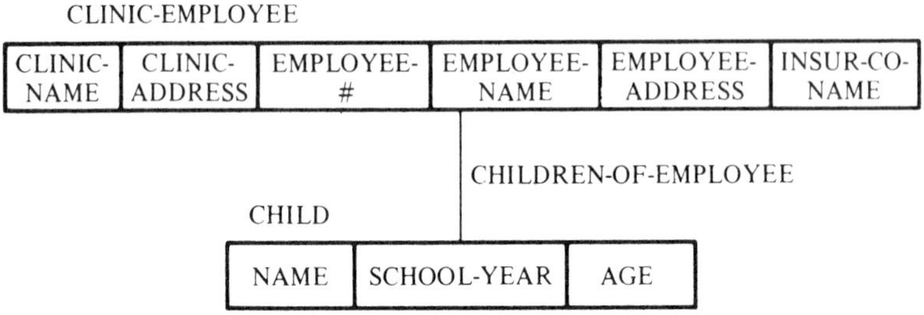

CLINIC-EMPLOYEE

CLINIC-NAME	CLINIC-ADDRESS	EMPLOYEE-#	EMPLOYEE-NAME	EMPLOYEE-ADDRESS	INSUR-CO-NAME

CHILDREN-OF-EMPLOYEE

CHILD

NAME	SCHOOL-YEAR	AGE

(b) Subschema as seen by the user or application program B

Figure 3.9.   *Two possible subschemas from the schema in Figure 3.7*

larly relational GDBMS, permit a rearrangement and subsetting of attributes from different entities into a "new entity" to be seen through a subschema; some may permit changing or subsetting the declaration of the data type of an attribute in the subschema; etc. Again, the complex task of the data base management system is to support subschemas and meet the objectives introduced in the previous section.

Relationships

From the conventional schema point of view, a relationship between two entities can be of four **degrees** or types:

1. One−to−one
2. One−to−N
3. N−to−one
4. M−to−N

Figure 3.10 shows examples of each type in the relationship between DOCTOR and EMPLOYEE. Note that at this logical level, intended to be free of machine and storage considerations, the tabular or relational approach has no concern for whether or not a relationship is of any of these four types; see Figure 3.8. In nonrelational technology one must be aware of the four types, thus entailing concern for storage considerations. The types of relationships that can be defined, how they can be defined, how they may be traversed

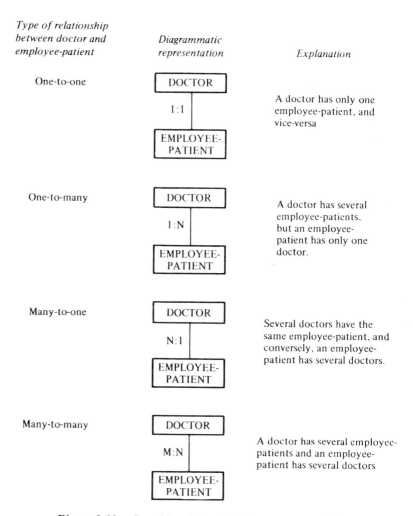

Figure 3.10. *Possible relationships between two entities*

within the data base, and so forth, vary from system to system and from interest group to interest group (e.g., CODASYL versus IMS versus relational systems).

Records, Repeating Groups, Segments, . . .

As we have repeatedly stated, the jargon and terminology in data base technology are not standardized and can be very confusing. Each competing data base technology implemented and proposed unfortunately seems to carry much jargon peculiar only to it. In this text we tend to use terms close to the

CODASYL, relational, and COBOL world. Figure 3.11 summarizes some of the main terms and their synonyms, or at least closest equivalent, among various implementations and competing groups.

Some GDBMS do not distinguish between repeating groups and records. For example, IBM's IMS and CICS refer to an individually addressable group of elementary data items as a segment; I/O statements retrieve whole segments

	Single Data Item	Data Aggregate	Record	Subschema	Schema or Data base
Conventional COBOL & PL/1	Field, Elementary Data Item	Group Item	Record	File	File
CODASYL DBTG	Field, Elementary Data Item	Group Item	Record	Subschema	Schema
IBM's IMS	Field	Segment	Segment	Sensitive Segments; Program Communication Block	Data Base (Physical, Logical)
Cincom's TOTAL	Data Item, Field	Data Element	Record	Data Base	Data Base
Informatics' MARK IV (File Management System)	Field	Segment	Segment	File(s)	Master File(s)
Honeywell's IDS	Data Field	Group Item	Record	**Subschema**	**Schema**
Software AG's ADABAS	Field	Group of Fields	Record	File of Files of Program	Coupled Files or Data Base
INTEL's SYSTEM 2000	Element	Repeating Group	Record	Application Program Data Base; Subschema	Data Base or Schema
In Use by Various Individuals	Attribute	Attribute Group	Entity	Entity Set	(Whole) Entity Set
Relational Data Base Systems	Domain, Column	Relation or Table	Relation or Table	User Data Base, Data Submodel, View	Data Base, Data Model

Figure 3.11. *Common terms and equivalencies in the data management world*

directly, but not individual items within the segment. CODASYL systems retrieve whole records or entities directly, and only afterward repeating groups or elementary data items of this record may be accessed in core.

Relational GDBMS do not permit a repeating group within a relation or table (record). This contributes to the relational data representation being called a **flat file** representation. Note that a repeating group can be split off as a separate but related file.

3.5 LOGICAL ORGANIZATIONS: HIERARCHIC OR TREE, NETWORK, RELATIONAL

Data base technology has introduced powerful logical data base structures or models made up of interconnected records. These can be classified generally into three categories, depending on the extent and type of relationships allowed in the schema:

1. **Tree** or **hierarchic model**, which includes the IMS hierarchic structures, the inverted hierarchic structures, and the CODASYL DBTG tree structures;
2. **Network model**, which includes the CODASYL DBTG network structures;
3. **Relational model**.

Realize that the hierarchic, network, and relational models are three alternative ways of organizing or viewing data at the logical level, irrespective of machine implementation and storage. In the following paragraphs we will discuss their differences. In the next chapters we will exemplify their description via data description languages of commercial GDBMS, whereas here we resort to block diagrams to show pictorially the logical structures and differences. Trees and networks predominated in commercial systems up to the mid-1980s. In the early 1980s GDBMS supporting the relational model were successfully introduced commercially, after much debate on already established GDBMS.

The difference between the relational and nonrelational data based models was presented in the previous section and is illustrated in Figure 3.8. A network or a hierarchic data model can be converted to a relational model by transforming the explicit relationships into implicit relationships.

A tree is a special case of a network structure. Any network structure can be converted to a tree or to a set of trees, although redundant data values may have to be introduced. We shall illustrate this later.

The nature of the data organization and relationships in most practical situations is such that either trees or networks or relations can handle the majority of situations without difficulty; an exception is the representation of M−to−N relationships, as we shall see.

There has been considerable debate on the pros and cons of trees versus networks versus relations since the emergence of data base technology in the late 1960s. Since the mid- and late 1970s, the relational approach is being compared and favored at the logical level over either trees or networks by many individuals. However, virtually all commercial data base systems available as of 1980 accepted and managed data assuming a tree or network form only. The expectation of many individuals is that some of these systems should also provide in the future a relational view interface for users.

Hierarchies or Trees and Relationships (CODASYL Sets)

Tree structures have been used for many years. Trees are used in both logical and physical data descriptions and organization. In logical data descriptions they are useful in denoting the logical structure of data, from simpler single file record structures (e.g., the record in Figure 2.4) to more complex multifile organizations focused upon in subsequent paragraphs. Trees have been used a great deal in physical data organizations, for example, the doubly-chained tree organization in Section 2.6. Various types of trees have been discussed by numerous authors, particularly in physical organization. Our interest in trees here is in logical data base description.

For the convenience of the reader, let us review the nature of trees. A tree consists of a number of nodes arranged in a hierarchy. Figure 3.12 shows a tree. Every node represents a data element. Every node is related to another node at the next higher level; the latter is called the **parent** node. Every parent may have one or more elements at the lower level: these are called **children**, and the connection to a parent is called a **branch**. A child node cannot have more than one parent. The height of the tree is the number of hierarchic levels involved. The topmost node is called the **root** and the elements at the lowest levels which have no children are called **leaves**. Thus reviewing the conventional COBOL or PL/1 record description (e.g., the record in Figure 2.4), the name of the record is the root, the elementary data items are the leaves, and a group item name or substructure name is a parent of one or more data items. A binary tree is an example of a tree in which a parent can have at most two children.

Our interest in logical data base terms is to view each node of a tree as a record, that is, a tree shall now be a hierarchy of records or files. This has led to the term **hierarchic data base** in reference to a tree or hierarchy of linked files. IMS uses this hierarchic approach, where each node is a **segment** or set of fields. CODASYL introduced in its 1971 DBTG report the term **set** for a

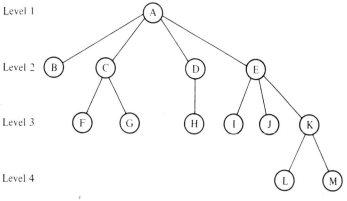

Tree: 4 levels
13 nodes including 8 leaf nodes (B,F,G,H,I,J,L,M) and 5
data aggregates (A,C,D,E,K)

NOTE: In conventional COBOL record description a leaf
node is an elementary data item; other nodes are
only data aggregates of leaf nodes. In data base
technology every node represents a record or file

Figure 3.12. *A hierarchy or tree (no element or node has more than one parent)*

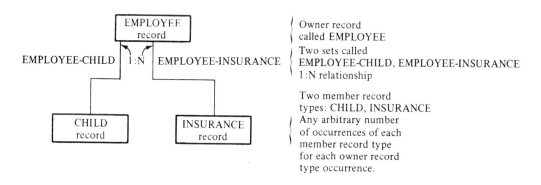

CODASYL DBTG set: A two-level tree of records with one owner record
and one or more member record types. M-to-N
relationship not allowed within a set occurrence.

Figure 3.13. *An example of CODASYL DBTG sets*

103

relationship denoting a two-level tree of records. An arbitrary number of instances of a set of the same type is a two-level hierarchy. The parent record is called the **owner**. The owner may have one or more child records, each of which is called a **member** record. Each occurrence of a set *must* contain one occurrence of its owner record and may contain an arbitrary number of occurrences of each of its member record types. The owner-member relationship, or the parent-child relationship in the hierarchic model, can be 1:1 and 1:N, but not $M:N$. A set, following tree rules, can have only one owner record type *within* the given set. An owner record and a member record could be structurally the same. The set is given a name and must be defined via the data declaration language. Figure 3.13 shows two CODASYL sets.

A data base is described by a schema consisting of one or more sets arranged in a multilevel tree fashion. Thus a record can be both a member of a set and an owner of another set. For example, in Figure 3.7 the EMPLOYEE record is a member of the set owned by DOCTOR and is also the OWNER of the set with member CHILD. Details on DBTG sets and schema will be presented in Section 5.2.

Networks

The classical tree structure does not allow a child or member record in a given relationship to have more than one parent or owner. A network structure is one which does allow it, and is thus a more general data organization. It is important to realize that in the DBTG approach a member can have one or more owners as long as each owner is in a *different* set. Thus CODASYL DBTG proposes capabilities of defining network structures directly, except those involving $M:N$ relationships within the same set. Note in Figure 3.13 that if two EMPLOYEE records, let us say, husband and wife, each have the same CHILD(ren), then husband and children must be a different set instance than wife and children. The CODASYL group was much inspired by the pioneering work of Bachman and the resulting IDS (Integrated Data Store) GDBMS at Honeywell (General Electric at the time) based on network structures.[5,10] the network approach has been advocated since the earliest data base efforts in the mid-sixties leading to today's data base technology.

Figure 3.14 shows two examples of networks. The nice hierarchic visual structure of trees tends to be lost now, although the levels may be preserved to a great degree in most cases with proper arrangement of the network. Compare the logical meaning of Figure 3.14(a) and 3.14(b). Figure 3.14(a) shows the same record type CHILD in two relationships, CHILD OF EMPLOYEE and CHILD OF DOCTOR. But in Figure 3.14(b) the meaning is different. The CHILD record type now is connected to DOCTOR as the relationship DOCTOR_OF_CHILD. This is called a cycle, that is, one in which a child of

(a) A network:

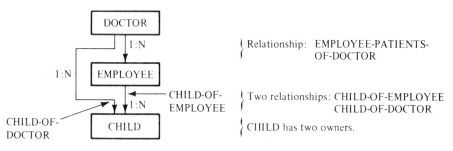

(b) A network which is a cycle:

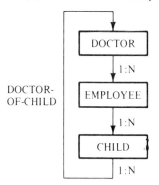

Note: Some data base systems can represent cycles directly;
others can not.

Figure 3.14.   *Examples of networks*

a node becomes a parent of an ancestor of said node. Some commercial data base systems cannot represent cycles.

A cycle could perhaps contain only one record type, that is, the child record type and the parent record type are one and the same. This could be the schema for a family-tree data base. Many commercial systems do not allow such a singular cycle.

Transformation of Networks to Trees

Any network structure can be transformed into a single tree or several trees by introducing redundancy of nodes. The transformation is easy and no new tree levels need to be added if the relationships are not *M:N*. Figure 3.15

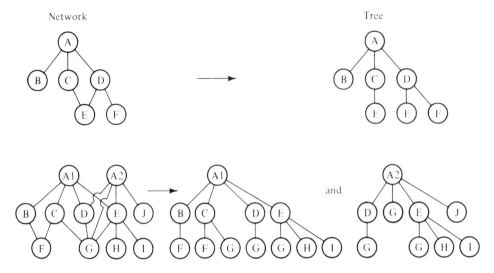

Figure 3.15. *Transforming networks into trees, no M:N relationships*

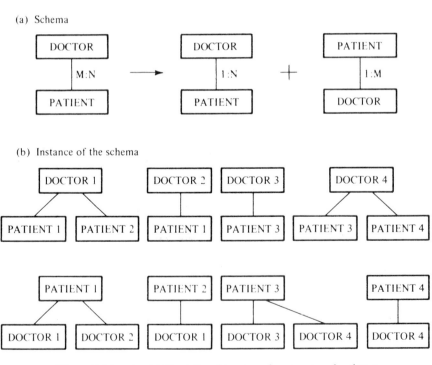

Figure 3.16. *An M:N relationship viewed as two two-level tree relationships*

illustrates how a network may be transformed to one or more trees by introducing duplicate nodes.

An $M{:}N$ relationship is in reality a network by itself. Transformation of an $M{:}N$ relationship between two records in a network or a tree data base is more complex and adds another tree level. For example, consider the $M{:}N$ DOCTOR_PATIENT relationship of DOCTOR records and PATIENT records in Figure 3.16. Any DOCTOR record can be associated with one or several PATIENT records, and any PATIENT record can be associated with one or several DOCTOR records. Note the potential storage redundancy problem if the relationship is actually implemented as in Figure 3.16(b). We shall see in subsequent chapters how $M{:}N$ relationships are best handled to avoid such problems in CODASYL systems and IMS and how it is nicely handled and not of such concern in relational systems.

Transformation of Networks and Trees to Relations

The transformation of networks and trees to relations involves transforming every explicit relationship into an implicit relationship as illustrated in Figure 3.8. An implicit relationship is established when a common attribute is stored in the two relations. Beyond this, the normalization algorithm presented in Chapter 9 guides the transformation process.

On Implementations to Support Trees, Networks, and Relations

Most implementations oriented toward effectively supporting tree structures cannot support (define *and* process) network structures or relations directly. Thus, some GDBMS handle only trees. However, in the preceding paragraphs we stated how one can transform a network to a tree structure at the logical level so that it is possible to use a tree oriented GDBMS to handle a network. Most GDBMS oriented toward network structures will undoubtedly be more effective in processing a given network data base than will a tree-oriented GDBMS, but not more than a hierarchic inverted GDBMS in handling the tree data base that is the equivalent of the network. However, as it has been discussed in the previous chapter, the access time performance of physical data organizations is entirely dependent on and highly sensitive to many factors, including availability of indexing, processing requirements, and data base contents, so generalizations are dangerous.

Some of the originally hierarchic or network GDBMS may provide some ability to view data relationally. However, GDBMS specifically designed to *process,* and not just view, data relationally will undoubtedly be more effective than such nonrelational systems.

No two GDBMS implementations are alike. The difference in implementation approaches begins increasing the moment that access paths or secondary data organizations start to be considered. Many differences exist also from the functional point of view at the logical level. Some systems have the capability of establishing only one relationship between one record type and another. Some can handle more easily a single relationship between a parent record and two or more child record types. Some can handle M:N relationships more directly. These are just a few of the many differences to be encountered in functional capability in systems already implemented.

Classification of GDBMS

Due to the type of data base accessing and processing, and not just the type of relationships in the data base model, GDBMS may be classified primarily into four categories:

1. Hierarchic;
2. Network;
3. Inverted, some of which are either hierarchic or network in terms of the data base model; and
4. Relational

This is the classification of GDBMS that we shall follow. As an example, IMS is a hierarchic system that is vastly different from the inverted System 2000 which also follows the hierarchic data base model.

3.6   CONSTITUENTS AND FUNCTIONING OF GENERALIZED DATA BASE MANAGEMENT SYSTEMS

Let us trace what general steps occur in processing an I/O statement or query requesting access to a record from a GDBMS. Figure 3.17 outlines the functions that come into play:

1. The I/O statement or query (e.g., DELETE EMPLOYEES WHERE AGE ≤65 AND DEPARTMENT = ECONOMICS) is detected and analyzed syntactically and semantically by the GDBMS. The compiler of the language of the program containing the I/O statement does not process any of the GDBMS I/O or data definition statements that may be referring to data not in the subschema.
2. The GDBMS checks to see if the subschema associated with the particular I/O statement is defined in its directory, is supported by

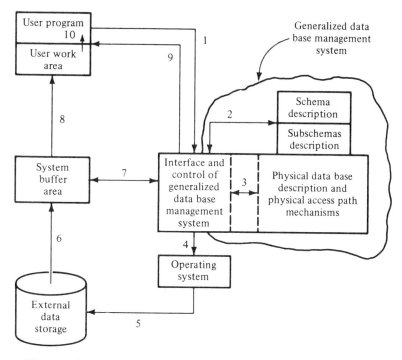

Figure 3.17. *Conceptual data base system and sequence of events to service a data base I/O request*

the GDBMS, and can be accessed by the particular issuer of the I/O command (e.g., correct password, DELETE allowed, access on the basis of AGE and DEPARTMENT allowed).

3. The GDBMS, based on its analysis of the request, uses its access path mechanisms (e.g., inverted mechanisms) in the best possible way to determine which records qualify under the query or are needed in order to answer the query, and exactly where they are in the physical storage. The physical records or blocks that need to be accessed are determined. The GDBMS attempts to minimize the number of blocks to be accessed. How minimal this is depends both on the inherent access path efficiency of the GDBMS and the extent to which the data base administrator set-up the optimum physical organization and access paths.

4. The GDBMS issues physical I/O commands to the host operating system to access the specific physical records or blocks needed containing the desired records. The operating system has no notion of what is stored in each of the blocks, whether it is control data, real data, garbage, or empty space.

5. The operating system searches the external storage devices and accesses the physical records requested.

6. The operating system transfers the data from secondary storage to the system buffer area in core, accessible only by the GDBMS. The system buffer area is shared by all application programs under the control of the GDBMS.

7. The particular records requested by the application program are derived by the GDBMS from all the physical records that had to be transferred to the system buffers. Data transformation and processing needed by the particular subschema(s) are made by the GDBMS so that the application program may see only its specific records.

8. The GDBMS transfers the required records from the system buffer area to the buffer area of the application program.

9. The GDBMS provides status information to the calling program or terminal on the outcome of its call.

10. The application program now can manipulate in core the records given to it by the GDBMS.

This is obviously a generic and global trace of what happens. Available GDBMS differ in implementation approaches, techniques, and details of these steps in achieving their goals. Most GDBMS appear to the host operating system as simply application programs, no matter how complex or sophisticated they might be. Thus a high degree of operating system independence is achieved.

A major difference between GDBMS and GFMS or report writers is the efficiency with which multifile situations may be searched to accomplish the query. A GFMS does not offer relatability between files nor the access path sophistication of a GDBMS. A GFMS has essentially only the sophistication of the basic access methods of the operating system; thus data searching will be invariably exhaustive in the sense that all records in the files referred to will be scanned. For a single-file data base the GFMS may perform comparably to the GDBMS, but not for multifile cases.

In the 1960s software systems based on multilist structures, tree organizations, and so forth were developed in-house with the attempt to provide more cost-effective access to subsets of data in a growing file environment and to achieve many of the goals of shareability, data independence, and such, outlined in Section 3.3. Files had to be linked and integrated. Conventional data management facilities in operating systems did not satisfy the needs. Thus, a body of data management software began to grow on top of regular compilers and operating systems and operate in the fashion described above. Attempts were made to generalize the special software built, for example, to easily define and load any record structure in a number of files, to interconnect any of a limited number of files, and to index any field easily. Most of these in-house efforts were very expensive, were in a constant state of flux, and only partially achieved some of the goals. These needs and problems led vendors and software houses to develop today's GDBMS. It is interesting to note that a number of these in-house systems did flourish and are used successfully only in-house, although most of them would be difficult if not impossible to replace with a truly generalized DBMS without extensive or prohibitive reprogramming of application programs and data reformatting. In many cases this is mostly due to the fact that these in-house systems were not designed to appear as application programs to the host operating system.

Constituents of DB/DC Systems and GDBMS

A GDBMS may be used alone or it may be coupled with a generalized **Data Communications (DC) system**. A coupled GDBMS and generalized DC system is generally referred to as a DB/DC system. Other commonly used terms for generalized DC system are: generalized **TeleProcessing (TP) monitor, terminal management system** and **teleprocessor**. The term GDBMS/TP monitor is equivalent to the term DB/DC system. We will use these terms interchangeably. The terminology problem existing in practice is evident. The word "generalized" when applied to TP means that the TP facilities have a high degree of independence with respect to types of users, terminals and specific operating system on which the TP facilities are used.

Let us look at the constituents of the more encompassing DB/DC system, particularly since most GDBMS may be interfaced to an external data communications processor in the host operating system. Deletion of all comments on data communications reduces the following paragraphs to a short description of the makeup of a GDBMS. Subsequent sections and chapters do not address data communications aspects.

Generalized DB/DC systems are those in which data base management and data communication management facilities have been highly developed as an "integrated" system, or at least on an "aware-of-each-other" basis. Among the prime examples are IBM's IMS[7] DB/DC and Cincom's TOTAL-ENVIRON/1 (TOTAL is the GDBMS and ENVIRON/1 is the DC System).[11] IBM's CICS (Customer Information Control System) embodies some data base capability (but not to the extent of a GDBMS) with much DC capability on a highly integrated and essentially inseparable basis. In a nutshell, data communications make the data base available so that it may be accessed and/or modified from computer terminals. These might be typewriter-like terminals or visual display CRT terminals which are connected to the computer by means of leased or private telephone lines. These terminals may be either remotely located or nearby; in either case the data communications facility allows a number of users to interact with the central data base at the same time.

GDBMS have been developed because of insufficient or inadequate capabilities of the basic file management facilities of the host operating system in dealing with the more demanding modern data management needs. Similarly, generalized TP monitors have evolved (more recently than GDBMS) because of insufficient or inadequate capabilities of the basic data communication facilities of the host operating system (i.e., the *basic* TP or DC facilities) in dealing with the more demanding modern data communication needs such as:

Terminal independence, that is, the ability to change terminal characteristics without requiring modification of the TP application programs;

Efficiency and control in dealing with a large number of terminals and high volumes of data communication;

Task control, that is, scheduling of message or transaction processing programs according to message priority, authorization, and availability of resources;

Control over communication between different message processing programs or terminals;

Formatting of terminal messages and displays

TP monitors are designed to be over and use (or augment or replace) the basic data communication facilities of the host operating system. Unfortunately, there is no standard for TP monitors, analogous to the DBTG report for GDBMS, and so the capabilities and jargon vary widely across vendors.

If the data communication demands in accessing a data base are low, then the TP facilities of the host operating system may suffice. If not, then the generalized TP should be considered. GDBMS can be used from remote keyboard terminals and display CRT terminals if an interface to the basic TP monitor of the host operating system is available and the proper TP programming is done by the application-systems programmer.

SYSTEM 2000's generalized TP monitor feature allows the use of the complete set of SYSTEM 2000's capabilities from various teletypewriters and a variety of hard copy terminals and CRT terminals.[12] This system has been interfaced with several basic TP monitors. As another example, TOTAL (without its ENVIRON/1 DC companion) and a few other GDBMS have been interfaced to several generalized TP systems, including Turnkey Systems' TASK/MASTER, and IBM's TSO. However, GDBMS using basic teleprocessors or generalized TP monitors of other vendors perhaps may not benefit from all the highly developed and productive data communication facilities in an integrated DB/DC system developed by the same vendor.

We can better understand the needs that data base/data communications systems serve if we examine their evolution. The TP systems installed in the 1960s were relatively simple. They usually involved a single application (e.g., an accounts receivable program) and had files and terminals dedicated to that application. If a second application was developed, it too generally had its own set of dedicated files and terminals. These TP application programs interfaced directly with the operating system and were normally written in a basic assembly language because there was no practical alternative. In the majority of cases, the application approaches were quite elementary and were often limited to simple inquiry. The programmer also had to develop his or her own communications control program, generally with very basic and hard to use special languages, such as IBM's BTAM (Basic Telecommunications Access Method) and QTAM (Queued Telecommunications Access Method).

The early TP environment required costly special skills, training, and programming ingenuity. Data processing needs included running many applications on-line concurrently, all sharing the same terminal network and the same data base. In other words, the need was for a DB/DC system. Operating systems of the late 1960s and early 1970s did not support the new needs and, as a result, many installations attempted to solve the problems in-house in order to establish the desired new processing. Most of these efforts proved to be overly expensive and many settled for partial implementation and implementations in a state of flux; most were not modular enough to allow the programmer to easily expand or change the system. These pioneering efforts led to today's DB/DC technology designed to significantly alleviate the problems. Flynn[13] provides a brief history of early TP developments, problems, and solutions by programmers and vendors (notably the milestones of single-thread processing, first hardware and then software front-ends, task monitoring, paging, and hardware buffering).

Figure 3.18 outlines the global constituents of a DB/DC system:

1. Data Base Management function,
2. Terminal (Teleprocessing or Data Communication) Management function,
3. System Control function,
4. Language Interface function, and
5. Operating System function.

The objectives and characteristics of the data base management function have been discussed in previous sections. The **terminal management** function includes the objectives briefly mentioned earlier in this section and shields application programmers from the complexities of the communications network. As a result, application programmers can operate without the burden of programming for polling, addressing, queuing, code conversion, and other such factors encountered in the TP environment (whereas in a GDBMS programmers have all the programming and scheduling burden of the basic TP monitor of the operating system). Applications programmers need only a basic

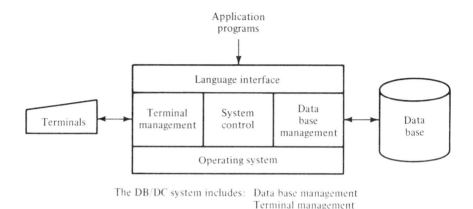

The DB/DC system includes: Data base management
Terminal management
System control
Language interface

Figure 3.18.   *Global constituents of a data base/data communications (DB/DC) system*

conceptual understanding of TP in order to do their job. As the name indicates, the terminal management function enables terminals to operate together efficiently so that any terminal in the network may communicate with any other terminal or with any application program in the DB/DC system. This function also handles interactive processing, fast response to inquiries, and terminal security. It fosters system modularity so that program and network changes can be handled without major disruption to TP application programs and ongoing operations.

As can be seen from the services provided, the terminal management function is much more than a sophisticated TP access method. It builds on the access method (such as IBM's BTAM, QTAM and VTAM) using its line and terminal control code as a base for broader, easier to use, and more comprehensive services. This is entirely analogous to the data base management function that builds on top of the basic access methods of Figure 2.1.

The presence of independent functional modules for data base management and terminal management leads to the need for efficient system control. This is where the **system control** function comes in. This function interfaces the DB/DC system to the operating system and also coordinates the multitude of other elements. This function is essential, whether it is a GDBMS or a DB/DC system. The system control function is an intelligent administrator that has to optimize the use of the system's storage and processing resources and schedule operation of application programs according to user-defined properties. A complete system should include many facilities required to support data bases in day-to-day operations. These facilities are also referred to as **utilities** or

system support routines and can be thought of as a part of the fuzzy system control function:

1. Dump, edit and print routines;
2. Data base load routines;
3. Garbage collection routines;
4. Statistical gathering and analysis routines;
5. Reorganization and tuning routines;
6. Audit trail routines;
7. Check point/restart and recovery routines;
8. Start up and shut down routines;
9. Error handling routines; and
10. Data compression.

Other necessary system services must also be provided. It is in these areas that every commercially available system differs a great deal. No standards have been widely proposed for what should be provided or how it should appear to the user or programmer. This has been the realm of individual implementors.

A large GDBMS or DB/DC system has in its own right a great deal of the elements and complexity of an operating system. This is evident when one considers that a system like IMS carries with it its own basic file access methods (HSAM, HDAM, HISAM, HIDAM) and its own TP access methods, beyond the basic file and TP access methods of the host operating system. All GDBMS and DB/DC use a standard host operating system, except for a few that venture to use a (sometimes highly) modified operating system.

The **language interface** function has the task of simplifying the application developer's use of the system. It permits use of transaction-oriented languages such as COBOL and PL/1 as well as its nonprocedural, high-level English-flavored query language to interface easily and directly to the DGBMS or DB/DC system (Figures 3.18 and 3.2). Interfaces have been also built by vendors of GFMS to allow their systems to communicate with and use all the facilities of the GDBMS, just like any other programming language. These interfaces are modules of the GFMS and are sold by the vendor as an extra option, for example, ASI-ST's IMS(DL/1) Interface and TOTAL Interface and Mark IV's IMS (DL/1) Interface.

IBM's Data Base/Data Communications
IMS—System Flow

Let us now take a look at the normal flow of actions involved in a specific system. We will look at IBM's IMS first as a DB/DC system and then as a

GDBMS (excluding the DC function). In subsequent sections and chapters we do not focus on the DC side of a DB/DC system. The interested reader may pursue further details in available general references and specific references on a given implementation.

The following paragraphs and related figures have been extracted from reference 7.

Teleprocessing System. Once the region or partition containing the IMS/VS control program and one or more regions or partitions to be utilized for the message processing have been initialized by the job management facilities of the operating system, the following system flow occurs as per Figure 3.19:

1. The telecommunication facility (event 1) requests restart instructions from the master terminal. After the completion of restart, the master terminal enables communication from all user terminals (event 2).

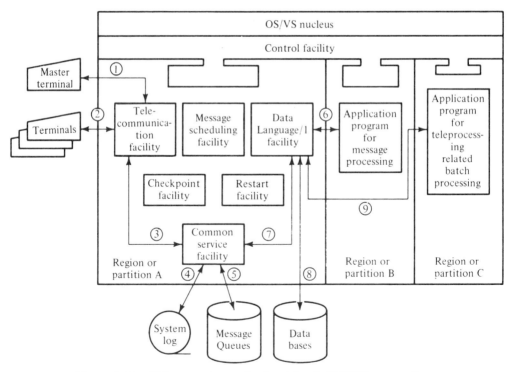

Figure 3.19.   *Teleprocessing and related batch IMS/VS system flow*
             (Courtesy IBM Corp.)

2. When an input message or message segment is received (event 2), the telecommunication facilitiy invokes the common service facility (event 3) and the input message is logged (event 4) and queued (event 5).

3. When there are input messages pending for processing, and a message processing region or partition of the required class is available for scheduling, control is passed to the scheduling facility to determine the application message processing program to be scheduled. The application program is loaded into region or partition B and given control.

4. The application program subsequently makes requests for the input message and/or data base references (event 6). Control passes to the Data Language/1 (DL/1) facility for either message reference (event 7) or for data base reference (event 8). The message reference is accomplished through the common service facility.

5. During application program execution, modifications can be made to the data base (event 8) and/or output messages may be queued (events 5 and 7).

6. When the application program terminates or requests another input message, all output messages queued are transmitted to the designated output terminal (events 3 and 2).

Batch Processing of Teleprocessing Data Bases. Once the IMS/VS region or partition associated with teleprocessing has been initiated by the operating system, a batch region or partition can be initiated. The application program in the batch region or partition is scheduled by operating system job management. This batch region or partition may contain an application program for processing against teleprocessing data bases. The Data Language/1 facility of IMS is used for data base reference and update. See Figure 3.19. Any data reference is initiated by the batch application program (event 9).

Data Language/1 (DL/1) Data Base Batch Processing. Whether or not the teleprocessing capabilities of IMS/VS exist within the jobs operating under the operating system, the Data Language/1 facility of IMS can be used in a batch-only data base environment following Figure 3.20.

1. The application program for batch-only data base processing is initiated through the job management routine of the operating system (event 1).

2. The DL/1 facility is invoked by the application program (event 2). The highest DL/1 module analyzes the data base call request. Depending on the I/O function requested in the call request, the insert (event 3), the retrieve (event 4), or the delete/replace function

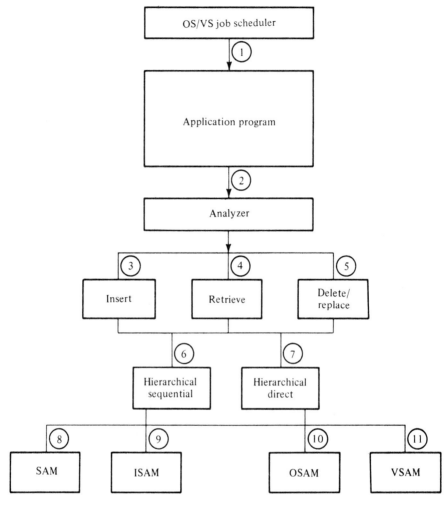

Figure 3.20.   *Data Language/1 data base batch system flow*[7]

(event 5) is invoked. These functions subsequently invoke functions unique to either the hierarchical sequential (event 6) or the hierarchical direct organization (event 7). These functions subsequently invoke access method modules for ISAM (event 8), SAM (event 9), OSAM (event 10), or VSAM (event 11).

We examine IMS and DL/1 processing in Chapter 7.

3.7   DATA DESCRIPTION, DATA MANIPULATION, AND QUERY LANGUAGES

Six languages or command facilities are involved in data base technology:

1. The standard procedural programming languages (COBOL, PL/1, PASCAL, etc.);
2. I/O language or data manipulation language;
3. Query language;
4. Subschema description language;
5. Schema description language; and
6. Physical data description language.

We will describe them below. Examples from specific systems will be given in subsequent chapters.

Procedural Programming Languages

The application programmer still uses a standard programming language such as COBOL for all processing of data in core (including program buffers) excluding I/O. Sometimes such a language is also called misleadingly a data manipulation language, including at times all I/O statements communicating with a data base system. COBOL, FORTRAN, and PL/1 are the most widely acceptable languages by data base systems and are often called **host languages**.

It has been discussed in Section 3.2 that the highly nonprocedural language of a generalized file management system may displace the conventional highly procedural programming language. Thus various GFMS are interfaced to communicate with a data base system. The data base system neither modifies nor executes non-I/O statements of the programming languages of GFMS.

I/O Language or Data Manipulation Language

An application program communicates its data needs to the data base system via an I/O language, referred to as **Data Manipulation Language**, **DML**, by the CODASYL DBTG. DML commands and host language commands are mixed in an application program. This I/O language can be viewed as

1. An extension of the host programming language or
2. A separate I/O language of the data base management system.

As an extension of the programming language, it could be conceivably independent of the particular data base management system used. As a facility of the data base management system, it could be independent of a particular programming language.

It turns out that most data base management systems have an interface fairly common (although not identical) to any programming language, i.e., instead of seeing several language interfaces the user sees essentially one. CODASYL, as part of its standardization motives, defined in the 1970s an extension to COBOL (introducing the term data manipulation language, DML) with the intent of being the standard interface to any data base management system. CODASYL GDBMS generally support this DML.

The current state of matters is that an application program must have all I/O language commands tailored to the expectations of the particular GDBMS. It is well known that in many cases application programs can become so tied down to the initial data base management system that to change systems would unfortunately involve extensive reprogramming.

Differences in the kind of logical data model used impair transferability of programs even more. In Section 3.5 the hierarchic, network, and relational models were briefly introduced. Different I/O commands and particularly different degrees of data independence accompany each type of model. Transferability of application programs from a data base management system to another using a different data model usually involves complete reprogramming (e.g., changing a COBOL application from CODASYL to IMS or vice versa).

Examples of the DML of CODASYL and other systems will be given in subsequent chapters.

Query Language

Practically every data base management system offers its own query language. No query language standard has been proposed. However, languages are rather similar in that most are nonprocedural and natural language oriented. The query language is intended to:

1. Handle spontaneous on-line information retrieval and maintenance;
2. Provide a convenient nonprocedural, English-flavored, and nonprogrammer-oriented means to use the system;
3. Handle low volumes of data; and
4. Access subsets of the data base satisfying a set of data content qualifications.

Query language commands are generally self-standing, that is, they are generally considered to be unrelated and are processed individually by the data base management system. In some systems query language commands can appear embedded in a program written in a programming language. In relational

GDBMS a unique feature is that the DML and the query language are essentially one language: a query language in which the same command issued in an on-line terminal can be embedded in a program.

Subschema Description Language

The data base management system must have the means for a DBA to describe the logical subschemas allowed to each program or user, data types, access permits, and so forth. At the same time, query language users and application programmers must have the means to describe their views of the data. The term **Subschema Data Description Language**, DDL, introduced by CODASYL, refers to these means. As already stated, other terms are also often used, such as the "sensitivity" of a program in the IMS environment and the user "view" in relational systems.

Just as in the DML case, the DDL can be considered either an extension of a host programming language or a separate data definition language. However, because each programming language system has its own conventions and peculiarities, user subschema DDLs tend to be dedicated to a particular programming language. The subschema DDL of the DBTG Report is for COBOL. The DBA DDL should be independent of what programming languages will be used. Functionally, a subschema DDL should include the ability to:

1. Select the record-types or fields within a record-type from the schema to make up the subschema;

2. Establish the correspondence between the schema and subschema descriptions of elementary data items and intrarecord organizations; and

3. Describe the structure, format, representation, and other general characteristics of data base data consistent with the data description facilities of the host language.

The model of data of the data base management system is a prime determinant of the particular subschema DDL. Subschema data descriptions for a hierarchic data base system differ from those for a network data base management system; transfer of programs from one system to another entails respecifying data base data descriptions.

The rules for correspondence between data items and data aggregates declared for a record in the schema and data items and data aggregates in the subschema are not standardized. The DBTG report proposes an encompassing set of such rules for its architecture.

Schema Description Language

The Schema **Data Description Language**, *DDL*, is the language used by the data base administrator to describe the whole logical data base. The data base administrator is the individual(s) who has the task of developing a common data base for a number of users. A major task of the data base design process is to define the data base such that it accommodates all intended users, some of which may have conflicting needs. The emerging functions of data base administration are discussed in Chapter 13.

It is important to have one single way and set of conventions for specifying a schema, independent of particular programming languages and GFMS that may be using subsets of the data base. Every data base management system has its own DDL language, reflecting the particular logical model for viewing data on which the information world of the users is to be organized.

A schema DDL should not include references to either physical organization or physical devices or media space. A schema written in the DDL is the logical description of the data base and is not affected by physical organization or the devices and media used to store the data. The data base may thus be stored on any mix of external storage devices which are supported by the system. Some devices, such as tapes, because of their sequential nature and limitations, may not allow taking full advantage of the facilities in the DML.

Examples of schema definitions will be provided for specific GDBMS in subsequent chapters.

In current practice there are many differences in the DDL's, DML's/ query languages, and particularly the underlying storage structures, across data base management systems. This is already of much concern. In many organizations the commitment to some of the more complex systems has already been so large that many data base administrators acknowledge that to change to a different data base management system would be prohibitively disruptive to application systems and costly. Thus, in the more global sense, data independence is nil, although within the realm of a given data base management system there is a varying degree of data independence.

Physical Data Description Language

A data base must be physically organized and mapped on storage devices. Of concern are many details of storage devices, data layouts, basic access methods, and higher-level physical data organizations (inverted files, chained trees, etc.). Many complex alternatives arise for each of these architectural levels of physical data organization. The following section examines these levels. A **physical data description language** would be one to describe such aspects. The CODASYL DBTG Report coined the term **Device/ Media Control Language** for the language to assign, for example, data to devices, and to specify buffering, paging, and overflows. However, CODASYL left this to the realm of individual implementations until the late 1970s when it proposed a **Data Storage Description Language, DSDL**, for consideration.[14]

GDBMS available today use widely different means and conventions by which data base designers specify access paths and logical to physical mappings. In some cases, specification of certain access path aspects or physical organization concerns appear at the schema description level, for example, the specification of the key-names to invert or index for faster access.

The ideal goal is, of course, to develop enough intelligence in GDBMS such that the choice of access paths, logical to physical mapping, and all physical organization is done automatically and cost-effectively. Thus, data base designer-administrators would not be burdened by physical data descriptions and would not have the many headaches that they have with current systems. But we are very far from having such needed automated capability. This is one of the biggest challenges for data base system researchers and developers for the next few years.

3.8   ARCHITECTURAL LEVELS OF DATA BASE ORGANIZATION—THE DIAM FRAMEWORK

3.8.1   Data Organization Levels and Issues

The organization of data in a data base management system may be viewed at four architectural levels, as it proceeds from its logical data organization to its equivalent physical organization and mapping in storage devices. In parallel with Figure 2.1, which shows the hierarchy of data management software facilities discussed in previous chapters, Figure 3.21 shows the four architectural levels at which data organization may be viewed in a data base management system. At the top level, only logical considerations enter into the picture. There are alternative logical models of data. They include the hierarchic or tree, network, and relational models introduced in Section 3.5. The top level may represent in reality two logical realms. The higher user level may involve entities or objects and their functional relationships. The next realm underneath it would then involve logically equivalent hierarchic, network, or tabular or relational constructs (which may be derived with an eye toward level 3) needed to support the higher-level requirements. This realm is described via schema and subschema data description languages The highest-level realm would be the realm at which an information system and all its flows and transformations are specified, perhaps via a problem statement language independent of any particular data base management system.

The lower levels outlined in Figure 3.21 reflect machine considerations and dependency in increasing degrees. The interface between levels 3 and 4

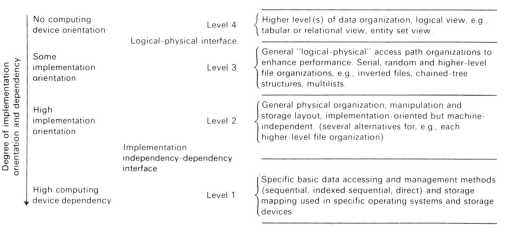

Figure 3.21. *Architectural levels of data in a data base management system*

may be called the *logical-physical* interface. Level 3 is a first-order performance-oriented level at which the general presence and limitations of computing devices are taken into account. The issues at hand are alternative access path strategies to enhance the performance of data handling (retrieve, update, etc.), for example, serial versus basic random access versus secondary data base organizations (inverted, chained-tree, etc.) and their possible variations. These organizations have been amply discussed in Chapter 2.

Level 2 reflects that there are usually alternative physical organizations and storage layouts of data in linear storage for any of the physical organizations viewed at level 3. To be specific, consider an example using the doubly-chained tree organization. Figure 2.12(a) shows values of a subset of key-names of a set of records. This is the logical view at level 4. Figure 2.12(b) shows its doubly-chained tree organization, illustrating level 3 alternatives. The chained-tree example in Figure 2.12(b) can be mapped into linear storage in two ways: (1) following a top-to-bottom left-to-right approach, Figure 2.12(c), or (2) following a level-by-level layout. The few authors who recognize only three levels essentially consider levels 2 and 3, in our four-level hierarchy, to be one single level.

Level 1, the lowest level of data organization, refers to specific physical storage device characteristics and aspects. These are at the root of the whole data base system and are usually different from computer system to computer system. The interface between levels 1 and 2 is a device independency-dependency interface. The concern at this low level includes: the organization of physical devices into subdivisions such as blocks and tracks; the mapping of data into the physical device subdivisions; the allocation and accounting of overflow areas; garbage collection; and other machine dependent and microscopic characteristics such as the placement of the recorded key of a record, of control fields of a record, and so forth in external storage (i.e., at the level of detail illustrated by Figure A.7 for IBM Systems).

Before continuing with a formal and more detailed discussion of these levels, it needs to be said that unfortunately these distinct levels have not been generally envisioned in much of actual practice and data base management systems implemented—although recognition of the levels now is increasing as data base know-how advances in great strides. This has led to difficulty in identifying and differentiating between conceptual, implementation-oriented, and implementation-dependent aspects permeating systems implemented. Specific alternatives and trade-offs are hardly identifiable. Thus physical data base design is largely done in an ad hoc and unsystematic manner, leading to costly problems of performance, tuning, and transferability or migration of data from one environment to another.

3.8.2   DIAM (**D**ata **I**ndependent **A**ccessing **M**odel)

The **Data Independent Accessing Model, DIAM** is a formal conception of data organization in a data base management system.[15-17] The DIAM encompasses and adds detail to the four levels previously presented qualitatively. We will use the encompassing formalism of the DIAM and framework to trace data base organization from the logical to the physical device realms. We have dropped the DIAM's original "entity set" logical model. We have modified the original terminology to coincide with more conventional logical models and terms used in practice (the original DIAM terminology[15] is difficult to follow). The term DIAM will be used from now on to mean the phrase "DIAM with our modification."

The four levels of the DIAM are outlined in Figure 3.22 and encompass the following data models:

1. Logical (Entity) Model;
2. String Model;
3. Encoding Model; and
4. Physical Device Model.

These correspond to the architectural levels of Figure 3.21. Each level has specific elements and parameters. Specifications of each level are recorded in an associated **catalog** or **directory**. A language, or software procedures, exists at each level for manipulating primitive elements and parameters peculiar to the level or model.

The entity model is a very general logical conceptualization of the conventional models of data already introduced. This level deals only with *entities*.

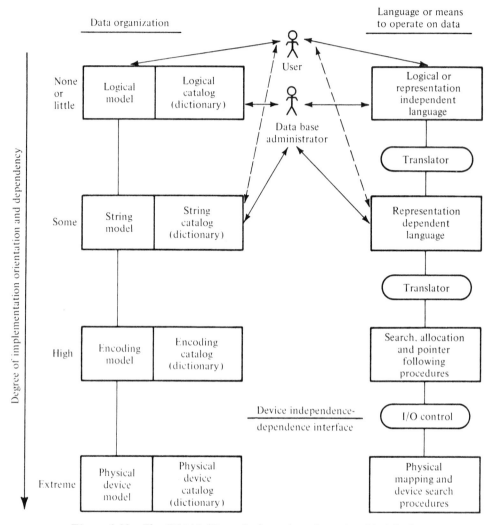

Figure 3.22   *The DIAM (Data Independent Accessing Model) data*
organization levels

An **entity** is a real world concept or object about which information is recorded. The associated language deals with logical aspects; it is the DML and/or the query language in which users formulate their data base requests reflecting their logical conceptualization of the data in the realm of the logical model used, but with no reference to physical access path matters.

Below the top level there are three distinct "languages" (Figure 3.22). The language(s) and procedures of the two lower DIAM levels are what we earlier termed globally physical data description language. The language associated with the string or access path model will be called the **Representation Dependent Language**, **RDL**. It deals with access paths interconnecting attribute values and collections of attribute values by means of unidirectional operators called **strings** (thus the term string model). Typical operations in the RDL might involve creating an access path (e.g., inverting a given key-name), or following one access path from among those available. However, the logical data structure is also expressed in the string model. Available data base management systems differ greatly as to how and to what extent a physical data base designer and application programmer deals with such aspects. Note that no device dependent factors are involved at the access path level.

No formal language has been developed *and* widely accepted to express data operations in terms of the encoding or physical device models. In actual practice these "languages" take the form of collections of standard procedures internal to the GDBMS and are designed to accomplish requests for data formulated at the higher levels. CODASYL developed a preliminary data storage description language (1978),[14] subsequent to their introduction of the idea of a device/media control language in the 1971 DBTG Report. Still, the ideal goal is to shield data base designers and particularly application program designers from having to deal with these lower-level machine considerations. The intent of these low-level languages is to provide a common framework and yardstick for the elements and parameters involved in all data base systems of concern to GDBMS designers.

Some kind of language translation facility must be provided between the levels as illustrated in Figure 3.22. Operations expressed in the language of any model must be translated eventually into procedures that manipulate the physical representation of data. Thus a statement in the logical level language will be converted to a set of statements in the RDL. This set will in turn be used to generate calls to procedures at the encoding level which will finally be translated into execution of physical device-oriented procedures. Realize that a request to retrieve a certain data item at the logical level would be translated into commands to follow the appropriate path to the data item (which path to follow is to be determined by the translator, or the user if the translator lacks the necessary intelligence). At the encoding level the path-following commands would be translated by the system into a series of symbolic pointer retrievals, since pointers are used to encode the paths. Finally, at the lowest level pointers would be converted into addresses of the physical device(s) where the data is actually stored.

Languages such as DML of DBTG and DL/1 of IMS really involve representation dependent-oriented notions, as we shall see in Chapters 5 and 7. In the following sections we focus on the functions of DIAM's three top levels and provide detailed examples.

3.8.3 Logical (Entity) Model

The intent of this level is that (1) only the logical aspects of data be viewed and (2) user and application program formulate retrieval, update, insertion, and so forth of data items in terms of the logical structure of the entity model (without concern for whether the underlying structure is a network or a tree). We will not use the formal "entity" model terminology; we will use instead the following more conventional terminology. The atomic element is the **attribute name** or **field name**, e.g., COLOR, AGE. Each attribute name may assume any one of several values called **attribute values** or **field values** e.g., RED, BLUE, GRAY. The basic form of information in the entity set model is the **entity**, which is a real-world object or concept about which information is recorded. An entity is made up of a collection of attribute name/attribute value pairs as conceptualized in Figure 3.23. An **identifier name** is that attribute name each of whose values, called identifier values,

EMPLOYEE entity

EMPLOYEE #/291
NAME/TURNER
DEPT/C.S.

Figure 3.23.   *An entity made up of a collection of attribute name/attribute value pairs*

identifies uniquely a particular entity. Two or more attribute names could be used as an identifier if needed. A set of entities with the same structure but with differences in attribute values is the conventional file. In Figure 3.7 four entity descriptions could be visualized: DOCTOR, EMPLOYEE, CHILD, and INSURANCE_CO; or perhaps the user might like to think of it as one large entity. The entity description catalog (or data base dictionary) for the four entities is shown in Figure 3.24. This catalog would be derived from a schema data description command. Note that if one set of entities is associated with another (or the same) set of entities in a many-to-one relationship, take EMPLOYEE patients of a DOCTOR, then the DOCTOR association (say) must be recorded in the entity description of the many EMPLOYEE entities. This is done so as to represent the relationship and also to maintain the same structure for all DOCTOR records.

An example of the representation-independent language is a query type of language in which physical access path notions are not involved as illustrated by

PRINT DOCTOR DATA
WHERE CLINIC.ADDRESS = ENCINO AND SPECIALTY = EAR

The equivalent representation-dependent language commands at the access path level might be

```
     I = 1;
A:   READ DOCTOR IN FILE (X) WHERE KEY = I;
     IF CLINIC.ADDRESS = ENCINO AND
     DOCTOR.SPECIALTY = EAR THEN
     PRINT DOCTOR FILE (PRINTER);
     I = I + 1;
     GO TO A;
```

if no direct paths exist to records on the basis of ADDRESS and SPECIALTY. These statements are now crawling through an access path to records, searching them one by one for the matching criteria and writing them if qualified. Only when the data base system has the intelligence to decide how to answer a query at the representation-independent realm by choosing appropriate access path(s) does the user avoid dealing with access path notions.

As a more complex case, consider the logical schema in Figure 3.7. Let us take a request for information contained in the INSURANCE_CO entity concerning insurance companies that have more than 20 insured employees whose individual $OWED_TO_DOCTOR is greater than $10,000. The subset could be described in the following access-path independent way:

FORM TROUBLE SET FROM INSURANCE_CO WHERE COUNT
OF (FORM TEMPORARY SET FROM EMPLOYEE SUCH THAT
TEMPORARY.INSUR_CO_NAME = TROUBLE.INSUR_CO_
NAME AND TEMPORARY.$OWED_TO_DOCTOR > 10000) > 20.

Conceptually, the subset of INSURANCE_CO called TROUBLE is formed, such that for each entity in TROUBLE, a temporary subset of EMPLOYEES called TEMPORARY can be formed meeting the desired conditions. The TEMPORARY specifications illustrates a recursive nesting of subset specifications. The entities that qualify for inclusion in TEMPORARY are those for which the employee's INSUR_CO_NAME is the same as the INSUR_CO_NAME of the selected TROUBLE entity and the employee's $OWED_TO_DOCTOR is greater than 10000. The condition on TEMPORARY is that it contain more than 20 entities. COUNT would be a built-in function provided

Name	*Function*	*Identifier*
DOCTOR	Entity Name	DOCTOR-NAME
DOCTOR-NAME	Attribute	—
CLINIC-NAME	Attribute	—
CLINIC-ADDRESS	Attribute	—
DOCTOR-SPECIALTY	Attribute	—
EMPLOYEE	Entity Name	EMPLOYEE #
EMPLOYEE #	Attribute	—
NAME	Attribute	—
ADDRESS	Attribute	—
DEPARTMENT	Attribute	—
AGE	Attribute	—
SPOUSE-NAME	Attribute	—
*INSUR-CO-NAME	Attribute	—
*DOCTOR-NAME	Attribute	—
$OWED-TO-DOCTOR	Attribute	—
CHILD	Entity Name	EMPLOYEE # .CHiLD-NAME
CHILD-NAME	Attribute	—
*EMPLOYEE #	Attribute	—
CHILD-AGE	Attribute	—
SCHOOL-YEAR	Attribute	—
INSURANCE-CO	Entity Name	INSUR-CO-NAME
INSUR-CO-NAME	Attribute	—
ADDRESS	Attribute	—
CLAIM-CYCLE	Attribute	—

* These attributes provide the relationship link to other entities.

Figure 3.24. *Entity description catalog (or data base logical directory) of the schema in Figure 3.7 (relationships not cataloged) derived from the definition of the schema in the data description language*

by the data base system which returns the number of entities in the given set.

Note that the previous query does not entail access path considerations by the user. In order to process this query automatically, the data base system will have to have powerful access path mechanisms and enough logical intelligence. Not many commercial data base systems available can answer this query directly and the user may be forced to deal with the data base at the access path-oriented level and/or in-core data manipulation commands. But, imagine how many COBOL or PL/1 statements would be required to answer the above query when using only the basic access methods available in a conventional operating system.

Most so-called query languages or immediate access languages in commercial systems are representation-independent languages, within some bounds of query complexity particular to each system. In contrast, many of the data manipulation languages of commercial systems are access path-oriented in that they involve "Get Next Record and Test" notions, e.g., CODASYL's DML, TOTAL's DML, and IMS's DL/1. However, a number of data base specialists might contend that "Get Next" notions as defined in a number of systems are essentially logical structure dependent. The relational model and its associated languages are far from any physical access path considerations, further than other models (CODASYL, IMS, etc.). Needless to say, there is much controversy on representation-independent languages and models (and even on what the representation independence yardstick is!).

3.8.4   DIAM String Model and Catalog

The string model represents the first step toward representing entity sets in computer storage, independent of particular computer systems. Access paths will be specified by interconnecting attribute values and collections of attribute values by means of unidirectional operators called **strings**. The string model is independent of the many possible **encodings** of the strings. As has been shown in the previous chapter, for any given string structure specification a variety of ways of encoding or laying out the structure exists. The failure of some data base efforts to recognize this level of independence (i.e., the separation of logical access path specification from the encoding specification) accounts in great part for the frequent inability of these efforts to achieve total storage generality (i.e., independence from particular storage devices).

With three basic types of strings and associated parameters, any access path structure can be specified (e.g., sequential files, multifile secondary indexing organizations). The three types of strings arise naturally out of existing file organizations and the types of associations involved in existing logical models of data. Alternatively, it would be possible to define one general kind of string with a large set of possible parameters that would allow specifying a path from any data element to another in the data base. In specific situations those parameters not appropriate would be left undefined. This is not as convenient as the three DIAM strings. Another reason for not selecting one general kind of string is that the three types of strings make it relatively simple to specify paths that normally make sense and to bias the model against the selection of possible but impractical (from the practical machine efficiency point of view) paths.

The following paragraphs will describe the functions of each of the three types of DIAM strings and how the strings are defined, leaving the details of parameter and catalog specifications to subsequent paragraphs. The schema in Figures 3.7 and 3.24 will be used as a basis for examples.

A-String (Attribute String)

An **A-string** (*A*ttribute string) is defined on a single entity. Each instance of a given named A-string connects a specified subset of an entity's attribute values in a specified order, as illustrated in Figure 3.25. A given named A-string is equivalent to the CODASYL record, the relational model relation, and the IMS segment. More than one type of A-string can be defined over an entity. Thus, A-strings may define subschemas over an entity type, and a particular entity may have more than one representation stored in the data base (and perhaps incur redundancy in storage).

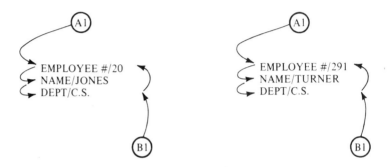

Two instances of two A-String types (subschemas) A1 and B1 over one entity (schema)

Figure 3.25.   *A-string (Attribute string) instances*

E-String (Entity String)

Instances of a specified named string type with the same type description are interconnected by an **E-string** (*E*ntity string). If the specified component

E-String called E-EMP has as components A1 instances with DEPT = C.S. and are in order by NAME value

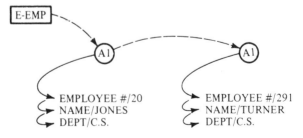

Figure 3.26.   *An E-string (Entity string)*

type is an A-string, a subset representation of an entity may result, perhaps involving a subset of the entity's attributes, as shown in Figure 3.25. The conventional file is an E-string. A named string of any of the three types may be specified as the basis of an E-string collection. Parameters allow specification of conditions for inclusion of an instance of the component string as well as specification of an access order among the elements of the collection, as illustrated in Figure 3.26.

A **partitioned E-string** may also be specified based on the values or range of values of an attribute of a component A-string, as shown in Figure 3.27. For each discrete value of the attribute, an E-string instance is formed connecting the component instances which contain that value. A second E-string might

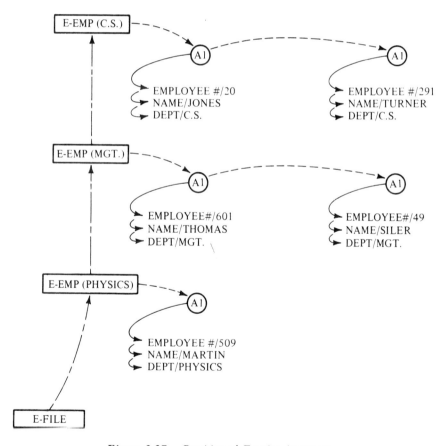

Figure 3.27.   *Partitioned E-string instances*

then connect instances of the first in an order based on the attribute value, as shown in Figure 3.27, the E_FILE string. In traditional terminology, an E-string might correspond to the ordered collection of records of a sequential data file, the COBOL repeating group, or to the records of a hash addressed file.

L-String (Link String)

An **L-string** (*L*ink string) connects instances of any of the three types of string in a specified order, based on a match among attribute values from the same attribute domain occurring within A-strings within the component strings. For example, in Figure 3.28, if we have a second set of entities INSURANCE_CO, then an L-string, say L-REL, can be specified to connect an A-string, say A_INS, with the corresponding E-string named E_EMP; the A-string A_INS is connected to the corresponding E-string named

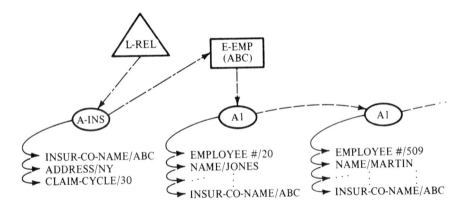

L-REL links A-INS instances with corresponding E-EMP instances on the basis of matching attribute values from the INSUR-CO-NAME. It is a 1-to-N relation as shown.

L-REL corresponds to a DBTG set:

Figure 3.28.   *L-string (Link string)*

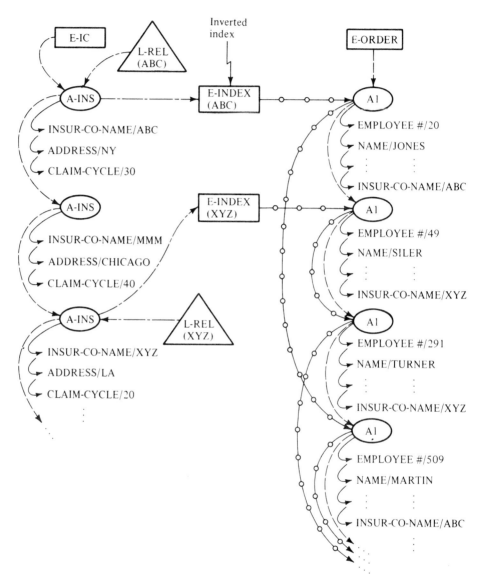

Figure 3.29. *Inverted indexes and sequential access paths, represented in DIAM strings*

E_EMP (ABC) because the latter contains all the EMPLOYEE entities where INSUR_CO_NAME = ABC. The conceptual schema involved is that made up of the EMPLOYEE and INSURANCE_CO entities included in Figure 3.7.

L-strings provide the linking among structurally different collections of strings required to form such structures as DBTG sets, IMS hierarchies, indexes, and rings. See Figure 3.28 again.

Figure 3.29 shows an example of a one-level inverted index and sequential access paths. Employee A-strings A1 are connected in EMPLOYEE # order by E-string E_ORDER and are indexed (inverted) on INSUR_CO_NAME by the other E-strings E-INDEX shown. A-string A_INS defines another entity type and includes INSUR_CO_NAME attribute. The E-string E_IC selects only unique A_INS instances and provides access to them in order by INSUR_CO_NAME. A1 instances having the same value of INSUR_CO_NAME are collected by the partitioned E-string E_INDEX and linked to the corresponding A_INS instance by the L-string L_REL.

All string information is centralized in the string catalog (access path directory). The string catalog is the entity set catalog augmented by this string information. The string parameter specifications are discussed in subsequent paragraphs.

Figure 3.29 illustrates the search path problem posed by the existence of multiple access paths to information. A request in the Representation Independent Language for information about a subset of the Employee entities contains nothing about how to find the desired entities. The system must determine from the catalog that the A1 (and perhaps other) A-string instances contain the desired information and that they can be reached by paths starting with E_ORDER and E_IC. If the system does not have such intelligence, then the user must give access path-oriented commands. The most efficient path must be chosen depending on the characteristics of the incoming query and the strings available. A simple optimization for a single query might take into account only the String Model specifications. A more thorough optimization for a request to be repeated many times would also take into account the specifications of the next two lower levels.

The following paragraphs present the details of the string parameters and the makeup of the string catalog.

String Model Parameters and Catalog

An A-string specification has three parameters:

1. The *Entity Set Name*, ESN, which specifies the universe of the attributes of the entity, call it the *entity set*, over which the A-string is defined.

2. The *Attribute List*, AL, parameter containing an ordered list of the specific attribute names making up the A-string.
3. The ON parameter indicating the names of other strings of which this string is a member.

The general form of an A-string is

A-string Name   ASG   ESN = (Entity Set Name)
                           AL = (Attribute name 1, Attribute name 2,...)
                           ON = (String name 1, string name 2,...)

Consider the entity set

EMPLOYEE(EMPLOYEE # , NAME, ADDRESS, DEPARTMENT, AGE, SPOUSE_NAME, INSURANCE_CO, DOCTOR_NAME, $OWED_TO_DOCTOR)

with EMPLOYEE # the identifier. These two A-strings could be defined over the entity set:

1. AA   ASG   ESN = (EMPLOYEE)
                   AL = (EMPLOYEE #, NAME, DEPARTMENT, AGE)
2. AB   ASG   ESN = (EMPLOYEE)
                   AL = (EMPLOYEE #, ADDRESS, SPOUSE_ NAME, INSURANCE_CO, DOCTOR_ NAME, $OWED_TO_DOCTOR).

If, for example, the majority of transactions referring to the entity EMPLOYEE are directed to EMPLOYEE #, NAME, DEPARTMENT, and AGE, but not against the other attributes of EMPLOYEE, the data base designer might want to store the AA portion of EMPLOYEE on a relatively high-speed storage device, whereas the less frequently used AB portion might be stored in a lower-speed device. The identifier attribute EMPLOYEE # is needed in both strings for the reconstruction of the entire EMPLOYEE entity. The AA and AB strings would be specified as an initial basis for the desired physical structure organization.

The E-string is used to connect together all instances or subsets of instances of strings of the same type. The particular subset is established on the basis of quantitative properties of the members of the collection. Each E-string specification has five parameters:

1. The Attribute List parameter AL which contains the name of the one and only base string over which the E-string is being defined.

2. A *sel*ection SEL criterion which specifies the qualification of an instance of the base string. There are, of course, many qualification criteria. In general, a data base designer-administrator will specify qualification based on attribute values. The possible qualifications would be those defined in Appendix B: in practice, the qualification is not too complex. The example AL = A1 SEL = (A1. DEPART-MENT = FINANCE) would then qualify for inclusion within the collection being defined those instances of the A1 string for which the value of the DEPARTMENT attribute is FINANCE.

3. An optional *parti*tion parameter PART which partitions the collection of qualified instances defined by the E-string. A partition parameter contains a list of attributes. As many partitions will be formed as there are unique combinations of values for these attributes within the set of qualified string instances. For example, AL = A1 PART = (A1. DEPARTMENT, A1.INSUR_CO_ NAME). If there were four unique values for the attribute DE-PARTMENT and four unique values for the attribute INSUR_CO_ NAME within the set of qualified A1 instances, then the collection of these instances would be partitioned into 16 uniquely identifiable subcollections.

4. An *or*dered *on* parameter ORO identifying those attribute names on which the qualifying collection or partitions of base strings will be ordered.

5. An ON parameter indicating the names of other strings of which this string is a member.

The form of an E-string specification statement is

E-string Name   ESG   AL = ( )   SEL = ( )   PART = ( )
                        ORO = ( )   ON = ( )

As examples consider the specification of the two E-strings diagrammed in Figure 3.27:

1. E_EMP   ESG   AL = (A1)   PART = (A1. DEPT)
                  ORO = (none)   ON = (E_FILE)
2. E_FILE   ESG   AL = (E_EMP)   SEL = (All)
                   ORO = (E_EMP. DEPARTMENT)

The L-string provides access paths connecting a finite number of structurally different string instances. Functionally, an L-string is similar in nature to an A-string, the difference being that each instance of an L-string connects not attribute values but rather instances of other A-, E-, or L-strings of any complexity. A DBTG set and an IMS parent segment-child segment two-level hierarchy correspond to an L-string.

Each L-string type involve three parameters:

1. An attribute list AL containing an ordered list of string names, instances of which are to be connected by the L-string being defined.
2. A matched-on-criterion, MC, which indicates how instances of the component strings in the AL are to be related together to form an instance of the L-string being defined.
3. An ON parameter indicating the names of other strings of which this string is a member.

The general L-string form is

L-string Name   LSG   AL = ( )   MC = ( )   ON = ( )

As an example, the definition of the L-string L_REL in Figure 3.28 is

L_REL   LSG   AL = (A_INS, E_EMP)
MC = (A_INS. INSUR_CO_NAME
= E_EMP.INSUR_CO_NAME)

Here the L-string L_REL connects the A-string A_INS [the parent (master) segment (record) representation] to the matching E-string E_EMP. E_EMP connects a collection of A-string A1's which are leaf or detail segment (record) representations. Hierarchies or networks with more levels and more types of records or segments at the same level are easily represented. At the string model level, the hierarchic structures of IMS, TOTAL, IDS, and so forth, look essentially alike.

Each A-, E-, and L-string specification is derived from data base design consideration and is centralized in the *string level* catalog. Each string will contain its parameterized information plus a list of all those other strings in whose attribute list it appears. This facilitates the identification of search paths in processing a given transaction.

Example

An example with the use of all three types of strings is now in order. Consider the data base shown in Figure 3.24 disregarding the DOCTOR entity. Suppose that the transactions consist primarily of a request for an EMPLOYEE followed by a request for information on the children of this employee and/or a request for the insurance company of this employee. In this case, the data base designer-administrator would want to establish several access paths, each of which would connect an employee to his child(ren) and insurance company.

Access paths are specified by means of an adequate language or commands. Sometimes access paths are specified by one single language which involves logical structure notions as well as physical organization notions (e.g., attribute names to invert). Sometimes it is done via two languages, one to specify structure and another primarily for physical structuring (the latter usually not a formal language but a rather awkward means to specify it).

The following string specifications would be involved in our example:

1. A1   ASG   ESN = (EMPLOYEE)
                AL = (EMPLOYEE #, NAME,ADDRESS,
                     DEPARTMENT,AGE,SPOUSE_NAME,
                     INSUR_CO_NAME,DOCTOR_NAME,
                     $OWED_TO_DOCTOR)
2. AINS ASG   ESN = (INSURANCE_CO)
                AL = (INSUR_CO_NAME,ADDRESS,
                     CLAIM_CYCLE)
3. ACH   ASG   ESN = (CHILD)
                AL = (CHILD_NAME,EMPLOYEE #,
                     CHILD_AGE,SCHOOL_YEAR)

for each of the three entities of interest, i.e., EMPLOYEE, INSURANCE_CO, and CHILD. The next specification creates appropriate subcollections of the ACH instances. Each subcollection of ACH instances is the child(ren) of a given employee:

4. ECH   ESG   AL = (ACH)
                PART = (ACH. EMPLOYEEE #)
                ORO = (ACH. CHILD_NAME)

The next specification would create the access paths linking a person to his child(ren) and his insurance company:

5. L   LSG AL = (A1, ECH, AINS)
                MC = (A1. EMPLOYEE # = ECH. ACH.
                EMPLOYEE #,
                A1. INSUR_CO_NAME = AINS.
                INSUR_CO_NAME)

Finally:

6. EDB   ESG   AL = (L)
                ORO = (L.A1.EMPLOYEE #)

represents a single E-string characterizing the access path connecting all the instances of the L-string L, thus accounting for the whole data base.

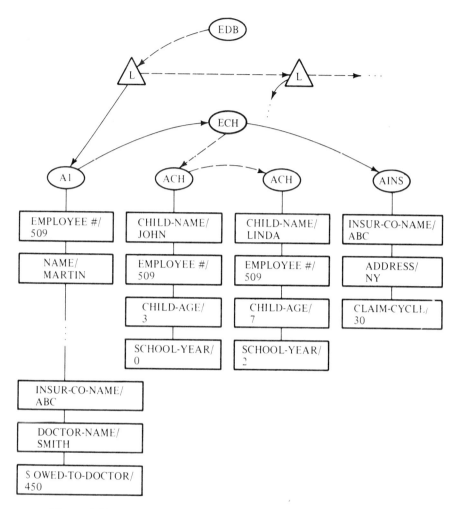

Figure 3.30.   *DIAM string structure of the employee-child-insurance data base*

The string structure of the data base is shown in Figure 3.30. It involves a 1:1 relationship between the EMPLOYEE entity and the corresponding INSURANCE_CO entity and a 1:N relationship between the EMPLOYEE entity and the corresponding subcollection of CHILD instances. In order to access this hierarchy, one enters via EDB (enter data base), finds the appropriate instance of L on the basis of the EMPLOYEE # in A1, and then accesses the corresponding ACH and AINS subcollections. The string catalog involved is shown in Figure 3.31. Note that the catalog is free of any information regarding the physical encoding of the strings.

EMPLOYEE	ENTITY NAME	IDENTIFIER = EMPLOYEE #
	A1 ASG	ESN = (EMPLOYEE)
		AL = (EMPLOYEE #, NAME,
		ADDRESS, DEPARTMENT, AGE, SPOUSE-NAME,
		INSUR_CO_NAME, DOCTOR_NAME,
		$OWED-TO-DOCTOR)
		ON = (L)
	L LSG	AL = (A1, ECH, AINS)
		MC = (A1, EMPLOYEE # = ECH.ACH.
		EMPLOYEE #, A1.INSUR_CO_NAME =
		AINS. INSUR_CO_NAME)
		ON = (EDB)
	EDB ESG	AL = (L) ORO = (L.A1.EMPLOYEE #)
EMPLOYEE #, NAME	Attributes	ON = A1
ADDRESS, DEPARTMENT	Attributes	ON = A1
AGE, SPOUSE_NAME	Attributes	ON = A1
INSUR_CO_NAME	Attribute	ON = A1
DOCTOR_NAME	Attribute	ON = A1
$OWED_TO_DOCTOR	Attribute	ON = A1
CHILD	Entity Name	IDENTIFIER = EMPLOYEE #. CHILD_NAME
	ACH ASG	ESN = (CHILD)
		AL = (CHILD_NAME,
		EMPLOYEE #, CHILD_AGE, SCHOOL_
		YEAR) ON = (EINS)
	ECH ESG	AL = (ACH) PART = ACH. EMPLOYEE #
		ORO = (ACH. CHILD_NAME) ON = (L)
CHILD_NAME	Attribute	ON = ACH
EMPLOYEE #	Attribute	ON = ACH
CHILD_AGE	Attribute	ON = ACH
SCHOOL_YEAR	Attribute	ON = ACH
INSURANCE_CO.	Entity Name	IDENTIFIER = INSUR_CO_NAME
	AINS ASG	ESN = (INSURANCE_CO)
		AL = (INSUR_CO_NAME,
		ADDRESS, CLAIM_CYCLE)
		ON = (L)
INSUR_CO_NAME	Attribute	ON = AINS
ADDRESS	Attribute	ON = AINS
CLAIM_CYCLE	Attribute	ON = AINS

Figure 3.31.   *DIAM string catalog (dictionary) of the employee-child-insurance data base*

The hierarchic or level-by-level DIAM structure and accompanying catalog description can be used to define both an encoding similar to that used in the IMS system and an encoding similar to that used in CODASYL systems. For the particular storage structure developed, it is not the logical-physical nature of the structure, i.e., access paths, where the systems are different; it is only in the actual access path encodings where differences arise. We shall illustrate this later in this section.

3.8.5   DIAM Encoding (Physical Structure)
Model and Catalog

The encoding level is concerned with the specific encoding, with the specific physical layout, and with the bit-level encoding of the access paths in the data base. All storage devices have the common characteristics of bit or byte streams, and thus it is desirable to extract these common characteristics for another level, the encoding level, and leave consideration of physical device-dependent and complicated parameters to a separate and lower level, the physical device model.

Three basic concepts are involved in the encoding model: *linear address spaces*, *basic encoding units*, and *factoring*.

Linear Address Spaces. A **L**inear **A**ddress **S**pace, **LAS**, is a uniquely named, one-dimensional bit stream of arbitrary length. Each bit within an LAS is uniquely addressable. It is with a view toward these bit strings that data is encoded; it is from these bit streams that transformation onto physical storage devices is accomplished.

Basic Encoding Units. Every instance of every defined string represents an explicit information unit and should therefore have an explicit stored representation. In deciding on a sufficient representational form, it is important to realize that in existing data organizations and data management systems space is set aside for actual attribute values and for the following three types of control information:

1. Names for files, records, fields, and so forth, placed so that a program may derive the nature of the component to be decoded;
2. Length indication for files, records, and fields; and
3. Physical pointers to the next component to be decoded.

Each of the control information components looks like a field-value. It would be possible to define a model that considers each control field as a pseudo-attribute and then define its characteristics (e.g., length) in the same way as is done for actual attributes. General models of this type have been proposed by a few authors. A more systematic and simple model that gives sufficient generality with a few well-defined parameters is preferred. To arrive at it, consider similarities and differences in, for example, Figure 3.30.

Note that there are four essential characteristics appropriate to each instance of each defined string:

1. The name of the string,
2. For each ordered collection of which the string instance is a member, an indication of the location of the next member of the collection. In

Figure 3.30, for example, an indication of the location of an ECH instance would be a characteristic of an A1 instance with respect to the collection L;

3. An indication of the location of the first member of the collection making up the string instance. In Figure 3.30, for example, an indication of the location of an instance of A1 would be a characteristic of L; and

4. A means for determining the end of the collection making up the string instance.

The stored representation of a string instance must contain information corresponding to each of these characteristics. These features appear at all levels of existing data base structures. Files, records, and fields are simply names for particular kinds of collections of smaller units that are connected into one or more larger collections. In addition, the encoding scheme must be sufficiently general so that a wide range of physical encodings is attainable.

The fundamental unit for encoding all the relevant information for a string instance is the **Basic Encoding Unit, BEU**. The general BEU format is given in Figure 3.32 and its components are in direct correspondence with the characteristics listed above. Thus, STRING LABEL is that portion of the representation containing the name of the collection of information that the string or the attribute name defines. Each *Association Pointer*, APTR, portion of the representation contains the information necessary to determine the LAS location of the next member of the collection, of which this BEU is a member. There is one APTR for each distinct collection of which this BEU is a member. The *Value Pointer*, VPTR, portion of the representation contains the information necessary to determine the LAS location of the first member of the collection defined by the string that owns this BEU. In the case of an attribute name, the collection consists of its attribute value. In the case of an A-, E-, or L-string, the collection consists of the set of BEUs linked by it. The *Termination TERM* contains the information to determine the end of the collection defined by the string corresponding to this BEU. All instances of a given string have the same BEU representational format. The representations differ only in the values for the various components.

The catalog entries (in addition to those for the string model) required to support the notion of BEUs consist of sets of specifications (one set for each defined string) by means of which the various components of the BEU can be

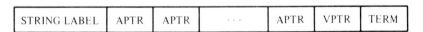

| STRING LABEL | APTR | APTR | · · · | APTR | VPTR | TERM |

General BEU Format

Figure 3.32. *DIAM BEU (Basic Encoding Unit) format*

isolated within the bit stream and decoded. The nature of these specifications will be exemplified after discussing the notion of factoring.

Factoring. In general, each string structure instance will contain, within its encoded bit stream representation, i.e., its BEU, information regarding each of the components mentioned above. In some situations, however, certain information is common in all of the instances of a particular string. In these situations, that information which is common can be removed from the representations or data stream and placed within the BEU portion of the catalog description of the string itself. This process is called **factoring**.

Factoring systematically achieves any encoding combination from generalized list structures (unfactored BEUs) to serial fixed-length record files (completely factored BEUs). Systematic and explicit factoring places at the disposal of the data base designer-administrator a spectrum of possible factorings, and therefore of possible encodings. In present-day file and data base organization schemes, factoring is made an integral and nonmodifiable part of

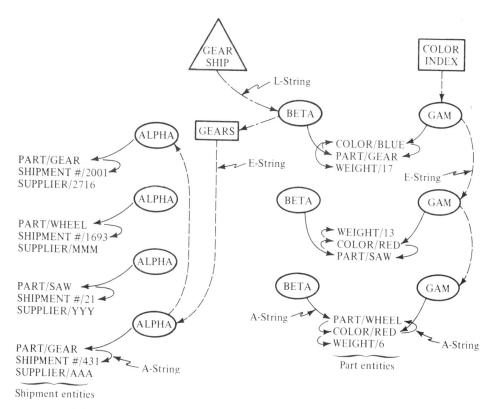

Figure 3.33. *DIAM string structure of the part-shipment data base*[15]

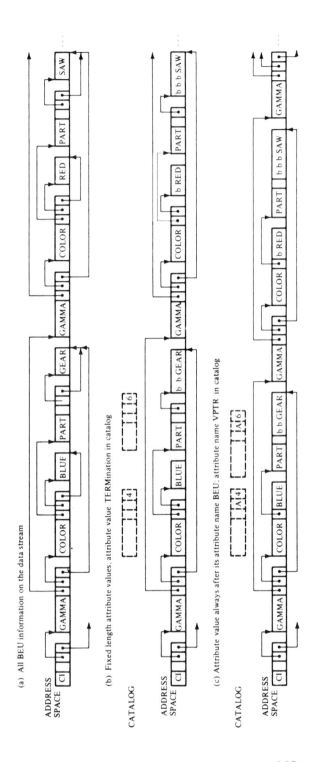

(a) All BEU information on the data stream

(b) Fixed length attribute values; attribute value TERMination in catalog

(c) Attribute value always after its attribute name BEU; attribute name VPTR in catalog

146

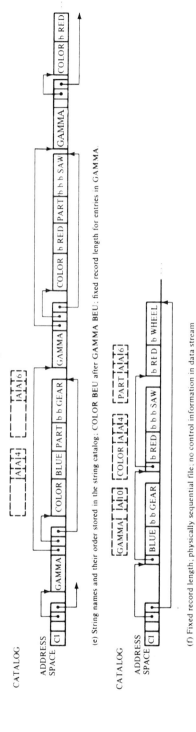

Figure 3.34. *Factoring of the Basic Encoding Unit (BEU)*[15] *(Courtesy IBM Corp.)*

(d) PART BEU always after its COLOR BEU; APTR of COLOR BEU in catalog

(e) String names and their order stored in the string catalog; COLOR BEU after GAMMA BEU; fixed record length for entries in GAMMA.

(f) Fixed record length; physically sequential file; no control information in data stream

147

the total file or data base system: to alter the factoring even slightly requires major reprogramming or creation of a totally new file or data base package.

Let us illustrate the process of factoring with an example. This is the example from reference 15. Consider the E-string COLOR INDEX over GAM A-strings shown in Figure 3.33 for a data base with PART entities and SHIPMENT entities. Figure 3.34(a) shows the stream of the unfactored BEU, for the collection COLOR INDEX (a list of GAM A-strings). The BEUs are placed next to each other for convenience, but it should be realized that any element connected by pointers may appear at any position (LAS) on the data stream (as for example in the chained-tree organization, Figure 2.12).

The BEU components are stored in the order LABEL, APTR, VPTR, TERM. Note that in Figure 3.34(a) BEUs for the following strings and attribute names appear in this order: COLOR INDEX, GAMMA (denoted as GAM in Figure 3.33), COLOR, PART, GAMMA, COLOR, PART.

If all of the attribute values of COLOR have a fixed length of four bytes and those of PART have a fixed length of six bytes, then the terminator parameters can be removed from the data stream and placed in the type description in the catalog. This factoring is shown in Figure 3.34(b).

If the attribute name is considered to be always physically followed by the associated attribute value in every BEU of this attribute name, then its VPTR can be factored. The result appears in Figure 3.34(c).

If the PART BEU is always after its associated COLOR BEU, then the APTR in the COLOR BEU can be factored. The result is shown in Figure 3.34(d).

If the order of the GAMMA string instances is specified, for example, ordered on the basis of part COLOR and in addition every COLOR BEU always follows its associated GAMMA A-string BEU, then the factoring shown in Figure 3.34(e) can be obtained. Note that the A-string GAMMA record is fixed length, 10 bytes long, and is indicated in the catalog.

Finally, if every A-string instance is to be physically followed by its next A-string instance in the collection COLOR INDEX, then we have a fixed-length record sequential file representation of the collection COLOR INDEX; the layout is shown in Figure 3.34(f). Note that at this point no control information appears in the data stream.

Now consider the two-level hierarchy, 1:n relationship between the BETA record and its detail ALPHA records represented by the L-string GEAR SHIP. Figure 3.35(a) − 3.35(c) (adapted from reference 15) shows IDS and IMS representations for this hierarchical collection. Figure 3.35(a) shows the IDS GEARS collection with a back pointer; IDS uses chained or network data structures. Note that this catalog is not too different from that in Figure 3.34(e), except that the string length (e.g., 13 bytes for BETA) is stored in both the catalog and data stream. In Figure 3.35(b) the catalog is essentially the same as 3.35(a) but with the redundant length field of BETA and ALPHA

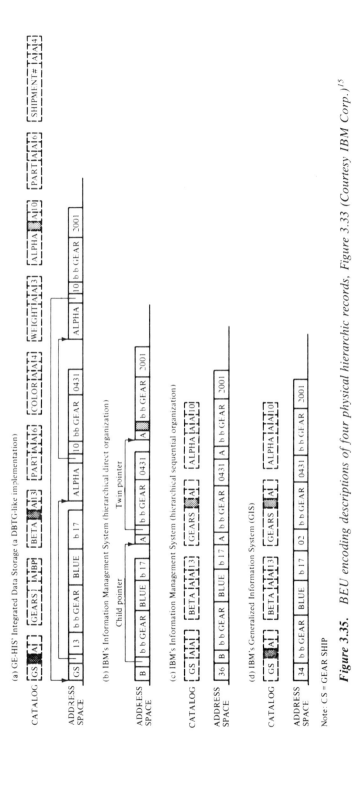

Figure 3.35. *BEU encoding descriptions of four physical hierarchic records, Figure 3.33 (Courtesy IBM Corp.)[15]*

Note: CS = GEAR SHIP

149

BEUs removed from the data stream. In Figure 3.35(c) it may appear that pointers in the IMS Hierarchical Sequential organization have been omitted. However, the pointers for connecting pieces or records together are not really a property of the IMS segments; they are a property of the physical record structure of IMS and thus do not appear at this encoding level.

The information of this encoding level resides in a catalog or dictionary. This catalog is the string catalog augmented by entries that specify the encoding level aspects just discussed. Further details on encoding level specifications appear in references 16 and 17.

3.8.6 Physical Device Level Model

The Entity Set, String Structure, and Encoding specifications provide a basis for describing features of data base organizations in high-speed storage and in virtual address systems. However, these specifications neither take into consideration the periodic structures and heterogeneous access times characteristic of large-capacity DASD nor express storage organization strategies to avoid the often serious penalties incurred in random accessing. For example, it is desirable to have a mechanism that automatically inserts new records near related old records so as to minimize physical access time.

Existing systems like ISAM, IMS, and IDS involve a rather complex set of parameters to describe the physical device level. A discussion of actual physical file organizations and device level considerations is provided in Chapter 2 and Appendix A. There is a wide range of functions at the device level in existing systems.

Broadly speaking, the physical device level requires at least the following:

1. Physical subdivision type specification—to define properties of named physical subdivision types such as types of blocks, pages, or tracks. For example, ISAM has four types of physical subdivisons: prime, overflow, track index, and higher-level index.

2. Physical device formatting—to provide for formatting specific physical storage devices in terms of physical subdivision types.

3. Address space allocation—to provide a means for correlating named Linear Addresses Spaces, LAS, used in the encoding level model with the formatted device addresses. A named address space may be discontinuous with respect to the physical device address space, may be multidimensional, and may span portions of one or more storage devices (e.g., an E-string may span across several disks).

4. Placement specifications—to define a physical record and describe the system strategies for placing it in storage.

We shall not delve further into this device-dependent physical level. Some of the parameterization suggested by the DIAM effort and some details appear in reference 15. However, the DIAM model at this level is sketchy and was not completed by its pioneering authors. No complete models are available. This area invites much research and development.

3.9 THE ENTITY-RELATIONSHIP-ATTRIBUTE ERA LOGICAL DATA BASE MODEL

The **Entity-Relationship-Attribute, ERA**, is a model originally proposed by Chen[19] for expressing in very high-level and graphical terms the logical content or structure of a data base or schema. The ERA model is a logical conceptualization of the conventional hierarchic, network, and relational data models. Using the DIAM framework, the ERA model is at the higher user-level realm involving entities and their functional relationships. Practitioners' jargon refers to the ERA model, and its derivatives and extensions, as a *logical data base model*, *conceptual data base model*, and *information model*.

In the early 1980s many authors, practitioners, and vendors started endorsing the ERA model as a very attractive model to express conceptually the logical structure of a data base, independent of any one GDBMS and without the constraints of hierarchic, network, or relational models. At the same time, however, a few individuals have proposed the relational model as an appropriate conceptual model. The original ERA model has given rise to a variety of derivatives and extensions, and it has been extensively applied.[20] It is used as part of several proposed data base design methodologies. In particular, various meanings or semantics and integrity controls have been added to the model.

Let us illustrate the ERA model through examples and avoid defining all its formalisms and semantics.

Example

Consider the schema in Figure 3.7, and in Figure 3.24 for the DIAM model. Figure 3.36 shows graphically the ERA model of such schema. The fact that this ERA schema is self-explanatory to most readers is evidence that the ERA is an attractive model. Note that:

1. *Entities* are represented by squares or rectangles, with an appropriate and unique entity name placed inside. The key attribute(s) or identifier name(s) uniquely identifying each entity instance is usually placed inside.

2. The *attributes* may be also placed inside the box and clearly differentiated from the key attribute(s). The entity attributes are not included in the example herein.

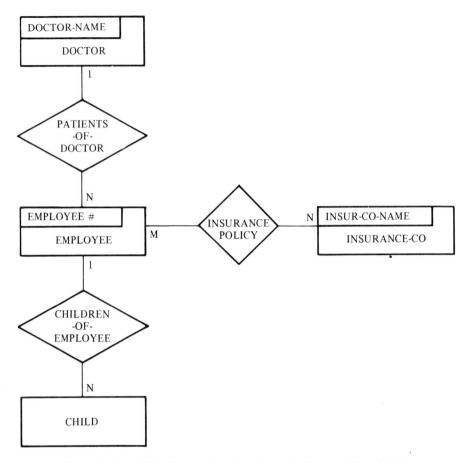

Figure 3.36. *ERA diagram for the schema in Figures 3.7 and 3.24*

3. Any *relationship* of interest is *explicitly* defined, and uniquely named, as in the CODASYL model and as opposed to implicitly defined as in the relational model. The relationships are to be names using terms as indicative of the meaning as possible. The name of the relationship is placed inside a diamond.

4. The degree of the relationship is indicated, whether it is 1:1, 1:N, or M:N (it is usually implied that a given instance of an entity may be related to zero instances of another entity).

5. A clear textual description of each entity and of the meaning of each relationship should be included with each ERA diagram.

This ERA model may then be mapped or transformed to a network, relational, or hierarchic model. As an exercise, the reader should try it.

Example

Let us consider another example involving attributes in a relationship and additional semantics. Suppose that we wish to define a data base that deals only with "persons who are over 50 years old and who work in projects with project names COBRA and ZEBRA for 20 percent or more of their time." Figure 3.37 shows the ERA model. In this case, % OF-TIME is an attribute of the relationship WORKS-IN, AGE is an attribute of PERSON, and PROJECT-NAME is an attribute of PROJECT. Note how semantics and integrity controls have been expressed independent of any particular GDBMS specifics.

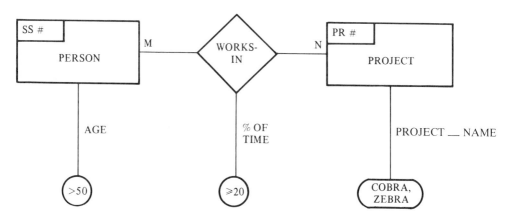

Figure 3.37. ERA diagram example

3.10 SUMMARY

In the late 1960s and particularly the 1970s data management technology evolved into file management and data base management technologies. Generalized file management systems (GFMS) and generalized data base management systems (GDBMS) have been designed to serve a wide spectrum of users. Each of these types of systems has its own distinct objectives. GFMS strive to provide facilities primarily for report writing and sorting, superior to those available in conventional programming languages. GDBMS strive to provide facilities to achieve data independence (both logical and physical), data shareability, nonredundancy of data stored, relatability between records, integrity, access flexibility, security, performance and efficiency, and administration and control. These objectives are delineated in Section 3.3. They are achieved in varying degrees by the various commercially available GDBMS.

Fundamental and common to all data base systems is the ability to define schemas and subschemas and to separately manipulate this defined data. Each subschema represents the particular view or schema of a given application program or user and is formed by a particular subset of the fields, records, and relationships composing the schema. A schema data description language (DDL) and a subschema data description language are provided by a GDBMS. The two languages are usually very similar. A separate data manipulation language (DML) and a natural-language-oriented query language are provided for accessing the data base.

Three different approaches for logically representing data, that is, three different data base models may be considered: the hierarchic or tree model, the network model, and the relational or tabular model. Section 3.5 provides an introductory view of these logical organizations. Commercial GDBMS support one or two of these categories. The hierarchic model does not allow a child or member record type to be related to more than one owner or parent record type, although it can have any number of children record types. A network model is one that allows this; in fact, in the general network model any record may be related to any other record. Thus the network model is a more general organization. The relational model is essentially a network model in which a relationship is implicitly established by storing a common attribute (typically a unique identifier) in the two relations or tables (record types).

Considering the type of data base accessing and processing, and not just the data model, commercial GDBMS may be classified into four classes: hierarchic, network, inverted (and which are either hierarchic or network in terms of the data base model), and relational. The sole exponent of the classical hierarchic model is IBM's IMS, one of the GDBMS in widest use. The network approach has been advocated since the earlier data base efforts in the sixties leading to the milestone 1971 Data Base Task Group (DBTG) architecture authored by the CODASYL DBTG. The DBTG architecture is followed by an increasing number of commercial GDBMS. A network GDBMS can of course represent any hierarchic data base also.

The inverted approach uses an inversion implementation mechanism (inversion has been covered in the previous chapter) in conjunction with a network or hierarchic model so as to provide the capability of accessing data by content. Access is on the basis of any logical qualification on the inverted fields. In contrast the strict hierarchic and network GDBMS do not provide such a high degree of access by content; they are more oriented toward following pointer access paths from record to record, that is, toward "navigating" a data base. A number of inverted GDBMS are available commercially.

The relational approach is a more recent proposal claiming a number of advantages, particularly greater user convenience in dealing with a data base, one integrated high-level query language for accessing data on-line or from within programs (in COBOL, PASCAL, etc.), and greater data independence and security controls. Data is viewed as a set of two-dimensional or "flat" tables. The relational approach is being followed by an increasing number of commercial GDBMS, starting in the early 1980s.

Six types of languages or command facilities are usually involved in using a GDBMS: the schema DDL, the subschema DDL, the DML, the conventional programming language(s) (e.g., COBOL), a query language, and the physical data organization description language. The DML is used by an application program written in a programming language or by a user on a stand-alone basis (without the need of using a programming language) for all accessing of the data base under the control of the GDBMS. The GDBMS uses in turn the computer's operating system. A query language may be also provided with the GBDMS for low-volume English-oriented type of requests or simple report writing, usually on-line. A wide variety of mechanisms are found in use by GDBMS for describing how the data base contents are actually physically organized and laid out in storage devices; usually these mechanisms are not provided as a clean-cut physical data organization description language. Section 3.7 addresses these six most important types of languages for setting up and using data bases.

The organization of data in a data management system may be viewed at four architectural levels, as it proceeds from its logical data organization to its equivalent physical organization and mapping in storage devices. The mappings from level to level achieve a number of data base objectives, such as data independence and access flexibility. The data independent accessing model DIAM is a formal conception or model of data organization in a data management system. DIAM encompasses and details the four architectural levels. It has not been implemented as a commercial system. Section 3.8 uses the convenience and thoroughness of DIAM to explore data organization, the fundamental issues and alternatives, without a biased dependence on the details and idiosyncracies of any one commercial GDBMS. The particulars of commercial systems portraying each of the fundamental data models previously indicated are the subject of subsequent chapters.

The entity-relationship-attribute (ERA) model expresses in very high-level and graphical terms the logical structure of a data base or schema. The ERA model is a logical conceptualization of the conventional hierarchic, network, and relational data models followed by commercial GDBMS. It is classified as an information model or logical data base model.

REFERENCES

1. "Data Analyzer, General Information Manual," Program Products Inc., Nanuet, NY.

2. "Mark IV Systems, Technical System Description," Informatics, Inc., Document No. SM-7406 T76A, Canoga Park, Calif., June 1974.

3. "Mark IV," DataPro Research Corporaton, Report # 70E-500-01a, Delran, N.J., May 1975.

4. "ASI-ST, An Advanced Approach to Data Management," Applications Software Inc., Form MA-003.

5. IDS Reference Manual, General Electric Information Systems Division, CPB (565A), Phoneix, Ariz., September 1969.

6. Bleir, R. F., "Treating Hierarchical Data Structures in the SDC Timeshared Data Management System (TDMS)," *Proceedings, 22nd ACM National Conference*, 1967, pp. 41−49.

7. "Information Management System Virtual Storage (IMS/VS), General Information Manual," IBM Corporation, Form Number GH20-1260.

8. CODASYL, "Data Base Task Group (DBTG) Report, 1971," April 1971, Association for Computing Machinery, New York.

9. "Data Base Management System Requirements," GUIDE/SHARE Data Base Requirements Group, November 1971.

10. Bachman, C. W., and S. S. Williams, "A General Purpose Programming System for Random Access Memories," *Proceedings, 1964 Fall Joint Computer Conference*, Vol. 26, AFIPS Press, pp. 411−422.

11. "TOTAL Reference Manual," Cincom Systems Inc., Cincinnati, Ohio.

12. "SYSTEM 2000 Reference Manual," INTEL Corp., Austin, Texas.

13. Flynn, R. L., "A Brief History of Data Base Management," *DATAMATION*, August 1974, pp. 71−77.

14. CODASYL, "Draft Specification of a Data Storage Description Language," BCS Data Base Administration Working Group, Data Description Language Committee, *Journal of Development*, Secretariat of the Canadian Government EDP Standards Committee, January 1978.

15. Senko, M. E., E. B. Altman, M. M. Astrahan, and P. L. Fehder, "Data Structures and Accessing in Data Base Systems," *IBM Systems Journal*, Vol. 12, No. 1, 1973, pp 30−93.

16. Astrahan, M., et al., "Concepts of a Data Independent Accessing Model," IBM Research Report RJ 1105, San Jose, California, October 1972.

17. Altman, E. B., "Specifications in a Data Independent Accessing Model." IBM Research Report RJ 1141, San Jose, California, January 1973.

18. Fry, J. P., and E. H. Sibley, "Evolution of Data Base Management Systems," *Computing Surveys*, Vol. 8, No. 1, March 1976, pp. 7−42.

19. Chen, P. P., "The Entity Relationship Model: Toward a Unified View of Data," *ACM Transactions on Data Base Systems*, Vol. 1, No. 1, March 1976, pp. 9−13.

20. *Proceedings International Conference on the Entity-Relationship Approach to Information Modeling and Analysis* (held every two years since 1979 in different cities), ER Institute, Saugus, Calif.

EXERCISES

1. "In most applications you absolutely have to use *both* a generalized file management system in conjunction with a generalized data base management system." Do you agree with this statement? Under what circumstances might this be (a) the case; (b) not the case? Show the breadth of your understanding of available technologies.

2. Consider the following set of relations:

    Employee (<u>Man #</u>, Name, Birthday, Job_History, Children)

    Job_History (<u>Jobdate</u>, Title, Salary_History)

    Salary_History (<u>Salarydate</u>, Salary)

    Children (<u>Childname</u>, Birth_Year)

    (a) Translate this data base into a DIAM entity set data base and its directory. Show *all* A-, E-, and L-string definitions in the directory, linking the above relations. Clearly define the entities as shown above.

    (b) Suppose that an inverted index is to be established so that the Employee data may be easily retrieved on the basis of either of three possible titles: manager, technical staff, or enemy-spy. Show these access paths in the DIAM data base and directory.

3. Consider the DBTG set defined below, relating INSURANCE to EMPLOYEE. Can it be represented by the DIAM string model? If so, describe in detail how this is done.

    Can the DIAM string model represent inversions in a generalized GDBMS (like SYSTEM 2000 or ADABAS)? How is this done assuming we want to invert on the basis of RATING and CLAIM-CYCLE?

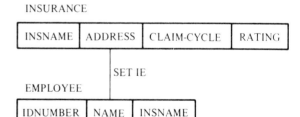

4. In the case of a typical GDBMS on a typical operating system, does the operating system "know" what is inside the blocks or pages that it stores (and retrieves) on (from) external storage devices for the GDBMS (i.e., does the operating system know if the blocks have data values or control information)? Explain, showing your understanding of the interaction between the GDBMS and the operating system.

4

GENERALIZED DATA MANAGEMENT SYSTEMS COMMERCIALLY AVAILABLE

The basic concepts and architecture of GDBMS have been introduced in Chapter 3. This chapter presents a brief survey of the commercial market place. Names of GDBMS, vendors, prices, hardware support, and functional features are summarized. A review of Sections 3.1 through 3.7 is advisable at this point.

An examination of the marketplace shows that there are between 30 and 50 commercially available generalized file management systems (GFMS) and data base management systems (GDBMS). This count excludes a number of (GFMS- or GDBMS-oriented, but not truly generalized nor as encompassing) systems developed by small vendor companies or in-house by some user organizations over a number of years and which have enjoyed success within the particular organization. It is difficult to establish a more exact count of systems available. Some systems have enjoyed little or no success at all due to technological and/or marketing reasons, although they have been publicized and their existence is known. Some systems have appeared and disappeared already. Others have come into the marketplace rather recently, particularly a number of GDBMS. Section 3.2 traced the chronology and functional relationships of basic report writers, GFMS, GDBMS, and programming language processors.

Informatics' Mark IV, Application Software's ASI-ST, and Program Products' Data Analyzer account for at least 80 percent of the installed GFMS. As of the early 1980s there were probably at least 4000 installed GFMS. In addition, there are hundreds of installations of IBM's GIS[20] which embodies many of the ingredients of GFMS, but not all (and thus we do not classify it as a GFMS).

The GDBMS market is somewhat more evenly shared. The top sellers include IBM's IMS[8] and Cincom's TOTAL,[19] each one with over 2000 installations; Cullinet's IDMS;[3] Intel's SYSTEM 2000;[14] and Software AG's ADABAS.[15] Among micro-GDBMS the leader is Ashton-Tate's dBASE II[23] with over 150,000 installations. This is a very fast-growing market. The large majority of the systems appearing in the commercial marketplace in the 1970s were based on the CODASYL DBTG architecture, the subject of Chapter 5. A significant number of the systems introduced commercially in the 1980s are relational systems, the subject of Chapters 9 through 11.

Figure 4.1 outlines the main available systems and their characteristics. Although it is not a complete list, it does include the systems that account for at least 80 percent of the installed population, excluding micro-GDBMS. Prices and characteristics change with time and options included. The price data in Figure 4.1 is approximate as of 1983–84. Price data in this text is as of 1983–84.

The following observations may be made:

1. The large majority of GFMS are marketed by software houses.
2. A large portion of GDBMS are marketed by software houses.

3. The majority of the data management systems produced by software houses operate primarily on IBM 360/370, 30XX, and 4XXX computers, although support for other computers is slowly expanding.

4. The sale price ranges from about $15,000 to $200,000 depending on the particular vendor, versions of the system, and options included.

A typical GFMS example is ASI-ST. It comes in three versions: Mini ASI-ST (a basic report writer), $14,000; COMPACT ASI-ST, $24,000; and ASI-ST, $34,000. The interactive access facility is an additional $16,000. In addition, 13 special option modules are available, totaling $74,000; for example, the TOTAL and IMS (DL/1) interfaces at $12,000 each. An average installation might cost in the $50,000–$70,000 range. The average Mark IV installation falls also in this cost range.

A GDBMS example is SYSTEM 2000 and its modules: the basic data management module, $35,000; the interactive query language, $25,000; $15,000 first procedural language interface, $7,500 second interface, and $5,000 each additional; complex report writer, $15,000; sequential file processing, $15,000; teleprocessing monitor, $12,500–$32,500; multithread or asynchronous command processing, $20,000.

The detailed pricing schemes for ASI-ST, SYSTEM 2000, and ADABAS are shown in Figures 4.2, 4.3, and 4.4. We have arbitrarily chosen to include price details for these products; this choice should not be interpreted as indicative of the author's preferences or market dominance.

Most systems available may ascend to over $100,000 if most of the additional options are included. The capabilities of each module and the number of modules offered are constantly being expanded by the vendors; hence pricing schemes vary.

5. The pricing scheme of GDBMS from mainframe vendors is usually quite different and frequently lower than that of GDBMS marketed by software houses. Tie-ins with hardware sales affect greatly the pricing of a GDBMS, like any other software package "bundled" with hardware.

6. Most systems, particularly the earlier GDBMS, require at least a small to medium computer with significant core and sufficient random access devices to hold most, if not all, of an application data base. Support for sequentially organized data bases on tape devices is also available in a number of systems, e.g., IMS, SYSTEM 2000. Traditionally, GDBMS were initially developed only for medium and large-scale computers. GDBMS started appearing for powerful minicomputers, e.g., Digital Equipment Corp. and Hewlett-Packard "minicomputers," in the late 1970s and early 1980s.

RELATIONAL DATA BASE MANAGEMENT SYSTEMS

Supplier*	Name	Classification†	Computer Used‡	Minimum Memory and Operating System	Programming Host Language(s)	Query Self-contained Language	Secondary Indexing	Cost,§ Approximate, 1983–84
Burroughs	DMS-II	Network	B1700–7800 series	80 k words MCP	COBOL, PL/1, Algol	Yes	Bit vectors; Partial inversion	$400–1100/mo. $14,000–39,000
Computer Corporation of America	Model 204	Inverted network-oriented	IBM 360/370, 30XX, 43XX	DOS/VSE, OS/VS1, OS/VS2, CMS, VM, MVS 250 k	COBOL, FORTRAN, PL/1, BAL	Yes	Full to partial inversion	$2730–8190/mo. $155,000–235,000
Control Data	DMS-170	CODASYL DBTG	Cyber 70, 170 CDC 6000	SCOPE NOS	COBOL, FORTRAN Algol, Assembly	Yes	Partial inversion	
Cincom	TOTAL	Network	Burroughs 2500–4800 IBM 360, 370 IBM System 3 Honeywell 200, 2000 Univac Series 70, 9400/9700 NCR Century 101 CDC 6000	MCPV, 80k words 3K to 32K bytes DOS, OS, VS1, VS2 Mod1, Mod2, OS/2000 OS4, OS7, OS9 B1-B4	COBOL, RPG II, PL/1, FORTRAN, BAL in most computers	Yes	No	$500–1500/mo. $15,000–40,000
Cullinet Software	IDMS	CODASYL DBTG	Cyber 70–74, 170–175 DEC PDP 11 IBM 360/370, 43XX, and 30XX	SCOPE, KRONOS, NOS RSX-11D, IAS DOS, OS, VS1, VS2, MVS, 55K	COBOL, FORTRAN, PL/1	Yes	No	$600–4000/mo. $55,000–115,000
DEC	DBMS/10	CODASYL DBTG	DEC PDP 10	DEC-10 Monitor 64K words	COBOL, FORTRAN	No	No	$900–1600/mo.
Honeywell	IDS II DM-IV	Ringed predecessor of DBTG CODASYL	H400 H60/6000	GCOS	COBOL for DML and DDL	Yes	No	
IBM	CICS	Interactive communications control system	IBM 360, 370, 43XX, 30XX	DOS 48K OS/VS 2000K	COBOL, PL/1, BAL	No	Partial inversion	$1200/mo.
IBM	IMS2 IMS/VS	Hierarchical	IBM 360/370 Models 40 and 145 and up; 43XX and 30XX series	DOS 98K bytes IMS 2 DB: 128K IMS 2 DB/DC: 512K IMS/VS DB: 2000K IMS/VS DB/DC: over 2000K	FORTRAN, COBOL, PL/1, and BAL	No	Partial inversion	$950–3700/mo.

Vendor	System	Type	Computers	Operating system / memory	Language			Cost
IBM	GIS/2	Information retrieval— report writing	IBM 360, 370, 43XX, 303X	OS/VS 500K		Yes	No	$900–1900/mo.
INTEL	SYSTEM 2000	Hierarchic, inverted	IBM 360, 370, 43XX, 30XX; CDC 6000 Cyber 70, 170 Univac 1100	DOS, OS/VS 160K SCOPE/KRONOS/NOS 20K 60-bit words EXEC 8 31K 36-bit words	COBOL, FORTRAN, PL/1, BAL	Yes	Full to partial inversion	$1200–5800/mo. $30,000–140,000
Phillips	PHOLAS	CODASYL DBTG	Phillips P1000	64K, P1000 OS		No	No	
Software AG	ADABAS	Network-oriented inverted	IBM 360, 370, 30XX SIEMENS 4004 Univac 9000 ICL System 4 DEC PDP11	OS/DOS 110K	COBOL, FORTRAN, PL/1, BAL	Yes	Full to partial inversion	$2500–5000/mo. $40,000–132,000
Univac	DMS 1100	CODASYL DBTG	Univac 1100 series	60K 36-bit words	COBOL, FORTRAN, PL/1	Yes	No	$750/mo.
GENERALIZED FILE MANAGEMENT SYSTEMS								
Applications Software	ASI-ST	Generalized file management system	IBM 360, 370, 43XX, 30XX	DOS 44K, DOS/VS OS 65K, OS/VS1, OS/VS2	Replaces host programming languages	Yes	No	$560–2800/mo. $14,000–72,000
Informatics	Mark IV	Generalized file management system	IBM 360, 370 43XX, 30XX UNIVAC 90 series Siemens 4004	DOS, OS, OS/VS1, OS/VS2 48K TDOS, DOS, OS/4 65K	Replaces host programming languages	Yes	No	$400–$1500/mo. $15,000–80,000
Program Products	Data Analyzer	Generalized file management system	IBM 360/370	40 K DOS 85 K OS	Replaces host programming languages	Yes	No	

* Although this is not a complete list of vendors, it includes those that account for at least 80% of the installed population. Figure 4.5 covers the population on mini-micro/personal computers.

† All systems are Generalized Data Base Management Systems except those classified as Generalized File Management Systems, Information Retrieval, or Communications Control Systems (Data Communications systems).

‡ Availability of a system on IBM 360/370 computers usually also means availability on IBM 43XX and 30XX series and on IBM-compatible computers such as AMDAHL computers.

§ Costs are approximate since prices vary frequently. Costs vary depending on the computer system hardware involved. The sale costs indicated as a range reflect the cost of the basic system and its various optional modules. These costs do not include the data communications systems or options. The monthly lease cost indicated as a range reflects also the different costs depending on the duration and nature of the lease (lease/purchase option, lease/no purchase option), and the version of the system.

Figure 4.1. Generalized data management systems commercially available

Supplier	Name	Classification	Computer Used	Minimum Memory and Operating	Programming Language(s)	Query Language	Secondary Indexing	Cost Approximate, 1983–84
IBM	SQL/DS	Relational	IBM 370, 30XX, 43XX	CICS/DOS/VS DOS/VSE/ICCF DOS/VSE 1-2 megabytes	COBOL, PL/1, Assembler	Yes	Partial to full secondary indexing	$300/mo.
IBM	Query-by-Example	Relational	IBM 370, 30XX, 43XX	VM/CMS 1.5 megabytes	PL/1, APL	Yes	Partial to full inversion	$325/mo.
Relational Software Inc.	ORACLE	Relational	DEC PDP-11 DEC VAX-11	RSX-11, MRSX-11 IAS, UNIX, RSTS VAX-VMS, VAX-UNIX 300K	COBOL, PL/1, FORTRAN, C, PASCAL, BASIC	Yes	Partial to full inversion	$12,000– 48,000 (DEC)
			IBM 360, 370, 30XX, 43XX	VM, MVS				$96,000 (IBM)
			DG MV8000 MV10000	AOS				$48,000
			ALTOS PC M68000-based	ZENIX				$600–2,000
Relational Technology Inc.	INGRES	Relational	DEC VAX-11 M68000	VAX-VMS, VAX-UNIX 68000/UNIX	COBOL, FORTRAN, C, PASCAL, BASIC	Yes	Partial to full secondary indexing	$800–2800/mo. for 1–5 year acquisition. $30,000
Mathematica Products Group	RAMIS II	Relational	IBM 370, 30XX, 43XX	MVS, OS/VS1, DOS/VSE, VM/CMS	COBOL, PL/1, FORTRAN, BAL	Yes	Partial to full secondary indexing	$40,000–$172,000

Figure 4.1. continued

		Monthly	
	Perpetual License	Lease/ Purchase Option	Non-Equity Lease

ASI-ST

Consists of comprehensive file and data element (field) definition facilities; permits retrieval of an unlimited number of reports as well as subfile output to other I/O devices, in one pass of a set of files; ability to perform calculations and manipulation of data in all phases of processing; processing of both fixed point and floating point data; provides an "automatic" facility for transaction-driven file creation and maintenance. Also includes a number of special features at no additional cost, including Procedural Directives; Extended Table Handling; ability to Catalog and Use ASI-ST Requests on a repetitive basis; Own Code Exits to programs written in other languages; ability to process sets of related (i.e., "coordinated") files with all I/O, collation logic and buffer synchronization performed by ASI-ST "automatically"; and a temporary working storage facility known as Temporary Variables.	$34,000	$1,700	$1,360

COMPACT ASI-ST

Differs from the full ASI-ST version in that the "automatic" facility for transaction-driven file maintenance of OS/DOS files plus Own Code Exits (may be acquired optionally) are excluded. All other features of the full ASI-ST version are included at no additional cost.	$24,000	$1,200	$960

MINI ASI-ST

The basic version of ASI-ST oriented to the function of report generation. It contains all of the reporting capabilities of ASI-ST and can produce an unlimited number of reports from multiple input files in one pass. Separately priced options are available to permit expansion to COMPACT ASI-ST	$14,000	$700	$560

SPECIAL FEATURES

Applicable to all three versions of ASI-ST:

IMS(DL/1) Interface*	$12,000	$ 500	$ 400
IMS(DL/1) Retrieval	9,000	350	300
TOTAL Interface*	12,000	500	400
TOTAL Retrieval	9,000	350	300
Free Form Language	6,000	300	240
Conversational ASI-ST (TSO or IMS DB/DC)	16,000	800	660
Conversational ASI-ST Macro Language	8,000	400	320
Automatic JCL (OS) Generator	2,000	200	180

Other Optional Features applicable to COMPACT or MINI ASI-ST versions

Own Code Exits (COMPACT & MINI)	$ 4,000	$ 200	$ 160
Request Cataloging (MINI only)	2,000	100	80
Output Subfiles (MINI only)	2,000	100	80
Input Coordinated Files (MINI only)	2,000	100	80
Extended Table Handling (MINI only)	2,000	100	80
Procedural Directives (MINI only)	2,000	100	80

ASI-INQUIRY

	$44,000	$2,200	No

* Requires the Procedural Directives Feature

NOTE: Annual service agreement is 6% of the Perpetual License.

Figure 4.2. *ASI-ST modules and prices. (Provided by Applications Software, Inc.)*

IBM (All Versions but DOS/VS)

Module	Paid-up License	Permanent Monthly Lease Plan Number of Monthly Payments 12	18	24	12 mo. Rental	Monthly Maintenance
Basic SYSTEM 2000 Plus one Host Language Interface	$70,000	$5,560	$3,845	$2,990	$2,475	$3,000
Each Additional Interface	10,000	795	550	430	355	
QUEST	30,000	2,385	1,650	1,285	1,065	
QUEX	20,000	1,590	1,100	855	710	
Report Writer,Genius, Graphics	35,000	2,780	1,925	1,495	1,240	
Accounting Log (*IBM only*)	10,000	795	550	430	355	
Multi-Thread (*IBM, UNIVAC*)	10,000	795	550	430	355	
XDD	30,000	2,385	1,650	1,285	1,065	

Univac (All Versions But 1100/60); CDC

Module License	Paid-up 12	Permanent Monthly Lease Plan Number of Monthly Payments 18	24	12 mo. Rental	Monthly
UNIVAC 1100/60					
Basic SYSTEM 2000 Plus One Host Language Interface	45,000	3,575	2,475	1,925	1,265	3,000
Additional Host Language Interface	10,000	795	550	430	285	
QUEST	15,000	1,195	825	645	425	
QUEX	20,000	1,590	1,100	855	565	
Multi-Thread	20,000	1,590	1,100	855	565	
Report Writer, Genius & Graphics	20,000	1,590	1,100	855	565	

IBM DOS/VS Version Only

Module	Paid-up License	Permanent Monthly Lease Plan Number of Monthly Payments 12	18	24	12 mo. Rental	Monthly Maintenance
Basic SYSTEM 2000 Plus One Host Language Interface, Multi-user, Accounting Log and QUEST	$49,500	$3,935	$2,720	$2,115	$1,395	$3,000
Each Additional Host Language Interface	9,000	715	495	385	255	
Report Writer	15,000	1,195	825	645	425	
Multi-Thread	20,000	1,590	1,100	855	565	

Multiple Copy Discount

Installation Number	Discount
1	0%
2-5	15%
6-10	20%
11 and greater	25%

Figure 4.3. SYSTEM 2000 modules and prices, 1984. (Provided by INTEL Corp.)

166

      Less robust and smaller GDBMS started appearing in the 1980s for the large microcomputer and personal computer market flourishing in the 1980s. Figure 4.5 shows a compendium of systems advertised as micro-GDBMS in trade publications. Many such micro-GDBMS lack the major facilities of a robust GDBMS, for example, the ability to define subschemas, concurrent use of a data base by more than one user, robust recovery mechanisms, high performance and efficiency, and so forth (and thus, in some cases, may not deserve being labeled GDBMS). Correspondingly, the sale price of micro-GDBMS ranges from hundreds of dollars to a few thousand dollars.

7. Most systems, particularly all those from software houses, use the underlying basic access methods of the standard host operating system. The data management systems themselves appear as application programs to the host operating system. Thus the systems remain relatively independent of internal operating system changes.

8. Most systems have: (a) a high-level query language of their own for interactive use (usually called a self-contained language), and (b) data definition and manipulation languages or commands to interface to the standard procedural programming languages, typically, COBOL, FORTRAN, PL/1 and PASCAL.

9. Most systems have their own particular way of linking files or record types and creating and retrieving the data base and their own peculiar data definition and manipulation languages. Many were actually conceived before the DBTG 1971 proposal was published and before standardization was widely discussed. Thus data base queries and application programs written to interface to a particular GDBMS are *not* directly transferable to other GDBMS; the exception is of course when going from one DBTG GDBMS to another.

10. The available GDBMS fall primarily into one of four categories with respect to (a) the type of data base model or structure that may be defined and (b) the type of data base accessing and processing: hierarchic, network, inverted (hierarchic or network-oriented) and relational.

      Figure 4.6 shows a data base structure space scale indicating some of the main exponents of each category. As an example, note that TOTAL[19] is a network data base system, whereas SYSTEM 2000 is the classical inverted hierarchic exponent. However, most of the more recent and robust systems being implemented follow the 1971 DBTG network standard. As of the early 1980s there were at least five large-scale DBTG-like products: Honeywell's DM-IV/IDS II,[1] UNIVAC's DMS 1100,[2] Cullinet's IDMS,[3] DEC's DBMS/

PURCHASE AND LEASE

Unrestricted "rights of use" are available for a specific computer for an unlimited time. This includes two training courses with subsequent training available at standard rates. Technical Services to include ADABAS enhancements, documentation updates and maintenance are included for one year and available for a fee per installation for each subsequent year.

PRICE LIST

Product	Purchase	M-T-M	24 Months	36 Months	48 Months	60 Months
GDBMS:						
ADABAS (DOS)	106,000	4,514	3,011	2,681	2,447	2,089
ADABAS (OS)	142,000	6,043	4,134	3,591	3,276	2,811
ADABAS (MVS)	172,000	7,321	4,886	4,350	3,969	3,392
ADABAS VM	24,000	1,021	682	607	554	473
ADABAS VTAM	24,000	1,021	682	607	554	473
Application						
Development System:						
NATURAL (DOS)	40,000	1,704	1,136	1,012	924	788
NATURAL (OS)	50,000	2,130	1,420	1,265	1,155	985
NATURAL (MVS)	60,000	2,556	1,704	1,518	1,386	1,182
DC System:						
COM-PLETE (DOS)	50,000	2,130	1,420	1,265	1,155	985
COM-PLETE (VS1)	60,000	2,556	1,704	1,518	1,386	1,182
COM-PLETE (MVS)	90,000	3,830	2,557	2,276	2,076	1,775

All lease contracts guarantee the purchase price even though the purchase price may increase in future years and contain a cancellation clause which specifies payment of 50 percent of the remaining payments. Technical Services as described above are provided for the term of the lease.

MULTIPLE INSTALLATIONS

If the rights for a first computer are obtained (purchase or lease), the same rights are available for additional computers at different locations, at discounted prices.

Installation	Purchase, off	Lease, off
2nd–4th	35%	20%
5th–10th	50%	50%
11th plus	60%	50%
percentage of 1st installation charges		

Multiple computers at the same location do not count toward multiple installation discounts. There is no charge for ADABAS on computers used exclusively for backup.

PRODUCT SPECIFICATIONS:

ADABAS includes the ADABAS Nucleus, Utilities, ADASCRIPT QUERY Language, ADACOM Reporting Language, ADAMINT Macro Interface, and ADABAS Data Dictionary.

Figure 4.4. *ADABAS pricing schedule for IBM 360, 370, 30XX, and 43XX computers, 1984. (Provided by Software AG.)*

10,[17] and Phillips' PHOLAS.[18] This standardization enhances the transferability of application programs from one GDBMS to another, besides reducing the confusion to those facing the wide number of choices of systems available.

11. The relational data base approach is an attractive and promising new approach originating in the 1970s and appearing commercially in the early 1980s. It is being introduced, debated, and investigated particularly with respect to its cost-effective implementation and performance (performance is its major problem for large-scale data bases). Query-by-Example[10] was the first commercial relational system.

   It should be noted that most existing GDBMS can support relational data bases, that is, sets of interrelated flat files or tables. However, what may be missing in most cases is a query language including the powerful relational operators, in particular the join operator, to access and process the data base. Consequently, such systems cannot be classified as relational.

   A significant number of the GDBMS being introduced in the 1980s are relational-oriented and tend to follow the approach of (a) IBM's QBE or (b) IBM's SQL/DS and RTI's/University of California, Berkeley's INGRES, which play the role of de-facto relational standards.

12. Inverted indexing or other types of indexing facilities for more flexible and cost-effective access to a subset of the data base selected on the basis of complex logical qualifications are featured in a number of GDBMS. The classical exponents are of course the inverted GDBMS, namely, SYSTEM 2000, ADABAS, Model 204, and DATACOM/DB, exhibiting powerful query languages. Now other types of GDBMS are incorporating some form of inversion capability, such as IMS, DMS-II, and, in particular, relational GDBMS. The DBTG implementations may try to provide some inversion capability, perhaps with a query language. CODASYL did not specify a query language for the DBTG system; implementors are now developing query languages which, unfortunately, are not fully compatible with each other due to a lack of a common standard.

13. The software investment in application programs interfacing to a particular GDBMS and the difficulty or cost of transferring them to other GDBMS is so large in many current installations that the transfer to any single GDBMS standard is almost a foregone possibility (the exception of course is when going from one DBTG GDBMS to another). The dependence of applications on a given GDBMS and on the particular data base structure chosen is very high in systems in which applications "navigate" or follow specific paths (e.g., DBTG sets, IMS parent-child hierarchic relationships) established by the

Company	DBMS Name	Type	Hardware	Price	Features
Advanced Data Management	DRS	Non-Codasyl/network, inverted	DEC PDP-11, VAX-11	$29,000	Report writer, dictionary, security package, transaction processor, graphics, development tool
Amcor Computer Corp.	AMBASE	Non-codasyl/network	DEC PDP-11	$23,500	Dictionary, report writer, security package, transaction processor, development tool
The Automated Quill, Inc.	Super English 1X	DMS/inverted	DG Nova, Eclipse	$11,000 to $16,000	Report writer, dictionary, security package, graphics
Cincom Systems, Inc.	TOTAL	Non-Codasyl/hierarchical	IBM System 3, System 4, Univac Series 70, DEC PDP-11, Harris Series 80-800, Varian V70, Perkin-Elmer 7/32, 8/32, all Prime series	$13,500 to $30,000	Report writer, dictionary, security package, transaction processor, graphics, development tool
Charles Mann & Associates	Business Data Base	DMS/inverted	TI 99/4, Radio Shack TRS-80	$89.95	Report writer
Complete Computer Systems	CREATE	DMS/inverted	DG Nova, Eclipse	$18,000	Report writer, data dictionary, security package, transaction processor
Condor Computer Corp.	Condor Series 20	Non-Codasyl/relational	Any Z80 μp	$695	Transaction processor, data dictionary, productivity tools
CRI, Inc.	RELATE 3000	Non-Codasyl/relational	Hewlett-Packard HP 3000	$11,000	Security package
Database Systems Corp.	TAGS	DMS/inverted	All Prime models	$35,000	Data entry, query language, forms design, transaction processor
Data General Corp.	DG-DBMS	Codasyl/hierarchical-network	DG Eclipse	$10,000	Query language, report generator, data dictionary, productivity tool
Data Management Systems, Inc.	DATASCAN	DMS/inverted	Datapoint 6000, 5500, 3800, 1800, IBM System 34, NCR 8000	$6250	Report writer, data dictionary, security package
Digital Equipment Corp.	DBMS-11	Codasyl/hierarchical-network	DEC PDP-11	$16,500	Query language, security package
ELS Systems Engineering	Product 3	DMS/inverted	DEC PDP-11	$2800 (Custom products from $13,500)	
Exact Systems & Programming Corp.	DNA-4	Non-Codasyl/inverted	DG MicroNova, Nova, Eclipse	$4000 to $40,000	Report writer, productivity tool, security package, data dictionary
Florida Computer, Inc.	Data Boss/2	Non-Codasyl/relational	DEC PDP-11	$20,000	Query language
	Data Boss/32	Non-Codasyl/relational	DEC VAX-11	$40,000	Query language, data dictionary, report writer, security package, transaction processor
Gemini Information Systems, Inc.	DDQUERY	Codasyl	Series 16, Perkin-Elmer 3200, IBM Series/1	$20,000	Report writer, query language, data dictionary, security package, transaction processor, productivity tools
Harris Computer Systems	Harris-AZ7	DMS/inverted	All Harris systems	$9500	TOTAL Interface, data dictionary, report writer

Company	Product	Data model	Computers	Price	Features
Henco, Inc.	INFO	DMS/inverted	All DEC VAX series, all Prime and Harris series, Honeywell Level 6	$14,700	Report writer, transaction processor, data dictionary, security package
Hewlett-Packard Co.	IMAGE	Non-Codasyl/hierarchical	HP3000, 1000, 250	Comes with hardware	Report writer, transaction processor, security package
International Computing Co.	RTFILE	Codasyl/relational	DEC LSI-11, PDP-11	$2500	Data directory, dictionary, CRT forms generation, transaction processor, command file, applications interfaces
International Data Base Systems, Inc.	SEED MICRO-SEED	Codasyl	DEC VAX-11, PDP-11, Z80 processors	$14,000 to $35,000	Query language, report writer, transaction processor
Micro-Architects	IDM-M2	DMS/inverted	Radio Shack TRS-80 Level II	$199	Report writer
Micro Data Base Systems, Inc.	MDBS	Codasyl	Any Z80, Z8000 or 8080/8086-based μp, DEC PDP-11	$1500	Report writer, query language, data dictionary, transaction processor, security package
Miller Microcomputer Services	DATAHANDLER	DMS/inverted	Radio Shack TRS-80	$49.95	Query language, datacom, data dictionary
Mini-Computer Systems, Inc.	FACTMATCHER	Non-Codasyl	MCS Micos 200	$90,000	
MRP Systems	INFOTRIEVE	DMS/inverted	DG Nova, all Point-4, Bytronics and Amtex series	$3000	Report writer, transaction processor, data dictionary, security package
Prime Computer, Inc.	DBMS	Hierarchical-network	All Prime series	$20,000	Report writer, security package
Quoda Corp.	QDMS	DMS/inverted	DEC PDP-11	$8175	Report writer
RLG Corp.	UNIBASE	Non-Codasyl/inverted	DEC PDP-11	$25,000	Report writer, transaction processor
Ross Systems, Inc.	INTAC	DMS/inverted	DEC PDP-11 VAX-11	$20,000	Report writer, transaction processor, data dictionary
RSI	ORACLE	Non-Codasyl/relational	DEC PDP-11, VAX-11	$30,000	Report writer, data dictionary, transaction processor, security package
Science Management Corp.	IDOL	DMS/inverted	All Basic-Four, Rexon, Pertec and Onyx series, IBM Series/1		Report writer, transaction processor, security package, data dictionary
Source Data Systems, Inc.	SDL	DMS/inverted	Honeywell Level 6, NCR 9020, IBM Series/1	$25,000	Report writer, transaction processor, security package
Software AG	ADABAS-M	Non-Codasyl/inverted	DEC PDP-11	$40,000	Report writer, transaction
The Software Store	Data 80	DMS/inverted	Any Z80 or 8080-based μp	$750	
	INFO-80	DMS/inverted	Any Z80 or 8080-based μp	$1040	
Tandem Computers, Inc.	ENCOMPASS	Non-Codasyl/relational	All Tandem series	$22,500	Report writer, data dictionary, security package, transaction processor
Texas Instruments, Inc.	DBMS-990	Non-Codasyl/inverted	TIDS990	$2650	Query log, data dictionary, report writer, security package
Warner-Edison Associates, Inc.	INMAGIC	DMS/inverted	DEC PDP-11, VAX, Hewlett-Packard HP 1000	$7200	Report writer, security package

Note: The accuracy of the information in this figure has not been checked by the author of this textbook. dBASE II, the leader in number of installations (as of the writing of this book), is not included in this figure.

Figure 4.5. *Generalized data management systems commercially available for mini-micro computers and personal computers (courtesy of Mini-Micro Systems, October 1981, reference 21)*

	Noninverted	Inverted
Hierarchical, Tree	IMS	SYSTEM 2000
		ADABAS
Network	IDS DBTG* TOTAL	

*DBTG includes: DMS 1100, IDMS, DEC DBMS/10, PHOLAS.

Figure 4.6. *Data base structure space in commercial nonrelational GDBMS*

data base designer. Transferability out of (or into) hierarchic (IMS) and network GDBMS is typically not as easy as out of (or into) inverted GDBMS (e.g., SYSTEM 2000, ADABAS) and relational GDBMS.

14. The capabilities of each module are frequently being enhanced and new modules are being introduced by vendors. Vendors are striving to somehow incorporate attractive features and strong points of competing data base systems (although such incorporation subsequent to the initial architectural design of the GDBMS is sometimes not very smooth from a user's point of view). As an example, IMS tries to provide a type of network data base facility via its logical data base facilities (as we shall see in Chapter 7) and also a type of inverted facility (introduced by IBM in subsequent releases). The inverted ADABAS, through its macro feature ADAMINT, now allows the programmer to view a series of inverted coupled files in a hierarchical fashion. As another example, relational interfaces to enhanced non-relational GDBMS have been introduced by some vendors, as in the case of DATACOM/DB.[20] Thus the position of a GDBMS in the nonrelational data base structure space in Figure 4.6 tends to cover more or shift in this space as new developments occur.

15. Enhancement and new options by a number of GDBMS vendors toward report writing, sorting, and so forth, are bringing closer together some GDBMS product lines with GFMS product lines. Recall Figure 3.1(e). The differences between report writer modules offered by a number of GDBMS vendors and GFMS products are mostly in degree and strength, rather than objectives. It is of interest to compare the price tag of some report writers, e.g., SYSTEM 2000's starting at $15,000, with the most basic module of GFMS which is typically a report writer, e.g., mini ASI-ST at $14,000.

16. GFMS vendors strive to take advantage of the most populous data base technology via good interfaces to existing GDBMS. The inter-

faces developed by GFMS vendors are typically to IMS and TOTAL costing on the order of $10,000 per interface.

17. With the emergence of the relational approach as a very user friendly approach, starting in the mid-1980s some vendors provide both a relational and nonrelational interface to an existing GDBMS. As an example, UNIVAC's UDS-1100 includes its CODASYL DMS-1100 and a data translation interface that permits viewing the CODASYL data base as a relational data base and performing some relational operations on it.[22]

18. No single GDBMS nor type of GDBMS (hierarchical, network, inverted, relational) accounts for the majority of the installed GDBMS. As distributed data and processing (the subject of Chapter 16) flourish along with computer networking and telecommunications, the need to communicate between different GDBMS emerges. Some vendors are producing load/unload interface modules between different GDBMS, such as between IMS and SQL/DS. More sophisticated couplings or interfaces are bringing closer together some GDBMS, for example, Informatics' DAG for a heterogeneous distributed set of IMS and SQL/DS data bases.

19. Data dictionary systems have evolved rather recently and have become an increasingly useful tool for DBAs, auditors, systems analysts, programmers, and users. In many organizations where data bases and information systems achieve a high degree of evolution and sophistication, the data dictionary becomes a practical necessity. The data dictionary is a specialized data base management system, or application of an existing GDBMS, in which the data base is a repository of descriptive information about the data bases, processing programs, and other entities associated with information systems practice. Chapter 14 is devoted to this subject.

More and more, GDBMS vendors are now marketing data dictionaries, with growing capabilities for use specifically with their GDBMS. However, some vendors who do not market a GDBMS have developed data dictionaries that are almost self-standing, that is, do not require the use of a GDBMS. At the same time, such products have interfaces to generate data descriptions specific to the most popular GDBMS available. The sale price range varies from about $15,000 to $40,000, depending on the particular vendor, versions of the system, and options included. Figure 4.7 summarizes the availability and main features of several of the major data dictionary systems. This choice is arbitrary and should not be interpreted as indicative of the author's preferences nor overall product ratings.

Supplier	Name	Computer* Used	GDBMS Required to Use the System	GDBMS for Which Data Definitions Are Generated	Cost Approximate[†] 1983–84
Cullinet	Integrated Data Dictionary (IDD)	IBM 360/370 43XX and 30XX	Yes, IDMS	IDMS	$15,000 $500–$1,300/mo.
IBM Corp.		IBM 360/370 43XX and 30XX	Yes, IMS or DL/1	IMS	—
Management Systems and Programming Ltd.	Datamanager	IBM 360/370 43XX and 30XX	No	IMS Total ADABAS SYSTEM 2000 IDMS	$13,500–$40,000 $13,500 basic system +25 options at (usually) $3,000 each for IBM OS/VS
TSI International	Data Catalog 2	IBM 360/370 43XX and 30XX UNIVAC 1100 Honeywell 66	No	IMS TOTAL ADABAS DMS-1100 DATA MANAGEMENT IV	$14,900 basic system plus $5,000 for each GDBMS interface $21,900–$35,000
UNIVAC	Data Dictionary (DDS)	UNIVAC 1100	Yes, DMS-1100	DMS-1100	$375/mo.

*Availability of a system on IBM computers usually means also availability on IBM-compatible computers such as AMDAHL computers.
[†]Costs are approximate. Those shown as a range reflect the cost of the basic system and its optional modules. Monthly costs indicated as a range also reflect the different costs depending on the duration and nature of the lease.

Figure 4.7. Sample of major data dictionary/directory systems

174

REFERENCES

1. "Data Management-IV Administration/Application Summary," Reference Manual DF74, Honeywell Information Systems, Waltham, Mass.

2. "Data Management System (DMS 1100), American National Standard COBOL Data Manipulation Language," Programmer Reference UP-7908 Sperry Univac Computer Systems, St. Paul, Minn.

3. "IDMS, System Overview," Cullinet Software, Westwood, Mass.

4. "CODASYL Data Base Task Group Report, 1971," CODASYL, Association for Computing Machinery, New York, April 1971.

5. CODASYL Data Description Language Committee, *Data Description Language Journal of Development*, Document C13.6, vol. 2, No. 113, U.S. Government Printing Office, 1973.

6. CODASYL, *CODASYL COBOL Journal of Development*, Department of Supply and Services, Government of Canada, Technical Services Branch, Ottawa, Canada, 1976.

7. Generalized Information System GIS/360, Application Description Manual, IBM-Reference Manual, Form GH20-0842.

8. Information Management System Virtual Storage (IMS/VS), General Information Manual, IBM Reference Manual GH20-1260.

9. Data Language/1 System 370 DOS/VS, General Information Manual, IBM Reference Manual GH20-1246.

10. "Query-by-Example, Terminal User's Guide," IBM Reference Manual SH20-2078.

11. SQL/Data system, Concepts and Facilities, IBM Reference Manual GH24-5013.

12. "ORACLE, Terminal Users' Guide," Relational Software Inc., Menlo Park, Calif.

13. "INGRES, Users' Guide," Relational Technology Inc., Berkeley, Calif.

14. "SYSTEM 2000 Reference Manual," Intel Corp., Austin, Texas.

15. "ADABAS Reference Manual," Software AG., Reston, Virginia.

16. "Model 204 Reference Manual," Computer Corporation of America, Cambridge, Mass.

17. "DECsystem-10, Data Base Management System DBMS/10, Version II," Programmer and Administrator Guides, Digital Equipment Corporation, Maynard, MA.

18. "PHOLAS, Phillips Host Language System," Phillips Data Systems, Apeldoorn, The Netherlands.

19. "TOTAL Reference Manual," Cincom Systems Corp., Cincinnati, Ohio.

20. "DATACOM/DB User's Guide," Applied Data Research Corporation, Princeton, N.J.

21. Weiss, H., "Which DBMS Is Right for You?" *Mini-Micro Systems*, October 1981, pp. 157–160.

22. "Universal Data System UDS-1100," Administrator's and User's Guides, Sperry-UNIVAC, Minneapolis, Minn.

23. "dBASE II Reference Manual," Ashton-Tate Inc., Culver City, Calif.

Preface to Chapters
5, 6, 7, 8, 9, 10, and 11

The following seven chapters present and illustrate the architecture, data base model, data definition facilities for the global data base and for the user views of it, and the data manipulation facilities of systems represent-ing each of the major types of GDBMS: network, hierarchic, inverted tree, and relational. Chapter 5 is devoted to the network approach of the CODASYL specifications, which is followed by many commercial systems. Chapter 6 is devoted to Cincom's TOTAL which portrays the network approach but deviates from the CODASYL specifications. Chapter 7 is devoted to IBM's IMS which portrays the hierarchic approach. Chapter 8 is devoted to INTEL's SYSTEM 2000, one of the main inverted tree GDBMS. Chapter 9 presents the relational data base approach. Chapters 10 and 11 present IBM's SQL/DS and QBE which are representative of the two types of relational GDBMS. The same data base and data accessing examples are carried throughout these chapters to illustrate the similarities, differences, advantages, and disadvantages of the approaches and the particular GDBMS—a major feature of this text.

Each of the following chapters is self-contained and does not require reading a preceding chapter. However, cross references to previous chap-ters are included in each for comparison purposes. Chapter 12, focusing on data base functional dependencies and normalization, does require that Chapter 9 be read first.

Each of the GDBMS that we shall treat is detailed by its vendor (or proponent) in hundreds or thousands of pages. Although we present a streamlined description of each GDBMS, we do present and exemplify its main concepts and facilities such that the reader may derive a good understanding of it for developing and using a data base and for compar-ing it with other alternative GDBMS.

The jargon in the data base technology world is unfortunately varied, and at times confusing and even inconsistent. We shall use the terminol-ogy particular to each system as we present it. However, we will provide frequent cross referencing to other equivalent concepts and terminologies; at this point review Figure 3.11 (same as Figure 1.8).

5

THE CODASYL DBTG SYSTEM

181

5.1 INTRODUCTION AND ARCHITECTURE

The specifications of the CODASYL Data Base Task Group (DBTG) for a generalized data base management system for defining and processing network-oriented data bases appear in the milestone 1971 CODASYL DBTG Report published in early 1971.[1] This proposal, written by a dedicated group of voluntary representatives from computer manufacturers and users in U.S. industry and government, and university researchers, has become the basis for a growing number of data base systems. The initial DBTG specifications have undergone subsequent development and refinement as reported by two CODASYL groups.[2,3,10,11] The changes are noticeable. However, the fundamental architecture and functional capability is the same as that specified in the 1971 Report. A number of commercially available systems have used one or more versions of the specifications as the implementation base. While these commercial implementations may show slight differences, they follow the same basic 1971 DBTG data model. As of the early 1980s, robust/popular DBTG-type systems commercially available included:

DMIV-IDS/II (Integrated Data Store/II), marketed by Honeywell Information Systems for use on Honeywell series 60 and 6000 computers; the initial IDS[4] implemented by General Electric in the late 1960s preceded and served as background for the 1971 DBTG specifications.

DMS/1100 (Data Management System/1100),[5] marketed by UNIVAC for use on UNIVAC series 1100 computers.

IDMS (Integrated Data Management System)[6] marketed by Cullinet Software for use on IBM 360/370 and 30XX and 43XX computers.

DBMS (Data Base Management Sytem),[7] marketed by Digital Equipment Corporation for use on DEC System 10 and VAX computers.

PHOLAS (Phillips Host Language System),[8] marketed by Phillips Electrologica of Holland for use on Phillips P1000 computers.

SEED,[9] marketed by United Telecom Group for use in a wide variety of large, medium, and micro computers.

Other implementations continue appearing on other computers. The effect of the 1971 DBTG report on the software marketplace has been similar to that of the CODASYL COBOL report in 1960: it is a widely followed standard.

In this chapter we will summarize the main features of the DBTG system following primarily the 1971−73 DBTG specifications followed by commercial GDBMS. We shall not delve into minor differences that exist between the original 1971 DBTG Report[1] and subsequent 1973 reports.[2,3] These differences are overshadowed by differences among the actual commercial DBTG implementations. However, we will cover the major changes/advances introduced by the 1978 CODASYL specifications,[10,11] and being considered by vendors.

The DBTG specifications propose three levels of data organization and associated data definition languages, plus a language for processing this data. The four languages are:

1. The schema *Data Definition Language*, schema DDL.
2. The subschema *Data Definition Language*, subschema DDL.
3. The *Data Manipulation Language*, DML.
4. The *Device/Media Control Language*, DMCL, subsequently renamed the *Data Storage Description Language*, DSDL.

The two DDLs and the DML have been detailed by CODASYL. The DMCL was originally only mentioned, leaving detailed physical and device-oriented data organization aspects to specific implementations. In 1978 CODASYL detailed the DSDL. The languages detailed fit or are compatible with COBOL. The stated intent of DBTG is that a functionally similar subschema DDL and DML be defined also for use with other programming languages. Subschema DDLs and DMLs have been defined by CODASYL for COBOL[1,11] and subsequently for FORTRAN.[13] The specification of these interfaces between a DBTG system and other languages such as PL/1, has been left up to the implementer of such systems. These implementations may differ, thus losing possible benefits of independence between application programs in such languages and the different DBTG implementations.

The **schema** is the logical description of the global data base. The schema is made up of a description of the various **record types** involved and of the **set types** relating these record types. A record type is made up of one or more **data items** (e.g., EMPLOYEE_NAME); the data item is the smallest unit of data in the data base.

The general architecture of a CODASYL DBTG system is illustrated in Figure 5.1. The intent is that the data base administrator set up the schema via the schema DDL, the subschemas for the various application programs via the subschema DDL, and the physical access paths and storage mappings via a DMCL. Although the intent is to not involve physical organization aspects at the schema definition level, a number of physical organization notions are involved at the schema level as has been indicated in the previous chapter and will be further discussed subsequently. For example, the general method to be used by the system to locate a record occurrence, indexing for the purpose of enhancing efficiency, and so forth, may be specified via the schema DDL, rather than via a DMCL. The 1978 CODASYL specifications shift many of these physical organization aspects from the DDL to the DSDL.

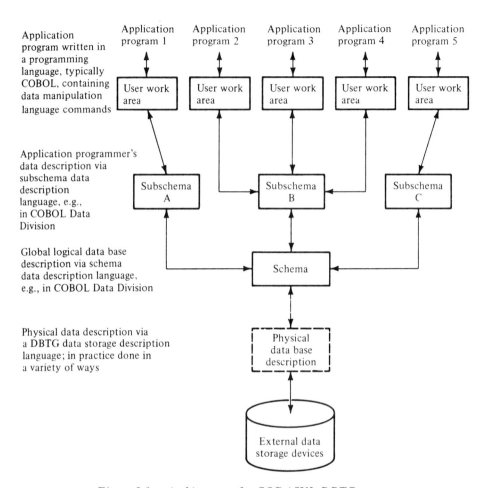

Figure 5.1. *Architecture of a CODASYL DBTG system*

A **subschema** is a logical subset of the schema, i.e., a subset of the defined sets, record types, and data items in these record types. Set types, record types, and data items not in the schema cannot be defined or introduced via a subschema. An arbitrary number of subschemas may be defined for a given schema.

An arbitrary number of users or programs may share a given subschema. The user or programmer declares his or her subschema (to the programmer it may be the whole data base) and communicates with the GDBMS through a buffer area called the *User Work Area*, UWA.

5.2   THE SCHEMA

A schema description in the DBTG DDL includes four types of declarations:

1. The schema name declaration, unique for each schema handled by the GDBMS;
2. One or more record type declarations, defining the data items for each record and the PICTURE details a-la-COBOL;
3. One or more set declarations, defining the relationships between defined record types;
4. One or more area declarations, defining the physical area(s) in which records will be stored.

We will illustrate the DBTG schema definition using the sample Employee-Child-Insurance data base used in Chapter 3.

Record Types

A record type is described in a fashion similar to COBOL, as illustrated by the record type EMPLOYEE described in Figure 5.2. The name of the record type must be unique. A data aggregate type CHILD is included, which can occur multiple times in the record. A data aggregate is just another name for subrecord or substructure in COBOL terms. The type and format of data items can be described by a TYPE clause or by the ubiquitous PICTURE clause similar to COBOL. A data type can be a character string, a bit string, or

```
RECORD NAME IS EMPLOYEE.
02 EMPLOYEENO; PICTURE 9(6).
02 NAME; PICTURE A(12).
02 ADDRESS; TYPE IS CHARACTER 20.
02 DEPARTMENT; PICTURE A(10).
 :         :
02 NOCHILD; PICTURE 99.
02 CHILD; OCCURS NOCHILD TIMES.
    03 CHILD_NAME; TYPE IS CHARACTER 10.
    03 CHILD_AGE; PICTURE 99.
    03 SCHOOL_YEAR; PICTURE 99.
 :
```

Figure 5.2. A DBTG record type description

arithmetic data which can be decimal or binary, fixed point or floating point, and real or complex.

An arbitrary number of record types and of occurrences of them may be used in a DBTG data base (as well as in other data base systems, of course).

Sets

A basic concept in DBTG is the set type. A **set type** is a named relationship between record types arranged as a two-level tree. Multilevel trees and network structures are built using multiple two-level trees. A large data base is thus composed of various record types and sets. The simplest set that may be defined involves two record types and is represented in Figure 5.3. The types of sets that may be defined are summarized in their pictorial representation in Figure 5.4. The main characteristics of DBTG sets are summarized in Figure 5.5. These fundamentals will now be the focus of our discussion.

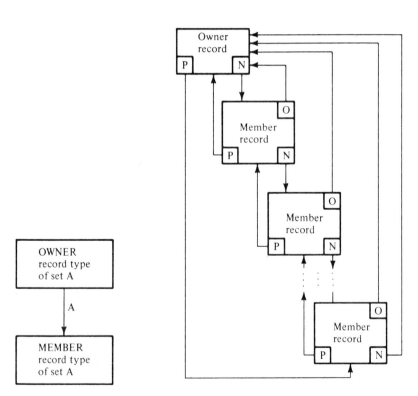

(a) CODASYL DBTG set representation   (b) Instance or occurrence of set A with owner (O), next (N) and prior (P) pointers

Figure 5.3.   *The CODASYL DBTG set*

A set type may be composed of only one owner record type and one or more member record types, as pictorially represented in Figures 5.3(a), 5.4(a) and 5.4(b). There may be an arbitrary number of occurrences of a member record type in a set but only one occurrence of its owner record type. Logical relationships (sets) may be implemented by pointer mechanisms linking all

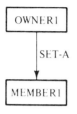

(a) Set representation, one
owner record type and
one member record type

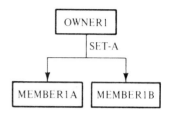

(b) Two record types as members
of a single set

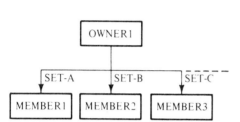

(c) A record type as owner
of two or more different sets

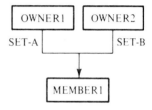

(d) A record type as member
of two or more sets (two
or more owner records,
each in a different set)

(e) A record type as member
of a set and owner of
another set

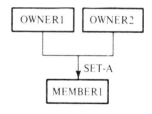

(f) A record type (or occurrence)
with two owner record types (or
occurrences) within the same
set is not allowed: transformation
to two two-level hierarchies, Fig. 3.16,
by passes this limitation on
record occurrences.

Note: The more detailed characteristics of areas, and of record and set placement, are highly
dependent on the particular GDBMS implementation (and CODASYL revision of the DBTG
report)

Figure 5.4.   *The CODASYL DBTG data model (Owner, Member, Set)*

1. A **set type** represents a unique relationship between unique record types.
2. A set type must be uniquely named, must have one *owner* record type, and contains one or more *member* record types, Figure 5.4(a), 5.4(b).
3. A **singular set** is a special type of set for which the owner is the "SYSTEM," where SYSTEM has only one occurrence.
4. A **dynamic set** differs from an ordinary set in that it does not have any record types declared for it in the schema. Any record may be made a member of it, or removed from it, at execution time by a data manipulation command. The 1978 CODASYL specifications removed the dynamic set.
5. An arbitrary number of set types may be declared in a schema.
6. Any record type may be the owner of one or more set types, Figure 5.4(c).
7. Any record type may be a member of one or more set types, Figure 5.4(d).
8. Any record type may be both an owner of one or more set types and a member in one or more different set types, Figure 5.4(e).
9. A record type with two or more owner record types within the same set type is not allowed, Figure 5.4(f).
10. A record occurrence with two or more owner record occurrences within the same set, that is, an *M:N* relationship, is not allowed, Figure 5.4(f); transformation to two two-level hierarchies bypasses this limitation, Figure 3.16.
11. A set occurrence involves only one occurrence of the owner record type.
12. An *empty set* is a set made up of only an occurrence of its owner record type and no occurrence of its member record type(s).
13. A set must have an occurrence of its owner record type and may have an arbitrary number of occurrences of each of the member record types.
14. A record type cannot participate as both owner and member record in the same set type; however, 1978 CODASYL specifications permit it.
15. Every set type must have an order specified for its member records in the schema, indicating the sequence in which they are to be maintained; several types of ordering may be declared.
16. Owner records in a set cannot have an order specified for them as owners. However, if these records are members of another set then they can be ordered under it. Only member records can have an order specified for them.

Figure 5.5. *Summary of main characteristics of DBTG sets*

record occurrences into a continuous chain. The DBTG specifications allow optional bidirectional chains as well as pointers in each member record occurrence to identify the owner record occurrence, as shown in Figure 5.3.

Figure 5.3(b), detailing the set representation in Figures 5.3(a) and 5.4(a), shows that the owner of the set contains a pointer N (next) which identifies the first member record occurrence. The first member record occurrence also contains a pointer N which identifies the second record occurrence in the set, and so on. In the last record occurrence the pointer N identifies the owner record. Thus these N pointers form a ring structure commonly called a **chain**. The N pointers establish a logical access path in the "next" direction. The concept of "next" is one of the bases for accessing the data base via the DML.

The pointers P (prior) establish a logical chain in the prior direction. The owner contains a pointer P which identifies the last member record occurrence in the set it owns. The last record contains a pointer P which identifies its predecessor, which in turn points to its predecessor, and so on. In addition, each member record occurrence may optionally contain a pointer O (owner) which identifies the owner record occurrence of the set. The "next" chain along with the prior chain and the owner pointers are considered an implementation of the set. Recall that a data base may contain any number of member record occurrences.

In the simple pictorial representation of the set in Figure 5.3(a), the arrow is the shorthand equivalent of all next, prior, and owner pointers shown in Figure 5.3(b). The name of the set (A) appears next to the arrow. The tail of the arrow always starts on the record type which is the owner of the set; the point of the arrow ends on the record type which participates as a member of the set. In practice, the V point of the arrow is sometimes left out with the understanding that a lower block going from top to bottom in the diagram is a member record type.

The set mechanisms are the building blocks which can be used to construct complex multilevel and network data bases. The main rules for the formation of sets are pictorially summarized in Figure 5.4 and are:

1. A set type must be uniquely named, must have one owner record type, and must contain one or more member record types within the set type.

2. Any record type may be the owner of one or more set types, Figure 5.4(c).

3. Any record type may be a member of one or more set types, Figure 5.4(d).

4. Any record type may be both an owner of one or more set types and a member in one or more different set types, Figure 5.4(e). Thus multilevel tree structures can be easily formed.

5. A record type with two or more owners within the same set type is not allowed, Figure 5.4(f).

6. One-to-one and one-to-N relationships between owner record and member record(s) in a set are allowed. An M-to-N relationship, that is, a record occurrence with two or more owner record occurrences within the same set occurrence, is not allowed. However, this limitation may be bypassed by transformation to two two-level hierarchies (three record types and two set types) as outlined in Figure 3.16. An example in the DBTG model will be detailed later (Figure 5.12).

As an example, Figure 5.6 shows a two-level DBTG schema composed of three record types: EMPLOYEE, CHILD, and INSURANCE_CO. The relationships between these record types are expressed in two set types: EMP_CHILD and EMP_INSUR.

The following is offered as a review of why the DBTG data model is said to be a network data model. As discussed in Chapter 3, the classical tree data organization does not allow a node at one level of the tree to have more than one parent node, Figure 3.12. If a node has multiple parents, then the tree becomes a network structure. In data base terms each node is a record. Since a DBTG record type can have more than one owner record type as long as each is in a different set, Figure 5.4(d), the DBTG data model is then a network model. However, in the case of a single occurrence of one DBTG set type, a member record type occurrence cannot have more than one owner record type occurrence; that is, an M to N relationship in terms of record occurrences within the same set is not allowed. Thus, in this single set respect, the DBTG does not handle a network structure. However, due to the former facility, the

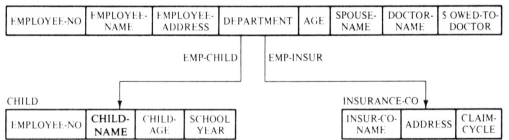

Schema contains three record types: EMPLOYEE, CHILD and INSURANCE-CO

Relationships between the record types expressed in two set types: EMP-CHILD and EMP-INSUR

Figure 5.6. *An Employee-Child-Insurance DBTG data base*

DBTG model is said to be a network model. [As already indicated, an M to N relationship such as that illustrated by the DOCTOR_PATIENT schema in Figure 3.16(a) can be accommodated by transforming it to a two two-level schema as illustrated in Figure 3.16(b). An illustration in DBTG terms will be provided later.]

Figure 5.5 is a summary of the main characteristics of DBTG sets. It includes the basic characteristics introduced in previous paragraphs and a number of others that we will now discuss.

Single Files

By now the reader might be wondering about the ubiquitous single, sequential-oriented files. A single file can be defined via a **singular set**. A singular set is a special type of set whose owner is declared in the schema to be the "SYSTEM," that is, the GDBMS; a singular set is the traditional file containing records of the same type. Any record type can be a member of a singular set at the same time that it participates in other (normal) sets. For example, in Figure 5.6 the record type INSURANCE_CO could be a member of also the singular set INSUR, and EMPLOYEE could also be a member of the singular set EMP. The ordering of the record occurrences in a singular set can be different to the ordering of the same records under a different set (ordering will be treated later). Thus, the singular sets INSUR and EMP materialize two independent single files, each of which can be ordered and searched independently of the rest of the schema.

Cycles

A cyclic schema such as the one shown in Figure 3.14 may be defined in the DBTG system. The special case of a cycle in which a record type is both an owner and a member of the same set type is allowed in 1978 specifications. This special case arises in a few major situations, such as a bill-of-materials data base and a family tree data base in which owner and member records have identical structure.

Dynamic Set

A **dynamic set** is a set that does not have member record types declared for it in the schema. A facility in the DBTG DML permits an application program to include at execution time any record occurrence in the data base as a member of the dynamic set, or remove it from the set. At the end of execution their membership in the dynamic set is canceled. The dynamic set was removed by the 1978 CODASYL specifications.

Ordering of Sets

Every set must have an ORDER specified for its member record occurrences, indicating the sequence in which they are to be maintained by the GDBMS. This logical sequence seen by the programmer is not necessarily the actual physical sequence in which the records are stored in the hardware. The same records may be members of different set types and their order may be different in each set.

Owner records in a set cannot have an order specified for them as owners. However, they can be ordered as member records of another set.

The following three ordering options may be specified in the set type description:

1. ORDER IS IMMATERIAL indicates that the order of member records is to be determined by the GDBMS.
2. ORDER IS SORTED indicates that records will be maintained in ascending or descending order of the value of the key declared in a subsequent clause. As an example, the subsequent clause ASCENDING KEY IS EMPLOYEE_NO, CHILD_NAME followed by DUPLICATES ARE NOT ALLOWED says that the order of member records is to be in ascending value of its two data items EMPLOYEE_NO and CHILD_NAME which together form the key, and that no member records (within a set occurrence) are allowed to have the same key-value.
3. The order may be the basis of time of insertion of the record or before or after a chosen record. ORDER IS LAST indicates that the record is inserted at the last record position in the (logical) sequence of member records; analogously, ORDER IS FIRST is self-explanatory. ORDER IS PRIOR or ORDER IS NEXT indicates that the record will be inserted (logically) before or after a particular member record occurrence identified by the application program.

Membership Class of Sets

The so-called **membership class** is an important characteristic of *each* set type defined in the schema. The membership class for each set type is:

$$\text{INSERTION IS} \left\{ \begin{array}{c} \text{AUTOMATIC} \\ \text{MANUAL} \end{array} \right\} \text{RETENTION IS} \left\{ \begin{array}{c} \text{FIXED} \\ \text{MANDATORY} \\ \text{OPTIONAL} \end{array} \right\}$$

The INSERTION rules are as follows:

1. If AUTOMATIC is specified, then when an occurrence of the member record type is created it must become a member of a set occurrence

(of this set type) owned by an owner record occurrence satisfying the selection criteria expressed in the appropriate DML command.

2. If MANUAL is specified, then when an occurrence of the member record type is created it does not have to become a member of any set occurrence (of this set type).

The RETENTION rules would be more appropriately called "integrity rules," which is what they really are:

1. If FIXED is specified, then a member record occurrence is constrained to a single set occurrence once it is stored into the data base. The member record occurrence cannot be moved to another set occurrence unless the record occurrence is first erased entirely from the data base and then stored again.

2. If MANDATORY is specified, then once a member record occurrence is made a member of an occurrence of this set type it cannot exist in the data base unless it is a member of some (possibly different) occurrence of this set type.

3. If OPTIONAL is specified, then a member record occurrence may exist in the data base either participating or not participating in an occurrence of this set type.

We shall see that the membership class option affects the action of various DML commands as they are used to process the data base.

Areas

The concept of areas is sometimes a debated issue of the DBTG approach. An **area** is a named portion of the storage space in which records are to be physically stored independent of their membership in sets. The storage space in which the data base is stored is divided into one or more areas. The DBTG approach states that the AREA(s) must be specified in the schema for the purpose of helping the GDBMS to provide a more efficient physical organization. Figure 5.7 summarizes the characteristics of areas.

A number of practitioners criticize the definition of areas at the logical schema level as counter to data storage independence; that is, logical and physical aspects are unnecessarily intermingled. The definition of areas at the logical schema level of course does not involve actual physical addresses, but it introduces at least an unnecessary concern for the description of schemas (and all subschema descriptions in the various application programs) whenever hardware devices or physical organization techniques and trade-offs change.

Practitioners disagree principally on the issue of where the concept of areas is to be defined (at the logical schema level or at the physical schema level) and not on whether or not the concept of areas or physical storage is

1. An area is a named subdivision of the storage space of a data base.
2. An arbitrary number of areas may be declared.
3. For each record type, the area(s) within which occurrences of the record type are to be placed when loaded into the data base is (are) defined in the schema.
4. Occurrences of a record type are assigned to areas independent of the set(s) in which they participate.
5. A record occurrence is stored within one area only.
6. Occurrences of a set type or of portions of a set type may be stored within one area.
7. Occurrences of a set type may span several areas.

Note: The more detailed characteristics of areas, and of record and set placement, are highly dependent on the particular GDBMS implementation (and CODASYL revision of the DBTG report).

Figure 5.7. *Summary of characteristics of DBTG areas*

eventually needed. The concept of areas is surely very important from the practical data base storage and retrieval performance point of view. The data base administrator, at the physical data base design phase, can subdivide the data base into areas and assign different records according to the limitations in Figure 5.7, and without introducing device dependent details, so as to improve access time. For example, the data base administrator or designer can place within the same area [or page(s)] occurrences of records, from the same record type or from different record types, commonly accessed together by programs, so as to minimize seek time (or page-jumping time). Less frequently used record types or occurrences can be assigned to slower areas of the device space. For example, in terms of disks having an area served by moving arm read-write heads and a smaller area by fixed heads, if the INSURANCE_CO record type in Figure 5.6 were the most frequently accessed data by the application programs, then one could specify that it be within the area served by the fixed-head tracks. The area name can be even specified as a variable or established as a procedure. The mapping of the area name used in the schema description to the actual device addresses is done supposedly via the DMCL, but in practice the mappings are accomplished in different ways peculiar to each DBTG implementation, since the DMCL was not defined in the DBTG specifications.

The declaration of areas is made before records and sets are described: AREA NAME IS. . . . The indication that a record is to be stored within an area called COSTLY is as follows: WITHIN [AREA] COSTLY. If the record is to be in the same area of its owner, then one would state: WITHIN [AREA OF] OWNER. This last option is very useful since one of the many reasons for using data base technology is to be able to relate different record types via sets in DBTG and then be able to access them together. However, if two record types are frequently accessed but not together in the same set where one is owner and one is member, then they should not be stored within the same area. If a record type is in two different set types as member, then the DBA should indicate which owner record type directs the area choice.

Data Base Keys

A **data base key** is a unique value that identifies every record occurrence and differentiates it from all other record occurrences in the data base. It is a symbolic key and not a physical record address. It is generated by the GDBMS for each particular user. All pointers as seen by the user of a schema are data base keys.

A program may obtain direct access to any record occurrence at any time via appropriate DML commands indicating the desired data base key. Data base keys remain constant, independent of physical storage or reorganization. The precise format and rules for using data base keys were originally confusingly specified in DBTG reports, and consequently are very dependent on the particular implementation.

In DBTG, the currency indicators are the data base key-values indicating the record occurrence most recently accessed by the program for each area, record type, and set type. The important currency indicators will be discussed in Section 5.6.

5.3   SAMPLE SCHEMAS AND THEIR DESCRIPTION

Three examples will illustrate the DBTG concepts presented and will introduce a number of additional characteristics of the DBTG system. The first two examples include the schema description in the DBTG DDL. The second example is an addition to the schema of Example 1. The third example details the DBTG representation of an M to N relationship and the necessary transformation to do so.

Example 1: Three Record Types and Two Set Types

As our first example, consider the Employee-Child-Insurance data base in Figure 5.6. This is shown also in Figures 3.30 and 3.31 in terms of the DIAM string data model with three differences: (1) the data item INSUR_CO_NAME, the key or field uniquely identifying each INSURANCE_CO record occurrence, does not appear as a part of the EMPLOYEE record type in Figure 5.6 (the set in DBTG corresponds to the DIAM L-string); (2) the three record types are related via two sets, EMP_CHILD and EMP_INSUR, in Figure 5.6, whereas in Figure 3.30 they are related via one DIAM L-string which is in effect a single set; and (3) the data field TOT_RECEIVABLES is introduced with the DOCTOR record in Figure 5.9. The description of the schema in Figure 5.6 via the DBTG data description language is shown in Figure 5.8. Let us examine it.

Statement 1 defines the name of the data base.

Statements 2 and 3 indicate the name of the areas in which the data base records are to reside. However, no indication of device address or other device dependent aspects are involved; these are the realm of physical structure and device mapping mechanisms of the particular GDBMS. Two areas are declared, EMP_CHILD_AREA which will contain all the occurrences of EMPLOYEE and CHILD, and EMP_INSUR_AREA which will contain all the occurrences of INSURANCE_CO.

Statement 4 declares a record type named EMPLOYEE.

1. SCHEMA NAME IS EMPLOYEE_CHILD_INSURANCE.
2. AREA NAME IS EMP_CHILD_AREA.
3. AREA NAME IS EMP_INSUR_AREA.
4. RECORD NAME IS EMPLOYEE;
5. PRIVACY LOCK FOR GET FIND IS 226D;
6. PRIVACY LOCK FOR MODIFY, INSERT, DELETE, REMOVE, STORE IS XXYYZZ;
7. LOCATION MODE IS CALC HASH-PROC-1 USING EMPLOYEE_NO IN EMPLOYEE;
8. DUPLICATES ARE NOT ALLOWED;
9. WITHIN EMP_CHILD_AREA.
10. 02 EMPLOYEE_NO;   PICTURE 9(6).
11. 02 EMPLOYEE_NAME;   PICTURE A(12).
12. 02 EMPLOYEE_ADDRESS;   PICTURE X(20).
13. 02 DEPARTMENT;   PICTURE A(10).
14. 02 AGE;   PICTURE 99.
15. 02 SPOUSE_NAME;   PICTURE A(12).
16. 02 DOCTOR_NAME;   PICTURE A(12).
17. 02 $OWED_TO_DOCTOR;   PICTURE 99999V99.
18. RECORD NAME IS CHILD;

19. WITHIN EMP_CHILD_AREA.
20. 02 EMPLOYEE_NO; PICTURE 9(6); IS VIRTUAL SOURCE IS EMPLOYEE_NO OF OWNER OF EMP_CHILD.
21. 02 CHILD_NAME;   PICTURE X(8).
22. 02 CHILD_AGE;   PICTURE 99.
23. 02 SCHOOL_YEAR.   PICTURE 99.
24. RECORD NAME IS INSURANCE_CO;
25. LOCATION MODE IS CALC HASH-PROC-2 USING INSUR_CO_NAME IN INSURANCE_CO;
26. DUPLICATES ARE NOT ALLOWED;
27. WITHIN EMP_INSUR_AREA.
28. 02 INSUR_CO_NAME;   PICTURE X(12).
29. 02 ADDRESS;   PICTURE X(20).
30. 02 CLAIM_CYCLE;   PICTURE 999.
31. SET NAME IS EMP_CHILD;
32. ORDER IS SORTED;
33. MODE IS CHAIN;
34. OWNER IS EMPLOYEE.
35. MEMBER IS CHILD INSERTION IS AUTOMATIC RETENTION IS MANDATORY;
36. ASCENDING KEY IS EMPLOYEE_NO, CHILD_NAME;
37. DUPLICATES NOT ALLOWED.
38. SET OCCURRENCE SELECTION IS THRU LOCATION MODE OF OWNER.
39. SET NAME IS EMP_INSUR;
40. ORDER IS SORTED;
41. MODE IS CHAIN;
42. OWNER IS EMPLOYEE.
43. MEMBER IS INSURANCE_CO INSERTION IS AUTOMATIC RETENTION IS MANDATORY;
44. ASCENDING KEY IS INSUR_CO_NAME;
45. DUPLICATES NOT ALLOWED.
46. SET OCCURRENCE SELECTION IS THRU LOCATION MODE OF OWNER.

Figure 5.8. *DBTG data description of the schema in Figure 5.6*

Statements 5 and 6 specify the privacy or access control locks to be used for controlling access to the record type EMPLOYEE. Only when the indicated privacy key (226D or XXYYZZ) is provided can a program or user have the defined access authority to EMPLOYEE.

Statement 7 defines the MODE for locating an occurrence of record type EMPLOYEE. CALC HASH-PROC-1 USING EMPLOYEE_NO IN EMPLOYEE says that the GDBMS is to take the value of the data item EMPLOYEE_NO and process it with the procedure HASH-PROC-1 (the procedure is intended to be some kind of key-transformation or hashing algorithm defined by the data base administrator or GDBMS) so as to derive the key that identifies or locates the corresponding occurrence of EMPLOYEE.

Statement 8 says that no occurrences of EMPLOYEE may have the same EMPLOYEE_NO value. This clause needs to be stated if LOCATION MODE IS CALC . . . for locating an EMPLOYEE record occurrence.

Statement 9 indicates that every EMPLOYEE occurrence is to be physically stored within the external storage area EMP_CHILD_AREA.

Statements 10–17 indicate the data items making up the record type EMPLOYEE. Their type and formats are also defined in a fashion similar to COBOL. The O1 level is not used for the record name as in COBOL.

Statements 18–22, excluding statment 20, define the record type CHILD as above, except that no privacy lock or access control is to be used for CHILD, and an occurrence of CHILD is not to be located via LOCATION MODE IS CALC. CHILD is a member record in the definition of the set EMP_CHILD in statements 31–39. Although the absence of CALC means that a CHILD occurrence cannot be located directly, it can be located by a more lengthy sequential search of the CHILD member chain of an occurrence of the set EMP_CHILD.

Statement 20 indicates that EMPLOYEE_NO is *virtual*, that is, the GDBMS does not physically store this data item in the CHILD occurrence (although the programmer sees it as if it were stored); the GDBMS makes sure that the value of EMPLOYEE_NO seen by the programmer is identical to the value of EMPLOYEE_NO actually stored in the EMPLOYEE record occurrence owning the particular occurrence of the set EMP_CHILD. Virtual fields are declared to insure data integrity and to avoid storage redundancy.

Statements 24–30 define the record type INSURANCE_CO in a manner similar to EMPLOYEE, except that no privacy lock is to be used for accessing INSURANCE_CO.

Statement 31 declares the set type EMP_CHILD.

Statement 32 indicates that the CHILD occurrences within each EMP_CHILD set occurrence are to be sorted (and maintained sorted) by the GDBMS according to the data item(s) selected as the sort-key. Statement 36 indicates that the sort key is the two data items EMPLOYEE_NO and CHILD_NAME together and that the sort order is on an ASCENDING basis.

Statement 33 indicates that the implementation mechanism by which member CHILD occurrences are related to the owner EMPLOYEE occurrence within every set occurrence is a chain (chains were introduced in Section 2.6). However, the particular MODE does not affect the application program, except for search time and storage performance. Other MODES are proposed in the 1971 DBTG report, but subsequent DBTG DDL publications[2,10] properly removed this set MODE clause to the DSDL since it involves physical organization efficiency notions that should not appear at the schema level intended to deal with purely logical descriptions.

Statement 34 declares the owner record type.

Statement 35 indicates the member record type and its membership class in the set type (each member type description must be accompanied by a membership class for each set type) as MANDATORY AUTOMATIC. MANDATORY means that once a CHILD occurrence X has been loaded as a member of an EMP_CHILD set, X can be assigned to another EMP_CHILD set occurrence or deleted completely from the data base via a DELETE command. AUTOMATIC means that when a CHILD occurrence is first stored in the data base via a STORE command, the GDBMS will insert it automatically into the corresponding set occurrence chosen by the application program; this is in contrast to the MANUAL option for which the programmer must identify explicitly the corresponding set occurrence and then insert the CHILD occurrence via an explicit INSERT command. More on set membership later.

Statement 36 indicates the sort key (two data items form the key in this case) and sort order, already explained in Statement 32.

Statement 37 indicates that within an EMP_CHILD set occurrence, every member CHILD occurrence must have a different CHILD_NAME value. Note, however, that all CHILD occurrences over the EMP_CHILD set occurrences do not have to be unique (i.e., the same name is usually given to a CHILD by several EMPLOYEEs), and thus in the definition of CHILD the clause DUPLICATES NOT ALLOWED does not appear.

Statement 38 defines that a particular EMP_CHILD set occurrence is chosen by locating the desired owner EMP record occurrence using the LOCATION MODE specified for the owner. The LOCATION MODE specified in Statement 7 indicates the use of the procedure

HASH-PROC-1 on the value assigned by the application program to the record's key data item EMPLOYEE_NO. Thus the following could be done via the DML:

MOVE 749 TO EMPLOYEE_ NO IN EMPLOYEE.
FIND EMPLOYEE RECORD.

to locate the EMPLOYEE occurrence whose EMPLOYEE_NO = 749. Notice that it would be more appealing to be able to say FIND EM-PLOYEE WHERE EMPLOYEE_NO = 749; unfortunately, the procedureness of COBOL influenced the DBTG proposal and consequently this more streamlined statement is not defined.

Statements 39–46 specify the EMP_INSUR set type similarly.

The set EMP_INSUR materializes a list of INSURANCE_CO records for each EMPLOYEE record occurrence. Note that if a list of EMPLOYEE record occurrences were very frequently desired for each particular INSURANCE_CO record occurrence, then it probably would pay off to define a "backward" set INSUR_EMP (different from the EMP_INSUR set) in which the INSURANCE_CO record type is the owner and the EMPLOYEE record type is the member record type.

Example 2: *Addition of a Record Type to the Schema—*
A Three-Level Schema

Suppose that it is desired to add a DOCTOR record type at the top of the schema in Figures 5.6 and 5.8 so as to relate each DOCTOR record occurrence to its corresponding EMPLOYEE patients. Figure 5.9 diagrams the new Doctor-Employee-Child-Insurance data base. Figure 5.10 shows the data description entries that must be added to the data description in Figure 5.8 to account for the addition of the DOCTOR record type as shown in Figure 5.9. Note that the DOCTOR record description, statements A1–A15, can be inserted before or after any of the record type descriptions in Figure 5.8 and, similarly, the DOC_ PAT set type definition can be inserted before or after any of the set type descriptions in Figure 5.8. The following observations are offered for clauses not previously used.

Statements A10 through A13: A10 defines an elementary data item which does not appear in the diagram in Figure 5.9, but which is introduced here for the purpose of allocating in statement A11 a variable number of occurrences (rather than a less efficient fixed number) of DOCTOR_SPECIALTY (statement A12) and associated YEARS_ EXPERIENCE data item (statement A13).

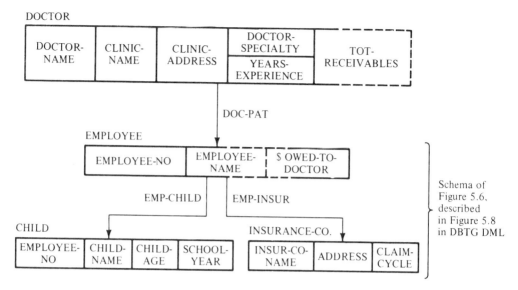

Figure 5.9. *A Doctor-Employee-Child-Insurance DBTG data base*

Statements A14 and A15 indicate that the data item TOT_
RECEIVABLES is virtual (it does not exist physically in the stored
DOCTOR record, but to the application program it appears as if it were)
and that its value is computed (when it is requested for use by a DML
command) for a DOCTOR occurrence by applying the procedure PRO-
CEDUREX to the members of this DOC_PAT set (when the DML
command is executed). In this example the procedure would sum the
$OWED_TO_DOCTOR values of the EMPLOYEE occurrences of
the particular DOCTOR occurrence.

The definition of the set type DOC_PAT in statements S1–S8 is
analogous to previous set type definitions in Figure 5.8, with the exception of Statement S5. Note that S5 specifies the use of the membership
class OPTIONAL MANUAL for the EMPLOYEE member records of
the SET DOC_PAT (in contrast with MANDATORY AUTOMATIC
for the EMP_CHILD and EMP_INSUR set types). This allows an
occurrence of EMPLOYEE to be removed from an occurrence of the
set DOC_PAT (typically by means of a DISCONNECT statement) but
without deleting it from the data base. This facility would be necessary if a
DOCTOR record occurrence had to be deleted (perhaps due to the
doctor's death) but its member EMPLOYEE record occurrences kept in
the data base for awhile until these were assigned to a new DOCTOR
owner or to an existing DOC_PAT set (whose owner is an existing
DOCTOR).

A1   RECORD NAME IS DOCTOR;

A2   PRIVACY LOCK FOR GET FIND IS DOCDOC;

A3   PRIVACY LOCK FOR MODIFY. INSERT, DELETE,
     REMOVE, STORE IS DDOOCC;

A4   LOCATION MODE IS CALC MAGIC USING DOCTOR_NAME
     CLINIC_NAME;

A5   DUPLICATES ARE NOT ALLOWED;

A6   WITHIN EMP_ CHILD_AREA.

A7   02 DOCTOR_NAME;   PICTURE A(12).

A8   02 CLINIC_NAME;   PICTURE A(15).

A9   02 CLINIC_ADDRESS;   PICTURE IS A(20).

A10 02 NUMB_SPEC;   PICTURE 9.

A11 02 XX; OCCURS NUMB_SPEC TIMES.

A12   03 DOCTOR_SPECIALTY;   PICTURE A(12).

A13   03 YEARS_EXPERIENCE;   PICTURE 99.

A14 02 TOT_RECEIVABLES;   PICTURE 999999V99;

A15   IS VIRTUAL RESULT OF PROCEDUREX ON MEMBERS OF
        DOC_PAT.

S1   SET NAME IS DOC_PAT;

S2   ORDER IS SORTED;

S3   MODE IS CHAIN;

S4   OWNER RECORD IS DOCTOR.

S5   MEMBER IS EMPLOYEE INSERTION IS MANUAL
     RETENTION IS OPTIONAL;

S6   DUPLICATES ARE NOT ALLOWED;

S7   ASCENDING KEY IS EMPLOYEE_NAME.

S8   SET OCCURRENCE SELECTION IS THRU LOCATION MODE
     OF OWNER.

Figure 5.10.   *DBTG data description addition to Figure 5.8 to incorporate the schema addition in Figure 5.9*

Example 3: *DBTG Representation of an M to N Relationship*

As already stated, an M to N relationship between records in one single set (one owner record type, one member record type, one set type) cannot be expressed directly in the DBTG schema. However, it is easily

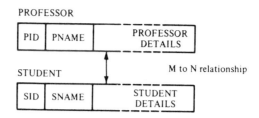

(a) A two-level schema with an M to N relationship

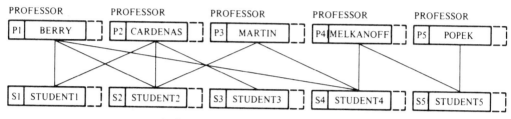

(b) Sample contents of the two-level data base

Figure 5.11. *A two-level schema with an M to N relationship between two record types*

accommodated by transforming it into a schema with three record types and two set types. As an example, consider the two-level data base structure shown in Figure 5.11 representing a PROFESSOR record type and a STUDENT record type in an M to N relationship. A PROFESSOR teaches a number of STUDENTS through several courses, and a STUDENT is taught by the PROFESSORS in charge of the courses that he is taking. The DBTG data model will handle this case only if the data base administrator transforms it into the equivalent data base shown in Figure 5.12.

Note that the transformation to fit the DBTG approach requires introducing duplication or redundancy, i.e., PID and SID now appear in two record types. Figure 5.12(b) shows why the transformation is often said to go from a two-level schema to a three-level schema. This three-level view is in fact the view that the programmer must take in order to properly search or "navigate" through the data base via the DML commands.

It would be a useful self-study exercise for the interested reader to draw up the schema declaration for this data base. Sufficient material has been provided already to accomplish this.

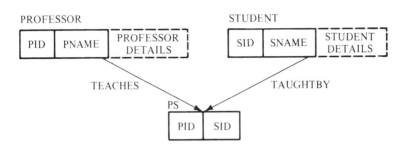

(a) Two-level, two-record schema in Figure 5.11 transformed to a three-record schema

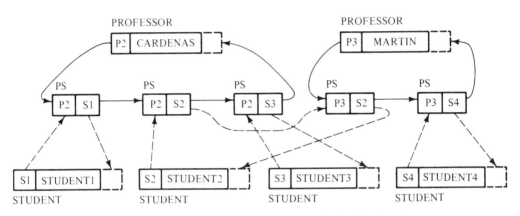

(b) Portion of the contents of the Professor-Student data base in
Figure 5.11 transformed to a three-record type data base

Figure 5.12.   *Schema of Figure 5.11 transformed to a DBTG schema*
representing an M to N relationship with three record types
and two set types

5.4 SELECTION OF SETS AND LOCATION
MODE OF RECORDS

Set selection refers to the process of identifying and locating a given
occurrence of a given set type. **Location mode** of records refers to the method
by which a record occurrence is to be identified and located. These are
fundamental storage and retrieval functions of a GDBMS, involving many
possible questions and options. The following is an introduction to it, not a
complete explanation.

The detailed techniques for searching for a record or set are the realm of the DML. However, at the schema level the data base designer specifies the general technique or access strategy indicating whether a routine included in the application program itself is to be used, whether a key is used, or whether accessing is to involve the use of another set. A SET OCCURRENCE SELECTION clause included in the set definition in the schema defines the set selection type. A LOCATION MODE clause accompanying a record definition in the schema defines the mode of locating the record.

Let us use the schema in Figures 5.6 and 5.8 to illustrate the set selection options that we shall now outline. Assume that the objective is to store the new CHILD occurrence "250, MICHAEL, 1, 0" for EMPLOYEE_NO = 250.

The following types of set selection may be declared:

1. Selection by a program procedure in an application program. For example, the clause SET OCCURRENCE SELECTION IS THRU PROCEDURE MAGIC.

2. Current occurrence of the set. Very simply,

    SET OCCURRENCE SELECTION IS THRU CURRENT OF SET

    tells the GDBMS to use the current occurrence of the set chosen by the procedural DML in the application program as follows:

    Statements (e.g., input, MOVE) to form CHILD occurrence "250, MICHAEL, 1.0" in UWA
    MOVE 250 TO EMPLOYEE_NO IN EMPLOYEE
    FIND EMPLOYEE RECORD
    STORE CHILD

3. Selection by means of the data base key of the owner record of the set(s) referenced. In this case, the owner record type description would have to include the clause LOCATION MODE DIRECT. The data item used as key may or may not be part of the record.

4. Selection by means of a CALCULATION using the data base key of the owner record of the set(s) referenced; the CALC key must be a part of the record. A CALC record type is stored in the data base using the value of one or more data items within the record occurrence to be stored. A procedure or hashing algorithm (or key transformation algorithm) uses the data item value, i.e., the key, to determine the logical storage position within the area in which the record is to be stored by the GDBMS. When a record occurrence is to be retrieved later, the application program supplies the named data item value or

key-value desired. Let us consider statements 7 and 38 in the schema description in Figure 5.8. The self-explanatory statement 38:

SET OCCURRENCE SELECTION IS THRU LOCATION MODE OF OWNER

states that the set occurrence is to be determined by the particular owner record occurrence using the location mode declared in the owner record type description (which may be either DIRECT or CALC). In our example, statement 7

LOCATION MODE IS CALC HASH-PROC-1 USING EMPLOYEE_NO IN EMPLOYEE

says that the GDBMS will calculate the location of the record occurrence by applying the procedure HASH-PROC-1 to the key EMPLOYEE_NO IN EMPLOYEE specified in the UWA by the application program. The programmer must provide the key-value before storing the new CHILD occurrence, for example, as follows:

Statements (e.g., input, MOVE) to form CHILD occurrence "250, MICHAEL, 1, 0" in UWA
MOVE 250 TO EMPLOYEE_NO IN EMPLOYEE
STORE CHILD

5. Selection by means of another set. For example, consider the three-level schema in Figure 5.9, and in Figure 5.8 replace statement 7 by

LOCATION MODE IS VIA DOC_PAT SET

and statement 38 by

SET OCCURRENCE SELECTION IS THRU LOCATION MODE OF OWNER USING EMPLOYEE_NO IN EMPLOYEE

where DOC_PAT is the set type defined in Figures 5.9 and 5.10. This means that in order to find an EMP_CHILD set occurrence the following occurs:

(a) The programmer must first identify the desired DOCTOR record occurrence.

(b) Then the GDBMS accesses its corresponding DOC_PAT set occurrence via the mode indicated in statements A4 and S8 in Figure 5.10.

(c) The GDBMS searches this DOC_PAT set occurrence for an occurrence of the record EMPLOYEE which has the EMPLOYEE_NO value indicated in EMPLOYEE_NO in EMPLOYEE in the UWA.

(d) Finally, the GDBMS obtains the EMP_CHILD set occurrence belonging to this EMPLOYEE record occurrence.

The SET OCCURRENCE SELECTION option with the form THRU LOCATION MODE OF OWNER USING EMPLOYEE_NO IN EMPLOYEE implies that the owner of the set being defined must be declared in the schema as a member of another set type (which in turn has its owner) and must have the LOCATION MODE:

LOCATION MODE IS VIA set name SET.

This convention or implication may appear to some readers as rather awkward and difficult to remember—DBTG has its faults.

5.5   THE SUBSCHEMAS

As discussed in Section 3.4 a subschema is a logical and consistent subset of the schema. Revisions of the 1971 DBTG proposal[3] and commercial implementations exhibit some variations among them with respect to the syntactic rules for forming subschemas.

The following are the main rules for subschemas (not an exhaustive list):

1. An arbitrary number of subschemas may be defined on a given schema.

2. Different subschemas can overlap.

3. An arbitrary number of programs can share a given subschema.

4. Any of the following schema declaration entries can be omitted in a given subschema: the declaration of one or more areas, sets, records, or data items.

5. Names specific to the subschema may be specified for areas, sets, records, and data items, i.e., such names in the schema may be replaced by synonyms.

6. The relative order of data items within their containing record may be changed.

7. The data type of data items may be changed.

8. Sets may be assigned different SET OCCURRENCE SELECTION clauses but not different LOCATION MODE of owner record types or membership class of member record types.

9. Privacy locks may be changed.

All this may be done within the limits of consistency. For example, a record declaration may not be omitted if a set declaration referring to it is included. Obviously, areas, record types, set types, and data items not in the schema cannot appear in a subschema.

It follows from the previous characteristics that expansions and changes to the schema are shielded so as not to affect application programs, except perhaps in terms of storage and access time performance. New record types, new data items for existing record types, and new areas may be accommodated. New sets may be added but only under certain conditions.

The DBTG proposal specifies the data description language for a COBOL subschema. This language fits in properly with COBOL in syntax and semantics. Two DBTG divisions are necessary to define the subschema:

1. The SUBSCHEMA IDENTIFICATION DIVISION

2. The SUBSCHEMA DATA DIVISION consisting of these four sections:
   (a) Renaming Section (Optional);
   (b) Area Section;
   (c) Record Section; and
   (d) Set Section (Optional).

Example

Figure 5.13 is a subschema from the schema in Figure 5.6.

Figure 5.14 shows the COBOL DBTG data description of this subschema, following the 1971 DBTG syntax.

In the definition of subschemas the syntactic differences are more noticeable between the 1971 Report,[1] subsequent CODASYL revi-

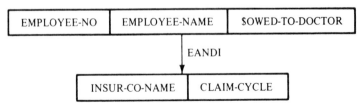

Figure 5.13.   *A subschema from the schema in Figure 5.6*

```
SUBSCHEMA IDENTIFICATION DIVISION.
  SUBSCHEMA NAME IS EMPANDINSUR OF SCHEMA NAME
    EMPLOYEE_CHILD_INSURANCE.
SUBSCHEMA DATA DIVISION.
  RENAMING SECTION.
    DATA NAME $OWED_TO_DOCTOR IN SCHEMA IS
    CHANGED TO DOLLARS_OWED.
    SET NAME EMP_INSUR IN SCHEMA IS CHANGED TO EANDI.
  AREA SECTION.
    COPY AREA EMP_INSUR_AREA.
    COPY AREA EMP_CHILD_AREA.
  RECORD SECTION.
    01 EMPLOYEE.
       02 EMPLOYEE NO;      PICTURE 9(4).
       02 EMPLOYEE_NAME;    PICTURE A(12)
       02 DOLLARS_OWED;     PICTURE 9(5)V99.
    01 INSURANCE_CO.
       02 INSUR_CO_NAME;    PICTURE X(12).
       02 CLAIM_CYCLE;      PICTURE 999.
  SET SECTION.
    COPY EANDI.
```

Figure 5.14.   *COBOL DBTG data description of the subschema in Figure 5.13*

sions,[2,3] and the various commercial DBTG implementations. For example, this 1971 DBTG statement syntax followed by most commercial DBTG GDBMS (e.g., DMS-1100,[5] IDMS[6]):

> SUBSCHEMA NAME IS EMPANDINSUR OF SCHEMA
> NAME EMPLOYEE_CHILD_INSURANCE

has the following syntax in the most recent DBTG revisions:[2,3]

> SS EMPANDINSUR WITHIN SCHEMA
> EMPLOYEE_CHILD_INSURANCE

Syntactic details may differ, but the architecture and functional capability remain the same: DBTG.

5.6   DATA MANIPULATION LANGUAGE (DML)

We will outline the main characteristics of the DBTG *Data Manipulation Language*, DML. We will focus on the main DML commands. There are many detailed options and implications in the DML that we will not address. Subsequent to the 1971 DBTG report,[1] proposed DBTG revisions modify a little the DML syntax and (the 1978 revisions) to some degree some of the DML functions.[2,3,11] We will follow the original 1971–73 DBTG DML which is the basis for most DBTG implementations.

The reader should cover the previous sections on the DBTG architecture and data model in order to understand the DML. We will use the previous data base examples, namely, the Doctor-Employee-Child-Insurance schema and the Professor-Student data base. The subschema that we will use is almost the same as the schema, and so we shall not differentiate between the two.

The DBTG DML is somewhat oriented for use within a COBOL application program. DML I/O commands are issued in the PROCEDURE Division of the COBOL program.

It should be noted that the DML is a rather procedural data retrieval language. It is a representation-dependent language in terms of the DIAM framework, as opposed to a representation-independent language or high-level query language. The DML is a language that expects users to *navigate* through the logical paths of the data base network and keep track of where in the insides of the network they are. Sometimes it is not easy for users to keep track of where they are inside the data base.

Currency

The so-called currency status indicators are central to the DBTG DML. A **currency status indicator** is a GDBMS variable identifying the data base key-value of the record occurrence most recently accessed (unless indicated otherwise, as will be shown) by the application program for each area, record type, and set type. The following currency status indicators are defined for the purpose of keeping track of where one is in the data base as one "navigates it":

1. "Current of area A" or "current of A" refers to the most recently accessed record occurrence within area A.
2. "Current of record type R" or "current occurrence of R" or "current of R" refers to the most recently accessed R record occurrence.
3. "Current of set type S" or "current occurrence of S" or "current of S" refers to the most recently accessed S set occurrence. The current of S is determined by an occurrence of either the owner or member record, whichever record occurrence was the most recently accessed via the DML. Note that the current of S refers to a record occurrence (owner or member).
4. "Current of run unit" refers to the most recently accessed record occurrence, independent of its involvement with areas and sets. Run

unit means the execution of the program. This fourth currency indicator is generally the most important of all, as will be illustrated.

We shall generally use the shorter of the synonyms of each of the preceding terms in our discussions.

Let us see an example of currency status setting. Consider the small data base Professor-Student of Figure 5.12. Note that Figure 5.12 is the transformation of the data base of Figure 5.11. Consider the following self-explanatory pseudostatements, focusing on Figure 5.12b:

FIND PROFESSOR RECORD WITH PNAME = MARTIN
FIND FIRST PS RECORD OF TEACHES SET
FIND OWNER IN TAUGHTBY OF CURRENT OF TEACHES SET

After execution of these three statements, the status of the currency indicators is:

Currency Indicator	*Status*
Current of run unit	STUDENT 'S2, STUDENT2'
Current of STUDENT	'S2, STUDENT2'
Current of PS	'P3, S2'
Current of PROFESSOR	'P3, MARTIN'
Current of set TAUGHT BY	The set owned by STUDENT 'S2, STUDENT2'
Current of set TEACHES	The set whose member is PS 'P3, S2'

The COBOL Data Manipulation Language

The COBOL DML is made up of three divisions in this order:

1. Identification Division;
2. Data Division; and
3. Procedure Division.

Figure 5.15 shows the skeletal structure of a COBOL application program with the additions for DBTG DML use. The reader might at this point review the nature and fundamentals of COBOL; however, a knowledge of standard COBOL is not necessary for our introduction to the DML. The DML statements do not modify or affect the standard COBOL statements.

A PRIVACY KEY entry defines the program and run-unit authority to execute DML executable commands. The GDBMS checks to see if it matches the authority locks declared in the schema or subschema for the program.

IDENTIFICATION DIVISION.

PROGRAM-ID.   Identification.

> PRIVACY KEY, DBTG Entries (Optional)

> Standard COBOL Entries

ENVIRONMENT DIVISION.

> Standard COBOL Entries.

DATA DIVISION.

SCHEMA SECTION.

INVOKE   SUB-SCHEMA Subschema Name OF SCHEMA Schema Name.

> Standard COBOL Sections

PROCEDURE DIVISION.

> Standard COBOL and DBTG DML
> Executable Commands

Figure 5.15.   *Skeletal structure of a COBOL application program using the DBTG DML*

An INVOKE SUBSCHEMA statement specifies the previously defined subschema that the program may access; the GDBMS sets up the appropriate user working area (UWA) storage for the execution of the program.

The following DML commands are defined:

OPEN,   which opens all areas that the "run unit (execution of the program)" is to use, specifying usage mode of RETRIEVAL or UPDATE, and other options.

CLOSE,   which closes or releases areas.

ORDER, which permits the user to specify for a given set a new ordering of its member records only for the duration of the program's execution where the ordering is different from that specified in the schema.

MOVE, which obtains the explicit value (a data base key) of any of the specified currency status indicators (run unit, record, set, or area). This DML special MOVE should not be confused with the encompassing and powerful standard COBOL MOVE statement.

IF, which causes a condition to be evaluated by the GDBMS so that it may then take action depending on whether the condition is true or false.

GET, which retrieves and presents for the programmer the current of the run-unit (the object record).

FIND, which locates (but *does not* retrieve) a record occurrence and sets it up as the current of run unit; FIND also causes the current of run-unit to become the current of the area, of the record type, and of the set(s) in which the current of run unit participates.

STORE, which creates a *new* record occurrence, stores it in the data base for all sets for which it is an AUTO-MATIC member, and establishes it as the current of run-unit; STORE also causes the current of run unit to become the current of the area, of the record type, and of the set(s) in which the current of run unit participates as an owner or AUTOMATIC member.

ERASE, which erases (deletes) the current of run unit, disconnects it from all set occurrences in which it is a member, erases all record occurrences which are MANDATORY members of set occurrences owned by it, and disconnects or optionally erases all record occurrences which are OPTIONAL members of set occurrences owned by it.

CONNECT, which connects (inserts) the current of run unit as a member of the occurrences of the specified set types, provided that it is declared as an OPTIONAL AUTOMATIC, OPTIONAL MANUAL, or MAN-DATORY MANUAL member of those sets.

DISCONNECT, which disconnects (removes) or cancels the membership of the current of run unit in the occurrence(s) of the specified set type(s) in which it participates as a member, provided that the current of run-unit is declared as an OPTIONAL member of the sets specified.

MODIFY,   which replaces the values of all or specific data items of the current of run unit, with values from the UWA; it may also change its membership from one set occurrence to another and position within a set occurrence so as to maintain the data base as per the set occurrence selection and ordering specified in the schema.

FREE, KEEP, and USE are additional DML statements that we shall discuss in Section 13.6. We will now illustrate the fundamental and major features of DML by means of examples of the main statements GET, MODIFY, FIND, STORE, ERASE, CONNECT, and DISCONNECT. Various options and implications of combinations of these statements will be left out; interested readers should consult the CODASYL DBTG reports. In the examples below a sample logical request is first stated, followed by its DBTG DML equivalent, and then by a brief explanation of it. The schema involved is the Employee – Child – Insurance schema shown in Figure 5.6 and defined in the DDL in Figure 5.8, except where indicated otherwise.

Get

Get all the information of EMPLOYEE 20

MOVE 20 TO EMPLOYEE_NO IN EMPLOYEE.
FIND EMPLOYEE RECORD.
GET EMPLOYEE.

Note that the FIND statement locates the desired record occurrence but does not retrieve it. The GET statement brings the located record into the EMPLOYEE location within the previously specified UWA (EMP_CHILD_AREA). If the current of run unit is not an occurrence of EMPLOYEE, then the statement fails and an ERROR STATUS will arise. ERROR-STATUS codes are suggested in the DBTG report for a number of abnormal conditions of the DML facilities; we shall ignore these and merely refer to any abnormal condition as an ERROR-STATUS condition.

Specific data fields of a record occurrence may be brought into the UWA, rather than the whole of it (which does not necessarily mean that physical transfer of the whole record occurrence is avoided). For example, GET EMPLOYEE; EMPLOYEE_NAME, DOCTOR_NAME, $OWED_TO_DOCTOR.

GENERAL FORMAT OF THE COMMAND FIND:

$$\underline{\text{FIND}} \text{ rse} \left[\underline{\text{SUPPRESS}} \begin{Bmatrix} \text{ALL} \\ \text{RECORD} \\ \text{AREA} \\ \begin{cases} \text{SET} \\ \text{set-name-1 [,set-name-2] ...} \end{cases} \end{Bmatrix} \begin{matrix} \text{CURRENCY} \\ \text{UPDATES} \end{matrix} \right]$$

General format of record-selection-expression (rse):

Format 1:

[record-name-1] <u>USING</u> identifier-1

Format 2:

$$[\underline{\text{OWNER}} \text{ IN set-name-3 OF}] \underline{\text{CURRENT OF}} \begin{Bmatrix} \text{record-name-2 } \underline{\text{RECORD}} \\ \text{set-name-4 } \underline{\text{SET}} \\ \text{area-name-1 } \underline{\text{AREA}} \\ \text{RUN-UNIT} \end{Bmatrix}$$

Format 3:

$$\begin{Bmatrix} \underline{\text{NEXT}} \\ \underline{\text{PRIOR}} \\ \underline{\text{FIRST}} \\ \underline{\text{LAST}} \\ \text{integer-1} \\ \text{identifier-2} \end{Bmatrix} \text{[record-name-3] } \underline{\text{RECORD}} \text{ OF } \begin{Bmatrix} \text{set-name-5-}\underline{\text{SET}} \\ \text{area-name-2 } \underline{\text{AREA}} \end{Bmatrix}$$

Format 4

<u>OWNER</u> RECORD OF set-name-6 SET

Format 5:

[NEXT <u>DUPLICATE</u> WITHIN] record-name-4 RECORD

Format 6:

record-name-5 <u>VIA</u> [<u>CURRENT</u> OF] set-name-7

   [<u>USING</u> data-base-identifier-3 [,data-base-identifier-4] ...]

Format 7:

NEXT <u>DUPLICATE</u> WITHIN set-name-8

   <u>USING</u> data-base-identifier-5 [,data-base-identifier-6] ...

Figure 5.16. *Definition of the DBTG DML command FIND (from the 1971 DBTG Report)*

Find

In order to give an idea of the many possibilities and richness of the FIND command, its full 1971 DBTG definition is shown in Figure 5.16. Seven formats are defined. We will give examples of each of them. The function of the FIND is to locate a record occurrence and establish it as the current of run unit, and at the same time as the current of the area, of the record type, and of the set(s) in which it participates (unless indicated otherwise by the SUPPRESS clause, which we shall not discuss).

FIND Format 1. Find the EMPLOYEE record identified by the current value of the data base key EMP_DB_KEY.

FIND EMPLOYEE USING EMP_DB_KEY.

The EMP_DB_KEY data item (local to the run unit but not a part of the data base) must be defined in the schema with a USAGE IS DATABASE-KEY clause.

FIND Format 2. Find the EMPLOYEE record occurrence which is the owner of the current of the INSURANCE_CO record.

FIND OWNER IN EMP_INSUR OF CURRENT OF
INSURANCE_CO RECORD

Note that Format 2 allows the OWNER record to be located for the current of a member record, current of a set, current of an area, or the current of run unit.

FIND Format 3. Considering the Professor–Student data base in Figure 5.12, find a student whose professor is Martin:

MOVE MARTIN TO PNAME IN PROFESSOR.
FIND FIRST PS RECORD OF TEACHES SET.
FIND OWNER IN TAUGHT BY OF CURRENT OF TEACHES SET.

This was previously presented when we introduced the concept of currency. As another example, using the Employee–Child–Insurance data base, retrieve the NAME and AGE of all the CHILDren of EMPLOYEE 20:

MOVE 20 TO EMPLOYEE_NO IN EMPLOYEE.
FIND EMPLOYEE RECORD.
IF EMP_CHILD SET EMPTY GO TO
NO_SET_OCCURRENCE.
NEXT   FIND NEXT CHILD RECORD OF EMP_CHILD SET.

> IF ERROR STATUS = no more member occurrences GO TO
> FINISH.
> GET CHILD; CHILD_NAME, CHILD_AGE.
> {PRINT IT}
> GO TO NEXT.

The second statement, FIND, locates the EMPLOYEE whose EMPLOYEE_NO is 20. This current of unit establishes the currency of the EMP_CHILD and EMP_INSUR sets, of the record EMPLOYEE, and of the area in which EMPLOYEE resides. The IF statement tests to see if there are no CHILDren for this EMPLOYEE. The statement FIND NEXT locates the next CHILD record occurrence within the current occurrence of the set EMP_CHILD. Recall that the ordering of CHILD occurrences is specified in the schema. After the first time that FIND NEXT is executed, the current of CHILD is the first CHILD record occurrence in the set of EMPLOYEE_NO = 20. The rest of the statements in the preceding example are self-explanatory.

Note that in the FIND Format 3 the word NEXT can be replaced by PRIOR, FIRST, LAST, an integer, or an identifier (data item name) whose value is an integer. These options call on the access paths that were defined earlier in Figure 5.3 for a set. In the last two options, the integer indicates the number of the desired record occurrence: if the integer is positive it is the number in the NEXT direction from the beginning of the set occurrence, and if negative it is the number in the PRIOR direction from the end of the set occurrence.

FIND Format 4.   Find the EMPLOYEE owner record occurrence of the current of set EMP_INSUR.

> FIND OWNER RECORD OF EMP_INSUR SET.

This format can be considered a special case of format 2 if the same set name is used in the OWNER IN and CURRENT of clauses of format 2: FIND owner in EMP_INSUR OF CURRENT OF EMP_INSUR SET.

FIND Format 5 (for CALC case).   This format is used when DUPLICATES are allowed for the CALC-key. As an example let us assume that in the Employee−Child−Insurance schema the following LOCATION MODE had been declared for the INSURANCE_CO record type, replacing statements 25 and 26, Figure 5.8:

> LOCATION MODE IS CALC HASH-PROC-2 USING
> INSUR_CO_NAME IN INSURANCE_CO;
> DUPLICATES ARE ALLOWED.

The following statements find all occurrences of INSURANCE_CO for INSUR_CO_NAME = 'EQUITABLE' via the FIND format 5 (CALC key):

> MOVE 'EQUITABLE' TO INSUR_CO_NAME IN
> INSURANCE_CO.
> NEXT   FIND NEXT DUPLICATE WITHIN INSURANCE_CO
> RECORD.
> IF ERROR STATUS = no more member records GO TO
> FINISH.
> {GET INSURANCE_CO and process it}
> GO TO NEXT.

These statements cause the GDBMS to first find the first record occurrence of INSURANCE_CO with the value INSUR_CO_NAME = 'EQUITABLE' specified in the UWA and then keep finding, one by one, the occurrences where INSUR_CO_NAME = 'EQUITABLE'.

FIND Format 6.   In Format 6, referring to the FIND definition in Figure 5.16, data base identifiers 3 and 4 must be the names of data items in record-name-5. Record-name-5 must be defined as a member of set-name-7. For example, to find the ADDRESS of the INSURANCE_CO whose name is 'EQUITABLE' which services EMPLOYEE number 20:

> MOVE 20 TO EMPLOYEE_NO IN EMPLOYEE.
> FIND EMPLOYEE RECORD.
> MOVE 'EQUITABLE' TO INSUR_CO_NAME.
> FIND INSURANCE_CO VIA CURRENT OF EMP_INSUR USING
> INSUR_CO_NAME.
> IF ERROR-STATUS = no occurrence with name = 'EQUITABLE'
> GO TO NOT-FOUND.
> GET INSURANCE_CO; ADDRESS

The FIND INSURANCE_CO statement searches automatically the EMP_INSUR set occurrence owned by EMPLOYEE_NO 20 for the first IN-SURANCE_CO occurrence with an INSURANCE_CO_NAME value equal to the value of the data item INSUR_CO_NAME established in the UWA (by the second MOVE statement above).

FIND Format 7.   In Format 7, with reference to the FIND definition in Figure 5.16, data base identifiers 5 and 6 must be names of data items in a record type defined as a member of set-name-8 (note the slight difference from Format 5). For example, for EMPLOYEE 20 find the INSURANCE_CO_

NAME of all the INSURANCE companies servicing him with a CLAIM_
CYCLE = 15:

```
              MOVE 20 TO EMPLOYEE_NO IN EMPLOYEE.
              FIND EMPLOYEE RECORD.
              MOVE 15 TO CLAIM_CYCLE.
              FIND INSURANCE_CO VIA CURRENT OF
              EMP_INSUR USING CLAIM_CYCLE.
      NEXT    IF ERROR STATUS = no occurrence with
              CLAIM_CYCLE = 15 GO TO NOT-FOUND.
              GET INSURANCE_CO; INSUR_CO_NAME.
              FIND NEXT DUPLICATE WITHIN EMP_INSUR USING
              CLAIM_CYCLE.
              GO TO NEXT.
```

The first four statements locate the first INSURANCE_CO occurrence for
EMPLOYEE 20 whose CLAIM_CYCLE is 15; these statements are similar
to the previous example using Format 6. Assuming there is one such IN-
SURANCE_CO occurrence, the Format 7 FIND NEXT DUPLICATE . . .
searches the current EMP_INSUR set occurrence for the NEXT INSUR-
ANCE_CO occurrence containing the same CLAIM_CYCLE value 15. This
Format 7 FIND scans in the forward direction (much like Format 5) from the
current of run unit, whereas Format 6 FIND does not go forward. The last four
statements are repeatedly executed until no occurrence with the condition is
found.

Store

Add the new CHILD record occurrence 'JOE, 1, 0' to EMPLOYEE
106's set of CHILDren

```
      MOVE 'JOE' TO CHILD_NAME.
      MOVE 1 TO CHILD_AGE.
      MOVE 0 TO SCHOOL_YEAR.
      MOVE 106 TO EMPLOYEE_NO IN EMPLOYEE.
      STORE CHILD.
```

The first three statements create the indicated values for the new CHILD
occurrence. The fourth MOVE gives the desired values to the UWA data item
EMPLOYEE_NO so that the STORE command may then store the correct
set occurrence. Note that EMPLOYEE_NO IN CHILD is a VIRTUAL field
whose SOURCE IS EMPLOYEE_NO OF OWNER OF EMP_CHILD,

Figure 5.8, line 20; thus EMPLOYEE_NO IN CHILD is automatically materialized when the STORE command is executed.

After the STORE above, the new CHILD occurrence is the current of run unit, the current CHILD occurrence, the current of area EMP_CHILD_AREA, and the current of the EMP_CHILD set. A new record occurrence STOREd becomes the current of all sets for which it is an owner or AUTOMATIC member, unless the SUPPRESS option is used. The STORE command updates the currency indicators as much as the FIND command.

Erase

The ERASE command has four options:

$$\text{ERASE [record-name]} \begin{bmatrix} \text{PERMANENT} \\ \text{SELECTIVE} \\ \text{ALL} \end{bmatrix}$$

The options function as follows:

1. ERASE R means to erase (delete) record R except when it is the owner of a set occurrence which is not empty.
2. ERASE PERMANENT means to erase the current of run unit and all record occurrences that are MANDATORY or FIXED members of set occurrences owned by it; the OPTIONAL member record occurrences are disconnected from each set occurrence owned by it but are not erased from the data base.
3. ERASE SELECTIVE means the same as ERASE PERMANENT except that now all record occurrences that are OPTIONAL members of set occurrences owned by it are also erased from the data base (unless these members participate in other set occurrences not owned by the current of run unit).
4. ERASE ALL means to erase the current of run unit as well as all member occurrences of every set occurrence of which it is the owner, no matter what membership class they have.

The current of run unit is null after execution of ERASE, but the other currency indicators remain as before. The GDBMS applies the original ERASE form to every erased member record occurrence that is in turn the owner of another set occurrence. Note the great impact of DELETE ALL!

As an example to erase the EMPLOYEE record 106 and all CHILD and INSURANCE_CO member record occurrences owned by it, any of the three options ERASE PERMANENT, ERASE SELECTIVE, or ERASE ALL suffices (since the set membership of CHILD and INSURANCE_CO is declared as MANDATORY, lines 35 and 43 in Figure 5.8).

Now consider the case of the Doctor-Employee-Child-Insurance schema in Figure 5.9:

    MOVE 'SHEINBEIN' TO DOCTOR_NAME.
    MOVE 'CLINIC AA' TO CLINIC_NAME.
    FIND DOCTOR RECORD.
    DELETE DOCTOR ONLY.

This means that the DOCTOR record occurrence whose key is SHEINBEIN CLINIC AA is to be erased. However, the EMPLOYEE record occurrences in the set owned by it are to be disconnected from the set but not erased entirely from the data base, since the membership class of EMPLOYEE in the DOC_PAT set is declared as OPTIONAL, line S5 Figure 5.10. If the EMPLOYEE membership class were MANDATORY, then all the EMPLOYEE occurrences owned by SHEINBEIN CLINIC AA would be erased entirely from the data base, but all the CHILD and INSURANCE_CO occurrences owned by each of these erased EMPLOYEE occurrences would be disconnected but not erased from the data base if the CHILD and INSURANCE_CO membership class were OPTIONAL.

Connect

CONNECT connects or inserts the current of run unit as a member of the occurrences of the specified set types, provided that it is declared as an OPTIONAL AUTOMATIC, OPTIONAL MANUAL, or MANDATORY MANUAL member of those sets.

In the Doctor-Employee-Child-Insurance schema, suppose that EMPLOYEE occurrence 106 is not currently a member of any occurrence of the set DOC_PAT (maybe it was initially stored but then disconnected from DOC_PAT). To connect this EMPLOYEE occurrence into the DOC_PAT set owned by the DOCTOR occurrence SHEINBEIN CLINIC AA, the following would do it:

    MOVE 'SHEINBEIN' TO DOCTOR_NAME.
    MOVE 'CLINIC AA' TO CLINIC_NAME.
    FIND DOCTOR RECORD.
    MOVE 106 TO EMPLOYEE_NO IN EMPLOYEE.
    FIND EMPLOYEE RECORD.
    INSERT EMPLOYEE INTO DOC_PAT SET.

The first three statements locate the desired occurrence of set DOC_PAT, the next two locate the desired EMPLOYEE occurrence (but the current of set DOC_PAT is not changed by the second FIND because employee 106 at that point is not a member of any occurrence of DOC_PAT), and the last performs the connection. The current of run unit, EMPLOYEE 106, then becomes the current of set DOC_PAT.

Disconnect

DISCONNECT is the opposite companion of CONNECT. It cancels the membership of the current of run unit in the occurrence(s) of the specified set type(s) in which it participates as a member, provided that the current of run unit is declared as an OPTIONAL member of the sets specified.

For example, to disconnect the EMPLOYEE occurrence 106 from the set DOC_PAT occurrence owned by DOCTOR occurrence SHEINBEIN CLINIC AA (a reversal of the INSERT action above):

```
MOVE 106 TO EMPLOYEE_NO IN EMPLOYEE.
FIND EMPLOYEE RECORD.
DISCONNECT EMPLOYEE FROM DOC_PAT.
```

EMPLOYEE record 106 is disconnected from its DOC_PAT set occurrence, but not erased from the data base. The current of set DOC_PAT is EMPLOYEE record 106 even though it no longer participates in a DOC_PAT occurrence.

Modify

MODIFY replaces the value of all or of specific data items of the current of run unit with values specified in the UWA; it may also change the membership(s) of the current of run unit from its set occurrence(s) to another set occurrence, as well as the position within a set occurrence so as to maintain the ordering specified in the schema.

For example, in the Employee-Child-Insurance schema to change the INSUR_CO_NAME of EMPLOYEE 106 from Puritan to Aetna and also his DOCTOR_NAME to Jones could be written as follows:

```
MOVE 106 TO EMPLOYEE_NO.
FIND EMPLOYEE RECORD.
MOVE 'JONES' TO DOCTOR_NAME.
MODIFY EMPLOYEE; USING DOCTOR_NAME.
MOVE 'PURITAN' TO INSUR_CO_NAME.
FIND INSURANCE_CO VIA CURRENT OF EMP_INSUR USING
INSUR_CO_NAME.
MOVE 'AETNA' TO INSUR_CO_NAME.
MOVE 'LOS ANGELES' TO ADDRESS.
```

MOVE 30 TO CLAIM_CYCLE.
MODIFY INSURANCE_CO.

The first two statements locate the desired EMPLOYEE; the next two update his DOCTOR_NAME; the fifth and sixth locate his INSURANCE_CO record for Puritan; the last three MOVEs form the new INSURANCE_CO record occurrence in the UWA; and finally the last statement replaces the Aetna INSURANCE_CO record with the new record just formed in the UWA.

Although the MODIFY and ERASE commands are modified somewhat by the 1978 CODASYL revisions, most commercial implementations stand as per the 1971–73 specifications herein.

5.7   1978 CODASYL CHANGES AND ADDITIONS

In 1978 CODASYL proposed a number of changes and significant additions to the original specifications in the CODASYL DBTG report[1] and interim revisions.[2,3] The 1978 CODASYL proposal has two parts:[10]

1. The 1978 CODASYL schema DDL specifications; and
2. An appendix by the British Computer Society (BCS)/CODASYL Data Base Administration Working Group (DBAWG) proposing a Data Storage Description Language (DSDL).

The 1978 DDL is very similar to the 1971 and 1973 DDL highlighted in the previous sections, except that several commands or clauses have been removed from the DDL and modified and repositioned as part of the DSDL. The DSDL is a new language for DBAs to map the logical schema into a physical storage schema, and it includes a rich variety of options (often overwhelming) for physical placement and optimization of the data base. The DSDL embodies the options referred to as the Device/Media Control Language (DMCL) but never specified in the 1971 or 1973 CODASYL reports.

The primary achievement of the 1978 specifications is increased potential for data independence by separating external or logical data description from internal storage considerations. Figure 5.17 shows conceptually the difference between the 1971 and 1978 CODASYL specifications.

In this section we summarize briefly the most important changes and additions at the level of the DDL. Miscellaneous syntactic changes and semantic clarifications have been made over the earlier specifications, but they are of no consequence to the purposes of this text. In the following section we highlight the major features of the DSDL.

It should be noted that as of the early 1980s, the most robust and

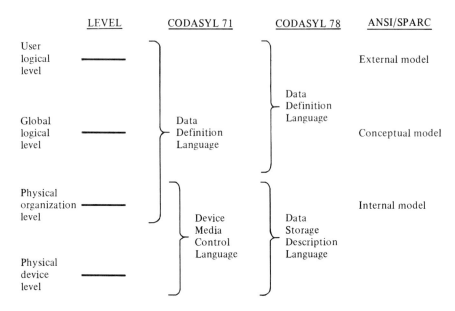

Figure 5.17. *Relationship of architectural levels of 1971 CODASYL,*
1978 CODASYL, and ANSI/SPARC architectures

well-established CODASYL GDBMS commercially available followed the
1971−73 CODASYL specifications and did not reflect the majority of the 1978
guide. The extent to which the 1978 DDL changes and especially the new
DSDL will be implemented by vendors remains to be seen.

The bulk of the following 1978 DDL changes and additions are aimed at
providing more data independence and more integrity controls. Record, data
items, and set description entries are affected.

Changes to Enhance Data Independence

Data independence is improved, although some may contend that it is
only slightly improved, in the 1978 DDL by removing 1971 and 1973 DDL
clauses that have internal structure and physical connotations. Some of these
clauses are modified and repositioned in the 1978 DSDL and others are entirely
omitted, as follows:

1. *Record entry*
   (a) The LOCATION MODE clause for a record is moved from the
       DDL to the DSDL. The PLACEMENT subentry within the
       storage record entry of the DSDL provides the LOCATION
       MODE CALC and VIA options addressed in Section 5.4. Thus
       such hashing matters and physical position of records are of no
       concern at the 1978 DDL level.

(b) A schema record can now have one or more data items or combinations of data items within a record type declared as record keys (via the new RECORD KEY clause) for the purpose of accessing, or ordering in ascending or descending sequence, record instances via these keys. However, this multikey access flexibility does not appear to be up to par with that of inverted and relational GDBMS. The RECORD KEY clause identifies which keys may be used as access paths by application programs, by referring to the record keys by name, whereas in inverted and relational GDBMS access keys and paths remain transparent to applications, thus enhancing data independence.

2. *Data item entry*
   (a) The specification ACTUAL versus VIRTUAL storage of a data item which is a RESULT of a data base procedure (see the example in Figures 5.9 and 5.10) or has as SOURCE a data base identifier (see the example in Figure 5.8) is removed from the DDL. This concern for whether or not a data item is physically stored is moved to the DSDL.
   (b) The DATABASE KEY has been redefined as a unique record reference within a single run unit, and prior references to direct, physical connotations are removed.

3. *Set entry*
   The 1978 DDL introduces a variety of changes to the set entry to enhance separation of logical and physical concerns. Two set clauses that are used in Sections 5.2 and 5.4 are affected as follows:
   (a) The SET SELECTION option to identify owner record occurrence by physical locator value, i.e., by either DATABASE-KEY or CALC-KEY value is removed from the DDL.
   (b) The MODE IS clause defining how the set occurrence is to be implemented, i.e., by either CHAIN or set index (pointer array), is moved from the DDL to the DSDL.

Data Integrity Enhancements

The 1978 DDL adds several clauses to enhance data integrity as follows:

1. The optional set membership description clause

STRUCTURAL CONSTRAINT IS

{data-identifier-of-member EQUAL TO data-identifier of owner}.

is added to insure the participation of a member record occurrence in a set occurrence such that the data identifier of the member is equal in value at all times to the corresponding data identifier of the owner occurrence. This insures the integrity of each set occurrence in view of occurrence changes and insertions.

2. The STRUCTURAL CONSTRAINT is also made explicit in the enhanced SET SELECTION clause of the 1978 DDL. The use of the clause SET SELECTION is by STRUCTURAL CONSTRAINT insures that the owner record occurrence selected satisfies the constraint that its data identifier is equal in value to the data identifier of the member.

3. Set membership retention class FIXED is added as an option to the MANDATORY and OPTIONAL set membership classes. The FIXED retention class constrains a member record occurrence to a single set occurrence once it is stored into the data base. The member record occurrence cannot be moved to another set occurrence unless the record occurrence is first deleted from the data base and then stored again.

The 1978 DDL structural constraint enhancements are unfortunately only a small subset of more general integrity constraints or controls that may be envisioned.

Recursive Set

A very significant addition in the 1978 DDL is the ability to define recursive sets. A **recursive set** is a set in which the owner record type and the member record type are the same. For example, the EMPLOYEE record type may be both the owner and member of a set type named MANAGES; this example defines an organization chart. The addition of recursive sets is a major addition for applications of this type which otherwise require the use of two record types and two set types. The inquisitive reader should try, as an exercise, to define the schema for the previous example without the use of a recursive set. A notorious type of data base facilitated by a recursive set is the bill of materials data base illustrated for IMS in Section 7.5.5.

Other Changes

Several other changes, of lesser concern and impact, include the following:

1. DYNAMIC SET cannot be defined any more;
2. The PRIVACY LOCK clause has been renamed the ACCESS-CONTROL LOCK clause;

3. The CONVERSION IS NOT ALLOWED clause is added as an option to specify that the schema and subschema formats for a data item must be the same. Note that in the subschema definition example in Section 5.5 there are allowed differences in some data formats with respect to the corresponding formats in the schema declaration.

5.8   1978 DATA STORAGE DESCRIPTION LANGUAGE (DSDL)

The 1978 CODASYL **Data Storage Description Language**, DSDL, provides the facilities for mapping the logical schema into a **physical storage schema**, and it includes a rich variety of options (sometimes overwhelming) for physical placement and performance optimization.[10] The DSDL includes the facilities referred to as the DMCL, but never specified, in previous CODASYL reports.[1,2] The DSDL also absorbed some commands with physical storage notions included in the earlier CODASYL DDL, as indicated in the previous section.

The DSDL is a unique and formal specification of physical storage strategies and controls expressed via high-level language constructs. It addresses the physical levels of data base organization envisioned in the DIAM framework (Section 3.8). The richness and formality of the DSDL stand out. As of the early 1980s, none of the implemented GDBMS, CODASYL or not, provided as much variety of physical organization controls to a DBA. The physical placement and organization issues dealt with by the DSDL apply to different degrees to non-CODASYL GDBMS. Many issues apply to any GDBMS. An example is whether or not a schema record is to be represented as a single storage unit or as several linked storage units. However, few GDBMS available provide a DBA with this degree of optimization flexibility.

The extent to which the DSDL will be implemented by vendors remains to be seen. Some version of a DMCL has been implemented independently by each CODASYL vendor. Because of this independence, the implemented DMCLs are incompatible with each other and show a wide range of options, language levels, etc. The DSDL provides a much richer variety of options than DMCLs previously implemented.

The implementation of the DSDL demands from a vendor a significant investment in internal GDBMS software and added GDBMS sophistication. At the same time, in order to deal with and take advantage of the full features of the DSDL, the DBA is expected to have a better understanding of GDBMS performance issues and of the characteristics of a data base and its users. Future implementations of the DSDL may involve a subset of it and may take a number of defaults to ease the task of defining the storage schema for less robust data bases and environments, where the full power of the DSDL is an overkill.

We will outline below the most salient features provided by the DSDL. We will close with an example combining these features.

There are five major types of DSDL entries or categories: Storage Schema, Mapping Description, Storage Area, Storage Record, and Index.

Storage Schema Entry

The **Storage Schema Entry** names the storage schema to which the logical schema specified via the DDL is mapped. This entry specifies the security controls (see Section 13.4) to access or modify the storage schema, as well as which schema records and sets are to be represented in the storage schema. The storage schema may represent a subset of the logical schema. This flexibility may be helpful in incremental data base implementation and in application and data base testing.

Mapping Description Entry

The **Mapping Description Entry** specifies the mapping between schema records and storage records. A schema record type may be mapped to one or

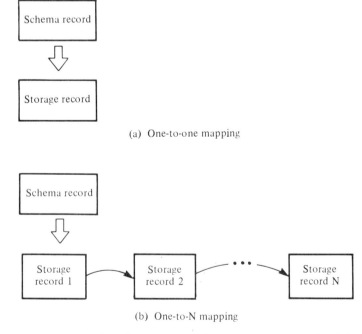

(a) One-to-one mapping

(b) One-to-N mapping

Figure 5.18.   *Mapping of schema record to storage record(s), CODA-SYL DSDL*

more storage record types. The storage records representing a single schema record are linked internally by pointers. Figure 5.18 illustrates these options pictorially. For example, the Employee data base schema in Figure 5.6 could be mapped to a storage schema as follows:

1. One-to-one mapping for CHILD and INSURANCE_CO record types; and

2. One-to-two mapping for EMPLOYEE record type such that the data items EMPLOYEE_NAME, EMPLOYEE_ADDRESS, DE-PARTMENT, and AGE reside in one storage record and SPOUSE_NAME, DOCTOR_NAME, and $OWED_TO_DOCTOR reside in another storage record.

A data item may be stored physically in a different position from which it appears in the schema record, and it may be stored redundantly in different storage records representing the schema record.

Different occurrences of a schema record type can be represented by storage records of different types. The mapping is conditionally controlled by values of data items in the schema record. For example, the EMPLOYEE record type in Figure 5.6 could be mapped as follows using the DSDL:

```
MAPPING FOR EMPLOYEE
    IF $OWED_TO_DOCTOR ≥ 10,000
            THEN STORAGE RECORD IS SINGLE_$OTD
    IF $OWED_TO_DOCTOR ≥ 0 AND < 10,000
            THEN STORAGE RECORDS ARE FIRST_$OTD,
            SECOND_$OTD
    IF $OWED_TO_DOCTOR < 0
            THEN STORAGE RECORD IS NEGATIVE_$OTD
```

The variety of mappings to storage records is available to enhance performance and data distribution. Splitting a schema record into two or more storage records permits storing data items most frequently accessed in a storage record that could be allocated to higher-speed, more reliable, or better protected external storage. The options also permit the physical separation of current data and history data while providing a single record view at the schema level. All mappings are entirely transparent to the application or user, except for differences in performance.

Storage Area Entry

The **Storage Area Entry** defines the physical characteristics of named portions of the storage space in terms of numbers of pages and page sizes. This schema area construct is repositioned from the DDL to the DSDL. For example:

> STORAGE AREA NAME IS AREAX
>
> > INITIAL SIZE IS 500 PAGES TO 100 PAGES
> > EXPANDABLE BY STEPS OF 50 PAGES
> > PAGE SIZE IS 512 WORDS

Storage Record Entry

A **Storage Record Entry** must be included for each storage record type named in the mapping entry previously addressed. The following subentries specify how its occurrences are to be physically placed in the data base:

(a) The storage record subentry names the storage record and defines the nature of the links (DIRECT or INDIRECT pointers) to other storage records for the same schema record.

(b) The placement subentry (one or more) defines in what storage area the record occurrences are to reside, conditionally defines the density of record occurrences stored on pages, and defines how occurrences are to be stored (hashed, sequentially, or clustered). This subentry includes the LOCATION MODE clause appearing in pre-1978 DDL. For example:

> STORAGE RECORD NAME IS EMPLOYEE
> DENSITY IS 40 STORAGE RECORDS PER PAGE
> PLACEMENT IS CALC USING EMPLOYEE_NO
> WITHIN AREAX FROM PAGE 1 THRU 200

(c) The set pointer subentry (zero or more) defines types of pointers (DIRECT or INDIRECT) to be contained in the storage record for implementing a set relationship and defines the type of pointer allocation (preallocation or dynamic).

(d) The data subentry (zero or more) defines format, alignment, and relative placement of a data item in the storage record.

Each of these subentries has a variety of options and gives much control to the DBA. For example, there is a set pointer subentry for each set in which the schema record type represented by the storage record participates as tenant (owner or member). Figure 5.3 shows possible pointers involved. The ALLOCATION options for pointers are:

(a) STATIC, in which the pointer space is allocated when the storage record is created; and

(b) DYNAMIC, in which the pointer space is allocated upon insertion in the set.

Index Entry

The **index entry** specifies characteristics of indexes that may be requested and stored in the storage schema to enhance access time performance. There are three types of indexes:

1. STORAGE KEY index to implement indirect pointers to storage records;
2. RECORD KEY index to implement a search index for a schema record key (note that a schema record may have multiple record keys for retrieval purposes); and
3. SET index to implement a set relationship as explained in subsequent paragraphs and outlined in Figure 5.19. There is one occurrence of the set index for each occurrence of the set.

Set indexes may be placed near the set owner or they may be hashed (using CALC) to a specific page. Indexes for record keys and storage keys may be placed within a specified range of pages of a specified storage area. This epitomizes the high degree of control provided for the DBA to optimize access time performance by allowing the DBA to store data and indexes to that data physically close or contiguously.

We will illustrate and clarify the use of these indexes in a subsequent example of a storage schema.

Set Implementation

A set type may be implemented using either:

1. A chain strategy, in which pointers are physically stored in the member record occurrences, as shown in Figure 5.3; or
2. A set index strategy, in which pointers are physically stored in a set index rather than in the member record occurrences, as shown in Figure 5.19.

There are obvious performance differences between these two set implementations. For example, the set index strategy provides faster retrieval of a member record near the middle of a set occurrence. Maintenance of some kind of order of member record occurrences is facilitated by a set index; only pointers in the set index need to be moved to reorder, whereas in the chain mode there is the need to relink record occurrences. On the other hand, the chain strategy provides faster overall retrieval when it is desired to obtain a list of most or all the members of a set occurrence.

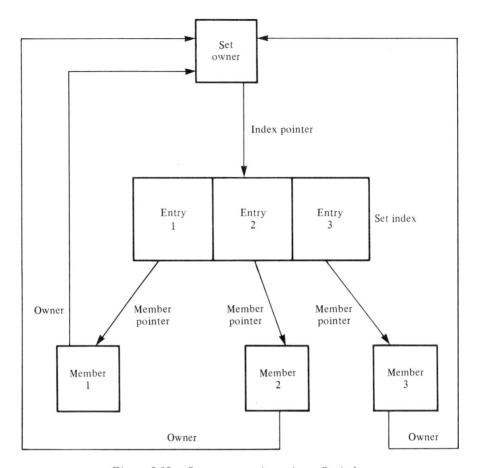

Figure 5.19.   *Set representation using a Set index*

Example: Storage Schema Definition

Consider the data base schema shown in Figure 5.9. Let us call it the DOC_EMPL schema. A storage schema is defined for it via the DSDL in Figure 5.20. Figure 5.21 shows a diagram of what is being defined. Let us examine each of the numbered DSDL statements used in Figure 5.20:

1. The STORAGE SCHEMA entry establishes the name DOCEMP for the storage schema being defined and corresponds to the schema DOC_EMPL. The REPRESENT clause is used to define a subset of the schema to be represented, in this case, DOCTOR and EM-PLOYEE records and the set DOC_PAT.

2. The schema record DOCTOR is mapped 1-to-1 to the storage record DOC. This 1-to-1 mapping would be the default if this clause were not specified, with the default storage record name being the same as the schema record.

3. The schema record EMPLOYEE is mapped conditionally to the two storage records ADULT1 and ADULT2 if the employee is more than 20 years old. It is mapped conditionally in a 1-to-1 correspondence to the storage record YOUNG in any other case.

4. This statement is self-explanatory. The storage area AREAX will be mapped to an operating system file or files in a separate command for the specific operating system.

5. The Storage Record entry specifies the links and set pointers associated with a storage record, the placement of a storage record, and the format of the data items of a storage record. This is probably the most complex entry to define because of the overwhelming variety of physical organization options. The specification is in terms of a storage record's four subentries:

   (a) STORAGE RECORD subentry. The storage record ADULT1 is to contain a link pointer to ADULT2, which is the other storage record of the split. ADULT1 and ADULT2 represent one EMPLOYEE schema record when AGE > 20. The STORAGE KEY IS REQUIRED clause indicates that a storage key index will be used to provide indirect pointers to ADULT1 for accessing (see the set index entry for DE_SET_INDEX).

   (b) PLACEMENT subentry. It specifies that an occurrence of the storage record ADULT1 will, if possible, be placed on the same page (CLUSTERED) as another occurrence of ADULT1 of the same DOC_EMP set occurrence. All pages are to be within AREAX.

   (c) SET subentry. The set for which the storage record ADULT1 is to have pointers is DOC_PAT. The pointer allocation is static rather than dynamic (at execution time). Two pointers are indicated: a pointer to the set index DE_SET_INDEX (see its Index entry) and a next pointer, which points to the next member of the set unless there is no next member (i.e., this is the last member of the set), in which case it points to the owner. The pointer clause is therefore specified twice, once for the case when the target record is a member (the schema record EMPLOYEE) and once for the case when it is an owner (the schema record DOCTOR). If the next pointer target is an occurrence of the schema record EMPLOYEE, the pointer is direct to the

STORAGE SCHEMA DEFINITION EXAMPLE

1. STORAGE SCHEMA NAME IS DOCEMP FOR DOC_EMPL
      SCHEMA
      REPRESENT ONLY DOCTOR, EMPLOYEE RECORDS AND
      ONLY DOC_PAT SETS
2. MAPPING FOR DOCTOR
      STORAGE RECORD IS DOC.
3. MAPPING FOR EMPLOYEE
      IF AGE > 20 THEN STORAGE RECORDS ARE ADULT1,
         ADULT2
      ELSE STORAGE RECORD IS YOUNG.
4. STORAGE AREA NAME IS AREAX
      INITIAL SIZE IS 500 PAGES
      EXPANDABLE BY STEPS OF 50 PAGES TO 1000 PAGES
      PAGE SIZE IS 512 WORDS.
5. STORAGE RECORD NAME IS ADULT1
         LINK TO ADULT2 IS DIRECT
         STORAGE KEY IS REQUIRED
      PLACEMENT IS CLUSTERED VIA SET DOC_EMP WITHIN
      AREAX
      SET DOC_PAT
         ALLOCATION IS STATIC
         POINTER FOR INDEX DE_SET_INDEX
         POINTER FOR NEXT RECORD EMPLOYEE IS
               INDIRECT TO ADULT1
               IS DIRECT TO YOUNG
         POINTER FOR NEXT RECORD DOCTOR IS DIRECT
            TO DOC
         02 EMPLOYEE_NO
         02 EMPLOYEE_NAME
         02 EMPLOYEE_ADDRESS
         02 $OWED_TO_DOCTOR
6. STORAGE RECORD NAME IS ADULT2
      PLACEMENT IS CLUSTERED VIA SET DOC_PAT WITH
      ADULT1 WITHIN AREAX
      02 AGE
      02 SPOUSE_NAME
      02 DOCTOR_NAME
7. STORAGE RECORD NAME IS YOUNG
         PLACEMENT IS SEQUENTIAL ASCENDING AGE WITHIN
            AREAX
         SET DOC_PAT
            POINTER FOR INDEX DE_SET_INDEX
            POINTER FOR NEXT RECORD EMPLOYEE IS

INDIRECT TO ADULT1
IS DIRECT TO YOUNG
POINTER FOR NEXT RECORD DOCTOR IS DIRECT
TO DOC
8. STORAGE RECORD NAME IS DOC
PLACEMENT IS CALC HASH-PROC-1 USING EMPLOYEE_
NO IN EMPLOYEE WITHIN AREAX
SET DOC_PAT
POINTER FOR INDEX DE_SET_INDEX
02 DATA ALL
9. INDEX NAME IS DE_SET_INDEX
POINTER FOR EMPLOYEE IS DIRECT TO YOUNG
IS INDIRECT TO ADULT1
USED FOR SET DOC_PAT
WITHIN AREAX
10. INDEX NAME IS ADULT1_INDEX
USED FOR STORAGE KEY ADULT1
WITHIN AREAX

Figure 5.20. *CODASYL DSDL definition of the storage schema DOCEMP for the schema in Figure 5.9*

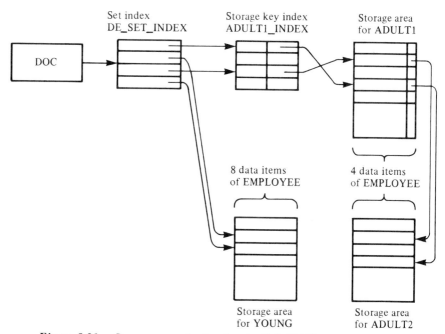

Figure 5.21. *Storage organization for the DOCEMP storage schema defined in Figure 5.20 in the CODASYL DSDL for the schema in Figure 5.9*

storage record YOUNG if the AGE was less than or equal to 20 and indirect to ADULT1 if the AGE was greater than 20. If the next pointer target is the owner, the pointer is to the storage record DOC, since the schema record DOCTOR is only mapped to one storage record, DOC.

(d) Data subentry. It specifies that only the four named data items of the schema record EMPLOYEE are placed in the storage record ADULT1. The other four data items of EMPLOYEE are indicated to be stored in the storage record ADULT2 (see its storage record entry). Since no data formats are indicated here, the formats are then as defined in the schema record.

6. The storage record ADULT2 has no storage key required, for no storage record or index points indirectly to it; and it has no reserved pointers, for it has no set pointers associated with it (notice the absence of the set subentry for ADULT2). It is placed clustered via its set DOC_PAT and is also placed near ADULT1 wherever possible. Like ADULT1, it is stored in the area AREAX. The data subentry specifies that only the four named data items of the schema record EMPLOYEE are placed in ADULT2. Their formats are as defined in the schema record.

7. The storage record YOUNG has no links, since EMPLOYEE was not split in the branch of the conditional mapping corresponding to YOUNG. It is pointed to only directly and so does not need a storage key. It is placed sequentially in ascending order of the data item value of AGE within the storage area AREAX. The set subentry is identical to that of ADULT1, because YOUNG and ADULT1 are both storage records of the conditional mapping of the schema record EMPLOYEE.

8. The storage record DOC occurrences are placed in pages within area AREAX. The CALC clause specifies that each DOC occurrence is stored in the page determined by the hashing algorithm specified by HASH_PROC_1, which uses EMPLOYEE_NO as the hash key. The set subentry defines that this storage record DOC is to contain a pointer to the set index DE_SET_INDEX used to implement the DOC_EMP set, relating each owner (DOCTOR) record occurrence with member (EMPLOYEE) record occurrences. See Figures 5.19 and 5.21. The pointer to the set index is always direct. The data subentry DATA ALL indicates that the data items and formats defined in the schema record DOCTOR are stored in DOC.

9. The first of the two indexes defined is DE_SET_INDEX. Its fine placement (as opposed to its gross placement within a storage area) is not specified, so the placement is implementor defined. The pointer

for the schema record EMPLOYEE is indirect to ADULT1 and direct to YOUNG. The pointer clause must include both types of storage records because EMPLOYEE was conditionally mapped into YOUNG and ADULT1 (and ADULT2, but since ADULT2 is linked to ADULT1, we need not worry about it). The used clause indicates that this is a Set index used to implement the set DOC_PAT. This index is placed within the storage area AREAX.

10. The second index defined is ADULT1_INDEX. Note that this name is not referred to anywhere, unlike DE_SET_INDEX, which was referred to in the Index clause of the Set subentry of the storage entries of ADULT1 and YOUNG. The association between a storage key index and its storage key is implicitly handled by the DBMS. As before, the fine placement is not specified. The used clause indicates that this is a storage key index for ADULT1. See Figure 5.21. The pointer clause is not specified because the pointers are only allowed to be direct. This index is then used by any storage or index record pointing indirectly to ADULT1. The index is also placed within the storage area AREAX.

5.9   DATA REPRESENTATION DEPENDENCY OF DML

Readers undoubtedly have had to spend much time keeping track of where they were as they navigated the data bases used in the previous examples. Proper navigation through the paths in a DBTG network data base via the ample options of the DML requires care and concentration. In fact, if readers do not look at the DML facilities for awhile, getting back to the previous examples will frequently demand frustrating overhead time to understand and follow them again. In a large data base with many record types, navigation through it involving commands other than the simpler FIND options may be quite intricate and tedious.

The procedurality and the representation-dependency of DML are very high. As a result, although a DBTG system does achieve much of the independence desired between application programs and the way that data is structured and stored, many examples can be shown in which data independence is violated. This is particularly obvious when the set relationships between record type A and record type B are changed from owner-A-member-B to owner-B-member-A. The correctness of many DML procedures depends highly on the path directionality and schema structure chosen. For example, the DML commands that permit users to easily find a list of all INSURANCE_CO records for EMPLOYEE 106 with the schema in Figure 5.6 do not provide

the same answer if the schema structure is modified so that INSURANCE‿
CO is the owner of the set in which EMPLOYEE is the member record type.
Another example is changing a 1:N relationship to M:N.

These same general critical remarks can be made with respect to TOTAL
and IMS, as readers will realize after examining the nature of their data
manipulation language. The same remarks apply to any representation-
dependent type of language in the framework of the DIAM model.

Query languages have emerged for DBTG systems. They are less representation-dependent and avoid a great deal of the procedurality and record-
at-a time attitude of the DML. Unfortunately, CODASYL did not specify a
query language and thus query languages of DBTG GDBMS are not identical.

5.10   SUMMARY

The DBTG architecture is the milestone architecture designed by
CODASYL and followed by an increasing number of commercial GDBMS. It
introduced the terms and concepts of schema, subschema, and data manipulation; the separation of data definition and data manipulation; and the separation between logical and physical organization. These concepts of course
permeate earlier GDBMS such as IMS and IDS. DBTG data bases may be
either hierarchic or network. A network data base is one in which a record type
may be related to more than one parent record type. Network data bases occur
often in practice. In DBTG a record type may be related to any number of
record types via sets. A relationship is established between an owner record
and a member record type via the set type. Various set types may be defined as
summarized in Figure 5.4; they can be used to form any kind of data base.
Various important types of controls need to be established by the DBA, such as
the set membership class of a record type, the particular field to be used as the
key field, and so forth. Sections 5.1–5.3 present the fundamentals of DBTG,
network schemas, and schema data definition facilities.

Any logical and consistent subset of the schema may be defined to be a
subschema via the subschema data definition language. A subschema may
include any subset of the fields of record types, any record type, and any set
type.

The DBTG data manipulation language, DML, is a procedural access
path-oriented language for navigating through the data base. The currency
status indicators are crucial for keeping track of where users are in the data base
by identifying the most recently accessed record occurrence for each record,
set, and area; knowing where they are, users can then go to the next or prior
record occurrence in the chain implementing the set occurrence. Direct access
via a hashing algorithm on a key field may be defined for any record type. A
different hashing algorithm may be provided by the DBA for each record type.

The DML includes a large number of commands and options for entering the data base through any record and for navigating through any set paths in the data base. Section 5.6 presents the main DML facilities.

Although a DBTG system does achieve much of the independence desired between application programs and the way that data is structured and stored, various examples can be shown in which data independence is violated. The same is true of other commercial GDBMS. In general, different GDBMS achieve in varying degrees the main objectives of data base technology: data independence, relatability, security, and so forth.

The physical data base organization realm was not specified in the 1971–1973 DBTG reports and thus left up to each implementation. The nature of the schema, subschema, and DML is such that various similarities in physical data base organization strategies and trade-offs are expected in the various implementations; e.g., the use of chain or doubly-chained structures or hashing. However, various significant differences in physical data base organization may exist between various DBTG implementations, since the 1971 report did not specify the physical organization realm. The 1978 CODASYL proposal specified a powerful and encompassing Data Storage Description Language (DSDL) with many options in physical organization and access paths. The extent to which vendors will implement the 1978 DSDL and the few DDL and DML changes proposed, presented in Sections 5.7 and 5.8, remains to be seen.

REFERENCES

1. "CODASYL Data Base Task Group Report, 1971," CODASYL, Association for Computing Machinery, New York, April 1971.

2. CODASYL Data Description Language Committee, Proposed Revision of the 1971 DBTG Report, February 1973.

3. CODASYL Data Base Language Task Group, Proposed Revisions of the 1971 DBTG Report, June 1973.

4. "IDS Reference Manual," General Electric Information Systems Division, CPB (565A), Phoenix, Ariz., September 1969.

5. "Data Management System (DMS1100), American National Standard COBOL Data Manipulation Language," Programmer Reference UP-7908 Sperry Univac Computer Systems, St. Paul, Minn.

6. "IDMS, Concepts and Facilities," Cullinane Corporation, Wellesley, Mass.

7. "DECsystem-10, Data Base Management System DBMS/10, Version II," Programmer and Administrator Guides, Digital Equipment Corporation, Maynard, Mass.

8. "PHOLAS, Phillips Host Language System," Phillips Data Systems, Apeldoorn, The Netherlands.

9. "SEED Reference Manual," United Telecom Group Inc., Philadelphia, Pa.

10. "CODASYL Data Description Language," *Journal of Development*, January 1978 (Secretariat of the Canadian Government EDP Standards Committee, 1978).

11. "CODASYL COBOL Data Base Facility," CODASYL COBOL Committee, *Journal of Development*, 1978.

12. Loomis, M. E., "The 78 CODASYL Database Model: A Comparison with Preceding Specifications," *Proceedings, SIGMOD Conference*, 1980, Santa Monica, Calif., pp. 30–44.

13. "Fortran Data Base Facility," CODASYL FORTRAN Committee, 1980.

EXERCISES

1. Answer the following TRUE-FALSE questions regarding the DBTG data model:

   _____ a. A set type is a named relationship between record types.

   _____ b. A schema consists of only one set type.

   _____ c. For each record type the schema specifies the area or areas into which the occurrences of that record are to be placed when they are entered into the data base.

   _____ d. A set type within a schema may be unordered.

   _____ e. Any record type may be declared in the schema as a member of one or more set types.

   _____ f. The capability for a record type to participate as both owner and member in the same set type is not supported by the data description language.

   _____ g. A singular set consists of an owner record and at least one member record.

   _____ h. An M:N relationship can be represented with only one set type.

   _____ i. A set may have an arbitrary number of occurrences of the member record types declared for it in the schema.

   _____ j. Any record type may be declared in the schema as the owner of one or more set types.

2. Give an example of a real-life data base that can be described in DBTG terms as follows (indicate the possible logical structure of each record type and the semantics of each set):

3. (a) Consider the Doctor-Employee-Child-Insurance DBTG data base in Figure 5.9. Indicate the DML commands to answer each of the following requests:

1. How many employees are there with children under X years old?

2. For each insurance company in the data base, obtain a list of the names of the clinics with associated doctors who service employees insured by the same insurance company.

(b) If you were the data base administrator, had the freedom to establish and delete relationships, and knew that the two preceding data base requests were among the most frequently made, what new relationship(s), if any, would you establish? Define such new relationship(s) using the DBTG schema DDL.

4. Refer to the Employee-Child-Insurance schema in Figure 5.6 and Example 1. Since an M:N relationship cannot be represented directly by a single DBTG set, and normally an insurance company insures many employees and a few employees may have more than one insurance company, the schema in Figure 5.6 (included also in the schema in Figure 5.9) may not be very realistic.

(a) Convert the schema to reflect the fact that an insurance company may insure one or many employees, but an employee may not be insured by more than one insurance company.

(b) Convert the schema to reflect the fact that an insurance company may insure one or many employees and that an employee may be insured by more than one insurance company, i.e., there is a M:N relationship.

(c) Modify the DBTG data description of the schema in Figure 5.6 to account for each of the previous (a) and (b) cases.

(d) If we absolutely did not want to modify the original schema of Figure 5.6 and absolutely wanted to store cases of type b even at the price of record storage redundancy and possible consistency problems, can we do it? If yes, describe how you would do it and indicate any storage redundancy and consistency problems that may arise.

5. Consider the data base sketched below with the indicated M:N and 1:N relationships:

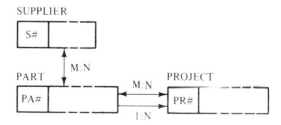

(a) Describe in detail, in English, an example of a real-life situation represented by such a data base sketch.

(b) Can a DBTG GDBMS handle this data base? If yes, first describe what transformation has to be done, then define the schema using the DBTG DDL, and then draw the DBTG links involved for a data base containing two to five instances of each of the three record types indicated.

6. Consider the data base in Exercise 5 and your answers to 5(a) and 5(b). Now describe in detail the membership class that you would use for each member of each set: OPTIONAL, MANDATORY, or FIXED (once a member occurrence is stored in a set occurrence, it can exist only in that set occurrence or else be deleted entirely from the data base).

7. Discuss the possible problems that may arise when updating a schema record that is conditionally mapped to different DSDL storage record types depending on some value(s) of data item(s) in the schema record.

8. Discuss the pros and cons of DYNAMIC and STATIC allocation of pointers in a storage record to implement a set. Consider chain pointers and set index pointers (see Figures 5.3 and 5.19).

9. Define a storage schema (using the DSDL options introduced in this chapter) for the Professor_Student data base in Figure 5.11. Explain the reasons for the mappings and strategies selected. The DSDL options in this chapter are a subset of the full DSDL options.

6
TOTAL

6.1 INTRODUCTION AND ARCHITECTURE

TOTAL is a GDBMS marketed by Cincom Systems, Inc. since 1968.[1,2,3] It is one of the two GDBMS enjoying the largest number of installations (close to two thousand as of the early 1980s), the other one being IBM's IMS, presented in the next chapter. Thus, TOTAL deserves a chapter in this book. However, it is a variation of the CODASYL DBTG architecture presented in the previous chapter, and therefore only an abridged presentation of it is included in this book.

TOTAL is currently available in a wider variety of hardware configurations than any other commercial GDBMS. The entry on TOTAL in Figure 4.1 summarizes its commercial availability: IBM System 3, 360/370, 30XX, and 4XXX; Honeywell 200, 2000; Univac Series 70, 9400, 9700; NCR Century; CDC Series 6000; DEC PDP-11; and Burroughs 1700, 3500. It was one of the few GDBMS available for small computer systems in the 1970s and was the pioneer of GDBMS for small computers. This wide available is undoubtedly a major reason for the success of TOTAL. There are small differences between the TOTAL versions for the various computers, but they will not concern us.

The basic TOTAL can be complemented by two major companion products: the report writer SOCRATES to facilitate the generation of reports from TOTAL data bases and the on-line teleprocessing or data communications system ENVIRON/1 highly integrated with TOTAL for accessing data bases via more demanding on-line multiterminal environments. Other smaller (and less costly) modules may complement TOTAL, namely, a data dictionary and a number of utilities specific to TOTAL data bases. Facilities of TOTAL's data dictionary are exemplified in Chapter 14.

TOTAL deals with network data base structures, much like DBTG. It is in reality a trimmed down variation of the DBTG specifications. Although TOTAL is not advertised by Cincom as a DBTG-like implementation, it could be envisioned as 60 to 80 percent DBTG conceptually, although syntactically it is very different (it has some of the flavor of IMS). A number of features in TOTAL have been highly optimized to provide the high performance in processing time and storage utilization reported by various TOTAL users. TOTAL carries its own terminology and set of conventions, as we shall see.

A TOTAL data base may be composed of the constituents indicated in Figure 6.1:

1. Data item or field, which is the smallest identifiable and accessible unit of data.
2. Data element, which is either a single data field or a group of commonly used data fields. This is the mode of communication with data under TOTAL.

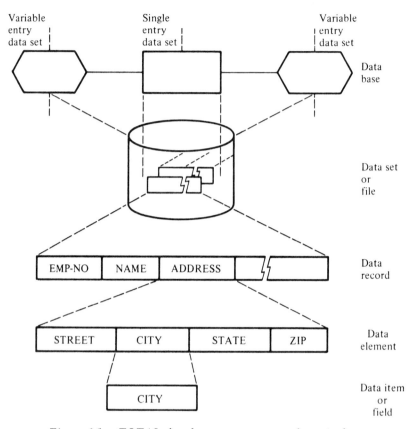

Figure 6.1.   *TOTAL data base components and terminology*

3. Data record, which is a collection of data elements and data fields. It is identifiable by a **record control key** or a **relative record number**.

4. **Data set**, which is a synonym of data file. It is a collection of data records. We will see that TOTAL deals with two types of data sets: **master data sets** and **variable entry data sets**, whereas DBTG sees the need for only one type.

5. Data base, which is a collection of data sets related by relationships called **linkage paths** (TOTAL's own terminology). An unlimited number of data bases may be defined, and any data set may be included in any number of different data bases. Thus the concept of schema and subschema is provided by TOTAL.

TOTAL embodies a *Data Base Definition Language*, DBDL, through which schemas and subschemas are defined. The terms schema and subschema are not utilized widely in the TOTAL jargon, but we will use them herein. The

DBDL is syntactically very different from DBTG's and from that of all other GBDMS, although in a few areas it has some of the flavor of IMS. In the following section we will provide a brief example of a TOTAL data base definition.

TOTAL's data manipulation language, DML, is syntactically significantly different from DBTG's. Furthermore, TOTAL DML does not include the many options and formats of the DBTG I/O commands, particularly the find command (Figure 5.16). Thus the overhead supporting the richness in options, especially those somewhat redundant, is avoided. TOTAL has placed a great deal of emphasis on achieving superior performance and efficiency, and thus trims down where possible without major sacrifices in capability. However, conceptually the TOTAL DML has close counterparts in DBTG; it is hashing-oriented and also oriented to navigate through logical linkage paths of the data base network.

TOTAL data bases may be accessed via the DML from COBOL, PL/1, FORTRAN IV, RPG II, and assembly language. It is one of the few GDBMS with an interface to RPG II, which is used mostly in smaller computers. As we shall see, the DML is in reality a series of CALL statements including a parameter list. Thus, it has some of the flavor of the IMS DML. We will provide examples of TOTAL DML commands.

6.2   THE SCHEMA AND SUBSCHEMAS

A TOTAL data set or file may be of either of two types:

1. **Single entry**, also called master, or
2. **Variable entry**, also called detail/transaction.

The availability of the two types undoubtedly stems in part from the practice of master file and detail file(s) in traditional data management. A brief discussion of these two types follows.

Single Entry Data Sets

Single entry data sets are intended to be relatively stable as to record content and number of record occurrences. Hence the synonymous term master data set that we shall use also. A single entry data set is used to store data efficiently for direct (random) access by an application program and to serve as an entry to related information contained in variable entry data sets. Each record in the single entry data set is uniquely identified by a **control key**. A data element in the record serves as the control key such that there is only one single entry record per unique control key and one unique control key per single entry record. No duplicate records for a key are permitted. The control key is used by TOTAL DML commands to locate a record directly, via a proprietary hashing algorithm internal to TOTAL. Entry to the data set is through its control key. Each single entry data set can be the parent of many variable entry data sets. This relationship is accomplished by establishing a linkage path to each variable entry data set. Each record within the single entry data set may be related to up to 2,500 variable entry data sets.

Variable Entry Data Sets

Variable entry data sets are data sets which may be accessed via a variable number of control fields. In contrast to master data sets, they contain a variable and highly volatile number of record occurrences. They contain descriptive supportive information of single entry data sets. Variable entry records are not randomly stored based on a control field, but rather in a chained manner. A control field defined for a variable entry data set establishes a relationship or linkage path to the single entry data set having that control field, and it directs TOTAL to relate all the variable entry records for the data set to form a chain. Each record is thus the member of the logical linkage path that is "owned" by the master record occurrence with a specific control field value. The variable entry nature of a variable entry data set is as follows:

1. A variable number of control fields may be defined for each record, whereas only one control field may be defined for each single entry record. Thus each record may be a member of a variable number of linkage paths or logical relationships to single entry records.
2. Each unique control field may have an arbitrary number of variable records; each record is linked to the previous and to the next record in the chain.
3. Each record is accessible via DML commands specifying the control key of the logically related single entry data set.
4. The variable entry data set may have up to 2,500 differently formatted record types. Each of these may have any number of control fields; in other words, each may have any number of unique relationships to single entry data sets. Although the records may have different formats and amounts of significant information, they are still of fixed length (blocked or unblocked).

Linkage Path: Data Set Relationship

A relationship called a **linkage path** may be established only between a single entry data set and a variable entry data set. A unique name is given to each linkage path when the data base is defined. Linkage paths are not established directly between data sets of the same type. The linkage path from

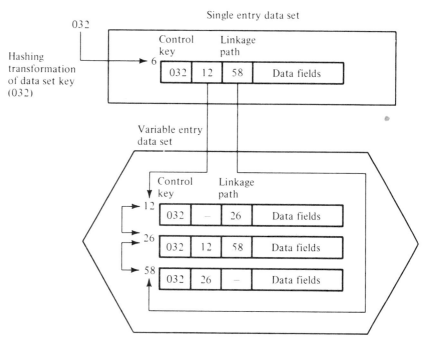

Figure 6.2. *A TOTAL linkage path: a relationship between a single entry (master) data set and a variable entry (detail/transaction) set*

a single entry to a variable entry data set is established by explicitly defining as part of the variable record the corresponding control key and two four-byte pointer fields. In each single entry record occurrence the first pointer points to the first record in its corresponding variable entry chain and the second pointer to the last record in this chain. In each variable entry record occurrence the first pointer points to the previous record in the chain and the second pointer to the next record in the chain. The concept of "next" is one of the bases for accessing the data base via the DML. Figure 6.2 illustrates a linkage path between two data set types. A square is used to denote a single entry and a hexagon to denote a variable entry in TOTAL data base diagrams.

The linkage path is the same as the DBTG set implementation of a relationship, Figure 5.3, except that TOTAL does not employ pointers from a record in the middle of the chain to the owner single entry occurrence. Unfortunately, the terminology is different.

Data Base Structure

Multilevel trees and network data base structures are built from data sets and linkage paths. The types of interconnections that may be established in the

TOTAL data base model are shown in Figure 5.4(a), (c), (d), and (e). Figure 5.4 outlines the DBTG possibilities and thus the similarity to TOTAL is obvious when one realizes the equivalence of the following terms:

DBTG		*TOTAL*
owner record type	→	single entry or master data set
member record type	→	variable entry data set
set	→	linkage path

We shall not discuss the meaning of the (a), (c), and (d) relationships in this chapter since they have already been discussed in Section 5.2, although in

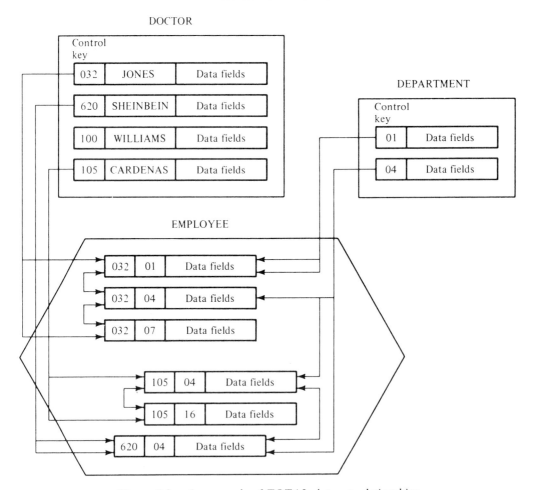

Figure 6.3. *An example of TOTAL data set relationships*

DBTG terminology. The three-level structure in (e) requires attention. In TOTAL a data set cannot be both single entry and variable entry at the same time. Therefore, a single entry data set connected to two variable entry data sets, or conversely, two single entry data sets connected to one variable entry data set are close equivalents to the DBTG structure in Figure 5.4(e).

As in DBTG, more than one linkage path may be established between two data sets, one for each desired relationship.

Figure 6.3 shows an example of TOTAL data set relationships. A variable entry data set (EMPLOYEE) may be related to an arbitrary number of single entry data sets (two in this example). This is a small example of a network data base since the "child" EMPLOYEE is owned by the two different record types DOCTOR and DEPARTMENT.

A TOTAL data base may be made up of several integrated data bases. Each of these integrated data bases may be viewed as the subschema for a particular application program or user. Figure 6.4 illustrates a TOTAL data base structure. All linkage paths are bidirectional. The data sets within the dotted (...) lines comprise one data base B1; those within the dashed ($- - -$) lines comprise another data base B2; and those within the asterisked (***) lines comprise a third data base B3. In general, any single entry or variable entry data set may appear in one or any number of data bases.

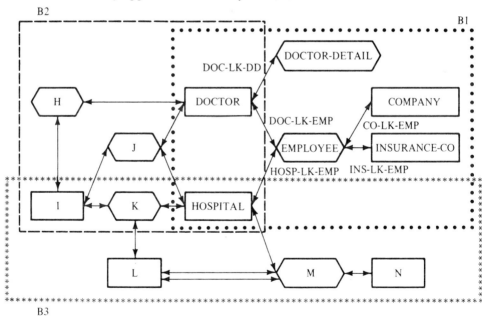

Note: B1, B2, and B3 are subsets (subschemas) of the integrated data base.

Figure 6.4. *A TOTAL network data base*

Figure 6.4 can be also interpreted to portray the evolutionary growth of a data base from an initial configuration B1 to B2 to finally B3. This growth is such that the impact on operational programs is little if any, i.e., data independence is achieved. Note that if a linkage path is broken and replaced by another single entry-variable entry-linkage path unit, then programs using the original linkage path deleted will be obviously affected and will have to be modified. However, data independence is maintained if the original linkage is also kept along with the new unit inserted. In this example the evolution from the structure B1 to B2 could have taken place by adding data sets H, I, J, and K and their linkages without affecting programs with schema or subschema B1. Similarly, evolution to structure B3 could be by the addition of data sets L, M, and N, and their linkages without affecting programs using B1 or B2.

Sample Data Base Definition

TOTAL has a special data base definition language DBDL for use by the DBA to define the data base and/or subdata bases within the overall data base. This is done in terms of names and types of data sets, data records, and data elements and in terms of the data set and data record relationships. TOTAL's DBDL is syntactically quite different from the DBDL of other commercial GDBMS. As we shall see, it has some of the flavor of the IMS DBDL illustrated in Chapter 7, namely, macroassembly language-oriented.

Let us illustrate the TOTAL data base definition. Consider the schema B1 in Figure 6.4 made up of four single entry data sets, two variable entry data sets, and the indicated linkages; no linkages to the outside of the B1 are to be considered. Figure 6.5 shows the data base definition for the master data set HOSPITAL and the variable data set EMPLOYEE. A brief explanation is included at the right-hand side of each statement that is not self-explanatory; this explanation is not part of the actual statement. The numbers preceding each statement are not part of TOTAL's syntax, but rather for explanation purposes below.

(a) Partial TOTAL data base definition:

1. BEGIN-DATA-BASE-GENERATION:
2. DATA-BASE-NAME = XXXXX
3. OPTIONS: LOG = N, OUTPUT = DISK
4. IOAREA = USERAREA $\Big\}$ Two I/O areas requested
5. IOAREA = USERAREA2
6. END-IO:
7. BEGIN-MASTER-DATA-SET:

8.	DATA-SET-NAME = HOSPITAL	
9.	IOAREA = USERAREA	
10.	MASTER-DATA:	
11.	HOSPROOT = 8	Eight-byte root required by TOTAL.
12.	HOSPCODE = 6	Hospital logical control key: unique hospital number
13.	HOSP-LK-EMP = 8	Link to EMPLOYEE variable entry records
14.	HOSPDATA = 88	Data fields follow:
15.	.1.HOSPNAME = 28	Hospital name
16.	.1.HOSPADDR = 28	Hospital address
17.	.1.HOSPCITY = 20	Hospital city
18.	.1.NUMBBEDS = 4	Hospital number of beds
19.	.1.NUMBROOM = 4	Hospital number of rooms
20.	.1.QUALRATE = 4	Hospital quality rating
21.	END-DATA	
22.	LOGICAL-RECORD-LENGTH = 110	
23.	LOGICAL-RECORDS-PER-BLOCK = 9	
24.	TOTAL-LOGICAL-RECORDS = 10800	200 tracks of storage on IBM5444 disk
25.	CONTROL-INTERVAL = 1080	
26.	END-MASTER-DATA-SET:	
27.	BEGIN-VARIABLE-ENTRY-DATA-SET:	
28.	DATA-SET-NAME = EMPLOYEE	
29.	IOAREA = USERAREA2	
30.	BASE-DATA:	
31.	HOSPCODE = 6	Control key to HOSPITAL chain
32.	HOSP-LK-EMP = 8	Link to HOSPITAL chain
33.	DOCCODE = 6	Control key to DOCTOR chain
34.	DOC-LK-EMP = 8	Link to DOCTOR chain
35.	INSURCODE = 6	Control key to INSURANCE-CO chain
36.	INS-LK-EMP = 8	Link to INSURANCE-CO chain
37.	COCODE = 6	Control key to COMPANY chain
38.	CO-LK-EMP = 8	Link to COMPANY chain

39. EMPDATA = 81   EMPLOYEE data fields follow:
40. .1.EMPNAME = 20   Employee name
41. .1.EMPADDR = 25   Employee address
42. .1.EMPCITY = 20   Employee city
43. .1.EMPDEPT = 8   Employee department
44. .1.EMPAGE = 4   Employee age
45. .1.EMPOWEDOC = 4 PACKED AMOUNT   Amount of money owed to
                                                doctor

46. END-DATA:
47. LOGICAL-RECORD-LENGTH = 137
48. LOGICAL-RECORDS-PER-BLOCK = 20
49. TOTAL-LOGICAL-RECORDS = 100000
50. END-VARIABLE-ENTRY-DATA-SET:

Definition of the DOCTOR-DETAIL
variable entry data set

Definition of the other master data sets
DOCTOR. DATE. INSURANCE-CO

(b) Partial TOTAL data base schema defined above:

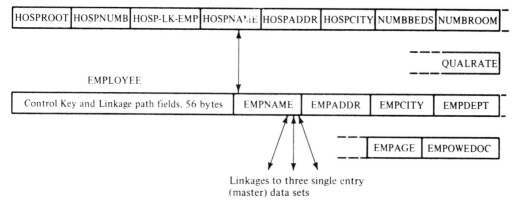

Figure 6.5. *Partial TOTAL data base definition of the schema B1 in Figure 6.4 (excludes linkages outside of B1)*

254

The purpose of the "root" field HOSPROOT in statement 11 is for hashing-collision storage management, to link all master records hashing to the same storage location. The DBA must explicitly define also the 8-byte linkage fields, e.g., statement 13. In most other GDBMS the DBA is not forced to explicitly define control fields.

Note the definition of the name of each field within a record along with a count of the number of bytes, e.g., statements 15 through 20. Statement 22 indicates the total number of bytes for the record HOSPITAL, including control fields and data fields.

For variable entry data sets the control field and the 8-byte linkage field for *each* linkage must be explicitly defined, e.g., statements 31 through 38.

6.3   DATA MANIPULATION

The TOTAL data manipulation language DML is the means for accessing and manipulating a TOTAL data base. As in DBTG and other GDBMS, the TOTAL DML functions in conjunction with a host programming language to form the application program. The DML may be invoked from COBOL, PL/1, FORTRAN IV, RPG II, or assembly language. As mentioned earlier, the TOTAL DML does not provide as many options and different command formats as DBTG DML; in this sense, it has some of the IMS flavor. Thus the overhead supporting the richness in options, particularly those highly redundant, is avoided.

TOTAL's DML commands use the EXIT or CALL facility of the host programming language. The EXIT or CALL command must include a parameter list which indicates exactly what is to be done. Communication between the application program and TOTAL is through the work area indicated as one of the parameters. Eleven parameters are available, some of which are used in every DML command, some of which depend on the particular type of data set being accessed (that is, master or variable), and a few that are used only in a number of specialized functions.

Figure 6.6 indicates the form of the CALL command and its parameters as it would appear in, for example, a COBOL program. Figure 6.6(a) using seven parameters applies to master data sets. Figure 6.6(b) using nine parameters applies to variable entry data sets; it includes the two parameters REFERENCE and LINKAGE-PATH not appearing in the CALL command for single entry data sets. The meaning of the nine DML parameters is summarized in Figure 6.7.

TOTAL provides an encompassing variety of DML commands to satisfy the needs of data base processing. Each of these commands is denoted by a brief code which is inserted by the user via the FUNCTION parameter in the DML CALL statement. Four commands are available for single entry data sets

(a) To access master data sets (seven parameters required): CALL 'DATBAS' USING FUNCTION, STATUS, DATA-SET, CONTROL-KEY, ELEMENT-LIST. USER-AREA. ENDP.

(b) To access variable entry data sets (nine parameters required): CALL ∙ 'DATBAS' USING FUNCTION, STATUS, DATA-SET, REFERENCE, LINKAGE-PATH, CONTROL-KEY, ELEMENT-LIST, USER-AREA, ENDP.

Note: The parameter names shown are replaced by numeric or nonnumeric values by the user (typically via standard COBOL MOVE statements preceding the CALL statement).

Figure 6.6. *TOTAL DML command formats for COBOL*

'DATBAS'	A TOTAL program that acts as the interface between the user program and TOTAL.
FUNCTION or OPERATION	Indicates the operation to be performed on the TOTAL data base, e.g., read a record in a master data set, read "next" record in a variable entry data set.
STATUS	Indicates the success or failure of the operation when the command is executed. TOTAL returns "****" as the value of STATUS if the command executed correctly. Other coded values are returned for various abnormal terminations of the command.
DATA-SET	Names the data set on which the operation is to be performed. Four characters maximum allowed.
REFERENCE	Indicates the Internal Reference Point (a number), which is the relative physical position of a record occurrence with respect to the beginning of the named variable entry data set; it may also refer by its LKXX code to the logical beginning or end of a chain of the variable entry data set XX; not applicable to master data sets.
LINKAGE-PATH	Names the linkage path to be processed; not applicable to master data sets. Eight characters maximum allowed.
CONTROL-KEY	Indicates the control key of the particular record in the named data set to be processed.
ELEMENT-LIST	Indicates the list of the names of the fields or data elements to be processed.
USER-AREA	Names the user work area where the values of the fields indicated in the ELEMENT-LIST are to be placed.
ENDP	Indicates the end of the command parameter list.

Figure 6.7. *Meaning of the TOTAL DML command parameters*

256

READM   Read Master. TOTAL randomizes the contents of the specific Control-Key field to locate the specific record. The fields specified in the Element List are then placed in the User Area.

WRITM   Write Master. TOTAL randomizes the contents of the specific Control-Key for retrieving the record to be updated. The data elements in the User Area are moved to the record which is then rewritten.

ADD-M   Add Master. TOTAL randomizes the contents of the specific Control Key to locate space, take the data elements specified in the Element List and residing in the User Area, and write the new record in the data set.

DEL-M   Delete Master. TOTAL randomizes the contents of the Control Key to locate the specific record. The record is deleted by filling it with blanks and the space freed is immediately released for reuse.

Figure 6.8.   *TOTAL DML command operations for single entry (master) data sets*

and nine for variable entry data sets. Figure 6.8 summarizes the single entry commands.

Records in a single entry or master data set are accessed on a direct basis via a proprietary and efficient hashing algorithm applied to the control key defined for the data set by the DBA. Records in variable entry sets may be accessed by specifying the particular master control key and its associated linkage path. The particular record desired is located by specifying a relative physical position with respect to the beginning of the variable entry data set (via the so-called Reference Point value), or a "next" or "previous" position as in DBTG. TOTAL actually uses the control key to access a master record and then follows its chain to the desired variable record.

Any of the parameters in the CALL statement may be a variable to which a literal value or storage location name is assigned before executing the CALL.

We will provide a few COBOL examples using DML commands for accessing single entry data sets and variable entry data sets. We will use the schema B1 in Figure 6.4 and its description in Figure 6.5. Some of these examples are asterisked on the right to mean that they are also illustrated for the DBTG model in the previous chapter.

Retrieve

1. Retrieve the name (HOSPNAME) and complete address (HOSP-ADDR followed by HOSPCITY) of the HOSPITAL master record whose identification is UCLA.

```
MOVE SPACES TO STATUS.
MOVE 'UCLA' TO CONTROL-KEY.
MOVE 'HOSPNAMEHOSPADDRHOSPCITY' TO
ELEMENT-LIST.
MOVE SPACES TO USER-AREA.
CALL 'DATBAS' USING 'READM', STATUS, 'HOSPITAL',
CONTROL-KEY, ELEMENT-LIST, USER-AREA, 'ENDP'.
IF STATUS ≠ '****' GO TO ERROR-ROUTINE.
PRINT HOSPNAME, HOSPADDR, HOSPCITY.
```

The first four MOVE statements are standard COBOL statements initializing the indicated TOTAL parameters. Other parameters in the CALL statement could be similarly initialized. TOTAL sets the STATUS area to '****' if the CALL command is executed successfully. TOTAL places the retrieved fields in the USER-AREA for subsequent use by the application program.

2. Obtain a list of all the EMPLOYEEs hospitalized at the UCLA HOSPITAL.

```
        MOVE 'READV' TO FUNCTION.
        MOVE SPACES TO STATUS.
        MOVE 'EMPLOYEE' TO DATA-SET.
        MOVE 'LKMP' TO REFERENCE.
        MOVE 'HOSP-LK-EMP' TO LINKAGE-PATH.
        MOVE 'UCLA' TO CONTROL KEY.
        MOVE 'EMPNAMEEMPADDREMPCITY' TO
        ELEMENT-LIST.
NEXT.   MOVE SPACES TO USER-AREA.
        CALL 'DATBAS' USING FUNCTION, STATUS,
        DATA-SET, REFERENCE, LINKAGE-PATH,
        CONTROL-KEY, ELEMENT-LIST,
        USER-AREA, 'ENDP'.
        IF STATUS = 'CHAIN TERMINATED' GO TO
        FINISH.
        IF STATUS ≠ '****' GO TO
        ERROR-ROUTING.
        PRINT EMPNAME, EMPADDR, EMPCITY.
        GO TO NEXT.
FINISH. PRINT USER AREA.
        FINISH.
```

Execution of the first CALL and PRINT command prints out the name (EMPNAME) and address (EMPADDR and EMPCITY) of

the first variable entry EMPLOYEE record in the chain of HOSPI-
TAL UCLA. The value of REFERENCE is set by TOTAL to the
Internal Reference Point or relative record number of the record
located. Subsequent execution of the CALL and PRINT pair results in
printing out the remaining records in the chain. "XX" in the REF-
ERENCE code 'LKXX' are the last two characters of the LINKAGE-
PATH parameter, "MP" in this case.

The READV command operates by logically following forward
pointers in the specified linkage path. If we use instead the command
READR (Read Reverse), then TOTAL will retrieve in reverse direction starting with the last record in the chain.

3. Print the name of all the INSURANCE companies servicing EM-
PLOYEE 20 (EMPLOYEE field EMPLOYEE-NO = 20) with
CLAIM-CYCLE = 15. INSURCODE is both the insurance name
and the control key of the INSURANCE master data set. Every
EMPLOYEE has a unique EMPLOYEE-NO; an INSURANCE-
CO does not service more than one EMPLOYEE with a given
EMPLOYEE-NO.   *

This query would be much more easily answered if EMPLOYEE
had been set as a master entry data set (with EMPLOYEE number as
its control key) and INSURANCE-CO as the variable entry data set;
this query sees EMPLOYEE as the master information and IN-
SURANCE-CO as the detail information. This query was answered in
Section 5.6 for the DBTG example. The query is answered as follows
using the schema in Figure 6.4.   *

```
              MOVE 'DNXT' TO FUNCTION.
              MOVE SPACES TO STATUS.
              MOVE 'INSURANCE-CO' TO DATA-SET.
              MOVE BEGN TO QUALIFIER.
              MOVE 'INSURCODECLAIM-CYCLE' TO
              ELEMENT-LIST.
NEXTINS.      MOVE SPACES TO USER-AREA.
              CALL 'DATBAS' USING FUNCTION,
              STATUS, DATA-SET, QUALIFIER,
              ELEMENT-LIST, USER-AREA, 'ENDP'.
              IF STATUS = 'CHAIN TERMINATED' GO
              TO FINISH.
              IF STATUS ≠ '****' GO TO ERROR-
              ROUTINE.
              IF CLAIM-CYCLE ≠ 15 GO TO NEXTINS.
NEXTEMP.      MOVE 'READV' TO FUNCTION.
              MOVE SPACES TO STATUS.
```

```
                    MOVE 'EMPLOYEE' TO DATA-SET.
                    MOVE 'LKMP' TO REFERENCE.
                    MOVE 'INS-LK-EMP' TO LINKAGE-PATH.
                    MOVE 'INSURCODE' TO CONTROL-KEY.
                    MOVE = 'EMPLOYEE-NO' TO ELEMENT-
                    LIST.
                    MOVE SPACES TO USER-AREA2.
                    CALL 'DATABAS' USING FUNCTION,
                    STATUS, DATA-SET, REFERENCE,
                    LINKAGE-PATH, CONTROL-KEY,
                    ELEMENT-LIST, USER-AREA2, 'ENDP'.
                    IF STATUS = 'CHAIN TERMINATED' GO
                    TO NEXTINS.
                    IF STATUS ≠ '****' GO TO
                    ERROR-ROUTINE.
                    IF EMPLOYEE-NO = 20 PRINT
                    INSURCODE.
                    GO TO NEXTINS.
        FINISH.     END.
```

The first execution of the first CALL in the NEXTINS loop obtains the record at the beginning (QUALIFIER set to BEGN) of the single entry INSURANCE-CO data set. The second, third, etc. execution of this CALL obtains the second, third, etc. record in the INSURANCE-CO data set, since TOTAL automatically sets the value of QUALIFIER to Internal Reference Point 2, 3, etc., even though the program did not explicitly re-set QUALIFIER.

Add

4. Add employee CARDENAS as the new EMPLOYEE patient of DOCTOR SHEIN. Store only 'CARDENAS' as the value of the EMPLOYEE-NAME field. SHEIN is the value of the DOCCODE control field of the DOCTOR master data set.   *

```
            MOVE 'ADDVC' TO FUNCTION.
            MOVE SPACES TO STATUS.
            MOVE 'EMPLOYEE' TO DATA SET.
            MOVE 'LKMP' TO REFERENCE.
            MOVE 'DOC-LK-EMP' TO LINKAGE-PATH.
            MOVE 'SHEIN' TO CONTROL-KEY.
            MOVE 'EMPLOYEE-NAME' TO ELEMENT-LIST.
            MOVE 'CARDENAS' TO DATA-AREA.
```

CALL 'DATBAS' USING FUNCTION, STATUS,
DATA-SET, REFERENCE, LINKAGE-PATH,
CONTROL-KEY, ELEMENT-LIST, DATA-AREA, 'ENDP'.
IF STATUS ≠ '****' GO TO ERROR-ROUTINE.

The FUNCTION 'ADDVC' and the REFERENCE code 'LKMP'
instruct TOTAL to store the new record at the end of the chain owned
by SHEIN. The FUNCTION could have been set instead to 'ADDVA'
and the REFERENCE to a number 'X' in order to insert the new
record right after the EMPLOYEE record whose Internal Reference
Point is 'X'. Alternatively, the FUNCTION 'ADDVB' would insert
the new record before the EMPLOYEE record identified by 'X'.

Recall that the Internal Reference Point is a relative physical
location with respect to the beginning of the variable entry data set; it
is not a relative location from the logical beginning of the chain. After
execution of the CALL statement with the FUNCTION 'ADDVC',
TOTAL puts in REFERENCE the Internal Reference Point of the
added record.

Write

5. Update (write over) the EMPLOYEE record of CARDENAS who is
the patient of DOCTOR SHEIN. Add his address 'Boelter Hall,
UCLA, Los Angeles, California'.

MOVE 'WRITV' TO FUNCTION.
MOVE SPACES TO STATUS.
MOVE 'EMPLOYEE' TO DATA-SET.
MOVE '17' TO REFERENCE.
MOVE 'DOC-LK-EMP' TO LINKAGE PATH.
MOVE 'SHEIN' TO CONTROL-KEY.
MOVE 'EMPADDREMPCITY' TO ELEMENT-LIST.
MOVE 'BOELTER HALL, UCLA, LOS ANGELES,
CALIFORNIA' TO USER-AREA.
CALL 'DATBAS' USING FUNCTION, STATUS,
DATA-SET, REFERENCE, LINKAGE-PATH,
CONTROL-KEY, ELEMENT-LIST, DATA-AREA, 'ENDP'.
IF STATUS ≠ '****' GO TO ERROR-ROUTINE.

The WRITV function updates the indicated fields of the variable
record where Internal Reference Point is in the REFERENCE field,
17 in this example. Note that it is assumed that the user knows that this
Internal Reference Point corresponds to CARDENAS; as in Example

4, after execution of a CALL with the FUNCTION 'ADDVC', TOTAL puts in REFERENCE the Internal Reference Point of the added record.

Delete

6. Delete the EMPLOYEE information of CARDENAS who is the patient of DOCTOR SHEIN. This is a reversal of the ADD action in Example 4. *

        MOVE 'DELVD' TO FUNCTION.
        MOVE SPACES TO STATUS.
        MOVE 'EMPLOYEE' TO DATA-SET.
        MOVE '17' TO REFERENCE.
        MOVE 'DOC-LK-EMP' TO LINKAGE-PATH.
        MOVE 'SHEIN' TO CONTROL-KEY.
        MOVE 'END' TO ELEMENT-LIST.
        MOVE SPACES TO DATA-AREA.
        CALL 'DATBAS' USING FUNCTION, STATUS,
        DATA-SET, REFERENCE, LINKAGE-PATH,
        CONTROL-KEY, ELEMENT-LIST, DATA-AREA, 'ENDP'.

The DELVD function deletes all fields of the variable record where Internal Reference Point is in the REFERENCE field, 17 in this example. Note that here it is assumed that the user knows that this Internal Reference Point corresponds to CARDENAS.

Add, write, and delete commands are similarly available for operating on master data sets. The previous variable entry examples are sufficiently close to their master data set counterparts so that there is no further need for illustrations.

6.4 STORAGE STRUCTURE

TOTAL performs efficiently, according to many of its users. The physical organization of records is based on a proprietary hashing algorithm internal to TOTAL and on highly dynamic garbage collection of space vacated by deleted records. TOTAL accesses master records only by randomizing the value of the mandatory control key. Collisions do occur, as in every known hashing method. The so-called root field is used to maintain a synonym chain to the home address. TOTAL accesses a variable record by randomizing the value of the control field indicated in the I/O command, and then following its linkage path to the desired variable entry record.

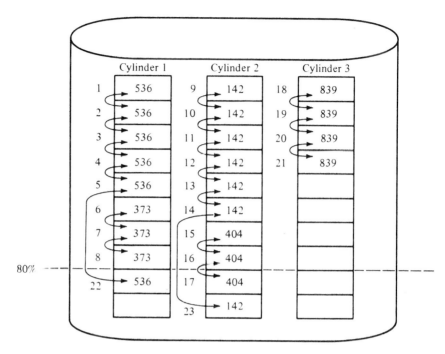

Note: Numbers 1–23 indicate the sequence
in which the records were loaded.

Figure 6.9.   *Example of TOTAL storage organization for variable entry
data set records*

Note that in the DBTG architecture any or all of the defined record types may be declared to be accessed on a direct hashing basis, using a hashing algorithm provided by the DBA. A different hashing algorithm may be used for each record type if desired.

It is interesting to note the TOTAL strategy for storing variable entry data sets on cylinders. Figure 6.9 indicates the storage layout of the records with the control keys shown after loading these records in the sequence indicated by the numbers 1, 2,..., N. A percentage of each bucket is set aside for "overflow," 20 percent of each cylinder in this figure. The main goal is to gain access time efficiency by attempting to keep a variable entry record on the same cylinder as the first record in the chain. No new chains are started in the overflow areas.

6.5   SUMMARY

TOTAL is one of the major GDBMS in terms of number installed. It is an advocate of the network data base approach. Conceptually, TOTAL may be envisioned as 60 to 80 percent DBTG, but syntactically it is very different. It has its own terminology. It does not have some of the COBOL syntactic flavor that DBTG has. TOTAL has trimmed down on many of the DBTG options and formats, particularly on DML commands. TOTAL trims down where possible without major sacrifices in capability in order to achieve its goal of superior performance and efficiency, in terms of storage and access time.

A TOTAL data base may be composed of two types of data sets (the TOTAL name for file): single entry or master data set and variable entry or detail/transaction data set. This is a follow-up to the practice of master file and detail file(s) in traditional data management. Single entry data sets are intended to be relatively stable as to record content and number of record occurrences, whereas variable entry data sets are intended to contain a variable and highly volatile number of record occurrences. Any number of relationships, called linkage paths, may be established between a single entry data set and variable entry data sets. Hierarchical and network data bases are built from data sets and linkage paths. An unlimited number of data bases may be defined, and any data set may be included in any number of different data bases. Thus the concept of schema and subschema is provided. Sections 6.1 and 6.2 present the basics of TOTAL and the definition of schemas and subschemas.

TOTAL provides direct access entry to any master data set record via a proprietary hashing algorithm applied to the field of the data set selected by the DBA as the identifier and control key. Access to a variable entry data set record is accomplished by specifying both the value of the particular control key of its related master data set and the name of the linkage path relating both data sets. A particular variable entry record may also be located either by specifying a relative position in the chain linking the variable entry record occurrences under a given control key or by specifying a "next" or "previous" position, as in DBTG. TOTAL actually uses the control key to access a master record in a hashing manner and then follows its chain to the desired variable record. Thus TOTAL's DML provides both hashing entry to the data base and access path navigation like DBTG. TOTAL's DML does not provide as many options and different overlapping command formats as DBTG. Thus the overhead supporting the richness in options, particularly those somewhat redundant, is avoided. The DML commands are call statements with arguments, much more like IMS DML than DBTG's DML. Section 6.3 outlines the TOTAL DML.

TOTAL prides itself on its highly efficient and proprietary algorithm for hashing and managing collisions, undoubtedly a major reason for the high efficiency achieved by various TOTAL users. Furthermore, storage utilization is optimized by highly dynamic garbage collection of space vacated by deleted records.

REFERENCES

1. "OS TOTAL Reference Manual—Application Programming," Publication No. PO2-1323, Cincom Systems Inc., Cincinnati, Ohio.
2. "TOTAL Data Base Administration," Reference Manual No. P02-1324, Cincom Systems Inc., Cincinnati, Ohio.
3. "TOTAL Print and Modify Statistics," Reference Manual No. P11-0002, Cincom Systems Inc., Cincinnati, Ohio.

EXERCISES

1. (a) Consider the TOTAL network data base in Figure 6.4. Indicate the DML commands to answer each of the following requests:
   1. How many employees are there with companies located in ABC?
   2. For each insurance company in the data base obtain a list of the names of the hospitals which have associated doctors who service employees insured by the same insurance company.

   (b) If you were the data base administrator, had the freedom to establish and delete relationships between records, and knew that the two preceding data base requests were among the most frequently made, what new relationship(s), if any, would you establish? Can you establish such relationship(s) in TOTAL? Compare the facility to establish new and arbitrary relationships in TOTAL versus DBTG. Define such new relationship(s) using the TOTAL schema DDL.

   This exercise is similar to Exercise 3 in Chapter 5, Exercise 3 in Chapter 7, and Exercise 3 in Chapter 8. Compare the solutions.

7
IMS

7.1   INTRODUCTION AND ARCHITECTURE

IBM's *I*nformation *M*anagement *S*ystem, IMS, is one of the major GDBMS, or generalized data base/data communications (DB/DC) systems when the DC option is included, on the market.[1-8] It had its beginning in the mid- to late-1960s. IBM and North American Aviation (now Rockwell International) developed the first IMS versions in order to manage the vast amount of information related to the Apollo moon program in the late 1960s. Soon thereafter, IBM developed it to be the first large-scale and truly generalized DB/DC.

A DB/DC system is one in which both the data base and the data communication (or teleprocessing) facilities have been highly developed in an integrated basis over and above those of a host operating system. At this point the reader should read or review Section 3.6 presenting the constituents of DB/DC systems versus GDBMS and a brief description of IMS DB/DC system flow. We shall not focus on the DC function of IMS. Interested readers may pursue this subject in the available references.

There are a number of versions or "releases" of IMS running under a number of IBM operating systems (OS/MFT, OS/MVT, OS/VS1, OS/VS2, MVS).[1-8] Our presentation of IMS applies to any of the versions of IMS/360 or the newer IMS/VS (on OS/VS1, OS/VS2). IMS is one of the largest and most complex GDBMS available. It has many options and trade-offs. It is being continuously enhanced by IBM in a variety of directions. The documented description of the full IMS details runs several thousand pages. It is often said that IMS is the most complex GDBMS to master and use. We will focus herein on the fundamentals of IMS.

The architecture of IMS is outlined in Figure 7.1. A schema, not an IMS term, is made up of one or more connected **physical data bases**. The logical structure of each physical data base is defined by a physical *D*ata *B*ase *D*escription, DBD. Each DBD also includes part of the specifications for the mapping of the data base into storage and access method specifications. Hence the term physical DBD is frequently used. However, the user does not see the data base as it is stored; IMS provides a high degree of data independence. A **logical data base** is composed of one or more linked physical data bases. Thus in IMS the term schema is equivalent to either one physical data base or to a logical data base composed of one or more linked physical data bases.

A *P*rogram *C*ommunication *B*lock, PCB, is a subset of the data base description. A set of PCBs for a given user or application program is called a *P*rogram *S*pecification *B*lock, PSB. The term subschema is not used in the IMS world. A PSB, a single PCB or a set of PCBs, is a subschema. A PSB may not be used by more than one application program, but two PSBs may contain

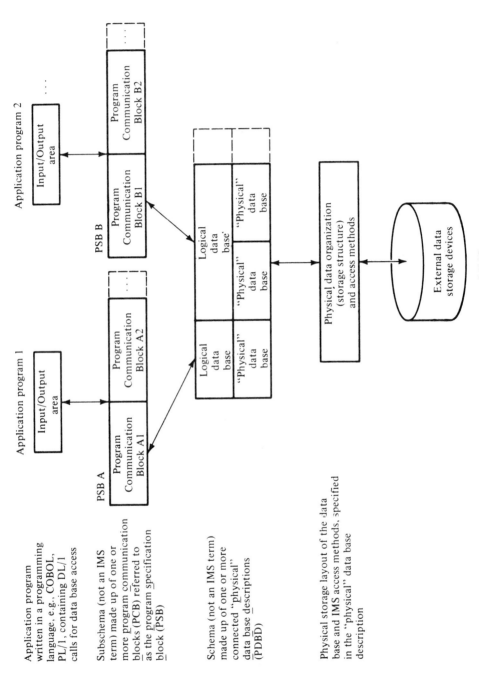

Figure 7.1. Architecture of IMS

Application program written in a programming language, e.g., COBOL, PL/1, containing DL/1 calls for data base access

Subschema (not an IMS term) made up of one or more program communication blocks (PCB) referred to as the program specification block (PSB)

Schema (not an IMS term) made up of one or more connected "physical" data base descriptions (PDBD)

Physical storage layout of the data base and IMS access methods, specified in the "physical" data base description identical information. The data base of an application program is the set of occurrences of a PCB or PSB.

Application programs written in COBOL, PL/1, or IBM basic assembly language communicate with IMS data bases via *Data Language/One*, **DL/1**. DL/1 is the common data access or data manipulation language. Transfer of data between the application program and IMS is via an Input/Output area. An *Interactive Query Facility*, IQF, was available for on-line retrieval but was subsequently retired by IBM.[4] It was a very nonprocedural query language primarily for read-only access.

7.2   THE PHYSICAL DATA BASE OR SCHEMA

Each IMS "*Physical*" *Data Base*, PDB, is made up of a hierarchic or tree structure composed of segment types. Again, bear in mind that the use of the term physical data base is misleading and should be thought of instead as the "logical" data base. A **segment** is made up of an arbitrary number of data fields. A segment corresponds to the record in conventional file management and to the DBTG record type. The smallest unit of data that may be accessed and transferred by DL/1 is a segment.

Figure 7.2 shows a hierarchic IMS data base containing five segment types: DOCTOR, CLINIC, EMPLOYEE, INSUR_CO, and CHILD. This is essentially the same data base used in exemplifying the DBTG systems, Figure 5.9; our IMS data base has in the segment type CLINIC some of the data elements in DOCTOR in Figure 5.9. This is also similar to data base B1 used in exemplifying TOTAL, Figure 6.4, except that our IMS data base uses the segment name CLINIC instead of DOCTOR-DETAIL and uses a CHILD

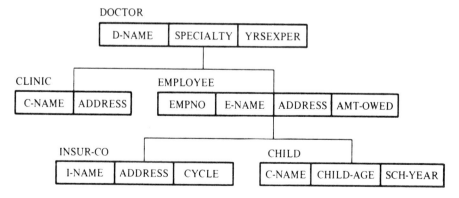

Figure 7.2.   *A Doctor-Clinic Employee-Insurance-Child IMS data base*

segment. In the early IMS versions segment names and field names are limited to eight characters to a name. The **root** segment type is the segment at the top of the tree; DOCTOR is the root segment. All other segments are dependent segments arranged in the tree structure in "physical" parent-child relationships. A **parent** segment type normally has at least one **child** segment type; e.g., the parent of EMPLOYEE is DOCTOR. A parent does not have to have at least one child, i.e., a root-only data base is valid. A child cannot have more than one parent. The segment types at the bottom of the tree are child segments which are not parents of any segment types, e.g., CLINIC, INSURANCE_ CO, and CHILD. The term parent always refers to the parent immediately above.

Each occurrence of a parent segment type may contain zero, one, or more occurrences of each of its child segment types. All occurrences of a child segment type that have a common parent occurrence are called **twins**; a better term would be siblings (brothers or sisters), which is used in non-IMS environments as such but which IMS uses to refer to segment types at the same level. This is one more example of confusing jargon.

There is a 1-to-N relationship between a parent segment type and each of its child segment types. M-to-N relationships cannot be defined directly. However, we have indicated previously how they can be defined by essentially introducing another level or segment type, Figure 3.16; we shall illustrate in Section 7.5 how M-to-N relationships can be defined in IMS by using "logical" data base pointer mechanisms.

Figure 7.3 shows a sample record occurrence. The DOCTOR root occurrence has two CLINIC occurrences and three EMPLOYEE occurrences. The first of the EMPLOYEE occurrences has two INSUR_CO occurrences and two CHILD occurrences. The same parent-child relationships for segment types hold for segment occurrences. We shall no longer use the terms type and occurrence unless it is necessary to avoid confusion.

The following list summarizes briefly the IMS hierarchic or tree data base structure:

1. There must be one and only one root segment type.
2. The root may have an arbitrary number of child segment types.
3. Each child segment of the root may have an arbitrary number of child segment types; a maximum of 255 segment types may be included, up to 15 segment types in any one hierarchical path.
4. No child segment type may have more than one parent segment type.
5. Each occurrence of a segment type may have an arbitrary number of occurrences of each of its child segment types.
6. No M:N relationship may be directly defined between a parent and a child segment type; that is, no child occurrence may have more than one parent occurrence.

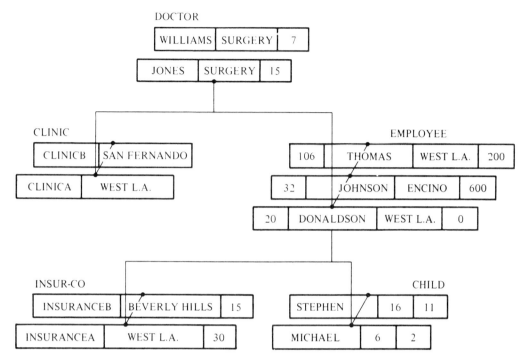

Figure 7.3.   *Sample data base record occurrences of the Doctor data base in Figure 7.2*

7. No child segment occurrence can exist without its parent.

8. Root segment occurrences must be ordered.

9. Occurrences of a child segment may be ordered.

Compare these IMS characteristics with those of the network DBTG approach summarized in Figures 5.4 and 5.5. In contrast to (7) in the above list, the DBTG approach allows a child record occurrence to exist alone if it is declared to be an OPTIONAL member of the set owned by its parent record (see Section 5.4).

The *DATA BASE DESCRIPTION*, DBD

Each IMS data base and part of its mapping to storage is defined by the DBA by means of a set of special System 360/370 assembly language macro statements that constitute the *Data Base Description*, DBD, "language." It is unfortunately a rigid and machine-oriented means of defining logical structures. We will disregard for now physical-oriented entries in the DBD constructs, such as physical access methods and storage mappings.

Example

Figure 7.4 shows the IMS DBD for the Doctor data base in Figure 7.2. Let us go through this example; the leading statement numbers are not part of the DBD syntax. The sequence of SEGM statements in the DBD explicitly indicates the hierarchic logical structure of the data base, according to a top to bottom, left to right mapping. This concept is central to the IMS hierarchic approach. IMS identifies each segment type according to its position in this hierarchic structure. Thus, in the Doctor PDB, DOCTOR has identifier 1, CLINIC has identifier 2, EMPLOYEE 3, INSUR_CO 4, and CHILD 5. The sequence of segment occurrences, a sequence which is central to the process of navigating through the data

```
 1  DBD      NAME = DOCTORDB
 2  SEGM     NAME = DOCTOR, BYTES = 26
 3  FIELD    NAME = (D_NAME, SEQ), BYTES = 16, START = 1
 4  FIELD    NAME = SPECIALTY,  BYTES = 8, START = 17
 5  FIELD    NAME = YRSEXPER, BYTES = 2, START = 25

 6  SEGM     NAME = CLINIC, BYTES = 41, PARENT = DOCTOR
 7  FIELD    NAME = (C_NAME, SEQ), BYTES = 16, START = 1
 8  FIELD    NAME = ADDRESS, BYTES = 25, START = 17

 9  SEGM     NAME = EMPLOYEE, BYTES = 49,
             PARENT = DOCTOR
10  FIELD    NAME = (EMPNO, SEQ), BYTES = 4, START = 1
11  FIELD    NAME = E_NAME, BYTES = 16, START = 5
12  FIELD    NAME = ADDRESS, BYTES = 25, START = 21
13  FIELD    NAME = AMT_OWED, BYTES = 4, START = 46

14  SEGM     NAME = INSUR_CO, BYTES = 45,
             PARENT = EMPLOYEE
15  FIELD    NAME = (I_NAME, SEQ), BYTES = 16, START = 1
16  FIELD    NAME = ADDRESS, BYTES = 25, START = 17
17  FIELD    NAME = CYCLE, BYTES = 4, START = 42

18  SEGM     NAME = CHILD, BYTES = 12,
             PARENT = EMPLOYEE
19  FIELD    NAME = (C_NAME,M), BYTES = 8, START = 1
20  FIELD    NAME = CHILD_AGE, BYTES = 2, START = 9
21  FIELD    NAME = SCH_YEAR, BYTES = 2, START = 11
22  DBDGEN
23  FINISH
24  END
```

Figure 7.4. IMS physical DBD for the Doctor data base in Figure 7.2

base via DL/1, is also thus determined. For example, a "get next" DL/1 command may step from the last CLINIC occurrence to the first EM-PLOYEE occurrence under the common DOCTOR segment occurrence.

Statement 1 gives the name of the DBD.

Statement 2 defines the root segment, DOCTOR, made up of fields taking up 26 bytes (in 360/370 hardware each alphanumeric character takes one byte, and each single precision numeric field may take 2 or 4 bytes). Note this unfortunate inclusion of machine-level byte counts in the logical definition.

Statements 3−5 define the fields making up the segment DOC-TOR. Notice again the need to have to indicate byte counts and offsets precisely. It would be much more convenient to simply specify data types and field lengths by means of PICTURE-like means as in COBOL, DBTG DDL, SYSTEM 2000's DDL, and so forth. By not including a data type definition, it might be easier (in terms of implementation) to later view a field with different data type declarations. Root segment occurrences must be sequenced. Sequencing must be on the basis of the first field appearing in the segment definition. Thus D_NAME is the sequence field so that PDB record occurrences will be arranged in ascending collating sequence of D_NAME. This is a logical ordering that does not necessarily mean physical ordering. Root segments are physically ordered, but not when the HDAM physical organization is used, as we shall see.

Statement 6 declares the segment CLINIC as the next one in the top to bottom, left to right hierarchical convention. It is a child of DOCTOR. Note that the parent-child relationship is implied by the hierarchical ordering convention, as well as by an explicit declaration of the relation-ship. In DBTG the relationship is an explicitly declared object: the set. Forty-one bytes are allocated to CLINIC.

Statements 7−8 declare the fields of CLINIC. A *seq*uence, SEQ, is declared for the first field C_NAME; it means that for each occurrence of the parent segment DOCTOR, its child CLINIC occurrences are ordered according to the ascending sequence of C_NAME, and C_NAME values must be unique.

Statement 9 declares EMPLOYEE as a child of DOCTOR.

Statements 10−13 declare the fields of EMPLOYEE. The EMP_NO is declared to be the sequence field.

Statement 14 declares INSUR_CO as a child of EMPLOYEE.

Statements 15−17 declare the fields of INSUR_CO.

Statement 18 declares CHILD as a child of EMPLOYEE.

Statements 19−21 declare the fields of CHILD. The indication M for the sequence field C_NAME is that twin CHILD occurrences may contain the same child name value; that is, an employee might have two children with the same name (for example, as the result of a second marriage).

Statement 22 indicates the end of the DBD generation control statements for this data base.

Statements 23 and 24 are termination instructions to the link-edit program and to the operating system.

7.3   THE IMS SUBSCHEMAS: PCBs AND PSB

A subschema is a logical and consistent subset of the Data Base Description (DBD) or schema. In IMS the Program Communication Block (PCB), or a set of PCBs which are collectively called a Program Specification Block (PSB), constitutes the subschema. The set of occurrences of a PCB or PSB constitutes the data base of the application program containing the PCB or PSB declaration. We shall talk in terms of a PCB.

Following are the main rules for forming a PCB (not intended to be an exhaustive list of rules):

1. A PCB is a subset of the hierarchic arrangement of DBD segment types. In forming a PCB, any DBD segment type may be masked out; however, all of its child segment types are also necessarily masked out from the PCB. For example, the PCB in Figure 7.5 may be derived from the DBD in Figure 7.2.

2. A PCB is a subtree or subhierarchy of a DBD; therefore the PCB root segment must be the same as the DBD root segment. Note that this is a restriction not found in other GDBMS systems, for example, in forming subschemas in a DBTG system, or TOTAL, or SYSTEM 2000, or a relational system.

3. Different PCBs can overlap.

4. An arbitrary number of PCBs may be defined over a DBD, as many as there are subtrees in the tree. Thus, for the schema in Figure 7.2, ten

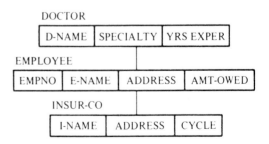

Figure 7.5.   *A subschema from the Doctor data base in Figure 7.2*

distinct IMS subschemas may be derived. Note that for a DBTG system, in which any two record types can be connected by a set, a much larger number of subschemas could be defined.

5. An arbitrary number of programs can share a given PCB (via different PSBs).

6. In the early IMS versions all data fields of a segment declared in the DBD had to be included in the PCB using that segment. The new IMS/VS releases allow masking out any fields. In DBTG, SYSTEM 2000, relational systems, and a number of other GDBMS, any of the schema fields can be omitted to form the subschema.

IMS does insulate application programs from a number of changes to the DBD, except perhaps in terms of storage and access time performance. For example, a new segment type may be added to a DBD as a child of an existing segment type as long as it does not intrude or break into any parent-child relationship. This will not affect existing PCBs. For the DBD in Figure 7.2, child segment types can be added under CLINIC, INSUR_CO, and CHILD, and under DOCTOR and EMPLOYEE as long as the existing connections are not broken to insert the new child segment(s). The addition of a segment type to a DBD generally requires unloading the whole data base and reloading it to reflect the new DBD; new IMS releases strive to minimize unloading.

The addition of a new field to a segment type normally necessitates changing the PCBs using this segment. DBTG, SYSTEM 2000, relational systems, and a number of other GDBMS show more data independence since new fields may be added to record types in a schema without affecting any of the subschemas.

In the IMS environment, the **sensitivity** of a program refers to the segment types that are seen by an application program. The sensitive segments are all those included in the PCBs declared for the program.

Figure 7.6 shows the PCB declaration for the subschema in Figure 7.5. The PCB consists of a set of System 360 assembler language macro statements, similar to the DBD macro statements. The numbered statements accomplish the following tasks (the statement number is not part of the PCB syntax).

```
1  PCB       TYPE = DB, DBDNAME = DOCTORDB, KEYLEN = 36
2  SENSEG    NAME = DOCTOR, PROCOPT = G
3  SENSEG    NAME = EMPLOYEE, PARENT = DOCTOR,
             PROCOPT = GI
4  SENSEG    NAME = INSUR_CO, PARENT = EMPLOYEE,
             PROCOPT = GIR
5  PSBGEN    LANG = COBOL, PSBNAME = ALFPSB
6  END
```

Figure 7.6.   *IMS PCB for the subschema in Figure 7.5*

Statement 1 indicates that this is a data base TYPE, not a data base/data communications TYPE. Recall that IMS options exist to configure it as a DB/DC also. The name of the underlying DBD is declared, DOCTORDB. The length of the so-called *key feedback area* is 36 bytes. The latter byte calculation is unfortunately required in each PCB. Let us analyze what the key feedback parameter is.

Proper communication between an application program and an IMS data base requires the use of a number of parameters for each PCB declared. These parameters are set automatically by IMS at execution time. We will address them when we introduce DL/1 in the following section. One such parameter is called the *key feedback area* which contains the concatenation of the sequence keys of the segments in the hierarchic path from the root segment to the segment occurrence last accessed. Let us call it in this discussion the *hierarchic concatenated key*, HCK. The HCK performs a function analogous to that of the record currency indicator in DBTG; namely, it keeps an indicator of where the user is while navigating the data base. If, for example, a DL/1 call retrieves the INSUR_CO occurrence for INSURANCEA in Figure 7.3, IMS places the value JONES 20 INSURANCEA in the key feedback area. IMS unfortunately expects the PCB designer to declare the maximum possible length of an HCK. Thus, in statement 1 KEYLEN = 36:16 bytes for DOCTOR, 4 bytes for EMPLOYEE, and 16 bytes for INSUR_CO are already declared in the underlying DBD.

Statement 2 declares the root segment and the type(s) of accessing allowed for this segment. The cryptic PROCOPT stands for "*proc*essing *opt*ions." The IMS code G indicates that get or retrieval DL/1 commands are allowed. Among the PROCOPTs that may be declared for a segment in various consistent combinations are: R for replace (modify), I for insert, and D for delete. In the new IMS/VS2 selected fields of the whole segments can be included in the PCB. That is, individual data fields can be masked out; the type of access can be defined on an individual field basis.

Statement 3 declares EMPLOYEE as the next sensitive segment, with get and insert access rights. The top to bottom, left to right hierarchical structure of the DBD must be followed. PARENT = DOCTOR declares the proper parent segment (if PCB and DBD syntax were to be consistent, then there should be no need to explicitly indicate PARENT in a PCB).

Statement 4 declares INSUR_CO as the last sensitive segment of the subschema with get, insert, and replace rights to segment occurrences.

Statement 5 states that the program using this PCB is written in COBOL and that the PSBNAME (Subschema name) is ALFPSB.

Masking out of Intermediate Segments in the IMS Hierarchy

Let us now see how IMS attempts, although not very elegantly, to mask out an intermediate segment in a DBD subtree. We mentioned the IMS drawback of PCBs having to deal with complete subtrees of the DBD. If a given segment is to be masked out from the view of the user, then the PCB designer must indicate PROCOPT = K (K stands for key sensitivity) for the segment. Thus if the sensitivity of a user program is to be Figure 7.5 minus the EMPLOYEE segment information, then the corresponding PCB would be that in Figure 7.6 but with PROCOPT = K in Statement 3. The PCB must still include EMPLOYEE segment information. Furthermore, the hierarchic concatenated key placed by IMS in the key feedback area after a DL/1 call accesses an INSUR_CO occurrence will include the value of the EMPNO key field of EMPLOYEE, even though EMPLOYEE is not a sensitive segment!

7.4   DATA MANIPULATION: DATA LANGUAGE/ONE (DL/1)

Application programs written in COBOL, PL/1, or System 360/370 assembly language communicate with IMS data bases via *Data Language/ One*, DL/1. DL/1 is the common data access and data manipulation language. We will outline only the main characteristics of DL/1. There are many detailed options and implications in the various DL/1 commands which we shall not address. Reference 3 defines DL/1.

DL/1 is a procedural data access language which is really a set of subroutine calls with a number of parameters. Thus the common term "DL/1 call" is more appropriate than the less frequently used term "DL/1 statement." Although DL/1 is the communication language for IMS data bases, the DL/1 processor is also available separately from the larger IMS configurations. Thus the DL/1 module and a portion of its language can be a stand-alone data base retrieval package for the smaller IBM DOS system, typically used on the smaller 360/370 type models.

An *Interactive Query Facility*, IQF, used to be available for on-line read-only retrieval.[4] It was subsequently retired by IBM.

For the convenience of readers, we shall introduce the fundamentals of the hierarchic approach and DL/1 functions without the heavy burden of the many rigid and idiosyncratic IMS syntax and other programming details. In the last part of this section we shall illustrate the programming details involved for COBOL and PL/1 applications.

Transfer of data and communication between an application program and an IMS data base described by a valid PCB(s) indicated in the program is via an I/O area; see Figure 7.1. There are nine parameters associated with each PCB of the program; they are stored in the I/O area. The value of most of these parameters is determined or updated by IMS after executing every DL/1 command. The function of each of these nine PCB parameters is summarized in Figure 7.7. Let us call them the "PCB parameters" (this is not an IMS term). The name of each parameter is arbitrarily declared as a program variable by the application programmer. We have chosen the names in Figure 7.7. Their meaning or function is as follows (examples indicated refer to the data base in Figures 7.2 and 7.3):

The variable name DBD-NAME indicates the name of the underlying DBD used throughout the execution of the program.

The variable SEG-LEVEL contains the hierarchical level number of the segment accessed by the most recent DL/1 call to this PCB. The root segment is level 1, all its children are at level 2, and so on.

STATUS-CODE indicates the success or error condition after every DL/1 call. This two-character value is the means by which IMS informs the user of success or unusual situations.

PROC-OPTIONS indicates the processing options for the segment just accessed (e.g., G for get or retrieval).

RESERVE-DL/1 is reserved for IMS' own use.

SEG-NAME contains the name of the segment last accessed.

Function or use	Parameter name (arbitrary)
Name of the underlying DBD used by the program in execution	DBD-NAME
Segment hierarchy level indicator	SEG-LEVEL
DL/1 results status code	STATUS-CODE
DL/1 processing options	PROC-OPTIONS
Reserved for IMS own use	RESERVE-DL/1
Segment name	SEG-NAME
Length of hierarchical concatenated feedback key	LENGTH-FB-KEY
Number of sensitive segments used by the program in execution	#SEN-SEGS
Key feedback area	KEY-FB-AREA

Figure 7.7. *Functions of the parameters involved for each IMS PCB used in an application program*

LENGTH-FB-KEY contains the current length of the hierarchic concatenated key of the segment just accessed.

\# SEN-SEGS indicates the number of sensitive segments seen by the program.

KEY-FB-AREA contains the hierarchic concatenated key of the segment just accessed. For example, if a DL/1 call accesses the INSUR-CO occurrence for INSURANCEA in Figure 7.3, then the value of KEY-FB-AREA set by IMS is JONES 20 INSURANCEA. This is the sequence of keys of the parent segments in the hierarchical path from the root segment occurrence to the segment occurrence last accessed (we avoid in our examples the IMS significance of blanks and left justification details).

DL/1 Commands

Figure 7.8 summarizes the main DL/1 operations and corresponding syntactic abbreviation used in a DL/1 call. The actual format of a DL/1 call is the ordinary subroutine call format shown in Figure 7.9. Its parameters give the following indications (the name PL1TDL1 is for calling from a PL/1 program):

1. The first parameter indicates the function to be performed, e.g., GU, GN, etc.
2. The second parameter indicates the name of the target PCB at which the DL/1 call is directed.

Function		Code
GET UNIQUE	Direct retrieval	GU
GET NEXT	Sequential retrieval in top to bottom, left to right sequence	GN
GET NEXT WITHIN PARENT	Sequential retrieval under the current parent occurrence	GNP
GET HOLD UNIQUE NEXT NEXT WITHIN PARENT	Same as above but permits subsequent DELETE or REPLACE	GHU GHN GHNP
REPLACE	Replaces an existing segment	REPL
INSERT	Inserts a new segment	ISRT
DELETE	Deletes an existing segment	DLET

Figure 7.8. *Main DL/1 commands (function codes)*

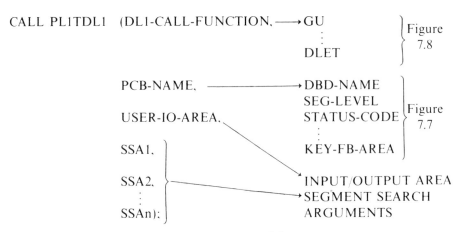

Figure 7.9.   *DL/1 call format*

3. The third indicates the address of the I/O area.
4. The fourth, fifth, . . . *n*th are optional and each indicates the *segment search a*rgument, SSA.

An SSA consists of a segment name optionally followed by the triplet:

⟨field name⟩ ⟨comparison operator⟩ ⟨field value⟩

or a series of this type of triplet connected by logical operators (AND, OR, NOT). The field name must be one of those in the segment. The comparison operators available are: $=, \neq, >, \geq, <, \leq$.

As an example, consider the DL/1 call

```
GU   DOCTOR     (D-NAME = JONES)
     EMPLOYEE (E-NAME = DONALDSON)
     INSUR-CO   (I-NAME = INSURANCEA)
```

aimed at the data base in Figure 7.3. This DL/1 command retrieves the whole INSUR-CO segment occurrence for INSURANCEA whose parent is the EMPLOYEE with E-NAME = DONALDSON and whose root segment is the DOCTOR with D-NAME = JONES. The GU (get unique command) accomplishes a top to bottom, left to right scan from the start of the data base. This is the conceptual logical view, although internally IMS does not necessarily store and access segments in such fashion, as we shall see in Section 7.6. The segment retrieved is the first encountered in the scan satisfying the three SSAs. The SSAs indicate the hierarchical path from the root segment to the segment desired. The preceding GU command causes IMS to search for the first DOCTOR occurrence with D-NAME = JONES, then to search for this DOC-TOR's child EMPLOYEE occurrences for the first whose E-NAME = DONALDSON, and then to search for this EMPLOYEE's child INSUR-CO occurrences for the first whose I-NAME = INSURANCEA. Only the segment occurrence at the bottom of the indicated hierarchy is retrieved.

If it is desired to retrieve into the I/O area the contents of all the segment occurrences in the hierarchical tree from the desired root occurrence to the segment occurrence at the bottom of the tree, then the so-called D ("data") command code may be used as follows:

```
GU   DOCTOR*D    (D-NAME = JONES)
     EMPLOYEE*D (E-NAME = DONALDSON)
     INSUR-CO    (I-NAME = INSURANCEA)
```

A number of other very useful (but syntactically cryptic) command codes are available in the recent IMS/VS versions. More on these codes is covered later.

The complete and actual DL/1 call format is as outlined in Figure 7.9. For the previous example, the DL/1 call coming from a PL/1 application program would be:

```
CALL PL1TDL1   (GU, DOC-PCB-NAME, USER-IO-A,
                'DOCTOR*D    (D-NAME = JONES)',
                'EMPLOYEE*D (E-NAME = DONALDSON)',
                'INSUR-CO    (I-NAME = INSURANCEA)');
```

Note that each SSA is actually a character string parameter of the subroutine call. If DL/1 and the IMS interface to the user were to be redesigned, obviously a much more convenient and less terse data manipulation language could be easily attained (possibly implemented by a translator from the more convenient DML to the present DL/1). As an example, the preceding call could be replaced by the more readable form:

```
FOR PCB = DOC-PCB-NAME, GET UNIQUE COMPLETE
    PATH FOR DOCTOR (D-NAME = JONES), EMPLOYEE
    (E-NAME = DONALDSON), INSUR-CO
    (I-NAME = INSURANCEA); PUT INTO USER-IO-A.
```

We shall avoid an unnecessary burden by not using the complete DL/1 call syntax in the following examples. Instead, only the pertinent function code and SSAs will be indicated. We will use the Doctor data base in Figures 7.2 and 7.3. The examples asterisked on the right are also illustrated for the DBTG and/or

TOTAL and/or SYSTEM 2000 and/or SQL/DS and QBE systems in other chapters.

Direct Retrieval

1. Retrieve all the data fields of employee 106 without concern for the particular DOCTOR parent segment occurrence: *

   ```
   GU   DOCTOR
        EMPLOYEE (EMPNO = 106)
   ```

2. Retrieve the first EMPLOYEE segment occurrence whose AMT-OWED > 600, starting at the beginning of the data base in a top to bottom, left to right conceptual fashion:

   ```
   GU   DOCTOR
        EMPLOYEE (AMT-OWED > 600)
   ```

   Any other EMPLOYEE occurrences meeting the criteria indicated are not scanned.

Sequential Retrieval

3. Retrieve all the CHILD segment occurrences of EMPLOYEE 106:

   ```
           GU   DOCTOR                                          *
                EMPLOYEE (EMPNO = 106)
                CHILD
      L    GN   CHILD
                check the hierarchic concatenated key (HCK) and
                stop when it does not contain the EMPNO value 106
                GO TO L
   ```

   Get unique and get next (and the insert DL/1 command) establish a current position in the data base. GU above retrieves the first CHILD occurrence for EMPLOYEE 106 and establishes the current position; the first execution of GN retrieves the next CHILD occurrence starting from this position; and so on.

4. Retrieve all the segment occurrences in the data base:

   ```
           GU   DOCTOR
      L    GN
                GO TO L
   ```

This retrieval is done in the usual top to bottom, left to right fashion, starting with the first DOCTOR segment occurrence and ending with the last CHILD occurrence of the last DOCTOR root occurrence. The user can find out what segment type has been retrieved after every execution of GN by examining the parameter SEG-NAME. Obviously the procedure can be expensive for large data bases. This would be the way to unload a data base and then perhaps load it by a series of insert commands or load utility.

5. Retrieve all the CHILD occurrences whose CHILD-AGE > 14 for the first EMPLOYEE occurrence whose AMT-OWED ⩾ 600:

         GU   DOCTOR
                 EMPLOYEE (AMT-OWED ⩾ 600)
                 record as EMPNO the EMPLOYEE key appearing
                    in the hierarchic concatenated key (HCK)
  L   GN   CHILD (CHILD-AGE > 14)
                 stop if EMPNO ≠ the EMPLOYEE key appearing in
                    the new HCK, or else continue
                 GO TO L

6. Retrieve all the CHILD occurrences whose CHILD-AGE > 14 for all the EMPLOYEE occurrences (not just the first occurrence as in Example 5) whose AMT-OWED ⩾ 600:

         GU   DOCTOR
                 EMPLOYEE (AMT-OWED ⩾ 600)
                 CHILD   (CHILD-AGE > 14)
  L   GN   EMPLOYEE (AMT-OWED ⩾ 600)
                 CHILD   (CHILD-AGE > 14)
                 GO TO L

Sequential Retrieval Within Parent

The function of "get next within parent," GNP, is the same as that of "get next," except that when all the segments meeting the SSA criteria have been retrieved for the current parent, the next try to execute GNP will produce a termination flag for the user via the STATUS-CODE parameter. The current parent is the last one retrieved by a get unique or get next, but not by a GNP command.

7. Get the name and claim cycle of every INSUR-CO of EMPLOYEE 106 for DOCTOR JONES:

```
   GU    DOCTOR (D-NAME = JONES) ˙
         EMPLOYEE (EMPNO = 106)
L  GNP   INSUR-CO
         extract NAME and CYCLE in I/O Area
         GO TO L
```

Replacement of a Segment

The segment to be replaced or modified must be first retrieved by a "get hold" command, then modified in the I/O area and then replaced. However, the segment sequence field cannot be modified by the replace command REPL.

8. For EMPLOYEE 106 change the ADDRESS of his insurance company INSURANCEA to DISAPPEARED and change the SPE-CIALTY of his DOCTOR JONES to QUACK: *

```
GHU   DOCTOR*D      (D-NAME = JONES)
      EMPLOYEE*D    (EMPNO = 106)
      INSUR-CO      (I-NAME = INSURANCEA)
      change DOCTOR'S SPECIALTY to QUACK in the
         I/O area
      change the INSUR-CO's ADDRESS for
         INSURANCEA to DISAPPEARED in the I/O
         area
      REPL
```

Note that if the D code had been placed only at the second level EMPLOYEE, then the DOCTOR occurrence would not have been retrieved and thus could not have been updated.

Insertion of a Segment

In IMS and in the hierarchic approach in general, no child can exist without a parent. Thus an insert command must specify the hierarchical path to the existing parent; otherwise the segment will be inserted following the current position (as determined by the last get unique, get next, or insert command). IMS will store the new segment in the correct sequence of the key field (if a sequence has been declared in the DBD).

9. Insert a new CHILD occurrence in EMPLOYEE 106's set of children: *

> Build the new segment in the I/O area
> ISRT   DOCTOR
>   EMPLOYEE (EMPNO = 106)
>   CHILD

10. Insert a new DOCTOR YOUNG together with his CLINICs:

> Build the DOCTOR YOUNG segment and the first subordinate CLINIC segment in the I/O area
>
> INSRT   DOCTOR*D
>   CLINIC
> L   Build the next subordinate CLINIC segment in the I/O area
> ISRT   CLINIC
>   GO TO L

The first ISRT command inserts the new DOCTOR root segment (in the correct position to maintain the root key sequence) and its first CLINIC. Without the D command, the root segment would not have been inserted and IMS would stop processing. Note that the second ISRT omits the hierarchic path and thus inserts the next CLINIC following the current position determined by the previous insert.

Deletion of a Segment

The segment to be deleted must first be retrieved by a get hold command, and then the deletion may be accomplished. The deletion at a segment occurrence normally results in the deletion also of all its subordinate segment occurrences. This is the case even if there are subordinate segments defined in the DBD but not sensitive to the PCB in force at the time that the delete command issued. Thus unsuspecting users might delete subordinate segments that they do not "see"! The DBA must exercise special care in this situation, i.e., tight control over who can delete segments.

11. Delete EMPLOYEE 106's EMPLOYEE segment and all its INSUR-CO and CHILD occurrences   *

> GHU   DOCTOR
>   EMPLOYEE (EMPNO = 106)
> DLET

Note the following inconsistency between DL/1 commands: a get unique retrieves only the desired segment occurrence, but none of its subordinates (unless one resorts to an accompanying series of get next commands), whereas a delete command deletes the segment occurrence and its subordinates.

DL/1 SSA Command Codes

IMS Version 2 and more recent versions extend the capability of DL/1 by means of SSA command codes. A *command code* is a one-character indicator placed after the segment name in the SSA. There are at least seven command codes (D, F, C, L, U, V, N, −).[5] We will illustrate the D and F commands.

D Command Code

The following example of the D command code has been previously given.

12. Retrieve into the I/O area the contents of all the segment occurrences in the hierarchic tree from the desired segment occurrence (DOCTOR whose name is JONES) down to the lowest segment occurrence indicated (INSUR-CO whose name is INSURANCEA):

```
GU   DOCTOR*D     (D-NAME = JONES)
     EMPLOYEE*D   (E-NAME = DONALDSON)
     INSUR-CO     (I-NAME = INSURANCEA)
```

D may be specified at any level desired. For example:

13. Retrieve only the EMPLOYEE segment and its indicated child INSUR-CO:

```
GU   DOCTOR       (D-NAME = JONES)
     EMPLOYEE*D   (E-NAME = DONALDSON)
     INSUR-CO     (I-NAME = INSURANCEA)
```

The D command may be used to easily update, insert, or delete a complete hierarchic path. Updating of segments along a path was illustrated in Example 8.

F Command Code

An example follows illustrating the utility of the command code F when users want to navigate through the data base somewhat counter to the top to bottom, left to right mode inherent in the IMS hierarchic world.

14. Get the name of an INSUR-CO of the first EMPLOYEE in the data base who has a CHILD with CHILD-AGE > 10:

> GU   DOCTOR
> L   GN   EMPLOYEE
> GNP   CHILD (CHILD-AGE > 10)
> If such CHILD is not found go to L
> GNP   INSUR-CO*F
> Extract the name of the INSUR-CO segment in the I/O
>   area and print it.

The get unique call stations us at the start of the data base. The get next identifies an EMPLOYEE as the current parent. The get next within parent looks for the desired CHILD. If no CHILD for the current parent has age > 10, then searching continues for a new EMPLOYEE parent until one is found with a CHILD whose age > 10. This EMPLOYEE becomes then the current parent. The get next within parent with the F command allows us to go backward or counter to the normal hierarchic scan. That is, IMS will start from the first occurrence of INSUR-CO under the current EMPLOYEE parent occurrence. Thus the result of this example is the output INSURANCEA.

Note that if GNP did not have the F command, the result would be a STATUS-CODE of "segment not found" because the search is forward and INSUR-CO occurrences (under the common parent) precede CHILD occurrences in the hierarchic sequence. If GNP INSUR-CO*F were to be replaced by a get next, then IMS would retrieve the first INSUR-CO occurrence of the subsequence occurrence (who does not necessarily have any CHILD occurrence whose age > 10!).

Searching on Relationships Between Segments at the Same Level and on Different Hierarchic Paths

Let us now use an example to illustrate the difficulties encountered in the hierarchic data base approach when data manipulation is required based on relationships between segments at the same level and on different hierarchic paths.

15. Get all the CHILD segment occurrences of every EMPLOYEE
    insured by INSURANCEA: *

	GU	DOCTOR
		EMPLOYEE*D
		INSUR-CO (I-NAME = INSURANCEA)
REP		Extract EMPNO from the EMPLOYEE in the I/O area
		Use it to build an SSA, assign it to VARIABLE
	GU	DOCTOR
		EMPLOYEE (EMPNO = VARIABLE)
NEC	GNP	CHILD
		If not found go to NOC
		Print the CHILD segment occurrence just retrieved
		GO TO NEC
NOC	GN	DOCTOR
		EMPLOYEE*D
		INSUR-CO (I-NAME = INSURANCEA)
		If not found then stop the search
		GO TO REP

For this type of request the hierarchy defined in Figure 7.2 is awkward. If the hierarchy were instead as shown in Figure 7.10, then the
requested information could be perhaps more easily obtained as
follows:

	GU	DOCTOR
		INSUR-CO (I-NAME = INSURANCEA)
		EMPLOYEE
NEC	GNP	CHILD
		Print the CHILD segment occurrence retrieved
		GO TO NEC
NIC	GNP	EMPLOYEE
		If not found go to NOC
		GO TO NEC
NOC	GN	DOCTOR
		INSUR-CO (I-NAME = INSURANCEA)
		EMPLOYEE
		If not found then stop the search
		GO TO NEC

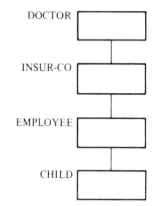

Figure 7.10. *Alternative Doctor IMS data base schema*

We have just illustrated the large changes that may be required on an IMS DBD to accommodate answering easily queries of the type addressed. To transform the data base from the PCB hierarchy of Figure 7.2 to that of Figure 7.10, the data base designer must modify the underlying DBD and reload the data base. This means that other application programs with the view of Figure 7.2 will have to be modified, thus violating data independence, or else resort to logical data base linking mechanisms addressed in Section 7.5. Recall that in the IMS hierarchic approach the only subschemas that may be derived from a physical DBD are any of the subtrees starting from the roots. The data base administrator has the data base design task of providing the best DBD logical view for the range of expected transactions.

DBTG and rational GDBMS do not pose the problem that we have encountered here in IMS. An additional DBTG set would be easily defined in Figure 7.2 in which INSUR-CO is the owner record type and CHILD is the member record type. If the set did not exist initially in the schema, the new schema including it would have to be declared and the data base reloaded. However, all other application programs would still be able to use the same subschemas as before, thus preserving data independence.

Current Position Indicators: IMS Versus DBTG

In the DBTG model the following currency indicators are set after executing every DML command so as to keep track of the navigation through the data base: the current of each record type, set type and area, plus the "current of run unit" which refers to or identifies the record most recently accessed (via a data base key value) no matter what record type it is or what set type or area it participates in.

The parent segment-child segment relationship is equivalent to the DBTG set. On this basis, IMS does not have an equivalent to the current of each record type, of each set type, or of each area. But it does have an equivalent to the current of run unit: the hierarchic concatenated key or concatenation of the key fields of all the parent segments in the tree from the root segment occurrence to the particular segment just accessed via DL/1.

The SEG-LEVEL and SEG-NAME parameters, set by IMS after executing every DL/1 call, are also a type of currency indicator. SEG-LEVEL contains the level number of the segment just accessed (where the root segment is level 1, its children level 2, etc.). SEG-NAME contains the name of the segment last accessed.

7.5   THE LOGICAL DATA BASE OR SCHEMA

7.5.1   Objectives of Logical Data Bases

In IMS a *Logical Data Base*, LDB, is composed of segments from one or more "physical" data bases, PDBs. We discussed physical data bases and their DBD description in Section 7.2. An LDB is described by its logical data base description. Each LDB record occurrence may be made up of segments from distinct occurrences of physical data base records (from one or several PDBs). An LDB is materialized by its underlying PDBs, each with its corresponding DBD. However, an LDB always appears to the DL/1 user as if it were just a single hierarchic PDB with its own DBD. This is the case for retrieval (Get) operations; but for update, insert, and delete type of operations the DL/1 user must be concerned with the underlying PDBs and the particular interconnections that provide the logical data base view.

Any number of consistent subschemas may be derived from each logical data base via the PCB mechanisms, just as if it were a PDB.

The IMS storage organization and access methods that we shall introduce in Section 7.6 apply to each individual PDB. We shall describe here how segments from different PDBs may be related or connected to give the added capability of logical data bases. Such interconnections are in addition to all storage mapping, organization, and linking mechanisms underlying each PDB.

Before delving into details, let us stress that the main reasons for using IMS logical data bases are:

1. To link or establish relationships between one physical data base and others, or within one physical data base in addition to the normal hierarchic relationships in the PDB.

2. To reduce redundancy in the data actually stored internally while at the same time providing apparent redundancy at the logical level for

the convenience of the logical data base DL/1 user; a segment will be stored only once but may participate in several logical data bases.

3. To provide a means for users to view the data in a variety of hierarchic ways in addition to the hierarchic view associated with each underlying physical data base; to permit handling network type of data bases.

The LDB mechanism is a step toward permitting the representation of fairly limited network data bases. As we shall see, it entails establishing so-called logical hierarchic relationships between different segments from one or more PDBs. However, the LDB view and all DL/1 calls are still inherently hierarchic in nature and not network (e.g., DBTG) oriented. In the following sections we shall illustrate how LDBs are established by means of logical relationships between segments to meet the objectives just listed.

In practical situations it may be necessary for some application systems to process two data bases separately, but for other application systems to access one data base from the other. Instead of having to integrate the two data bases into one huge data base and perhaps incur a number of internal data redundancies, as we shall illustrate, we integrate them into one logical data base while retaining the underlying PDBs. Seen in another way, a logical data base permits users to see data with a logical view and logical data redundancy conveniently, while internally actually avoiding such redundancy. By allowing a segment to exist only once, yet participate in a number of logical data bases, IMS allows the DBA to eliminate redundant data and facilitate processing.

7.5.2   General Approach to Forming Logical Data Bases

The basic approach to forming an IMS logical data base is to establish a relationship or link between any point in a physical data base hierarchy and a so-called **target segment** of another or perhaps the same physical data base. The target segment is commonly called the **logical parent segment**. This relationship or link is provided by establishing a link field as a new data field created for this purpose as:

1. Part of an existing segment in the PDB hierarchy, be it the root segment or any of its subordinate segments (although in most applications it is a subordinate segment).

2. Part of a new segment created as a subordinate in the PDB hierarchy and for the express purpose of containing the link field. Additional fields that collectively are referred to as **intersection data** may be included in this new segment. The intersection data is unique to the relationship between a pointer segment occurrence and a target segment occurrence.

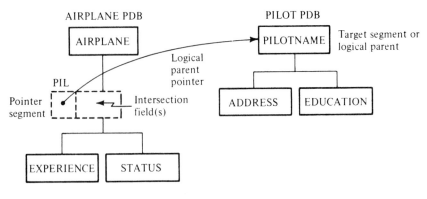

IMS Terminology:

Logical parent pointer goes from the pointer segment to the target segment

Logical child pointer goes from the target segment to the pointer segment

Logical parent segment is the target segment pointed at (inconsistent with e g , DBTG terminology)

Logical child segment is the pointer segment (inconsistent with e.g.. DBTG terminology)

Figure 7.11.   *Relating IMS physical data bases into one logical data base*

The segment with the link field becomes the so-called **pointer segment**.

Figure 7.11 outlines the general method of relating several physical data bases into one logical data base. Only segment names are shown for simplicity. Figure 7.12 indicates the appearance of this LDB to the DL/1 user; the LDB appears as if it were a single PDB with its own DBD (except for nonread operations which force the linked view of Figure 7.11 on the DL/1 user). In Figure 7.11 the PILOTNAME segment in the airplane inventory data base has been replaced by a pointer segment which directly addresses the PILOT-NAME segment. The PILOTNAME segment is the target or logical parent segment of the pointer segment PIL. Note the place of the optional intersection fields in Figure 7.11. They could be, for example, either the DATE on which this pilot last flew this airplane or the FLYING-HOURS of this pilot on this airplane.

A similar approach is used to define logical data bases within a single physical data base. We will illustrate this later.

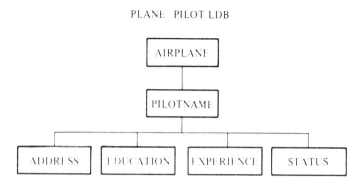

Figure 7.12. *The logical data base view of Figure 7.11 to the DL/1 user*

7.5.3   IMS Logical and Physical Relationship Terminology

The IMS terminology of logical and physical relationships commonly used deserves special consideration and clarification. It is a terminology not consistent with non-IMS GDBMS.

All relationships between segment types in a given physical data base defined via a DBD are referred to as physical relationships. A **logical relationship** in IMS is that established between two segment types by linking a segment in one PDB with the target segment in another PDB, or perhaps with the root segment or another segment of the same PDB. A logical data base thus may contain segments from different physical data bases, or from the same PDB not in the same PDB hierarchic order.

Let us review the terminology by means of the example in Figure 7.11. The PIL pointer segment is the physical child of AIRPLANE and is also the **logical child** of PILOTNAME. PILOTNAME is the logical parent of the PIL pointer segment. Note that in IMS the target segment or segment pointed at is considered the **logical parent**, not the child or member as is the case in most other GDBMS, e.g., DBTG. This is very important to remember in order to avoid confusion.

A major aim of logical data bases is to allow a segment occurrence to be physically stored only once, yet participate in several logical data base record occurrences, that is, attain a high degree of data shareability and nonredundancy of data. Thus a pilot may actually fly several airplanes at different times but his descriptive PILOT PDB segment will be stored only once. In a manner analogous to physical twins, all occurrences of a logical child with a common logical parent occurrence (stored only once) are called **logical twins**.

The so-called **connection segment** of the LDB that results from the pointer segment mechanism, e.g., PILOTNAME in Figure 7.12, is made up of the concatenation of:

1. The hierarchic concatenated key of the logical parent;
2. The intersection data fields; and
3. The logical parent, including the sequence field value of the logical parent.

This is in general the view to the DL/1 user. Alternatively, the DL/1 user may see, retrieve, and modify either the intersection data only (which must be always accompanied by the hierarchic concatenated key which serves as the pointer to the corresponding logical parent) or the logical parent only. Note that the pointer segment established at the PDB level is what materializes the connection segment at the LDB level.

Example

Let us now illustrate in more detail the IMS physical and logical relationships and redundancy considerations. Suppose that it is desired to have access to the information of therapists and clinics or rehabilitation centers as shown in Figure 7.13. The THERAPIST record consists of the therapist full name (assume this is the unique identifier), his specialty, and years of experience. The CLINPAT record shows in this order: the name of the clinic or rehabilitation center in which the therapist provides the treatment; the date of the treatment; the name of the patient and the type of treatment administered; the clinic's address; informative description, and so on. Other subordinate segments of THERAPIST may be included but are of no further relevance.

Notice that if a PDB were set up for this information, there would be much clinic data redundantly stored. Typically, several patients will be treated by a therapist at the same clinic (in fact in many cases a therapist

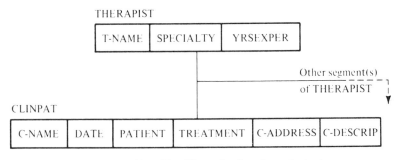

Figure 7.13.   *The Therapist data base desired*

will provide his services at only one clinic). Also, a number of therapists will share the same clinic. However, all the clinic information (C-NAME, C-ADDRESS, C-DESCRIP, etc.) would be actually stored for each patient treated instead of only once. The example in Figure 7.14 illustrates this (only the main sequence fields are shown). This inefficiency is very significant in terms of dollar cost of storage. It may be avoided by means of a logical data base as follows, while still providing the desired logical view of Figure 7.13 and apparent redundancy shown in Figure 7.14.

We will establish two physical data bases:

1. The CLINIC PDB in Figure 7.15.

2. The THERAPIST PDB with a link to the CLINIC PDB as shown in Figure 7.16. Figure 7.16 shows that the CLINPAT segment contains a pointer to the corresponding root segment in the CLINIC PDB. Now

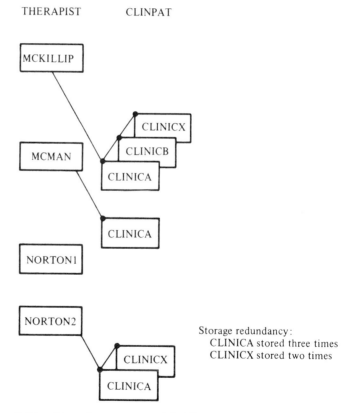

Figure 7.14.   *Record occurrences of the Therapist data base and storage redundancy*

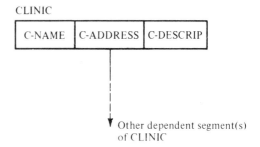

Figure 7.15.   *The Clinic data base*

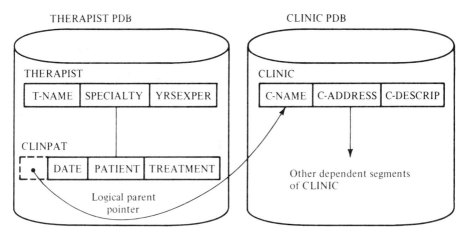

Note: Each PDB may be on the same or different direct access storage devices.

Figure 7.16.   *The linked Therapist and Clinic PDB's materializing the THERCLIN logical data base in Figure 7.18*

the actual, internally stored data is as shown in Figure 7.17, rather than as shown in Figure 7.14. However, from the DL/1 user's point of view he or she will see the data base as the LDB in Figure 7.18 with all the apparent (but not real) redundancy of Figure 7.14 that simplifies the task and avoids pointer and physical storage considerations. Note that the LDB in Figure 7.18 is the same as the data base desired shown in Figure 7.13 except for the repetition of the logical parent sequence key C_NAME; this redundancy will be real unless C_NAME is established as a virtual field (an option in IMS) in the THERAPIST DBD.

It is important to realize that DL/1 insert, delete, and update operations must be concerned with the physical connectivity of the underlying PDBs (see Section 7.5.7).

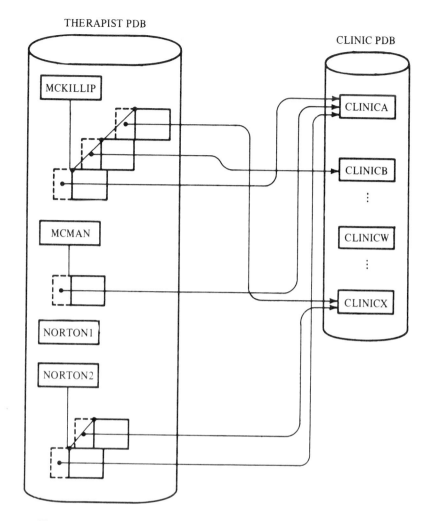

Note: Each PDB may be on the same or different direct access storage devices.

Figure 7.17. *Record occurrences of the linked Therapist and Clinic PDBs*

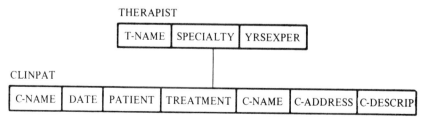

Figure 7.18. *The THERCLIN logical data base materialized by the linked physical data bases in Figure 7.16*

7.5.4   Physical and Logical Data Base Descriptions and Loading

Each LDB is defined via a logical data base declaration, logical DBD. An LDB is defined in terms of one or more physical data bases. However, the physical DBDs must indicate that they are involved in each LDB. The DBA is unfortunately forced to know what PDBs are involved and how they are to be connected to form an LDB when writing the DBDs. In the previous example, the DBA must have been aware that the THERAPIST and CLINIC PDBs were to later participate exactly as shown in Figure 7.16 to form the THER-CLIN LDB in Figure 7.18. If not, the DBA had to unload the established PDBs, change the DBDs, declare the logical DBD, and go through a complete reloading process. Complete reloading is an expensive process, but that is what has to be done in practice. The usefulness of logical data bases is thus impaired if the DBA does not foresee the requirements. Future IMS implementations will probably improve this situation.

Let us use our example in Figure 7.16 and 7.18 to illustrate the rather intricate IMS forms for defining linked PDBs and LDBs. Figures 7.19 and 7.20 show the skeletal DBDs for the THERAPIST and CLINIC PDBs in Figure 7.16. Figure 7.21 shows the logical DBD for the THERCLIN LDB. We will explain each figure. Readers should realize that the syntactic forms and means for defining PDBs and LDBs are intricate and tedious. Many practitioners indicate emphatically that they are unnecessarily intricate. Readers are thus urged to examine closely Figures 7.19−7.21 (which omit some more details of an actual case!) in order to understand the IMS definitional syntax. We will

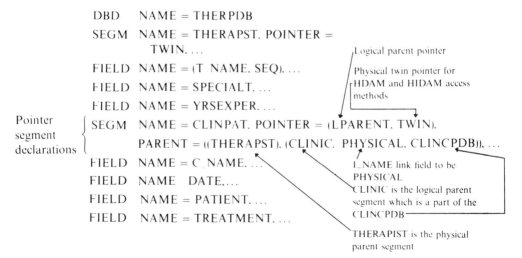

Figure 7.19.   *Physical DBD for the Therapist PDB (skeleton)*

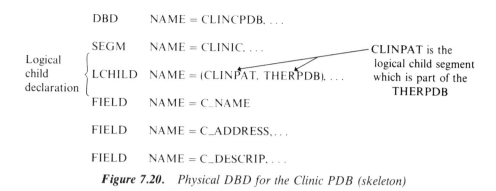

Figure 7.20. *Physical DBD for the Clinic PDB (skeleton)*

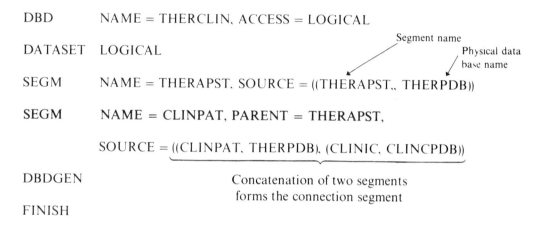

Figure 7.21. *Logical DBD for the THERCLIN LDB*

outline the following aspects that are not self-evident. We will shorten some names to conform to the eight-character IMS limit.

The declaration in Figure 7.19 for the pointer segment CLINPAT specifies that its prefix is to include a logical parent pointer (LPARENT) to the CLINIC segment which resides in the CLINCPDB PDB. Now let us account for some physical pointer concerns. LPARENT specifies a direct and fast pointer which can be used only if the logical parent is in an HDAM or HIDAM access organization (these access methods are presented in Section 7.6). If it is in a HISAM organization, then the pointer must be the logical parent hierarchic concatenated key (the concatenation of the key fields of the root of the logical parent and of its subordinates up to and including the logical parent); although this is a slower manner to access the logical parent, its advantage is that it allows the PDB containing the logical parent to be reorganized without affecting the logical child's PDB (THERPDB).

The inclusion of TWIN in the POINTER specification in Figure 7.19 calls for the use of physical twin pointers (as opposed to hierarchic pointers) to maintain the top to bottom, left to right DL/1 view. Physical twins and hierarchic options apply only to HDAM and HIDAM and are addressed in Section 7.6.

As illustrated in Figure 7.21, the logical DBD specifies the segments involved and how they are involved to produce the logical view of Figure 7.18. Segment names may be changed in the logical DBD. The second segment entry states that CLINPAT is a subordinate of THERAPST and is composed of the concatenation of the CLINPAT segment in the THERPDB PDB and the CLINIC segment in the CLINCPDB PDB (plus the implicit pointer field C_NAME).

Loading the Logical Data Base

The loading of an IMS logical data base involves two steps:

1. Loading each individual physical data base separately, most often through a specialized loading utility.
2. Creating the logical pointers and all necessary links to materialize the logical data base; this is done via IMS utility programs.

The loading process is rather elaborate. The creation of the many logical pointers that may exist in a logical data base is intricate and may be very costly (as a number of IMS users testify).

7.5.5   Logical Data Bases in One Physical Data Base

A number of logical data bases can be defined over a single physical data base for the purpose of: (1) reducing redundancy in the data actually stored and/or (2) allowing a DL/1 user to view the data base in hierarchic ways other than the one inherent in the physical data base. These two objectives are intertwined in IMS.

Recall that the segment occurrences making up an LDB occurrence are actually distinct occurrences of segments which may be part of one or more different PDBs; said in other words, an LDB occurrence is made up from several distinct physical data base occurrences and these in turn may belong to one or more PDBs. Let us illustrate this for a single PDB by means of two examples. We shall no longer delve into the IMS DBD programming mechanisms to set up the PDBs and LDBs. Sufficient flavor is given in Figures 7.19−7.21.

Example

Consider the bill of materials, <u>BOM</u>, data base in Figure 7.22. This data base indicates for each parent part (PART) its component part(s) (COMPONENT) . . . Visualize several PDB record occurrences. Notice the possible redundancy since a parent segment PART contains the fields PART # and NAME also appearing in its child segment COMPONENT. Figure 7.23 shows how a pointer segment SUB‑MAN including a logical pointer to PART can materialize the logical data base view shown in Figure 7.24, while avoiding the redundancy. No intersection data (such as the quantity of the subpart making up the parent part) are shown.

Note that the segment SUB‑MAN is actually *both* the physical child and the logical child of one segment, PART; or seen in a different way, PART is both the logical parent and the physical parent of SUB‑MAN. This should not be too confusing if readers realize that the IMS understanding is that no SUB‑MAN occurrence or COMPONENT occurrence can have the same PART occurrence as both logical and physical parent.

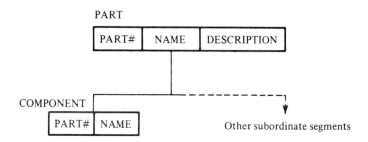

Figure 7.22.   *Bill of materials data base*

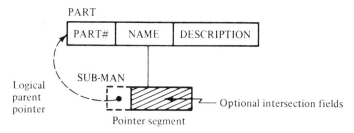

Figure 7.23.   *The BOMPDB physical data base with pointer segment materializing the BOMLDB logical data base in Figure 7.24*

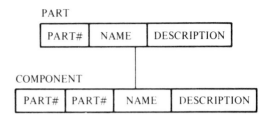

Figure 7.24. *The BOMBLDB logical data base materialized by the physical data base in Figure 7.23*

7.5.6   Network-Oriented Data Base Relationships

Relationships Between Segments Not in the Hierarchic Path. Let us illustrate how IMS permits users to link segments and establish logical relationships between segments not in the hierarchic path; that is, relationships that make the data base a network data base. Consider our ubiquitous Doctor data base in Figure 7.2. Suppose that we would like to be able to support for a class of users the logical view shown in Figure 7.25. We omit individual fields from here on and use segment names only. That is, we desire to find easily all the CLINIC segment occurrences in which a given EMPLOYEE has been treated by a given DOCTOR. This would be comparatively difficult to obtain using the data base in Figure 7.2. The desired view cannot be materialized by PCB subschema capabilities. However, it can be materialized by establishing the CLINIC segment as the logical parent of the pointer segment as shown in Figure 7.26. No intersection data fields are included in the example.

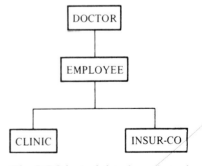

Figure 7.25. *The DEC logical data base desired*

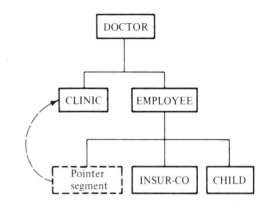

Figure 7.26. *The Doctor physical data base with pointer segment materializing the DEC logical data base (a subschema) in Figure 7.25*

Bidirectional Logical Relationships. Bidirectional relationshps can be established between segments (in the same PDB or in different PDBs). For example, Figure 7.27 shows how a pointer segment CE under CLINIC (establishing EMPLOYEE as the logical parent of CE) and a pointer segment EC under EMPLOYEE (establishing CLINIC as the logical parent of EC) permit deriving the two logical data base views shown. These two data base views cannot be defined via PCB subschema facilities using a PDB without the pointer segments indicated.

Representation of M to N Relationships Between Segments. An M to N relationship between two segments (be it on the same PDB or in different PDBs) can be easily represented in IMS by defining two bidirectional pointer segments, as in the previous example. Let us do this for the Professor-student data base of Figure 5.11. A professor teaches many students and a student is taught by several professors. This is the meaning of an M to N relationship. The goal is to be able to find all the STUDENT occurrences of a particular PROFESSOR as well as all the PROFESSOR occurrences of a particular STUDENT. The DBTG representation of M to N relationships is also shown for this data base, Figures 5.11 and 5.12.

Figure 7.28 shows the IMS representation of the Professor-student M to N relationship via two logical pointer segments, TEACHES and TAUGHTBY. TEACHES is declared as the physical child of PROFESSOR and the logical child of STUDENT. Conversely, TAUGHTBY is declared as the physical child of STUDENT and the logical child of PROFESSOR. This materializes the two indicated hierarchic logical data bases and the underlying physical storage-saving structure of the sample occurrences of the data base.

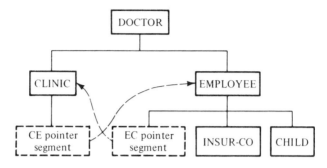

LDB materialized by the CE pointer segment   LDB materialized by the EC pointer segment

Figure 7.27. *The Doctor physical data base with bidirectional pointer segments materializing the logical data bases shown*

Intersection data could be included as part of the relationship between a particular PROFESSOR occurrence and a STUDENT occurrence; for example, the course in which the particular professor taught the student. This now raises the issue of whether or not this intersection data is stored twice, once in the TEACHES pointer segment and once in the TAUGHTBY pointer segment. IMS gives the DBA the option of physically storing it twice (in which case the two segments are said in IMS to be physically PAIRED) or of avoiding it by declaring one pointer segment to be a virtual of the other (in which case the two segments are said in IMS to be virtually PAIRED). The decision here for the DBA is one between achieving storage savings or achieving faster response. Access time is slower for DL/1 requests for intersection data via the physical parent whose physical child is the pointer segment declared virtual; additional pointers must then be followed to reach the real physical location of the intersection data. A number of IMS data base cases report that performance effects of pointer-following mechanisms heavily tax access time performance.

As far as the DL/1 user is concerned, virtual pairing looks exactly like physical pairing. Application programs are unaffected by the choice, except for performance effects.

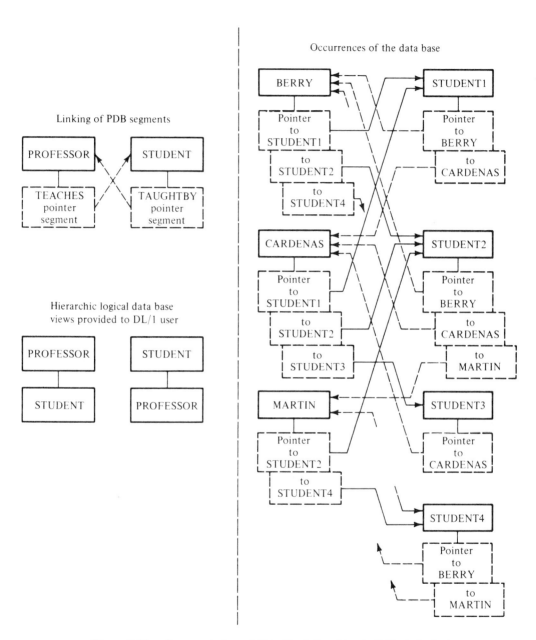

Figure 7.28. *Representation of M to N relationships in IMS via logical relationships*

Further Examples. Figure 7.29 shows six logical data bases that may be derived from the three physical data bases indicated using IMS logical pointer mechanisms. Only segment names are shown. Segments marked L are materialized in the LDB as shown via logical pointer segments. Readers should convince themselves that this can be done. A physical child and a physical parent of a logical parent can act as a subordinate of the concatenated pointer segment-logical parent segment in the LDB.

THREE PHYSICAL DATA BASES:

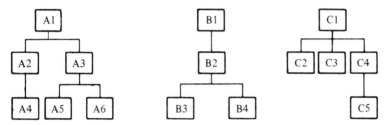

SAMPLE LOGICAL DATA BASES THAT MAY BE DERIVED:

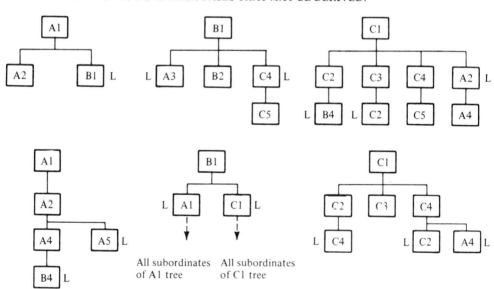

Note: Segments marked L are materialized in the logical data bases as shown via logical pointer segments.

Figure 7.29. *Examples of logical data bases that may be derived from physical data bases*

On Network Data Base Representation in IMS. The previous examples have shown that through pointer segment mechanisms relationships characteristic of network data bases can be established in IMS. At the physical data base level any network can be established since any segment (as logical parent segment) may be pointed at by any number of logical parent pointers and hence may participate in any number of logical data base record occurrences. However, some facts must be realized. First, the DBTG network mechanism, the set, is a more direct and general way to establish a network data base than the IMS pointer segment mechanism. Second, and more importantly, IMS has a limited network capability since the LDB view materialized and seen by the DL/1 user is still inherently hierarchic in nature. DL/1 calls will still operate only with a hierarchic view. The root of the LDB must be a root of a PDB. For DL/1 read-only (Get) operations only a hierarchic view is seen. However, for update, insert, and delete operations the DL/1 user must be concerned with the real underlying network, that is, the underlying hierarchic PDB(s) and the particular logical pointer relationships that provide the LDB view. More on this appears in the following section.

7.5.7   DL/1 Access to Logical Data Bases

An LDB behaves just like a PDB for DL/1 retrieval operations. However, for replace (REPL), delete (DLET), and insert (ISRT) operations the behavior of a logical parent, logical child, or physical parent of a segment that also has a logical parent depends on the IMS option declared by the DBA for that segment and that operation. The underlying PDB(s) and pointer relationships are not transparent for nonread operations; questions analogous to DBTG set membership therefore (Section 5.3) arise. Each such segment must have a specification of the replace, delete, or insert option in the SEGM statement in the corresponding PDB and LDB. Each of these options may have three further options: physical, virtual, or logical. The options specified apply to all nonread DL/1 operations on the segment, be it through the individual PDB view or through the LDB view.

The implications of these options in complicated logical data bases are complex and we will not delve into these matters. To attain a flavor, let us consider the THERCLIN LDB in Figure 7.18 and its two underlying PDBs in Figure 7.16.

Replace DL/1Commands. Updating or replacement of only a THERA-PIST root segment in the THERAPIST PDB takes place without affecting any other segments. Replacement of the intersection field values (DATE, PATIENT, and TREATMENT) also takes place without affecting other segments. However updating of the logical parent fields (CADDRESS and

CDESCRIP) in a CLINPAT segment (a logical child of CLINIC) is allowed only if the replace option of CLINIC is virtual; what happens is that the CLINIC segment is replaced, as well as the logical parent fields in all other CLINPAT occurrences having this same logical parent CLINIC occurrence.

Delete DL/1 Commands. Deletion of a THERAPIST occurrence removes this occurrence and all of its subordinate CLINPAT occurrences from the THERAPIST PDB. Deletion of a CLINPAT occurrence due to either direct deletion or to deletion of its physical parent THERAPIST takes place without affecting other segments. However, if this is the last CLINPAT occurrence for the CLINIC involved and CLINIC has a virtual delete option, this CLINIC occurrence will be also deleted from the CLINIC PDB.

Deletion of a CLINIC occurrence directly from the CLINIC PDB involves two aspects:

1. The physical option allows deleting a CLINIC occurrence only if there is no CLINPAT occurrence that has it as a logical parent.
2. The virtual and logical options allow deleting a CLINIC occurrence from the CLINIC PDB, but not from the THERCLIN LDB if there is at least one CLINPAT occurrence that has it as its logical parent. The moment that the last such CLINPAT occurrence is deleted, that logical parent CLINIC occurrence is deleted completely.

Insert DL/1 Commands. Insertion of a THERAPIST occurrence takes place without concern for other segments. Insertion of a CLINPAT occurrence involves these possibilities:

1. If the CLINIC occurrence to which the CLINPAT occurrence refers already exists in the CLINIC PDB, the CLINPAT occurrence is inserted in the THERAPIST PDB. Furthermore, if the insert option of CLINIC is virtual, the new CADDRESS and CDESCRIP field values from the CLINPAT occurrences (as seen by the LDB view) actually update these values in the corresponding CLINIC occurrence.
2. If the CLINIC occurrence to which the CLINPAT occurrence refers does not exist in the CLINIC PDB then there are two options:
    (a) If the insertion option of CLINIC is physical, the insertion is not allowed; or
    (b) If the insertion option of CLINIC is virtual or logical, then the insertion into the THERAPIST PDB takes place and in addition the CLINIC occurrence is actually inserted into the CLINIC PDB. Recall that insertion of a CLINPAT occurrence via the THERCLIN LDB that the DL/1 ISRT command sees includes all

the fields making up the corresponding CLINIC occurrence in the CLINIC PDB.

7.6   IMS ACCESS METHODS

7.6.1   Introduction

No presentation of IMS is complete without an introduction to its four alternative physical data organizations and corresponding access methods. The term access method is used to refer to the routines and guidelines internal to the GDBMS which store, access, and manage the data base in the particular physical data organization. Physical data organizations at the access method level are relatively transparent to schema and subschema user levels. See Figure 7.30.

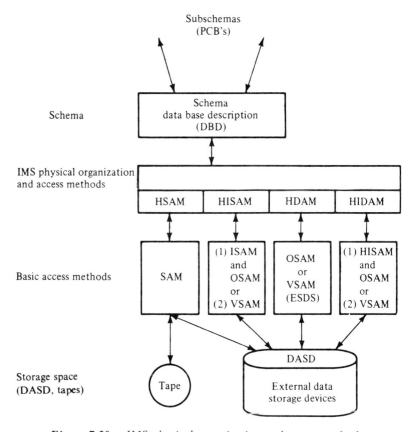

Figure 7.30.   *IMS physical organization and access methods*

The reason for the four alternatives to storing and processing IMS data bases is to help achieve better access time and storage performance. Physical data base designers have at their disposal four alternative physical organizations for the IMS physical data base. Each IMS access method has its own features, parameters (e.g., blockings, size of overflow areas), advantages, and disadvantages. The characteristics of the contents of each particular data base (e.g., number of hierarchic levels, length of segments, number of segment occurrences) and of the transaction load requirements (e.g., frequency of accesses versus updates and inserts, relative access frequency of segment types) must be examined to find the best or at least a "good" access method and setting of parameters. This is one of the main functions of data base administrator-designers. It is a challenging task as the amount of data integrated into a data base and as the number of application programs and users sharing the data base grow. Each application competes for resources and best performance. The reality is that only an overall good or optimum can be achieved, at a possible sacrifice of performance for a minority of applications.

No GDBMS provides a black box capable of examining the data base(s) and its application requirements and automatically choosing or maintaining the best physical data organization and access paths. This is a challenging goal for both researchers and developers, particularly when there is a wide range of alternatives and associated performance "knobs," as in IMS. In current practice, the choice of IMS alternatives and setting of performance "knobs" is done manually, on a trial-and-error basis and using many guesstimates. IMS has more performance knobs than any other GDBMS.

A dominant feature of IMS is that the applications programmer always views the data base as hierarchic, regardless of the access method employed or physical location of the data. Thus the four access methods and associated storage structures are all "hierarchic":

1. Hierarchic Sequential Access Method, HSAM.
2. Hierarchic Indexed Sequential Access Method, HISAM.
3. Hierarchic Indexed Direct Access Method, HIDAM.
4. Hierarchic Direct Access Method, IIDAM.

These access methods in turn use the following *basic* access methods:

1. OS/360/370 Sequential Access Method, SAM.
2. OS/360/370 Indexed Sequential Access Method, ISAM.
3. IBM Virtual Storage Access Method, VSAM.
4. IMS special Overflow Sequential Access Method, OSAM.

Figure 7.30 shows the relationships involved. Note that HISAM uses either ISAM and OSAM or VSAM, while HIDAM uses either HISAM and OSAM or VSAM. We will take an introductory look at HSAM, HISAM, HIDAM, and HDAM in this order. An introductory knowledge of IMS access methods requires an introductory knowledge of ISAM. A detailed understanding of IMS access methods requires an understanding of ISAM or VSAM to some level of detail. Since ISAM and VSAM appear the same externally (both are indexed sequential mechanisms), except that VSAM internally attempts to provide better access time and storage performance for insertions and deletions, we will refer to the traditional ISAM in most of the subsequent involvement of the indexed sequential method. The four hierarchic IMS access methods and storage structures are detailed in Reference 7.

Each "physical" data base described logically by the DBD is stored in any of the four storage structures. The choice of the storage structure is indicated in the DBD by means of the ACCESS clause. Each segment occurrence is stored

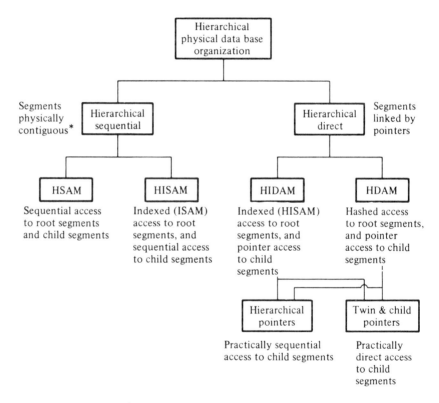

*Always true for HSAM; true for HISAM after initial loading.

Figure 7.31. *Overview of the IMS data organization and access methods*

internally preceded by a *prefix* containing control information, including deletion flags, pointers, etc. This prefix may include or be in addition to the control
information at the storage device level, e.g., Figures A.6(a) and A.6(b). The
user does not see this overhead information. The prefix takes up a significant
number of bytes and is thus a noticeable expense. A data base broken up into a
large number of segment types each with a few fields will incur a larger prefix
overhead than when organized into fewer segment types each with a larger
number of fields. The prefix is essentially the same for all the IMS storage
organizations.

It should be stressed that all pointer and linking mechanisms that we shall

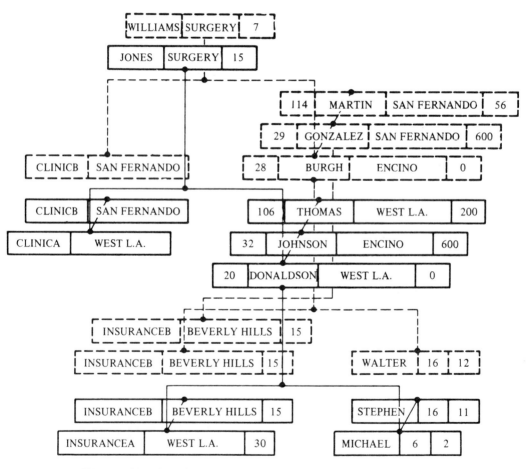

Figure 7.32. *Sample data base contents of the IMS Doctor data base in
Figure 7.2*

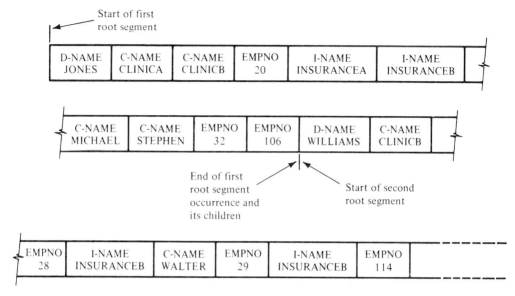

Figure 7.33. *Sample HSAM structure for the Doctor data base in Figure 7.32*

outline herein for each access method are in addition to all other logical link mechanisms described in the previous section to form logical data bases.

The hierarchic top to bottom, left to right approach and the use of DL/1 is essentially unaffected by the choice of access method. This is not entirely true for all situations (HDAM is a case that we shall illustrate); thus data independence may not be complete. The four physical organizations differ in the manner in which the data base contents are organized, linked, processed, and laid in physical storage. Figure 7.31 summarizes the nature of the four access methods; we shall illustrate each of these in the following sections.

For illustration purposes we shall use the Doctor data base described in Figure 7.2 and its sample contents in Figure 7.32. Figure 7.32 is a slightly expanded repeat of Figure 7.3 used in past IMS discussions.

7.6.2   HSAM

HSAM is strictly a physical sequential access method. An HSAM data base can be stored on tape or direct access storage devices. The top to bottom, left to right hierarchic sequence is maintained by physical contiguity. Figure 7.33 shows the HSAM physical organization for the sample data base in Figure

7.32. Here the hierarchic logical order seen by the user coincides with the physical order maintained at the storage level.

HSAM provides the traditional and ubiquitous sequential file processing. Once created, an HSAM data base can be accessed only sequentially as an input file via get DL/1 commands, i.e., only by get unique, get next, and get next within parent commands. As in traditional tape files, delete and insert commands cannot be performed unless the whole file is processed and recreated. An HSAM data base is loaded by means of a series of insert commands using as input the hierarchically sequenced segment occurrences of the data base.

An HSAM data base is stored into a series of fixed-length physical records or buckets. Each physical record may contain one or more segment occurrences. A segment occurrence must fit within this physical record. A stored segment occurrence cannot span across several physical records in HSAM or in any of the other IMS organizations. Thus a design consideration by the DBA is the choice of this fixed-length record, as well as the blocking of these fixed-length physical records into larger physical blocks. It should be stressed that a major performance parameter of all the IMS access methods is the size of the various blockings involved. The determination of the optimum blocking factors for the IMS access methods is indeed a more complex task than for individual basic access methods.

7.6.3   HISAM

As briefly indicated in Figure 7.31, HISAM provides indexed access to root segments, via the root sequence field, and sequential access to all dependent segments. The hierarchic segment relationships are maintained by physically recording the segments sequentially in a top-down, left-right manner. HISAM data bases are created from a hierarchic sequential source, e.g., an HSAM source. Access to new root segments inserted after loading is not as direct as to initially loaded roots, as we shall illustrate. Access to the mth subordinate segment of a given root involves scanning all the $(m - 1)$ subordinates that precede it.

HISAM provides two separate storage areas or data sets, either an ISAM area and an OSAM area, or a VSAM area composed of its KSDS and ESDS data set pair, each made up of a series of fixed-length physical records:

1. Main or prime ISAM area, or prime VSAM area, containing each root segment occurrence initially loaded and as many of each root's subordinate segments as can fit into the fixed-length physical record.

2. Overflow OSAM area, containing all subordinate segments that do not fit in the main area as well as all new root occurrences inserted subsequent to initial loading. For VSAM, the ESDS area replaces the OSAM area and contains all such segments.

Figure 7.34 shows the HISAM organization for the Doctor data base in Figure 7.32 just after loading. When the data base is loaded in the expected hierarchic sequence, each root segment is placed at the start of an ISAM fixed-length physical record. As many of its dependent segments as possible are then placed in the physical record. All the root's subordinates that can not fit in the ISAM record are then mapped into linked OSAM fixed-length records as shown in Figure 7.34. Thus, each root segment occurrence and all its subordinates are organized into one ISAM record and a series of zero or more linked OSAM records.

The length of the two fixed-length record types must be chosen judiciously by the DBA. It is a very important performance parameter. Spanning of segment occurrences is not allowed and thus there is usually some empty space at the end of each physical record.

IMS "deletes" HISAM segments by setting a deletion flag in the segment prefix. Thus every "deleted" segment generously occupies space, as much as an active segment. HISAM does not provide dynamic garbage collection when ISAM is underneath. When VSAM is underneath there is a higher degree of actual deletion of segments and dynamic garbage collection. ISAM and VSAM

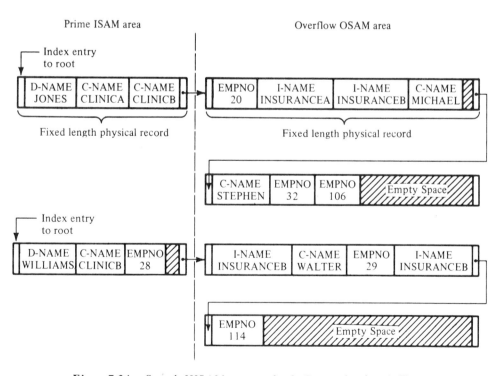

Figure 7.34.   *Sample HISAM structure for the Doctor data base in Figure 7.32*

appear the same externally, except that VSAM internally attempts to provide better performance for insertions and deletions.

Insertion of segments is more elaborate. Two cases are involved:

1. Subordinate segment insertion; and
2. Root segment insertion.

Subordinate Segment Insertion. Segment occurrences subordinate to a root segment are inserted at the proper point to maintain the hierarchic sequence. The segments following (in the hierarchic sense) the new segment(s) to be inserted are physically shifted within the ISAM physical record to make room for them. If these segments being shifted do not fit in the ISAM record, and normally they do not fit, then they are shifted into OSAM physical records created for this purpose. The necessary pointers are automatically set to preserve the hierarchic view. Figure 7.35 illustrates the state of the HISAM structure of Figure 7.34 after inserting the CLINIC segment with C-NAME = CLINICD as a child of the root segment occurrence with D-NAME = WILLIAMS. Only the affected root is shown in this figure.

Note in Figure 7.35 that shifting segments into an OSAM physical record may result in "wasting" a large portion of this newly created record. No garbage collection is performed by HISAM; that is, the hierarchy of segments from INSURANCE . . . INSURANCEB is not shifted "backward" to free

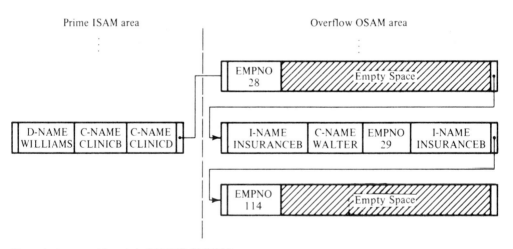

Dependent segment inserted: C-NAME CLINICD

Segment shifted into OSAM: EMPNO 28

Figure 7.35. *Insertion of a dependent segment in the HISAM structure of Figure 7.34*

the last fixed-length physical record for other uses. Thus, about half of the allocated OSAM area in Figure 7.35 is empty and is thus wasted.

Root Segment Insertion. Roots inserted after the initial loading of the data base are inserted in a new OSAM physical record, and not in the prime area (except in the case of inserting a segment with the same sequence field value as that of a previously deleted segment). No new root key is inserted into ISAM after the data base is loaded. Figure 7.36(a) shows the result of inserting the root segment TAYLOR into the HISAM structure of Figure 7.34; Figure 7.36(b) shows the result of inserting the root segments (TAYLOR and SHEIN-BEIN). The subordinate segments of these roots are not shown in Figure 7.36; in reality, the subordinates would be placed after their root in the same OSAM physical record, or other linked OSAM records as needed. Note that root segments are sequenced on the key field values by physical contiguity within ISAM and by chaining when OSAM is needed.

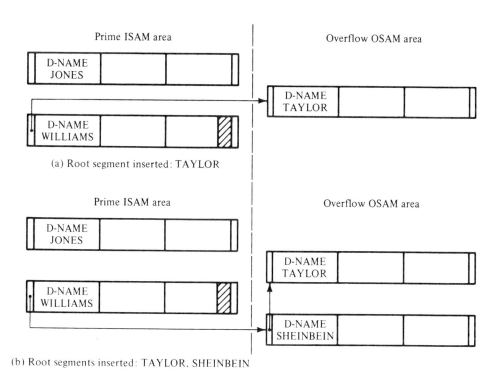

Figure 7.36.   Insertion of root segments in the HISAM structure of Figure 7.34

7.6.4   Hierarchic and Child/Twin
Pointers in HIDAM and HDAM

HIDAM and HDAM do not store the dependent segments under one root in a physically sequential manner necessarily, but rather use pointers to store these dependents to preserve the hierarchic DL/1 view. Direct pointers from parent(s) to children and among twins under a parent are established. In effect, each segment type becomes a file, as is essentially the case in other GDBMS such as DBTG systems and TOTAL. In HIDAM and HDAM all data segments are stored in an OSAM area, or in an ESDS area if VSAM is used. Internal to IMS, these pointers are carried in the segment prefix and indicate the byte offset position of a segment in the OSAM area.

The DBA may declare in the DBD two types of pointer strategies for dependent segments:

    1. Hierarchic pointers; and

    2. Child/twin pointers.

Figure 7.37 exemplifies the use of hierarchic pointers. Each segment has a pointer to the next one in the hierarchic sequence, except for the last dependent segment (thc one at the bottom right-hand corner of the hierarchy) which does not carry a pointer.

Figure 7.38 illustrates the use of child/twin pointers. Each parent segment occurrence has a pointer to the first occurrence of each of its child segment types. Each child segment has a pointer to its next twin.

A backward pointer chain can also be declared in addition to the forward chain. For the hierarchic pointer strategy each segment would also carry a pointer to its predecessor, and likewise for the child/twin pointer strategy. The

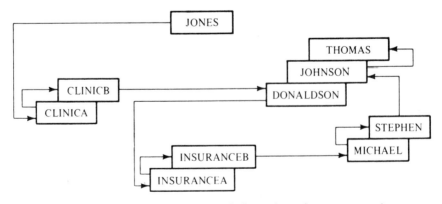

Figure 7.37.   *Hierarchic pointers linking dependent segments in a HIDAM or HDAM IMS data base*

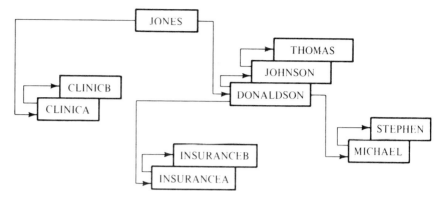

Figure 7.38. *Child/Twin pointers linking dependent segments in a HIDAM or HDAM IMS data base*

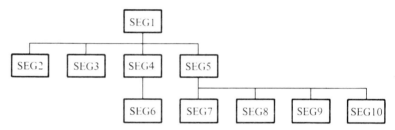

(a) If DL/1 requests are for rightmost, close to bottom segment types, the child/twin pointer strategy provides better access time performance than the hierarchical pointer strategy.

(b) Access time performance of hierarchical and child/twin pointers might not be too different in some cases; but if there are many segment occurrences at each level then child/twin pointers provide better performance when accessing segments at the lower levels.

Figure 7.39. *IMS data base hierarchy and pointer type performance*

backward pointer chain does include a pointer in a parent segment to the last occurrence of its appropriate dependent segment.

Root segment occurrences are linked by IMS with twin pointers, no matter how the dependents are linked. For performance reasons, the DBA may choose to use hierarchic pointers for some segment types in the hierarchy and child/twin pointers for other segment types. The nature of the particular DL/1 transactions should guide the choice of the pointer strategy. For example, suppose that there are many segment types and occurrences at each level of the hierarchic DBD as shown in Figure 7.39(a), and the DL/1 calls are for only occurrences of the rightmost and bottom segment types. In this situation it is much better to use child/twin pointers so as to avoid the IMS internal scanning of unrequested segments that would take place if hierarchic pointers were used. If, on one hand, hierarchic sequential data requests predominate, then hierarchic pointers are best. If, on the other hand, we had the extreme of an IMS data base with only one segment type at each level, as shown in Figure 7.39(b), then the performance of hierarchic and child/twin pointers might not be too different. However, the performance of hierarchic pointers versus child/twin pointers can be significantly different even for the "slim" data base of Figure 7.39(b) if there are many segment occurrences at each level and access requests are for occurrences of segment types close to the bottom of the hierarchy.

7.6.5   HIDAM

HIDAM provides indexed access to root segments via the root sequence field and pointer access to dependent segments. The HIDAM data base organization consists of:

1. An index containing root sequence values organized in effect either as a HISAM data base or as a VSAM data base (KSDS and ESDS).
2. All the actual segment occurrences organized either as an OSAM data base or as an ESDS area if VSAM is used.

Figure 7.40 illustrates this showing only segment key fields; the same root segment case in the HISAM Figure 7.36(b) is used.

The INDEX (this is the IMS name) is essentially like a HISAM organization with its own ISAM and OSAM area. However, only the root sequence field is stored in this INDEX, and not the whole root segment. There is one index entry for every root segment occurrence. Each index entry then contains a pointer to its corresponding root segment occurrence in the large OSAM area.

The large OSAM area is made up of fixed-length physical records (unblocked) into which each root and its corresponding dependents are mapped. At load time, the segments are mapped sequentially into the sequence of

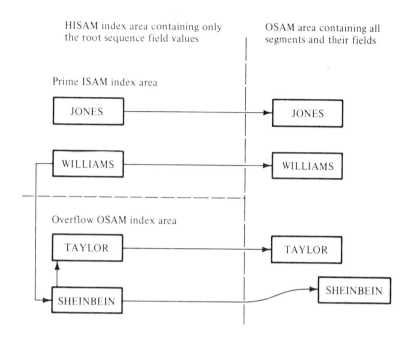

Figure 7.40. *Sample HIDAM structure after inserting root segments*

physical records according to the input hierarchic sequence, much like in HSAM. All pointers (hierarchic or child/twin) are set up by IMS. Root segments and dependent segments inserted subsequently are stored as close as possible (physically) to the immediate predecessor (logically) in the hierarchic sequence. Figure 7.40 exemplifies the addition of the root segments Taylor and Sheinbein subsequent to the initial loading. Insertion of a new segment in HIDAM and HDAM does not involve physically shifting other existing segments, whereas in HISAM there may be shifting. The use of pointers permits inserting a new segment at any physical location while still preserving the hierarchic sequence and the ability to access the segment.

When a segment is deleted in HIDAM and HDAM the space freed can be reused. This is a big advantage over HISAM in which a deleted segment is only flagged as deleted, as in ISAM, and its space cannot be reused (unless the new segment has the same sequence field value as the one causing the vacancy). If VSAM rather than ISAM is used with HISAM then there is a higher degree of actual record deletion and reclaiming of such space for subsequent use.

Note that as the number of segment deletions and insertions increases in HIDAM and HDAM, space freed may become scattered and the physical organization may become increasingly distant from the hierarchic organization. Pointer following may become increasingly expensive, especially when using moving arm random access storage devices. Thus access time performance will deteriorate. A number of IMS installations do report this problem and find that their transaction characteristics are better suited for HISAM (are highly hierarchic sequential, i.e., "get next"-oriented).

7.6.6 HDAM

HDAM offers direct access to root segments via the root segment sequence field and pointer access to dependent segments. Access to roots is direct via a hashing and chaining overflow technique, whereas in HIDAM the access is indexed via a (perhaps more time-consuming) HISAM mechanism. The HDAM data base organization consists of:

1. An OSAM or VSAM ESDS prime hashing area composed of M fixed-length physical records each containing one or more root segments, and perhaps but not necessarily the root's subordinate segments (depending on the loading sequence).
2. An OSAM or VSAM ESDS overflow area composed of fixed-length physical records containing roots and/or subordinate segments that do not fit in the prime area.

Figure 7.41 shows the HDAM structure and an example to be explained below. The size of the prime area is determined by the DBA by essentially indicating the parameter M in the DBD. The DBA is responsible for supplying and loading in IMS the hashing or key transformation procedure which has the crucial task of taking a value of the root sequence field and producing a "good" address, P, of a physical record within the prime range of 1 through M. The reader should be familiar with the basics and problems associated with hashing in general. The size of the physical record, the size of the prime area (the number of physical records), and especially the specific hashing method are three parameters which greatly affect access time performance in HDAM. IMS does not have an "intelligent black box" capable of determining these parameters for the DBA; the long-range goal of future systems would certainly be in this direction.

HDAM is the only one of the four IMS access methods that does not require loading the data base from a hierarchic sequential source (HSAM-like source). A parent root segment occurrence must be loaded before any of its subordinates may be loaded. Thus, as an example, all the root segment occurrences could be loaded ahead of all their subordinates, perhaps, so that root segment occurrences may be more optimally placed in the prime hashing area.

Let us examine first the organization of root segment occurrences and later the mapping of subordinate segment occurrences. We provide a simplified description of what is involved; the details are presented in Reference 7.

When a root segment comes for insertion, either as part of the loading process or subsequent to the initial loading process, it will be hashed by IMS

Entry via hashing algorithm, hashed address 30

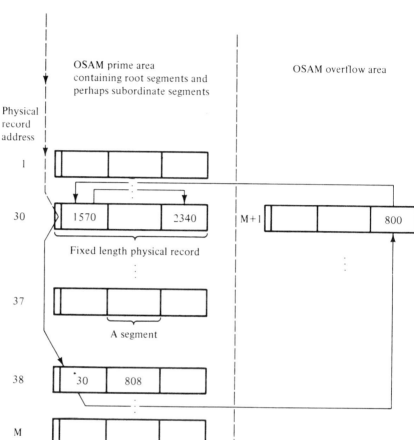

Figure 7.41.   Sample HDAM structure after inserting root segments (subsequent to initial loading)

into a physical record address P. The new root segment will be placed within it. If there is no room within P, then the new root will be placed in the physically nearest prime physical record which has enough room for it. If there is no space for it in any prime physical record, then it will be placed in the next position available in the overflow area. Let us now see how these hashed root segments are managed.

Any hashing method has the problem that different source key fields may hash to the same P address. HDAM uses a chaining overflow method to chain in ascending key field sequence all root segment occurrences that hash to the same P physical record. Note that the initial portion of this chain of segments may be in the physical record P, some may be in other prime physical records, and some may be in overflow physical records. Another characteristic of hashing is that any ordering of records on the basis of the source key field is usually lost upon hashing. Try an example to see the result of the division/ remainder hashing. Thus in HDAM the logical sequence of root segment occurrences may not be preserved (depends on the particular hashing routine) since two roots in logically consecutive hierarchic sequence may be on a different physical record and a different chain. Of course, it is possible that the hashing method may not "disorder" two or a few consecutive source segments. Note, however, that the hierarchic sequence of the subordinate segments under each root occurrence is always preserved by means of the hierarchic or child/twin pointers (Figures 7.37 and 7.38).

Let us look at an example using a division/remainder method where the divisor is the number of prime physical records, $M = 770$. This hashing consists of dividing the root sequence field by M and setting P equal to the remainder. The overflow chain of segments shown in Figure 7.41 would be obtained as a result of inserting root segments with the following sequence fields, subsequent to initial loading and after some roots have been deleted, thus leaving the vacated spaces used in this sequence:

1. Insert root 1570. Thus $P = 30$.
   This root fits in physical record 30 (in the first slot available left by a deleted segment).
2. Insert root 2340. Thus $P = 30$.
   This root fits in physical record 30.
3. Insert root 30. Thus $P = 30$.
   This root does not fit in record 30 because it is now full; this root fits in the nearest physical record with space available (vacated by a deleted segment, 38).
4. Insert root 808. Thus $P' = 38$.
   This root fits in its physical record 38. It does not belong in the previous chain since it hashes to a different physical record. Assume that 808 is the first that hashes to 38.
5. Insert root 800. Thus $P = 30$.
   The prime area is full. This root fits in the next available slot which is a record $M + 1$ in the OSAM overflow area.

The chain in Figure 7.41 results at the *end* of these insertions. Intermediate chain steps are not shown. Readers should perform these and be aware of the intermediate chaining and rechaining that has to be done after every previous step to preserve the ascending root segment field sequence.

As illustrated in Figure 7.41, overflow chains may jump across the storage space depending on what has been vacated by deleted records. Thus, to reduce access time it is important to choose a proper hashing algorithm that results in few synonyms, i.e., short chains. An ideal case is to have zero length overflow chains in which case HDAM access is very fast.

Now let us trace the insertion of subordinate segments. At insertion or load time HDAM places a segment occurrence as physically near its present root segment occurrence as possible (but without of course shifting any stored segments) to reduce access time. If the root is in physical record P, the new segment will be stored in P if there is room; if there is no room, the segment will be placed in the closest vacant slot in the prime area, or at worst in the overflow area. Note that if subordinate segments are not loaded initially in hierarchic sequence under its present root segment, and all root segments are loaded first, the subordinates may end up at a physically distant location. All subordinates of a root occurrence are still obtained via pointers.

7.6.7 Performance Degradation and Data Base Reorganization

Readers will realize that the access time and storage utilization performance of an IMS data base in HISAM, HIDAM, and HDAM will degrade as deletions, insertions, and updates take place. For example, in HISAM (ISAM-OSAM) deleted segments are only flagged as deleted and this essentially nonreusable space may become a noticeable expense; in HDAM the addition of a large number of root segments and their subordinates may result in long chains and/or expensive chains traversing "long DASD distances"; and so on. Sooner or later performance will degrade to the point where a reorganization will be required. Reorganization consists of retrieving all active segments and reloading them again as a new data base so as to improve the performance while maintaining data independence. It should be noted that most of the kinds of reorganization allowed in a GDBMS are those that gain performance but do not entail making changes to the application programs. However, if the access method is changed at reorganization time, then issues of data independence require some care, e.g., when converting to HDAM from other access methods, or converting to HSAM (which prohibits the use of insert, delete, and replace commands).

IBM utility programs are available to assist in reorganization. As a matter of fact, the INDEX of a HIDAM data base may be reorganized without necessarily reorganizing the data record space in the OSAM area. Alternatively, users could write their own reorganize program consisting of a series of "get next" DL/1 commands without SSA (without logical qualification) aimed at the old data base, each followed by its corresponding "Insert" DL/1 command aimed at the new data base. An example of this was given in Section 7.4. Note that if a series of "get next" calls does not indicate the root field and is not ordered by the user according to the root field sequence, HDAM will return the next physical segment which is not necessarily in hierarchic root sequence—as has been previously explained.

One of the biggest challenges for the DBA is the task of choosing the appropriate access method, the appropriate setting of parameters, and the appropriate reorganization point. There are many parameters that can be set for each access method at load time, usually declarable in the DBD, and which have a major effect on performance, for example, the length of the fixed-length physical record. Other performance considerations or parameters are not really declared in the DBD as such but are introduced by the DBA. For example, to prevent long pointer chains in a HDAM organization, at load time the DBA may input dummy root segments and subordinates, so that subsequent insertions may fall in these dummy allocated slots (this is what we would recommend also for direct access and indexed sequential single files). The intent of load and reorganize utilities is of course to establish parameters and easily request as many of these performance "knobs" as possible. IMS has many knobs that affect performance, but the optimum or even a good setting cannot be easily determined due to the multitude of interrelated performance parameters. IBM is actively pursuing the design of good IMS physical design aids, in the form of judicious DBA design methodologies and intelligent software modules to aid in determining good IMS physical data base designs.

In a number of dynamic IMS installations, data bases are reported to be reorganized every weekend at a considerable cost, in some cases consuming over $1,000 per reorganization. Usually a backup copy of the data base is also obtained as a byproduct for recovery purposes, so that the cost of reading the data base is shared by reorganization needs and backup/recovery needs. However, in loading or reorganizing a data base the largest cost is not in reading the records, but in writing them and setting up all the indexes, pointers, and so on. Thus, the largest portion of the bill still goes to reorganization when reorganization and backup are performed at the same time.

More on performance and tools available will be found in Chapter 11.

7.6.8   Data Set Groups

A *Data Set Group*, DSG, is a grouping of segment types. An HISAM, HIDAM, and HDAM data base can be spread over one primary data set group and several secondary data set groups. Each DSG is the usual ISAM-OSAM area (e.g., Figure 7.34) for HISAM. For HIDAM each DSG is an OSAM area, although the INDEX data base cannot be split since the INDEX entries are only the occurrences of the root sequence field. For HDAM each DSG is an OSAM overflow area, but only the primary DSG has the prime hashing area (i.e., provides hashed access to root segments). The primary DSG contains all the occurrences of at least the root segment. Each DSG contains all the occurrences of at least one segment type. Notice that the notions of a DSG are equivalent to the notions of the DBTG area summarized in Figure 5.7 (except that in DBTG all occurrences of a record type do not have to be within one area, although generally they would be).

The major reason for resorting to DSGs is to enhance IMS data base performance. The primary potential gains are:

1. Improvement of overall access time in HISAM, HIDAM, and HDAM data bases; and

2. Reduction of the amount of different-sized empty storage (caused by deletions and then insertions of different-sized segments) in HIDAM and HDAM. We shall not look at these intricate and implementation dependent aspects.

The determination of the best DSGs for a particular application is a task of the physical data base design process. We shall only summarize the basic access time considerations of DSGs. Details are found in Reference 7.

The access time performance of some direct access DL/1 calls can be expensive. For example, a "get unique" call for a segment occurrence close to the right-hand bottom corner of a hierarchy, e.g., segment SEG10 in Figure 7.39(a), involves traversing all segments that precede it in the hierarchic sequence. This is the case for HISAM and also for HIDAM and HDAM using hierarchic pointers to link subordinate segments of a root segment occurrence; use of child/twin pointers allowed in HIDAM and HDAM shortens access time in such a circumstance, Figure 7.39. In HISAM direct access to any segment type on the second level of the hierarchy can be achieved by means of DSGs. In HISAM any subtree of the hierarchy starting with a second-level segment can be in a separate DSG (whereas in HDAM and HIDAM any segment type can be in any DSG independent of its logical hierarchic position). For example, four possible DSGs are shown in Figure 7.42 [for the data base of Figure 7.39(a)]; other DSG groupings may be formed, of course, e.g., two DSGs.

Every HISAM DSG starts with a second-level segment. When first loaded, segments in the primary DSG are treated as if they were the only segments in the whole data base. Segments in each secondary DSG are treated as if they were the whole data base, except that the DSG's top segment (but a second-level segment from the overall data base point of view) is preceded by the key sequence field of the parent root segment. Direct access to this DSG is via this root field in the ISAM area (of the ISAM-OSAM pair of each DSG).

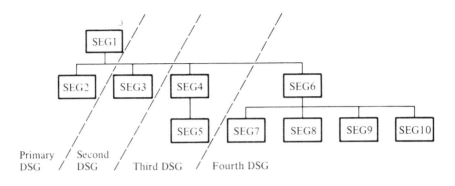

DSG: data set group

DSGs may be used to enhance data base performance in
HISAM, HDAM, and HIDAM; in HDAM and HIDAM any segment
type can be assigned to any DSG

Figure 7.42.   *Data set groups in an IMS data base*

Another advantage of DSGs is that different segments of the data base
may be clustered into a DSG, and the DSGs may be then judiciously stored in
various physical areas of the storage devices, or even in different storage
devices, so as to enhance overall access time. Access time can be enhanced if
those portions of the data base being most frequently used are placed physically
together. However, the internal overhead for linking DSGs may in some cases
offset these gains. The trade-offs are not clear.

In HIDAM and HDAM any segment type can be assigned to any DSG.
For example, in Figure 7.39, segments SEG1, SEG2, SEG3 may be the
primary DSG; and SEG4, SEG6, SEG7, and SEG8 the second DSG; and
SEG5, SEG9, and SEG10 the third DSG.

7.6.9   Definition of Access Methods and Storage Mapping in the DBD

The DBA indicates the desired access methods, storage organization,
and mappings as part of the DBD. These are the details at the two lower levels
in Figure 7.1, or essentially the two lower levels in the DIAM model framework, Figure 3.22. We will give a flavor of how the main options discussed in
previous sections are defined but will not delve into the many intricate IMS
means to declare the options. We shall use the Doctor DBD example of Figure
7.2 in streamlined form.

Entries in the DBD must indicate the following items:

1. The access method: HSAM, HISAM, HIDAM, or HDAM. If
   HIDAM is called for, then the DBA is burdened with having to define

two separate DBDs, a data DBD and an index DBD, and to indicate in a rather intricate way (that we shall not trace) that the index DBD is the logical parent of the root segment indexed in the associated data base.

2. The name of the hashing or randomizing procedure for the HDAM method. The procedure and its name are supplied by the DBA and placed in the IMS system library. The number of physical records comprising the HDAM prime area must also be indicated.

3. For HIDAM and HDAM data bases the type of internal pointers to use: hierarchic or child/twin, forward/backward pointers. An entry in each SEGM statement in the DBD indicates the choice: POINTER = HIER/HIERBWD/TWIN/TWINBWD. The BWD suffix indicates *backward* pointers.

4. The grouping of segments into one or more data set groups and the mapping onto specific symbolic storage device locations.

```
 1                     DBD   NAME = DOCTORDB, ACCESS = HISAM
 2  PRIME              DATASET   DD1 = JCL ddname of the ISAM data file,
                       OVFLW = JCL ddname of the overflow OSAM data file, . . .
 3                     SEGM   NAME = DOCTOR, . . .
 4                            ¦Field definition
 5                     SEGM   NAME = CLINIC, . . .
 6                            ¦Field definition
 7  SECONDARY DATASET   DD1 = JCL ddname of the ISAM data file,
                       OVFLW = JCL ddname of the OSAM data file, . . .
 8                     SEGM   NAME = EMPLOYEE, . . .
 9                            ¦Field definition
10                     SEGM   NAME = INSUR_CO, . . .
11                            ¦Field definition
12                     SEGM   NAME = CHILD, . . .
13                            ¦Field definition
                              ⋮
14  //ddname           DD   DSNAME = PRIMEDD1, . . .
15  //ddname           DD   DSNAME = PRIMEOVFLW, . . .
16  //ddname           DD   DSNAME = SECDD1, . . .
17  //ddname           DD   DSNAME = SECOVFLW, . . .
```

Figure 7.43. *Sample IMS DBD skeleton with access method and data set definitions (HISAM)*

The example in Figure 7.43 focuses on the syntax for defining access method and data set mappings for the main skeleton of the Doctor data base, Figures 7.2 and 7.4. Let us trace the definition.

Statement 1 indicates that this data base is to be organized as an HISAM data base.

Statement 2 is a DATA SET statement which indicates various aspects: that the segments defined in the next SEGM statements are part of the named data set group, the IBM Operating System Job Control Language "ddnames" (which in turn give the specific storage device details, statements 14, 15), physical record length, blocking factors (for HSAM and HISAM), and so forth. In this particular case the DOCTOR and CLINIC segments defined in statements 3–6 form the PRIMARY DSG. The DD1 parameter indicates for HISAM the ddname of the ISAM data file. The OVFLOW parameter indicates for HISAM the ddname of the overflow OSAM data file. Statements 14 and 15, in turn, specify the lowest-level details, such as the operating system data set name (DSNAME = . . .) in which the DSG is stored, the direct access volume (IBM 3330 etc.) containing this data set, and so on.

Statement 7 defines the SECONDARY data set group as being made up of the segments defined in the subsequent statements 8–13, EMPLOYEE, INSUR-CO, and CHILD. DD1 and OVFLW data names are specified for this DSG. Recall that each DSG has its own ISAM-OSAM pair for HISAM. If only one primary data set group were to be used, then this DATASET statement 7 would have to be deleted.

7.7   SECONDARY INDEXING

7.7.1   Overview

IMS provides **secondary indexing** facilities with the objective of reducing the amount of searching in the data base for some data requests for which such indexing is specifically set up. The reduction in searching is in terms of actual internal physical accessing of the data base by IMS and, in many cases, (but not always), in the amount of DL/1 calls or programming.

Overall, unfortunately, the secondary indexing facilities are very limited, disappointingly awkward, and difficult to set up and change, and, in most cases, they violate the precepts of data independence. Secondary indexing is undoubtedly a most noticeable weakness in IMS. Chapter 2 establishes the level of secondary indexing that one expects and that is implemented particularly by inverted GDBMS and relational GDBMS. The previous criticisms of the IMS secondary indexing are evident when compared to the indexing capabilities and benefits in other systems presented in this text.

Only the following indexes can be established in IMS:

1. An index to a root or dependent segment on the basis of any field of that segment.
2. An index to a root or dependent segment on the basis of any field in a physical (but not logical) dependent of that segment.

The field on which the index is based can be either a single field or up to five fields in the same segment concatenated in any order. A secondary index is implemented much like the INDEX in the HIDAM structure shown in Figure 7.40, except that it is implemented in VSAM and not ISAM/OSAM. HSAM data bases cannot be indexed, for obvious reasons. A logical data base may be also indexed, but then our previous criticisms of the IMS indexing are at their extreme.

We will illustrate the possible types of indexes that may be established in a physical data base, focusing on their use, impact, and data independence. We will spare the reader's having to look at the awkward DBD and logical child declarations, along the lines of Figure 7.20, that must be used to set up and change *each* index. We will address below first indexing to a root segment and then indexing to a nonroot segment.

7.7.2   Indexing to a Root Segment

Index to the root on a field in the root

As an example, in the schema in Figure 7.2 let us index to (point to) DOCTORs based on values of the SPECIALTY field. IMS then sets up an INDEX in which for each value of SPECIALTY in the data base it will point to the root segment occurrences (one or more) that are characterized by such value of SPECIALTY. Consequently, if one wishes to retrieve all DOCTOR occurrences whose SPECIALTY is SURGERY, the use of the index avoids the need for IMS to retrieve internally each DOCTOR occurrence and then check its SPECIALTY. If no index is available, or if an index is available but is not to be used, the DL/1 commands are:

```
        GU    DOCTOR (SPECIALTY = SURGERY)
   L    GN    DOCTOR (SPECIALTY = SURGERY)
        GO TO L
```

If an index is available and is to be used, the DL/1 commands must *explicitly* refer to the name of the index, let us say INDEX-SPEC, declared by the DBA in the DBD that must be set up for each index:

```
        GU     DOCTOR (INDEX-SPEC = SURGERY)
        Stop if not found
L       GN     DOCTOR (INDEX-SPEC = SURGERY)
        Stop if not found
        GO TO L
```

The DL/1 user may now see the data base in *secondary processing sequence* by ascending values of the SPECIALTY field as an alternative to the primary sequence which is on ascending values of the D-NAME field. Root segment occurrences cannot be inserted or deleted when using the secondary sequence.

The previous indexing *violates principles of data independence:* if the index is dropped, or modified in certain ways, the previous DL/1 commands and "get unique"/"get next" strategies are impacted and must be changed. This is also the case for the other types of indexes outlined below. This is not the case with robust inverted and relational GDBMS.

Index to the root segment on a field in a dependent

As an example, in the schema in Figure 7.2 let us index to DOCTORs based on values of the AMT-OWED field in the EMPLOYEE segment. IMS then sets up an INDEX in which for each value of AMT-OWED it will point to the corresponding root segment DOCTOR occurrences. Consequently, if one wishes to retrieve all DOCTORs who have EMPLOYEEs whose AMT-OWED ≥ 600, the use of the index avoids the need for IMS to retrieve internally each DOCTOR occurrence, then retrieve each of its EMPLOYEEs, and check its AMT-OWED:

```
        GU DOCTOR      (INDEX-AMT-OWED $\geq$ 600)
        Stop if not found
L       GN DOCTOR      (INDEX-AMT-OWED $\geq$ 600)
        Stop if not found
        GO TO L
```

Note that if the INDEX-AMT-OWED is not available, the previous program must be changed drastically to obtain the answer.

7.7.3   Indexing to a Nonroot Segment

Index to a nonroot segment on a field in that segment

Whenever an index to a nonroot segment is established, the impact is not only an enhancement in performance but also a restructuring of the hierarchy such that the nonroot segment appears as the root segment to the DL/1 user when the secondary processing sequence is used. If, however, the primary sequence is used, the hierarchy appears as it was originally without the index. In the restructured hierarchy the ancestors of the indexed segment become the leftmost dependents of this new root segment in reverse order.

As an example, in the schema in Figure 7.2, let us index to EMPLOYEEs based on values of AMT-OWED. IMS effectively restructures the schema to the *secondary structure or view* shown in Figure 7.44. By following the IMS restructuring rules,

1. The indexed segment appears as the new root.
2. The ancestors of the indexed segment appear as the leftmost dependents of this new root, in reverse order. Thus the original root appears at the leftmost bottom of the hierarchy.
3. The dependents of the indexed segment maintain the original structure, except that they stay to the right of the ancestors-turned-dependents.
4. All other segments are excluded. Note that the CLINIC segment is excluded in Figure 7.44.

The "get unique" and "get next" operations see the secondary view when the index is used, and they see the primary view when the index is not used. The secondary view does not permit insertion or deletion of the indexed segment (EMPLOYEE) or its dependents.

Using the secondary view of Figure 7.44, we see that the following retrieves all doctor names and the corresponding insurance company names for all EMPLOYEEs whose AMT-OWED $\geq$ 600 (to reduce coding, assume there is at most one INSUR-CO per EMPLOYEE):

```
        GU  EMPLOYEE (INDEX-AMT-OWED ≥ 600)
            DOCTOR
        stop if not found
        GN  INSUR-CO
        print D-NAME and I-NAME
L       GN  EMPLOYEE (INDEX-AMT-OWED ≥ 600)
        stop if not found
        GN  INSUR-CO
        print D-NAME and I-NAME
        go to L
```

If the secondary index is not used, then in order to obtain the answer, every DOCTOR and EMPLOYEE occurrence in the primary schema in Figure 7.2 must be retrieved. Try it as an exercise. It is precisely this exhaustive searching that the index avoids. Unfortunately, totally different DL/1 calls

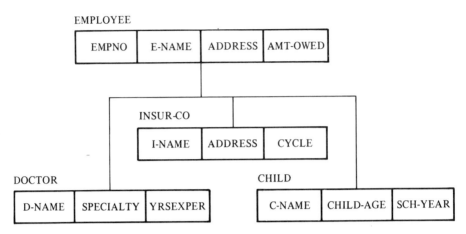

Figure 7.44. *Secondary view when indexing to the EMPLOYEE seg-ment on the basis of a field of a dependent of EMPLOYEE in Figure 7.2*

must be issued and even a different data base structure is involved, depending on whether or not an index is used. This is a serious lack of data independence. The presence or absence of indexes should not impact application program-ming, only performance, as well illustrated by robust inverted and relational GDBMS.

Index to a nonroot segment on a field in a dependent segment

As an example, in the schema in Figure 7.2 let us index to EMPLOYEE based on values of the CHILD-AGE field of its CHILD dependent segment. The schema now appears in Figure 7.44. The following retrieves all the CHILD occurrences whose CHILD-AGE > 14 for all the EMPLOYEE occurrences whose AMT-OWED ≥ 600 (to simplify coding, assume at most one child over 14 for an employee).

```
       GU     EMPLOYEE (AMT-OWED ≥ 600 AND INDEX-
              CHILD-AGE > 14)
       CHILD
       Stop if not found, else print CHILD
  L    GN     EMPLOYEE (AMT-OWED ≥ 600 AND INDEX-
              CHILD-AGE > 14)
       CHILD
       Stop if not found, else print CHILD
       GO TO L
```

Example 6 in Section 7.4 provides the same response, but using no indexing, a corresponding different set of DL/1 commands, and more internal searching. Thus, if no children over 14 exist in the data base, with indexing no segment occurrences are accessed; without indexing every EMPLOYEE occurrence must be retrieved and checked.

7.8   FAST PATH

The Fast Path option or facilities of IMS emerged as a result of the following:

1. The growing demands for very large data bases with very large volumes of on-line transactions requiring fast and reliable servicing.
2. The growing size of available main storage into dozens and eventually hundreds of megabytes.

Fast Path (FP) was introduced in the late 1970s and has been evolving since then as main memory technology and on-line processing demands of large data base users have been evolving. In a nutshell, Fast Path

1. Trades off functional capabilities of IMS and main storage use for fast access to highly active segments and higher throughput.
2. Is oriented for high-volume but limited on-line data base processing needs.
3. Improves performance with respect to regular IMS through reduced I/O, reduced resource contention, and increased parallel processing of concurrent users.

The more apparent and major capabilities of IMS not supported in FP are the logical data base mechanisms (Section 7.5) and secondary indices.

A characteristic of FP, and not of regular IMS, is that updates to the data bases are not made during processing by the application but are kept in a buffer in main memory. Actual update of the data base is delayed until the processing reaches a so-called synchronization point. This occurs when a message-driven application program (one that operates in wait-for-input mode) issues the next Get Unique call to its I/O PCB; for a nonmessage-driven application program, any new DL/1 call establishes a synchronization point. We shall not address the details and use of the synchronization point mechanism in maintaining the integrity of the data base in concurrent user operations and in recovery and restart procedures.

The DBA designs an IMS data base as either a regular full-function data base or a Fast Path data base. The IMS/VS communication facilities route appropriate terminal and program messages and DL/1 calls to the Fast Path data base(s) rather than to regular IMS data bases. There are two types of FP data bases:

1. **A Main Storage Data Base (MSDB)**, which consists of only a root segment and which resides in main memory.
2. **A Data Entry Data Base (DEDB)**, which contains a root segment and a limited number of dependent segments and hierarchic levels.

We shall address each of these two options below.

7.8.1 Main Storage Data Base (MSDB)

The MSDB option of FP permits the data base to contain only a root segment. All root occurrences reside in the main storage, thus reducing I/O activities. The size of the data base is limited only by the amount of main memory available. Two alternative MSDB options are provided for implementing applications: *terminal-related* and *nonterminal related*.

The terminal related MSDB has the following general characteristics:

1. Each segment is assigned to and "owned" by one logical terminal.
2. Only the owner terminal may update the segment. Other terminals may read but not update the segment.
3. The logical name of the owner terminal is the segment key, but the key does not reside in the segment.

The nonterminal related MSDB has the following characteristics:

1. Segments are not owned by specific logical terminals. Any terminal user can read and update the segments.
2. The key may be any identifier. If a logical terminal name is used as a key, it does not reside in the segment. If another identifier is used, it resides as a sequence field in the segment.

7.8.2 Data Entry Data Base (DEDB)

A DEDB is an HDAM-like data base containing a maximum of 15 hierarchical levels and up to 127 segment types (the initial version of the DEDB was limited to two hierarchical levels and eight segment types):

1. A root segment.
2. An optional sequential dependent segment.
3. From zero to 127 direct dependent segments (a maximum of 126 if the sequential dependent exists).

A DEDB is designed for:

1. Fast collection of detailed information in the sequential dependent segments.
2. Fast retrieval and update of summary information stored in the root segments.
3. Fast retrieval and update of the direct dependent segments.

Fast access to a DEDB is enhanced by its particular physical organization strategy versus the regular IMS strategy. In the regular IMS the logical data base is spread across an entire data set; or if multiple data sets are used, the data base is broken up on a segment basis, as discussed in Section 7.6.8. A DEDB is designed to use several data sets (operating system files), each of which contains instances from every logical segment in the data base (root, sequential, and direct dependent segments), as shown in Figure 7.45. A DEDB record occurrence (a root and its dependent segment occurences) cannot span data sets. A DEDB can be divided into dozens or hundreds such data sets, called *areas* (one more term in the IMS jargon!). Each data set or area is a VSAM file.

The DEDB features and controls of areas are oriented toward processing very large data bases with high performance. DEDB provides:

1. Increase performance through fine control over physical distribution. Areas can be stored on different DASD and can have different control interval sizes (basically the VSAM page size) and space allocation. Each area can be further controlled as indicated below.

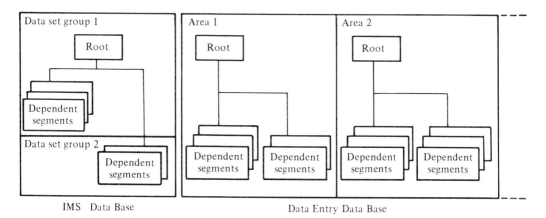

Figure 7.45.   *Physical distribution of an IMS data base and an IMS Fast Path Data Entry Data Base*

2. Increased availability and reliability of data by permitting reorganization and recovery concurrent with on-line processing. For example, if
an error occurs in an area and if it must be taken off-line for recovery,
or if an area must be reorganized to regain higher performance, the
rest of the data base is still available for processing. The only transactions that are temporarily held up are those that access the area being
reorganized or recovered.

3. Increased availability and reliability of data by permitting up to seven
multiple copies of the same areas operating concurrently. Multiple
copies can be created and destroyed dynamically on-line by the DBA.

Write, insert, and delete operations are automatically propagated to all the
multiple copies and are transparent to the user. A read operation may be
serviced by accessing several of the redundantly stored areas and by checking
for any inconsistencies between them. If an abnormal situation or inconsistency is detected, then a majority vote is taken to decide which copy is correct
and hence used to respond to the read request. For example, with three
multiple copies, if there is an error, the two copies that agree are considered the
correct ones. The incorrect version can then be destroyed and a new copy of the
correct version(s) created. This is all done on-line. Note that the multiple-copy
approach is also a recovery strategy, an alternative to the more traditional
backup and roll forward/backward recovery strategies. Recovery is discussed
in Chapter 13.

Physical Organization of the DEDB

Each DEDB area is physically divided into three portions, as shown in
Figure 7.46.

1. Root addressable (for roots and direct dependents).
2. Independent overflow (for roots and direct dependents).
3. Sequential dependent.

The root addressable portion is used to store root segments and their
direct dependents. If the direct dependent segment cannot be stored in the
same control interval as its root segment occurrence, the root addressable
overflow and then the independent overflow storage are searched for the
needed space. The initial placement and accessing of the root and direct
dependents are either through a randomizing algorithm, as in HDAM for the
whole DEDB, or for each individual area.

The sequential dependent portion resides at the end of each area. It is
specifically designed for fast data collection of a large volume of detailed data.
Sequential dependent segments are stored in the sequential dependent portion

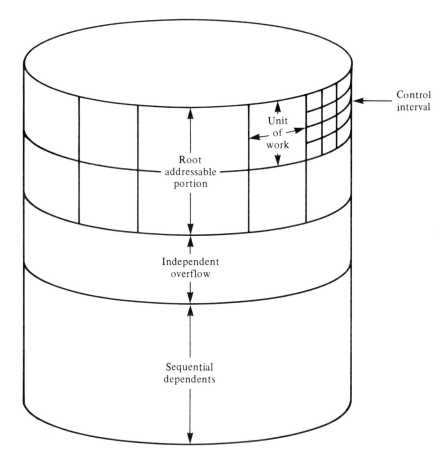

Figure 7.46. *Physical layout of an IMS DEDB area*

in time-of-entry sequence. They are chained off the root in a last-in, first-out (LIFO) manner.

Different DL/1 operations are available for:

1. Root and direct dependent segments that can be read, added, deleted, updated, and lengthened.

2. Sequential dependent segments that can be read and added in a LIFO sequence. A utility can be invoked to delete sequential dependent segments to free space.

Each portion of an area is divided into VSAM control intervals of 512, 1K, 2K, or 4K bytes as specified by the DBA. The Unit-of-Work (another term!) is made up of a number of contiguous control intervals, as specified by the DBA. The Unit-of-Work is the basic unit of space collection, reorganization, and overflow processing.

The control interval is the unit of resource allocation. Only one user can access or update a control interval at any one time. This control interval is very small and thus resource contention is kept low.

7.9 SUMMARY

IMS is perhaps the largest and most complex GDBMS available. It was one of the earliest GDBMS and today is one of the top two GDBMS in terms of numbers installed. It has a unique architecture and jargon, significantly different from that of all other commercial GDBMS. IBM is the only vendor of IMS. It is highly unlikely that other companies would venture to implement and market a system like IMS.

IMS is inherently a tree or hierarchic system. A parent to child relationship can be established between two segment (record) types. In a schema or subschema a given segment type can have only one parent segment type, and a given segment occurrence can be related to only one parent segment occurrence. No child can exist without a parent, although a data base can be made up of only one segment type. Section 7.2 is devoted to the IMS general architecture and schema definition.

A subschema may be defined over a schema as long as it is a subtree of the schema; that is, no segments in different subtrees may be related to form a subschema. In contrast, the network approach portrayed by DBTG systems and by TOTAL does not limit subschemas to subtrees of the schema. Section 7.3 is devoted to defining the user views or sensitive segments of a given application, as the subschema is called in IMS terms.

The IMS data manipulation language DL/1 is navigation- and access path-oriented, just as DBTG's DML and TOTAL's DML are. However, DL/1 is further molded by the IMS hierarchic approach. DL/1 navigates through a hierarchy based on a top to bottom, left to right storage layout of the hierarchy. The DL/1 user must be aware of this storage hierarchy in order to access an IMS data base. The "get unique" command appears essentially as a direct access (although internally it may be serviced in the top to bottom, left to right manner). The "get next" and "get next within parent" commands require the user to be aware of position within the hierarchic data base and of the top to bottom, left to right storage layout. The capability of DL/1 has been augmented significantly by the so-called command codes, which alleviate a number of navigation or access restrictions caused by the hierarchic rules. However, the user still has to be aware of the hierarchic and storage layout conventions.

The "logical" data base facilities make IMS a much more powerful GDBMS. Many of the problems of the hierarchic approach are alleviated. In summary, such "logical" data base facilities permit: (1) Linking or establishing relationships between one physical data base and another (perhaps previously established and used) physical data base, and defining subschemas using segments from the different data bases (although any subschema will still appear to the user as a hierarchy, at least as far as get operations are concerned). (2) Viewing the data in a variety of ways in addition to the hierarchic view of the physical data base(s) involved; however, any subschema will still appear to the user as a hierarchy for get operations, but will appear as the limited physical data base network that it really is internally, for insertion and deletion DL/1 commands particularly. (3) Reduction of redundancy of data actually stored while at the same time providing apparent redundancy at the logical level for the convenience of the logical data base DL/1 user; a segment will be stored only once but may participate in several logical data bases. IMS logical data base facilities are powerful, but they are intricate to establish and use. Section 7.5 presents the logical facilities. Note the specific significance in IMS of logical data bases in contrast to the physical data bases. This often confusing IMS terminology is not used in other GDBMS.

IMS provides four different access methods for physically organizing and accessing a data base. These access methods are peculiar to IMS. No GDBMS provides as many choices and performance "knobs" as IMS. Figures 7.30 and 7.31 summarize the four main access methods: HSAM, HISAM, HIDAM, and HDAM. Tape devices can support only HSAM. Direct access devices support all access methods. In an effort to further optimize the access to child segments in the heirarchy, child/twin pointer mechanisms may be used instead of hierarchic pointers (compare Figure 7.37 with 7.38). Further optimization may be possible (although not for HSAM) by grouping various segment types into so-called data set groups for the purpose of achieving these potential gains: (1) improvement of overall access time and (2) reduction of the amount of different-sized empty storage caused by segment deletions and then additions in HIDAM and HDAM. Section 7.6 details the access methods and strategies.

The view and functioning of all DL/1 operations is unaffected by the choice of physical organization and access methods, except of course for HSAM which allows only get-type of commands. However, the choice of physical organization may have a great effect on the storage utilization and access time of the data base, so that in actual practice physical organization is very important, as many IMS users will testify. Inevitably, any data base under any GDBMS will degrade in performance as insertions, deletions, and updates occur; the DBA will eventually have to physically reorganize the data base in order to improve efficiency.

IMS provides secondary indexing facilities for reducing the amount of searching in the data base for certain data accessing requests for which such indexing is specifically set up. The following indices can be established, as illustrated in Section 7.7: (1) an index to a root or dependent segment, on the basis of any field of that segment, and (2) an index to a root or dependent segment, on the basis of any field in a physical (but not logical) dependent of that segment. Whenever an index to a nonroot is set up, a secondary view of the original schema is effectively made available in which the indexed segment becomes the root, the original ancestors become the leftmost dependents of the new root, the original dependents of the new root remain to the right of the ancestors-turned-dependents, and all other former dependents of the previous root are excluded. The primary data base structure remains physically and can still be used but without the use of the secondary index. Overall, unfortunately, the secondary indexing facilities are very limited, awkward, and difficult to set up and change, and, in most cases, they violate the precepts of data independence.

The powerful IMS Fast Path (FP) facilities have emerged due to (1) the demand for large data bases with very large volumes of on-line transactions requiring fast and reliable servicing and (2) the availability of very large main memories. FP trades off functional capabilities of IMS and main memory use for fast access to highly active segments and higher throughput. Section 7.8 outlines the features of the two types of FP data bases: (1) Main Storage Data Base (MSDB), which is composed of only a root segment and resides in main memory, and (2) Data Entry Data Base (DEDB), which contains a root segment and a limited number of dependent segments and hierarchic levels. Fast access to a DEDB is enhanced by its particular physical organization strategy versus the regular IMS strategy, as illustrated in Figure 7.45. Higher availability and reliability are achieved in a DEDB by permitting reorganization and recovery concurrent with on-line processing and by permitting up to seven multiple copies of the same data base areas operating concurrently.

REFERENCES

1. Information Management System/360 Version 2, General Information Manual, IBM Reference Manual GH20-0765.

2. Information Management System Virtual Storage (IMS/VS), General Information Manual, IBM Reference Manual GH20-1260.

3. Data Language/1 System 370 DOS/VS, General Information Manual, IBM Reference Manual GH20-1246.

4. Interactive Query Facility (IQF) for IMS Version 2, General Information Manual, IBM Reference Manual GH20-1074. (This is no longer marketed.)

5. DL/1 DOS/VS Application Programming Reference Manual, IBM Reference Manual SH12-5411.
6. Information Management System/360 Version 2, Application Programming Reference Manual, IBM Reference Manual SH20-0912.
7. Information Management System/360 Version 2, System/Application Design Guide, IBM Reference Manual SH20-0910.
8. IMS/VS Fast Path Feature, General Information Manual, IBM Reference Manual GH20-9069.

EXERCISES

1. Answer each of the following as TRUE or FALSE for the IMS data model.

_____ a. An IMS PDBR contains a single type of root segment.

_____ b. A root segment has an arbitrary number of child segment types.

_____ c. No child segment occurrence can exist without its parent.

_____ d. A sequence field is optional for all IMS segments except the root.

_____ e. An M to N relationship can be represented only by using logical data base mechanisms (an LDB).

_____ f. An IMS LDBR root must be also a PDBR root.

_____ g. PROCOPTs may be defined for nonsequence fields of an IMS segment.

_____ h. Initial loading of an IMS data base need not be performed in root occurrence sequence (ordered by its sequence field) for HDAM.

_____ i. In HDAM the logical sequence of root segment occurrences is not lost.

_____ j. In HISAM only root segments may be placed in the ISAM data set (assuming no secondary data set groups).

_____ k. In HIDAM only root segment may be placed in the HISAM index data base (assuming no secondary data set groups).

_____ l. There is no restriction in HISAM and HDAM on the assignment of segment types to data set groups.

_____ m. Splitting an IMS data base into several data set groups increases the amount of storage fragmentation.

_____ n. In IMS access to any segment type may be established via secondary data set groups, except for HISAM and HSAM.

_____ o. A child segment type can have a physical parent type which is also at the same time the logical parent type.

2. Discuss in detail the main reasons for resorting to IMS logical data bases. Illustrate in some detail using suitable examples. A general and superficial answer will not suffice.

3. Repeat Exercise 3 in Chapter 5 (a DBTG exercise) but use instead the IMS data base in Figure 7.2. Discuss some of the problems and solutions of IMS in dealing with the need to establish any nonhierarchic relationships that you may deem necessary to handle efficiently the two types of queries indicated.

4. Explain what "storage fragmentation" is in data bases and the effect that IMS data set groups play on it. Give a clear example.

5. Consider the currency indicators in a DBTG data base. Does an IMS data base have similar or equivalent indicators? Discuss in detail and illustrate. Indicate first the types of DBTG currency indicators.

6. Explain the basic difference between hierarchic pointers and child/twin pointers in IMS, using a graphical example with segment occurrences in a small data base that you are to diagram. Indicate the types of DL/1 queries that would be best served by child/twin pointers.

7. Consider the HISAM structure in Figure 7.34 for the Doctor data base. Show the physical structure after inserting each of the following segments:

    (a) The new CHILD segment with C_NAME = WILLIAM for EMPNO = 20.

    (b) The new CLINIC with C_NAME = CLINICX along with two EM-PLOYEE patients EMPNO = 1 and EMPNO = 2 for DOCTOR WILLIAMS.

8. Transform the two IMS DBDs below to the equivalent DBTG DDL schema. Include all that is necessary, except PICTURE clauses. Draw up first a schema block diagram and then the DDL schema description. The two IMS DBDs are:

    (a) The physical DBD for the Therapist PDB, Figure 7.19.

    (b) The physical DBD for the Clinic PDB, Figure 7.20.

9. This exercise is exactly like Exercise 5.4 but convert it to refer to the IMS data base in Figures 7.2, 7.3, and 7.4. Do parts (a) through (b) of the exercise after you have covered Section 7.5 on the IMS logical data base mechanisms.

10. Suppose that the two hierarchic data base subschemas indicated below are to be provided from a single shared data base. Can this be provided in IMS? If so, explain and indicate clearly how to best do it. Do not show the syntactic details of the IMS schema or subschema DDL.

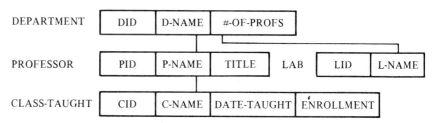

DEPARTMENT | DID | D-NAME | #-OF-PROFS

PROFESSOR | PID | P-NAME | TITLE | LAB | LID | L-NAME

CLASS-TAUGHT | CID | C-NAME | DATE-TAUGHT | ENROLLMENT

Subchema B:

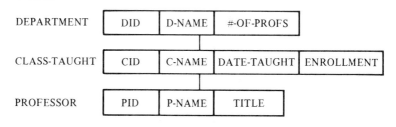

DEPARTMENT | DID | D-NAME | #-OF-PROFS

CLASS-TAUGHT | CID | C-NAME | DATE-TAUGHT | ENROLLMENT

PROFESSOR | PID | P-NAME | TITLE

8

SYSTEM 2000

8.1   INTRODUCTION AND ARCHITECTURE

INTEL's (formerly MRI's) SYSTEM 2000,®[1] is one of the most successful inverted data base systems commercially available since the early 1970s. Software AG's ADABAS,[2] CCA's Model 204,[3] and ADR's DATA-COM/DB[6] are the other major inverted data base systems. IBM's IMS, Burroughs network-oriented DMS II, and a few CODASYL GDBMS include some (but much less encompassing) inverted file options. A number of the relational GDBMS use extensively inverted file techniques internally to optimize relational data base accessing and processing.

We have chosen to focus on SYSTEM 2000 (S2K) as an exponent of inverted GDBMS. SYSTEM 2000 had its beginnings in one of the earliest GDBMS efforts: SDC's TDMS (*T*ime *S*hared *M*anagement *S*ystem), a fully inverted hierarchic GDBMS conceived in the late 1960s.[4]

S2K operates on several computer systems: IBM 360/370, 43XX and 30XX models, UNIVAC 1100 series, CDC 6000 series, and CYBER 70 and 170 series. The basic S2K can be complemented by several optional modules including: a nonprocedural query language for nonprogrammers; a procedural language interface to COBOL, PL/1, FORTRAN, and assembly language for programmers; sequential file processing capability; a multiuser capability, a multithread feature, and, for IBM 360/370 environments, a teleprocessing monitor.

S2K supports the concept of the schema and any number of subschemas. Each subschema can be made up of any subset of the data items or elements defined in the schema. The data base definition, as the schema is usually called in S2K publications, consists of data elements arranged in essentially the same manner as in COBOL or PL/1 records. There are no notions of DBTG sets and owner-member records. Thus S2K data bases are hierarchic structures.

The same architectural block diagram of the DBTG system in Figure 5.1 also applies to S2K. Beyond this similarity, S2K is very different, especially with respect to the way that a data base is organized and accessed. An S2K data base schema appears to the data base designer and users like a large COBOL or PL/1 record, that is, like a hierarchic structure. In addition, any or all of the fields can be inverted and established as access paths to the data base. The principle of the inverted data organization was introduced in Section 2.4. Readers are advised to review Section 2.4 and Figures 2.5–2.7 on the inverted approach. ADABAS and DATACOM/DB support network data bases.

8.2   THE SCHEMA OR DATA BASE

Let us illustrate the makeup of an S2K data base using the Employee-Insurance-Child data base used in the DBTG discussion in Chapter 5. This data base is included in the Doctor-Clinic-Employee-Insurance-Child data base used in the IMS discussion in Chapter 7. The Employee-Insurance-Child data base pictured in DBTG terms in Figure 5.6 and described by the DBTG DDL in Figure 5.8 can be structured and defined in S2K as shown in Figures 8.1 and 8.2, respectively. We have made some changes in the original DBTG schema to illustrate a few S2K features. Our S2K example is equivalent to the DBTG case in which INSURANCE-CO is the owner of the set in which EMPLOYEE is a member.

Figure 8.2 uses actual S2K syntax and format. The first line calls the DEFINE processor of S2K in order to define a new data base. The second line defines the new data base name INSURANCE-EMPLOYEE. Statements 1−18 declare the logical structure of the data base, the data types involved, and the inverted access fields required by the DBA. The numbers initiating each statement are a part of the S2K definition, but are not used in exactly the same way as in standard COBOL or PL/1 to specify the logical structure—as we shall see.

The Insurance-Employee data base.

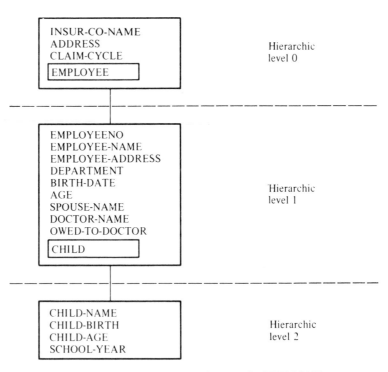

Figure 8.1. *Sample data base in SYSTEM 2000*

DEFINE:

NEW DATA BASE IS INSURANCE-EMPLOYEE:

1 * INSUR-CO-NAME (KEY NAME X(48)):

2 * ADDRESS (NON-KEY NAME X(40)):

3 * CLAIM-CYCLE (NON-KEY INTEGER 9(3)):

4 * EMPLOYEE (REPEATING GROUP):

5 * **EMPLOYEE-NO (KEY INTEGER 9(6) IN 4):**

6 * EMPLOYEE-NAME (KEY NAME X(25) IN 4):

7 * EMPLOYEE-ADDRESS (NON-KEY NAME X(40) IN 4):

8 * DEPARTMENT (KEY INTEGER 9(3) IN 4):

9 * BIRTH-DATE (NON-KEY DATE IN 4):

10 * AGE (INTEGER FUNCTION?((*FTODAY* – BIRTH-DATE)/365.25)?):

11 *SPOUSE-NAME (NON-KEY NAME X(10) IN 4):

12 * DOCTOR-NAME (KEY NAME X(25) IN 4):

13 *OWED-TO-DOCTOR (NON-KEY MONEY 9(5).9(2) IN 4):

14 * CHILD (REPEATING GROUP IN 4):

15 * CHILD-NAME (NON-KEY NAME X(10) IN 14):

16 *CHILD-BIRTH (NON-KEY DATE IN 14):

17 * CHILD-AGE (INTEGER FUNCTION? ((*FTODAY*-CHILD-BIRTH/365.25)?

18 *SCHOOL-YEAR (NON-KEY INTEGER 9(2) IN 14):

Figure 8.2. *Definition of an Insurance-Employee-Child data base in SYSTEM 2000*

No sets and no owner-member or parent-child relationships are explicitly defined in S2K. No undue concern for how to represent M to N relationships is forced; M to N relationships are handled equally as 1 to N relationships are. The basic components of a data base definition are data elements and repeating groups, which are in turn aggregates of data elements. A data element (a data item or field in other GDBMS terminologies) is also called a component in S2K. Repeating groups may be arranged and related only in a hierarchical fashion. Relationships may be 1 to N or M to N. The schema must be hierarchical.

In Figure 8.2 a repeating group is used to group a series of data items under it. Repeating groups also serve to implicitly link the levels of the hierarchy. The IN clause is used with each data element description to indicate the repeating group to which it belongs. For example, CHILD-BIRTH has the clause IN 14, meaning that it is under the repeating group name defined in line 14. Other data elements can be easily added, for example, by placing after statement 18:19* DEGREE (NAME X(4) IN 4).

A repeating group corresponds to the DBTG record type and the IMS segment. The use of repeating groups at the schema level does not mean that S2K stores physically together and must access a whole INSURANCE-EMPLOYEE record every time that any of its data elements are desired. To see this, look at the DBTG schema in Figure 2.16 and its possible realization in Figures 2.17 and 2.18. Now convert logically this schema to the S2K realm; Figure 2.19 shows the S2K inverted approach which shields the user from having to navigate through the intricate internal access paths. It is interesting to note that S2Ks logical data view is closer to the tabular or relational approach than either DBTG or IMS; this will surface as we discuss S2K.

By default, all data elements defined in the schema are automatically inverted when the data base is loaded. Any or all of the data elements can be declared to be noninverted by declaring the element to be NON-KEY, e.g., EMPLOYEE-ADDRESS NON-KEY. The concern for inverting is the result of access time performance considerations, and not of logical data considerations. The data base administrator has the responsibility of determining what data elements to invert. The considerations for determining what to invert were presented in Section 2.10. In S2K specific unique values of a data element cannot be selectively inverted, that is, either all or none of the values of an element are inverted.

A data element may be set up to be a *virtual* element whose value is determined at execution time by a computational procedure or function. For example, in Figure 8.2 AGE is determined by the integer function indicated which uses TODAY's date and the corresponding stored BIRTH-DATE. Thus when AGE is requested for any record, S2K materializes AGE when the request is executed; AGE is actually not physically stored at any time in external storage. The question mark and the asterisk are syntactic markers.

S2K data bases may consist of as many as 1,000 components and may be defined to 32 hierarchic levels. Our INSURANCE-EMPLOYEE data base has 16 data elements (the name of a repeating group is counted as a data element although it is not a data element in reality) and three hierarchic levels.

A data base is first defined by invoking the DEFINE processor of S2K. It is then loaded by means of special statements. Subschemas and types of accessing (read, update, etc.) are assigned by calling the CONTROL processor, as will be shown in the next section. Accessing of the data base through the subschemas allowed is discussed in Section 8.4.

Note that an S2K data base definition does not force the user to have to be concerned whether relationships between occurrences of repeating groups are 1 to 1, 1 to N, or M to N. As an example, the Professor-Student data base in

Figure 5.11 would be defined in the same way in S2K no matter what relationship there is between professors and students. Try it as an exercise. In DBTG we have to transform it as shown in Figure 5.12.

The S2K inherent hierarchic orientation is augmented with the LINK verb to permit network views of the data base. LINK allows the programming language programmer to establish relationships between any two record types based on common, or associative, keys. Links are dynamically established and do not require special utilities to establish, modify, or delete. Relationships can be established between any two record types in the same data base or in different data bases, allowing network-oriented data base processing while maintaining the inherent hierarchical schema structure. Retrieval of one record automatically retrieves the first record occurrence established by the LINK.

8.3   SUBSCHEMAS

The data base administrator may define as a subschema any logical and consistent subset of the data base. Let us trace how this is done.

After the data base has been named and defined, the DBA may define valid passwords and subsequently assign to each password the particular subschema and type of access to each data element. The first nine statements in Figure 8.3 define two subschemas and the type of access allowed, assuming that the INSURANCE-EMPLOYEE data base in Figure 8.2 has been previously defined. Let us trace the statements.

Statement 1 provides the DBA's master password which when recognized by S2K permits definition of subschemas and associated types of accesses. Only the holder of this master password can define and assign accessing rights to the data base.

Statement 2 indicates the schema or data base name. This data base name should be provided to users of any subschema defined over it.

Statement 3 calls the CONTROL processor of S2K so as to execute the next commands.

Statement 4 declares CARDENAS as a password. This password in conjunction with the data base name is essentially the subschema name.

Statement 5 says that all data elements in the data base definition of Figure 8.2 form the subschema associated with CARDENAS, and that CARDENAS has authority to read (R), update (U), and use in WHERE clauses (W) all data elements. The WHERE clause will be illustrated later; it is used for fast access via the inverted data elements specified.

Statement 6 defines GOODGUY as a password.

Statement 7 says that GOODGUY can read only the indicated data elements; the other elements cannot be accessed by GOODGUY.

Data base administration commands
{
1   USER, DB ADMINISTRATOR:

2   DATA BASE NAME IS INSURANCE-EMPLOYEE:

3   CONTROL:

4   VALID PASSWORD IS CARDENAS:

5   ASSIGN R, W, U TO ALL COMPONENTS FOR
    CARDENAS:

6   VALID PASSWORD IS GOODGUY:

7   **ASSIGN R TO INSUR-CO-NAME, EMPLOYEE-NO,
    EMPLOYEE-NAME, DEPARTMENT, OWED-
    TO-DOCTOR FOR GOODGUY:**

8   **ASSIGN W TO EMPLOYEE-NAME, EMPLOYEE-NO
    FOR GOODGUY:**

9   EXIT:
    :
}

User commands
{
10 USER, GOODGUY:

11 DATA BASE NAME IS INSURANCE-EMPLOYEE:

12 PRINT OWED-TO-DOCTOR, DEPARTMENT
    WHERE EMPLOYEE-NAME EQ RATKOVIC:

    { Printout of the requested information

13 CHANGE   INSUR-CO-NAME   AETNA   WHERE
    DEPARTMENT EQ 10:

    "Above statement not permitted to GOODGUY;
    GOODGUY has no authority to update nor to use
    DEPARTMENT with inverted access WHERE clause"
    :
}

Note.   The definitions in this figure assume that the INSURANCE-EMPLOYEE
data base in Figure 8.2 has been previously DEFINED; statements 11–13
assume that the data base has been previously LOADED.

Figure 8.3.   *Sample definition and on-line accessing of subschemas in
SYSTEM 2000*

Statement 8 says that GOODGUY can use EMPLOYEE-NAME and
EMPLOYEE-NO in a WHERE clause.

Statement 9 tells S2K that the DBA is terminating the interaction.

Statements 10–13 are self-explanatory. They show typical on-line accessing by GOODGUY. Note that statement 12 is executed by S2K, but not

statement 13 because GOODGUY is not allowed to update any elements or use DEPARTMENT in a WHERE clause.

8.4   DATA MANIPULATION

S2K provides five types of data manipulation facilities or modules to access and update data bases:

1. QUEUE query/update language;
2. QUEST query/ update language;
3. Report writer;
4. QUEX, query/update by example language; and
5. PLEX (Programming Language Extension), programming (procedural) language interface.

Figure 8.4 summarizes briefly their retrieval and updating features. We will discuss and illustrate the QUEUE, QUEST, and procedural language interface

SYSTEM 2000 Features	Retrieval	Updating
QUEUE Query/update Language	• Information production runs • Postprocessor input • Sequential processing • Standard queries • On-line with multiple terminals	• Data base creation • Maintenance • High volume (batch) updating • Update functions • On-line maintenance
QUEST Query/update Language	• Standard and ad hoc queries • Interactive browsing • System and user-specified functions • Nonrelated queries • Positional retrieval • On-line with multiple terminals	• Single and multiple element updates • Ad hoc updating • Positional updating • Small batch updates • On-line maintenance
QUEX Query/update Language	A menu-driven, formatted-screen, query and update language with some of the flavor of Query-by-Example	
Report Writer	• Standard reports • Ad hoc, one-time reports	• Changing of report format specifications
PLEX Programming Language Interface	Opens data bases to procedural programs for retrieval, updating, merging, and manipulating. Procedural programs may be written in COBOL, PL/1, Fortran, or assembly language.	

Figure 8.4.   *Facilities for retrieving and updating data bases in SYSTEM 2000*

PLEX facilities. We will use the sample data base and transactions or queries used in other chapters so that readers may realize the significant differences that we will point out between S2K and other GDBMS. The commands supported by QUEUE and QUEST make up the S2K self-contained query/update language, and they are highly nonprocedural and nonprogrammer user-oriented, in contrast to the more procedural language interface PLEX commands and the even more procedural DML of DBTG, TOTAL, and IMS.

QUEUE, Query/Update Language

The QUEUE query/update language or the Queued Access Feature is a part of the Basic S2K version; this term is peculiar to S2K. It provides facilities for data base loading, maintenance, and production of periodic reports. It is also used for ad hoc querying and updating involving a few data elements of the data base. However, queued access is designed for high-volume data base processing where the requirements may be organized into job queues and is suited for batch or remote-batch processing. Queued access might be used, for example, to perform all updates to a data base at the end of the day or week.

Queued access is designed to process a series of related transactions. All commands in a sequence are first examined and arranged by S2K into an internal sequence. For fast processing, all WHERE clause processing is completed taking advantage of the inverted data elements (indicated in the WHERE clause). Thus, all or a large portion of the queued or batched transactions can be processed in a single pass of only the relevant portions of the data base.

The major QUEUE commands enable the user to PRINT, LOAD, ADD, ASSIGN, APPEND, REMOVE, and CHANGE values in the data base. Values for single data elements, series of elements, repeating group and all of its logical descendants or trees or hierarchies, or an entire data base entry can be manipulated with a single command. Five of these statements are also available via the immediate access facilities. Loading of a data base and most data base maintenance in most installations will be done via the queued module or with the procedural language interface.

An example of the PRINT command is

PRINT EMPLOYEE WHERE EMPLOYEENO EQ 106

The command requests the full details of EMPLOYEE 106, i.e., data elements 5–18 in Figure 8.2.

Use of Inverted Indexes, WHERE Clause, and IF Clause

S2K fundamental inversion techniques allow complex logical access criteria and very fast retrieval via inverted data elements. The WHERE clause permits expressing complex access criteria using data elements and comparison operators such as EQ, NE, GT, GE, LT, LE, SPANS, FAILS, and EXISTS; comparison expressions may be combined with the logical operators AND, OR, and NOT. For example,

> PRINT EMPLOYEE-NAME, ADDRESS WHERE INSUR-CO-NAME
> EXISTS AND (DEPARTMENT EQ COMPSCI OR DEPARTMENT
> EQ MGT) AND OWED-TO-DOCTOR EXISTS.

is self-explanatory, in which EXISTS tests for the existence of a nonnull value for the data element indicated. Try this in DBTG DML, TOTAL DML, or IMS DL/1 to see the large difference between this nonprocedural communication and the procedural counterpart.

The data elements to be inverted are selected by the data base administrator when he or she defines a data base, e.g., Figure 8.2. Inverted and noninverted fields may be used in the WHERE clause to establish access criteria. In the basic S2K, QUEUE access mode qualification using noninverted values is also available via the IF clause as follows:

> IF ⟨some conditions are true⟩ THEN ⟨perform operation 1⟩
> [ELSE ⟨perform operation 2⟩]
> WHERE ⟨inverted data qualification⟩

The WHERE clause is typically used to screen out a major portion of the irrelevant data. The IF clause further qualifies the data and may screen it on both inverted and noninverted data elements. In the foregoing IF construct, operation 1 will operate on all data that satisfies both the WHERE clause and the IF clause criteria; operation 2 operates on all data that satisfies the WHERE clause but not the IF cause. Two examples are:

> IF OWED-TO-DOCTOR GE 1000* THEN PRINT INSUR-CO-NAME,
> PRINT EMPLOYEE-NAME WHERE BIRTH-DATE LT 1/1/30*:
> IF RATE OF PAY LT 3.75* THEN ASSIGN BONUS EQ 150.00*
> ELSE ASSIGN BONUS EQ 175.00*
> WHERE ALL OF (RATE-OF-PAY GE 3.25*, RATE-OF-PAY LE 4.50*):

The last command assigns a bonus of $150 to all those earning between $3.25 and $3.75 an hour; all those earning between $3.75 and $4.50 receive a bonus of $175.

QUEST Query/Update Language

The S2K QUEST query/update language is suited for standard and ad hoc queries, low-volume processing, single and multiple element retrieval and updating, interactive browsing, and on-line use of a data base via keyboard terminals. Each command is processed individually and independently of the next command. The performance objective is fast access to selected portions of a data base.

The major QUEST commands are summarized in Figure 8.5. Values for single data elements, series of elements, repeating group and all of its logical descendants or tree, or an entire data base entry can be manipulated with a single command. Figure 8.6 illustrates the use of these commands for the INSURANCE-EMPLOYEE data base defined in Figure 8.2. These same eight examples of data manipulation are also shown in Section 5.6 for a DBTG system and its DML (except Example 4 which is intricate to carry out in

DESCRIBE	to retrieve a copy of the data base definition, or of a portion of it.
TALLY	to obtain statistical information about the values of data elements stored in the data base (e.g., number of unique values, frequency of occurrence).
PRINT*	to retrieve specified data sets that satisfy the "WHERE clause" and output the data in a simple sequential list.
LIST	to retrieve specified data sets that satisfy the "WHERE clause" and output the data in (simple) report format.
ADD*	to add data values within existing data sets where no data values currently exist.
CHANGE*	to change data values within existing data sets where data exists.
ASSIGN*	to assign data values within existing data sets whether or not the existing data sets contain data values.
REMOVE*	to remove data values from selected data sets.
REMOVE TREE*	to remove the values from each selected data set and *all* of its hierarchic descendant data sets.
ASSIGN TREE	to replace current data trees with new data trees.
INSERT TREE	to add new data trees where data trees do not exist.

*Also available in the QUEUE query/update language.

Note: Data set refers to an occurrence of a repeating group.

Figure 8.5. *Main SYSTEM 2000 QUEST query/update commands*

DBTG), in Section 7.4 for IMS and DL/1, in Section 10.3 for SQL/DS, and in Section 11.3 for QBE; most of these examples are also shown in Section 6.3 for TOTAL and its DML. The examples in Figure 8.6 are self-explanatory. Notice the convenience of this nonprocedural query communication versus the burdensome procedural network and hierarchic counterparts. Reference to a query in the following paragraphs will be to those in Figure 8.6.

1. Get full details of employee 106.
    PRINT EMPLOYEE WHERE EMPLOYEE-NO EQ 106

2. Retrieve the NAME and AGE of all children of employee 106.
    PRINT CHILD-NAME, *CHILD-AGE* WHERE C5 EQ 106

3. Retrieve the ADDRESS of the insurance company whose name is EQUITABLE which services employee 20.
    PRINT ADDRESS WHERE INSUR-CO-NAME EQ EQUITABLE AND EMPLOYEE-NO EQ 20

4. Retrieve the name, age, and school year of all children of employees insured by PURITAN.
    PRINT   CHILD-NAME,   *CHILD-AGE*,   SCHOOL-YEAR WHERE INSUR-CO-NAME EQ PURITAN

5. Indicate employee 106 has a policy with AETNA (and previously had no policy).
    ADD INSUR-CO-NAME EQ AETNA* WHERE EMPLOYEE-NO EQ 106

6. Employee 106 has changed insurance company from PURITAN to AETNA, and has acquired a new doctor named JONES.
    CHANGE INSUR-CO-NAME EQ AETNA* WHERE C5 EQ 106: CHANGE DOCTOR-NAME EQ JONES* WHERE SAME

7. Add a new child to employee 106
    INSERT TREE CHILD EQ 15 * JOE * 16 * 1.12.76 * 18 * 0 * END * AFTER EMPLOYEE-NO EQ 106

8. Delete employee's 106 information, that is, all data elements owned by this employee.
    REMOVE TREE EMPLOYEE WHERE EMPLOYEE-NO EQ 106

Note: These queries are directed at the full INSURANCE-EMPLOYEE data base described in Fig. 8.2.

Figure 8.6.   *Sample data base accessing in SYSTEM 2000, QUEST Query/Update Language*

Query 2 shows the use of a data name whose value is calculated at execution time; enclosing asterisks indicate it: *CHILD-AGE*.

The name of a data element may be replaced in a command by its corresponding sequence number indicated when the data base was first defined. Thus, queries 2 and 6 use C5 in the WHERE clause to denote EMPLOYEENO.

The results of WHERE clause processing may be reused with the SAME operator so that WHERE clause access criteria need not be reprocessed. For example, see query 6.

BEFORE/AFTER Data Manipulation

Access of data by logical or by physical position in the data base is a capability available in QUEST and in PLEX. A BEFORE or AFTER keyword may be used to navigate based on relative logical position in the data base. BEFORE or AFTER must be used with INSERT TREE instead of a WHERE clause to refer to the data located before or after the data selected by the BEFORE/AFTER clause. This facility is a counterpart to the "get next" data base navigation commands in DBTG and IMS.

SYSTEM 2000 also permits access based on the relative physical position of the data in the data base. The capability enables the user to list the most recent values that have been entered for a repeating group's element regardless of the element's logical content; for example, in a skills inventory data base it permits listing the most recent skills that each person has acquired.

Programming Language Interface and Processing

S2K data bases may be accessed and processed by programs written in COBOL, PL/1, FORTRAN, or assembly language via the PLEX procedural language interface applicable to each language. Processing via programming languages is warranted when the costs of programming and error correction of procedural programs are offset by economies achieved through frequent use, such as in the repetitive processing of large master files. It is essential that a GDBMS have interfaces to these languages since most organizations have substantial investments in programs coded in these languages (sometimes hundreds of thousands of lines of code).

The interfaces provide facilities for opening the portion or subschema(s) of the data base to be processed by the program, screening and ordering the data in the sequence expected by the procedural program, retrieving selected data from the data base, reloading procedurally processed data into the data base, and closing the data base. The invocation of S2K is through code inside a source program. A COBOL source program would be first passed through a S2K precompiler where first the subschema(s) intended to be used are checked and then all S2K procedural statements are converted to the appropriate call statements to the procedural language interface. The COBOL compiler then compiles the source program. At execution time the compiled program calls the procedural language interface, which in turn calls S2K to access the desired portion of the data base. Data may be assessed using the WHERE clause or an ordering clause, in a manner equivalent to the QUEST access mode.

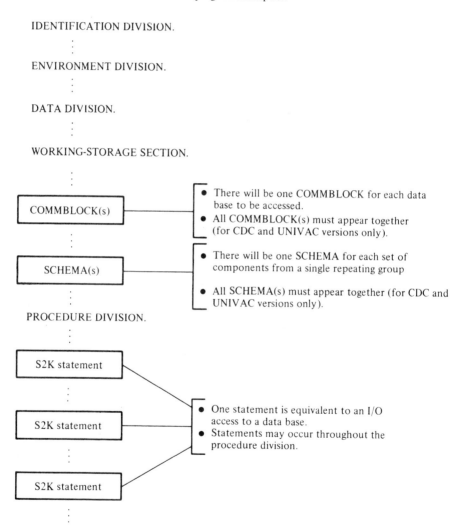

COBOL program description

IDENTIFICATION DIVISION.

ENVIRONMENT DIVISION.

DATA DIVISION.

WORKING-STORAGE SECTION.

COMMBLOCK(s)
- There will be one COMMBLOCK for each data base to be accessed.
- All COMMBLOCK(s) must appear together (for CDC and UNIVAC versions only).

SCHEMA(s)
- There will be one SCHEMA for each set of components from a single repeating group
- All SCHEMA(s) must appear together (for CDC and UNIVAC versions only).

PROCEDURE DIVISION.

S2K statement

S2K statement
- One statement is equivalent to an I/O access to a data base.
- Statements may occur throughout the procedure division.

S2K statement

Figure 8.7. *Skeletal structure of a COBOL application program using SYSTEM 2000*

Working Storage Statements in Data Division

COMMBLOCK — to define, for each data base to be accessed, the WORKING-STORAGE communication area for status flags, return codes, and identification information necessary for proper communication between SYSTEM 2000 and the user program.

SCHEMA — to identify and describe those elements of a repeating group for which values will be retrieved or updated during the processing of a procedural language command within the user's program.

Procedure Division Statements

OPEN — to make a data base available to the user program.

CLOSE — to logically "close" the data base.

START S2K — to signal the SYSTEM 2000 precompiler to perform initialization procedures.

GET1 — to retrieve one and only one data set occurrence from the entire set.

LOCATE — to create a scratch file containing the pointer(s) for one or more data sets qualified by the conditions in a WHERE clause.

GET — to retrieve a data set using one of the pointers collected by a LOCATE statement.

ORDER — to order the data sets collected by the LOCATE statement.

INSERT — to create a new data set occurrence in the data base.

MODIFY — to add, change, or remove one or more data values within a data set. The assumption is that the user has retrieved the data set occurrence to be modified prior to issuing the MODIFY statement.

REMOVE — to remove one or more data values from a data set occurrence.

REMOVE TREE — to remove a complete data set occurrence and all of its hierarchic descendants.

Note: Data set refers to an occurrence of a repeating group.

Figure 8.8.   *SYSTEM 2000 PLEX language commands for use in a program written in COBOL, PL/1, etc.*

The interfaces permit extracting data from one data base, retaining the data, and combining it procedurally with data from a second data base. Data from several data bases may be merged and manipulated and the results reflected in the appropriate data bases.

Let us examine the COBOL interface and then a complete COBOL application program. Figure 8.7 shows the typical invocation of S2K in a COBOL application program. The schemas are declared in the COBOL Working Storage section. There is one COMMBLOCK for each data base to be accessed. Note that there must be one schema in the application program for each set of components from a single repeating group in the original data base definition. Recall that, as shown in Figure 8.3, an application program will not be allowed by S2K to access data elements not assigned to the password that the program must provide.

Figure 8.8 summarizes the PLEX commands for use in a program written in COBOL, PL/1, etc. Some of these commands will now be used in an example.

Example: Use of S2K in a COBOL Application

The INSURANCE-EMPLOYEE data base defined in Figure 8.2 will be used by the following COBOL application. The task is:

1. Read a TRANS record from a TRANSACTION sequential file not under the control of S2K.

2. Determine from a code in the TRANS record how the INSURANCE-EMPLOYEE data base is to be affected: remove a given EMPLOYEE tree, insert a new CHILD, or change the insurance information.

3. Repeat (1) and (2) for every record in the TRANSACTION file.

Figure 8.9 shows the complete COBOL application program and S2K subschema definition, control and data manipulation commands to accomplish the preceding tasks. The program should be essentially self-explanatory for most readers (if not, remedial reading in COBOL is advised). S2K commands start in column 7 before the start of the COBOL A margin so as to differentiate S2K commands from COBOL (COBOL usually has a number of margin restrictions for placing certain COBOL constructs). We will artificially precede S2K commands herein with an asterisk (*).

The COMMBLOCK of the INSURANCE-EMPLOYEE data base is an area in WORKING STORAGE that provides pertinent communication and information between the S2K data base and the program. This information is provided via the indicated variable names with the 02

```
IDENTIFICATION DIVISION.
PROGRAM-ID. COBOL-S2K.
REMARKS. EXAMPLE OF A COBOL PROGRAM AND SYSTEM
   2000 INTERACTION.
ENVIRONMENT DIVISION.
DATA DIVISION.
FILE SECTION.
FD   TRANSACTION   RECORD CONTAINS 159 CHARACTERS
                   RECORD MODE IS F
                   LABEL RECORD IS STANDARD
                   DATA RECORD IS TRANS.

01   TRANS.
     02  I-CODE            PIC 9.
     02  I-INS-NAME        PIC X(48).
     02  I-INS-ADDR        PIC X(64).
     02  I-EMP-NUMBER      PIC 9(6).
     02  I-CHILD.
     03  I-CHILD-NAME      PIC X(32).
     03  I-CHILD-BIRTH     PIC 9(6).
     03  I-CHILD-SCHOOL    PIC 9(2).

WORKING-STORAGE SECTION.
*COMMBLOCK OF INSURANCE-EMPLOYEE.
01   INSURANCE-EMPLOYEE.
     02   SCHEMA-NAME.
     02   RETURN-CODE.
     02   FILLER.
     02   LAST-DATA-SET.
     02   PASSWORD VALUE IS 'ABRA'.
     02   NUMBER-OF-DATA-SETS.
     02   DATA-SET-POSITION.
     02   LEVEL.
     02   CYCLE-TIME.
     02   CYCLE-DATE.
     02   CYCLE-NUMBER.
     02   SEPARATOR-SYMBOL.
     02   END-TERMINATOR.
     02   DAMAGE-STATUS
     02   PARENT.
```

(continued)

```
*SCHEMA INSURANCE OF INSURANCE-EMPLOYEE.
01  INSURANCE.
    02  INSUR-CO-NAME    PIC X(48).
    02  ADDRESS          PIC X(64).
*SCHEMA EMPLOYEE OF INSURANCE-EMPLOYEE.
01  EMPLOYEE.
    02  EMPLOYEE-NO      PIC 9(6).
*SCHEMA CHILD OF INSURANCE-EMPLOYEE.
01  CHILD.
    02  CHILD-NAME       PIC X(32).
    02  CHILD-BIRTH      PIC 9(6).
    02  SCHOOL-YEAR      PIC 9(2).
*END SCHEMAS.
PROCEDURE DIVISION.
*START S2K.
    OPEN INPUT TRANSACTION.
*OPEN INSURANCE-EMPLOYEE.
MORE.
    NOTE THIS PARAGRAPH ACCESSES THE NON-S2K
        SEQUENTIAL FILE.
    READ TRANSACTION AT END GO TO COMPLETE.
    IF I-CODE EQUAL TO 1 THEN GO TO DELETION.
    IF I-CODE EQUAL TO 2 THEN GO TO NEW-CHILD.
    IF I-CODE EQUAL TO 3 THEN GO TO CHANGE-INS.
DELETION.
    MOVE I-EMP-NUMBER TO EMPLOYEENO.
    NOTE NEXT STATEMENT ACCESSES THE DATA BASE.
*GET1 EMPLOYEE WHERE EMPLOYEENO.
    IF RETURN-CODE NOT EQUAL TO 0 THEN GO TO ERROR.
    NOTE PREVIOUS RETURN-CODE CHECKING IS
        NECESSARY, BUT IS NOT SHOWN FURTHER.

*REMOVE TREE EMPLOYEE.
    GO TO MORE.
NEW-CHILD.
    MOVE I-EMP-NUMBER TO EMPLOYEE-NO.
*GET1 EMPLOYEE WHERE EMPLOYEE-NO.
    MOVE I-CHILD TO CHILD.
*INSERT CHILD.
    GO TO MORE.
```

(continued)

```
CHANGE-INS.
    MOVE I-INS-NAME TO INSUR-CO-NAME.

*GET1 INSURANCE WHERE INSUR-CO-NAME.
    MOVE I-INS-ADDR TO ADDRESS.

*MODIFY INSURANCE.
    GO TO MORE.
COMPLETE.
    CLOSE TRANSACTION.

*CLOSE INSURANCE-EMPLOYEE.
    STOP RUN.
ERROR.
    DISPLAY 'ERROR DURING PROCESSING'.
    STOP RUN.
    END.
```

Figure 8.9.   *Sample COBOL program using SYSTEM 2000 to access the INSURANCE-EMPLOYEE data base in Figure 8.2*

level: SCHEMA-NAME through PARENT. It includes status flags, return and identification information to keep the user appraised of the S2K data base. This information is the counterpart of that provided by IMS for an application program, Section 7.4. The information is provided by S2K after the execution of every S2K command, except PASSWORD which must be provided by the program before opening the data base. PASSWORD is initialized to 'ABRA' in this case.

Three application program schemas are declared based on the INSURANCE-EMPLOYEE data base: INSURANCE, EMPLOYEE, and CHILD. One schema must be declared for each set of data elements from a single repeating group.

If the proper PASSWORD has not been provided, then S2K does not obey the OPEN INSURANCE-EMPLOYEE command.

The first statement in paragraph MORE reads the first or the next record in the TRANSACTION file. The next three statements determine from the I-CODE in the record just read what to do, i.e., what paragraph to invoke.

Paragraph DELETION retrieves from EMPLOYEE-INSUR-ANCES via GET1 the EMPLOYEE occurrence and all of its tree (logical dependents) for the EMPLOYEENO indicated. If the EMPLOYEE desired exists in the data base, as indicated by zero value for RETURN-CODE, then that EMPLOYEE record occurrence and all its data elements and its CHILD repeating group are removed from the data base. This will be executed if the correct password has been previously indicated and it has been given update rights to all elements under the EMPLOYEE repeating group.

Paragraph NEW-CHILD retrieves via GET1 the EMPLOYEE tree for the EMPLOYEENO indicated. The following MOVE modifies in memory one of the CHILD occurrences. The INSERT command inserts or creates the new CHILD occurrence for the particular EMPLOYEE.

Paragraph CHANGE-INS retrieves from the data base via GET1 the stored INSUR-CO-NAME and its ADDRESS for the given I-INS-NAME. The next MOVE replaces in memory the ADDRESS by the new I-INS-ADDR. The elements denoted by INSURANCE stored in the data base for this insurance company are then modified by the MODIFY command.

At the end of each paragraph a return to MORE is made. Processing terminates when no more records appear in the TRANSACTION file.

The use of the COMMBLOCK indicators is not illustrated in this example, except for PASSWORD and RETURN-CODE. In practice it is important to check the RETURN-CODE provided by S2K after execution of every S2K statement in the PROCEDURE DIVISION and take proper action when the RETURN-CODE value indicates abnormal conditions.

REFERENCES

1. "SYSTEM 2000 Reference Manual," INTEL Corp. Austin Texas.
2. "ADABAS Reference Manual," Software AG., Reston, Va.
3. "Model 204 Reference Manual," Computer Corporation of America, Cambridge, Mass.
4. Bleir, R. F., "Treating Hierarchical Data Structures in the SDC Time-shared Data Management System (TDMS)," *Proceedings, 22nd ACM National Conference*, 1967, pp. 41–49.
5. "SYSTEM 2000 Extended Procedural Language Feature," INTEL Systems Corp., Austin, Texas.
6. "DATACOM/DB User's Guide," Applied Data Research Corp., Princeton, N.J.

EXERCISES

1. Define the SYSTEM 2000 schema for the IMS data base shown in Figure 7.2. Use the SYSTEM 2000 schema DDL.

2. Define a SYSTEM 2000 subschema based on the schema that you defined in Exercise 1. Include only the key fields D_NAME,C_NAME, E_NAME, and I_NAME with read and write rights to each field. Use the SYSTEM 2000 SUBSCHEMA DDL.

3. Using the SYSTEM 2000 QUEST access query language, service each of the following questions. These are among the questions exemplified for IMS using DL/1 in Section 7.4. Assume that you have access to the whole schema that you defined in Exercise 1.

   (a) Retrive all data files of EMPLOYEE 106 without concern for the particular DOCTOR involved.

   (b) Retrieve all repeating groups in the data base.

   (c) Retrieve all the CHILD information for each child whose age > 14 and whose parent has AMT_OWED $\geqslant$600.

   (d) Retrieve the name and claim cycle of every insurance company of EMPLOYEE 106.

   (e) For EMPLOYEE 106 change the address of his insurance company to DISAPPEARED and change the SPECIALTY of his DOCTOR to QUACK.

   (f) Delete all fields of EMPLOYEE 106, all of the related CHILD information, and all information on the company that insures him.

   (g) Retrieve the names of the insurance companies insuring employees with children older than 10.

4. Suppose that there are three separate data bases each with several fields: $A_1, A_2, \ldots$ for data base A; $B_1, B_2, \ldots$ for data base B; and $C_1, C_2 \ldots$ for data base C. Consider that they are to be implemented using an inverted GDBMS such as SYSTEM 2000. Is it possible to answer queries in which the qualification part (following the WHERE clause) involves fields of several data bases, for example: LIST A_1, A_2, and A_3 WHERE ($A_4 = x$ AND $B_1 = y$ AND $C_1 = 2$) OR $B_2 = 60$? If yes, define three SYSTEM 2000 data bases, show clearly what you would invert, and explain how the query or queries would be posed to SYSTEM 2000. Use real SYSTEM 2000 syntax and semantics.

5. Consider the Insurance-Employee SYSTEM 2000 data base in Figure 8.1. Indicate the QUEST access query language command(s) to service each of the following requests:

   (a) How many employees are there with children under X years old?

(b) For each insurance company in the data base, obtain a list of the names of the departments whose employees are insured by the insurance company.

(c) Obtain the names of the insurance companies that insure employees whose AGE is greater than 65 and who have at least one child under 3 years old.

(d) Delete all the employee information, along with the children, for which the amount OWED_TO_DOCTOR >5000.

(e) Delete all children from parents whose AGE is greater than 65, are insured by PURITAN, and the amount OWED_TO_DOCTOR >5000.

(f) Change the name of the C.S. DEPARTMENT to Computer Science wherever it appears in the data base.

9

THE
RELATIONAL
DATA BASE
APPROACH

9.1   INTRODUCTION AND ARCHITECTURE

Four previous chapters have focused on the main data base structures and associated data manipulations supported by commercially available nonrelational GDBMS; the network approach is exemplified by the CODASYL DBTG system, Chapter 5, and TOTAL, Chapter 6; the hierarchic approach, as exemplified by IMS, Chapter 7; and the inverted hierarchic approach as exemplified by SYSTEM 2000, Chapter 8. We showed how a data base may be defined and manipulated by such representative GDBMS while striving to achieve the stated objectives of data base technology: data independence, nonredundancy, relatability, and so forth. We saw that these goals are achieved by the GDBMS in various degrees and forms.

A data base system must be able to represent and manipulate entities (records or segments) and their relationships easily and conveniently. In the IMS hierarchic or tree approach, the relationship between two segments is represented by the relative top to bottom position of the segment types involved. In the network approach, relationships are represented by pointer-oriented set mechanisms tying an owner record type with a member record type. For a large and complicated data base the logical model and the manner in which users may access it via a data manipulation language (e.g., DBTG's DML and IMS's DL/1) may become very complex, in fact, too complex for casual programmers. Furthermore, data accessing becomes very access-path oriented in terms of the links or hierarchic positions established by the data base designer. Thus a number of changes to the data base may violate data independence and affect application programs. A review of the DBTG, TOTAL, and IMS examples shows this. The inverted approach, exemplified by SYSTEM 2000 particularly, with its query language(s) (Chapter 8), avoids to a greater extent many such problems.

The relational data base approach conceived by E. F. Codd[1-4] and evolving since 1970 is a significantly different approach to the *logical* description and manipulation of data. It strives to avoid many of the drawbacks mentioned and to provide advantages in data independence, ease of use and user friendliness, data base processing power, and security controls.[19] In a nutshell, it views the logical data base as a simple collection of two-dimensional tables called **relations**. These tables are flat in that no repeating groups are involved. They are easily understood and handled by users with little or no training in programming, and they involve no consideration of positional, pointer, or access path aspects. A simple table such as that in Figure 3.8(b) seems easier to visualize and manipulate than its equivalent conventional form in Figure 3.8(a). Just as a network data base can be transformed into a tree data base by introducing redundancy, so can any data base be transformed into a relational or flat table data base by introducing additional redundancy.

In this chapter we will outline the fundamentals of the relational approach. Chapters 10 and 11 present the SQL/DS and QBE relational systems, which illustrate the two major relational approaches commercially available. Chapter 12 will focus on the functional relationships of data in a data base, concepts fundamental to the semantics of data which have also evolved as part of the relational approach but which are actually applicable to other data base models.

Codd suggested two data manipulation languages, called **data sublanguages**, for relational data bases.[3] We shall outline them. They are very high-level query languages that operate at the logical level. They are very access path independent.

It should be stressed that we shall deal herein with the logical data base realm and not with the powerful access paths and physical data structures that are obviously essential to support the logical features and expected capabilities advocated by the relational approach. The ultimate test of the cost-effectiveness feasibility of the relational approach in a real and very large commercial data base environment is being performed in the 1980s. Relational systems have been greatly successful in smaller scale data base environments. Readers should be aware that successful commercial GDBMS are largely the result of practical compromises that have to be made between (1) desired features and capabilities for the convenience of users and (2) what can be implemented at an acceptable cost and performance. Practical compromises and advances in hardware horsepower are leading to the success of commercial relational GDBMS. One of the biggest challenges to the relational approach is its efficient and cost-effective implementation for large data bases.

An increasing number of data base efforts center on the relational data base model. Many publications and conference activities have been inspired by Codd's specifications in the early 1970s. As of 1975, over 150 articles had been written on relational data base matters;[12] Date's textbook presented the first overall introduction to the relational approach.[14]

The relational approach unfortunately carries a terminology of its own and a tendency to use unconventional terms which are rather mathematically oriented. The relational approach is based on the mathematical theory of relations. It thus has a good theoretical foundation. However, the relational theory terms have been adopted for the data base environment, thus presenting at times perhaps intricate terminology for rather simple ideas.

Figure 9.1 shows the relational architecture advocated. The overall level-by-level architecture is the familiar one of most GDBMS. The global data base is a collection of relations generally referred to as the **relational data model**, **stored relations**, **base relations**, or **relational data base**. The term schema is infrequently used. The data model is defined by the data base administrator (DBA) via a **relational data model description language**.

A particular user's data model extracted from the global data model is

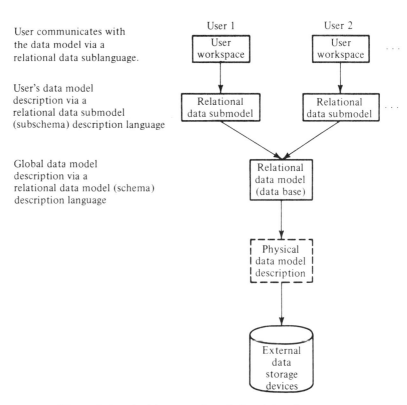

User communicates with
the data model via a
relational data sublanguage.

User's data model
description via a
relational data submodel
(subschema) description language

Global data model
description via a
relational data model (schema)
description language

Figure 9.1. *Architecture of a relational data base system*

called a **relational data submodel** or **view** (the term view is more frequently used). The term subschema is infrequently used. The data submodel is defined by the DBA and/or called by the user via a **relational data submodel description language**. The data submodel is a collection of relations that may be derived from those in the data model by a number of **relational operations**. The data submodel description language will include the necessary relational operations or mechanisms to form permissible submodels from the model. In fact, the submodel description language is basically the data sublanguage itself, with some data definition augmentation.

An arbitrary number of submodels may be defined over a given data model. A submodel could be the whole data model (this will be the case in most of our examples). An arbitrary number of users may share a given data model via the submodels. The submodels may overlap.

Each user has one or several **workspaces** to hold temporarily a reasonable amount of data being accessed from or being stored in the data model.

9.2   THE RELATIONAL DATA MODEL (SCHEMA)

In less formal terms, a **relation** is a two-dimensional table with n-columns and made up of a set of n-tuples. Each row is an n-tuple. Each of the columns in a relation is a set of values of one data item type (field type or attribute) and is referred to as a **domain**. In the formal mathematical language, given sets D_1, $D_2...$, D_n (not necessarily distinct), R is a relation on these n sets if it is a set of n-tuples each of which has its first element from D_1, its second element from D_2, and so on. If the relation has n domains or columns, the relation is said to be of degree n. Relations of degree 2 are called binary, of degree 3 are called ternary, and of degree n are called n-ary. The term **table** refers to a collection of tuples of a given relation. Hence the terms table and relation are used interchangeably (note that the word table is the term used in COBOL to denote an array!).

Figure 9.2 shows a relation called DOCTOR formed by the domains DOC# (doctor identification number), DOC-NAME (doctor name), SPECIALTY and CLINIC (in which the doctor practices). The notational representation of this structure of the relation is

DOCTOR (DOC#, DOC-NAME, SPECIALTY, CLINIC).

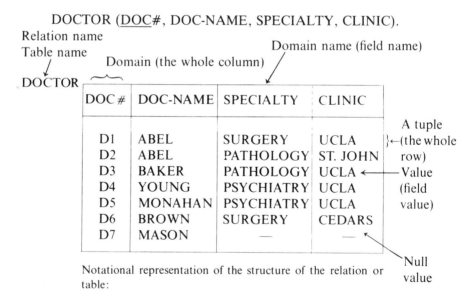

Notational representation of the structure of the relation or table:

DOCTOR (DOC#, DOC-NAME, SPECIALTY, CLINIC)

Key domain

Figure 9.2.   *A relation (or table)*

A relation or table is a two-dimensional array with the following characteristics:

1. Each entry in the table is one data item; there are no repeating groups. Said in other words, each domain D_i must be a simple domain; that is, it does not represent another relation. A relation is said to be **normalized** (perhaps "flat" might have been a much better term) if it has no repeating groups; otherwise it is said to be unnormalized.

2. Each column, the domain, is assigned a distinct name, a domain name, and is made up of values of the same data item.

3. All rows or tuples are distinct; duplicates are not allowed.

4. The rows and the columns can be ordered in any sequence at any time without affecting the information content or the semantics involved.

We can visualize the following approximate correspondence with IMS and the more traditional COBOL and DBTG terminology;

Relational	DBTG	IMS
Attribute, field, column	Data item	Field
Attribute value, field value	Data item value	Field value
Domain	—	—
Relation, table structure	Record type	Segment type
Tuple, row	Record (occurrence)	Segment (occurrence)
Relation, table	File	File
Interrelation relationship	Set type	Parent-child relationship
Degree of a relation	Number of items in the record type	Number of fields in the segment type

It is important to keep these correspondences in mind. They are a good basis for comparison. One of the difficulties in understanding the relational approach is that its terminology is so different from that of nonrelational practice.

For a given assortment of data different users perceive different relations and relationships. It is necessary to derive subsets of the table columns to form tables of smaller degree for some users and to join tables together to form tables of larger degree for other users. Codd suggested two languages to carry out these operations in logical terms: the **relational calculus** and the **relational algebra**,[3,4] which we will address later. A relational data base is viewed by programmers and users as a time-varying collection of normalized relations of various degrees manipulated by powerful operators for extracting columns and joining them. These operations call for a high degree of logical data manipulation not readily available in conventional network and hierarchic data base systems.

Each tuple of a relation must have a **key** by which the tuple can be uniquely identified and differentiated from other tuples of that relation. The key is either a simple domain (field) or combination of domains. A key made up of a combination of domains is **nonredundant** if no domain of the key can be deleted without destroying the ability to uniquely identify each tuple. There may be more than one set of domains which may be a key, that is, that uniquely identifies each tuple and is nonredundant. These sets are called **candidate keys**. The **primary key** is the set of domains chosen to identify the tuples. Normally it should be the one with the smallest number of domains.

As an example, the primary key of the relation DOCTOR shown in Figure 9.2 is DOC#. DOC-NAME could not be the key since it is possible that two different doctors may have the same name. The key is indicated by underlining it in the notational representation of the relation:

DOCTOR (DOC#, DOC-NAME, SPECIALTY, CLINIC)

Normalization

Normalization is the process by which any nonflat data structure, such as a COBOL, network, or tree data base, can be transformed by a data base designer into a set of **normalized relations**, that is, a set of flat relations that have no repeating groups. Just as a network data base can be transformed into a hierarchic data base by introducing redundancy (as shown in Figure 3.15), so can any data base be transformed into a relational data base by introducing additional redundancy. A nonflat relation is said to be **unnormalized**. An unnormalized relation has at least one domain which is in reality another relation. A normalized relation has only simple domains, that is, domains that are not in turn another relation.

A file which is flat except for a repeating group is normalized by removing the repeating group into a separate relation. (Recall that a repeating group is actually a 1 to N relationship; compare the following with the representation of a 1 to N relationship in DIAM.) This new relation must be named and must have a key. Figure 9.3 shows this normalization for a two-record type data base (same as Figure 3.8). Note that the key field DEPT # must be repeated in the new relation PROFESSOR and combined with PROF # to form the key of PROFESSOR. Duplication is introduced by the need to use some fields in more than one relation in order to uniquely identify the tuples. Although this duplication does not necessarily mean real storage redundancy internal to the GDBMS, it does pose the burden on the GDBMS of trying to avoid large redundancies. Logical redundancy does not necessarily mean physical redun-

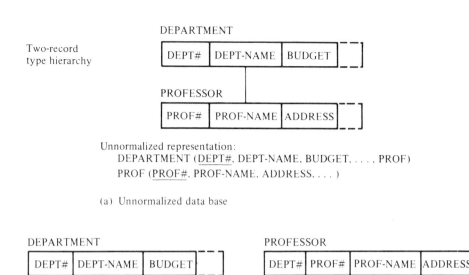

(a) Unnormalized data base

(b) Normalized relational data base

Figure 9.3.   *Conversion of a two-record type hierarchy into a normalized relational data base*

dancy, but it definitely means at least some overhead cost to avoid physical redundancy.

Note that if repeating groups are not separated from record types by normalization when a data base is initially designed, it is possible that they may need to be separated later due to the way in which the data base may evolve. For example, if a new record type needs to be related to instances of a repeating group embedded in a record type of the original design, then this repeating group may have to be separated. If it is separated, then the application programs using the original record type may have to be modified. Normalization enhances data independence, i.e., the insulation of an application program to changes in the data structures.

Let us describe formally the normalization process, using as an example the hierarchic Doctor data base shown in Figure 9.4 that we have used in past chapters (Figure 7.2). Normalization proceeds as follows:

1. Starting with the relation at the top of the tree, remove each of its subordinate relations (the nonsimple domains) into a separate relation augmented by the primary key of the top relation.

(a) The hierarchic scheme:

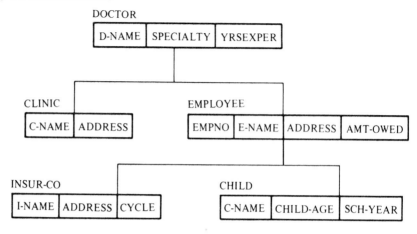

DOCTOR   (D-NAME, SPECIALITY, YRSEXPER, CLINIC, EMPLOYEE)
CLINIC   (C-NAME, ADDRESS)
EMPLOYEE   (EMPNO, E-NAME, ADDRESS, AMT-OWED, INSUR-CO, CHILD)
INSUR-CO   (I-NAME, ADDRESS, CYCLE)
CHILD   (C-NAME, CHILD-AGE, SCH-YEAR)

(b) The equivalent normalized relational data model:

DOCTOR   (D-NAME, SPECIALITY, YRSEXPER)
CLINIC   (D-NAME, C-NAME, ADDRESS)
EMPLOYEE   (D-NAME, EMPNO, E-NAME, ADDRESS, AMT-OWED)
INSUR-CO   (D-NAME, EMPNO, I-NAME, ADDRESS, CYCLE)
CHILD   (D-NAME, EMPNO, C-NAME, CHILD-AGE, SCH-YEAR)

Figure 9.4. *Normalization of a hierarchic data base*

2. The primary key of each separated relation must be made up of the primary key before separation concatenated with the primary key of the parent relation.

3. Delete all the nonsimple domains in the parent relation.

4. Remove this top parent relation from further normalization activity.

5. Repeat steps 1–4 on each remaining subtree.

The end result of the previous steps is a set of normalized relations. The result of applying this procedure to the unnormalized data base in Figure 9.4(a) is shown in Figure 9.4(b). The primary key of each normalized relation is underlined. Note that data redundancy is introduced by the new keys that must be used.

Any network data base may be converted to a normalized set of relations by first transforming it to its equivalent tree (or set of trees) representation and then normalizing each of these trees.

Representation of M to N Relationships

The relational model avoids problems that we have seen for the network model and particularly the hierarchic model of data in dealing with so-called M to N relationships between record types. The question of M to N relationships arises because of the preoccupation for chain or pointer-oriented physical implementation considerations which actually should not burden the logical model of data. Figure 9.5(b) shows the normalized relational form of a two-record type professor-student data base shown in unnormalized form in Figure 9.5(a). The data base indicates for each professor (PID) every student (SID) that he has taught and the COURSE involved. Figure 9.5 shows how simple it is to take an unnormalized data base having an M to N relationship between record types and transform it to a normalized relational data base.

In order to represent the professor-student data base of Figure 5.11(b),

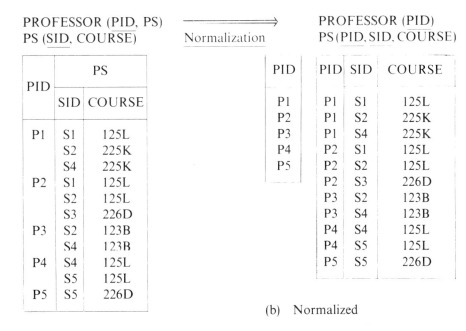

Figure 9.5.   *Normalized relational representation of a two-record type data base with an M to N relationship*

the DBTG model necessitates the use of two sets and the transformation and complication outlined in Figure 5.12. The IMS hierarchic model requires the use of so-called logical relationships necessitating the definition of pointer segments, as outlined in Figure 7.28.

Problem of Pointer-Oriented Linking of Record Types

The use of pointer-oriented mechanisms in the network and hierarchic data models to link or establish relationships between record types is a result of the subtle intermingling of the logical description of data with the physical organization description entailing physical pointers and chaining mechanisms. This may lead to two difficulties that we want to point out: complicated logical data descriptions and the so-called interconnection trap.

In most data bases there may be many logical associations between records. The representation of all these associations with lines (e.g., DBTG sets) may result in a complicated network of connections. See, for example, Figures 5.12 and 7.28. The use of these physically oriented connecting paths by conventional data manipulation languages (e.g., DBTG DML, IMS DL/1) may be complex. Furthermore, it opens the door to violating the insulation of application programs from various changes to the data base requiring modification of such links.

A relationship between two record types may be represented by a relation of degree 2, a binary relation. For example, the relationship between DOCTOR and CLINIC in Figure 7.2 may be represented by the binary relation: DOC-CLIN (D-NAME, C-NAME). Suppose that we were to establish two different relationships between DOCTOR and CLINIC, let us say, to represent the relationship of a DOCTOR to FOREIGN CLINICs in which he has served and also his relationship to U.S. CLINICs in which he normally serves. Using the DBTG approach we would resort to two different sets or links. Using the relational approach we would easily represent this via a ternary relation: DOC-CLIN(D-NAME, C-NAME, US?).

When links are drawn from one record type to another and then to a succeeding record type, the user might tend to follow these links and assume that they represent a ternary relation, thus leading to the so-called *connection trap*. This is the result of an invalid attempt by an unsuspecting programmer or user to represent a ternary relation as two binary relations. Let us use and paraphrase Codd's[1] classical relational example of the SUPPLIERS data base shown in Figure 9.6. Suppose that each SUPPLIER is linked to the description of each PART supplied by that supplier, and that each PART description is in turn linked to the description of each PROJECT which uses that PART. The user may erroneously conclude that if all the paths are followed from a SUPPLIER via the PARTs one will *always* obtain a valid list of the PROJECTS supplied by the SUPPLIER. Due to the links shown in Figure 9.6(a),

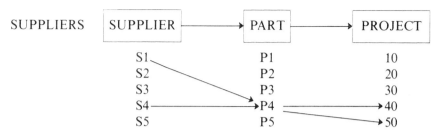

SUPPLIERS

The connection trap: inferring that PROJECT 50 is necessarily supplied by SUPPLIER S4; it is clear below that this is not true, in this example.

(a)   The linked data base

SUPPLIERS	SUPPLIER	PART	PROJECT
	:	:	:
	S1	P4	40
	S1	P4	50
	:	:	:
	S4	P4	40
	S5	P5	50

(b)   The relational data model

Figure 9.6.   *The connection trap*

the user may infer from the links that Project 50 has SUPPLIER S4 as one of its SUPPLIERs. This may not be true. The real situation could be unambiguously represented by the ternary relation in Figure 9.6(b), thus avoiding the connection trap.

9.3   DATA MANIPULATION: DATA ACCESSING AND OPERATIONS ON RELATIONS

9.3.1   Overview

The result of any data retrieval request or query is a relation derived in some fashion from the relational data base. Fundamental to the relational approach is the ability to manipulate relations via powerful and logical operators so as to extract from the data model the desired relation(s) or to form new relations from existing relations. These operators are at the heart of relational thinking.

A relational data base is viewed by the DBA and users as a time-varying collection of normalized relations of various degrees. It is necessary to derive subsets of the table columns to form tables of smaller degrees as well as to join tables together to form tables of larger degrees.

Codd suggested two data manipulation languages, called in relational terms **data sublanguages**: the relational algebra sublanguage and the relational calculus sublanguage.[3,4] Three levels of data handling facilities are envisioned:

1. **Relational calculus sublanguage.** It is a nonprocedural query language by which users state what they need without having to indicate the procedural manipulation steps that must be performed on the data model to obtain desired results. The data base system is thus expected to carry out these procedural steps to answer a query in the relational calculus.

2. **Relational algebra sublanguage.** It is a procedural query language by which users manipulate the relations of the data model using relational algebra operators to derive what they want. These operators are high-level logical data manipulation operators involving no physical access-path notions.

3. **Tuple by tuple language.** This would be a low-level language used by programmers to go from one tuple (or record) to another at a time so as to derive the data requested.

The popular phrase "navigating through the data base" refers to going through a data base record or segment at a time. Both the calculus and algebra sublanguages are aimed at avoiding the procedurality, physical access-path dependency, and programming orientation of navigation languages such as DBTG DML and IMS DL/1. Query languages of a number of inverted systems such as the QUEST Query Language of SYSTEM 2000 (outlined in the previous chapter) and ADASCRIPT/NATURAL of ADABAS do have much of the logical power of the relational languages for a great portion of today's real data bases. The use of high-level operators would be more difficult on a complex data base with network or hierarchic structures with repeating groups than on a relational data base. The relational model route is thus advocated to enhance the ability of using and implementing high-level operators that easily manipulate data.

9.3.2   Relational Algebra

We shall now present the basic relational algebra operators involved: **projection**, **join**, **composition**, **restriction**, and **division**. A relational algebra operator takes one or more relations as its operand(s) and produces a relation.

The notation used for these operators is in a state of flux in relational data base writings, and so is the syntactic notation for data definition and manipulation.

The **projection operator** on a relation A over specified domains D results in a relation B. B is a relation with only the specified domains and with no duplicate tuples or rows. It is thus a subsetting operation. This operation is available in commercial GDBMS. Figure 9.7 shows the two relations EMPLOYEE and EXPER derived via two projection operations on the base relation EMP-EXP. Let us use the original Codd symbol for projection II.[1] The two projections are then derived as follows:

EMPLOYEE = II EMP-EXP (<u>EMP#</u>, E-NAME, EXPERTISE,
          AGE)
EXPER   = II EMP-EXP (<u>EXPERTISE</u>, <u>LOCATION</u>)

where

EMP-EXP (<u>EMP#</u>, E-NAME, EXPERTISE, AGE, LOCATION)

The **join operator** denoted by * does the opposite of the projection operator. It takes two relations that have a common domain D and joins them to form a new relation. Each tuple of the new relation consists of a tuple of the first relation concatenated with each tuple from the second relation which has the same domain D (field) value. Figure 9.7(c) shows the resulting EMP-EXP' relation that may be derived from the relations EMPLOYEE and EXPER via a join over EXPERTISE, denoted as follows:

EMP-EXP' = EMPLOYEE* EXPER (EXPERTISE)

Note that EMP-EXP' does contain all the actual information of EMP-EXP, but it also contains additional information which is not actually true (e.g., THOMAS is in CHICAGO) and is indistinguishable from the real information. The creation of this possibly false information by a series of projections and joins is a serious problem, referred to as the **lossy join problem**.

The **composition** of two relations A and B is a relation C obtained by first joining A and B over a common domain D and then taking this intermediate relation and applying a projection so as to exclude the domain D. Thus the composition of EMPLOYEE and EXPER in Figure 9.7 is EMP-EXP' without the domain EXPERTISE (on which EMPLOYEE and EXPER were initially joined). The composition operator is not really a basic one, because it is implemented by a join and a projection.

The **restriction operator** takes two relations and produces one relation. The restriction of A by B on the common domain(s) D, where B is composed of domain(s) D, is a relation A' which has all the domains of A and all of those tuples whose D values match the D values of the tuples of B. We are purposely

(a) EMP-EXP

EMP#	E-NAME	EXPERTISE	AGE	LOCATION
1	JONES	ACCOUNTING	30	CHICAGO
2	MARTIN	COMP-SCI	35	LOS ANGELES
3	GOMEZ	MGT-SCI	42	MEXICO CITY
4	CHU	COMP-SCI	34	LOS ANGELES
5	DAMES	ACCOUNTING	40	CHICAGO
6	THOMAS	ACCOUNTING	52	LONDON
7	WATSON	MGT-SCI	39	LOS ANGELES

(b) EMPLOYEE

EMP#	E-NAME	EXPERTISE	AGE
1	JONES	ACCOUNTING	30
2	MARTIN	COMP-SCI	35
3	GOMEZ	MGT-SCI	42
4	CHU	COMP-SCI	34
5	DAMES	ACCOUNTING	40
6	THOMAS	ACCOUNTING	52
7	WATSON	MGT-SCI	39

(b) EXPER

EXPERTISE	LOCATION
ACCOUNTING	CHICAGO
COMP-SCI	LOS ANGELES
MGT-SCI	LOS ANGELES
MGT-SCI	MEXICO CITY
ACCOUNTING	LONDON

(c)   EMP-EXP'

EMP#	E-NAME	EXPERTISE	AGE	LOCATION
1	JONES	ACCOUNTING	30	CHICAGO
1	JONES	ACCOUNTING	30	LONDON
2	MARTIN	COMP-SCI	35	LOS ANGELES
3	GOMEZ	MGT-SCI	42	LOS ANGELES
3	GOMEZ	MGT-SCI	42	MEXICO CITY
4	CHU	COMP-SCI	34	LOS ANGELES
5	DAMES	ACCOUNTING	40	CHICAGO
5	DAMES	ACCOUNTING	40	LONDON
6	THOMAS	ACCOUNTING	52	CHICAGO
6	THOMAS	ACCOUNTING	52	LONDON
7	WATSON	MGT-SCI	39	LOS ANGELES
7	WATSON	MGT-SCI	39	MEXICO CITY

EMPLOYEE and EXPER derived from EMP-EXP via two projections.
EMP-EXP' derived from EMPLOYEE and EXPER via a join over EXPERT-
ISE

Figure 9.7.   *Manipulation of relations: projection and join operation*

avoiding being mathematically rigorous. Figure 9.8 illustrates the restriction of
PS by STUDENT resulting in PS'. In a sense, the restriction operator is a join
of A and B where all of B's domains are a part of A.

The **division operator** takes two relations A and B and produces one
relation C: C = A/B. Let us look at the simplest format division: it takes a
binary relation A (call it the dividend) and a unary relation B (call it the divisor)
and produces a unary relation C (call it the quotient). Let A be composed of
domains S and T, and B of domain T; the single domain of the divisor must be
the same as one of the domains of the dividend. The result C is made up of the
single domain S whose entries are all those values of S in A whose corresponding values of T (in A) include all the values of T in B. Figure 9.9 provides three
examples of relational algebra division.

The join, division, and composition operations can be performed over
multiple domains.[3] We mention this for completeness but do not explain this
facet further, as it is somewhat confusing, the advantages are not worth the
effort, and future relational algebra languages probably will not support directly the more confusing multiple-domain operations.

In the algebra sublanguage, relations are considered as sets of n-tuples.

PS   (PID   SID   COURSE)   STUDENT   (SID   COURSE)

PID	SID	COURSE
P1	S1	125L
P1	S2	225K
P1	S4	225K
P2	S1	125L
P2	S2	125L
P2	S3	226D

SID	COURSE
S2	125L
S2	225K
S3	226D

PS'   (PID   SID   COURSE)

PID	SID	COURSE
P1	S2	225K
P2	S2	125L
P2	S3	226D

PS' = Restriction of PS by STUDENT

Figure 9.8. *Manipulation of relations: restriction operation*

Thus the following set formalisms would perform the following insert, delete, and update operations on individual tuples at a time.

To insert a new row in a table, the set Union operator would be used. For example, to add the new tuple for employee 7 to relation EMPLOYEE one could perhaps state:

Union (EMPLOYEE, ⟨8, THOMAS, ACCOUNTING, 40⟩)

To delete an existing row from a table, the set Difference operator would be used. For example, to delete from EMPLOYEE the tuple for employee 5 one could perhaps state:

Difference (EMPLOYEE, ⟨5, ?, ?, ?⟩)

where ? means that the tuple with EMP# = 5 is to be deleted no matter what values its other domains have.

To update a record, in the strict set sense, one would use a suitable combination of the set difference and the set union operations.

Obviously, in practice these three previous operations would be done in a more attractive notational form, as we shall illustrate in Chapters 10 and 11.

We shall return to exemplifying the use of relational operators. Subsequent to the following introduction of the relational calculus approach, we will compare queries expressed at both the algebra and calculus level.

Base relations:

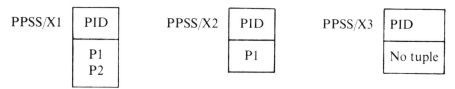

Division operations:

PPSS/X1	PID
	P1
	P2

PPSS/X2	PID
	P1

PPSS/X3	PID
	No tuple

Sample queries answered:
Derive a table of all professor PID's who have taught student S1: PPSS/X1
Derive a table of all professor PID's who have taught both S2 and S4: PPSS/X2
Derive a table of all professor PID's who have taught S1, S2, S3 and S4: PPSS/X3

Figure 9.9.   *Manipulation of relations: division operation*

9.3.3 Relational Calculus

A relational calculus is a mathematically oriented notation for defining a relation to be derived from existing relations in the data base. It permits users to indicate what they want to obtain without indicating many details of how to obtain it. The GDBMS is supposed to determine what relational algebra steps or equivalent operations would be required to derive the relation; the GDBMS is assumed to have powerful capabilities for generating automatically the detailed steps corresponding to every calculus language command.

Codd defined in detail a language based on the so-called first-order predicate calculus for accessing a relational data model.[4] It is called the "data sublanguage ALPHA." He showed that any query request expressed in a calculus expression can be converted into an equivalent algebra expression.[4] Experimental and commercial relational GDBMS are heavily based on the relational calculus logical capability.

In using the relational calculus, it is assumed that users each have one or more workspaces or buffer areas (in core) to communicate with their data model. Thus, for example, it is expected that they can retrieve some (or maybe preferably all) tuples from a relation into a portion of a workspace and some tuples from other relations into other portions of the workspace(s); these tuples from several relations will be concurrently available to users. The number of tuples concurrently available will obviously be directly dependent on the particular implementation. What we have just described is what is essentially done in all available nonrelational GDBMS. Once a tuple is in the workspace, the host language (PL/1, COBOL, FORTRAN, PASCAL, etc.) may operate on it.

Figure 9.10 summarizes the relational calculus notation and meaning. The syntax details that we will use in expressing queries in the relational calculus will be artificial and independent of any commercial implementation.

A typical query in the calculus has two parts: a **target**, which indicates the specific domains of the particular relation which are to be returned, and a **qualification part**, which selects specific tuples from the target relation by indicating a condition that they must satisfy.

Let us use a simple example to illustrate the basic calculus approach. Consider that the relational data model is the single relation EMP-EXP in Figure 9.7(a). The following calculus query produces a relation called X made

Symbol	Meaning
R.D	The unary relation made up of the set of data values of domain D of relation R.
$X(R_1.D_1, R_2.D_2,...$	A relation named X composed of the domains made up of the sets of data values $R_1.D_1, R_2.D_2,...$
$\exists$	Existential quantifier: "there exists."
$\forall$	Universal quantifier: "for all."
:	Such that. The expression to the left of the colon states what is to be retrieved from the data base and the expression to the right of the colon is the predicate or qualifier.
$\wedge, \vee, \neg$	The standard logical operators AND, OR, NOT to form qualifiers.
$=, \neq, <, \leq, >, \geq$	The standard operators equal, not equal, less than, less than or equal, greater than, greater than or equal.

Figure 9.10. *Relational calculus notation and meaning*

up of the set of employee name values and age values for every employee whose expertise is accounting and is located in Chicago:

X (EMP-EXP.E-NAME, EMP-EXP.AGE):EMP-EXP.EXPERTISE = 'ACCOUNTING' ∧ EMP-EXP.LOCATION = 'CHICAGO'

The expression in parentheses indicates the desired output and in general may contain domain names (as shown), relation names, or both. Domain names have to be qualified if necessary to avoid ambiguity, for example, to differentiate between the same domain name appearing in more than one relation of the data model. The colon stands for "such that" or "where" and the expression following it is the logical qualification or "predicate." The term **predicate** is not used in commercial GDBMS jargon. The predicate may be of arbitrary logical complexity and may include the usual comparison operators =, ≠, <, ≥, >, ≤, and the Boolean operators ∧, (AND), ∨, (OR) and ¬(NOT). A predicate takes the usual form of logical expressions in programming languages.

9.3.4   Query Examples: Relational Calculus and Algebra

Let us direct a number of queries at the data model shown in Figure 9.11 consisting of the relations PS (Professor-Student relation), PROFESSOR and STUDENT, plus the four special constant relations X1, X2, X3, and X4 set up to answer the queries in the relational algebra. Readers should compare the following relational examples with their counterparts using DML in the DBTG model (Figure 5.12) and DL/1 in the IMS model (Figure 7.28). The greater procedurality and dependency on links available of both DML and DL/1 is readily apparent. The query languages of inverted systems like SYSTEM 2000 (see Section 8.4 for examples) and ADABAS are as nonprocedural and high-level as calculus and algebra for many queries; according to many practitioners this is true for a large portion of commonly occurring queries in real data base applications.

Examples 1−7: Relational Queries (Read-Only)

1. Obtain the professor number PID for all professors who taught student S1, and call the result relation X.

    Calculus: X (PS.PID):PS.SID = 'S1'
    Algebra has two possibilities:
          a.   Join PS with X1 over SID.
               Project the result over PID.

PS

PID	SID	COURSE
P1	S1	125L
P1	S2	225K
P1	S4	225K
P2	S1	125L
P2	S2	125L
P2	S3	226D
P3	S2	123B
P3	S4	123B
P4	S4	125L
P4	S5	125L
P5	S5	226D

X1

SID
S1

X2

COURSE
125L

X3

COURSE
125L

X4

GOAL
PH.D.

PROFESSOR

PID	PNAME	DEGREE-FROM
P1	BERRY	BROWN
P2	CARDENAS	UCLA
P3	MARTIN	UCLA
P4	MELKANOFF	UCLA
P5	POPEK	HARVARD

STUDENT

SID	SNAME	GOAL
S1	STUDENT 1	PH.D.
S2	STUDENT 2	M.S.
S3	STUDENT 3	M.S.
S4	STUDENT 4	PH.D.
S5	STUDENT 5	PH.D.

Figure 9.11. *A Professor-Student relational data model (data base)*

      b.   Project PS over PID and SID.

          Divide the result by X1.

Result: X   PID

               P1

               P2

It is possible that the answer to a relational calculus query may be expressed in more than one way using the lower-level algebra, as just shown. Likewise, it is possible to express any query in more than one way at the calculus level; different predicates may be written to express the same qualifications.

2.   Obtain a list of the names of all professors who taught student S1.

Calculus: X (PROFESSOR.PNAME): ∃ PS (PS.PID = PROFESSOR.PID ∧ PS.SID = 'S1').

Algebra: Join PS with X1 over SID.

             Join the result with PROFESSOR over PID.

             Project the result over PNAME.

Result: PNAME

             Berry

             Cardenas

The calculus query makes use of the *existential quantifier* ∃. The query says: obtain the list of PNAME values from the relation PROFESSOR which are such that there exists a PS tuple whose PID value is the same as that in the PROFESSOR tuple and whose SID value equals S1. Note that in this example we are making use of the PID link between the relations PS and PROFESSOR. Thus, even in the relational approach there are notions of links, but they are very logically oriented.

3.   Same retrieval query as in Example 2 but using the relational *range* variable. Obtain a list of the names of all professors who taught student S1.

Calculus: RANGE PS R.

             X (PROFESSOR.PNAME): ∃ R (R.PID = PROFESSOR.PID ∧ R.SID = 'S1').

The relational "range" variable, R in this example, is used for two reasons: first, as a shorthand convenience (for example, if the relation PS were called PROFESSOR-STUDENT); and second, and most important, as an aid in stating the query when it involves the use of the existential quantifier ∃. Furthermore, the intent is for the range to be determined at execution time so that different relations may be used according to execution time criteria programmed.

4. Obtain a list of the names of the professors who did not teach course 125L or 226D.

Calculus: X (PROFESSOR.PNAME): ¬∃ PS
(PS.PID =
PROFESSOR.PID ∧ (PS.COURSE =
'125L' ∨ PS.COURSE = '226D')).

or   X (PROFESSOR.PNAME: ∀PS(PS.PID ≠
PROFESSOR.PID ∨ ¬ (PS.COURSE =
'125L' ∨ PS.COURSE = '226D')).

Algebra: Read a PS tuple at a time and produce a relation in which COURSE is not equal to either 125L or 226D. Join the result with PROFESSOR over PID. Project the result over PNAME.

Result: X PNAME
           ‾‾‾‾‾‾‾
           Martin

The second calculus alternative includes the universal quantifier ∀ meaning "for all"; the predicate shown says: for all PS tuples either the professor PID is not the one we want, or the course is neither 125L nor 226D.

The algebra approach for "does not exist" type of queries involves exhaustive-oriented searching, e.g., PS search above. This is due to the nature of the algebra operators defined.

5. Obtain a list of the professor numbers PID for all professors who taught students whose goal is a Ph.D. degree, and the list of courses involved.

Calculus: RANGE STUDENT R1.
X (PS.PID,PS.COURSE): ∃ R1 (R1.SID =
PS.SID ∧ R1.GOAL = 'PH.D').

Algebra: Join STUDENT with X4 over GOAL.
Join the result with PS over SID.
Project the result over PID and COURSE.

Result: X PID   COURSE
              ‾‾‾   ‾‾‾‾‾‾
              P1   125L
              P1   225K
              P2   125L
              P3   123B
              P4   125L
              P5   226D

6. Obtain a list of the professors (names) who taught students whose goal is a Ph.D. degree.

Two general calculus ways may be followed to answer this query, as well as in general more complex queries: (a) break it down into several smaller queries or (b) express it in a single predicate. We will not consider alternative relational algebra procedures.

(a) *Broken down into two simpler queries.* Service query in Example 5 resulting in relation X and then state the following query to get the corresponding professor names:

Calculus: XX (PROFESSOR.PNAME):
            ∃ X(X.PID = PROFESSOR.PID).
Algebra: Join X with PROFESSOR over PID. Project
            the result over PNAME.
Result: XX PNAME
            _____
            Berry
            Cardenas
            Martin
            Melkanoff
            Popek

Note that we are showing that a relation in the user workspace may be used for read-only access just as if it were part of that user's data model, i.e., his or her submodel subschema.

(b) *Query in a single predicate.* It is possible to express any query in a single predicate. In general, for the more complex queries, many alternative and equivalent predicates may be written to express a given logical qualification. For this example the two following predicates are equivalent:

RANGE STUDENT R1.
XX (PROFESSOR.PNAME):
    ∃ R1 (R1.GOAL = 'PH.D.' ∧
    ∃ PS (PS.PID = PROFESSOR.PID ∧
    PS.SID = R1.SID)).

and

XX (PROFESSOR.PNAME):
    ∃ PS (∃ R1 (R1.GOAL = 'PH.D.' ∧
    PS.PID = PROFESSOR.PID ∧
    PS.SID = R1.SID)).

A predicate may be converted into another one by a series of allowed modifications such as interchanging the two constructs around an "and" operator and shifting a quantifier and its associated variable to the left as is shown in (b) above. The quantifier and its variables can be shifted all the way to the left. Such a format is called the "prenex normal form."

7. Produce a relation X showing the identification number and name of students who are taught by every professor in the data base.

Calculus: X (STUDENT.SID,STUDENT.SNAME):
∀ PROFESSOR ∃ PS (PS.SID
= STUDENT.SID
∧ PS.PID = PROFESSOR.PID).

Algebra: Project PS over PID and SID.
Divide this result by the projection of PROFESSOR over PID.
Join the result with STUDENT.
Project the result over SID and SNAME.

Result: <u>SID</u> <u>SNAME</u>
no tuples satisfy the query

The calculus predicate above can be read as: for *all* professors there exists a PS tuple in which its SID matches the SID of a tuple in STUDENT and its PID matches the PID of the tuple in PROFESSOR.

Examples 8-10: *Relational Calculus Updating*

Let us now look at update operations in the calculus. Such operations in the algebra world have been illustrated already and thus we shall not provide any more algebra examples.

8. Change the degree goal of student S3 to Ph.D.

Calculus: HOLD X (STUDENT.SID.STUDENT.
GOAL):STUDENT.SID = 'S3'.
X.GOAL = 'PH.D.' done in workspace.
UPDATE X.

The HOLD retrieves values of a data model so as to then change them in the workspace and then store them back in the data model by means of an UPDATE command. The HOLD is intended to warn the GDBMS and perhaps temporarily lock out other users from seeing this data to be modified. The HOLD data holds in the workspace; the UPDATE actually updates the data. If several tuples were to be updated, e.g., change all degree objectives to NONE, then the updates would be formed in the workspace and a single update would update all tuples of the relation with the tuples formed in the workspace. This two-step process of updating is followed in a number of GDBMS, e.g., IMS DL/1 "get hold" operations.

9.   Delete Professor P2.

Calculus: DELETE (PROFESSOR:
PROFESSOR.PID = 'P2').

Note that the PS tuples for professor P2 are not deleted by this.

10.   Insert the new tuple in the STUDENT relation (6/DUMB/?):

Calculus: X.SID = '6'
X.SNAME = 'DUMB'
X.GOAL = '?'
PUT X (STUDENT).

Both the calculus and the algebra sublanguages have been shown by Codd[3] to be *complete* (a relational term), meaning that any relation that may be derived from the data model may be derived by a single calculus or algebra statement. The languages are simple, yet they are complete. Note that the complexity of a statement in the calculus language or in the algebra language is directly determined by the complexity of what the user wishes to do; simple requests are expressed very simply. In contrast, this may not be the case with other languages such as DML and DL/1. Both calculus and algebra are highly data independent; that is, they do not contain any reference to storage layout, pointers, and so forth. As we have said before, the calculus language is less procedural than the algebra. Relational advocates are hopeful that calculus features will be provided in some form or another in all future GDBMS languages for easier person–machine communication.

9.4   THE RELATIONAL DATA SUBMODEL (SUBSCHEMA)

Definition (Derivation) of the Data Submodel

A **data submodel** is a particular user's **view** (called a subschema in DBTG terms) or collection of relations that may be derived by the DBA from the global data model. The relations of the data model are called **stored** or **base relations** because they are actually physically stored by the GDBMS somehow as such, as opposed to derived relations of the submodel. An arbitrary number of submodels may be defined over a given data model (see Figure 9.1). A submodel could be identical to the whole model, as we have assumed in the examples of the previous section. An arbitrary number of users may share a data model via the submodels. The submodels may overlap.

The **data submodel definition language** is the language or means for defining a submodel as a collection of relations. The definition of a submodel or view is simply the process of deriving the submodel relations from the set of data model relations, and this process is similar to stating a query. Each submodel definition must be derivable by means of the calculus or algebra. The calculus and algebra query languages themselves can be used as the base to define the views. In contrast with nonrelational GDBMS, we are not burdened by entirely different languages to state queries and to define the global data base and the various views. This is possible because the relational query languages have the property of **closure**; that is, they operate on relations to form or define new relations. Thus, in the relational approach, unlike the conventional approaches, there is no submodel data definition language per se entirely separate from the query language.

A relation of the submodel or view can be a subset of a stored relation (a data model relation), or it may include elements of more than one relation (as a result of a join). Once a submodel is defined, read-only queries can be directed at the submodel as if it were the model made up of stored relations. Updates, inserts, and deletes to the data base made via derived submodels necessitate a number of restrictions and pose complicated questions still being researched; we will say more on this later.

Let us illustrate the definition of a single-relation submodel by using a hypothetical calculus-based submodel derivation language. Considering the Professor-Student data model of Figure 9.11, we can derive the relation X showing the name of the professors who taught students whose goal is a Ph.D. degree and the list of courses involved (essentially the query in Example 6 in the previous section).

RELATION X (PROFESSOR.PNAME,PS.COURSE)
$\left\{\begin{array}{l}\text{Definition of data type, precision, authorization, etc.,}\\ \quad\text{of each domain.}\end{array}\right.$
DERIVATION ∃ STUDENT (STUDENT.GOAL = 'PH.D.' ∧ ∃ PS
                              (PS.PID = PROFESSOR.PID
                              ∧ PS.SID = STUDENT.SID))

The first statement defines the submodel relation X as composed of the domains PNAME from PROFESSOR and COURSE from PS. The next lines would define its data type, precision, authorization (read-only, update, etc.), and so forth. The last line defines the derivation of X from the data model relations.

This example illustrates the purported flexibility of defining views beyond that provided by a number of nonrelational GDBMS:

   1.   The ability to make up views composed of (a) any subset of domains from a relation and/or (b) domains from different relations. In IMS, fields from different segments cannot be combined into a single

segment (except perhaps in the special case of the pointer segment and its logical parent segment in IMS logical data bases). In the DBTG system any data items from different record types cannot be combined into a single record type for a subschema. Inverted GDBMS generally provide the most flexibility in this respect among nonrelational systems but fall short of the relational flexibility.

2. The ability to readily define views as composed of subsets of the set of tuples of the data model selected according to arbitrary logical qualification on the basis of data content. For example, the view in this example includes only tuples for which the student goal is a Ph.D. degree. Such data selectivity is not directly available in DBTG, TOTAL, IMS, SYSTEM 2000, or most GDBMS.

Note the higher degree of data independence of the relational approach to changes in the data model such as these caused by growth of the data base and new applications: (1) addition of a new relation, and (2) restructuring of domains from an existing relation to another relation. Neither of these changes will affect any current users of the data model who have no need for such additions. However, users updating the data base through derived views formed through joins of different relations may be impacted as indicated subsequently. In IMS, segments may not be freely added to the hierarchy without impacting some users (as outlined in Section 7.3). Among nonrelational GDBMS, inverted GDBMS probably show the highest data independence.

Differences in Model and Submodel Domains

The domain of a submodel relation may further differ from its corresponding domain in the data model as follows (according to relational proponents):

1. Either all or only a subset of the values in the data model domain may be included; the previous example specifies including in the submodel relation X the domain GOAL (from STUDENT) including only the value PH.D. This is not possible in most GDBMSs without the need to write a special program.

2. The domain names may differ, as in many commercial GDBMS.

3. The computer representation for the domain values may differ; for example, in the model it could be plain numeric (as in COBOL) and in the submodel it could be float binary for a PL/1 application. This may be done in a number of commercial GDBMS.

4. The units may differ for numeric values or there may be a codificationdecodification step between the model/submodel interface. For ex-

ample, the domain DISTANCE could be in miles in the model and yet appear in kilometers in a submodel; this assumes that the DBA will provide to the GDBMS a definition of the procedure that it will have to apply when going to/from the model realm. This may be done in many commercial GDBMS.

5. The submodel domain may be *virtual* with respect to the domains actually stored in the data model; that is, it may be computed according to some programmed procedure (defined by the DBA) applied to domains of (perhaps different) relations. For example, a submodel from our Professor-Student data model could be a relation showing PNAME and the virtual domain COURSE-COUNT indicating for each professor name the number of different courses taught. Many commercial GDBMS provide the capability of defining virtual data items in the model as a function of other data items actually stored in the model (see the SYSTEM 2000 example in Figure 8.2 showing the two virtual data items AGE and CHILD-AGE). The capability of defining for a view a virtual field which is not already virtual in the data model is generally not allowed in nonrelational GDBMS.

Sublanguage Operations on Relations Derived from the Stored Relations

Any read-only calculus or algebra operation can be performed on any submodel that can be derived from a data model (the submodel in turn must be derivable from a data model via the calculus or algebra). A **derived relation** is generally defined as one formed by the use of the join operator on two or more relations; a derived relation is not physically stored as such. All the read-only query examples in Section 9.3 hold whether any or all the relations at which the query is aimed are really derived or actually stored. However, for update, delete, and insert operations, such flexibility for derived relations raises a number of issues currently being researched. The flexibility must then be curtailed for nonread operations as follows:

1. Every submodel relation must be exactly like the corresponding data model relation, except that (a) individual tuples can be omitted, and (b) nonkey domains can be omitted.
2. Key domains cannot be omitted.
3. The nonread operations may not be applied to derived relations, that is, those formed by the use of the join operator on two or more relations.

4. The nonread operations may not be applied to virtual domains.

Obviously, if users try to insert a tuple containing a key value not in their submodel, but present in the stored relation, then the GDBMS is expected to notify them that this is prohibited (since every tuple in a relation must be unique). Just as in various commercial GDBMS, the insertion of a new tuple in a data submodel relation will cause the GDBMS to insert some kind of null marker for that tuple's value for any domain omitted from the submodel but present in the corresponding stored relation.

9.5 RELATIONAL GDBMS IMPLEMENTATIONS

Although many authors attracted by the relational approach have written about it, only a handful of researchers (primarily) in the 1970s initiated development of relatively small and experimental relational systems aimed at establishing the promising feasibility of full-fledged relational GDBMS.[5-7,11,13] The experimental IBM IS/1 system showed the feasibility of supporting the relational algebra.[6] The INGRES system at the University of California, Berkeley,[7] the efforts at the University of Toronto,[13] and the Query-by-Example effort at the IBM T. J. Watson Research Center[16] can be cited as pioneering efforts aimed at a number of relational aspects. The experimental System R developed at the IBM Research Laboratory, San Jose, California,[11] was perhaps the most encompassing implementation effort of the relational approach.

Query-by-Example, introduced commercially in 1980 by IBM,[17] became the first commercial GDBMS. It was then followed in the early 1980s by major commercial versions of INGRES, introduced by Relational Technology Inc., and of System R, introduced commercially by IBM as SQL/DS. ORACLE, from Relational Software Inc., is another initial commercial GDBMS striving to be logically identical to SQL/DS. While these larger and more robust systems were initially aimed at larger IBM and DEC computers, a number of smaller and less robust relational systems are being implemented for the large and burgeoning microcomputer and personal computer market. The user-friendliness and simplicity of relational implementations for microcomputer and personal computers have led to their popularity. dBASE II, introduced by Ashton-Tate Inc. in the 1980s,[20] was one of the first micro-GDBMS, and it is possibly the most widely used micro-GDBMS in a variety of microcomputers and personal computers.

Chapter 4 and especially Figures 4.1 and 4.5 outline the commercial availability of relational (as well as nonrelational) GDBMS, both large and micro-GDBMS. It should be stressed that there is no industry-wide relational standard (although SQL/DS, INGRES, and QBE may be considered by many as de facto standards); thus almost all relational GDBMS unfortunately exhibit differences.

Chapter 10 introduces IBM's SQL/DS, which represents one of the two relational flavors. It is representative of INGRES, ORACLE, and the likes. Chapter 11 introduces IBM's Query-by-Example, which represents the other relational flavor. Most relational micro-GDBMS have the flavor of SQL/DS (due to the early System R and INGRES prototypes).

The success of the relational approach in a real and large commercial data base environment depends greatly on the ability of a relational GDBMS to handle the bulk of the variety of requirements in such environments with a performance comparable to the established nonrelational GDBMS. Data base machines are now being introduced for such large data base and high transaction environments, thus providing more direct hardware support and operating systems tailored to data base management needs. Chapter 15 is devoted to data base machines.

Research and development is being pursued toward very high-level artificial intelligence-oriented languages and means for interfacing with relational systems. Codd's Rendezvous efforts[15,18] may be cited. Rendezvous strives toward natural language interactive dialog.

9.6   ATTRACTIVE FEATURES OF THE RELATIONAL APPROACH—SUMMARY

The following features are frequently acknowledged as the primary attractions of the relational approach (particularly involving third normal forms, addressed in the next chapter) versus primarily the hierarchic and network approaches:

1. *Simplicity and ease of use.* Relations, being two-dimensional tables, are undoubtedly easier to comprehend and deal with for the large number of not-so-programming oriented users. Users are presented with a single and consistent data model or structure. There need be no undue concern for 1 to N versus M to N relationships. Users formulate their requests via powerful languages (calculus, algebra, and their descendants) in terms of information content with no reference to storage-oriented access paths. The clarity of the relational approach is even more noticeable as the number of record types and their relationships increases. Relationships between relations are easily expressed and established implicitly by including a common field or attribute in the two relations. However, it is fair to

say that for data bases that are not so complex, and even sometimes for those that are complex, hierarchic structures and network structures are not distasteful to many practitioners.

2. *Data independence.* The immunity of application programs to changes in the data model, submodel, and physical organization and physical access paths is greatly enhanced. The elimination from the user interface (calculus, algebra, and their descendants) of many considerations of physical structure and access paths, such as physical position and pointers, is noteworthy. A higher degree of data independence can be achieved more easily with relations than with most tree or network structures.

3. *Symmetry.* Data models involving connections between records may give undue preferential treatment to those access requests matching the connected structures of the data base. For example, in the hierarchic approach the easiest questions to pose are those which start at the root of the tree and move down the hierarchy (a positional concern) to the leaves, applying qualifications at each level. Questions counter to the hierarchy order are awkward to ask, at best. In the relational model all information is represented by data values and there is no preferred type of question at the user interface level. However, this does not necessarily force symmetry on the internal physical structures of a relational data base. For example, due to the more frequent use of a certain type of query and query content, the relational data base designer might establish a certain type of indexing to enhance performance.

4. *Flexibility and data base processing power.* Powerful algebra operations such as join and projection on easy to understand tables permit deriving easily (from a user's point of view, although most likely not so easily from the point of view of machine performance) a wide variety of tables. Such flexibility permits satisfaction of a wide variety of users and their changing needs. The power of the join operator stands out. An even higher-level language is the relational calculus, which has inspired commercial relational GDBMS.

5. *Security.* The ability to define any view as a result of an algebra or calculus query gives the relational approach unsurpassed security controls. Users can be constrained to any subset of not only data types (specific relations and attributes) but also subsets of data instances (specific instances of relations and attributes) based on data content.

6. *Good theoretical foundation.* The relational data model relies on the well-developed mathematical theory of relations and on the so-called

first-order predicate calculus. This theoretical base permits the definition of relational completeness and facilitates the formal study of good data base design (in terms of normalization). The mathematical background will not necessarily burden pragmatic users in an actual implementation and the potential benefits of the sound foundation may be accrued.

Other attractive features or overtones derived from the previous ones may be noticed by readers and cited in the large body of writings on the relational approach.

Note that features 1–4 may be cited in various degrees when comparing inverted systems such as ADABAS and SYSTEM 2000 with CODASYL DBTG systems, TOTAL, and IMS over a spectrum of applications.

These are the main challenges to the relational approach:

1. Efficient and cost-effective implementations, involving automated physical design and reorganization advances, and perhaps necessitating advances in hardware technology (e.g., associative hardware mechanisms). The commercial emergence of data base machines is an indicator.

2. Cost-effectiveness and success in a real and large commercial data base environment involving the variety of challenges posed on and being satisfactorily met by earlier nonrelational GDBMS.

The 1980s have shown the commercial attractiveness and feasibility of relational GDBMS for a significant portion of the marketplace, particularly initially for the small computer and personal computer market.

REFERENCES

1. Codd, E. F., "A Relational Model of Data for Large Shared Data Banks," *Communications of the ACM*, Vol. 13, No. 6, June 1970, pp.377–387.

2. Codd, E. F., "Normalized Data Base Structure: A Brief Tutorial," *Proceedings, 1971 ACM SIGFIDET Workshop on Data Description, Access and Control*, San Diego, Calif., November, 1971.

3. Codd, E.F., "Relational Completeness of Data Base Sublanguages," in *Data Base Systems*, edited by R. Rustin, Vol. 6 of the Courant Computer Science Symposia, Prentice-Hall, Englewood Cliffs, N.J., 1972.

4. Codd, E.F., "A Data Base Sublanguage Based on the Relational Calculus," *Proceedings, 1971 ACM SIGFIDET Workshop on Data Description, Access and Control*, San Diego, Calif., November 1971.

5. Whitney, V. K. M., "A Relational Data Management System (RDMS)," *Proceedings, Fourth International Symposium on Computer and Information Sciences*, Miami Beach, Fla., December 14−16, 1972, Plenum Press, New York, N.Y.

6. Notley, M. G., "The Peterle IS/1 System," IBM UK Scientific Center Report UKSC-0018, March 1972.

7. Held, G. D., Stonebraker, M. R., and E. Wong, "INGRES: A Relational Data Base System," *Proceedings, National Computer Conference*, Anaheim, Calif., May 1975.

8. Chamberlain, D. D., and R. F. Boyce, "SEQUEL: A Structured English Query Language," *Proceedings, 1974 ACM SIGFIDET Workshop*, Ann Arbor, Mich., May 1974.

9. Boyce, R. F., and D. D. Chamberlain, "Using a Structured English Query Language as a Data Definition Facility," IBM Research Report RJ1318, San Jose, Calif., December 1973.

10. Astrahan, M. M., and D. D. Chamberlain, "Implementation of a Structured English Query Language," IBM Research Report 1464, San Jose, Calif., October 28, 1974.

11. Astrahan, M. M., et al. (14 authors), "System R: A Relational Approach to Data Base Management," *ACM Transactions on Data Base Systems*, June 1976, Vol. 1, No. 2; appears also as IBM Research Report RJ1738, San Jose, Calif., February 27, 1976.

12. Codd, E. F., "Relational Data Base Management—A Bibliography," IBM Research Laboratory, San Jose, Calif., August 19, 1975.

13. Mylopoulos, J., Schuster, S. A., and D. Tsichritzis, "A Multi-Level Relational System," *Proceedings, National Computer Conference*, Anaheim, Calif., May 1975.

14. Date, C. J., *An Introduction to Database Systems*, Addison-Wesley, Reading, Mass., 1977, 1981.

15. Codd, E. F., "Seven Steps to Rendezvous with the Casual User," *Proceedings, IFIP TC-2 Working Conference on Data Base Management Systems*, Cargese, Corsica, April 1−5, 1974, North-Holland Publishing Co., Amsterdam, Holland.

16. Zloof, M. M., "Query by Example," *Proceedings, National Computer Conference*, Anaheim, Calif., May 19−22, 1975.

17. "Query-by-Example, Terminal User's Guide," IBM Corporation, IBM Reference Manual SH20−2078.

18. Codd, E. F., Arnold, R. S., Cadiou, J. M., Chang, C. L., and N. Roussopoulos, "RENDEZVOUS Version 1: An Experimental English Language Query Formulation System for Casual Users of Relational Data Bases," IBM Research Report RJ2144, January 26, 1978, 94 pages.

19. Codd, E. F., ACM Turing Award Lecture, "Relational Data Base: A Practical Foundation for Productivity," *Communications of the ACM*, Vol. 25, No.2, February 1982, pp. 109−117.

20. "dBASE II Reference Manual," Ashton-Tate Inc., Culver City, Calif.

EXERCISES

1. Consider the following relational data base:

PART

PART (NUMBER	NAME	COLOR	WEIGHT)
78	Gear	Red	12
125	Wheel	Green	65
617	Chain	Blue	21

PART

SUPPLIES (NUMBER	SUPPLIER #	QUANTITY)
78	4	33
617	3	46
617	2	51
125	1	4
76	2	128

SUP-

PLIERS (SUPPLIER #	CITY	SUPPLIER-NAME)
1	Los Angeles	Jones
2	New York	Smith
3	Houston	Johnson
4	Miami	Richards
5	Chicago	Davis

Demonstrate by an appropriate combination of joins and projections how to get information on what parts (names) can be supplied from what city. Give the answer as a series of steps showing the intermediate relations and their contents. Indicate the query in relational calculus.

2. Consider again the relational data base in Exercise 1. Indicate the relational algebra operations and the relational calculus query to answer each of the following questions:

(a) What parts (names) can be supplied by suppliers located in Miami?

(b) What suppliers (names) can supply wheels and in what quantity?

(c) What cities have suppliers supplying red or green parts?

10

SQL/DATA SYSTEM

10.1 INTRODUCTION AND ARCHITECTURE

During the 1970s and early 1980s much was written about the relational approach, and frequently it was favorably compared with the nonrelational GDBMS approaches as indicated in the previous chapter. Several major efforts and prototype systems that were developed showed the feasibility of the relational approach. One of the most encompassing and successful implementations was the experimental System R developed by the IBM Research Laboratory,[1-4] San Jose, California, starting in the early mid-1970s. In 1982 IBM made commercially available what is essentially System R under the name of Structured Query Language/Data System (SQL/DS), initially for the IBM 30XX and 43XX computers using the operating system DOS/VS, [5-7] as per Figure 4.1.

In the early 1980s, Relational Software Inc. introduced commercially another relational GDBMS called ORACLE which strived to be almost identical to SQL/DS at the logical user level.[8] ORACLE is available for DEC VAX and IBM environments as per Figure 4.1. Since IBM published in the mid-1970s the specifications of the high-level Structured English Query Language (SEQUEL) as System R's relational interface, other vendors may implement SEQUEL or SQL/DS look-alikes. It is expected that other SQL/DS-like relational products will become available in the 1980s from IBM and non-IBM vendors for other machine environments, particularly for the minicomputer, and microcomputer or personal computer market.[3]

INGRES was another of the pioneering relational GDBMS and originated in the 1970s at the University of California, Berkeley.[9] It is now commercially available from Relational Technology Inc. for DEC VAX computers,[10] as per Figure 4.1. It is similar to SQL/DS, although there are some noteworthy differences (particularly in programming language interface, multirelation updates and mechanisms for performing joins).

QBE was another pioneering relational GDBMS, but it is significantly different from SQL/DS, INGRES, and others. QBE, introduced by IBM in 1980, was the first truly fully relational GDBMS commercially available. The next chapter is devoted to QBE.

Other relational GDBMS recently introduced or expected to be introduced by other vendors tend to show the SQL/DS and INGRES flavor. Thus the coverage of SQL/DS in this chapter should provide a good understanding of such GDBMS as well.

The following sections will present the features and capabilities of IBM's SQL/DS and will follow the same outline as for the GDBMS presented in this text. Ample illustrative examples will be given, including the same data bases and most of the data base accessing and processing examples used for other systems. Thus readers may easily compare the relational approach with the

three main nonrelational approaches offered in today's marketplace and presented in previous chapters. The majority of the SQL/DS examples are also
shown for the QBE relational approach in the next chapter. We will use most of
the terminology of SQL/DS, except in a few cases, to avoid burdening the
reader with jargon.

Architecture

Figure 10.1 shows the functional architecture of SQL/DS (System R).
Compare it with Figure 9.1. The *Relational Data Base Storage Interface*,
RDBSI, is an internal facility for a user or programmer to access single tuples of
the base or (physically) stored relations making up the data base. The relational *Data Base Storage System*, DBSS, supports the RDBSI; together they
provide a subsystem that manages storage devices, storage allocation, buffers,
transaction and system recovery, and so forth. The DBSS maintains the sophisticated access path mechanisms that must be available to support efficiently
the relational data manipulation operations; it maintains indexes on selected
fields of base relations.

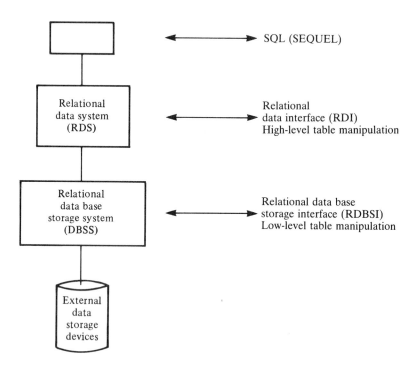

Figure 10.1. Macroscopic Architecture of the Relational SQL/DS (System R)

The *Relational Data Interface*, RDI, is the main external interface. It provides high-level data-independent facilities for relational data access, definition, and control. The RDI consists of a set of operators which supports the high-level relational interface. The high-level *Structured Query Language*, SQL (formerly SEQUEL) is SQL/DS's (formerly System R's) relational interface. SQL is part of RDI and is used for all data definition and manipulation. The *Relational Data System*, RDS, supports the RDI and alternative views (subschemas) of data. The RDS includes the following major functions: parsing, authorization, query optimization, and binding. The RDS contains a powerful optimizer which strives to choose an appropriate access path to service any user request from among those paths provided by the DBSS.

We shall focus on the use of SQL for data definition, manipulation, and communication with a host programming language. SQL is a relational nonprocedural data sublanguage with ideas from both the relational calculus and algebra. However, it does not make use of calculus quantifiers ($\forall$, $\exists$) or other mathematical concepts (unattractive to the bulk of practitioners); rather, it is a structured query language with English keywords.

10.2   THE SCHEMA OR DATA BASE

In accord with the relational approach, an SQL/DS data base consists of one or several tables (relations). Each table consists of columns (domains) and rows (tuples). A column corresponds to a field or attribute and a row corresponds to a record instance in nonrelational terminology.

Figures 10.2 and 10.3 show the relational Doctor-Employee data base that we will use to illustrate SQL/DS. This same data base schema is used in other chapters to illustrate the relational QBE approach and, in its nonrelational or "un-normalized" hierarchical form shown in Figure 9.4, the CODASYL, IMS, TOTAL, and SYSTEM 2000 approaches. The standard notational form for relational data bases is used to denote the logical schema structure in Figure 10.2. Underlined attributes or domains are key attributes, which uniquely identify a row or tuple of a table or relation. The sample data

> DOCTOR (D-NAME,SPECIALTY,YRSEXPER)
> CLINIC (D-NAME, C-NAME,ADDRESS)
> EMPLOYEE (D-NAME ,EMPNO,E-NAME,ADDRESS,AMT-OWED)
> INSUR-CO (D-NAME,EMPNO,I-NAME,ADDRESS,AMT-OWED)
> CHILD (D-NAME,EMPNO,C-NAME,CHILD-AGE,SCH-YEAR)

Figure 10.2.   *The Doctor-Employee data base in relational form*

DOCTOR	D-NAME	SPECIALTY	YRSEXPER
	JONES	SURGERY	7
	WILLIAMS	SURGERY	15
	WONG	EAR-NOSE	4
	YOUNG	CARDIOLOGY	20
	ZLOOF	CARDIOLOGY	10

CLINIC	D-NAME	C-NAME	ADDRESS
	JONES	CLINIC A	WEST L.A.
	JONES	CLINIC B	SAN FERNANDO
	WILLIAMS	CLINIC B	SAN FERNANDO
	WONG	CLINIC A	WEST L.A.
	YOUNG	CLINIC C	BEVERLY HILLS
	ZLOOF	CLINIC C	BEVERLY HILLS

EMPLOYEE	D-NAME	EMPNO	E-NAME	ADDRESS	AMT-OWED
	JONES	20	DONALDSON	WEST L.A.	0
	JONES	32	JOHNSON	ENCINO	600
	JONES	106	THOMAS	WEST L.A.	200
	WILLIAMS	28	BURGH	ENCINO	0
	WILLIAMS	29	GONZALEZ	SAN FERNANDO	600
	WILLIAMS	114	MARTIN	SAN FERNANDO	56
	WONG	29	GONZALEZ	SAN FERNANDO	1800
	YOUNG	320	FIRESTONE	ENCINO	2400

INSUR-CO	D-NAME	EMPNO	I-NAME	ADDRESS	CYCLE
	JONES	20	INSURANCE A	WEST L.A.	30
	JONES	20	INSURANCE B	BEVERLY HILLS	15
	WILLIAMS	28	INSURANCE B	BEVERLY HILLS	15
	WILLIAMS	29	INSURANCE B	BEVERLY HILLS	15
	WONG	29	INSURANCE C	SAN FRANCISCO	20
	YOUNG	320	INSURANCE D	CHICAGO	15

CHILD	D-NAME	EMPNO	C-NAME	CHILD-AGE	SCH-YEAR
	JONES	20	MICHAEL	6	2
	JONES	20	STEPHEN	16	11
	WILLIAMS	28	WALTER	16	12
	YOUNG	320	CHRISTOPHER	20	B.S.
	YOUNG	320	LINDA	22	M.S.
	YOUNG	320	DIANE	24	M.S.

Figure 10.3. *Sample data base contents of the relational Doctor-Employee data base in Figure 10.2*

414

base contents that we will use, shown in Figure 10.3, include the same data base contents that are used in other chapters.

Let us now see how the user or data base administrator defines or creates tables composing a data base schema via the SQL *D*ata *D*efinition *L*anguage (DDL) commands. The CREATE TABLE command is used to create a new stored table, also called a **base table**. This is done usually interactively on a terminal, but it may also be done from an application program. A base table may be (1) created from scratch or (2) derived from existing tables via SQL but converted (using the KEEP statement) to a base table. For each column of the created table, the column name and data type are specified. The data types supported (by IBM's SQL/DS) are integer (both half-word and full-word binary integer), decimal, float, and character string (both fixed and varying length).

The following creates the EMPLOYEE table:

```
CREATE TABLE EMPLOYEE
        (D-NAME      VARCHAR (20) NOT NULL,
         EMPNO       INTEGER NOT NULL,
         E-NAME      VARCHAR(20),
         ADDRESS     VARCHAR(25),
         AMT-OWED    INTEGER)
```

The two clauses NOT NULL indicate that blanks or empty spaces are not permitted for D-NAME or EMPNO. However, this does not mean that these two fields concatenated are the key for EMPLOYEE. Unfortunately, a key cannot be declared as directly as in other GDBMS. But we do want such a key as per Figure 10.2. SQL/DS, contrary to the early relational proposals and other relational GDBMS such as QBE, does not require that a table have a unique key (one or several concatenated columns). Thus a table may contain duplicate rows. However, SQL/DS does provide the "unique index" mechanism outlined in subsequent paragraphs through which uniqueness may be enforced if desired. Unfortunately, such enforcement requires defining an index, which is an access time performance mechanism. A base table may be deleted from the data base schema by means of a DROP TABLE statement: DROP TABLE EMPLOYEE.

Once a table is fully defined, data may be entered interactively via an INSERT command (one row per INSERT command), as shown in the next section, or via an INPUT command (several data rows per input command). For mass loading, it is best to use a special mass-loading facility available in batch mode.

Adding and Deleting Columns

Columns may be added to, or deleted from, a table that was previously defined. This can be done at any time, even after loading the data base and processing it. For example, let us add the column STATUS to the EMPLOYEE relation:

ALTER TABLE EMPLOYEE ADD STATUS INTEGER

Right after this command is executed, all values in the new STATUS column are either null or blank. Subsequently, a user or program will fill in values for the desired rows.

The addition or deletion of columns to a data base does not affect the correct functioning of SQL query commands unconcerned with the columns added or deleted. SQL/DS thus provides such data independence not provided by network or hierarchical GDBMS.

Indexes

To improve the access time performance of an SQL/DS data base, **indexes** may be defined for tables. An index is implemented in SQL/DS as a B-tree. A table can have zero, one, or several indexes. In practice, establishing a table having no indexes is seldom justified. An index is defined over one table. Each index can reference up to 16 columns of a table; thus a single index could be defined for the EMPLOYEE table with all its columns concatenated. Either ascending or descending sequence can be specified for each column. An index considers every data value in a column. Every index is named uniquely. For example:

CREATE INDEX OWED ON EMPLOYEE (AMT-OWED)
CREATE INDEX DOCEMP ON EMPLOYEE (D-NAME, EMPNO)

Note that the index DOCEMP is on two columns that are concatenated, not a separate index in each of the two columns.

None of the SQL query commands reference indexes to access a data base. The RDS, Figure 10.1, has an optimizer that analyzes each SQL command and all the available indexes, and then it decides which of the several possible access paths that may be available is the best one to use.

An authorized user or program can easily create or drop an index at any time. Indexes can be created or dropped while others are using SQL/DS. For example:

DROP INDEX OWED

Indexes are also a mechanism for ensuring that all values in the specified column(s) are unique if desired [since rows do not have to be unique on any given column(s)]. For example, we can specify that each row of the EMPLOYEE table is to be unique with respect to D-NAME and EMPNO (concatenated together):

CREATE UNIQUE INDEX DOC EMP ON EMPLOYEE (D-NAME, EMPNO)

This is the way in which a unique key is effectively defined for a table in SQL/DS.

Indexes also aid users or programs that desire to see data ordered or grouped by values of specific columns. Data may be received from SQL/DS in the desired order by creating the index(es), as opposed to users having to order data after SQL/DS presents it in unordered format.

Data Base Administrators, User(s), and Ownership of the Data

The creator or owner of a table (a terminal user, programmer, or DBA) controls all access to the table and its contents. The owner may create and drop indexes and may exercise all SQL commands on the table. The owner may grant to specific users some or all of the data base access rights that we shall discuss in the following sections and thus may share the data. The owner may also grant to some users the right of further granting the rights that they may receive. This will be illustrated in Section 10.5.4.

In SQL/DS there are three different classes of special authority or privileges that may be granted to one or several individuals (listed in increasing authority level):

1. CONNECT authority for users authorized to log onto SQL/DS and access data interactively or via a program.
2. RESOURCE authority for users authorized to create tables and acquire physical storage to hold their contents. A user having RESOURCE authority can ACQUIRE "private" data base space used for data to be accessed by only one user at a time, i.e., nonconcurrently; users not having DBA authority cannot CREATE TABLES in this space. RESOURCE authority also permits creation of tables in "PUBLIC" data base spaces acquired only by a user having DBA authority for data to be shared by more than one user at the same time, i.e., concurrently.

3. DBA authority for users having the highest authority. A DBA automatically has CONNECT and RESOURCE privileges. In addition, only users having DBA authority can do the following:

(a) Access and perform all operations on all tables created and stored by any user, i.e., remain immune from security controls established on data bases (Section 10.5.4).

(b) GRANT and REVOKE CONNECT, RESOURCE, and DBA authority to/from any user. Any user having DBA authority may GRANT or REVOKE DBA authority from any other users. In this respect, there is no DBA hierarchy in SQL/DS. Revocation applies only to previously granted rights by the same DBA.

(c) ACQUIRE, CHANGE, or DROP public data storage areas for data bases to be shared concurrently.

(d) Create a table in a private data base space owned by another user.

The highest authority is the DBA. When SQL/DS is first generated or activated at an installation, there is only one user having CONNECT, RESOURCE, and DBA authority. This initial user having such full authority may then create other users and grant them CONNECT and RESOURCE authority, as well as DBA authority. It is interesting to note that a data base may be created by any user having RESOURCE authority but without requiring DBA authority.

Thus in the typical SQL/DS data base environment there may be any or all of the following scenarios:

1. A data base with one user (the creator or owner) and one DBA, with the same individual actually being both the user and the DBA.

2. A data base with several users, in addition to the owner or creator, and one DBA.

3. A data base with several or many users, in addition to the owner or creator, and several DBAs.

10.3 DATA MANIPULATION

For illustration of the data manipulation commands of SQL, we shall first use the relational Doctor-Employee data base shown in Figures 10.2 and 10.3 that we also used to illustrate the CODASYL, IMS, TOTAL, and SYSTEM 2000 approaches in previous chapters and the other relational alternative QBE in the next chapter. Thus the relational SQL approach may be compared for the same data base and queries. The query examples asterisked are also shown for other GDBMS in other chapters. The actual output from a query will be shown only when helpful for the data base contents used. Subsequent examples will use another data base that is also used in illustrating QBE in the next chapter.

Readers will note the obvious advantage of the relational approach over the procedural DBTG DML, TOTAL DML, and IMS DL/1. The Query Language of SYSTEM 2000 appears just as powerful as SQL for these examples: compare Examples 1–9 that follow with the similar examples using SYSTEM 2000 shown in Figure 8.6. However, subsequent examples illustrate the advantages of SQL. Figures 10.2 and 10.3 show the normalized data base tables that we will use first.

10.3.1   Read-Only Queries (Nonjoin Operations)

Example 1*

Obtain the employee name, address, and amount owed for employee 106.

```
SELECT   E-NAME, ADDRESS, AMT-OWED
FROM     EMPLOYEE
WHERE    EMPNO = 106;
```

This illustrates the basic structure of an SQL query:

(a) SELECT clause: specifies the columns of the target result, which is always a table (null, one row, or many rows) or relations

(b) FROM clause: specifies the table(s) from which the target result is to be obtained

(c) WHERE clause: specifies the logical condition(s) or predicate on which the result is to be obtained. The range of logical conditions described in Appendix B can be specified. The WHERE clause is optional.

Example 2*

Obtain the full EMPLOYEE, INSUR-CO, and CHILD details of EMPLOYEE 106.

```
SELECT   *
FROM     EMPLOYEE
WHERE    EMPNO = 106;
```

```
SELECT   *
FROM     INSUR-CO
WHERE    EMPNO = 106;
SELECT   *
FROM     CHILD
WHERE    EMPNO = 106;
```

The asterisk in the SELECT clause means to retrieve all columns of the relation in the FROM clause.

Example 3*

Obtain the name and age of all the children of employee 106.

```
SELECT   C-NAME, CHILD-AGE
FROM     CHILD
WHERE    EMPNO = 106;
```

Example 4*

Obtain the address of the insurance company whose name is EQUITABLE which services employee 20 (it is assumed that an employee may be serviced by more than one insurance company and each insurance company has different office locations servicing different employees).

```
SELECT   ADDRESS
FROM     INSUR-CO
WHERE    EMPNO = 20 AND I-NAME = 'EQUITABLE';
```

Nesting of Queries

Let us illustrate the SQL facility of nesting SELECT commands so as to immediately use the result of an inner SELECT as the logical qualification of the WHERE clause of the next outer SELECT. We resort to this nesting when there is the need to retrieve or update rows in a relation on the basis of values of fields of other related relations. Users need to become accustomed to this jumping from one relation to another.

Example 5*

Obtain the name, age, and school year of all children of employees insured by PURITAN.

```
SELECT   C-NAME, CHILD-AGE, SCH-YEAR
FROM     CHILD
WHERE    EMPNO =
         SELECT   EMPNO
         FROM     INSUR-CO
         WHERE    I-NAME = 'PURITAN';
```

This query is particularly awkward to answer in DBTG, TOTAL, and IMS because of the need to navigate access paths to the three record or segment types EMPLOYEE, INSUR-CO, and CHILD. See in particular the IMS problem of navigating counter to the hierarchic top-to-bottom, left-to-right storage arising when INSUR-CO is the left child of EMPLOYEE and CHILD is the right child of EMPLOYEE (Example 15 in Section 7.4). SYSTEM 2000 answers the query actually more easily than SQL, Figure 8.6. In the SQL relational approach users may have to jump from one relation to another, whereas in inverted systems such as SYSTEM 2000 and ADABAS, they may not have to be concerned with jumping from one "logical structure" to another within the same data base. Thus inverted systems may turn out to be more convenient for many queries in a number of data base configurations.

10.3.2   Update Queries (Modification Operations)

Modification operations (update, insert, delete) can be performed only on base tables. Every modification user must view each table exactly like the corresponding base table, except that (a) individual rows can be omitted and (b) columns can be omitted, including those declared as non-null. More on the subject is addressed in Section 10.5.

In the following examples the user view coincides with the schema or base tables of Figures 10.2 and 10.3.

Example 6*

Update the data base to show that employee 106 is now insured by AETNA and previously was not insured by any company.

```
UPDATE   INSUR-CO
SET      I-NAME = 'AETNA'
WHERE    EMPNO = 106 AND I-NAME = NULL.
```

Here it is assumed that the name of the insurance company I-NAME is not part of the key of the INSUR-CO relation and may be null. The last part of the WHERE clause is redundant but is used for checking consis-

tency. If it is not true that INSUR-CO.I-NAME = Null, then the update
will not be performed and the inconsistency will have to be checked.
Aspects of consistency or integrity will be addressed in Chapter 13.

Example 7

Insert a new doctor JONES row into DOCTOR and also his corresponding clinic information into CLINIC.

> INSERT INTO DOCTOR VALUES ('JONES', 'SURGERY',
> 16).
> INSERT INTO CLINIC VALUES ('JONES',
> 'CEDARS', 'LOS ANGELES').

Example 8*

Employee 106 has changed his insurance company from PURITAN to
AETNA and has a new doctor named JONES. Assume that JONES has
just been inserted into the data base as in the previous example.

> UPDATE   EMPLOYEE
> SET   D-NAME = 'JONES'
> WHERE   EMPNO = 106;
> UPDATE   INSUR-CO
> SET   D-NAME = 'JONES', I-NAME = 'AETNA'
> WHERE   EMPNO = 106;
> UPDATE   CHILD
> SET   D-NAME = 'JONES'
> WHERE   EMPNO = 106;

Notice that if the user or the system is not aware that the CHILD relation also contains the doctor name for each employee and the last update
is not performed, then an inconsistency will be introduced. Similarly,
because of the way that we have set up the base relations, we must also
indicate the new doctor and insurance name in the INSUR-CO row
involved (we did not update the address and cycle in this row since
we assumed that they are the same for the new insurance company).
SQL/DS does not implement the *assertion* or integrity mechanisms proposed in the early SEQUEL writings[2] that would depict such inconsistencies, notify the user, and enforce specified update requirements. The
reason for not implementing them was undoubtedly the possibly prohibitive overhead of checking the assertion for each UPDATE.

Example 9*

Add a new child to employee 106.

INSERT   INTO CHILD VALUES ('DUMMY', 106, 'JOE', 1,0)

In the base table CHILD the doctor name D-NAME is part of the key and may not be null. Thus we must put some fictitious doctor name, DUMMY, if we do not know who the doctor is.

Example 10*

Delete employee 106 and all his children and insurance company information (insurance information of other employees is not to be affected).

```
DELETE   EMPLOYEE
WHERE    EMPNO = 106;
DELETE   CHILD
WHERE    EMPNO = 106;
DELETE   INSUR-CO
WHERE    EMPNO = 106;
```

Example 11*

Delete all children whose school year is > 12 and whose parent owes $> \$1000$ and whose doctor is a psychiatrist with practice at UCLA (clinic name). This is a particularly difficult request for a user to formulate for DBTG, TOTAL, or IMS. Undoubtedly, it is also a time-consuming request for any relational system.

```
DELETE   *
FROM     CHILD
WHERE    SCH-YEAR > 12
         AND D-NAME =
         (SELECT D-NAME
         FROM    DOCTOR
         WHERE   SPECIALTY = 'PSYCHIATRY' AND
                 D-NAME = (SELECT D-NAME
                 FROM CLINIC WHERE
                 C-NAME = 'UCLA'))
         AND
         EMPNO =
         (SELECT EMPNO
         FROM    EMPLOYEE
         WHERE   AMT-OWED > 1000);
```

Example 12

Increase by 10 percent the amount owed by employees insured by AETNA or PURITAN:

```
UPDATE   EMPLOYEE
SET      AMT-OWED = 1.10 * AMT-OWED
WHERE    EMPNO =
         (SELECT  EMPNO
         FROM     INSUR-CO
         WHERE    I-NAME = 'AETNA' OR I-NAME =
                  'PURITAN');
```

The SET clause may include an expression involving constants, operators, and field names, as illustrated here.

10.3.3 Join Operations

Let us now move on to another data model and illustrate the join operator. We illustrate some of the particular attractiveness and simplicity of the SQL/DS relational approach compared to most nonrelational approaches in handling data bases and queries of the following types. Most of these queries are also shown for QBE in the following chapter. Consider the data base in Figure 10.4 relating employees to department(s) and to their manager(s).

EMPLOYEE (EMPNO, E-NAME, DEPTNO, SALARY, MGRNO)
DEPARTMENT (DEPTNO, D-NAME, NEMPS)

EMPLOYEE	EMPNO	E-NAME	DEPTNO	SALARY	MGRNO
	1	JONES	1	35,000	5
	2	MARTIN	2	35,000	4
	3	GOMEZ	3	40,000	7
	4	CHU	2	42,000	250
	5	DAMES	1	50,000	250
	6	THOMAS	1	28,000	5
	7	WATSON	3	38,000	250
	8	PARKER	2	14,000	4
	250	GOPHER	4	65,000	0

DEPARTMENT	DEPTNO	D-NAME	NEMPS
	0	CEO	4000
	1	ACCOUNTING	75
	2	COMP-SCI	32
	3	MGT-SCI	12
	4	FINANCE	140

Figure 10.4. *The Employee-Department data base*

Join in a Single Table

Example 13*

List the names of all employees whose salary is more than that of their managers; also list the corresponding manager names.

```
SELECT   X.E-NAME, Y.E-NAME
FROM     EMPLOYEE X, EMPLOYEE Y
WHERE    X.MGRNO = Y.EMPNO
         AND X.SALARY > Y.SALARY;
```

Output from the query:

X.E-NAME	Y.E-NAME
GOMEZ	WATSON

This query involves the power of the relational **join** operator applied in a single table. The FROM clause indicates that different rows (named with cursor X and Y) of the same table EMPLOYEE are to be joined (in the past we had addressed only the join between different tables). The basis for joining rows is given in the WHERE clause, in this case X.MGRNO = Y.EMPNO AND X.SALARY > Y.SALARY. Field names in a query may stand alone or may be qualified by a table name (EMLOYEE.SALARY) or by a cursor name (Y.SALARY, as is necessary in this example).

Example 14

Print the names and salaries of all employees whose salary is more than that of their managers and who work in a department that has less than 15 employees; also list the corresponding manager names.

```
SELECT   X.E-NAME, X.SALARY, Y.E-NAME
FROM     EMPLOYEE X, EMPLOYEE Y
WHERE    X.MGRNO = Y.EMPNO
         AND X.SALARY > Y.SALARY
         AND DEPTNO =
             (SELECT DEPTNO
             FROM DEPARTMENT
             WHERE NEMPS < 15);
```

Output from the query:

X.E-NAME	X.SALARY	Y.E-NAME
GOMEZ	40,000	WATSON

Output from More Than One Table; Joining of Several Tables

A query may select data from more than one table and see this output data as one table. This is done by applying the *join* operation on the tables. In SQL/DS a **join** is invoked by listing the names of the tables in the FROM clause; SQL/DS logically joins these tables and then extracts the data qualified by the SELECT and WHERE clauses.

Example 15

Obtain a list of the names, salaries, and department names for employees who earn less than $15,000.

```
SELECT   E-NAME, SALARY, D-NAME
FROM     EMPLOYEE, DEPARTMENT
WHERE    EMPLOYEE.DEPTNO =
            DEPARTMENT.DEPTNO
         AND EMPLOYEE.SALARY < 15,000;
```

Output from the query:

E-NAME	SALARY	D-NAME
PARKER	14,000	COMP-SCI

10.3.4 Temporary Tables

The result of a query may be placed via the SQL assignment statement into either a temporary or a permanent relation in the data base. A temporary table is destroyed when the user who created it terminates interaction with the system. A temporary table may be manipulated just as any base relation. Let us illustrate the creation of a temporary table.

Example 16

Create a new temporary table called POORPEOPLE made up of the names and salaries of employees who are in the computer science department and earn less than $15,000.

```
ASSIGN TO POORPEOPLE (E-NAME, SALARY):
    SELECT   E-NAME, SALARY
    FROM     EMPLOYEE
    WHERE    SALARY < 15000
             AND DEPTNO =
             (SELECT  DEPTNO
             FROM     DEPARTMENT
             WHERE    D-NAME = 'COMP-SCI');
```

The new table POORPEOPLE is formed from EMPLOYEE and DE-PARTMENT at the moment that the assignment statement is executed. POOR PEOPLE then becomes an independent relation and will not be affected by any subsequent changes to EMPLOYEE and DEPART-MENT. For example, if the salary of a computer science department employee is changed from below $15,000 to over $15,000 a moment after the execution of the above assignment, this will not be reflected in POORPEOPLE. The user will have to take steps to maintain the consistency, for example, by deleting the POORPEOPLE row for the particular employee receiving the salary increase. The temporary table can be manipulated just like any base relation of the user's submodel.

A temporary table may be converted into a permanent table for subsequent use by that user by means of the KEEP TABLE command. Thus users can act as DBAs of their own relations.

The ASSIGN TO statement was implemented in the prototype System R but was not carried over to the commercial SQL/DS.

10.3.5   Ordering, Grouping, Built-in Functions, and Duplicate Rows

Duplicate Rows

The result of a query may include rows which are duplicates. The elimination of duplicates may be necessary in some cases but not in others. Duplicates are eliminated only if explicitly requested.

Example 17

Obtain a list of salaries and the corresponding department numbers.

1. Return duplicate rows: SELECT DEPTNO, SALARY
                             FROM EMPLOYEE;
2. Return only unique rows: SELECT UNIQUE DEPTNO,
                             SALARY FROM EMPLOYEE;

Built-in Functions

Several built-in functions may be used to operate on the values of a specific column at a time: average, maximum, and minimum of the values (AVG, MAX, MIN); sum of the values (SUM); and count of the number of values (COUNT). The argument of each of the functions may optionally include UNIQUE to specify that duplicate values should be considered only once when the function is applied. The function COUNT(*) counts all rows in a table without eliminating duplicates.

Arithmetic and logical expressions involving column names and built-in functions may also be used in the SELECT and WHERE clauses, as well as in other clauses subsequently introduced. Examples below illustrate it.

Example 18

Count the number of different salary values in the EMPLOYEE table.

SELECT COUNT(UNIQUE SALARY) FROM EMPLOYEE;

Example 19

Compute the average salary of employees over all departments.

1. Use duplicate salary values:

SELECT AVG (SALARY) FROM EMPLOYEE;

Output from this query: AVG(SALARY)
                              $38,555

2. Do not use duplicate salary values:

SALARY AVG(UNIQUE SALARY) FROM EMPLOYEE

Output from this query: <u>AVG(SALARY)</u>
                               $39,000

Example 20

List the name, department number, and salary of the employee(s) having the largest salary:

```
SELECT   E-NAME, DEPTNO, SALARY
FROM     EMPLOYEE
WHERE    SALARY =
         (SELECT MAX (SALARY)
         FROM EMPLOYEE)
```

Output from the query:

E-NAME	DEPTNO	SALARY
GOPHER	4	65,000

Example 21

List the highest and lowest salaries and the difference between them.

```
SELECT   MAX (SALARY), MIN (SALARY), MAX
         (SALARY) − MIN (SALARY)
FROM     EMPLOYEE
```

Output from the query:

MAX (SALARY)	MIN (SALARY)	MAX (SALARY) − MIN (SALARY)
65,000	14,000	51,000

Ordering Operations

SQL provides ordering facilities for basic reporting needs. Information may be produced in either ascending order or descending order. Major and minor sort priorities allow ordering output on the basis of a major column first, then on a second or minor column, then on a third or minor column, and so on. Several examples below illustrate this.

Example 22

List the employee names and department names in descending salary order, and for the same salary in ascending alphabetic order by employee name, for the computer science and management science departments.

```
SELECT   SALARY, E-NAME, D-NAME
FROM     EMPLOYEE, DEPARTMENT
WHERE    EMPLOYEE.DEPTNO = DEPARTMENT.
            DEPTNO
         AND (D-NAME = 'COMP-SCI' OR
             D-NAME = 'MGT-SCI')
ORDER BY SALARY DESC, E-NAME
```

Output from the query:

SALARY	E-NAME	D-NAME
42,000	CHU	COMP-SCI
40,000	GOMEZ	MGT-SCI
38,000	WATSON	MGT-SCI
35,000	MARTIN	COMP-SCI
14,000	PARKER	COMP-SCI

The ORDER BY clause is always placed at the end of the SELECT command and operates on the information resulting from the SELECT command. In the previous example the result is obtained from the two source tables EMPLOYEE and DEPARTMENT via a join. Ordering can be either in ascending sequence by default or in descending (DESC) sequence.

Grouping Operations and Built-in Functions

In previous examples the built-in functions were applied to single groups of rows obtained via the SELECT command. SQL provides the GROUP BY clause as an option in a SELECT command to permit the formation of multiple groups having in common the same row value for a given column or columns. Furthermore, a HAVING clause can then SELECT specific groups meeting some specified content criteria. Let us use several illustrations.

Example 23

List the average salary of employees by department number except for departments 0 and 4.

```
SELECT   DEPTNO,AVG(SALARY)
FROM     EMPLOYEE
WHERE    ¬ (DEPTNO = 0 OR DEPTNO = 4)
GROUP BY DEPTNO
```

Output from the query:

DEPTNO	AVG(SALARY)
1	37,666
2	30,333
3	39,000

The output of this query is developed conceptually as follows (although this is not necessarily what is physically done internally):

1. The FROM and WHERE clauses obtain a copy of the EMPLOYEE table consisting of rows for all department numbers except 0 and 4.
2. The GROUP BY clause partitions this table by DEPTNO and then applies the average built-in function to each set of SALARY values in each group.
3. Output each of the grouped department numbers and the corresponding average salary SELECTed.

A SELECT clause that contains column names with group functions may not contain column names that do not apply to groups. For example, SELECT E-NAME, AVG(SALARY) would be in error.

Example 24

List the average salary of employees and order the output in ascending order by department and then by manager. Also show the corresponding department number and manager number.

```
SELECT    DEPTNO, MGRNO, AVG(SALARY)
FROM      EMPLOYEE
GROUP BY  DEPTNO,MGRNO
ORDER BY  DEPTNO, MGRNO
```

Output from the query:

DEPTNO	MGRNO	AVG(SALARY)
1	5	31,500
1	250	50,000
2	4	24,500
2	250	42,000
3	7	40,000
3	250	38,000
4	0	65,000

A group is formed for every manager within every department, and then the average salary for each group is computed. In a query the GROUP BY clause may be followed by the ORDER BY clause to obtain the desired order in the output.

Example 25

List the department number and average salary of its employees for those departments in which the average salary of its employees is greater than $35,000.

```
SELECT       DEPTNO, AVG(SALARY)
FROM         EMPLOYEEE
GROUP BY     DEPTNO
HAVING       AVG(SALARY) > 35,000
```

Output from the query:

DEPTNO	AVG(SALARY)
1	37,666
3	39,000
4	65,000

The HAVING clause is a predicate (i.e., a type of WHERE clause) that is applied only to the groups formed by the GROUP BY clause, so as to choose specific groups and disqualify others. In contrast, the WHERE clause applies to individual rows of a table. The GROUP BY and HAVING clauses are always used after the initial data is selected via the SELECT...FROM...WHERE clauses.

Example 26

List the department number and average salary of its employees for those departments in which the average salary of its employees is greater than the average salary over all employees.

```
SELECT      DEPTNO, AVG(SALARY)
FROM        EMPLOYEE
GROUP BY    DEPTNO
HAVING      AVG(SALARY) >
            (SELECT AVG (SALARY)
            FROM EMPLOYEE);
```

Output from the query:

DEPTNO	AVG(SALARY)
3	39,000
4	65,000

This query illustrates that a subquery or nested query can be used in a HAVING clause to compare an attribute of the group (the average salary of the department) with a computed attribute of another group (the average salary over all departments, which in this case is $38,555). As explained in the previous example, the HAVING clause selects the desired group(s) (DEPTNO) formed by the GROUP BY clause from the result of the SELECT...FROM...WHERE...clauses.

Combined Join, Ordering, Grouping, Nesting, and Built-in Functions

Example 27

List the name, average salary, maximum salary, and number of employees for each department, except the CEO department, having an average salary greater than the average salary over all employees; list the result in ascending alphabetic order by department name (this is an expanded variation of the previous example).

```
SELECT                  D-NAME, AVG(SALARY),
                        MAX(SALARY), COUNT(*)
FROM                    EMPLOYEE, DEPARTMENT
```

WHERE   EMPLOYEE.DEPTNO =
                         DEPARTMENT.DEPTNO
                         AND D-NAME ¬ = 'CEO'
GROUP BY   DEPTNO
HAVING   AVG(SALARY) >
           (SELECT AVG (SALARY)
           FROM EMPLOYEE)
ORDER BY D-NAME;

Output from query:

D-NAME	AVG(SALARY)	MAX(SALARY)	COUNT(*)
FINANCE	65,000	65,000	1
MGT-SCI	39,000	40,000	2

This query illustrates the use of the various clauses that have been gradually introduced in previous examples. Such clauses can be used with a join operation in the same query, as shown in this example. Here the EMPLOYEE and DEPARTMENT tables are being joined. Let us review what each of the clauses is doing as the answer is being developed (this conceptual development does not necessarily coincide with how SQL/DS is physically and internally obtaining the answer):

1. The first FROM and WHERE clauses generate a "virtual" table X formed by the join of the EMPLOYEE and DEPARTMENT tables and composed of rows meeting the criteria in the WHERE clause (the CEO department is excluded as well as any other DEPTNOs that do not appear in both tables).

2. The GROUP BY clause groups the rows of table X by DEPTNO.

3. The HAVING clause eliminates from table X those groups whose average salary is not greater than the average salary over all employees, which was computed earlier by the nested SELECT AVG(SALARY) FROM EMPLOYEE.

4. The first SELECT obtains the D-NAME from table X, takes the average and the maximum of the salaries for each DEPTNO group, counts the number of rows for each DEPTNO, and arranges these four types of information into the desired output table Y.

5. Finally, table Y is printed in ascending D-NAME order, as specified in the ORDER BY clause (the last clause to be invoked).

10.3.6   Storing of Queries and Subsequent Invocation

Any SQL command or set of commands can be stored and subsequently invoked. This is available only in the interactive SQL (ISQL). A name is given to the query when storing it for subsequent recall. Variables or parameters may be used in the stored query; the invocation may then provide the actual values.

Example 28

Using the name Q-PERS, store, and subsequently invoke, the query in Example 27.

⟨Place here the SQL command from the previous example⟩
STORE Q-PERS;

Subsequently the stored query can be retrieved and executed by stating:

START Q-PERS;

Example 29

Store the following query so that you may subsequently be able to activate it in order to update the salary (increase or decrease) for any desired department.

        HOLD UPDATE   EMPLOYEE
        SET   SALARY = &1 * SALARY
        WHERE   DEPTNO =
                           (SELECT DEPTNO
                           FROM DEPARTMENT
                           WHERE D-NAME = '&2');
        STORE SAL-UPDATE;

The HOLD command prevents the execution of the UPDATE command since the parameter values &1 and '&2' are to be provided when the query is subsequently activated. The query is STORED under the name SAL-UPDATE.

Example 30

Activate the SAL-UPDATE query to increase by 25 percent the salary of employees in the computer science department.

START SAL-UPDATE (1.25 * COMP-SCI)

10.3.7   Simple Reports from Query Results

SQL/DS provides some elementary facilities for interactively adjusting the format of data returned from a SELECT command and then printing a report. These facilities are available only in the interactive SQL (ISQL). Included are facilities to:

1. Display a top title, bottom title, and page length to be used in the printout.
2. Rename column headings and adjust the spacing between them (by default the column names provided in the user's view are used).
3. Exclude displayed columns from a report.
4. Remove the repetition of values in a given column which has been grouped.
5. Display totals and subtotals by groups.

These purely reporting facilities in SQL/DS and other GDBMS query languages are minimal and elementary in comparison to the batch facilities of report writers and GFMS. However, such facilities, coupled with the ordering, grouping, interactive features, and powerful multifile or true relational data base querying facilities, are unique to GDBMS technology and cannot be matched by batch-oriented report writers and GFMS.

Example 31

List the employees name and department names in descending salary order, and for the same salary in ascending alphabetic order by employee name, for the computer science and management science departments (this is the same as Example 22). Furthermore, remove the repetition of values in the department name column, and then calculate the subtotals of the employees' salaries by department and the total of the salaries of employees in the two departments.

```
SELECT      D-NAME, E-NAME, SALARY
FROM        EMPLOYEE, DEPARTMENT
WHERE       EMPLOYEE.DEPTNO =
                DEPARTMENT.DEPTNO
            AND (D-NAME = COMP-SCI OR
            D-NAME = MGT-SCI)
ORDER BY    SALARY DESC, E-NAME
FORMAT      GROUP D-NAME
FORMAT      SUBTOTAL SALARY
```

Output from the query:

D-NAME	E-NAME	SALARY
COMP-SCI	CHU	42,000
	MARTIN	38,000
	PARKER	14,000
		———
****		91,000
MGT-SCI	GOMEZ	40,000
	WATSON	38,000
		———
****		78,000
		═══
		169,000

10.4 PROCEDURAL PROGRAM INTERFACE (EMBEDDED SQL)

Application programs written in major procedural program languages such as PL/1 and COBOL can access data bases managed by SQL/DS by embedding SQL commands in the application program. These embedded SQL commands are essentially the same as the SQL commands that are used in an interactive environment (with only minor syntactic alterations). In fact, one of the major design goals of relational systems has been that the data manipulation language be the same whether one is accessing the data base from an interactive console or from within a program written in a procedural programming language and being processed either in batch or interactive mode. This desired commonality is not achieved in a number of nonrelational GDBMS that have a procedural data manipulation language and a query language with significant syntactic and perhaps even significant semantic differences between the two languages.

Any host application program that contains any SQL DDL or DML command must be first preprocessed by SQL/DS. The SQL/DS preprocessor locates every SQL command, replacing each by the original SQL statement as a comment, and a standard procedure (or subroutine) call in the host programming language to the appropriate SQL/DS routines. It then sends the program to the standard programming language compiler for compilation and subsequent execution. At execution time SQL/DS is in control when the procedure calls that it generated are activated.

Let us first focus on data declarations, the binding of SQL and host language variables, and single row or record occurrence processing. Then we shall focus on multiple row retrieval and processing.

Declaration and Binding of Variables and Single Row Processing

An embedded SQL DML command may contain the name of the host language variables for communication between SQL/DS and the host program. Such variables must be declared for proper binding.

Example 32

Figure 10.5 shows an example for both PL/1 and COBOL. The numbers preceding each statement are used for our identification pur-

(a) PL/1 Example:

Other PL/1 and/or SQL statements

```
1 EXEC  SQL BEGIN DECLARE SECTION;
2           DCL PL-E-NAME CHAR (20) VAR;
3           DCL PL-SALARY FIXED BINARY (31);
4           DCL PL-EMPNO FIXED BINARY (15);
5 EXEC  SQL END DECLARATION SECTION;
```

Other PL/1 and/or SQL statements

```
6 EXEC  SQL SELECT E-NAME, SALARY INTO:  PL-E-NAME, :PL-SALARY
           FROM EMPLOYEE
           WHERE EMPNO = :  PL-EMPNO;
```

Other PL/1 and/or SQL statements

(b) COBOL Example:

IDENTIFICATION and ENVIRONMENT Divisions of COBOL

DATA DIVISION.

File Section of COBOL

WORKING-STORAGE SECTION.

```
1       EXEC SQL BEGIN DECLARE SECTION VAR.
2  77   PL-E-NAME PICTURE X(20).
3  77   PL-SALARY PICTURE S9 (9) COMPUTATIONAL.
4  77   PL-EMPNO PICTURE S9 (4) COMPUTATIONAL.
5       EXEC SQL END DECLARE SECTION VAR.
```

Other COBOL and/or SQL working storage declarations

PROCEDURE DIVISION

Other COBOL and/or SQL statements

```
6       EXEC SQL SELECT E-NAME, SALARY INTO: PL-E-NAME, :PL-SALARY
                FROM   EMPLOYEE
                WHERE  EMPNO = :  PL-EMPNO.
```

Other COBOL and/or SQL statements

Figure 10.5.   *Declaration and binding of variables and single row processing using SQL/DS in PL/1 and COBOL*

439

poses and are not part of the syntax. The SELECT statement 6 in
Figure 10.5 retrieves from the EMPLOYEE table in Figure 10.4 the
employee name and salary for a single employee whose employee number is contained in the host language variable PL-EMPNO. The employee name and salary are then stored by SQL/DS in the host language
variables PL-E-NAME and PL-SALARY, respectively. The host language variables are declared in the DECLARE section statements 1–5,
and they are differentiated from SQL column names by a colon (":")
preceding the DECLAREd variable name. Host language variables must
be compatible in data type and length with the SQL fields with which they
are compared or to/from which data is transferred; if not, SQL/DS
returns one of several diagnostic messages to the program. The example
in Figure 10.5 is compatible with the following EMPLOYEE table definition.

```
CREATE   TABLE EMPLOYEE
         (EMPNO SMALLINT NOT NULL,
         E-NAME VARCHAR(20),
         DEPTNO SMALLINT,
         SALARY INTEGER,
         MGRNO SMALLINT)
```

Multiple Row Processing and Cursors

Embedded SQL accesses data from multiple rows in a table via so-called
cursors. A cursor is a name used to identify a set of rows which, for example,
might be the result of a query, and also to keep an indicator to one of the rows
of the set. The rows may then be materialized and retrieved as they are needed,
one at a time, by the FETCH operator. This row-at-a-time processing facility is
necessitated by the orientation of the common programming languages toward
dealing with only one record at a time. Note that in the example in Figure 10.5
the SELECT command interfacing to the host program refers to only one row
(if not, SQL/DS returns a message). If a SELECT command retrieves more
than one row, then the cursor facility and the associated SELECT command
format must be used.

If the SQL command to be embedded in the host program is an UP-
DATE, DELETE, or INSERT command, then it does not matter whether it
processes zero, one, or many rows at a time: the cursor mechanism is not
necessary. The command format then is exactly as in our earlier examples.
However, one-row-at-a-time processing can still be done for the DELETE
and UPDATE operations via the cursor mechanism, as we will illustrate
subsequently.

Example 33

Figure 10.6 shows an example of multiple row and cursor use in a PL/1 program section. This program produces a display showing the names and salaries of the employees in department 10, ordered by employee name in ascending sequence. SQL commands start with the words EXEC SQL. The numbers preceding each statement are not part of the statement syntax. Let us see what each numbered statement is doing:

Statement 1 is a PL/1 assignment statement assigning to the PL/1 variable DEPT-NUMBER the department number for which we wish the display.

Statement 2 names and binds the PL/1 cursor CURS1 with the table that results from the SELECT query. At this point no rows are actually retrieved in response to the SELECT command.

Statement 3 activates CURS1. The input variable DEPT-NUMBER is used to qualify the set of rows desired. At this point no rows are retrieved by the OPEN command. The cursor is set to a position just before the first row of the output table. The optimizer in the SQL RDS, Figure 10.1, chooses an appropri-

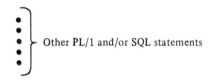

Other PL/1 and/or SQL statements

```
1 DEPT-NUMBER = 4;
2 EXEC SQL DECLARE CURS1 CURSOR FOR
      SELECT E-NAME, SALARY
      FROM EMPLOYEE
      WHERE DEPTNO = : DEPT-NUMBER
      ORDER BY E-NAME;
3 EXEC SQL OPEN CURS1;
4 EXEC SQL FETCH CURS1 INTO: PL-E-NAME, : PL-SALARY;
5 DO WHILE (SQLCODE=0);
6     PUT SKIP LIST (PL-E-NAME, PL-SALARY);
7 EXEC SQL FETCH CURS1 INTO: PL-E-NAME, : PL-SALARY;
8 END;
9 EXEC SQL CLOSE CURS1;
```

Figure 10.6.   *Sample PL/1 program using SQL/DS to access via cursor multiple rows of the Employee-Department data base in Figure 10.4*

ate access path and sets up the necessary mechanisms by which each row is to be subsequently materialized.

Statement 4 materializes the first row or next row of the desired table and assigns the data to the host variables PL-E-NAME and PL-SALARY.

Statement 5 checks the reserved PL/1 variable SQLCODE in which SQL/DS indicates various possible outcomes of processing. SQLCODE = 0 denotes success; success in this case means that FETCH did materialize a row. Statements 5 and 8 delimit a DO loop which executes statements 6 and 7 WHILE SQLCODE = 0.

Statement 6 prints out the name and salary of the most recently materialized row.

Statement 7 materializes the next row of the output table.

Statement 8 deactivates the use of the cursor.

A given application program may have several cursors active at any one time, either in one table or in several tables. Each SELECT command has its own cursor. Each cursor remains active until the command CLOSE OR KEEP is stated. KEEP takes the set of rows identified by the cursor referenced and forms a new permanent table in the data base.

The reader will note that one cursor identifying a single row is similar to the CODASYL currency status indicator (Chapter 5) identifying the last referenced occurrence of a record type. Most GDBMS provide some similar position status indicator.

Embedded update and delete SQL commands may refer to a single row referenced by the current position of the cursor. Thus the update or delete may be constrained to one row at a time.

Example 34

Decrease by 20 percent the salary of the employee in the row referred to by cursor CURS2:

```
UPDATE    EMPLOYEE
SET       SALARY=0.80* SALARY
WHERE     CURRENT OF CURS2
```

UPDATE does not affect the position of the cursor.

Dynamically Defined SQL Commands

Previous sections describe how SQL commands are embedded and communicate with a host program. The examples show SQL commands that are defined before the program is preprocessed by SQL/DS and the host language compiler and then subsequently executed. However, there are some applications in which the structure (not just the value of an embedded parameter value, Examples 28–30) of an SQL command is not known until the program is running. This situation occurs particularly in on-line application programs that support user access to the data base via interactive terminals. While the on-line program may have some predefined SQL commands, at execution time the user may wish to introduce some other SQL commands. Thus there is the requirement that SQL/DS, or any other GDBMS supporting an on-line application program environment, be able to support the construction and execution of data base commands dynamically defined by the user at run time. SQL/DS provides such facilities through the PREPARE, DESCRIBE, and EXECUTE commands. We shall not dwell on such details. Interested readers may consult the SQL/DS references.[5,6] Some other GDBMS, like QBE, provide equivalent facilities to support such dynamic requirements.

10.5   THE USER VIEWS OR SUBSCHEMAS

In SQL/DS a subschema consists of one or several selected base or stored tables and/or a view which results from projecting, joining, and grouping base tables.

In the subsections below we will address and illustrate in this order: the definition of views, queries on views, derivation of views on views, access controls over base tables directly or through views, and restrictions on update operations through views.

10.5.1   Definition of Views

In accord with the relational approach, the SQL DML is used to define or create a **user view** or subschema as one or several tables derived from one or more source tables. The result of a SQL query is always a table. The full power of the SQL DML SELECT command is used to define a view. The table(s) produced by any of the retrieval (SELECT) examples in Section 10.3 are possible user views. The only restrictions are that the ORDER BY clause and references to query variables (Examples 28 and 29) are not permitted in defining a view. View tables are *not* stored. Any number of views can be defined.

A view is created by the SQL DDL statement CREATE VIEW:

CREATE VIEW ⟨view name⟩
    [(column-name[,column-name]...)]
        AS ⟨any SELECT statement⟩

A view may be deleted by simply stating:

DROP VIEW ⟨view name⟩

No new columns may be added to a view. The view would have to be dropped and a new view would have to be defined to include any new column(s) desired in the view.

Example 35

Create a view on the Doctor-Employee data base in Figure 10.2 constrained to see the name, age, and school year of all children of employees insured by Puritan.

```
CREATE   VIEW PURITAN-CHILDREN
         AS SELECT  C-NAME, CHILD-AGE, SCH-YEAR
            FROM    CHILD
            WHERE   EMPNO =
                    (SELECT EMPNO
                    FROM INSUR-CO
                    WHERE I-NAME = 'PURITAN');
```

Another alternative is to use a join:

```
CREATE   VIEW PURITAN-CHILDREN
         AS SELECT  C-NAME, CHILD-AGE, SCH-YEAR
            FROM    CHILD C, INSUR-CO I
            WHERE   C.EMPNO = I.EMPNO
                    AND INAME = 'PURITAN';
```

This may be better because it doesn't tell the SQL/DS optimizer as much how to obtain the result.

The SELECT command used in deriving this view is the same as that used in the retrieval Example 5. The table in the PURITAN-CHILDREN view uses as column names those used in the schema table. However, if desired, any column name in a view may be renamed as shown in the next example. The data types and lengths appearing in a view are the same as those in the source tables.

Example 36

Create a view on the Employee-Department data base in Figure 10.4 composed of the name, salary, and department name for employees who earn less than $15,000.

```
CREATE   VIEW POOR-GUYS(NAME,SALARY,DEPT-
                                    NAME)
         AS        SELECT      E-NAME, SALARY,
                                    D-NAME
         FROM      EMPLOYEE, DEPARTMENT
         WHERE     EMPLOYEE.DEPTNO =
                   DEPARTMENT.DEPTNO
                   AND EMPLOYEE.SALARY < 15,000
```

Note that this view is derived by using a join of two tables. The SELECT command is the same one as used in the retrieval Example 15.

Example 37

Create a view on the Employee-Department data base in Figure 10.4 composed of the department number and average salary of its employees for those departments in which the average salary of its employees is greater than $35,000; also include the average monthly salary (the column SALARY in Figure 10.4 is the annual average salary).

```
CREATE VIEW RICH-DEPTS
            (DEPTNO, AVE-SAL-Y, AVE-SAL-M)
        AS  SELECT DEPTNO, AVG(SALARY),
            AVG(SALARY)/12
            FROM EMPLOYEE
            GROUP BY DEPTNO
            HAVING AVG(SALARY) > 35,000
```

Calculated or virtual fields may be included in a view, for example, the average department salary per year AVE-SAL-Y and per month AVE-SAL-M. The SELECT command is the same one as used in the retrieval Example 25, except for the additional virtual field AVE-SAL-M.

A view may be used just as a basic table is used:

1. Queries may be written on it subject to some restrictions for update operations addressed in Section 10.5.5.
2. Other views may be derived from it.

The following subsections address and illustrate each of these cases.

10.5.2   Queries on Views

Example 38

Retrieve all the information in the RICH-DEPTS view.

SELECT *
FROM RICH-DEPTS

This shows that a view is a way of storing a SELECT query which can be subsequently invoked by a SELECT * command as illustrated here. Examples 28−30 illustrate the other alternative, perhaps the more common one, for storing queries and subsequently invoking them.

Example 39

Using the RICH-DEPTS view (defined in Example 37), obtain a list of the average annual salaries of the employees for each department in which this average exceeds $50,000, excluding department 10; order the result in descending salary order.

SELECT   DEPTNO, AVG-SAL-Y
FROM   RICH-DEPTS
WHERE   AVE-SAL-Y > 50,000 AND DEPTNO ¬ 10
ORDER   BY AVE-SAL-Y DESC;

In processing a query on a view, the following happens inside SQL/DS and it is transparent to the user:

1. When the view is created, the contents of the view are not materialized or stored, that is, the SELECT command defining the scope of the views is not executed, but is instead saved by SQL/DS as part of the view definition.
2. When a query is issued over a view, the SQL RDS essentially combines the query with the view's SELECT and then identifies an

optimum or appropriate access path to access the data base and service the query. Thus for the previous query, what is actually considered by the SQL/DS optimizer internally is how best to obtain the answer to the following query:

```
SELECT   DEPTNO, AVG(SALARY)
FROM     EMPLOYEE
WHERE    DEPTNO ¬ = 10
GROUP    BY DEPTNO
HAVING   AVG(SALARY) > 50,000
```

This type of optimization and processing of queries on views is not unique to SQL/DS. Other intelligent GDBMS having powerful query languages, especially other competing relational GDBMS and inverted GDBMS, also exhibit such an approach to various degrees.

10.5.3   Derivation of Views on Views

Example 40

Create the view VERY-RICH-DEPTS consisting of the department number and the average annual salary of the employees for each department in which this average exceeds $50,000 (exclude department 10). The view RICH-DEPTS defined in Example 37 is used as the source for the new view.

```
CREATE   VIEW VERY-RICH-DEPTS
         AS SELECT DEPTNO, AVE-SAL-Y
         FROM RICH-DEPTS
         WHERE AVE-SAL-Y > 50,000 and DEPT ¬ = 10
```

This view includes the same information retrieved in Example 39, which uses a query on the view RICH-DEPTS. The only difference is that in this example the ORDER BY clause, which was used in Example 39 for ordering in descending salary order, cannot be used in deriving a view.

The derivation of a view using another view can be carried on recursively, that is, a view can be created on a view, which in turn has been created on a view, and so forth.

Any query may be written on a view which has been derived from another view. When the query is received by SQL/DS, the query is combined for execution with the SELECT of the view (the view seen by the issuer of the query), the SELECT of the underlying source table(s) (the view of the creator of the view), and so on.

Any views derived from a view being dropped are also automatically dropped. Deletion of the underlying stored table(s) causes all views derived from these table(s) to be automatically dropped.

10.5.4   Access Controls (Security Controls)

An SQL/DS user (terminal user, programmer, or DBA) who creates a table is the "owner" of the table. Initially, this owner is the only one authorized to access the table and derive views on it [except for the DBA(s) who have access authority over all tables—see Section 10.2]. However, the owner may then use the GRANT command to:

1. Grant to other users the right to access the table.
2. Grant to other users the right to access views created by this owner.
3. Grant to some users the right to further grant the rights that they receive.

The following privileges can be issued to or revoked from tables and views:

1. From tables and views: SELECT, INSERT, DELETE, and UPDATE.
2. From tables: ALTER and INDEX.

We will illustrate all of this with several examples below.

The view mechanism is used to establish access and control to specific columns and rows of any table. A view may be established and constrained to each or any combination of the commands SELECT, INSERT, DELETE, and UPDATE.

It is interesting to note that SQL/DS does not require that the creation of a table and the definition of new views be done only by a user possessing DBA authority. Users are also allowed to derive new tables and views from the original view granted to them initially by another user or DBA, and, of course, from the tables that authorized users create from scratch. Users have complete authority to perform any operation on what they have derived, so long as it is within the authority limits of the original view. Only the user who creates a table or view, or a user having DBA authority, may drop it.

For each right that a user may be given for a table or view, the user may be optionally given by the grantor of that right the authority to further grant or revoke the capability to/from other users.

A privilege that has been granted may be subsequently revoked by the REVOKE command. When one user's privilege is revoked, the privilege is automatically revoked for all users to whom that user granted it, unless the privilege was granted independently by another user who maintains the GRANT privilege.

Example 41

Authorize Parker and Popek to read and insert on all the columns of the table EMPLOYEE.

GRANT SELECT, INSERT ON EMPLOYEE TO PARKER,
    POPEK;

Example 42

Authorize all users, i.e., the "public," to read the table DEPART-MENT.

GRANT SELECT ON DEPARTMENT TO PUBLIC;

Example 43

Give all privileges (SELECT, INSERT, DELETE, UPDATE, ALTER, INDEX) to Melkanoff on the EMPLOYEE and DEPART-MENT tables, with the right to grant these privileges, except ALTER and INDEX, on EMPLOYEE to other users.

GRANT ALL PRIVILEGES ON DEPARTMENT TO
    MELKANOFF;
GRANT ALTER, INDEX ON EMPLOYEE TO MELKANOFF;
GRANT SELECT, INSERT, UPDATE, DELETE ON
    EMPLOYEE
        TO MELKANOFF WITH GRANT OPTION;

The key word ALL PRIVILEGES refers to all six privileges when granting or revoking them.

Example 44

Revoke the right to ALTER and INDEX the EMPLOYEE and DEPARTMENT tables and the right to grant any privileges given to Melkanoff in Example 43.

REVOKE ALTER, INDEX ON DEPARTMENT, EMPLOYEE
  FROM MELKANOFF;
REVOKE ALL PRIVILEGES ON EMPLOYEE
FROM MELKANOFF;
GRANT SELECT, INSERT, UPDATE, DELETE
ON EMPLOYEE TO MELKANOFF:

The last two statements are a more wordy alternative to revoking any of the listed rights that Melkanoff may have given to other users on EMPLOYEE as follows:

REVOKE GRANT OPTION ON EMPLOYEE FROM
  MELKANOFF

Unfortunately, this is not allowed in SQL.

Security controls can be set up on specific columns and rows through the view mechanism by granting users privileges on the view, instead of on each whole table, as was the case in previous examples. The creator of the view may grant for any column(s) any one or any combination of the SELECT, INSERT, UPDATE, and DELETE rights (ALTER and INDEX rights cannot be granted to views, only to tables); or the creator may decide what columns are not accessible at all.

Example 45

Give Gilbert the right to SELECT the name, age, and school year of all children of employees insured by Puritan, previously defined as the PURITAN-CHILDREN view over the schema in Figure 10.2; give Gilbert the right to grant only the SELECT privilege to others.

GRANT SELECT ON PURITAN-CHILDREN TO GILBERT WITH
                          GRANT OPTION.
GRANT UPDATE ON PURITAN-CHILDREN TO GILBERT

Example 46

Give Weber the right to retrieve the name and department name of employees who earn less than $15,000 (refer to the schema in Figure 10.4). This can be granted on either:

1. A new, tailor-made view to be created; or
2. The existing view POOR-GUYS that was defined earlier (in section 10.5.1) but masking out the salary column via the GRANT command.

1.   Creating a new view:

CREATE   POOR-GUYS-WEBER (NAME, DEPT-
               NAME)
AS   SELECT   E-NAME, D-NAME
               FROM   EMPLOYEE, DEPARTMENT
               WHERE   EMPLOYEE.DEPTNO =
                              DEPARTMENT.DEPTNO
                              AND EMPLOYEE.SALARY <
                              15,000;

GRANT SELECT ON POOR-GUYS-WEBER TO
WEBER

2.   Using the existing view POOR-GUY:

GRANT SELECT NAME, DEPT-NAME ON POOR-GUYS TO
WEBER;

10.5.5   Restrictions on Insert, Delete, and Update Operations Through Views

Any read-only query may apply to any view that may be derived in SQL. For nonread operations ("modification" operations), however, there are some restrictions and cautions. In Section 9.4, which addressed the original relational architecture, we outlined the general restrictions applying to the base tables of a view if we are to modify (i.e., that is, update, insert, or delete) rows in the view. As briefly mentioned earlier in this chapter, the specific conditions under which SQL/DS permits any of these modifications are that each table viewed:[6]

1.   Must look exactly like the corresponding base table, except that (a) individual rows can be omitted and (b) columns can be omitted, except that for the INSERT command those declared non-null cannot be omitted.
2.   Must not be derived from a join of two or more tables or views.
3.   Must not contain virtual columns that are calculated by some built-in function [e.g., AVG(SALARY)].
4.   Must not be derived by using the GROUP BY clause.

If the above conditions are met, then any modification query is actually performed on the base relation and immediately reflected in any view(s) using such information. Updates must be done directly on the base tables stored.

For views containing virtual columns calculated by some expression such as SALARY/12, SQL/DS does not permit (a) UPDATE on the virtual columns or (b) INSERT on the view. However, DELETE commands are allowed.

When the INSERT command is applied to a view that does not include all the columns of the base table, any column stored but not included in the view receives the null value. INSERT is not allowed on a view if a column declared non-null is missing from the view.

The following example illustrates some of these regulations and the caution that must be exercised when updating tables through views that may contain duplicate rows.

Suppose we wish to grant modification rights on the view consisting of the name, age, and school year of all children of employees insured by Puritan, as previously defined in Section 10.5.1 as the PURITAN-CHILDREN view on the schema in Figure 10.2. Note that in the base table CHILD, the columns D-NAME, EMPNO, and C-NAME are key columns, declared in SQL/DS as NON-NULL and with a UNIQUE INDEX. Figure 10.7 shows possible sample contents of the stored table and the corresponding contents of the PURITAN-CHILDREN view. Note that:

1. INSERTs into the VIEW are not allowed since the columns D-NAME and EMPNO in the base table cannot be NULL.
2. DELETE and UPDATE are allowed.

Stored Table :

CHILD	D-NAME	EMPNO	C-NAME	CHILD-AGE	SCH-YEAR
	ZAP	400	CHRISTOPHER	20	B.S.
	ZAP	400	LINDA	22	M.S.
	ZAP	400	DIANE	24	M.S.
	ZONK	450	LINDA	2	
	ZOO	30	DIANE	24	M.S.

PURITAN-CHILDREN Table View:

PURITAN-CHILDREN	C-NAME	CHILD-AGE	SCH-YEAR
	CHRISTOPHER	20	B.S
	LINDA	22	M.S.
	DIANE	24	M.S.
	LINDA	2	
	DIANE	24	M.S.

Figure 10.7.   *Sample contents of the stored CHILD of the Doctor-Employee data base in Figure 10.2 and of the view PURITAN-CHILDREN*

3. Since D-NAME and EMPNO are not included in the view, and many children may have the same name, and even the same age and school year, as shown in Figure 10.7, the user cannot tell which specific child corresponds to a given row of the view. If an update is performed using C-NAME = 'LINDA', the user cannot control which child is updated since not all of the key columns D-NAME, EMPNO, and C-NAME are included in the view. Hence, although SQL/DS permits such updating, and also deletion, this use of views requires much caution and care and should be avoided if possible.

Because of the absence of semantic integrity controls in SQL/DS, insertion and updating through views derived using the WHERE clause require much caution. It is possible to insert and update rows of a base table of a view such that they violate the definition of the view. For example, consider a view X consisting of all the columns in the EMPLOYEE table in Figure 10.4 but including only employees earning less than $30,000. SQL/DS permits inserting rows in X having a SALARY value greater than $30,000, but these rows will not be visible in the view X because now the resulting rows do not satisfy the definition of X! This appears to be a dangerous door opening to data base inconsistencies.

The inquisitive reader should think through why update rights cannot be granted in SQL/DS to the views POOR-GUYS and RICH-DEPTS, defined earlier in Section 10.5.1, and why and under what conditions modification may make sense even though SQL/DS does not allow it.

The issues and problems of updating through views are referred to in research circles as the "view update problem" and are still the subject of research, further work, and differing opinions. Various authors have suggested more systematic, concise, and well-founded general rules of updating.[11-15] Some have suggested much more freedom in updating and letting selected DBAs define the updating "do's" and "dont's" for each particular data base.[16] Relational and nonrelational GDBMS reflect this range of attitudes, with SQL/DS possibly favoring more of a fixed-rule and update-laxity attitude. The view update rules in SQL/DS are fixed and at times very lax, with the consequent dangers.

In practice, for any GDBMS, any rules desired for updating a data base may always be enforced by tailor-made applications software (usually preprocessor-type) that may be constructed by the DBA group. This is in fact done in practice very frequently, via "validation" or "preprocessing" software.[17] It would be more desirable to have a wide range of alternative updating rules, concisely and consistently thoughtout, provided as part of the GDBMS facilities from which one could choose the desired set of rules to be enforced. These facilities would be part of the integrity controls available in a GDBMS.

10.6   DATA INDEPENDENCE

The ample flexibility of SQL in forming and using views that was presented in Section 10.5 provides a very high degree of data independence. In
comparison to other nonrelational GDBMS, the relational SQL/DS GDBMS
provides unsurpassed data independence. In fact, the major advantages that
may be claimed by the relational approach are the superior view definition and
access controls, data independence, and high-level query facilities.

In summary, the flexibility of relational view definition, beyond that of
nonrelational GDBMS consists of the following:

1. The ability to make up subschemas consisting of any subset of col-
    umns of any table and to arrange the subset into any arbitrary set of
    tables (without the constraint of being structurally identical to a
    column-subset of the schema tables).

2. The ability to define subschemas consisting of subsets of the rows of
    the schema selected according to arbitrary logical qualifications on
    the basis of data content.

3. The ability to provide security controls to specific rows selected
    according to arbitrary logical qualifications on the basis of data
    content.

Let us review the data independence capabilities and limitations in SQL
for column additions and deletions and for restructuring of tables.

The addition of columns is probably the most frequent data base structure change. Columns and rows may be added to the base tables without
affecting the functioning of any of the existing views and the structure of
existing queries. However, it should be noted that the SELECT * command
will now include all new columns in the table to which it refers. Actually, an
application program would not be changed until it is recompiled, even though
the table's definition has changed. To prevent these problems, SELECT *
should be avoided in application programs. The addition of a column may be
for the purpose of establishing a new relationship between two tables. The
addition of new relationships is transparent to existing applications. This is not
necessarily the case in hierarchic-oriented GDBMS.

The deletion of columns and rows is infrequent. When done, any view or
query referring to the deleted columns will have to be changed to avoid
reference to the deleted column.

Restructuring of the base tables requires care. It is with respect to this
type of change that the relational systems provided unsurpassed data independence, but with restrictions involving updates. Suppose that the initial data

base tables include a table that we now need to break down into two smaller tables. For example, let us say we started with the following table:

EMP-EXP (<u>EMP#</u>, E-NAME, EXPERTISE, AGE, LOCATION)

We develop various subschemas, including the view VIEWX (EMP#, E-NAME, EXPERTISE). Due to the normalization reasons addressed in Chapter 12, we now decide to replace EMP-EXP with two new equivalent base tables:

EMPLOYEE (<u>EMP#</u>, E-NAME, AGE, LOCATION)
OFFICE (<u>LOCATION</u>, EXPERTISE)

We can now provide the original base table EMP-EXP as a view VIEWX on EMPLOYEE AND OFFICE, as follows:

CREATE VIEW VIEWX
        AS SELECT EMP#, E-NAME, EXPERTISE
        FROM EMPLOYEE, OFFICE
        WHERE EMPLOYEE.LOCATION =
        OFFICE.LOCATION

All original read-only uses of VIEWX are unaffected. Thus data independence is maintained. However, any updating uses of VIEWX are now prohibited. No updates are allowed on views derived from two or more tables. Thus data independence is not provided for updating operations. To avoid this limitation, although only partially, updating rights would have to be given directly on the base tables.

EMPLOYEE (<u>EMP#</u>, E-NAME)
OFFICE (<u>LOCATION</u>, EXPERTISE)

In other words, two separate tables must be seen, including the column LOCATION, if the updating user using the original VIEWX wishes to update at all. This is not a very satisfactory situation.

It should be noted that in a nonrelational DGBMS changes to a schema table or record type such as the above cannot be shielded from either read or nonread operations using the original record type. Data independence fails in these cases. The major advantage of the relational approach here is in the data independence for read-only operations. Fortunately, in many real-life data bases the majority of users need primarily read-only access.

10.7   SUMMARY

SQL/DS was introduced commercially by IBM in the early 1980s. It is the commercial version of System R, one of the most encompassing relational research and development prototypes that initiated the interest in, and showed the feasibility of, relational GDBMS in the 1970s. Other SQL/DS look-alikes or derivatives are being introduced in the 1980s, particularly for the mini-computer, microcomputer, and personal computer marketplace. A popular micro-GDBMS is dBase II.

SQL/DS and closely related relational GDBMS, such as INGRES (INGRES and System R were perhaps the most encompassing relational prototypes in the 1970s), represent one of the two major branches of the relational approach. The other branch is the QBE approach.

SQL/DS represents a data base as a series of relations or tables. This is done via a convenient data definition language, in either on-line or batch form. A relationship is established logically between two tables by defining two fields in common in each table.

The data manipulation language SQL is a prime exponent of the relational data accessing approach, in particular, of the relational calculus. Read, insert, modify, and delete statements are supported. The optional predicate (or where clause) for each statement can have basically any logical qualification (see Appendix B). SQL permits deriving from a data base any desired vertical or horizontal subset of each table, via the SELECT command. Ordering, grouping, and built-in functions available as optional clauses in the SELECT command add much functionality to SQL.

The powerful join operator is provided by SQL as an option of the select command. The join operator is perhaps the most powerful operator beyond nonrelational GDBMS. In a nutshell, a join is the merging of two (or more) tables on the basis of two common fields, resulting in a single table. A join is usually performed on two or more different tables, but it is also applicable to joining rows within one table.

Several features of SQL are noteworthy and are often considered advantages over nonrelational GDBMS:

1. The ability to apply any of the relational operations dynamically (on-line) or in a batch environment from an application program (COBOL, PL/1, etc.) using one common language, SQL;

2. The overall capability of the join operation; and

3. The ability to use the output of any operation as the input to any operation, e.g., a table resulting from a join can be used as an input to a join with another table.

The flexibility of SQL/DS in forming subschemas or user views is a major feature beyond nonrelational GDBMS. This flexibility translates in added degrees of data independence and security control. Specifically, any SQL query can be used to define a user view. Thus the flexibility of defining views beyond that provided by a number of nonrelational GDBMS is:

1. The ability to make up views consisting of
   (a) not only any subset of fields from a table
   (b) but also fields from different tables
   In nonrelational systems fields from different record types cannot be combined into a single record type for a subschema.
2. The ability to readily define views as consisting of subsets of the set of rows of the data base tables, according to arbitrary logical qualification on the basis of data content. Such horizontal data selectivity or partitioning is generally not directly available in nonrelational systems.

The security controls of relational systems stand out. A view X can be established on a view Y by the DBA or user who is given the right to use and, in turn, grant access rights to the data in Y. Furthermore, the user of X can, if allowed, establish any views over X, and so on.

Note the high degree of data independence due to the previous subschema flexibility: virtually any change to the schema structure can be made transparent to the user, since all that has to be done is redefine the subschema to maintain the same user view as before. In nonrelational systems a restructuring of the schema involving interchanging fields from one record type to another is not transparent to subschemas. However, in relational systems this type of schema restructuring is not totally transparent to insert, delete, and updating operations. The so-called "view update" problem arises. In an effort to maintain the integrity of the data base, SQL imposes various restrictions on insert, delete, and update operations performed through complex views. However, the use of complex views for nonread operations requires much care and in certain complex view cases should be avoided if possible.

One of the biggest challenges to the relational approach is acceptable performance in terms of CPU cycles and memory requirements. SQL provides powerful B-tree indexing facilities by which the definer of a table can index any or all of the fields of the table. An index can be established on single or concatenated fields. Powerful software optimization algorithms of the RDS develop several strategies to service the query; the RDS optimizer then selects the "best" one.

REFERENCES

1. Chamberlin, D. D., and R. F. Boyce, "SEQUEL: A Structured English Query Language," *Proceedings, 1974 ACM SIGFIDET Workshop*, Ann Arbor, Mich., May 1974.

2. Chamberlin, D. D., et al., "SEQUEL 2: A Unified Approach to Data Definition, Manipulation and Control," *IBM Journal of Research and Development*, Vol. 20, No. 6, November 1976.

3. Astrahan, M. M., and D. D. Chamberlin, "Implementation of a Structured English Query Language," IBM Research Report 1464, San Jose, Calif., October 28, 1974.

4. Astrahan, M. M., et al., "System R: A Relational Approach to Data Base Management," *ACM Transactions on Data Base Systems*, Vol. 1, No. 2, June 1976; also appears as IBM Research Report RJ1738, San Jose, Calif., February 27, 1976.

5. "SQL/Data System, Concepts and Facilities," IBM Corp., Reference Manual GH24-5013.

6. "SQL/Data System, Terminal User's Reference," IBM Corp. Reference Manual SH24-5017.

7. "SQL/Data System, Logic," IBM Corp., Reference Manual LY24-5217.

8. "ORACLE, Terminal Users' Guide," Relational Software Inc., Menlo Park, Calif.

9. Held, G. D., M. R. Stonebraker, and E. Wong, "INGRES: A Relational Data Base System," *Proceedings, National Computer Conference*, Anaheim, Calif., May 1975.

10. "INGRES, Users' Guide," Relational Technology Inc., Berkeley, Calif.

11. Dayal, U., and P. Bernstein, "On the Updatability of Relational Views," Harvard University, Cambridge, Mass., 1978.

12. Bancilhon, F., and N. Spyratos, "Update Semantics of Relational Views," *Rapport d. Recherche*, No. 329, October 1978.

13. Furtado, A. L., K. C. Sevcik, and C. S. Dos Santos, "Permitting Updates Through Views of Data Bases," *Information Systems*, Vol. 4, 1979, pp. 269–283.

14. Jacobs, B., "Applications of Data Base Logic to the Data Base Uniformization Problem," Research Report, University of Maryland, 1982.

15. Cosmadakis, S. S., and C. H. Papadimitriou, "Updates of Relational Views," *Proceedings, Symposium on Principles of Database Systems*, ACM, Atlanta, Ga., March 21–23, 1983.

16. Furtado, A. F., "A View Construct for the Specification of External Schemas," Departmento de Informatica, Pontificia Universidade Catolica, Rio de Janeiro, Brazil, 1978.

17. Grafton, W. P., Data Base Administration, Continental Airlines, personal communication, 1982.

18. Keller, A. M., "Update to Relational Data Bases Through Views Involving Joins," IBM Research Report RJ3282, San Jose, Calif., October 1981.

19. Blasgen, M. W., and K. P. Eswaran, "On the Evaluation of Queries in a Database System," IBM Research Report RJ1745, San Jose, Calif., April 1976.

20. Selinger, P. G., et al., "Access Path Selection in a Relational Database Management System," *Proceedings, ACM SIGMOD Conference on the Management of Data*, Boston, Mass., May 1979, pp. 23–34.

21. Yao, S. B., "Optimization of Query Algorithms," *ACM Transactions on Database Systems*, Vol. 4, No. 2, June 1979, pp. 133–155.

22. Kim, W., "On Optimizing an SQL-like Nested Query," *ACM Transactions on Database Systems*, Vol. 7, No. 3, September 1982, pp. 443–469.

EXERCISES

1. For each of the following requests for access rights to the relational data bases in Figures 10.2 and 10.4, indicate how it is done on SQL/DS. Show the commands. If it cannot be done in SQL/DS, indicate the possible reasons why it cannot be done.

   (a) Decrease by 20 percent the salary of employees in the computer science and planning departments in the schema in Figure 10.4.
   (b) Give Gilbert the right to access via SELECT the DOCTOR table in Figure 10.2 for doctors to whom no employee owes more than $5,000 and the employee is insured by 'ABC'.
   (c) Give Gilbert the right to grant to others the SELECT rights in (b), but do not give Gilbert the right to see any of the contents of DOCTOR.
   (d) Give Weber the right to retrieve and update the name, salary, and department name for employees who earn less than $15,000 in the schema in Figure 10.4.

2. Indicate how to obtain the following information using SQL/DS from the Employee-Department data base in Figure 10.4:

   (a) List the names and salaries of employees whose salary is less than 50 percent of the average of all salaries.
   (b) List the names of the departments in which the average salary is greater than $35,000. Also list the average salary.
   (c) List the manager number for each department in which there are two or more employees who have different salaries.
   (d) List the name, department name, and salary of the employee who has the highest salary.
   (e) List the names of employees who manage nobody.

3. For the Employee-Department data base in Figure 10.4, is the following command correct? SELECT E-NAME, MAX(SALARY) FROM EMPLOYEE. Explain.

4. Indicate what restrictions, if any, are placed on update operations (insert, delete, update in place) through subschemas or views in a relational data base. Under what conditions are what updating operations allowed on a relational data base? Discuss the issues and problems clearly and in depth. Give specific examples. Do not use any of the example data bases used in this chapter. Make up your own, but be realistic.

5. Consider Example 5. Can the answer be obtained by means of a join in SQL? If yes, explain how.

6. Consider the data base defined in block diagram in Exercise 5 in Chapter 5, with the 1:N and M:N relationships indicated. How can you represent it in the SQL/DS relational model? Define the data base using the SQL/DS DDL and indicate the tables involved for a data base containing two to five rows in each table.

11
QUERY-BY-EXAMPLE

462

11.1   INTRODUCTION AND ARCHITECTURE

Query-by-Example (QBE) represents an alternative relational approach to SQL/DS, ORACLE, INGRES, and other similar relational systems presented in Chapter 10. During the mid-1970s Zloof suggested the QBE approach as a different way to access and process a relational data base.[1] The logical view of the QBE data base is relational. However, the way to access and process the data base is significantly different in comparison to other relational and nonrelational architectures. Several human factors studies have shown apparent advantages of the QBE approach versus other relational approaches.[2]

The first QBE implementation was made available by IBM in 1980 for the IBM 30XX and 43XX computers.[3-5] IBM's QBE operates only on IBM's operating system CMS. QBE data bases can be accessed through its unique very high-level interactive language via on-line terminals or through its interface from PL/1 and APL programs. Other QBE-like systems are appearing in the 1980s as either prototypes or commercial systems. Novel types of data base systems such as pictorial or graphics data base management systems have been proposed with some of the flavor of the QBE approach.[6,7]

The following sections will present the features and capabilities of QBE, as implemented by IBM, following the same outline as for SQL/DS and other nonrelational systems in previous chapters. Ample illustrative examples will be shown using the same data bases and most of the data base accessing and processing examples used for other systems.

11.2   THE SCHEMA OR DATA BASE

Figure 11.1 shows the relational Doctor-Employee schema that we will use for illustrating most of the QBE facilities in this chapter. This schema was also used to illustrate SQL/DS and, in its nonrelational or "unnormalized" hierarchical form, to illustrate the nonrelational GDBMS. The standard notational form for relational data bases is used to denote the logical schema structure. Underlined attributes or domains are key domains to uniquely identify a row or tuple. Every stored relation or table must have a key (one attribute or several attributes concatenated).

Figure 11.2 shows the sample data base contents that we will use. It includes the same data base contents that were used in previous chapters.

Let us now trace step by step how the user or data base administrator defines interactively on a terminal table or relation composing a data base. We

DOCTOR (<u>D-NAME</u>, SPECIALTY, YRSEXPER)
CLINIC (<u>D-NAME</u>, <u>C-NAME</u>,ADDRESS)
EMPLOYEE (<u>D-NAME</u> ,<u>EMPNO</u>,E-NAME,ADDRESS,AMT-OWED)
INSUR-CO (<u>D-NAME</u>,<u>EMPNO</u>,<u>I-NAME</u>,ADDRESS,AMT-OWED)
CHILD (<u>D-NAME</u>,<u>EMPNO</u>,<u>C-NAME</u>,CHILD-AGE,SCH-YEAR)

Figure 11.1.   *The Doctor-Employee data base in relational form*

will detail how this is done for one of the tables, for the EMPLOYEE table. To define a table, the following steps are performed:

1. Issue the command P._, resulting in a blank skeleton table as shown in Figure 11.3 which is displayed on the interactive screen. The command may be entered in the screen through the interactive console keyboard or else by pressing a program function key.
2. Insert the name of the table in the first column through the insert command: I. EMPLOYEE (see Figure 11.4).
3. Insert the names of the columns (attributes or domains) by placing the insert command I in the first column and the desired column names in their corresponding columns (see Figure 11.4).
4. Press the ENTER key on the interactive console keyboard.

At this point QBE assigns a series of data definition attribute defaults. To see the defaults assigned, the query shown in Figure 11.5 is issued. The two print operators P.P. request (1) the list of the attribute keywords and (2) the row of values for each keyword. Note that the information is presented as a table. In the column entries the hyphen (-) means a null value, (DEF) indicates the default suggested by QBE, and Y means YES and N means NO. Any or all of the defaults can be changed. The null entries are to be filled in by the table definer using several of the available QBE alternatives. Figure 11.6 summarizes the meaning of each keyword.

Once a table is fully defined, data may be entered via interactive commands as shown in the next section. For mass loading it is best to use a special table definition and mass loading facility available in batch mode.[5]

Adding and Deleting Columns

Columns may be added or deleted from any table previously defined. To delete a column, place the operator D. before the column name; Figure 11.7(a) indicates to delete AMT-OWED from EMPLOYEE. The operator D. placed in front of the table name would delete the whole table definition.

DOCTOR	D-NAME	SPECIALTY	YRSEXPER
	JONES	SURGERY	7
	WILLIAMS	SURGERY	15
	WONG	EAR-NOSE	4
	YOUNG	CARDIOLOGY	20
	ZLOOF	CARDIOLOGY	10

CLINIC	D-NAME	C-NAME	ADDRESS
	JONES	CLINIC A	WEST L.A.
	JONES	CLINIC B	SAN FERNANDO
	WILLIAMS	CLINIC B	SAN FERNANDO
	WONG	CLINIC A	WEST L.A.
	YOUNG	CLINIC C	BEVERLY HILLS
	ZLOOF	CLINIC C	BEVERLY HILLS

EMPLOYEE	D-NAME	EMPNO	E-NAME	ADDRESS	AMT-OWED
	JONES	20	DONALDSON	WEST L.A.	0
	JONES	32	JOHNSON	ENCINO	600
	JONES	106	THOMAS	WEST L.A.	200
	WILLIAMS	28	BURGH	ENCINO	0
	WILLIAMS	29	GONZALEZ	SAN FERNANDO	600
	WILLIAMS	114	MARTIN	SAN FERNANDO	56
	WONG	29	GONZALEZ	SAN FERNANDO	1800
	YOUNG	320	FIRESTONE	ENCINO	2400

INSUR-CO	D-NAME	EMPNO	I-NAME	ADDRESS	CYCLE
	JONES	20	INSURANCE A	WEST L.A.	30
	JONES	20	INSURANCE B	BEVERLY HILLS	15
	WILLIAMS	28	INSURANCE B	BEVERLY HILLS	15
	WILLIAMS	29	INSURANCE B	BEVERLY HILLS	15
	WONG	29	INSURANCE C	SAN FRANCISCO	20
	YOUNG	320	INSURANCE D	CHICAGO	15

CHILD	D-NAME	EMPNO	C-NAME	CHILD-AGE	SCH-YEAR
	JONES	20	MICHAEL	6	2
	JONES	20	STEPHEN	16	11
	WILLIAMS	28	WALTER	16	12
	YOUNG	320	CHRISTOPHER	20	B.S.
	YOUNG	320	LINDA	22	M.S.
	YOUNG	320	DIANE	24	M.S.

Figure 11.2. Sample data base contents of the relational Doctor-Employee data base in Figure 11.1

465

Figure 11.3. *A blank skeleton table or relation*

Insertion of the table name EMPLOYEE

Insertion of the column names

I. EMPLOYEE I.	D-NAME	EMP-NO	E-NAME	ADDRESS	AMT-OWED

Screen display after pressing ENTER key:

EMPLOYEE	D-NAME	EMP-NO	E-NAME	ADDRESS	AMT-OWED

Figure 11.4. *Definition of a data base table*

EMPLOYEE	D-NAME	EMP-NO	E-NAME	ADDRESS	AMT-OWED
P.P.					

(a) Query: Print the attributes of the EMPLOYEE table

EMPLOYEE	D-NAME	EMP-NO	E-NAME	ADDRESS	AMT-OWED
KEY	Y (DEF)	Y (DEF)	Y (DEF)	Y (DEF)	Y (DEF)
DOMAIN	–	–	–	–	–
TYPE	–	–	–	–	–
IMAGE	–	–	–	–	–
ICW	6 (DEF)	6 (DEF)	6 (DEF)	7 (DEF)	8 (DEF)
OCW	–	–	–	–	–
POSITION	1	2	3	4	5
INVERSION	Y (DEF)	Y (DEF)	Y (DEF)	Y (DEF)	Y (DEF)

(b) Answer to the query above: a table showing defaults assigned by QBE

Figure 11.5. *Data definition attributes and defaults assigned by QBE to a data base table (IBM implementation)*

466

Keyword	Meaning and Default
Key	Specifies if each column is a key column or not. Options are Y for Yes and N for No. At least one column must be a key. By default, all columns (concatenated) are assumed as the table key.
DOMAIN	Essentially a synonym for a column name.
TYPE	Data type of the column: character, fixed, float, date (month/day/year), time (hour/minute/second).
IMAGE	Editing specifying the desired output appearance for the stored data for that column; many edits are available.
ICW	Input column width defining how many characters or numbers can be entered into that column without having to widen the column. The default ICW is the length of the column name.
OCW	Output column width defining the width of the column on output for character data only.
POSITION	Defines the position where QBE is to put the column when QBE produces column headings.
INVERSION	Specifies whether an inversion or index is to be created for the column to enhance data base performance. Y means Yes, N means No. By default, all columns are inverted.

Figure 11.6. *Meaning of keywords in the QBE table definition*

EMPLOYEE	D-NAME	EMP-NO	E-NAME	ADDRESS	D.AMT-OWED

(a) Deletion of the column AMT-OWED

EMPLOYEE	D-NAME	EMP-NO	E-NAME	I.STATUS	ADDRESS

(b) Insertion of the column STATUS

Figure 11.7. *Deletion and addition of columns in a QBE table*

467

To add a new column, place the cursor at the position desired, press a reserved program function to get a blank column, and then enter in the blank column the insert operator I. followed by the name of the column. See Figure 11.7(b). After the column is added, the column attributes are then defined as indicated above. Actual deletion or addition from the table takes place after the ENTER key is pressed.

The deletion and addition of columns from tables that hold actual data are done through other means.[4]

QBE System Administrator, Data Base Administrator(s), and Users

In the QBE framework, as implemented by IBM[5], the following people are involved:

1. The **system administrator** who is responsible for the installation and implementation of QBE and for controlling (a) what data bases are to be private (defined and accessed by one user) or shared (defined and accessed by one user but accessed by others), (b) which user id's or passwords to assign to data base administrators and to end users, and (c) which user id's have access to shared data bases. The system administrator can exercise all the QBE commands and access all QBE data defined by anybody at that installation.

2. The **data base administrator(s)** (DBA) who can (a) logically define a private or a shared data base and assign user views and authorization, (b) invoke data storage areas and load the data tables, and (c) control internal QBE system tables. Specifically, major DBA functions are to: implement and maintain data storage areas, tune the data base, design bulk load specifications for user data loading, and execute recovery procedures. A data storage area is assigned to a DBA user id to be formatted and loaded with data tables. The DBA needs good knowledge of QBE logical and physical organization facilities.

3. The **end user(s)** who can create a table for either a private or shared data base and assign user views and access rights for a shared data base, as we will show in Section 11.4. A DBA can do everything that an end user does, but not always vice versa, as explained below. An end user can avoid having to define and deal with physical storage aspects with the help of a DBA.

A private data base is created, loaded, and accessed by only one user id and/or a DBA. The only time that the DBA and the single user of a private data base are not the same person is when the system administrator defines it as such, for example, for private data bases in which the single user needs a professional DBA to deal with data storage initialization, tuning, loading, recovery, and so forth. The DBA still has unrestricted access to all tables in the data base.

A shared data base can be accessed by several end users, perhaps concurrently, and by a DBA. A shared data base is assigned to a DBA to create and maintain the data storage area and system tables. The DBA has unrestricted access to all tables in the data base, even those owned or created by another user. The DBA may also grant access authority to other users for any table in the data base, including system tables.

11.3 DATA MANIPULATION

The primary and by far the most attractive way to access and process a QBE data base is through the unique and highly interactive query-by-example language. The language can be also processed in batch mode, but this is seldom done in actual practice. There is also a variation of the query language complemented by procedural constructs and row-at-a-time processing to fit with a programming language to access a QBE data base. IBM's QBE has an interface for PL/1 and APL.

It is the unique nature of the query language that differentiates QBE from the relational approach of SQL/DS, INGRES, and others and from other nonrelational systems. At the data base schema level QBE appears essentially like any other relational system.

We shall use the relational Doctor-Employee data base shown in Figure 11.1 and also another one which we used to illustrate in previous chapters the approaches of CODASYL, IMS, TOTAL, SYSTEM 2000, and the other relational alternative, SQL/DS. Thus the QBE approach can be compared for the same data base and queries. The asterisked query examples are also shown for SQL/DS in the last chapter and in many cases for nonrelational GDBMS in previous chapters. The actual output from a query will be shown only when helpful for the data base contents used. Subsequent examples will use another data base that was also used in illustrating SQL/DS in Chapter 10.

11.3.1 Read-Only Queries (Nonjoin Operations)

We will first sign in as a valid QBE user. We then request a blank skeleton table by pressing a program function key or entering P. _. When we put the name of the desired table into the first column, QBE displays the corresponding columns that we are authorized to see. Now we are ready to issue the QBE query(ies).

To perform an operation on the data base, the user fills in an example of a possible solution to that operation in blank skeleton tables that are associated with the actual tables. The normal output to a retrieval query is one or more tables containing the requested information.

Example 1*

Print the employee number, name, address, and amount owed for employee number 106.

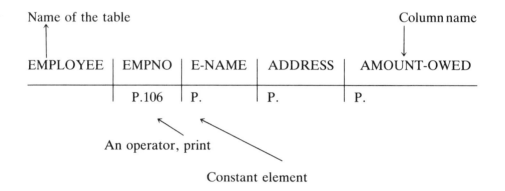

Example 2*

Obtain the EMPLOYEE, INSUR-CO, AND CHILD entity details of employee 106.

EMPLOYEE	D-NAME	EMPNO	E-NAME	ADDRESS	AMT-OWED
P.		106			

INSUR-CO	D-NAME	EMPNO	I-NAME	ADDRESS	CYCLE
P.		106			

CHILD	D-NAME	EMPNO	C-NAME	CHILD-AGE	SCH-YEAR
P.		106			

Note that when an operator, P. in this case, is placed under the table name, it applies to all the columns of the tables.

Example 3*

Obtain the name and age of all children of employee 106.

CHILD	D-NAME	EMPNO	C-NAME	CHILD-AGE	SCH-YEAR
		106	P.	P.	

Example 4*

Obtain the address of the insurance company whose name is EQUITABLE which services employee 20 (it is assumed that one employee may be serviced by more than one insurance company and each insurance company has different office locations servicing different employees).

INSUR-CO	D-NAME	EMPNO	I-NAME	ADDRESS	CYCLE
		20	EQUITABLE	P.	

Multiple tables with an example element

Example 5*

Obtain the name, age, and school year of all children of employees insured by PURITAN.

CHILD	D-NAME	EMPNO	C-NAME	CHILD-AGE	SCH-YEAR
		_20	P.	P.	P.

INSUR-CO	D-NAME	EMPNO	I-NAME	ADDRESS	CYCLE
		_20	PURITAN		

This operation may be paraphrased as follows: print the name, age, and school year for the child of an employee, as an example _20, where this same employee is insured by Puritan. The same example element _20 must be used in both tables to **link** the two tables and navigate from one table to another. Employee 20 may or may not exist in the data base.

It is just an example. **Example elements** are defined with a leading underscore character and establish **links** between two or more tables (as in this example), between two or more entries in the same row, or between two or more rows of the same table, as we will illustrate subsequently.

11.3.2 Update Queries

*Example 6**

Update the data base to show that employee 106 is now insured by AETNA and previously was not insured by any company.

INSUR-CO	D-NAME	EMPNO	I-NAME	ADDRESS	CYCLE
		106	P.		

If the resulting table has no entries, then do the following:

INSUR-CO	D-NAME	EMPNO	I-NAME	ADDRESS	CYCLE
		106	U.AETNA		

*Example 7**

Insert a new doctor Jones row into DOCTOR and also insert his corresponding clinic information into CLINIC.

DOCTOR	D-NAME	SPECIALTY	YRSEXPER
I.	JONES	SURGERY	16

CLINIC	D-NAME	C-NAME	ADDRESS
I.	JONES	CEDARS	LOS ANGELES

*Example 8**

Employee 106 has changed his insurance company from PURITAN to AETNA and has a new doctor named JONES. Assume that JONES has just been inserted into the data base as in Example 7.

EMPLOYEE	D-NAME	EMPNO	E-NAME	ADDRESS	AMT-OWED
	U.JONES	106			

INSUR-CO	D-NAME	EMPNO	I-NAME	ADDRESS	CYCLE
	U.JONES	106	U.AETNA		

CHILD	D-NAME	EMPNO	C-NAME	CHILD-AGE	SCH-YEAR
	U.JONES	106			

Note that if the user or the QBE system is not aware that the CHILD table also contains the doctor name for each employee and the last update is not performed, then an inconsistency will be introduced. Similarly, because of the structure of the base relations we must also indicate the new doctor and insurance name in the INSUR_CO row involved.

Example 9*

Add a new child to employee 106.

CHILD	D-NAME	EMPNO	C-NAME	CHILD-AGE	SCH-YEAR
I.	DUMMY	106	JOE	1	0

A blank entry is not allowed in the key, which is any column or group of columns that insures the uniqueness of a row from all other rows. Thus we must put some fictitious doctor name, DUMMY, since the key is D-NAME, EMPNO, C-NAME.

Example 10*

Delete employee 106 and all the related children and insurance company information; the child and insurance information of other employees is not to be affected.

EMPLOYEE	D-NAME	EMPNO	E-NAME	ADDRESS	AMT-OWED
D.		106			

INSUR-CO	D-NAME	EMPNO	I-NAME	ADDRESS	CYCLE
D.		106			

CHILD	D-NAME	EMPNO	C-NAME	CHILD-AGE	SCH-YEAR
D.		106			

Example 11*

Delete all children whose school year is more than 12, whose parent owes more than $1000, and whose doctor is a psychiatrist with a practice at UCLA (clinic name).

CHILD	D-NAME	EMPNO	C-NAME	CHILD-AGE	SCH-YEAR
D.	_DOC	_007			>12

DOCTOR	D-NAME	SPECIALTY	YRSEXPER
	_DOC	PSYCHIATRY	

CLINIC	D-NAME	C-NAME	ADDRESS
	_DOC	UCLA	

EMPLOYEE	D-NAME	EMPNO	E-NAME	ADDRESS	AMT-OWED
	_DOC	_007			>1000

This is a rather difficult request for a user to formulate for CODASYL, TOTAL, and IMS. This example highlights in particular the two-dimensional, by-example approach of QBE versus the linear and nested syntax approach of SQL/DS, INGRES, and similar relational systems illustrated in Chapter 10.

11.3.3 Join Operations

Let us now move on to another data base and illustrate the join operation and additional facilities of QBE. Let us illustrate some of the particular

EMPLOYEE (EMPNO, E-NAME, DEPTNO, SALARY, MGRNO)
DEPARTMENT (DEPTNO, D-NAME, NEMPS)

EMPLOYEE	EMPNO	E-NAME	DEPTNO	SALARY	MGRNO
	1	JONES	1	35,000	5
	2	MARTIN	2	35,000	4
	3	GOMEZ	3	40,000	7
	4	CHU	2	42,000	250
	5	DAMES	1	50,000	250
	6	THOMAS	1	28,000	5
	7	WATSON	3	38,000	250
	8	PARKER	2	14,000	4
	250	GOPHER	4	65,000	0

DEPARTMENT	DEPTNO	D-NAME	NEMPS
	0	CEO	4000
	1	ACCOUNTING	75
	2	COMP-SCI	32
	3	MGT-SCI	12
	4	FINANCE	140

Figure 11.8.   *The Employee-Department data base*

attractiveness and simplicity of QBE compared to most nonrelational approaches in handling queries of the following types. Most of these queries are also shown for SQL/DS in Chapter 10. Consider the data base in Figure 11.8 that relates employees to department(s) and to their managers.

Join in a single table

Example 12*

Print the names and salaries of all employees whose salary is more than that of their managers; also list the corresponding manager's name.

EMPLOYEE	EMPNO	E-NAME	DEPTNO	SALARY	MGRNO
		P.		P.>_100	_20
	_20	P.		_100	

The query may be paraphrased as follows: print the name of every
employee whose manager number may be, for example, _20 and who
earns more than, for example, _100 when employee _20 earns _100;
print also the corresponding manager name. Here the same example
element _20 is used to link the manager in the first row to the employee
number in the second row; another example is used to link and compare
the salaries. Note that the salary of the manager is not to be printed.

Output from the query:

EMPLOYEE	E-NAME	SALARY
	Gomez	40,000
	Watson	

This query involves the power of the relational join operator applied
to rows of the same table. Undoubtedly, this may be an expensive query
to answer, depending on the QBE implementation and data base tuning.
At worst, exhaustive searching may be done, requiring N(N-1) comparisons where N is the number of rows in the table.

Example 13*

Print the names and salaries of all employees who earn more than
their managers and who work in a department that has fewer than 15
employees.

EMPLOYEE	EMPNO	E-NAME	DEPTNO	SALARY	MGRNO
	_20	P	_10	P.>_100 _100	_20

DEPARTMENT	DEPTNO	D-NAME	NEMPS
	_10		<15

Output from the query:

EMPLOYEE	E-NAME	SALARY
	GOMEZ	40,000

Condition box

The **condition box** is used to store the logical qualifications or where-clause conditions that are not easily expressed in the table skeletons. This is the case for more logically complex qualification expressions (see Appendix B). This condition box is a one-column table invoked by pressing a special program function key. An example element is used to link the condition on the condition box with the desired column in the table being qualified. The following example illustrates it.

Example 14

Print the table made up of the names and salaries of employees who are in the computer science or in the accounting department and who earn less than $15,000.

EMPLOYEE	EMPNO	E-NAME	DEPTNO	SALARY	MGRNO
		P.	_10	P.<15,000	

DEPARTMENT	DEPTNO	D-NAME	NEMPS
	_10	_NEGLECTED	

CONDITIONS
_NEGLECTED=(ACCOUNTING OR COMP-SCI)

Output from the query:

EMPLOYEE	E-NAME	SALARY
	PARKER	14,000

Example 15a

Decrease by 20 percent the salary of the employees in department 2.

EMPLOYEE	EMPNO	E-NAME	DEPTNO	SALARY	MGRNO
U.				0.80 * _1	
			2	_1	

This operation can be paraphrased as follows: take an employee who works in department 2, find his salary, say _1, and update his salary to 0.80 * _1 (the asterisk means multiplication).

Example 15b

Decrease by 20 percent the salary of the employees in the computer science and planning departments.

EMPLOYEE	EMPNO	E-NAME	DEPTNO	SALARY	MGRNO
U.				.80 * _1	
			_0	_1	

DEPARTMENT	DEPTNO	D-NAME	NEMPS
	_0	_P	

CONDITIONS
_P=(COMP-SCI OR PLANNING)

Output from more than one table (user output tables) and joining of several tables

Up to now we have been using print operators in only one table, even though the query may refer to several data base tables. QBE can collect data from several source tables resulting from a QBE query into one or more new tables called **user output tables**. A user output table is not stored as an actual physical table in the data base schema. A physical table for a data base is created through the schema creation facilities as in Section 11.2. A user output table is formed by requesting a blank skeleton table, inserting any table name and column names, and then defining the content with example elements in the source tables. This is effectively the use of the join operator applied to different tables. Example 16 illustrates this.

Example 16

Create a new temporary table POORPEOPLE made up of the names and salaries of employees and their departments for employees who earn less than $15,000.

EMPLOYEE	EMPNO	E-NAME	DEPTNO	SALARY	MGRNO
		_X	_Y	_W	

DEPARTMENT	DEPTNO	D-NAME	NEMPS
	_Y	_Z	

CONDITIONS
_W < 15,000

POORPEOPLE	NAME	WAGES	DEPT-NAME
	_X	_W	_Z

Output from the query:

POORPEOPLE	NAME	WAGES	DEPT-NAME
	PARKER	14,000	COMP-SCI

11.3.4   Report Ordering, Grouping, and Built-in Functions

QBE provides ordering facilities and built-in functions for simple reporting needs. Information may be produced in either ascending or descending order. Major and minor sort priorities allow ordering output on the basis of a major column first, then on a second or minor column, then on a third or minor column, and so on. Some built-in functions may be used also: sum, count, average, maximum, and minimum. An example, which was also shown for SQL/DS in the previous chapter, is provided below. Additional examples are shown only for SQL/DS illustrating the ordering, grouping, and application of built-in functions. Such functions work in a conceptually similar manner in QBE (although syntactically they appear differently). Interested readers may refer to the additional examples for SQL/DS.

*Example 17**

Print the average salary for all employees. Then print the average salary and order the output, in ascending order, by department and then by manager. Also show the corresponding department number and manager number.

EMPLOYEE	DEPTNO	MGRNO	SALARY
P.	A0(1).G	A0(2).G	P.AVG.ALL AVG.ALL
	↑	↑	↖
	Ascending order, major	Ascending order, minor	Group-by, operator

Output from the query:

EMPLOYEE	DEPTNO	MGRNO	SALARY	
			38,555	average of all salaries
	1	5	31,500	
	1	250	50,000	
	2	4	24,500	
	2	250	42,000	
	3	7	40,000	
	3	250	38,000	
	4	0	65,000	

Note that QBE allows the use (if desired) of only a subset of the columns of the actual table in the user view and that the desired columns may be in a sequence different from that in the actual table. The order of the columns in the output will now be in this sequence. Let us see what each line in the query does:

1. The first line says compute the average of all the salaries in the table and then print it.
2. The second line says produce two ascending order (AO) sorts: major (1) by department and minor (2) by manager. The group by operator G. defines the groups of output desired. The average salary is computed for all employees grouped by department and manager. This group-by operator functions in the same manner as in SQL. This example shows that in a single QBE query one can mix column and row operators, have multiple requests, order columns as desired, and retrieve a part of the table.

11.3.5   Storing of Queries and Subsequent Invocation

Any QBE query can be stored and subsequently invoked. A name is given to the query and it is stored and invoked via the command box. The command box is invoked by pressing a special program function key. Let us illustrate it.

Example 18

Store the query in the previous example to produce printer output (as opposed to print on the on-line display terminal as in all previous queries).

Query:

EMPLOYEE	DEPTNO	MGRNO	SALARY
			P.AVG.ALL
P.	AO(1).G	AO(2).G	AVG.ALL

Command to store the query with the name Q-PERS-60 and indicate that its output on execution should be printed on paper:

COMMANDS
I.Q-PERS-60
PRINTER

Example 19

Display (print) stored query Q-PERS-60 on the terminal screen, and then execute it.

COMMANDS
P.Q-PERS-60
X.Q-PERS-60

The first command P. results in the display of the original query on the screen, and the second command X. executes the query which produces printed output as requested when the query was stored in Example 18.

11.4   THE USER VIEWS OR SUBSCHEMAS

In accord with the relational approach, QBE allows definition of user views or subschemas to include the whole data base or any subset of the data types or data base contents as may be expressed via a QBE query. Specifically, subschemas may be composed of:

1. Any subset of columns of any table, rearranged into any arbitrary set of tables, without the constraint of being logical subtables of the particular schema tables.
2. Subsets of the set of rows of the schema tables selected according to arbitrary logical qualifications on the basis of data content as may be expressed by a QBE query.

As examples, any of the retrieval QBE queries in Section 11.3 may be basically used to define views, as we will illustrate below.

In general, the wide range of flexibility and access controls for subschemas defined in Section 9.4 for the relational approach applies in QBE. The reader is advised to review Section 9.4 at this point.

The creator of a data base table is the owner of the table and can perform any operation on it. No one else, except a DBA, can access or use the table unless the creator gives the authority by defining authority constraints. The owner (and the DBA) can delegate or revoke print, insert, update, and/or delete authority to any user. A subschema is defined by indicating:

1. The type of authority and the user to receive the authority under the column of the table(s) for which the constraint is being defined; and
2. The query expression indicating what can be seen.

The query expression is like any other query and can include example elements, links to other tables, and conditions in the condition box. If more than one table is involved in the query, then the grantor of the authority must be the owner or have at least read authority over all tables involved. If a user identification is not specified, then any user can access the table(s) according to the rights and query defined.

Example 20

Give Cardenas the authority to:

1. Read the EMPLOYEE table including only employee number, name, and amount owed, as long as the amount is less than $2,000.
2. The INSUR-CO table including only insurance company name and claim cycle.

EMPLOYEE	D-NAME	EMPNO	E-NAME	ADDRESS	AMT-OWED
I.AUTH(P.)CARDENAS		_007	_MARTIN		< 2,000

INSUR-CO	D-NAME	EMPNO	I-NAME	ADDRESS	CYCLE
I.AUTH(P.)CARDENAS			_AETNA		_15

I.AUTH(P.)CARDENAS inserts the authority to print for Cardenas only the table columns indicated with the for-example elements and qualifications as long as the qualifications are adhered to. A blank entry in a column prohibits display of even the column name. Note that this user view does not have the knowledge of what employee is insured by what insurance company since EMPNO has been masked out of the INSUR-CO table for this view. For this view, INSUR-CO has the name and claim cycle of all insurance companies, even those insuring employees who owe $2,000 or more. The user view is thus:

EMPLOYEE	EMPNO	E-NAME	AMT-OWED
	20	DONALDSON	0
	32	JOHNSON	600
	106	THOMAS	200
	28	BURGH	0
	29	GONZALEZ	600
	114	MARTIN	56
	29	GONZALEZ	1800

INSUR-CO	I-NAME	CYCLE
	INSURANCE A	30
	INSURANCE B	15
	INSURANCE C	20
	INSURANCE D	15

Note that the view is not sorted. To sort the view we would have to define the desired sorting, e.g., Example 17. This sorting would not affect the order in which the data is actually stored in the schema.

Example 21

Give everybody the authority to read all employee and department information, except salary, but give Popek the right to update the salaries of employees who are in the computer science or accounting departments and who earn less than $15,000.

(a) The read authority for all, including Popek, is established as follows:

EMPLOYEE	EMPNO	E-NAME	DEPTNO	SALARY	MGRNO
I.AUTH(P.)	_1	_AL	_10		_50

DEPARTMENT	DEPTNO	D-NAME	NEMPS
	_10	_FATSOS	_5

(b) The desired update authority for Popek cannot be established. In QBE the authority definition can be expressed only in the row operator area under the table name column, EMPLOYEE. Thus, due to the qualification desired on department, an example element must be used under DEPTNO which automatically gives POPEK the authority to update DEPTNO also (and this is not wanted):

EMPLOYEE	EMPNO	E-NAME	DEPTNO	SALARY	MGRNO
I.AUTH(U.)POPEK			_10	<15,000	

DEPARTMENT	DEPTNO	D-NAME	NEMPS
	_10	_NEGLECTED	

CONDITIONS
_NEGLECTED=(ACCOUNTING OR COMP-SCI)

Example 22

Print the print authority constraints for Cardenas for the EMPLOYEE table.

EMPLOYEE				
P.AUTH(P.)CARDENAS				

Response from the above:

EMPLOYEE	EMPNO	E-NAME	AMT-OWED
AUTH(P.)CARDENAS	_007	_MARTIN	<50,000

The owner of a table or DBA can print any authority constraints defined for any user of the table. A user can print only those constraints that have been delegated to that specific user. A user cannot see another user's authority constraints. Thus the above request is accepted by QBE only if the issuer is either the owner of the EMPLOYEE table, Cardenas who received the authority, or the DBA.

11.5 DATA BASE TUNING AND PHYSICAL ORGANIZATION

We will outline some of the most important tuning and physical organization features of QBE as implemented by IBM.[5] QBE is written in OS/VS assembler and PL/1 optimizer languages and executes under the IBM VM operating system using facilities of the Conversational Monitor System (CMS).

Each QBE data base is stored in a "data storage area" owned and controlled by a DBA. A storage area is made up of disk buckets or pages of 4,000 bytes. Data definitions, internal control information, and the contents of a data base are stored in the disk pages composing a data storage area. Readers interested in actual page layout and mapping, overflow areas, page searching, and so forth, are referred to reference 5 or similar references for other QBE implementations.

Any column in a QBE table may be inverted or "indexed." The inverted technique used is as indicated in Chapter 2. This is a strategy for optimizing access time. It is also the fundamental strategy for the so-called inverted-oriented GDBMS such as SYSTEM 2000 and ADABAS and for other relational systems such as ORACLE. When a table is created, by default, IBM's QBE inverts or indexes every column in the table. Either the table creator or the DBA then has the task of deciding what to keep inverted and what not, as shown in Section 11.2. While 100 percent degree of inversion optimizes processing time for perhaps most read queries, it penalizes nonread queries. So an intermediate degree of inversion should be chosen depending on the query profile. Some guidelines for selecting inversion levels are given in Chapter 2.

EMPLOYEE	TUPLEID	D-NAME	EMP-NO	E-NAME	ADDRESS	column inverted AMT-OWED
	1	JONES	20	DONALDSON	DOMID3	0
	2	JONES	32	JOHNSON	DOMID1	600
	3	JONES	106	THOMAS	DOMID3	200
	4	WILLIAMS	28	BURGH	DOMID1	0
	5	WILLIAMS	29	GONZALEZ	DOMID2	600
	6	WILLIAMS	114	MARTIN	DOMID2	56
	7	WONG	29	GONZALEZ	DOMID2	1800
	8	YOUNG	320	FIRESTONE	DOMID1	2400

Internal table for column inverted:

Internal table for reducing storage:

AMT-OWED	VALUE	TUPLEIDS
	0	1,4
	56	6
	200	3
	600	2,5
	1800	7
	2400	8

ADDRESS	DOMID	ACTUAL DATA
	DOMID1	ENCINO
	DOMID2	SAN FERNANDO
	DOMID3	WEST L.A.

Figure 11.9. *Physical structures for optimization in a QBE table*

This is a very important tuning parameter and a challenge to a DBA.

Figure 11.9 shows an example of the EMPLOYEE table stored with the column AMT-OWED inverted. One inversion table is created for every column inverted. Internally, every stored table has a tuple or row identifier (TUPLE ID). Furthermore, to reduce primarily storage consumption, QBE does automatically for every column with character data type, of length greater than four characters, what is shown done for the ADDRESS column. DOMID1, DOMID2, and DOMID3 represent internal identifiers. Thus, if at least a small percentage of data values are repeated in different rows, in the character column, a net savings in storage is obtained. This strategy is aimed at reducing potentially large storage consumption in relational data bases. Storage consumption can be significantly larger than for nonrelational data bases due to the way that relationships are established between entities: in the relational approach, columns are redundantly stored (although it is not strictly necessary, in practice they are) to accomplish the relationship, whereas in nonrelational data bases the relationship is accomplished by a pointer mechanism consuming no more than a computer word.

11.6   SUMMARY OF COMMANDS

Let us summarize the QBE commands available. We have illustrated most of them through examples in this chapter.

Figure 11.10 summarizes the language operators.

Figure 11.11 summarizes the command functions invoked through the commands box.

Figure 11.12 summarizes the program function keys, some of which are referred to in previous sections. Note the program function keys for viewing any portion of a table definition or table contents that does not fit on the screen. This is done by scrolling the viewing window (the screen) up, down, right, or left across the table.

TYPE	OPERATOR	MEANING
System	P.	Print, display
	U.	Update
	I.	Insert
	D.	Delete
	X.	Execute
	G.	Group by
	AUTH.	Authority
	ALL.	Set definition
	AO.	Sort in ascending order
	DO.	Sort in descending order
Built-in Functions	SUM.	Sum
	CNT.	Count
	AVG.	Average
	MAX.	Find the maximum
	MIN.	Find the minimum
	UNQ.	Use unique values only
Comparison	=	Equal to
	¬	Not
	¬ =	Not equal to
	>	Greater than
	>= or =>	Greater than or equal to
	<	Less than
	<= or = <	Less than or equal to
Arithmetic	+	Add
	-	Subtract
	*	Multiply
	/	Divide
	**	Exponentiation
Logical	&	And
	AND	And
	|	Or
	OR	Or

Figure 11.10. *QBE language operators (Courtesy of International Business Machines Corporation)*

COMMAND	FUNCTION
PRINTER	Print results.
DISK	Store results on CMS file.
SAVE	Apply the results of update processing to the data base now.
MESSAGE	Control type and length of message displays.
CANCEL	Stop query processing (do not apply updates if any).
CMS	Enter CMS subset.
DESCRIBE	Store the definition of a table on a CMS file.
I. *name*	Store a query.
P. *name*	Display a query.
X. *name*	Execute a query.
CONTINUE	Continue query processing.
D. *name*	Delete a query.
U. *name*	Update a query.
P.-	Display a blank skeleton.
P.*	Display initial query.
P.	Display list of valid commands.
END	Terminate QBE session.

Figure 11.11. QBE command functions (IBM, Reference 5)

KEY	USE
PF1	Erases a table, column, row, column entry, or box, depending on cursor position.
PF2	Moves the physical screen down over the logical screen; cursor dependent by table.
PF3	Moves the physical screen up over the logical screen; cursor dependent by table.
PF4	Displays a blank table skeleton.
PF5	Moves the physical screen to the right over the logical screen.
PF6	Moves the physical screen to the left over the logical screen.
PF7	Adds a column or row to a table skeleton or a row to a box, depending on the cursor position.
PF9	Adds a continuation (folded) row.
PF10	Widens a column or a box.
PF11	Displays the condition box.
PF12	Displays the command box

Figure 11.12. QBE program function keys (Courtesy of International Business Machines Corporation)

11.7   SUMMARY

QBE was introduced commercially by IBM in 1980. It was the first fully relational commercial GDBMS. QBE represents one of the two branches of the relational approach, the other branch being represented by SQL/DS, ORACLE, INGRES, and the likes.

QBE represents a data base as a series of tables. This is done via a data definition language, primarily on-line. A relationship is established logically between two tables by defining two fields in common in each table.

QBE is unique in its highly interactive user-machine dialog in that the user indicates "by-example" what is to be retrieved, inserted, deleted, or modified in the data base. Hence the name Query-by-Example, QBE. Human engineering studies have shown advantages of this approach over SQL/DS and the likes. The QBE data base manipulation language is very different from that of any other relational or nonrelational GDBMS: it is a "two-dimensional" or tabular form-oriented language, as opposed to the usual one-dimensional and linear syntax. QBE permits deriving from a data base any desired vertical or horizontal subset of each table. Predicates for each table can be expressed with all the logical qualification shown in Appendix B. Ordering, grouping, and built-in functions are available.

The powerful join operator is provided. It is perhaps the most powerful operator beyond nonrelational GDBMS. A join is essentially a merging operation of two tables, or rows within a table, on the basis of two common fields. A join results in one table.

QBE's flexibility in forming subschemas or user views is a major feature that nonrelational GDBMS do not have. This flexibility translates into added degrees of data independence and security control. Specifically, any QBE query can effectively define a user view. Thus the flexibility of defining views beyond that provided by a number of nonrelational GDBMS is:

1. The ability to make up views consisting of the following:
   (a) Any subset of fields from a table; and/or
   (b) Fields from different tables.
   In nonrelational systems fields from different record types cannot be combined into a single record type for a subschema.
2. The ability to readily define views as composed of subsets of the set of rows of the data base tables, according to arbitrary logical qualification on the basis of data content. Such horizontal data selectivity or partitioning is generally not directly available in nonrelational systems.

The security controls of relational systems stand out. A view X can be established upon a view Y by the DBA or user who is given the right to use and, in turn, grant access rights to the data in Y. Furthermore, the user of X can, if allowed, establish any views over X, and so on.

Note the high degree of data independence due to the previous subschema flexibility: virtually any change to the schema structure can be made transparent to the user, since all that has to be done is redefine the subschema to maintain the same user view as before. In nonrelational systems a restructuring of the schema involving interchanging fields from one record type to another is not transparent to subschemas. However, in relational systems this type of schema restructuring is not totally transparent to insert, delete, and updating operations. The so-called "view update problem" arises. QBE imposes several restrictions on insert, delete, and update operations through complex views, in an effort to maintain the integrity of the data base. However, the use of complex views for nonread operations requires much care and in certain complex view cases should be avoided if possible.

One of the greatest challenges to the relational approach is acceptable performance in terms of CPU cycles and memory requirements. QBE provides inverted indexing facilities by which the definer of a table can invert any or all of the fields in the table. Long character fields are treated in a special way by forming a special internal table to reduce storage requirements of such fields.

REFERENCES

1. Zloof, M. M., "Query-by-Example," *Proceedings, National Computer Conference*, AFIPS Press, Arlington, Va., May 1975, pp. 431–437.
2. Reisner, Phyllis, "Human Factors Studies of Database Query Languages: A Survey and Assessment," *Computing Surveys*, Vol. 13, No. 1, March 1981.
3. "Query-by-Example," IBM Corp., Form 5796-PKT.
4. "Query-by-Example Terminal User's Guide," IBM Corp. Form SH20-2078.
5. "Query-by-Example Program Description and Operations Manual," IBM Corp., Form SH20-2077.
6. Chang, N. S., and Fu, K. S., "A Relational Data Base System for Images," *Pictorial Information Systems*, New York, Springer-Verlag, 1980, pp. 288–321.
7. Chang, N. S., and Fu, K. S., "Picture Query Languages for Pictorial Data Base Systems," *Computer*, Vol. 14, No. 11, IEEE Computer Society, November 1981, pp. 23–33.

EXERCISES

1. Consider the Employee-Department data base in Figure 11.8. Draw the organization chart implied by the contents of this data base, i.e., who is the boss of whom and what are the corresponding department names.

2. Indicate how to obtain the following information using QBE from the Employee-Department data base in Figure 11.8:
   (a) List the names and salaries of employees whose salary is less than 50 percent of the average of all salaries.
   (b) List the names of the departments in which the average salary is greater than $35,000. Also list the average salary.
   (c) List the manager number for each department in which there are two or more employees having different salaries.
   (d) List the name, department name, and salary of the employee having the largest salary.
   (e) List the names of employees who do not manage anybody.
3. For the Employee-Department data base in Figure 11.8, is the following command correct? Explain.

EMPLOYEE	E-NAME	DEPTNO	MGRNO	SALARY
	P.			P.MAX.ALL

4. Explain clearly and illustrate via diagrams how IBM's QBE system stores a column-type character which is inverted, say EXPERTISE, and one which is not, say E-NAME. Indicate all tables involved "underneath" for the table below. What do you gain and lose with this strategy?

EMP#	E-NAME	EXPERTISE
1	JONES	ACCOUNTING
2	MARTIN	COMP-SCI
3	GOMEZ	MGT-SCI
4	CHU	COMP-SCI
5	DAMES	ACCOUNTING
6	THOMAS	ACCOUNTING
7	WATSON	COMP-SCI
8	JONES	WHO-KNOWS

12

DATA BASE FUNCTIONAL DEPENDENCIES AND NORMALIZATION

12.1 INTRODUCTION

This chapter is devoted to the subject of normalization, which deals with important issues of data base semantics, functional dependencies, and logical design. Codd's significant proposal of the relational approach to data base definition and manipulation via powerful operators, addressed in Chapter 9, was accompanied by the equally significant introduction of the formal and systematic normalization approach toward sound data base design. The normalization approach actually applies to both relational as well as to nonrelational data bases. The issues and ideas of normalization apply to nonrelational GDBMS in which fields are grouped into two-dimensional structures, for example, DBTG or IMS in which simple fields are grouped into records (with no repeating groups) or segments.

(Normalization does not involve aspects of physical data base organization. It is concerned with the realm of logical data base design. Normalization properties are solely dependent on the semantics of the data base, particularly functional relationships between its fields, as visualized (perceived) *by* the data base designer. Normalization is of significant importance to data base administration-design.)

The concepts of normalization arise as a result of the observation that certain collections of relations have attractive properties in a changing environment in terms of protection from certain changes in the data base contents and its usage; other "equivalent" collections of relations containing the same information do not have these attractive properties. Three types of so-called **normal forms** may be defined for a data base: **first, second**, and **third** normal forms. These forms provide increasing improvement in the properties of the data base with respect to data base changes.

The basic ideas of functional dependencies and normalization first appeared in a series of papers by Codd.[1,2,4] Hundreds of other authors have subsequently contributed to the subject. Most of these publications have taken a very rigorous and formal approach to the basic concepts, which are essentially simple and very attractive. We will avoid "mathematism" (excessive formalism) in presenting the issues and concepts. It should be stressed that the subject matter is the object of much current research and development, and as a result is in a state of flux as new insights and proposals appear; furthermore, most of the new developments are largely theoretical.

A relation is said to be in **first normal form** if all of its domains are simple, that is, if it is a two-dimensional table or flat table. A relation with nonsimple domains, i.e., a nonflat table, is called an unnormalized relation. In Section 9.2 we show how any unnormalized set of relations can be converted to an equivalent normalized set. Every normalized relation is automatically in first normal form. A further process of normalization may take a first normal form relation and split it into simpler relations said to be in **second normal form**. Still a further step of normalization may take a second normal form relation and split it into even simpler relations said to be in **third normal form**. As we shall see, third normal form properties are the most attractive in a dynamic data base environment. Second normal form is a stopover on the way to the third normal form. Figure 12.1 portrays the levels of normalization.

To summarize, all normalized relations are in first normal form. Some first normal form relations are also in second normal form. Some second normal form relations are also in third normal form. The classification of a relation into any of the three categories is directly determined by its semantics as reflected by the so-called functional dependencies between domains or fields. This chapter is devoted to functional dependencies and normalization.

It should be stressed that everything that has been said in previous chapters applies equally whether the relations are in first, second, or third normal form. The definition and manipulation of relations via the calculus, algebra, or SQL/DS or QBE expect normalized relations in any of the three forms.

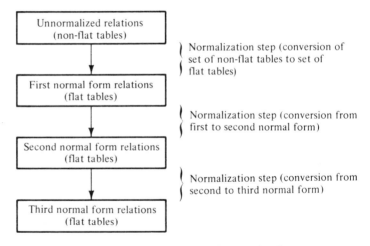

Figure 12.1.   *The normalization levels*

12.2 FUNCTIONAL DEPENDENCY AND KEYS

The classification of a relation into first, second, or third normal form rests on the functional dependencies existing among the attributes or domains particular to a relation. Functional dependencies are directly determined by the meaning or semantics of the data contents as interpreted by a data base designer.

Given a relation R, the attribute B is said to be **functionally dependent** on attribute A if at every instant of time each value of A has no more than one value of B associated with it in the relation R. More formally, if two rows in R agree on the A column, they must agree on the B column. Stating that B is functionally dependent on A is equivalent to stating that A **identifies** or **determines** B which may be denoted as $A \rightarrow B$ (that is, if A has a certain value "a" then B must have a value "b"). A is then called a **determinant**.

For example, in the EMP-EXP relation in Figure 12.2(b) we show that the nonkey domains E-NAME, EXPERTISE, AGE, and LOCATION are functionally dependent on the key domain EMP#. That is, given an EMP# value there is only one corresponding value for each of the other four domains. We also show that LOCATION is functionally dependent on EXPERTISE, that is, a given EXPERTISE is practiced at only one LOCATION; but, in general, several EXPERTISEs may be practiced at a given LOCATION. Functional dependencies between attributes are established strictly by the meaning of the data. Saying that AGE is functionally dependent on EMP# means that each given employee identified by EMP# must have only one age. However, AGE is not functionally dependent on E-NAME because we are assuming that there may be two or more employees of different age with the same name; and as a result of this interpretation E-NAME thus cannot identify any domains (thus E-NAME could not be used as a key). No other functional dependencies can be visualized here. There may be more than one employee with a given EXPERTISE value, with a given AGE value, and with a given LOCATION value.

Clearly, in every relation every nonkey attribute is functionally dependent on at least the key attribute. If a relation has more than one key attribute, then all its attributes are dependent on each key attribute. The dependence is trivial if the relation contains only the key attribute(s).

12.3   ANOMALIES DUE TO UPDATES, INSERTIONS, AND DELETIONS, AND THE NORMALIZATION APPROACH

The concern for normalization and the interest in using third normal form relations arise as a result of observing that in a dynamic data base environment possibly undesired side effects referred to as **anomalies** in relational jargon may result due to insertions, deletions, and updates. The following anomalies may be encountered, as an example, in the EMP-EXP relation in Figure 12.2:

1. *Insertion anomalies.* Suppose that we wish to insert the information that a new office has just been approved for RIO DE JANEIRO and that its EXPERTISE will be COMP-SCI. If no single employee has

(a)   The EMP-EXP relation:

EMP-EXP

EMP#	E-NAME	EXPERTISE	AGE	LOCATION
1	JONES	ACCOUNTING	30	CHICAGO
2	MARTIN	COMP-SCI	35	LOS ANGELES
3	GOMEZ	MGT-SCI	42	MEXICO CITY
4	CHU	COMP-SCI	34	LOS ANGELES
5	DAMES	ACCOUNTING	40	CHICAGO
6	THOMAS	TENNIS	52	LONDON
7	WATSON	MGT-SCI	39	MEXICO CITY

(b)   Diagrammatic representation of functional dependency:

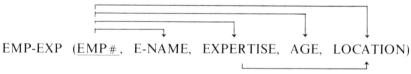

EMP-EXP (<u>EMP#</u>, E-NAME, EXPERTISE, AGE, LOCATION)

Functional dependency within a relation R:

$A \rightarrow B$ denotes that attribute B is functionally dependent on attribute A (A identifies B) meaning that: at every instant of time each value of A has no more than one value of B associated with it in the relation R.

Figure 12.2.   *Functional dependency and examples in the EMP-EXP relation*

been assigned yet for this office, this fact cannot be entered in the data base. In the relational system and in a number of nonrelational systems we would be unable to store this fact because null values are not permitted in the primary key; the fact could be stored if a fictitious primary key value were created.

2.   *Deletion anomalies.* Suppose that we wish to temporarily delete employee 6 from the data base. If we delete this employee, then we will delete the information that there is an office in LONDON, and that its EXPERTISE is TENNIS. If there were in the data base other employees who were tennis players in the London office, then there would be no problem. The side effect of deleting employee 6 could be

undesirable. This kind of preoccupation burdens the user with making sure that the tuple deleted is not the last tuple in some "category" (LOCATION) carrying important information on the category (EXPERTISE).

3. *Update anomalies.* Suppose that the EXPERTISE of the Chicago office is to be renamed as "AUDITING". Note that CHICAGO appears in several tuples; and in general in a large data base it would appear a large and varying number of times. Thus such updating would be costly since all tuples concerned must be identified and updated. A worse situation would be not to go through such expense and allow inconsistencies in the relation, i.e., store ACCOUNTING in a CHICAGO tuple and AUDITING in another CHICAGO tuple.

We have been leading to a very simple principle that good data base designers have advocated for a long time: do not represent more than one "concept" or "entity" in a single relation, record, or segment, otherwise you will face the previous difficulties. An important objective of normalization is to eliminate these anomalies by splitting a relation into simpler but equivalent relations. If we split our EMP-EXP relation via two projections into the two simpler relations EMPLOYEE and EXPER shown in Figure 12.3 we avoid the previous anomalies. Note the functional dependencies shown. We are splitting

EMPLOYEE

EMP#	E-NAME	EXPERTISE	AGE
1	JONES	ACCOUNTING	30
2	MARTIN	COMP-SCI	35
3	GOMEZ	MGT-SCI	42
4	CHU	COMP-SCI	34
5	DAMES	ACCOUNTING	40
6	THOMAS	TENNIS	52
7	WATSON	MGT-SCI	39

EXPER

EXPERTISE	LOCATION
ACCOUNTING	CHICAGO
COMP-SCI	LOS ANGELES
MGT-SCI	MEXICO CITY
TENNIS	LONDON

EMPLOYEE   (EMP#,   E-NAME,   EXPERTISE,   AGE)

EXPER   (EXPERTISE,   LOCATION)

Figure 12.3.   *The relations EMPLOYEE and EXPER and functional dependencies*

the concept of employee and the concept of office into two separate but connected (via EXPERTISE) relations.

Having illustrated the basic concept of normalization, let us now examine the details of first, second, and third normal forms.

12.4   FIRST, SECOND, AND THIRD NORMAL FORMS

Ideally, we would like to be able to state the functional dependencies when we define the data base and have the GDBMS police the data base contents at every instant. Any attempt by any given user to violate defined functional dependencies would then be aborted by the GDBMS. Difficulties arise in enforcing functional dependencies involving nonkey attributes.

An attribute can be functionally dependent on a group of attributes rather than on a single attribute. For example, in the relation PS in the Professor-Student data base shown in Figure 9.11, COURSE is functionally dependent on the concatenated key formed by PID and SID. An attribute or a collection of attributes, *B*, of a relation R is said to be **fully functionally dependent** on another collection of attributes, *A*, of relation R if *B* is functionally dependent on the whole of *A* but not on any subset of A. Now we can define second normal form: a relation is in **second normal form** if and only if the nonkey domains are fully functionally dependent on the primary key. If the primary key is a single attribute key, not a concatenated key, then there is no need for the second normal form; or, said in other words, the relation is in both first and second normal forms in such case.

Any normalized relation is in first normal form, but not necessarily in second normal form (and hence not in third normal form either) if the key is made up of several attributes. Let us illustrate this and show anomalies that can be prevented by converting the relation to two relations in second normal form each. Consider the Professor-Student data base shown in Figure 12.4 and its functional dependencies. COURSE is fully functionally dependent on PID and SID, both of which form the primary key. The degree GOAL of a student is *not* fully functionally dependent on the primary key because while it is functionally dependent on the whole primary key, it is also functionally dependent on SID which is a subset of the whole key. This relation is not in second normal form because it violates the formal properties of a second normal form relation:

> A relation R is in second normal form if it is in first normal form and also every nonprime attribute (an attribute which forms no part of a candidate key) is fully functionally dependent on the whole of each candidate key of R.

PROF-STUD	PID	SID	COURSE	GOAL
	P1	S1	125L	Ph.D.
	P1	S2	225K	M.S.
	P1	S4	225K	Ph.D.
	P2	S1	125L	Ph.D.
	P2	S2	125L	M.S.
	P2	S3	226D	M.S.
	P3	S2	123B	M.S.
	P3	S4	123B	Ph.D.
	P4	S4	125L	Ph.D.
	P4	S5	125L	Ph.D.
	P5	S5	226D	Ph.D.

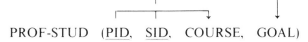

PROF-STUD   (PID,   SID,   COURSE,   GOAL)

Figure 12.4.   *The first normal form relation PROF-STUD but not in second normal form*

Three anomalies can arise in the PROF-STUD relation because it is not in second normal form:

1. *Insertion.* A new student and associated degree goal cannot be inserted until the professor(s) of the course(s) to be taken is (are) determined, unless a fictitious PID is made up for the new student.

2. *Deletion.* If professor P2 were to cease teaching course 226D and we decided to delete the tuple involved, we would destroy the information that there is a student S3 whose goal is an M.S. degree.

3. *Updating.* If a student advances to a Ph.D degree goal, it would be necessary to search and update the many tuples associated with this student, or else inconsistencies might arise (due to updating only one or a few of this student's tuples).

These irregularities are avoided by splitting the relation into the two relations in second normal form shown in Figure 12.5. The two relations are derived by two projection operations. As we shall see, these two relations also happen to be in third normal form.

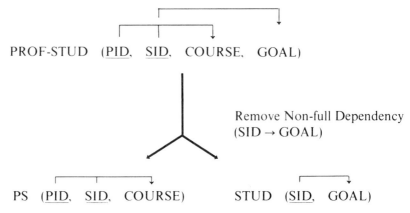

Figure 12.5. *Conversion of the PROF-STUD relation to two relations
in second normal form (these happen to be in third normal
form also)*

Third Normal Form

Anomalies similar to the previous ones can occur in a relation which is in second normal form. Recall that all those relations with single attribute keys, which is the case in most data bases, are in both first and second normal form. To remove these anomalies we employ another normalization step, converting from second normal form to third normal form. **Third normal form** has been defined in a variety of ways. The original definitions were given by Codd.[2] Subsequent writings, including those of Codd,[4] Date,[7] and Sharman,[5] have proposed definitions in other (but not always equivalent) terms:

Codd:[4]   A relation R is in third normal form if it is in first normal form and, for every attribute collection *C* of R, if any attribute not in *C* is functionally dependent on *C*, then all attributes in R are functionally dependent on *C*.
           This was unfortunately renamed by some writers as the **Boyce/Codd Normal Form (BCNF)** because it is actually more restrictive than Codd's original third normal form definition.[2] BCNF avoids some anomalies that may be present (although infrequently in actual practice) in the early third normal form.

Date:[7]   A relation R is said to be in third normal form if and only if the nonkey domains (domains not participating in the primary key) of R, if any, are both (1) mutually independent and (2) fully functionally dependent on the primary key of R. This is not necessarily BCNF.

> Sharman:[5] A relation is in third normal form if every determinant is a key, either the primary key or just a candidate key. If attribute B is functionally dependent on A, then A is said to be the determinant ($A \rightarrow B$). This is BCNF also.

We will use the term third normal form using Sharman's simple definition, keeping in mind that some writers also call it BCNF (this shows the confusing jargon problems!).

All definitions that we can cite are formal ways (and for a number of practitioners perhaps rather intricate ways) of expressing a very simple idea:

> Each relation (record or segment) should describe a single "concept," "fact," or "entity"; and if more than one is involved in a relation, then each should be split into a separate relation. Otherwise anomalies of the type that we have indicated will arise as we insert, delete, or update tuples.

Consider that the EMP-EXP relation in Figure 12.2 reflects at some point in time the fact that every office LOCATION has only a single EXPER-

EMP-EXP-2

EMP#	E-NAME	EXPERTISE	AGE	LOCATION
1	JONES	ACCOUNTING	30	CHICAGO
2	MARTIN	COMP-SCI	35	LOS ANGELES
3	GOMEZ	MGT-SCI	42	MEXICO CITY
4	CHU	COMP-SCI	34	LOS ANGELES
5	DAMES	ACCOUNTING	40	CHICAGO
6	THOMAS	ACCOUNTING	52	LONDON
7	WATSON	COMP-SCI	39	LOS ANGELES

EMP-EXP-2   (EMP#,   E-NAME,   EXPERTISE,   AGE,   LOCATION)

Reason for not in third normal form

Figure 12.6.   *The EMP-EXP-2 relation in first and second normal form but not in third normal form*

TISE (note that *now* we are looking at office as an entity in addition to the employee entity in the relation), because employee 6 was retrained to AC-COUNTING and employee 7 was moved to LOS ANGELES to practice COMP-SCI (the employee was retrained). In other words, we are saying that EXPERTISE appears to be functionally dependent on office LOCATION and not just on the employee EMP #. Figure 12.6 portrays this situation; the relation is renamed as EMP-EXP-2. Note that it could happen that just by chance employee 7 was moved to LOS ANGELES to practice COMP-SCI, *but* that an office LOCATION does not necessarily have to have a single EXPER-TISE. Thus whether or not there is in fact a real as opposed to a coincidental functional dependency has to be determined by the data base designer. EMP-EXP-2 is not in third normal form because EXPERTISE is functionally dependent on LOCATION, a nonkey attribute.

The problems that will arise as we try to insert, delete, or update various tuples are those already observed in Section 12.3. To avoid such side effects, we must convert the EMP-EXP-2 relation to its two simpler and equivalent relations in third normal form, EMPLOYEE and OFFICE, shown in Figure 12.7. These two relations would be preferred intuitively because information about offices will be needed independently of employee information, and we assume that EXPERTISE is primarily a fact about an office rather than about an employee (who, for example, might actually be in operations research but classified under his office charter MGT-SCI).

Let us look at the following changes that could be introduced to the data base and see that by converting relations EMPLOYEE and OFFICE to the third normal form we avoid the anomalies that arise with the original nonthird normal form EMP-EXP-2.

1. *Insertion.* We can now insert the information that a new office is in RIO DE JANEIRO whose EXPERTISE is COMP-SCI by adding this as a tuple to OFFICE. We no longer have the previous constraint of having to have at least one employee in an office to record such a fact.

2. *Deletion.* We can delete employee 6 from the relation EMPLOYEE without destroying the information that there is a LONDON office whose EXPERTISE is ACCOUNTING.

3. *Update.* We can change the EXPERTISE charter of the CHICAGO and London offices to AUDITING by introducing this change to only the two concerned tuples in the relation OFFICE, whereas in EMP-EXP-2 we would have to do much searching and updating of redundant information to enter this change and maintain consistency. Another benefit is that we can enter the fact that an employee has moved to another office by simply updating accordingly the

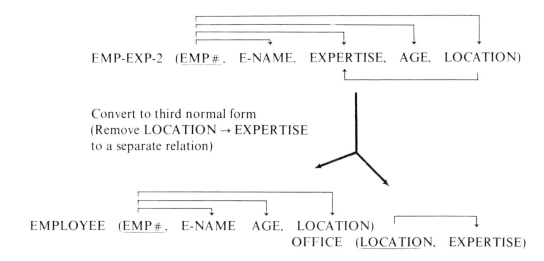

EMP-EXP-2 (EMP#, E-NAME, EXPERTISE, AGE, LOCATION)

Convert to third normal form
(Remove LOCATION → EXPERTISE
to a separate relation)

EMPLOYEE (EMP#, E-NAME   AGE, LOCATION)
                                        OFFICE (LOCATION, EXPERTISE)

EMPLOYEE   OFFICE

EMP#	E-NAME	AGE	LOCATION
1	JONES	30	CHICAGO
2	MARTIN	35	LOS ANGELES
3	GOMEZ	42	MEXICO CITY
4	CHU	34	LOS ANGELES
5	DAMES	40	CHICAGO
6	THOMAS	52	LONDON
7	WATSON	39	LOS ANGELES

LOCATION	EXPERTISE
CHICAGO	ACCOUNTING
LONDON	ACCOUNTING
LOS ANGELES	COMP-SCI
MEXICO CITY	MGT-SCI

Figure 12.7.   *The third normal form relations EMPLOYEE and
OFFICE equivalent to the first and second normal form
relation EMP-EXP-2*

LOCATION value of the employee's tuple; there is no need to
update an EXPERTISE value as is the case with the EMP-EXP-2
relation.

Note that while conversion to higher normal forms avoids the various
anomalies cited, it introduces two concerns: (1) duplicate recording of a key
field of one of the split relations and (2) as a result of duplicate recording, we
now face the burden of policing interrelation consistency; for example, every

LOCATION value appearing in EMPLOYEE must also appear in OFFICE. Note that if we delete LOCATION from EMPLOYEE we do not have an equivalent data model of EMP-EXP-2 (we have lost information). We would no longer be able to join EMPLOYEE and OFFICE and obtain back EMP-EXP-2. We shall discuss these concerns further in Section 12.7.

12.5   FURTHER FUNCTIONAL DEPENDENCY CONSIDERATIONS: TWO OR MORE CANDIDATE KEYS

Let us now point out a number of other functional dependencies that could actually exist within a relation involving several single-attribute or multi-attribute candidate keys. As an example, these will arise as a result of certain further semantic interpretations of the relations we have examined in previous sections. We will see what effect these semantics have with respect to the type of normal form classification, update anomalies, and normalization that may be necessary.

Example: *Single-Attribute Candidate Keys*

Suppose that for the EMPLOYEE relation in Figure 12.7, it is now semantically acknowledged that each employee will have a unique E-NAME as well as a unique EMP #. This leads to the result shown in Figure 12.8. There are two candidate keys, EMP # and E-NAME, either of which can be chosen as the primary key. Furthermore, the candidate key EMP # and the nonkey attributes AGE and LOCATION are functionally dependent on the now-candidate key E-NAME.

The EMPLOYEE relation with the functional dependencies indicated in Figure 12.8 is still in third normal form.

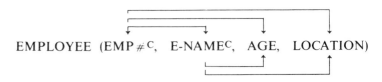

EMPLOYEE (EMP #^{C},   E-NAME^C,   AGE,   LOCATION)

"c" denotes a candidate key.

Figure 12.8. *Possible functional dependencies in the EMPLOYEE relation in third normal form*

We should distinguish between candidate key and prime attribute before proceeding to the next example. A **prime attribute** is an attribute which is a member of at least one set of attributes making up a multiattribute candidate key. In the case of Figure 12.8, each candidate key is made up of a single attribute, and therefore each prime attribute is at the same time a candidate key.

Example: *Multiattribute Candidate Keys*

Consider the relation EMP-LOC composed of the attributes EMP #, LOCATION of office, and EXPERTISE; EMP-LOC states for each employee number, EMP #, the various locations in which the employee practices a certain expertise, Figure 12.9. The nature of the situation is this:

1. An employee may work in several areas of expertise in different office locations; he is restricted to the expertise of the particular office and he may not practice the same expertise at more than one office. Thus the functional dependencies: (EMP #, EXPERTISE) → LOCATION; (EMP #, LOCATION) → EXPERTISE.

EMP-LOC	EMP #	LOCATION	EXPERTISE
	E1	LOS ANGELES	COMP-SCI
	E2	LOS ANGELES	COMP-SCI
	E2	SANTA BARBARA	MGT-SCI
	E3	LOS ANGELES	COMP-SCI
	E3	SAN DIEGO	AUDITING
	E4	SEATTLE	AUDITING

EMP-LOC (EMP # P,   LOCATION P,   EXPERTISE P)

"P" denotes a *prime attribute* (a member of the set of attributes making up a multiattribute candidate key)

Candidate keys: EMP # - LOCATION, EMP # - EXPERTISE

Figure 12.9.   *Possible functional dependencies in the EMP-LOC relation, not in third normal form (BCNF)*

2. An office location may practice in only one type of expertise, not several. Thus the functional dependency: LOCATION → EXPERTISE.

3. Each type of expertise of the company may be practiced at several office locations.

These functional dependencies are diagrammed in Figure 12.9. Note that the candidates keys are the multiattribute keys: EMP #-LOCATION and EMP #-EXPERTISE. Here all three attributes are prime attributes since each participates as an attribute of a candidate key. Either EMP #-LOCATION or EMP #-EXPERTISE may be chosen as the primary key. The relation is still in third normal form (BCNF) no matter what the primary key is (although it is in the early third normal form originally defined by Codd![2]). If we choose EMP #-LOCATION as the primary key the relation will be in first normal form, and not in second or third normal form. It is not in second normal form because EXPERTISE is not fully functionally dependent on the primary key. Viewed in another way preferred for its simplicity, it is not in third normal form (BCFN) because the determinant LOCATION is not a candidate key; it is just a prime attribute. The fact that all determinants are prime attributes tells us that this relation is in the early third normal form originally defined by Codd.[2] If EXPERTISE were not a prime attribute, then we would have a first normal form relation.

Since EMP-LOC is not in third normal form, it exhibits the side effects that we pointed out for first and second normal forms. For example, the fact that an ANAHEIM office will be opened with AUDITING expertise cannot be recorded without introducing a null employee EMP #. If we delete employee E3 we lose the information that the SAN DIEGO office is an AUDITING practice. We can avoid these possible anomalies by splitting the relation into the two relations EL and LE as shown in Figure 12.10, both of which are in third normal form. Without going through the functional dependency formalisms, we could intuitively realize the simple fact that we are representing two entities or concepts, employee and office, in the EMP-LOC relation; and that hence we should better break the relation into the two relations, each representing one of the concepts.

We could have split EMP-LOC into the two relations EL'(EMP #, EXPERTISE) and LE'(LOCATION, EXPERTISE) rather than into the EL and LE relations shown in Figure 12.10. It would have achieved the same results. Try it.

Note that if it is allowed that an employee may practice the same EXPERTISE at different office locations, then EMP #-EXPERTISE cannot be used as a key and there is no functional dependency (EMP #, EXPERTISE) → LOCATION. The relation is still not in third normal

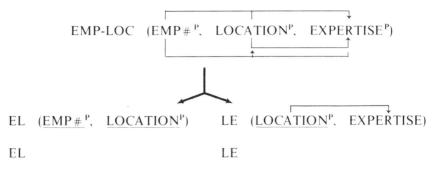

EL

EMP#	*LOCATION*
E1	LOS ANGELES
E2	LOS ANGELES
E2	SANTA BARBARA
E3	LOS ANGELES
E3	SAN DIEGO

LE

LOCATION	*EXPERTISE*
LOS ANGELES	COMP-SCI
SAN DIEGO	AUDITING
SANTA BARBARA	MGT-SCI
SEATTLE	AUDITING

"P" denotes a prime attribute.

Figure 12.10.   *Functional dependencies in the relations EL and LE in third normal form*

form or in second normal form, since EXPERTISE becomes nonprime and is thus not fully functionally dependent on the only possible key, EMP #-LOCATION. The relation is still in first normal form. The same anomalies as before may arise and the same previous normalization will avoid them: convert to the pair of third normal form relations shown in Figure 12.10.

In general, how can one decide which specific pair of relations to derive from a relation, if there are several alternative splits? The approach is to take out of the original relation that concept or entity causing the anomaly; the domains most related to the concept or entity should accompany the entity. However, choosing the appropriate split from a relation with several domains might not be easy due to a large number of possible splits.

Further Normal Forms

Data base theory has extended normalization to further refinements and more restrictive normal forms: fourth normal form (multivalued dependencies), fifth normal form (project-join normal form—join dependencies), domain-key normal form, etc.[6,7] Their payoff in actual data base practice remains to be seen/proven and thus we will not pursue them.

12.6 SUMMARY OF THE NORMALIZATION PROCESS

The normalization process of converting a first normal relation to an equivalent set of third normal form (BCNF) relations may be summarized as follows:

1. Take the first normal form relation and remove any nonfull functional dependencies by taking appropriate projections. This results in a set of second normal form relations. If every candidate key consists of a single attribute, then the first normal form relation is automatically in second normal form also.

2. Take projections of the first normal form relations or of the second normal form relations such that in the resulting relations every determinant is a candidate key but not just a prime attribute (a prime attribute is one which is a member of the set of attributes making up a multiattribute candidate key).

Figure 12.11 diagrams these steps, including conversion from unnormalized relations to first normal form relations.

In general, the set of third normal form relations corresponding to a first normal form relation may not be unique; that is, more than one set of equivalent third normal form relations may exist if the first normal form relation involves more than one candidate key.

A third normal form relation may still exhibit possible insert, delete, and update anomalies usually eliminated by normalization. The simple reason is that two concepts or entities, rather than one, may still be represented even in a third normal form relation. The anomalies may be eliminated by further splitting them into a set of equivalent third normal form relations, each relation holding only one concept.

12.7 NORMALIZATION AND DATA BASE DESIGN PRACTICE

The concept of normalization and the desirability of achieving third normal forms in a data base are of significant importance in data base design and use. Although primarily evident in the relational approach, the idea of

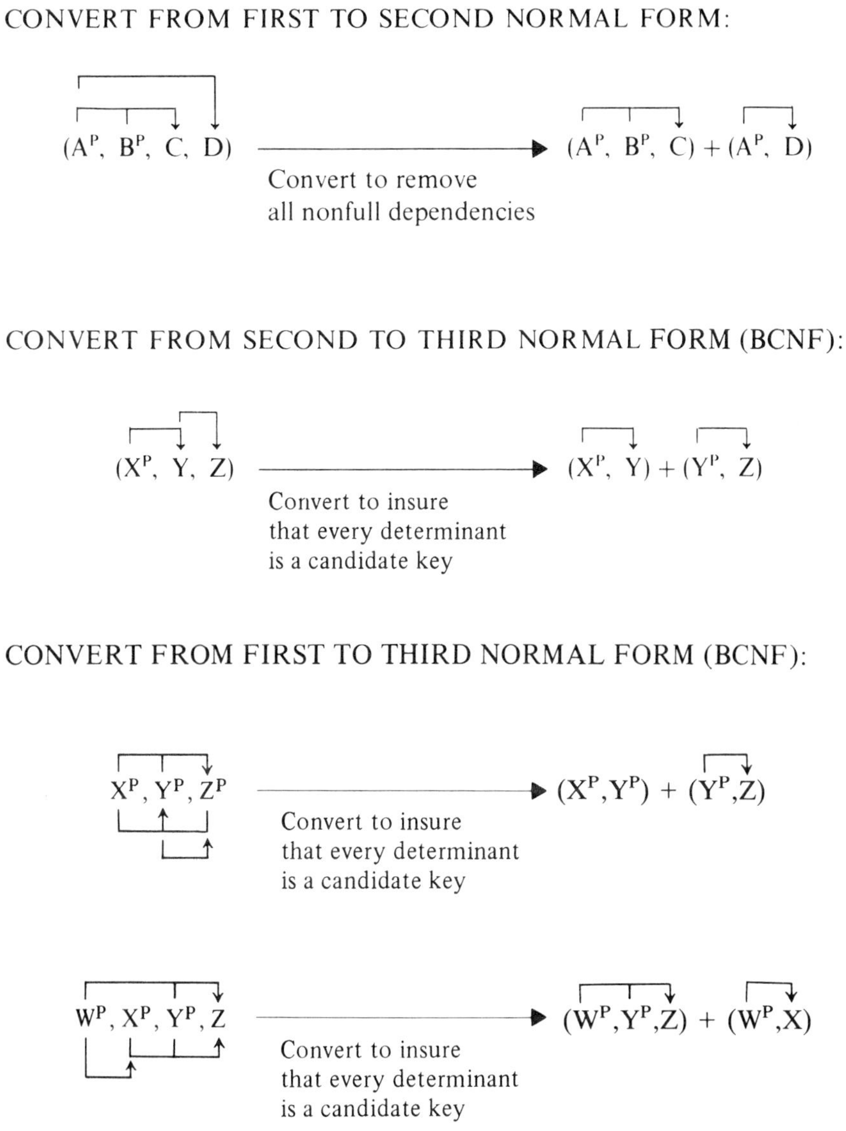

CONVERT FROM FIRST TO SECOND NORMAL FORM:

(A^P, B^P, C, D) $\longrightarrow$ $(A^P, B^P, C) + (A^P, D)$

Convert to remove
all nonfull dependencies

CONVERT FROM SECOND TO THIRD NORMAL FORM (BCNF):

(X^P, Y, Z) $\longrightarrow$ $(X^P, Y) + (Y^P, Z)$

Convert to insure
that every determinant
is a candidate key

CONVERT FROM FIRST TO THIRD NORMAL FORM (BCNF):

X^P, Y^P, Z^P $\longrightarrow$ $(X^P, Y^P) + (Y^P, Z)$

Convert to insure
that every determinant
is a candidate key

W^P, X^P, Y^P, Z $\longrightarrow$ $(W^P, Y^P, Z) + (W^P, X)$

Convert to insure
that every determinant
is a candidate key

"P" denotes a prime attribute (member of a candidate key).

Figure 12.11. *Outline of the normalization process*

normalization and its benefits can be applied in conventional nonrelational GDBMS. Existing GDBMS allow defining third normal form data base structures.

We shall now focus on normalization concepts, the advantages, and the concerns in actual data base practice.

The DBA starts with the task of examining all pertinent collections of information so as to identify the fundamental entities to be put in the data base. The DBA then has to put all this into some integrated logical structure, while considering the interests of users. The concepts of normalization and the third normal form should be valuable to avoid possible anomalies of the logical data base structures due to insertions, deletions, and updates. As we have seen already, we can convert any set of unnormalized relations into an equivalent set of normalized relation(s), and these in turn into a set of simpler and equivalent third normal form relations, each of which encapsulates one entity or concept of interest to the DBA and users. A useful self-study exercise of this whole process from unnormalized form to third normal form free of anomalies is to go through Exercise 1 at the end of this chapter; the Doctor-Employee data base used in previous chapters is treated.

All base relations, records, or segments making up the schema as well as all user views could be designed in third normal form. The DBA could define the schema and all user subschemas with such an understanding. All users would also have this understanding, so that if they have the facility of combining or interpreting different base relations, segment or record types, they do not come up with nonthird normal forms. The design of a data base in third normal form depends on the knowledge of the functional dependencies among the attributes in the data base. This knowledge cannot be discovered automatically by a GDBMS (at least not in current and near-future commercial GDBMS), but must be explicitly provided by a data base designer who understands the semantics of the information. As an example, just by looking at the table in Figure 12.6, can you as a user of a view, or can a programmed GDBMS, tell whether EXPERTISE is actually functionally dependent on LOCATION of office (and hence a violation of third normal form) or whether it is just a coincidence at that particular point in time that EXPERTISE appears as functionally dependent on LOCATION? What if the user view is this table which specifically excludes EXPERTISE and LOCATION values actually appearing in the data base that show no functional dependency? The only one who can tell is the data base designer or user who understands the real-world situation that is being represented by the data base.

Facilities in a GDBMS for policing the integrity constraint that all relations be in third normal form would be very helpful. We want to be told when a new relation formed by the DBA for the user, or by a user for another user, has the potential to violate third normal form. Suppose the EMP-EXP-2 table in

Figure 12.6 is formed at some point in time. Integrity proponents call for the ability to state and assure:

ASSERT: COUNT (SELECT UNIQUE LOCATION, EXPERTISE
         FROM EMP-EXP-2) = COUNT (SELECT UNIQUE
         LOCATION FROM EMP-EXP-2)

so as to be told when this potential third normal form violation occurs, i.e., LOCATION → EXPERTISE. A negative response to this assertion means that the relation is not in third normal form. The response to this assertion is positive for the table EMP-EXP-2. The data base designer or user should then interpret whether or not EXPERTISE is in fact, rather than coincidentally, functionally dependent on LOCATION; if it is, then the relation should be split again so as to end up with equivalent third normal form relations.

Note that checking for potential third normal form violations via the previous assertion mechanisms may be impractical if done indiscriminately in a real-life large data base. This is particularly true if users are going to be employing all the high-level language facilities (calculus, algebra, etc.) to generate all sorts of relations, which they may in turn assign as views to other users under their control. Note that the previous assertion mechanism involves forming a binary relation, then a unary relation made up of the possible identifier attribute, then counting the tuples in each relation, and comparing the count. If the count does not match, then EXPERTISE definitely is not functionally dependent on LOCATION. However, this does not rule out the possibility that in the binary relation the attribute LOCATION might be functionally dependent on EXPERTISE, as the case is in Figure 12.12. If the relation has a sizable number of attributes then it is impractical to test out all possible dependencies. In fact, even for a few attributes in a relation representing data about a situation whose semantics one does not know, but which one is trying to test out for third normal form, the number of possible functional dependencies is too large. Figure 12.13 shows this rapid growth with the number of attributes. In the majority of real-life cases it would be impractical to go through this mechanical procedure. Thus, the understanding of the semantics of the data so as to identify functional dependencies and avoid such exhaustive and costly mechanical means is invaluable. If the DBA and users are to exercise all the relational data manipulation capabilities and form all sorts of relations, then they are going to have to be more aware of data base design, normalization, and anomaly aspects than if they are not given all such manipulation capabilities. Perhaps a number of the current restrictions of GDBMS in forming views and manipulating data would in fact be advisable to prevent users from becoming exposed to anomalies.

We can take the usual anomaly argument to the extreme of even a binary

EXP-LOC

EXPERTISE	LOCATION
ACCOUNTING	CHICAGO
COMP-SCI	LOS ANGELES
MARKETING	NEW YORK
MGT-SCI	MEXICO CITY
PSYCHOLOGY	NEW .YORK

EXP-LOC (EXPERTISE, LOCATION)

Figure 12.12. *The binary relation EXP-LOC showing a possible functional dependency*

Number of Attributes in the Relation	Known Functional Dependencies (from single-attribute key to other attributes)	Additional Potential Functional Dependencies to Search for Mechanically
2	1	1
3	2	4
4	3	9
5	4	16
⋮	⋮	⋮
a	a − 1	$(a-1)(a-1)^*$

Situation: Single attribute key
* Formula valid for $a \geq 2$

Figure 12.13. *Number of possible functional dependencies in a relation to search for mechanically if semantics of the data are not known*

relation. Take the LE relation in Figure 12.10. We can say that we still have plenty of anomaly; for example, if we decide to bring in a new EXPERTISE value (e.g., OBSOLETE) into the data base but we have not decided where to open the office with such charter, then we can't insert this fact because we have no LOCATION key-value. You might guess that the way out is to form the only two relations showing lots of redundancy:

LE(<u>LOCATION</u>, EXPERTISE) and EL(<u>EXPERTISE</u>, <u>LOCATION</u>)

However, this does not avoid our problem since EL has a multiattribute key and both attributes must be specified for a tuple to exist. So there is no way out of our dilemma. What we have just illustrated is that you cannot eliminate all anomalies. However, good data base design should strive to do so using normalization principles. Most anomalies certainly can be eliminated in the large majority of real-life data bases.

Interrelation Consistency

We have mentioned only the pluses of normalization. We must now face a potential problem introduced by normalization: interrelation consistency. Every time that a relation is split for the sake of normalization we end up with the determinant attribute(s) stored in both relations acting as the key in one of the relations. The concern now is to maintain the consistency between normalized relations. For example, for the EMPLOYEE and OFFICE data base in Figure 12.7 the consistency concern would be to make sure that any LOCATION value in the EMPLOYEE relation has a corresponding entry in the OFFICE relation. We would then face these anomalies due to change:

1. If we insert a new employee with a new LOCATION value, then we have to make sure that there is a corresponding tuple in the OFFICE table.
2. If we delete an employee whose location value is the last one in EMPLOYEE, then we have the worry of deleting the corresponding tuple in the OFFICE table.
3. If we change the LOCATION value of an employee we have to worry about whether or not (a) the corresponding tuple in OFFICE should also be deleted because there are no other employees with such LOCATION value and (b) a new tuple with the new LOCATION value should be inserted in OFFICE. Furthermore, if we want to change MEXICO CITY to CUERNAVACA in the OFFICE relation then we must search for all affected EMPLOYEE tuples and make the change. Note that if we had a hierarchic or DBTG structure with OFFICE as a parent record and EMPLOYEE as a child record (without LOCATION as a field since it is unnecessary in these other data models), the desired change could be easily introduced: just update the single affected OFFICE record occurrence. Thus we see this advantage of the nonrelational approach.

Thus there is concern for maintaining interrelation consistency when we reduce the undesired intrarelation functional dependencies. We shall address the issue of data base integrity and consistency further in the next chapter.

Storage Considerations

The relational join operation, although powerful and attractive, may result in large tables whose materialization requires large amounts of storage; one of the most challenging tasks of the relational approach is the practical and efficient implementation of this operation. Transformation to third normal form is just the opposite of the join operation and thus reduces the amount of storage required in most cases, although not in all cases. (In what cases is it not reduced? See, for example, that the normalization in Figures 12.9 and 12.10 does not reduce storage.) Transformation of a relational data base into third normal form results in storing each fact at only one place. Third normal form and further avoidance of potentially harmful intrarelation functional dependencies minimize redundancy at the fact level.

Let us now look at the other side of the coin. Consider the question of all the duplication of keys introduced by normalizing from an unnormalized data base. The example in Figure 9.4 shows the proliferation of storage redundancy of the key attributes as we normalize a hierarchic data base. This key redundancy worsens with the height of the tree being normalized. However, this logical redundancy as seen by the user does not necessarily have to be real. That is, the access paths and storage mechanics underneath a relational interface could be, in fact, not that different from those used in nonrelational systems. For example, underneath the relational user interface a hierarchic record organization could conceivably exist to factor out key-values and store them only once. A key attribute could be "physical" at one place and "virtual" at several other places (by means of pointer mechanisms).

For the example in Figure 9.4, users would have the normalized view with the key redundancies shown, but underneath and transparent to them the physical structure could be more like the hierarchic unnormalized version. This unnormalized hierarchic organization underneath could then easily take care of, for example, a change to the D-NAME value (recall the DBTG, IMS, and SYSTEM 2000 example). This change at the user normalized level is much more difficult to introduce because it necessitates a change to every relation, since D-NAME participates as part of the key of every relation. But how about if the relational interface is designed with the understanding that if we change a D-NAME value in the DOCTOR relation, then the GDBMS will automatically introduce such change in all other relations affected? The point that we are making is that perhaps a convenient relational view could be provided highly insulated from internal structures which would not be that different from those in nonrelational systems. It appears that a relational interface could be provided more readily on top of an inverted GDBMS than on top of a network or hierarchic GDBMS because of the great flexibility of the inverted approach in obtaining any specific attributes based on the data content of any attributes.

REFERENCES

1. Codd, E. F., "Normalized Data Base Structure: A Brief Tutorial," *Proceedings 1971 ACM-SIGFIDET Workshop on Data Description, Access and Control*, San Diego, Calif., November 11–12, 1971.

2. Codd, E. F., "Further Normalization of the Data Base Relational Model," Courant Computer Science Symposia, Vol. 6 "Data Base Systems," New York, 1971; Prentice-Hall, Englewood Cliffs, N.J., 1972.

3. Heath, I. J., "Unacceptable File Operations in a Relational Data Base," *Proceedings 1971 ACM-SIGFIDET Workshop on Data Description, Access and Control*, San Diego, Calif., November 11–12, 1971.

4. Codd, E. F., "Recent Investigations in Relational Data Base Systems," *Proceedings 1974 IFIP Congress*, Stockholm, Sweden, August 5–10, 1974, North-Holland Publishing Company, Amsterdam, Holland.

5. Sharman, G. C. H., "A New Model of Relational Data Base and High Level Languages," Technical Report TR.12.136, IBM Hursley Park Laboratory, England, February 1975.

6. Kent, W. B., "A Simple Guide to Five Normal Forms in Relational Data Base Theory," IBM Technical Report TRO3.159, Santa Teresa Laboratory, San Jose, Calif., August 1981.

7. Date, C. J., *An Introduction to Data Base Systems*, 3rd ed., Addison-Wesley, Reading, Mass., 1981.

EXERCISES

1. Consider the Doctor-Employee data base in Figure 7.2 and in normalized form in Figure 9.4. For the contents shown in Figure 7.32:

(a) Indicate what functional dependencies appear in the normalized form.

(b) Show what splits, if any, are needed to convert the whole data base to third normal form.

(c) Indicate what updates to the contents of the data base in the original normalized form (a) would turn it into a different type of normal form (first, second, or third normal form).

2. Indicate if and to what extent normalization and functional dependencies apply and are relevant to nonrelational GDBMS, specifically (a) IMS and (b) CODASYL systems.

3. Consider the following entity (relation, record type, file, etc.) RELA ($\underline{D1}$, D2, D3, D4, D5):

RELA	$\underline{D1}$	D2	D3	D4	D5
	1	J	A	40	C
	2	M	C	39	LA
	3	G	M	42	M
	4	C	C	39	LA
	5	D	A	40	C
	6	T	A	52	LO
	7	W	C	39	LA

(a) Indicate below the functional dependencies for the above entity by drawing the appropriate arrows in the domains involved.

RELA ($\underline{D}1$, D2, D3, D4, D5)

(b) Convert the entity RELA to its equivalent entities in third normal form.

13
DATA BASE DESIGN AND ADMINISTRATION

13.1   INTRODUCTION

Most of the preceding chapters have focused on a specific GDBMS and data base architecture, its DDL for defining schemas and subschemas, and its DML. This most important chapter does not deal with a single GDBMS, but rather spans over all data base technology. It discusses issues arising in data base practice and GDBMS facilities for dealing with them. Examples are provided throughout on IMS, DBTG, TOTAL, SYSTEM 2000, and SQL/DS practice. The subject matter in this chapter is of utmost importance to the data base administrator-designer, called the DBA, who has the primary responsibility of dealing with it.

First, Section 13.2 outlines the process of designing data bases, detailing the various steps and decisions that the DBA must face. The importance of this section is obvious.

A major criterion for the acceptance of data base technology is reasonable performance in terms of resource utilization. Thus Section 13.3 is devoted to quantitative performance aids and technology for good data base design.

Section 13.4 deals with data base security.

Section 13.5 presents the integrity concerns and Section 13.6 the data sharing and locking concerns. The main aim is to prevent a data base from being maligned in the manner indicated therein by inadequate integrity and concurrent data sharing constraints.

Section 13.7 reviews the sources of errors that may cause a data base to fall into an incorrect state. A data base cannot be guaranteed always to be shielded from such errors. Consequently, recovery mechanisms are a must in practice in order to restore data base correctness. Section 13.7 addresses recovery practice.

When dealing with a data base, many tasks need to be performed in addition to schema and subschema definition and data manipulation. Many of these tasks may be performed by so-called data base utilities which are an important complement, and in reality an inseparable part, of the GDBMS. Section 13.8 discusses utilities.

Last, Section 13.9 is devoted to reviewing the primary responsibilities of the DBA. Technical and nontechnical tasks of the DBA are presented. The place of the DBA in the organization is addressed.

A study of data base technology is incomplete without consideration of the subjects in this chapter. It is in these realms that data base administrators are most likely to spend the majority of their time in actual practice. Readers should examine carefully the many issues herein.

13.2   THE DATA BASE DESIGN PROCESS

File and data base design is the process of synthesizing the collection and associations of data to satisfy the information storage, retrieval, and reporting requirements of users cost-effectively, while meeting a number of constraints (not always mutually compatible) such as access time, flexibility of use, storage, security, auditing, and recovery. The design of data bases is in actual practice usually an iterative process, often involving trial and error, just like the design of the information systems which the data bases are intended to support. Three major stages or phases are involved in this order:

1. Logical data base design;
2. Physical data base design; and
3. Data base loading and operation.

Various steps comprise each of these major phases. Figure 13.1 summarizes the design process. The separation is not always clear cut between various steps, for example, the separation between data base description in a DDL and access path determination in most commercial GDBMS. Figure 13.2, essentially a repeat of Figure 1.6, summarizes the data base organization realms covered in the design process.

The DBA has the responsibility of carrying out and managing this data base design process, which we shall now review in some detail, phase by phase, step by step. Further details on various steps may be found in references 1−3.

The Logical Data Base Design Phase

System Analysis and Statement of Requirements. The starting point is the identification of information needs via systems analysis techniques leading to at least the following:

1. Identification of information flows;
2. Reports that must be generated and queries or transactions that must be satisfied;
3. Individual data items, entities or records (characterized by highly related data fields) and relationships forming the conceptual data base in user forms (top of Figure 13.2); and
4. Performance criteria and justification for the application(s).

There are no industry-wide standards for systems analysis tools, forms, or languages. Organizations and information system designers employ various systems analysis methods. In an effort to systematize the information system development process, more and more of the larger organizations are establishing some kind of systems analysis standards. However, a challenge to both researchers and practitioners is to devise better systems analysis practices and tools, perhaps a futuristic computer language and processor for system analysis through which the computer itself may assist in checking for the consistency, completeness, and so forth, of the information system. So-called requirements specification or problem statement languages, such as the University of Michigan's PSL/PSA (Problem Statement Language/Problem Statement Analyzer), have been pioneering efforts in this direction.

A major aim of the initial systems analysis effort is to arrive at a conceptualization of the data base, independent of computer aspects (top of Figure 13.2). A possible means or model for expressing this conceptualization is the Entity-Relationship-Attribute model presented in Section 3.9. For a given application environment, various conceptualizations of the data base may result; not every DBA will visualize the conceptual data base in the same way (the conceptualization depends on the "eyes of the beholder").

Some initial measure of expected performance criteria should be developed for the data base to be designed. It could include ranges of access time and storage requirements, degree of expandability to accommodate future users while maintaining data independence, security needs, integrity constraints, and so on. Furthermore, the application(s) should be justified based on return on investment criteria; this is a crucial must.

Logical Data Base Structure in a Given Data Base Model. The second step consists of transforming the conceptual data base to an equivalent data base using a particular data model for computer definition, storage, and processing. Previous chapters have shown the three alternative data base models in the four alternative types of GDBMS: the IMS hierarchic approach, the DBTG and TOTAL network approach, the inverted hierarchic approach, and the relational approach. For each of these approaches, various specific "logical" data base structures may be established which are equivalent to a given conceptual data base. The choice of the particular data base structure is a major task of the DBA. Let us review what is involved.

Figure 7.2 shows a data base structure used in illustrating IMS in Chapter 7. The same structure may be established in a DBTG GDBMS, as was done in Chapter 5, Figure 5.9; it may be also established in an inverted-hierarchic system or in a relational system, Figure 9.4. Readers are encouraged to review at this point the facilities and rules of the game for defining data base structures in each of the data models that have been detailed in previous chapters. Note that some access path elements may appear at this logical level; specifically, the relationship or access path between the DOCTOR and EMPLOYEE established as a parent-child segment relationship in IMS or as an owner-member record relationship via a set in DBTG. The inverted GDBMS and particularly the relational GDBMS strive to avoid including such a high degree

Phase 1 Logical Data Base Design			Phase 2 Physical Data Base Design			Phase 3 Data Base Operation and Reorganization	
Statement of requirements (information flows, data transformation, reports— queries, performance criteria)	Logical or conceptual data base structure in a given information model	a) Data base schema definition via the schema data description language. b) Subschema definition via the subschema data description language	Access path determination (e.g., secondary indexing)	Mapping and representation of logical data on physical data structures (e.g., DBTG areas)	Physical layout of data on storage devices available and determination of low level data management parameters (e.g., buffers, blocking, device areas)	Actual data base loading and installation	Tuning and retuning or redesign due to changing requirements

Note: There is a definite separation between logical and physical data base design. The separation is not always clear between various steps comprising physical data base design.

The data base design process, like the information system design process, tends to be an iterative process.

File and data base design is the process of synthesizing the collection and associations of data to satisfy the information storage, retrieval and reporting requirements of users cost-effectively, while meeting a number of constraints (not always mutually compatible) such as: access time, flexibility, recovery, storage, security, auditing, etc.

Figure 13.1. The file and data base design process

524

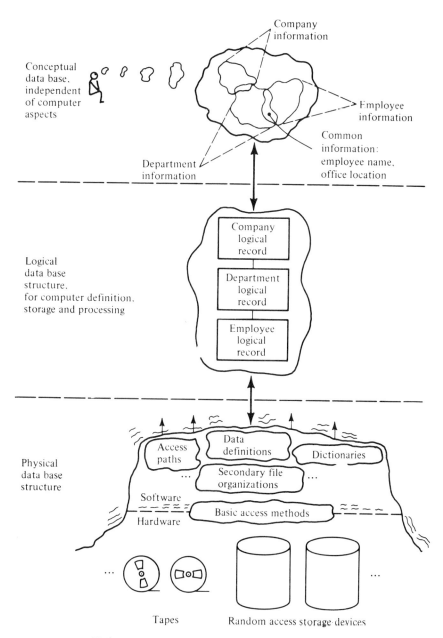

Figure 13.2. *The data base organization realms*

of access path considerations. The main concerns of the subsequent data base design steps are access paths and physical organization.

Figure 13.3 now shows two equivalent data base structures, B and C, that may be established in any commercial GDBMS as an alternative to the initial A structure. Why would a DBA choose the structure A as we did? Here is where the DBA's ingenuity comes into the picture, which involves careful consideration of both the semantics of the data base and the main factors that were shown in earlier chapters to affect processing time and storage performance in a major way:

1. The contents of the data base;
2. The characteristics of the users' data accessing requirements;
3. The characteristics of the particular data base structure and GDBMS used; and
4. The characteristics of the hardware used.

Let us see why we might prefer structure A over the other alternatives.

First, the conceptualization of the data world by the DBA and users might be predominantly more like A. DOCTOR information might be primarily considered the master entity and everything else the details in the traditional master file and detail file practice. Thus, due to this reason, and irrespective of everything else, structure A will be most attractive.

Second, an analysis of data base contents and dominant data accessing requirements may lead to A. Let us consider storage and access time performance in IMS, DBTG, and TOTAL. If the number of DOCTOR (record) instances is very small relative to the number of EMPLOYEE instances, an IMS or DBTG or TOTAL data base with structure A will result in fewer storage requirements than one with structure B or C. Readers should convince themselves on this point, recalling the 1:N relationship and storage aspects involved.

As far as access time is concerned, structure A will tend to be more effective in access time for IMS applications seeking DOCTOR fields. The nature of IMS is such that those segments more frequently accessed should be placed close to the top of the tree in order to optimize access time. This reasoning does not apply to other GDBMS. The reason is that direct entrance to any of the records in the data base is possible in DBTG systems through a key-to-address transformation algorithm and in inverted and relational systems through powerful indexing mechanisms. A TOTAL data base may be accessed via any of the record types defined as a master data set (which is directly accessed by the TOTAL internal key-to-address transformation).

Alternative A is used as one of the major example schemas in the DBTG, IMS, SQL/DS, and QBE chapters. The SYSTEM 2000 example carried through Chapter 8 is essentially alternative C. Review the SYSTEM 2000 data base examples in Figures 8.1 and 8.2 for quick reference.

Alternative
structure A:

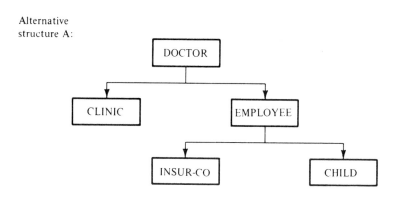

Alternative
structure B:

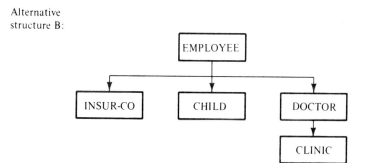

Alternative
structure C:

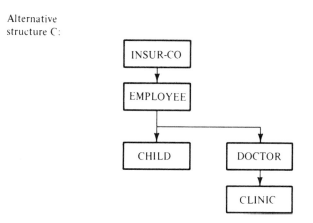

Figure 13.3. *Alternative data base structures for a given conceptual data base*

Data Base Schema Definition via the Schema Data Description Language. The third step consists of taking the result of the previous creative step and defining the data base using the specific data description language DDL of the GDBMS. DDLs vary from system to system with respect to syntax, semantics, and degree to which specification of physical data base design details is expected. Only systems following the DBTG standard have similar DDLs. Previous chapters have illustrated the DDLs for the five systems presented.

Subschema Definition via the Subschema Data Description Language. Subsequent to the schema definition, the DBA may define the subschemas desired. The DBA may be able to define them at any subsequent time, not only immediately after schema definition. The definition of the subschemas usually requires a great deal of thought, planning, and coordination. If the subschemas are to have only read access rights, then the definition is relatively straightforward. On the other hand, if at least one of the subschemas is to have further rights, particularly insert and delete rights, then there are challenges. Let us review one of the major challenges. The DBA must address the issues represented by the DBTG set membership characteristics of a member record discussed in Chapter 5: optional/mandatory and manual/automatic. This deals with what happens when a record occurrence (or tuple in a table in a relational data base) is to be inserted, deleted, or moved in the data base. Each record occurrence X may be related to other Y record type occurrences. Y could be within the same subschema of X or outside it. What should happen when, for example, X is deleted? Will all related Ys be deleted? What about all Z occurrences related to Y but not directly related to X?

These issues arise whenever a multiuser data base is created. They appear in various shades in all data base models. We discussed such aspects for IMS, particularly for IMS logical data bases, in Section 7.5. The DBTG report addresses these issues elegantly and in detail. Any DBA should be thoroughly familiar with them, no matter which data base system is involved. The issues are not of a physical organization nature, but rather of a logical relatability and integrity nature.

When a subschema is defined the DBA must define the access rights that each user has to each record type and perhaps to each field in that subschema. The types of access rights include: read, update (write in place), insert, and delete. In relational systems like SQL/DS and QBE, access rights can be given to any selected field on the basis of data content, whereas in nonrelational systems, access usually cannot be given on the basis of data content. Section 13.4 addresses security control over all systems.

The definition of the various subschemas and aspects just mentioned is done via the subschema data definition language. The subschema DDL is in practice usually a variation of the schema DDL which excludes physical structure details and which includes the mechanisms for specifying the matters in the previous paragraphs. In relational systems the subschema DDL is based heavily on the query language to express the user view.

The Physical Data Base Design Phase

Determination of Access Paths. The fourth step may be considered primarily as the first step of the physical data base design phase. This step is initiated to a certain extent in the "logical" design phase. Access path is a term used primarily to refer to a "road" that may be used to enter a data base, or to go from one place to another in the data base, i.e., navigate in an IMS or DBTG environment. In IMS the "physical" parent-child segment relationships (Section 7.2) and the "logical" parent-child relationships (Section 7.5) are navigation-oriented access paths, as are the DBTG sets and TOTAL linkage paths that may be established between an owner record and member record(s). Such relationships are actually determined during the logical data base design phase.

Perhaps the first major issue that must be resolved is what basic access method to use. In most systems the choices are a sequential method (on tape or direct access devices) or a random access method. If the predominant applications have a significantly high hit ratio (the percentage of the total number of records in the data base actually needed), typically more than 10 percent, then quite possibly the best access path choice is the sequential organization. If the hit ratio is low, as the case is in the large majority of data base applications, then the random method is selected. A difficult question is what this breakeven hit ratio is. Section 2.10 addresses this question in detail.

Once the random method is chosen, the following important alternatives must be faced next:

1. In inverted and relational systems, the degree of inversion or indexing and the specific fields to invert or index. The choice of fields to invert or index establishes the fastest access paths to the data base contents.

2. In DBTG systems, the records to which hashed entry is needed, and the field through which this entry is to be made. The fastest entry to a DBTG data base is usually through a hashing mechanism. The hashing or key-to-address transformation algorithm(s) to each record type may have to be devised by the DBA and provided to the GDBMS if the GDBMS vendor does not supply one. Readers should be aware of the uncertainty of the performance of hashing techniques.

3. In IMS, three alternatives are actually available: HISAM and HIDAM, which use underneath the ISAM or VSAM basic access

methods, and HDAM, which is a hashed access path approach (as in DBTG and TOTAL). The initial access path is to the top of the data base tree. A summary of the characteristics of the access paths is shown in Figure 7.31. So-called data set groups may be also set up for the purpose of directly entering segments appearing at the second level of the tree or at other levels (for HIDAM and HDAM). Some inversion capability is also provided for faster direct entry to segments at any level. IMS provides many alternatives for physical data base design, as detailed in Section 7.6. This variety poses a challenge to the DBA: which one(s) to use.

4. In IMS, and possibly in other future GDBMS, the portions of the data base that are to reside in main storage and those to reside in external storage. The IMS Main Storage Data Base facility provides the fastest possible access to that portion of the data base selected to reside in main storage at all times.

If a GDBMS provides a choice between the various types of secondary indexing methods discussed in Chapter 2, then this step would involve deciding which method to use (e.g., inverted method, doubly-chained tree method).

Previous chapters have illustrated what statements are used in the various DDLs for indicating the various access paths.

Mapping on Physical Data Structures. This fifth step is not always distinguishable from the previous step or the next one. This is particularly true for those systems in which logical and physical structure realms are not so cleanly separated. For example, IMS assumes from the start a top to bottom, left to right mapping of the data base.

A design decision involved in this step is the determination of the physical groups into which the record types will be placed. In DBTG this refers to the determination of the areas and the specific record types that will be physically placed in each area. An area is made up of physically-close external storage locations. In IMS this refers to the data set groups that may be formed. There are several performance reasons for establishing such groupings:

1. To reduce overall access time. Access from one record type to another in the same area is faster (due to physical proximity) than to another record in another area.

2. To reduce the amount of storage fragmentation, that is, different-sized empty storage, caused by deletions and then insertions of different-sized segments. Ideally, storage fragmentation is reduced if each group contains records of the same size only.

3. To assist in data base integrity and recovery needs. More frequent snapshots of the more dynamic data base areas may be taken to allow

faster recovery of the data base should an error occur. Subsequent sections address integrity and recovery.

Another important decision concerns the nature of the overflow areas. Dynamic environments will always force the use of overflow areas. The questions include: what percentage of overflow areas will be used for what, what type of overflow if a choice exists, and so on.

Physical Layout on Storage Devices and Detailed Physical Parameters. The sixth step includes all those aspects not treated in previous steps that must be specified by the DBA before loading the data base. The major ones are:

1.   The specific external storage device(s) that will be used.
2.   The specific cylinders and perhaps specific tracks to be used.
3.   What records, areas, or data set groups will go into what tracks and cylinders (GDBMS rarely allow such say-so to the track level).
4.   The physical location of the overflow areas.
5.   The kind of pointer-chaining mechanisms to use if a choice is available (e.g., child-twin pointers versus hierarchic pointers in IMS).
6.   The blocking factors and buffer areas to use.
7.   The fields that will be virtual images of physically stored fields (e.g., in the DBTG data base definition, Figure 5.8, EMPLOYEE_NO in the CHILD record is a virtual of EMPLOYEE_NO in the EMPLOYEE record).
8.   The procedure for calculating fields not actually stored in the data base (e.g., AGE in the SYSTEM 2000 data base definition, Figure 8.2).
9.   The details of the format of the data fields.
10. The codification/decodification (encryption/decryption) algorithms, if any, for data fields to be highly protected.
11. Data compression schemes, if any.

This is not an exhaustive list. There may be others that readers may recall from our previous chapters or from actual experience.

There is no industry-wide standard format or standard language for communicating all the physical details and storage mappings to a GDBMS. Every GDBMS has different mechanisms and conventions for indicating them. The 1971 DBTG committee recognized the need for a Standard Device Media/ Control Language, but did not design it. Thus, even DBTG implementations differ with respect to how and what physical structure details are indicated, although there will tend to be similarities due to the common DBTG logical (or logical-physical) architecture. The Data Storage Description Language (DSDL) designed by CODASYL initially in 1978 is practically the only and most significant, encompassing, and formal means proposed to specify all the physical organization details and storage mappings in a CODASYL (DBTG) data base. Section 5.8 presents the DSDL. The 1980s should show the level of acceptance of the DSDL by DBTG vendors specifically.

In actual practice this step may be the most challenging and time-consuming for nonsimple data bases, and perhaps the most frustrating. There are many parameters whose interrelationships in determining performance (access time, storage, and so forth) are very difficult to grasp.

The Data Base Loading and Operation Phase

Data Base Loading. The seventh step is the actual loading of the data base. It is the start of the third phase. Usually so-called utilities (special-purpose programs) that are provided with the GDBMS are the most cost-effective to use in loading a whole data base. It is possible to use DML statements to load a whole data base, but this is generally a more expensive route.

The loading of a data base is not necessarily a simple and quick step. The actual data base values may have to be placed in a certain format or with certain markers in the data stream (e.g., IMS expects a top to bottom, left to right ordering of the segments; SYSTEM 2000 expects some markers in the data stream). For complicated data bases, various time-consuming steps may have to be taken for loading. For example, an IMS "logical" data base involving two or more physical data bases will require loading each physical data base separately and then subsequent use of a utility program to "set up" the logical pointers between segments.

Tuning, Operation, and Reorganization. A design task of the DBA is to design the data base initially so that performance is satisfactory. It is costly to adjust the design and also to adjust performance parameters after the data base is loaded. The adjustment may require total or partial reloading. In practice, a significant degree of retuning may be necessary following the loading step. Although the intent is to do enough design homework before loading to avoid postloading changes, there are so many design parameters and their interrelationships may be so complex that a good design may not be achieved on the first try.

It is a fact of life that most information systems and their supporting data bases are dynamic. Data bases undergo updates, deletions, and additions of record occurrences. The rate of additions normally exceeds the rate of deletions. Data bases seldom diminish in size. The access time and storage performance will start deteriorating during operation as these changes occur, as the use of overflow areas and extra storage becomes significant, unexpected user requirements arise, and so on. Sooner or later the DBA will have to retune, restructure (physically), or reload the data base.

Information systems are dynamic in the sense that they evolve through time and new user requirements or new users appear, for example, the need for a new record type and its relationships to the original record types. Systems evolution often leads to some logical redesign of the data base and not only to physical restructuring. Logical redesign normally entails consideration of most of the steps of the whole data base design process, Figure 13.1.

The following section focuses on quantitative performance aids toward good data base design.

13.3 QUANTITATIVE PERFORMANCE AIDS AND TECHNOLOGY FOR DATA BASE DESIGN

The Goals

The designer faces a challenging goal after the logical data base has been identified: determining the best physical data base structure for the particular situation. A number of steps, each involving various complex design parameters and alternatives, comprise the physical file and data base design process. Figure 13.1 outlines the minimum steps that encompass the data base design process, as discussed in the previous section. Obviously, the determination of the best data base structure for a number of interrelated files is a much more complex task than for a single file.

Data base design and performance are of increasing concern as the amount of information, the number of users, and different subschemas and types of accesses increase. Inappropriate designs and deterioration of performance now represent more sizable and unacceptable cost factors. Unfortunately, the technological know-how and the existing software aids for helping to easily achieve the best data base design and performance for the specific situation need much further development and sophistication.

The ideal goal of data base technology research is to conceive an automatic data base designer, a software black box capable of choosing, generating, and maintaining the best data management system structure (both logical and physical), access paths, and storage structure mappings for the particular data base contents, transaction traffic, and computing and device characteristics. Figure 13.4 outlines the inputs and output of this ideal black box. Each input arrow represents a large number of parameters. The goal is to automate the design process as much as possible. In current practice, design is done manually in a trial-and-error mode, with the help of a few analytical tools, at best, and a few insights gained through hard-earned experience.

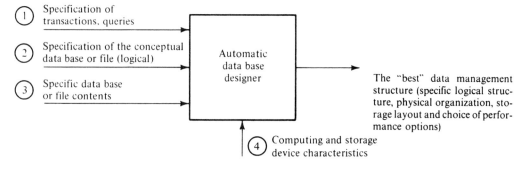

● Functions of the
  automatic designer:

  (1) Design and organize automatically based on ①, ②, ③ and ④
  (2) Reorganize automatically as ①, ②, ③, ④ change sufficiently

● Problems:

  (1) Elusive multitude of parameters, trade-offs,
      interrelationships, etc.
  (2) Very dynamic and volatile environments
  (3) Inflexible software and data structures

Figure 13.4.   *The ideal black box for automatic data base design—a goal*

More immediate and achievable goals (short of a "dream" black box capable of determining, generating, and maintaining automatically both the best data base design and associated application programs) are to conceive:

1. Easy to use, quantitative aids to enhance the design, performance, and cost-effectiveness of data management systems, all the way from simpler single file systems to integrated data base/data communication systems. These aids should be available at the level of very high-level languages and not at low- and intricate levels of an operating system command language level (the latter is portrayed in unfortunately too many initial aids).

2. Technology and methodology for more systematic and productive development and maintenance of *both* data bases and application programs.

A number of inroads are being made and much research and development is under way by vendors and practitioners toward these ends. The following section provides a picture of commercially available aids for file and data base design.

Another source of aids is a number of insights and guidelines derived by vendors and particularly by a growing number of authors interested in understanding, automating, and optimizing file and data base design. These aids usually appear in conference proceedings and journal publications. Some overview texts and references may be cited.[1-3] Various specific pioneering works are cited in Chapter 2.

Among the many functions discussed and attributed to the emerging function of file or data base administration are the following:

1. Select and set up the logical and physical data structures. This includes the schema, the subschemas, and the underlying physical structures and access paths.
2. Monitor the performance in terms of a number of factors, such as access time, storage, integrity, and so forth.
3. Reorganize the data base so as to maintain an acceptable level of performance as the history of record updating, insertion, and deletion inevitably degrades performance.

File and data base administrators need quantitatively based tools to help them cope with the variety of factors and interrelationships which they cannot easily understand all at once. A number of analytical and trial-and-error oriented tools are available for dealing with the spectrum of data management technology: basic file access methods, generalized file management systems (GFMS), and generalized data base/data communication systems. An increasing number of tools are being offered by mainframe vendors, and now software houses, as pressure from data base designers mounts. The following paragraphs provide an idea of the tools available.

Design Aids Available

Design Aids for Basic File Organization. When dealing with the basic access methods of file management provided by the common programming languages, a number of parameters that influence access time and storage costs must be considered. The designer must decide on loading factors, size of overflow areas, location of prime and overflow areas, and so on.

A number of vendors provide various software aids dealing with external storage to assist in initial design and in maintenance. For example, IBM's OS ISAM utilities can maintain statistics on:[4]

1. The number of cylinder overflow areas that are full;
2. The number of unused tracks in the independent overflow area;
3. The number of references to nonfirst overflow records; and
4. The number of records tagged as deleted (recall that in many ISAM implementations, records are only *flagged* as deleted while not actually deleted).

CDC's utility programs for SCOPE operating system indexed sequential files, SIS files,[5] are attractive. For example, the ESTIMATE utility program

ESTMATE

****

ESTMATE,NR = 8000,KS = 10,MR = 500,MI = 450.

THE PERCENTAGE OF PADDING IN THE INDEX BLOCK WAS NOT SPECIFIED
THE SIS DEFAULT VALUE OF 5 IS ASSUMED

INDEXED SEQUENTIAL FILE ESTMATE

NUMBER OF RECORDS = 8000   KEY SIZE = 10 CHARACTERS

MINIMUM RECORD SIZE = 45 WORDS   MAXIMUM RECORD SIZE = 51 WORDS

NUMBER OF INDEX LEVELS	ACCESS MODE	INDEX BLOCK SIZE	DATA BLOCK SIZE	MINIMUM BUFFER SIZE	SUGGESTED BUFFER SIZE
*2,10,,20					
2	RANDOM	127	511	896	896
2	SEQUENTIAL		511	573	573

****

SIS
                        STATISTIC OUTPUT
                        FILE FILTRY2

FILE FORMAT (IN WORDS)
                        INDEX BLOCK SIZE = 63
                        DATA BLOCK SIZE = 127
                        KEY TYPE = S
                        KEY SIZE = 2

TOTAL TRANSACTIONS
            NUMBER OF:
                        INSERTS = 25
                        DELETES = 10
                        REPLACES = 20

536

```
                    STORAGE ALLOCATION
                       NUMBER OF:
                              INDEX LEVELS = 1
                              INDEX BLOCK = 1
                              EMPTY INDEX BLOCKS = 0
                              DATA RECORDS = 15
                              DATA BLOCKS = 3
                              EMPTY DATA BLOCKS = 0

            NUMBER OF UNUSED ENTRIES IN THE PRIMARY INDEX = 28

            TOTAL MASS STORAGE USED BY SIS FILE = 576 WORDS
```

Figure 13.5. *Sample statistics report produced by CDC's ESTIMATE utility program for a SCOPE indexed sequential file (from reference 5)*

can take a description of records and keys and produce suggested sizes for data blocks, index blocks, and buffers based on different file designs, such as padding factors, blocking factors, and number of index levels. Designers can then consider these suggestions to define their best strategy. Figure 13.5 shows a sample report that may be obtained from the ESTIMATE package.

Some software houses have produced packages to monitor disk storage utilization, for example, the Panda disk file usage analysis system for the larger IBM operating systems.[6] It provides reports with information on: total number of tracks and extents allocated; number of tracks used, unused, and available for extension; dead space which could be recovered by reallocation or compression; percentage of allocated space in use; and data set characteristics (block size, data set organization, logical record length, and so forth). Information that the package may obtain about each storage volume includes: the percentage of tracks available on each volume that are allocated; volume table of contents; total number of dead tracks; defective track information; and the availability of space remaining on each volume.

Design Aids for Generalized File Management Systems. Most of the aids designed for dealing with the basic access methods (sequential, ISAM, and random) can be used when dealing with a generalized file management system since the latter invariably uses the standard basic access methods of the operating system involved. The GFMS may then have a few tools of its own to aid designers in dealing with its own performance parameters and characteristics.

Design Aids for Generalized Data Base Management Systems. GDBMS involve a much larger and more complex variety of factors and interrelationships than conventional single-file systems, which data base designers cannot easily understand all at once. How the logical data structures defined by the

DDL are mapped on the actual computing and storage devices depends on the specific GDBMS. The basic storage management and access path methods are not exactly the same across vendors. In the case of IMS, it even has its own access methods (HSAM, HISAM, HDAM, and HIDAM) at the operating system level; they are a part of IMS and hence IMS itself is rightly considered to have many of the ingredients of an operating system. Thus the rules of the game, parameters, knobs, trade-offs, and so forth, vary from system to system, particularly as one nears the depths and options of the data management system, operating system, and hardware. As already stated, the task of achieving optimal or highly cost-effective data base design and maintenance is a challenging task.

Fortunately, a number of GDBMS follow the same general architecture and have in common a number of important access time and storage performance parameters. For example, most DBTG implementations should have in common a number of performance "knobs." Better examples of the similarity of performance knobs are inverted and relational GDBMS. The degree of inversion or other indexing is a most important performance parameter. The basic considerations and approaches presented in Section 2.10 for determining what data fields to index apply to any GDBMS using inverted or index structures as the underlying structures. It is at the detailed level of parameter values that GDBMS differ due to their particular implementation, e.g., the actual time to retrieve and update a record, the actual storage incurred per inverted field, and so on. We have selected SYSTEM 2000's actual design and maintenance aids to describe in some detail in the following paragraphs. Other GDBMS have a growing number of design aids with various capabilities (usually insufficient for the more complex data base designs, according to most observers); they will not be surveyed.

SYSTEM 2000's Performance Measurement and Design Aids

Most of the following material on SYSTEM 2000 has been derived and interpreted from references 13.7 and 13.8.

SYSTEM 2000 provides the data base administrator with a variety of tools and methodologies to assist in making decisions on data base application optimization and reorganization/restructuring.

Execution Analysis. SYSTEM 2000 has a statistics-gathering function. During execution, counters are maintained to indicate accumulated central processor time, real time, and I/O operations for each opened data set (a repeating group or group of fields within a repeating group). The user of any of the SYSTEM 2000 data manipulation languages can enable or disable the external logging of these counters on a DML command-by-command basis.

For instance, suppose "AGE" is an indexed or inverted item in the following typical SYSTEM 2000 query:

PRINT NAME WHERE AGE GT 20

The user issuing the command above can obtain from SYSTEM 2000 the CPU time and mass storage accesses during each phase of execution (index searching and interrogation).

Storage Structure Analysis. Information which is perhaps more directly applicable to the data base designer's task is provided by a set of DBA-oriented features incorporated within SYSTEM 2000. These are used to analyze the data base storage structure and print selected reports concerning:

1. *Storage structure integrity.* That is, internal consistency of pointer structures, indexes, and so on.
2. *Data base statistics.* Examples: for a given character-type field, print the frequency distribution of values by length of value; print the number of occurrences of a repeating group or a field in the repeating group; print the number of distinct values (index entries) for an indexed field; and so on.
3. *Storage structure evaluation measures.* Examples: print the amount of unused space created by record deletion; indicate the degree of "skewedness" in linked lists and indexing structures; indicate the probability of accessing overflow areas when retrieving specific field values; and so on.

Data Base Reorganization/Restructuring. Data base performance inevitably degrades with a history of data base changes and with changes in the nature of the transaction requests (e.g., logical complexity and number of access keys). Facilities are provided to help the DBA take corrective action. The degree of inversion may be changed; that is, any data item may be inverted and any data item previously inverted may be changed to a noninverted status. In SYSTEM 2000, either none or all of the unique values of a data field over the whole data base must be inverted. Note that there is a need to invert only certain specific values of a data item in cases in which the data base access requests use only a small subset of the unique values of the particular data field, or when most data base entries fall under one unique value.

Changing the degree of inversion is a rather minor kind of reorganization in SYSTEM 2000. More significant reorganization is represented by the REORGANIZE command. The RELOAD command is essentially an unload and newload of the data base. These commands are described here as they appear in Reference 4, Section 6.1.

REORGANIZE Command

The purpose of the REORGANIZE command is to reorder various data base tables (directories) whose entries have become scattered due to incremental loads, many updates, or both. The directory tables include the three briefly exemplified in Figure 2.7. The format of REORGANIZE is:

REORGANIZE $\langle n \rangle$;

$$\text{where } \langle n \rangle = \begin{cases} \text{DIR,} & \text{reorganize the value directory and table of unique values} \\ \text{MOT,} & \text{reorganize the multiple occurrence table} \\ \text{ALL,} & \text{reorganize all three} \end{cases}$$

When the data base tables are first constructed, and following this first loading of data, the tables are in their most optimized state. If the data base is static, with no updates or additions to the data, the tables will remain in this organized condition. If the data base is dynamic, with updates to the data tables consisting of additions and/or deletions, the tables will lose their highly organized state and increased I/O activity will be experienced, suggesting it is time to reorganize. Reorganizing will usually substantially reduce the number of disk accesses to the reordered tables if the tables have become highly scattered.

When n = DIR, entries in the key-value directory are reordered so that all entries for a particular field are contiguous. Since the page in the table of unique values associated with each directory entry is implied by the position of the directory entry, this table is also reordered.

This organization will reduce the number of disk accesses to the key-value directory in a data base which has many entries for the field being referenced and which are spread over several pages of the directory. It may be most effective when changes to the data base have been largely changes to KEY elements whose values are unique or occur infrequently (e.g., employee numbers or last names in a personnel data base).

When n = MOT, the multiple occurrence table is reorganized. All the scattered blocks for the same values are collapsed into one block or several contiguous blocks of maximum size. This type or reorganization is effective if updates to the data base involve fields for which a single value occurs many times (e.g., changes of address where the same address occurs in many data base records).

When n = ALL, all three tables are reorganized. This method is more efficient than issuing two separate REORGANIZE commands (with n = DIR and n = MOT) since some of the necessary work is common to both algorithms.

Only the DBA who knows the master password for the data base may issue the REORGANIZE command.

RELOAD Command

The purpose of the reload command is to reorganize the data base tables of the attached data base. The command formats are:

1. RELOAD:
2. RELOAD WHERE ⟨where clause⟩:
3. RELOAD ORDERED BY ⟨ordering clause⟩ WHERE ⟨where clause⟩:

Examples of ⟨where clause⟩ : PRICE GT 20 AND DUE_DATE
                                                 LT 1/1/88
              ⟨ordering clause⟩ : COMPANY_NAME

The RELOAD command effectively unloads, releases, and loads a data base. The resulting data base, accordingly, is arranged optimally with no unused space and all related data stored together. Reloading is appropriate when:

1. The data base has been updated heavily to the extent that the data base files are unnecessarily large due to unused reusable space or access times are excessive.
2. The inverted index has been damaged. (Many, but not all damaged data bases may be repaired in this manner.)
3. It is desirable to reorder the logical entries in a data base.
4. It is desirable to eliminate a large percentage of the logical entries, i.e., extract a "subdata base."

The first command format listed, when issued, reconstructs the entire data base. If a WHERE clause is used, only the qualified logical entries are retained in the reconstructed data base. The data base size will be reduced accordingly. If an ordering clause is used, the logical entries will be ordered as specified in the reconstructed data base.

The use of RELOAD requires a considerable scratch file space. This is equivalent to the amount of scratch storage which would be required to do a LOAD of the entire data base.

Only the DBA who knows the master password may issue this command.

On the Use of Design Tools. Quoting Lowenthal: "As with all tools, merely processing them is not enough; one must understand how to use them to derive the greatest benefit. MRI has developed various techniques for using these tools to understand data base deficiencies and translate this understanding into specific corrective alternatives. These methodologies are presented in various documents as well as in the Applications Analysis Methods Course and the Data Base Design and Administration Course offered by MRI [INTEL]."[8] One cannot emphasize sufficiently the need to understand the capabilities, limitations, and applicability of design tools.

IMS Data Base Design

IMS is perhaps the largest and most complex system commercially available. This does not necessarily mean that it is the most sophisticated and powerful, as the readers may have already realized. However, it does mean, as is generally conceded by most observers, that the use of IMS usually requires more sophistication on the part of both the DBA and users. Four alternative access methods are available (HSAM, HISAM, HDAM, and HIDAM) for the DBA to choose from, each with a host of interrelated and hard-to-understand performance "knobs." Furthermore, application programmers using an IMS data base must have a good understanding of the particular files with which their application program is involved, and they must construct their programs and sequence of DL/1 calls wisely; otherwise poor performance will be experienced.

The complexity of IMS demands that the DBA pay ongoing attention to maintain an acceptable level of performance. This is of course true in all GDBMS. IMS involves more complex parameters and provides more "knobs" and adjustments for use by the DBA to tune a data base than other GDBMS. If performance is poor (and this is easily experienced in IMS), then tuning via the tools and mechanisms available in the IMS repertoire can result in significant improvements, often in the range of several orders of magnitude. All this should not be interpreted as meaning that the performance of an application and a data base is better under IMS than under other GDBMS. Often the opposite is reported, perhaps due in part to the IMS overhead required to meet the wide spectrum of needs of IBM's large customer base.

IBM has developed a number of software packages to assist IMS data base designers. IBM terms these packages IMS productivity aids. Some of them are available for users and others only for IBM personnel. Some of them have been highly successful. Three aids may be cited for estimating various performance factors of alternative data base designs, usage loads, and system configurations: DBDA (Data Base Design Aid), DBPROTOTYPE, and DBDCPERF. DBDCPERF is a simulation package for estimating performance.[9] The inputs to this simulator and the outputs estimated by it are indicated in Figure 13.6.

IMS DB/DC was perhaps the first integrated generalized data base/data communications system. Design aids are particularly needed for DB/DC environments. A number of tools are appearing, e.g., IMS DC MONITOR and DBDCPERF.

● INPUTS

HARDWARE CONFIGURATION INCLUDING CPU TYPE, NUMBER AND TYPE OF CHANNELS AND DASD DEVICES

NUMBER AND SPEED OF TELECOMMUNICATION LINES AND TERMINALS

OPERATING SYSTEM TYPE AND NUMBER OF MESSAGE PROCESSING REGIONS

APPLICATION PROGRAM SIZE AND NUMBER OF INSTRUCTIONS

DATA BASE DEFINITION, INCLUDING NUMBER OF DATA BASES AND DATA SETS, ACCESS METHOD(S) USED, DATA BLOCK LENGTHS, AND NUMBER OF CYLINDERS OF STORAGE NEEDED

TRANSACTION TYPE(S), RATES, AND RELATIVE FREQUENCY

TRANSACTION COMPLEXITY, INCLUDING NUMBER, TYPE AND SEQUENCE OF IMS DL/1 CALLS FOR EACH DATA BASE

● OUTPUTS

TRANSACTION RESPONSE TIMES (SERVICE AND WAITING)

CPU UTILIZATION REFLECTING PROCESSING OF OPERATING SYSTEM, IMS AND APPLICATION PROGRAMS

TELECOMMUNICATION LINE UTILIZATION

DASD CHANNEL USE AND DEVICE RESPONSE TIME

MESSAGE QUEUEING STATISTICS

Figure 13.6. *Typical inputs and outputs of IBM's IMS performance estimator package DBDCPERF for DB/DC environments*

13.4 SECURITY

Introduction

The term **security** refers to the protection of the data base against unauthorized or illegal access, modification, or destruction. There is a high degree of interest in the security aspects of data bases. One of the major goals of GDBMS is to provide a high degree of data security. We shall review the security realm and then the security facilities of IMS, DBTG, SYSTEM 2000, SQL/DS, and QBE.

The term **privacy** is sometimes heard as a complement to security, and often as a synonym for security. There is no clear-cut and widely agreed-upon definition of privacy, so we shall not use the term except in DBTG.

How does the concern for security stand out particularly in data bases? Recall two of the main objectives of data base technology: data shareability and nonredundancy of data stored. These objectives open the door for security concerns. Consider the data base that has been formed in Figure 3.4. The view of each application (an application program or an interactive terminal user) AP, PO, and RMI is shown, indicating a high degree of data shareability. In actual practice, the applications sharing a record or a data field do not and should not have the same access rights. Typically, one application (or at most a few) has complete authority over a given field, repeating group or record, whereas others have more restricted access; for example, application AP may have the right to read, add, delete, or update any field of records F_1, but PO may be restricted to only reading F_1.

Imagine the headaches that might arise if everybody had the same data rights. First, who could then be held responsible for the introduction of erroneous data or the deletion of critical information? Second, how could we enforce consistent quality control of the data when so many users might be involved in changing it? Third, would you share some of your sensitive data with others if sharing it meant giving others the same rights that you have over it (e.g., changing it)? We could go on and on. The point is that powerful mechanisms are needed for security control of data bases, mechanisms more powerful than the primitive ones provided for files by the operating system. The security mechanisms are thus provided by the data management system for use by the DBA. One of the major responsibilities of the DBA is to assign the subschemas and the access rights of each user to each subschema and fields within the subschema.

In general, the security foundation that we can consider initially is portrayed by an access control matrix shown in Figure 13.7. The use of this matrix approach has been suggested and is used in varying degrees and forms (e.g., a dictionary table) in various existing data management systems (both file management and data base management). There is one control matrix for all schemas. Each column represents, let us say, one user U_i of the set of users U_1, U_2, ... authorized by the DBA. The value of U_i is some password which is given by the user and examined by the system at execution time when the actual data items are to be accessed, and at compilation time if the user is a program to be compiled first.

If the total data base is composed of the set of data fields $D_1, D_2, D_3, ...,$ D_m, then there may be as many data base views or subschemas, or possibly files, as there are distinct subsets of $D_1, D_2, ..., D_m$. For each of the D_m items and for each of the data base views there can be any number of passwords. Each entry in the matrix may include four types of authorizations: read, update,

insert, delete. Other types of authorization could be
ability to use a field in statistical calculations but
calculate average salary over a department).

The access control matrix or its equivalent is ⸳
DBA using facilities generally provided with the ᴑᴜ⸜
description language(s). We shall review the IMS, DBTG, SYꜱ⸜ʟ⸜
SQL/DS, and QBE facilities. Some security proponents have suggested that
users also be allowed to create their own data bases (e.g., for temporary data or
permanent data over which the user will act as its DBA) and to define new
subschemas. The relational SQL/DS and QBE systems illustrated in Chapters
10 and 11 permit users to derive new relations and views (subschemas) from
their original view (granted to them initially by the DBA) or from relations that
users create from scratch. Users have complete authority to perform any
operation (read, update, insert, delete) as long as it is within the authority
limits of the original view (e.g., users cannot have and cannot delegate update
rights to any field if they were granted only read rights). Users may grant other
users these rights for each table or view that they derive: read, update, insert,
and delete for each field, and delete the view.

More demanding access control could be of interest: control based on
data field values, not just on field names. Here are a few examples. Suppose
that a data base includes a record type EMPLOYEE composed of the fields
EMPNO (employee number), NAME, SALARY, MGRNAME (name of the
employee's manager), DOCNAME (name of the employee's doctor). The
following controls could be considered for a given user who might be assigned a
given password:

1. Read rights to EMPLOYEE records only when SALARY < 35,000.

2. Read rights to all EMPLOYEE fields when SALARY < 20,000, but
   read rights only to these fields corresponding to a given MGRNAME
   for 10,000 < SALARY ≤ 30,000.

3. Read, update, delete, and insert rights to all of EMPLOYEE when
   MGRNAME = JONES OR MARIN OR DAVIS (these could be
   the managers within a given division) AND SALARY < 30,000.

4. Read rights to all EMPLOYEE fields; and update, insert, and delete
   rights to DOCNAME only if its corresponding employee NAME
   value equals the name of the current user sitting at the terminal.

5. Apply statistical operators to the SALARY field (for example,
   to obtain the average salary over all employees) under a given
   MGRNAME; individual SALARY values are not to be seen.

These are just a few examples of possible security requirements based on
data content. Data content security controls are expensive. In fact, they can
easily become prohibitively expensive in terms of access time overheads. Thus

		U_1	U_2	U_3	...
DATA FIELDS	D_1	READ	READ	READ	
		UPDATE	X	UPDATE	...
		INSERT	X	X	
		DELETE	X	X	
	D_2	X	READ	X	
		X	X	X	
		X	X	X	
		X	X	X	
	D_3	X	READ	READ	
		X	X	X	
		X	X	X	
		X	X	X	
	D_i	⋮	⋮	⋮	
	D_M				
DATA BASE VIEW, SUBSCHEMA OR FILE	DB_1	READ	X	READ	
		UPDATE	X	X	...
		INSERT	X	X	
		DELETE	X	X	
	DB_2	X	READ		
		X	UPDATE		
		X	X		
		X	X		
	DB_j	⋮			
	DB_N				

D_i: Data field, e.g., SALARY, DEPT_NO

$D_1, D_2, ..., D_M$:   Fields making up the total data base defined by the Data Base Administrator

DB_j: A data base view, subschema or a file which may be made up of any consistent subset of the D_M data items; DB_j is seen by the application program

546

U_i: A password (either an execution-time password or a compilation-time password)

ACCESS RIGHTS:

READ: Can read the data field D_i or all the data fields of DB_j

UPDATE: Can change field D_i or all data fields of DB_j

INSERT: Can insert new instances of D_i or DB_j

DELETE: Can delete instances of D_i or DB_j

Note: An X in the matrix means that the authority represented by the missing word is not granted for that password U_i

Figure 13.7.   *Data base access control matrix*

essentially only the more recent relational GDBMS provide most of the previous security capabilities.

A number of special-purpose data management system applications such as in military, criminology, and clinical environments do include a variety of sophisticated security controls. Security experts have designed complex security mechanisms specific to the data base application(s). These mechanisms have usually been implemented in software, often involving many months of design and programming.

The more complex the security requirement is, the more expensive it is to meet in terms of access time, storage, and perhaps implementation. The more difficult that we make our security mechanisms to break by the "enemy," or the more deterrents that we include against the "enemy," the more expensive they are. The more difficult that we make it for the "enemy" to break a security mechanism, the more likely that security will be maintained. It all boils down to achieving a satisfactory security level at a satisfactory cost.

Deterrents are sometimes used against violators. For example, a log file of all attempted security violations for a given sensitive area of the data base may be kept. This file could be checked subsequently or conceivably even immediately after a violation to see if the current violator has exceeded a violation threshold in which case a signal could be given immediately to a security guard.

Before reviewing the specifics of IMS, DBTG, SYSTEM 2000, SQL/DS, and QBE let us review the minimal steps that a data base user will experience in regard to security checking in current practice:

1.   *Access the computer system.* A valid job control or accounting control number must be provided by the user. A further level of checking may be required for the system to verify that the one providing such a number is in fact an authorized user, and not one who "stole" the

number. A certain secret password may now be required from the user. As another example, in an interactive environment a transformation mechanism may be involved: the computer system provides a random number or code x; the user and the system perform on the spot a transformation function T on x and the user gives the result $y = T(x)$ to the system; if the user's y matches the y calculated by the system, then the user is determined to be a valid user. The transformation function can be as simple as reversing the digits or code, or something more complicated (both more difficult for a legitimate user to remember and use, and more difficult for an illegitimate user to break).

2. *Access the GDBMS and a particular schema.* In a manner analogous to the one described above, the GDBMS will determine the validity of the user identification or password and whether or not the user can have access to some part of a data base under the control of the GDBMS.

3. *Access a particular subschema with a particular logical structure.* Using information stored in some internal and highly protected directories, the GDBMS determines if the name of the subschema, the named fields, and the logical structure indicated by the user via the user's subschema DDL is correct and may be accessed by the user.

4. *Access particular records and fields and conduct a number of operations (read, update, insert, etc.) appearing in the DML or query command.* Using information stored in some internal and highly protected area, the GDBMS determines if the specific fields and records may be accessed and subjected to the indicated operations. This security checking is performed for each DML or query command.

Thus several steps or **levels** of security control may be exercised.

IMS

Chapter 7 covered IMS. Access from a program to an IMS data base is via the appropriate program communication block, PCB. The following levels of protection are involved. The program must first provide a valid PCB name. Second, the program may access only the sensitive segments included in the PCB. Third, the program can perform on a segment only the operations authorized by the DBA via the PROCOPT (processing option) parameter. The PROCOPTs that the DBA may specify for a given segment for a given PCB include the common operations get, insert, delete, and replace in any combination.

IMS does not provide direct facilities for access control based on data base value content.

If the data communications system is included, IMS DB/DC, additional security controls may be exercised, for example, the ability to specify that a password be supplied to use certain application programs or certain commands from a given subset of available terminals; and the ability to specify that certain programs may be used and certain commands issued only from specified terminals.

DBTG

The CODASYL DBTG architecture specified in the 1971 DBTG and 1978 reports includes an extensive repertoire of security mechanisms, in addition to the subschema mechanisms which themselves provide the initial layer of security. A DBA has the flexibility of masking out from a given subschema not only any records but also any of the fields of any record (other GDBMS). See, for example, the subschema in Figure 5.13 derived from the schema in Figure 5.6.

A comprehensive set of mechanisms is provided in DBTG via PRIVACY *LOCKS* and PRIVACY *KEYS*. PRIVACY LOCKS are specified by the DBA in the schema or subschema. PRIVACY KEYS are specified by the user in the application program. Figure 5.8 contains a sample data base description and illustrates the use of some of these mechanisms as follows. Statement 5 specifies therein that read types of access (FIND and GET commands) to the record EMPLOYEE will be possible only if the application program specifies: PRIVACY KEY FOR FIND, GET OF RECORD EMPLOYEE IS 226D. Statement 6 specifies that the MODIFY, INSERT, DELETE, REMOVE, and STORE DML commands may operate on EMPLOYEE only if the application program specifies: PRIVACY KEY FOR MODIFY, INSERT, DELETE, REMOVE, STORE OF RECORD EMPLOYEE IS XXYYZZ.

It is interesting to note the use of the term "PRIVACY" in DBTG instead of "SECURITY" and the subsequent 1978 CODASYL report renaming of "PRIVACY" as "ACCESS-CONTROL." In this text we do not differentiate between security and privacy, although some individuals may attempt to differentiate between the two.

The application program must provide the exact key(s) defined by the DBA in order to access the data included in the subschema. All security keys must be provided by the user in the IDENTIFICATION DIVISION of the COBOL application program, as per Figure 5.15. The actual data accesses take place via DML commands appearing in the PROCEDURE DIVISION.

In DBTG a privacy lock may be specified to be a "literal" (the COBOL term for a number or character string), a data item or lock variable, or a procedure. The actual value of the lock is derived from the variable or from the procedure written by the DBA when the application program issues a request to access the "locked" object. If the value of the key provided by the application program does not match the lock, the GDBMS prevents the access to the locked object.

A privacy lock may be also a sequence of literals and/or lock variables and/or procedures connected by logical ORs. This lock is satisfied when an entry in the ORed string is satisfied.

A privacy key may also be a literal, key variable, or procedure. The value of the key variable or procedure is obtained by the application program when the operation on the locked object is attempted by the application program. The value of the key has to match the value of the lock for the particular operation (GET, DELETE, etc.); otherwise the GDBMS will prevent such an operation on the locked object.

Figures 13.8–13.11 show the privacy control mechanisms specified in the CODASYL 1971 DBTG and 1978 reports. We will now review a few of the many options shown. Readers interested in further details should refer to the CODASYL reports.

For the schema the DBA may lock the following operations: DISPLAY (display the schema), COPY (define a subschema based on the schema), and ALTER (alter the logical structure of the schema) and LOCKS (display the privacy locks in the schema). See Figure 13.8(a). In a similar manner, a subschema may be locked for DISPLAY, LOCKS, and ALTER, or for COMPILE (allow the use of the subschema in the compilation of the application program). See Figure 13.8(b). The GDBMS module(s) or utilities that are to perform DISPLAY, LOCKS, and ALTER operations must specify the proper privacy key; and likewise the application program must provide the proper privacy key for COPY and COMPILE.

A record may be locked for each of the DML statements (except KEEP and FREE) as indicated in Figure 13.8(c). Furthermore, note that individual fields, repeating groups, and vectors (arrays) within a record may be locked for GET, MODIFY, and STORE operations via Format 2.

A set may be locked for each of the DML statements which include a set name as one of the operands, namely, ORDER, FIND, INSERT, and REMOVE. See Figure 13.8(d).

An area may be locked for six so-called USAGE MODES: RETRIEVAL/UPDATE, PROTECTED RETRIEVAL/UPDATE, and EXCLUSIVE RETRIEVAL/UPDATE. See Figure 13.9. We discuss the meaning of these usage modes in Section 13.6 on data sharing. Again, security checking takes place when the application program attempts to open the area by providing a matching security key.

In addition, the CODASYL reports suggest the use of locks for major data base functions provided by a given implementation, for example, data base reorganization, audit trail logging, and so forth.

FUNCTION: To define the privacy lock(s) for the operations LOCKS, DISPLAY, COPY, and ALTER on the schema.

FORMAT:

$$\underline{PRIVACY}\ LOCK\ \left[FOR\ \left\|\begin{matrix}\underline{LOCKS}\\\underline{DISPLAY}\\\underline{COPY}\\\underline{ALTER}\end{matrix}\right\|\right]\ IS \begin{Bmatrix} \text{literal-1}\\ \text{lock-name-1}\\ \underline{PROCEDURE}\ \text{data-base-procedure-1} \end{Bmatrix}$$

$$\left[\underline{OR}\begin{Bmatrix} \text{literal-2}\\ \text{lock-name-2}\\ \underline{PROCEDURE}\ \text{data-base-procedure-2} \end{Bmatrix}\right] \dots$$

(a) Locks that may be established for the schema in the schema declaration

FUNCTION: To define and name a subschema within a schema:

1. Specifies the privacy lock(s) for the operations LOCKS, DISPLAY, COMPILE, and ALTER which applies to the use of a subschema.
2. Specifies the key for accessing a schema which includes a privacy lock on its use for deriving a subschema, i.e., it includes a PRIVACY LOCK FOR COPY clause.

FORMAT:

SUB-SCHEMA IDENTIFICATION DIVISION

SUB-SCHEMA NAME IS sub-schema-name OF *SCHEMA* NAME schema-name

$$\left[\underline{PRIVACY}\ LOCK\ \left[FOR\ \left\|\begin{matrix}\underline{LOCKS}\\\underline{DISPLAY}\\\underline{COMPILE}\\\underline{ALTER}\end{matrix}\right\|\right]\ IS\begin{Bmatrix} \text{literal-1}\\ \text{lock-name-1}\\ \underline{PROCEDURE}\ \text{data-base-procedure-1} \end{Bmatrix}\right.$$

$$\left.\left[\underline{OR}\begin{Bmatrix} \text{literal-3}\\ \text{lock-name-2}\\ \underline{PROCEDURE}\ \text{data-base-procedure-2} \end{Bmatrix}\right]\dots\right]\dots$$

(continued)

551

$$\left[\underline{PRIVACY\ KEY}\ \text{FOR COPY IS} \begin{Bmatrix} \text{literal-5} \\ \text{implementor-name-1} \end{Bmatrix}\right].$$

(b) The subschema declaration and locks that may be established for the subschema

FUNCTION: To define the privacy lock(s) for the operations indicated on a record (Format 1) or on subordinate data items or data aggregates included in a record (Format 2).

FORMAT:

Format 1

$$\underline{PRIVACY}\ \text{LOCK}\left[\text{FOR}\left\|\begin{array}{l} \underline{INSERT} \\ \underline{REMOVE} \\ \underline{STORE} \\ \underline{DELETE} \\ \underline{DELETE\ ONLY} \\ \underline{DELETE\ SELECTIVE} \\ \underline{DELETE\ ALL} \\ \underline{GET} \\ \underline{MODIFY} \\ \underline{FIND} \end{array}\right\|\right]\ \text{IS}$$

$$\begin{Bmatrix} \underline{PROCEDURE}\ \text{data-base-procedure-1} \\ \text{literal-1} \\ \text{lock-name-1} \end{Bmatrix}$$

$$\left[\text{OR}\begin{Bmatrix} \underline{PROCEDURE}\ \text{data-base-procedure-2} \\ \text{literal-3} \\ \text{lock-name-2} \end{Bmatrix}\right]\dots$$

Format 2

$$\underline{PRIVACY}\ \text{LOCK}\left[\text{FOR}\left\|\begin{array}{l} \underline{STORE} \\ \underline{GET} \\ \underline{MODIFY} \end{array}\right\|\right]\ \text{IS}\begin{Bmatrix} \underline{PROCEDURE}\ \text{data-base-procedure-3} \\ \text{literal-5} \\ \text{lock-name-3} \end{Bmatrix}$$

$$\left[\underline{OR} \left\{ \begin{array}{l} \underline{PROCEDURE} \text{ data-base-procedure-2} \\ \text{literal-7} \\ \text{lock-name-4} \end{array} \right\} \right] \cdots$$

(c) Locks that may be established for a record or for a data aggregate in the schema or subschema declaration

FUNCTION: To define the privacy lock(s) for the operations on a set.

FORMAT:

$$\underline{PRIVACY} \text{ LOCK} \left[\text{ FOR} \left\| \begin{array}{l} \underline{ORDER} \\ \underline{FIND} \\ \underline{INSERT} \\ \underline{REMOVE} \end{array} \right\| \right] \text{IS} \left\{ \begin{array}{l} \text{literal-1} \\ \text{lock-name-1} \\ \underline{PROCEDURE} \text{ data-base-procedure-1} \end{array} \right\}$$

$$\left[\underline{OR} \left\{ \begin{array}{l} \text{literal-3} \\ \text{lock-name-2} \\ \underline{PROCEDURE} \text{ data-base-procedure-2} \end{array} \right\} \right] \cdots$$

(d) Locks that may be established for a set in the schema or subschema declaration

Figure 13.8.   *Privacy locks that may be established in DBTG for schemas, subschemas, records, and sets (from the CODASYL 1971 DBTG and 1978 Reports)*

FUNCTION: To specify privacy and data sharing locks for the use of an area.

FORMAT:

$$\left[\underline{PRIVACY} \text{ LOCK} \left[\text{ FOR} \left\| \begin{array}{l} \left[\begin{array}{l} \underline{EXCLUSIVE} \\ \underline{PROTECTED} \end{array} \right] \underline{RETRIEVAL} \\ \left[\begin{array}{l} \underline{EXCLUSIVE} \\ \underline{PROTECTED} \end{array} \right] \underline{UPDATE} \\ \text{support-function-1 [,support-function-2]} \cdots \end{array} \right\| \right] \text{IS}$$

$$\left\{\begin{array}{l}\text{literal-1}\\\text{lock-name-1}\\\underline{PROCEDURE}\text{ data-base-procedure-1}\end{array}\right\}$$

$$\left[\underline{OR}\left\{\begin{array}{l}\text{literal-3}\\\text{lock-name-2}\\\underline{PROCEDURE}\text{ data-base-procedure-2}\end{array}\right\}\dots\right]\dots$$

Figure 13.9. *Privacy and data sharing locks that may be established in DBTG for areas in the schema and subschema declaration (from the 1971 DBTG Report)*

FUNCTION: To provide the program and run-unit authority to execute the classified DML imperative statements in accordance with the locks declared in the schema or subschema.

FORMAT:

$$\left[\underline{PRIVACY\ KEY}\text{ FOR }\underline{COMPILE}\text{ IS}\left\{\begin{array}{l}\text{literal-1}\\\text{implementor-name-1}\end{array}\right\}\right]$$

$$\left[\underline{PRIVACY\ KEY}\left|\text{FOR}\right|\left|\left|\begin{array}{|c|}\underline{EXCLUSIVE}\\\underline{PROTECTED}\end{array}\right|\underline{RETRIEVAL}\right|\right.$$
$$\left.\left|\begin{array}{|c|}\underline{EXCLUSIVE}\\\underline{PROTECTED}\end{array}\right|\underline{UPDATE}\right|\right]\text{ OF}$$

$$\left\{\begin{array}{l}\text{area-name-1 [,area-name-2]}\dots\underline{AREA}\\\text{ALL }\underline{AREAS}\end{array}\right\}\text{ IS}$$

$$\left\{\begin{array}{ll}\underline{PROCEDURE}&\left\{\begin{array}{l}\text{procedure-name-2}\\\text{literal-6}\\\text{identifier-6}\end{array}\right\}\\\text{literal-2}\\\text{identifier-2}\end{array}\right\}\dots$$

554

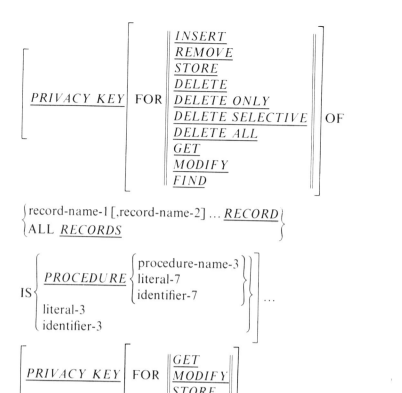

$$
\left[\underline{PRIVACY\ KEY} \quad FOR \left\| \begin{array}{l} \underline{INSERT} \\ \underline{REMOVE} \\ \underline{STORE} \\ \underline{DELETE} \\ \underline{DELETE\ ONLY} \\ \underline{DELETE\ SELECTIVE} \\ \underline{DELETE\ ALL} \\ \underline{GET} \\ \underline{MODIFY} \\ \underline{FIND} \end{array} \right\| \right] OF
$$

$$
\left\{ \begin{array}{l} \text{record-name-1}\,[,\text{record-name-2}]\ldots \underline{RECORD} \\ \text{ALL}\ \underline{RECORDS} \end{array} \right\}
$$

$$
IS \left\{ \begin{array}{l} \underline{PROCEDURE} \left\{ \begin{array}{l} \text{procedure-name-3} \\ \text{literal-7} \\ \text{identifier-7} \end{array} \right\} \\ \text{literal-3} \\ \text{identifier-3} \end{array} \right\} \ldots
$$

$$
\left[\underline{PRIVACY\ KEY} \left[FOR \left\| \begin{array}{l} \underline{GET} \\ \underline{MODIFY} \\ \underline{STORE} \end{array} \right\| \right] \right]
$$

OF data-base-identifier-1 [,data-base-identifier-2] ... $\underline{DATA\text{-}ITEM}$

$$
IS \left\{ \begin{array}{l} \underline{PROCEDURE} \left\{ \begin{array}{l} \text{procedure-name-4} \\ \text{literal-8} \\ \text{identifier-8} \end{array} \right\} \\ \text{literal-4} \\ \text{identifier-4} \end{array} \right\} \ldots
$$

$$
\left[\underline{PRIVACY\ KEY} \left[FOR \left\| \begin{array}{l} \underline{ORDER} \\ \underline{FIND} \\ \underline{REMOVE} \\ \underline{INSERT} \end{array} \right\| \right] OF \left\{ \begin{array}{l} \text{set-name-1}\,[,\text{set-name-2}]\ldots \underline{SET} \\ \text{ALL}\ \underline{SETS} \end{array} \right\} \right]
$$

$$
IS \left\{ \begin{array}{l} \underline{PROCEDURE} \left\{ \begin{array}{l} \text{procedure-name-5} \\ \text{literal-9} \\ \text{identifier-9} \end{array} \right\} \\ \text{literal-5} \\ \text{identifier-5} \end{array} \right\} \ldots
$$

Figure 13.10. *Privacy and integrity keys that may be provided by an application program using the DBTG system (from the 1971 DBTG Report)*

555

FUNCTION: To specify the USAGE MODE of an area and to interrupt further run-unit execution until such usage may be permitted in accordance with the USAGE MODE declared in the Schema and Subschema.
To invoke the checking of the run-unit's variable PRIVACY clauses.

FORMAT:

OPEN AREA area-name-1 [,area-name-2] ...

$$\left[\underline{USAGE\text{-}MODE}\ \text{IS}\ \begin{bmatrix} EXCLUSIVE \\ PROTECTED \end{bmatrix} \begin{Bmatrix} RETRIEVAL \\ UPDATE \end{Bmatrix} \right]$$

> ***Figure 13.11.*** *Data sharing (concurrency) options to an application program using the OPEN command in DBTG DML (from the 1971 DBTG Report)*

Figure 13.10 indicates the privacy keys for the subschema (COMPILE option), areas, records, data items, and sets that may be specified by an application program, e.g., in COBOL in the Identification Division. Usage modes of areas may be also specified. Recall that the keys provided must match the locks specified by the DBA in order for this program to access the data base.

SYSTEM 2000

Inverted and relational systems exhibit data base directory structures which may assist greatly in implementing security controls to the field level and even to the field value level. Let us discuss some implementation aspects now. Previous sections have not covered implementation aspects; all we have said is that security mechanisms are expensive. Consider the data base whose directory is shown in Figure 2.6. The directory includes the following information: the inverted field (key) names, the values of each inverted field, and the location of the records satisfying each value. Thus we can conceive adding to each key-name and to each key-value the information of what users can perform what operation on all records characterized by the key-name or key-value. This information could be thought of as a compact two-dimensional matrix A (user identification, operation type) whose values are 1 or 0 (i.e., the given user can or cannot perform such an operation on all records with the corresponding key-value).

When a user requests information on the basis of data value content, the system will use its directory mechanisms to the fullest. Perhaps some special program statements maybe needed in addition to directory mechanisms for the more complex types of data security, as the case might be for: user X requests updating all fields of EMPLOYEE for SALARY > 40,000 AND

MGRNAME = JONES. There are many ways of implementing security mechanisms, so that in spite of the architectural similarities of inverted systems, a given type of security may be implemented by different inverted systems in different forms.

SYSTEM 2000 provides a comprehensive set of security facilities, typical of inverted systems such as ADABAS and METABASE. Figure 8.3 illustrates some of the facilities in the on-line accessing mode of SYSTEM 2000. The first nine commands are invoked by the DBA to set up the subschemas, user identification, and security controls to the field level. The remaining commands are invoked by the user to access the data base. The first of the DBA commands must indicate the highly secret DBA password (DB-ADMIN-ISTRATOR in the example) so that the system may determine if the issuer is in fact a DBA. If the issuer does not provide the proper DBA password then the subsequent DBA commands are not allowed. Thus a given installation must exercise a great deal of care with the DBA password. The rest of the DBA commands are self-explanatory.

The first three user commands in Figure 8.3 indicate the user password GOODGUY and the desire to access a portion of the data base INSURANCE-EMPLOYEE. Notice that the user password is at the same time the name of a subschema. If the DBA had not created the GOODGUY password specifically for INSURANCE-EMPLOYEE, then the user would be considered illegitimate after statement 11 [e.g., GOODGUY defined only for other data base(s)]. Statement 12 is legitimate. Statement 13 is not legitimate because GOODGUY is not allowed to CHANGE the field INSUR-CO-NAME; the user has been assigned only read rights to this field.

SQL/DS and QBE

Relational GDBMS provide generally the most powerful security controls since they additionally provide security controls on the basis of data content. Section 10.5.4 presents and illustrates fully the robust security controls of SQL/DS. Section 11.4 describes the security controls in QBE.

Further Security Concerns and Measures

Since most GFMS and GDBMS appear to an operating system as an application program, an illegitimate user may completely bypass this application program and go directly to the operating system to break the security measures. No operating system can provide today complete security. Operating systems provide minimal security measures which have been shown to be breakable. Thus the degree of security of a data base under a GDBMS is largely dependent on the security of the underlying operating system software unless encoding/decoding schemes or physical security measures are employed.

Encoding/decoding schemes involve encoding every source field value via some encoding algorithm and storing the value in coded form. When the value is requested by the user, then a decoding algorithm must be applied to convert the value from its stored form back to the user form. If an illegitimate user is able to obtain a dump of the medium holding the data base by breaking the operating system security, or by physically stealing the medium and dumping it, all that the dump will contain is unintelligible coded data. Thus a high degree of protection is achieved. However, it is very expensive. Every time any value is to be stored or retrieved, a price will be paid in executing the transformation algorithm. ADABAS is one of the very few GDBMS providing encoding/decoding security mechanisms. Only a few of today's sensitive data bases have justified such a degree of security and its corresponding cost. Military applications are obviously attracted to such a level of security.

An intelligent intruder would consider breaking the encoding/decoding security by going after the encoding/decoding algorithm(s). If the intruder obtains the algorithm then the security mechanism is lost. Thus it is of utmost importance to protect the algorithm and perhaps have it reside in the GDBMS. Conceivably, the program statements of the algorithm could be themselves subjected to some codification.

Encoding/decoding schemes may be used for achieving security in communications-oriented uses of data bases. A communication line (be it a short one or a long one connecting a data base with a user miles away) may be wiretapped by an intruder. The intruder can then see any uncoded information passed between a user and a data base, and even perhaps become the user in place of the original user. The intruder could even sign-off the original user by appearing as the GDBMS for the sign-off protocol. The counter measure against wiretapping is encoding/decoding. The algorithm is then kept at the terminal and highly protected. It should not be transmitted via the communications line. Thus an intruder who wiretaps will only see unintelligible coded streams of data.

Due to the possibilities of still breaking all software measures and even hardware-oriented measures, physical security might even be used. For example, if a critical data base or file and a critical application are to be processed, then a computer system and its software including the GDBMS could be completely dedicated in a locked and shielded room to the cleared persons hand-carrying the data base devices and the program(s) themselves. All communication lines would be physically cut off; all other users would be barred from the machine and the room. Does it sound like too extreme a situation to take place in real life? There are a number of such situations taking place today!

13.5   INTEGRITY

Introduction

The term data base **integrity** has evolved to refer to the qualities of validity, consistency, and accuracy of the data base. Integrity is concerned with protection against improper data base access and modification, whereas security is concerned with illegal data base accessing and modification. Obviously, in some cases the distinction between "improper" and "illegal" is unclear and arbitrary. One of the objectives of data base technology is to provide means to maintain control over and preserve the integrity of the data base. The intent is for DBAs to be able to set up a number of integrity constraints on the data base via special facilities available to them, and then have the GDBMS monitor the usage of the data base and make sure that the integrity constraints are satisfied. In this section we will introduce a number of commonly considered integrity constraints and then outline how IMS, DBTG, and SYSTEM 2000 can deal with what constraints.

Integrity is somewhat like security as far as the extent to which it is achieved and the cost of achieving it. The higher the degree of integrity, generally the higher the cost of achieving it in terms of the necessary software, access time, and storage cost. Thus the intent is to achieve a satisfactory degree of integrity for a satisfactory cost. It is a fact of life that many of today's data bases are somewhat "polluted," that is, there are invalid data values, inconsistencies, and so on. It is difficult and costly to avoid such pollution. In some cases, it may be practically impossible to avoid it; for example, there may be no way of realizing that an input volume of sales of $1,250 should really be $1,350, although a volume of sales of $1,250,000 for the particular situation may be a detectable error.

There is no industry-wide standard for integrity. The closest to a standard might be the CODASYL proposals which include a number of integrity features as part of the architecture. Other GDBMS provide a number of integrity facilities. We will illustrate those of IMS, DBTG, SYSTEM 2000, and SQL/DS. A number of proponents of the relational approach have suggested more powerful integrity mechanisms than those available in today's systems. Today's operating systems and common programming languages provide only a few primitive constraints, and as a result the designers of application systems have had to design, program, and maintain their integrity mechanisms as preprocessors and/or postprocessors to the file management facilities. In most large conventional applications, system designers have masterminded at least some degree of data value validation at input time for some critical fields; for example, salary range should be between x and y. In some cases the validation mechanisms that have had to be developed are exceedingly specialized and sophisticated. Data validity has been of concern for many years, even before data base technology started to evolve. The intent of data base technology is to provide a wide range of easy to use generalized integrity mechanisms and avoid much of the traditional effort of implementing the mechanisms themselves, using them and enforcing them.

Integrity mechanisms fall in two categories: **data validity** and **consistency**. A few authors indicate that integrity entails primarily consistency, and not data validity. However, as the concepts of integrity evolve into the important role they play in real-life data base applications, both data validation and consistency are being included under integrity, whose ultimate goal is the correctness of the data base. We will now outline some of the most important data validity and consistency constraints, indicating which are provided by the GDBMS discussed in previous chapters.

Validity

1. Data types and format

A data field may be allowed to contain only values whose type and format must exactly match the characteristics declared for the data field in the schema via a PICTURE clause or equivalent. Some data base systems have gone further than conventional file and programming language technology in that further data types and formats may be defined. For example, SYSTEM 2000 allows definition of a "date" data type whose format is expected to be XX/XX/XX, for example, 3/10/79. During data base processing, only values with such a format may be assigned to a data field. Both conventional systems and GDBMS indicate automatically when data type and format violations occur during processing.

2. Value ranges

The value of a particular field may be required to fall within a certain range. For example, the MONTHLY-SALARY field must have values between 500 and 5,000. IMS and SYSTEM 2000 do not provide this integrity aid. DBTG provides it via the CHECK clause definable for a numeric data item or for a vector repeating group:

⟨data-item-name⟩ CHECK RANGE OF a THRU f

where a and f are numeric literals.

A field may be required to take only specified values. For example, DEPARTMENT-NAME can take only one of the five department names. This is a variation of the value range concept usually implemented as a main part of the input data validation step prior to processing in traditional nondata base environments.

3. Value ranges of related fields

The values of two or more particular fields may be related and may have to observe some constraints. For example, the field OFFICE-LOCATION may be constrained to be "LOS ANGELES" if the field EXPERTISE has the value "OVER-THE-HILL," and either LOS ANGELES, SAN

DIEGO, or SANTA BARBARA if EXPERTISE has any other value. A mechanism to permit definition and enforcement of this type of constraint is obviously costly. No commercial GDBMS provide it as yet. Where enforcement of these constraints has been necessary, application designers have had to develop custom software.

Since this situation is concerned with value relationships between different fields, it is included as part of data base consistency. We shall not argue definitional aspects. We have mentioned the terminology problems in the data management world, particularly in areas such as integrity and recovery.

4. Uniqueness of a key field

It may be required that occurrences of a given record have a unique identification field or combination of fields. For example, each employee record must have a unique IDNUMBER. Practically all GDBMS provide means to enforce this; in fact, some of them, particularly relational GDBMS, require that each record type have a unique key field.

In IMS a unique sequence field may be defined in the DBD for each segment. A sequence field is required for the root segment. If a segment is declared to have a sequence field, and if M (multiple value) is not specified, IMS will not permit two occurrences of the segment under a parent to have the same value in the sequence field. IMS will prohibit any DL/1 command that tries to introduce a duplicate.

DBTG provides various uniqueness checks via the DUPLICATES ARE NOT ALLOWED clause. It may be specified in the schema for CALC-keys, sort keys, and member record fields:

(a) *CALC-keys.* For each CALC-key the DUPLICATES ARE NOT ALLOWED clause may be specified, e.g., statements 8 and 26 in the sample schema of Figure 5.8. The GDBMS will void any addition or modification of a record occurrence if the new CALC-key value is the same as one already in the data base.

(b) *Sort-keys.* For each set name the DUPLICATES clause may be specified in reference to the uniqueness of the sort key of the member record occurrences within a given set occurrence. For example, statements 32, 36, and 37 in Figure 5.8 call for a unique multiple key (the EMPLOYEE-NO and CHILD-NAME fields concatenated) for the EMP-CHILD set. Thus for a given set occurrence, the GDBMS will prohibit any DML command resulting in two members (CHILD) having the same sort-key value (EMPLOYEE, CHILD-NAME).

(c) *Member record fields.* The DUPLICATES ARE NOT AL-
LOWED clause may be specified for each member record in its
set declaration, indicating which field or combination of fields
of the member must be unique within a given set occurrence.

Consistency

The broad term **consistency** has been used to include different aspects by
various authors. It normally entails some constraint in some relationship
between data objects in the data base. There is no standard for data base
consistency requirements. Two very important consistency constraints are:

1. The values of a data field in a given record may be required to appear
    also as values in some field of another record (or even perhaps in the
    same record). This requirement may be materialized in most com-
    mercial GDBMS.

    Consider the Employee-Child-Insurance data base in Figure
    5.6. It is reasonable to expect that any given value of EMPLOYEE-
    NO in CHILD must have a corresponding EMPLOYEE-NO value
    in EMPLOYEE. We can assure this in a DBTG system via a VIR-
    TUAL SOURCE clause. Statement 20 in the DBTG schema decla-
    ration appearing in Figure 5.8 corresponding to Figure 5.6 indicates
    that the field EMPLOYEE-NO IS VIRTUAL and that its SOURCE
    IS EMPLOYEE-NO OF OWNER OF EMP-CHILD set; in other
    words, the source is the record EMPLOYEE. This accomplishes two
    very important tasks that we shall now discuss.

    First, whenever the EMPLOYEE-NO field value is changed or
    added to the data base by a DML command referring to either the
    EMPLOYEE or CHILD records, the GDBMS will automatically
    introduce the same effect at both places. In general, if there are M
    virtual appearances of a field, the GDBMS will reflect the change at
    the physical location and all its M virtual locations. Imagine what
    could happen if this integrity restriction were not declared in our ex-
    ample and we had a program or user updating EMPLOYEE occur-
    rences. The EMPLOYEE-NO might be updated in EMPLOYEE
    without necessarily updating this corresponding field in the CHILD
    record. This could be an oversight, particularly in a large data base
    schema, that would introduce serious integrity problems.

    Second, the VIRTUAL mechanism provides apparent storage
    redundancy to application programs or users for their convenience
    while actually avoiding internally the apparent storage redundancy.
    Internally the field is stored only once physically; all other appear-
    ances of the field are virtual and are materialized via some pointer

mechanisms. In DBTG the DBA is given the ACTUAL option for requesting ACTUAL physical storage redundancy, for example, EMPLOYEE-NO IS ACTUAL SOURCE IS EMPLOYEE-NO OF OWNER OF EMP-CHILD.

Another way to insure this type of consistency but incurring redundancy is through the 1978 CODASYL DBTG set membership integrity clause STRUCTURAL CONSTRAINT IS data-identifier-of-member EQUAL TO data-identifier-of-owner. This insures the participation of a member record occurrence in a set occurrence such that the data identifier of the member is equal in value at all times to the corresponding data identifier of the owner occurrence.

IMS provides some consistency mechanisms via logical data bases. As an example for those recalling IMS logical data bases, Section 7.5, consider the Professor-Student data base in Figure 7.28 materialized as a logical data base to account for the M to N relationship between the PROFESSOR and STUDENT segments. Intersection data could be included as part of the relationship between a particular PROFESSOR occurrence and a STUDENT occurrence, e.g., the course in which the particular professor taught the student. This now raises the issue of whether or not this intersection data is stored twice, once in the TEACHES pointer segment and once in the TAUGHTBY pointer segment, Figure 7.28. IMS gives the DBA the option of physically storing twice or of avoiding this redundancy by declaring either pointer segment to be a virtual of the other (note that a whole segment may be a virtual of another). Whether or not actual redundancy is chosen, when the user affects an occurrence of either of the paired segments, IMS will introduce automatically the same effect to the other.

SYSTEM 2000 permits establishing any field as a virtual of any other field. The next consistency constraint will exemplify this.

2. The value of a data field in a record may be required to be the result of a procedure using actual values of other fields. This is a frequent requirement which some authors may classify as a consistency constraint while others may not. This case reduces to the previous one when the task of the procedure is simply to take the value of a single field and set it as the value of the result field. A result field is materialized only at execution time and the value is not actually stored in the data base. The procedure is provided by the DBA to the GDBMS.

In DBTG, SYSTEM 2000, and robust relational systems any field may be declared to be the result of a procedure applied to any field(s) of the data base. In the Doctor DBTG data base shown in Figure 5.9, the field TOT_RECEIVABLES will have a value materialized at execution time as the result of a procedure applied to the value of fields in the record EMPLOYEE. More specifically, statements A14 and A15 in the schema declaration in Figure 5.10 indicate that the value of the field TOT_RECEIVABLES for a particular DOCTOR record occurrence is to be the result of applying PROCEDUREX to the members of the DOC_PAT set owned by the DOCTOR occurrence; for example, PROCEDUREX could sum the values of the field $OWED_TO_DOCTOR of all the EMPLOYEE occurrences owned by the particular DOCTOR occurrence.

In the Insurance-Employee SYSTEM 2000 data base shown schematically in Figure 8.1 and declared in Figure 8.2, two fields are calculated result fields. The field AGE of EMPLOYEE is to be the result of the integer function defined in DDL statement 10; FTODAY is a SYSTEM 2000 built-in function that provides the data at the time of execution and BIRTH-DATE is a field of EMPLOYEE. Similarly, CHILD-AGE is calculated based on the CHILD-BIRTH field. Thus the AGE value is always up to date. This mechanism avoids the need to have a special program update periodically the age fields.

In SQL/DS and QBE it is through the creation of a user view that any fields may be virtual and the result of a procedure executed when the query requesting the field is executed. For the Employee-Department relational data base shown in Figure 10.4, in Section 10.5.1 an SQL/DS view is created composed of the department number and the annual average salary and monthly average salary for those departments in which the annual average salary of its employees is greater than $35,000.

Would you expect a result field to be allowed to be indexed, e.g., inverted? The answer is no. The value of the result field is not physically stored anywhere; it is only calculated at execution time. Furthermore, it would be expensive and difficult to update inversion directories involving result field values changing very frequently; nevertheless, this cost would be justified if the rate of read-only access based on such fast-changing fields were high enough.

It is conceivable that a data base could be made up of X fields, of which only one field is real and the rest $X - 1$ fields are virtual fields materialized at execution time. In actual practice the number of real fields is usually much greater than the number of virtual fields, of course.

Maintenance of data validity and consistency constraints entails much data checking. All update, insert, and delete operations on the portion of the data base with the constraints will have to be monitored. It may be very expensive for extensive constraints; this is the main reason why more extensive integrity controls that have been proposed,[10] particularly for relational systems, have been seldom implemented. Thus, the appropriate checking may be more cost-effectively done by means of a special utility program run periodically to perform the checking, rather than whenever the update operations occur. Such off-line auditing of the data base contents is becoming popular. GFMS, with all their report writing capabilities, are reported being used in a number of cases for auditing the data validity and consistency of large data bases. An important concern of the DBA is setting up all these checking/ monitoring means.

In spite of all the checking, some loss of integrity may take place. Recovery mechanisms must then be available for recuperating the integrity of the data base. Section 13.7 addresses the recovery process.

A situation classified under the category of both consistency concerns and data shareability concerns (which will be discussed in the following section) is that in which a **transaction** is implemented as a series of actions, each of which may change the data base. Once started, *all* of these actions may be required to set the data base to a consistent state. For example, a particular transaction may debit one account and credit another. This transaction consists of two actions, one to debit and one to credit. After the completion of the debit and before completion of the credit, the accounts are out of balance. After the completion of the credit the accounts are again in balance, and the data base is again consistent with the requirement that the total value of all accounts remain constant.

In general, a transaction may consist of many complex steps introducing changes to various record types. It is necessary that each transaction see a consistent view of the data base. The view must not be polluted by the actions of other *concurrently running transactions* sharing the data base. Thus it is necccssary to impose "locks" on records before they are accessed and to hold them until no further changes to those records are possible. All this leads us to the topic of **data shareability**, also known as **concurrency**, and **locking mechanisms** taken up in the following section. We stress that the locking procedures for maintaining consistency in multioperation and multiuser transaction environments must be set up by the DBA using a number of facilities available, unless the GDBMS provides default procedures.

It is in the area of integrity, concurrency, and recovery that robust GDBMS excel, and in which micro-GDBMS usually fall way short. Specifically, micro-GDBMS seldom support more than one user at a time on a data base.

13.6   DATA SHARING (CONCURRENTLY) AND LOCKING

Let us now address some of the potential problems and approaches to solutions in *shared* data base environments in which there are users *concurrent-*

ly operating, each with transactions involving multiple operations on the data base. This is the typical data base situation. We will concentrate on tools provided in the DBTG architecture and SQL/DS to handle such situations.

At the end of the previous section we introduced the integrity problem of concurrent users issuing transactions involving multiple updating operations. In most commercial GDBMS it is usually necessary to prevent or **lock out** (a term that has evolved with data bases) users from accessing that portion of the data base affected by any of the updating operations of the multiple-operation transaction currently being serviced; otherwise these other users may use the data base in a temporarily inconsistent state. Another consideration is that a given user may require total and exclusive control of some portion of the data base and lock out all other concurrent users from it, even though the user's transaction does not involve updating operations. If such a constraint is not exercised, then there is the danger that the initially consistent state with which the user starts may be suddenly converted to an inconsistent state by another user.

The DBA has the responsibility of coordinating the sharing of the data base by the various users and ascertaining that data integrity and correct interpretations of the data predominate. The DBA needs a number of powerful tools to set up the mechanisms and procedures toward this end. A number of problems arise in shared environments, and a number of solutions have been proposed.[11-17] Different GDBMS provide different tools and capabilities. Unfortunately again, there is no industry-wide standard for such an important concern. Much remains to be done. This is an active area of research and development for both centralized and distributed data bases. The problem becomes more complicated in a distributed data base environment (see Chapter 16).

Major Data Sharing (Concurrency) Strategies

Data sharing or concurrency strategies that have been envisioned to preserve consistency in a data base generally fall into the following major categories, as summarized and illustrated in the macroscopic models in Figure 13.12 and 13.13:

1. **Early consistency checking.** A transaction starts its service as soon as it arrives, unless the capacity or throughput of the GDBMS is such that the transaction must wait until the GDBMS has the capacity. The consistency of all the data objects are checked before accessed by the transaction. If a data object accessed is held by another transaction, then it may not be consistent, and therefore the transaction has to wait; otherwise it continues its service. Consider that the transaction stream T_1, T_2, T_3, T_4, ..., T_i, ... arrives in this time

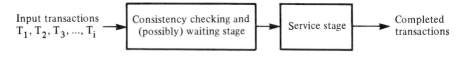

Order of service in service stage:

1. Time stamp order: $T_1, T_2, T_3, T_4, ..., T_i, ...$

or   2. Nontime stamp order or locking: e.g., $T_2, T_1, T_3, ..., T_i, ...$

Figure 13.12.   *Model of early-consistency-checking concurrency strategies (time stamp order, and nontime stamp order or locking)*

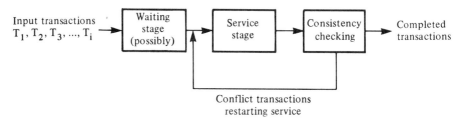

Conflict transactions
restarting service

Figure 13.13.   *Model of late-consistency-checking concurrency strategies (time stamp order, nontime stamp order)*

sequence where T_i is a particular transaction arriving at time i. There are then two major alternative early consistency strategies:

(a)   **Time stamp order.** Transactions are actually serviced in the same time sequence in which they arrive for consideration.

(b)   **Nontime stamp order** or **locking.** Transactions are not necessarily serviced in the same time sequence in which they arrive for consideration. For example, the actual sequence of servicing may be $T_2, T_1, T_3, T_4, ..., T_i, ..., T$. Locking is the most common term used.

2.   **Late consistency checking.** The arriving transactions are not checked for consistency upon arrival. A transaction starts being serviced as soon as it arrives, unless the capacity or throughput of the GDBMS is such that the transaction must wait until the GDBMS has the capacity. A transaction either (a) completes its service and leaves or (b) some other transaction being serviced conflicts with it, and it is then restarted from the beginning. Note that failed transactions restarting service start ahead of those in wait due to insufficient GDBMS throughput.

A GDBMS attempts to make any such consistency checking and solution approaches transparent to concurrent users, although not necessarily transparent to a DBA. This is generally so, except for the service time delays that may be incurred.

Each of the major concurrency strategies has a wide range of variations and refinements, as evidenced by many conference and journal publications. Most commercial GDBMS supporting concurrency use some type of implicit or explicit locking strategy or protocol. We shall now focus on locking and see various issues and variations involved through the locking strategies in DBTG systems and other systems.

The so-called **granularity of locking** or **sharing** can be at the level of the whole data base, an area, a record type, a page of record occurrences, a record occurrence, or even a field occurrence. Robust GDBMS provide the highest throughput by locking usually at the record occurrence level.

It has been shown that all transactions must be **well-formed** and locking must be **two-phased** in order to preserve data base consistency.[13] A transaction is well-formed if it:

1. Locks a resource before accessing it;
2. Does not lock a resource that is already locked by another transaction; and
3. Before terminating it unlocks every resource it locked.

Two-phased locking is one in which, within each transaction, no resource is unlocked before all resources are locked; thus the first phase is lock acquisition and the second phase is lock release.

DBTG

We will summarize the main facilities of the DBTG architecture for dealing with data sharing issues. DBTG implementations can be expected to follow generally the DBTG specifications. However, this is an area where there might be some variations. For example, UNIVAC's DMS/1100, one of the main DBTG implementations, provides locking facilities differing somewhat from the DBTG specifications.[14]

DBTG specifies control and management of data sharing by concurrent users (run units) based on the concept of areas. There can be one record type per area or a subset of record type occurrences per area. However, robust DBTG implementations usually lock at the level of pages or record occurrences (the use of areas in DBTG has been a controversial issue). First the DBA must establish the desired coordination "locks" for each area of each concurrent subschema. This is done for each area via the PRIVACY LOCK command outlined in Figure 13.9; the concurrency choices are EXCLUSIVE,

PROTECTED, RETRIEVAL, and UPDATE. Notice how these data sharing locks are tied to the security locks.

When an application program or user desires to use the subschema(s) for which privacy locks and/or concurrency controls have been set up by the DBA, it must include (if it is a COBOL program, in Identification Division) the proper lock keys in order to use the subschema. The types of integrity keys that may be provided are outlined in Figure 13.10. The skeleton of a COBOL application program is shown in Figure 5.15.

Next, when operating in the Procedure Division in COBOL, the OPEN command may call for the allowed types of data sharing. The form of the OPEN command is shown in Figure 13.11. The DBTG system will assure at execution time that the user does not violate the rules of the road for data sharing imposed originally by the DBA via the lock mechanisms.

The data sharing options are stated for each area via the OPEN statement USAGE MODE Clause and may be any of the following six, based on the DBTG specifications shown in Figure 13.9: RETRIEVAL, UPDATE, PROTECTED RETRIEVAL, PROTECTED UPDATE, EXCLUSIVE RE-TRIEVAL, and EXCLUSIVE UPDATE. These are the rules:

1. The OPEN statement is used to set up any usage mode for areas. The close statement is used to disable usage modes.

2. The EXCLUSIVE phrase prevents concurrent users (run units) from processing the same areas in any usage mode.

3. The PROTECTED phrase prevents concurrent updating but allows concurrent retrieval for the same area.

4. The USAGE-MODE IS RETRIEVAL phrase (without the EX-CLUSIVE or PROTECTED phrases) permits concurrent users to open the same area with any usage mode except EXCLUSIVE.

5. The USAGE-MODE IS UPDATE phrase (without the EXCLU-SIVE or PROTECTED phrases) permits concurrent users to open the same area in RETRIEVAL or UPDATE mode but not in EX-CLUSIVE or PROTECTED.

6. A concurrent user trying to execute an OPEN statement on an area which violates the usage mode already specified for the area will be placed in a wait state, and the GDBMS will provide a message of "privacy breach attempted."

7. The USAGE-MODE IS UPDATE clause (without the PRO-TECTED or EXCLUSIVE phrases) permits a concurrent user to also update records in the same area concurrently. However, this opens the door for the possibility of loss or consistency since the following DBTG specifications do not provide true locking or other attractive concurrency controls transparent to the user discussed

earlier. Thus DBTG implementations seldom provide for users the following DBTG specifications: KEEP and FREE statements to help avoid conflicts. Execution of the KEEP statement by a run unit (user) places the current of the run unit (a given record occurrence) in a "keep status" for the run unit; this status is released by executing the FREE statement on the same record. It is noted that the current of run unit is automatically in a keep status until it ceases to be current. The GDBMS will prevent a run unit from changing a record in keep status if that record has been changed by a concurrent run unit since it was placed in keep status. A change may be performed by any of these statements: INSERT, DELETE, REMOVE, and MODIFY. If the record has been changed, the GDBMS provides an appropriate ERROR status. The run unit must then FREE the record involved, thus removing the record from keep status and also the error condition. The run unit is now able to proceed. It is advisable that the run unit, before continuing processing, examine the record to see how it was changed by a concurrent user. Note that if the run unit only wants to read the record that it originally placed in keep status, the only way it can know if a concurrent run unit changed it since it was placed in keep status is by examining the record itself and comparing it to its past status! KEEP and FREE are controversial and seldom implemented.

Deadlock

The use of EXCLUSIVE or PROTECTED locks or access rights may in some special cases result in what is known as a **deadlock** between concurrently executing users. This often-mentioned deadlock results if the following sequence of actions occurs:

1. User U1 opens area A1.
2. User U2 opens area A2.
3. User U1 tries to open A2 in order to continue processing and eventually be able to close (release) A1 but has to wait because U2 is holding A2.
4. User U2 tries to open A1 in order to continue processing and eventually be able to close (release) A2 but has to wait because U1 is holding A1.
5. Neither U1 nor U2 can proceed: they are deadlocked.

A deadlock may occur in any GDBMS providing EXCLUSIVE or PROTECTED locks whenever certain resources are shared concurrently by two or more users. Note that a deadlock could occur while trying to share concurrently record occurrences within a single file, record types within an area, or any other resource. Just replace the words "open area" in the four-step deadlock listed above by "acquire resource." GDBMS provide the highest throughput by locking usually at the level of record occurrence. In practice, deadlock occurs very infrequently.

Deadlock Solution Strategies

The major deadlock solution strategies are:

1. **Prevention**, which involves locking required resources from given a priori information. This has the difficulty of determining and obtaining a priori the necessary information.
2. **Detection**, which involves detecting deadlock during execution and rolling back (backing out) a run unit or process selected as the "victim."

Various solutions based on run unit scheduling or rollback have been suggested and implemented by GDBMS and other systems where deadlock may occur. One of the most common solutions that may be adopted by the DBTG implementation is that of prohibiting a user from opening any area in EXCLUSIVE or PROTECTED mode if the user already has EXCLUSIVE or PROTECTED control of some other area. The user is then required to open all needed areas in a single OPEN statement. The GDBMS then grants control over the areas only when all of them are not under the control of another user. A user controlling some area(s) who wishes control over some other area(s) must first release this control and then request control over all areas in one OPEN command.

Thus the DBTG solution to the deadlock of the preceding four-step sequence is as follows in step (4): User U2 tries to open A1 in order to continue processing and eventually be able to close A2. Instead of waiting in a dead-locked contention, U2 releases control of A2 so that U1 may terminate processing completely. U2 then can have control over both A1 and A2.

In DMS/1100 deadlock is resolved by backing out the run unit that has made the fewest number of updates. At system generation time, the DBA can override this deadlock resolution with his or her own priority. Can you think of any other priority basis?

13.7 INCORRECT STATES AND RECOVERY

Incorrect States

A data base may fall into an incorrect state, that is, end up with some erroneous data, due to any of the following reasons:

1. *Loss of data validity or consistency.* The previous section indicated some of the main types of validity and consistency constraints that may be required in an application. It is possible that the DBA did not set up all the necessary mechanisms to prevent violating the requirements, or that an error occurred in the software implementing the prevention mechanisms. Thus the data base falls into an incorrect state. Furthermore, it is possible that after a period of operation of a data base, there may arise a requirement for a new integrity constraint. After checking the data base, the DBA may find this new requirement missing from the data base. Thus, the data base may now be in an incorrect state as far as the new requirement is concerned.

2. *An error in an application program.* Various kinds of errors may be incurred, all the way from the wrong application program being applied by a user at the wrong time, to a new and previously undiscovered error in the logic of the program. Errors in application programs probably account for the largest percentage of incorrect states in data bases. Users usually introduce most of the errors that persist in large and complex data bases. Due to this fact, and to the growing size and complexity of data bases in organizations, internal and external auditors are increasing their activities in attempting to detect errors introduced by users which bypass all error or integrity checks.

3. *An error introduced by a terminal user.* This is perhaps the most likely source of errors for many data bases. Terminal users may be very attracted by highly interactive and easy to use query languages to make quick decisions affecting the data base. The possibility of introducing errors when the user is making decisions quickly is obviously higher. Errors of course are avoided if a terminal user is given only read rights. This explains the tendency to limit the number of terminal users who have broad rights to data bases. The DBA has the important task of deciding which terminal users to allow and what update, delete, and insert rights to grant to each.

4. *An error introduced by a computer operator.* Computer operators do make mistakes. The wrong application program or utility program may be used, the wrong disc may be used, the wrong version of a backup tape could be used in reinitializing the data base, an error could occur in loading steps, and so on. Some of these possible errors may seem farfetched to some readers. But they do happen. In a few installations computer operators' mistakes are cited among the most frequent sources of errors.

5. *An error introduced by the GDBMS or the operating system.* Software is not perfect. GDBMS and operating systems are very complex

packages. Bugs do get through all the quality tests performed by the vendor. A bug in the GDBMS may result in an incorrect data base. Imagine the problems if a pointer is set to an erroneous value; it is probably a worse error than setting a data field to an erroneous value. Hundreds of thousands of pointers may be manipulated by GDBMS for a data base. It is surprising that relatively few pointer errors actually arise.

6. *An error introduced by a hardware failure.* An electronic failure may occur, and so may a more mechanically oriented failure (e.g., a disc may be physically scratched).

7. *An error introduced by the environment.* Electric power failures do occur. There may be a complete power failure. Voltage variations may exceed the tolerance of the electronic circuitry; in some countries this is not uncommon. Temperature control of the computer room might fail. When temperature and voltage limits are exceeded, unexpected random errors may occur.

8. *An error introduced by malicious mischief and catastrophe.* Some data bases may be the target of malicious mischief, all the way from "pulling the plug" to physical attacks on the hardware. Major catastrophes may occur, such as fire, earthquake, and war, resulting in partial or total destruction of the data base in operation.

Recovery

Any or all of the previous types of errors may victimize a data base, particularly large and complex data bases shared by many users. The term **recovery** has evolved to refer to the process of undoing the effects of a detected error and of restoring the correct state of the data base. The subject of recovery is of utmost importance in real-life data base technology practice. Recovery is one of the most time-consuming and difficult responsibilities of the DBA. Four ingredients and activities are involved:

1. *Error detection routines.* A GDBMS provides a number of error detection routines or utilities. Although the number and capability of such routines grows each day, most likely it will be up to the DBA and/or user to mastermind the largest portion of the detection mechanisms for the large variety of errors that might occur, particularly those caused by humans (as opposed to the computer), unconsciously or maliciously. Much concern and activity are being devoted now to the subject of error detection in large data bases.

2. *Routines for taking snapshots or copies of the data base.* It is important to take a snapshot or backup copy of the data base, or of a portion of it, at a certain point in time. The backup should be one

whose correctness has been certified, or at least "satisfactorily" certified. The backup copy is usually stored on a tape (e.g., in a HSAM fashion for an IMS data base). Backup routines are provided as part of the recovery mechanisms of a GDBMS. A copy of a data base may be taken after a certain volume of update, insert, and delete transactions is serviced. Alternatively, the copy may be taken periodically. In some cases, policy decrees that backup copies be taken every week, perhaps coinciding with periodic reorganizations of the data base so as to reduce overall recovery and reorganization costs. In other cases, copies are taken very frequently, perhaps every few hours or even minutes for very dynamic on-line data bases, and stored on disk.

Usually only a few backup copies covering the most recent time periods are kept by an installation. However, in a number of cases (for example, accounting and financial applications), perhaps hundreds of backup copies may be necessary to recreate past states for auditing, taxation, claims, and so forth, covering several years.

Copies of highly sensitive data bases are usually closely guarded. In case of major problems, such as fire and war, copies may be physically stored away from the installation using the operating data base.

Not all areas of a data base experience equal update activity in an application environment. Thus, more frequent snapshots of the highly active areas may be necessary. GDBMS provide various means for such strategies. For example, DBTG systems include the areas which may be copied relatively independent of other areas. IMS provides data set groups, which are analogous to DBTG areas.

3. *Audit trail routines.* Audit trail routines are sometimes called *log routines or journalizing routines.* Their task is to record on the audit trail file complete information on every transaction affecting the data base. The information recorded usually includes: the identification of the issuer of the transaction (program, terminal, etc.); a time and day of issue; a unique identification issued by the GDBMS for the transaction; the exact transaction as issued; and, for transactions causing a change to the data base, the address of all the data affected as well as a copy of its value just before and just after the change. A just-before-change copy is called a **preimage** or **before-look**, and a just-after-change copy is called a **postimage** or **after-look**.

4. *Recovery routines.* Recovery routines are used to set a data base to its correct state after an incorrect situation has been detected. The correct data base could be any of the following:

   (a) An earlier snapshot or backup taken and certified to be correct;

(b)   The data base content just before the transaction or situation causing the error was introduced; or

(c)   The up-to-date data base with the error corrected.

Recovery procedures may be of two types: (1) **forward**, also called "**rollforward**," and (2) **backward**, also called "**rollback**." Forward recovery routines are used to replace all or part of the data base with data taken from a backup copy of the data base certified to be correct. Subsequent changes to the data base, namely, those logged in the audit trail tape or log tape since the backup, are then reapplied to the backup copy to restore the data base to some recently existing correct state (typically to the state just before the error was incurred).

Recovery routines may be able to roll back a data base or portions of it detected to have an error. Rollback means to undo changes introduced in the data base, namely, those suspected to be erroneous. Rollback recovery is used when a transaction consisting of a sequence of changes to the data base aborts before successful completion. Rollback could perhaps be all the way back to a correct backup copy of the data base.

Historically, recovery automatically became an implicit part of EDP practice when data bases consisted of magnetic tape files. A tape file is not updated in place; that is, old values are not overwritten by new values. A distinction is made between input and output tapes. The existing version of a file to be modified is read from input tape(s). The modifications are read from a transaction or change file. The updated version of the file, incorporating the changes, is written on separate and distinct tape(s). In tape EDP, both backward and forward recovery are simple. When an updating run aborts before completion, a form of rollback is performed: reposition tapes backward and set uncompleted output tapes to blank. When the updating run completes successfully, the output tape is saved for normal future use, and so are the input and transaction files, just in case something incorrect may be introduced to the output tape(s). With the input and transaction files available, the original updating run may be rerun partially or completely to recover any or all output tapes. All this is standard practice.

With the advent of data base systems which process transactions from many application programs and on-line terminals concurrently and which update large interconnected files on direct access storage devices, many new complexities and requirements arise for recovery procedures. For example, backup copies of the whole or of a portion of the data base must be explicitly created, since records are changed in place. The changes themselves have to be explicitly written on a journal file. For each change, either or both preimages and postimages of the data base must be written. Preimages are used for backward recovery and postimages for forward recovery.

The actual forward recovery procedure employs the backup copy and the journal file. It is necessarily a very special GDBMS program. Forward recovery is not a rerun of the original updating process. Recovery is possible because the GDBMS recovery routines know precisely how the backup copy and the journal file are synchronized and related to changes in the data base. It should be stressed that the original updating process involved a network of resources no longer necessarily available when recovery takes place.

It is important to confine rollback to the effects of a single transaction coming from a single source (program or terminal), without affecting the ongoing processing of many concurrent transactions coming from elsewhere. At this point recovery requirements join and extend the requirements of data integrity, which involve the prevention of destructive interaction between concurrent transactions attempting to update the same data in the data base. So there is the need to define precisely the concept of a transaction, to define precisely the data to be locked for a transaction, and to define a protocol for imposing and releasing locks.

What portions of the data base should be put on a backup, and when? These are very important questions under current investigation and worrying many data base administrators.

There is unfortunately no industry-wide standard on recovery. Every GDBMS has its own mechanisms designed by the vendor. There are many similarities among GDBMS, of course, namely, the general ingredients and considerations herein discussed. However, the differences are considerable.[17-20] Terminology differences are a problem. It is to be expected that various DBTG implementations share more similarities in recovery matters among them than with respect to other GDBMS architectures; and the same can be said for relational GDBMS. There are wide differences in capability and flexibility of recovery between robust GDBMS and less powerful GDBMS, particularly micro-GDBMS. Recall that one of the objectives of GDBMS is to provide mechanisms for achieving integrity (the mechanisms have been reviewed in the previous section) and for maintaining it or recovering it should it be lost. We would all benefit by some industry-wide standard framework for recovery. This is a challenge to both data base researchers and developers.

Let us realize that although recovery is a cure for an incorrect data base state, it may not cure many of the bad effects that an incorrect state may have already caused to users who assumed a correct state. Certain actions or commitments (e.g., issue purchase orders or production orders, mail delinquency notices) could have been made by users heavily dependent on the specific data assumed to be correct but actually found subsequently to be incorrect. You can recover data by rollback and rollforward procedures, but you cannot correct actions and commitments this way. Thus it is of utmost importance to set up the first main line of defense around error detection and prevention rather than around recovery, which is essentially a remedial action.

13.8   DATA BASE UTILITIES

The term **utility** is used to refer to a special and optimized program provided with the system software which is of general use to a wide spectrum of users. Utilities provide system support functions. All operating systems include a number of high-efficiency utility programs for a variety of tasks, for example, tape to tape copying, disk dumping, and so on. Likewise, GDBMS vendors provide a number of utilities specifically for the data base environment. Such utilities complement the facilities of the GDBMS. The GDBMS vendor usually provides most of them, if not all, as necessary modules of the GDBMS.

When is a facility considered a utility and when an integral and inseparable part of the GDBMS? It is a thin and nebulous line. For example, the "insert a record" facilities of a GDBMS could be arbitrarily separated out from the DML and arbitrarily classified as part of a utility package for high-volume insertion or loading.

There is no industry-wide standard specifying what utilities must be provided with a GDBMS, their detailed capabilities, and the languages or syntactic forms for using them. The CODASYL DBTG Committee only suggested a number of utilities and made the decision that it would not attempt to specify them, but rather leave it in the realm of individual implementors. Thus no two GDBMS provide the same utilities in the same shape, form, or ease of use.

Utilities for the following functions are a necessity and are provided by almost all major GDBMS (this is not an exhaustive list):

1. Statistical gathering and analysis for data base design and reorganization.
2. Editing and error detection.
3. Recovery—data base snapshots, checkpoint, audit trail or logging, and rollforward and rollbackward.
4. Data base loading/unloading/reloading.
5. Modification of the structure of schema, subschemas, records, and relationship types.
6. Assignment of data to devices and media; definition of buffers, blockings, overflows, and so forth.

Section 13.3 addressed the functions of the utilities, or aids as they were referred to therein, for data base design and reorganization.

Section 13.7 addressed the functions of the utilities for editing-error detection and for recovery.

Utilities for data base loading/unloading are a must. These utilities are optimized for the specific task. These functions could also be performed via the normal DML facilities for record insertion, deletion, and modification. For example, the IMS DL/1 insert command could be used for loading a whole data base (although not an IMS logical data base which requires use of the load utility). However, the DML route is a much less cost-effective means than the highly optimized utility.

Typically, file sizes, record lengths, field definitions, device types, and so forth, change as the information needs of a company evolve. Thus there is the need to rapidly unload all or a selected portion of the data base previously loaded, reformat the data, and then reload it in the appropriate location. Facilities are provided to restructure, modify, extend, and initialize data fields. The unloaded portions of the data base can be written to either tape or disk for subsequent reloading while meeting a number of reloading requirements. Loading, unloading, and reloading are executed as close to serial processing speeds as possible, and all relationship and pointer processing is done automatically.

Is there any difference between *reloading* and *reorganization*? We do differentiate between the two, but sometimes there is not a clear distinction. The term data base reorganization tends to be used more to refer to the reloading of all or selected portions of the data base necessitated by storage and/or access time degradation because of transaction or data base content changes. Reloading tends to be used in the broader sense. Earlier we discussed SYSTEM 2000 data base design aids which include a REORGANIZE command and a RELOAD command. REORGANIZE is used to reorder various data base tables or directories whose entries have become scattered due to incremental loads, many updates, or both. RELOAD effectively unloads, releases, and loads the data base; it is applied, for example, to replace a damaged inverted index; to replace a large percentage of the logical entries, that is, to extract a subdata base; and so on.

Utilities or some DDL editing means are a must for easy modification of the structure of a schema, subschema, record type, or relationship. If the declaration for these objects is dozens of lines long, as is typically the case in medium to large data bases, then we need mechanisms that permit us to easily and conveniently introduce changes without the need for another complete redefinition and that protect us from introducing a number of possible errors (e.g., introduce a new record type without defining its relationship to other existing records). These utilities may be closely tied to loading/reloading utilities.

A sixth category of utilities includes those needed for a DBA to assign data to storage devices and computing media; define hardware resources; and define buffers, blockings, and overflows. The means for these tasks are a subset of the encompassing data storage description language defined by CODASYL. Loading/reloading can proceed only after the DBA has performed such tasks. It is in this area that a DBA devotes much time and thought in order to achieve and maintain good data base performance. GDBMS differ greatly in the form, shape, convenience, and ease of use of these facilities. A number of GDBMS provide some kind of "physical data definition and layout language" as opposed to a "utility." Data base practice would benefit if there were a common, high-level, and easy to use "physical data definition and layout" language, or at least one for each of the major types of GDBMS, rather than the large variety of unusually uncomfortable mechanisms provided with current GDBMS.

13.9   THE DATA BASE ADMINISTRATION FUNCTION

Introduction

Throughout this text we have been attributing to the so-called **data base administrator (DBA)** and to the **data base administration (DBA) function** a number of tasks, in fact, a large number of complex tasks. The DBA is crucial to the introduction of data base concepts and technology in any enterprise. The DBA is not necessarily one individual, but rather several individuals in the case of large organizations. This section reviews the importance of data as a resource to be managed, the tasks and responsibilities of the DBA function, and its place in the organizational structure—its importance has been stressed by the CODASYL DBA Working Group,[21] the growing number of writings on the subject,[22,23,24] and actual practice.

The data base is a large repository of data crucial to a growing number of application systems and users. The data base is a costly and important resource of any organization. It is costly to form a data base, to administer it, and to manage it—more costly than many writings on data bases seem to portray. However, the potential benefits of data base technology can exceed by far its costs; more importantly, it can exceed by even more the benefit factor of conventional file technology and associated means. The data base requires proper design, administration, and control—and these tasks fall on the DBA.

The DBA function must not be diffused among the many users and information system specialists. Why? The reason is that there will be situations requiring much coordination among the various users, and frequently even conflicting demands on the data base. The functions of the DBA have not been standardized and as a result there are significant differences in DBA practice. Wide differences are also noticeable between written charters of the DBA and the tasks actually consuming most of the time of the DBA.

It should be noted that at the other extreme of the multiuser and complex data base environment addressed herein is the case of the single-user and simple data base environment. In such a case, the single user may be at the same time most or all of the DBA, but facing only a small subset of the following responsibilities. This is the usual microcomputer environment.

The DBA functions include those that must be taken away from any one application system or user for the overall good. The DBA has a wide number of responsibilities, all the way from managerial realms to highly technical realms. We have presented in this chapter and in previous ones the majority of the technical responsibilities and decision-making falling on the DBA. We shall now review them as we outline also the many not-so-technical responsibilities of the DBA.

Responsibilities

1. *Spread and sell data base concepts and technology.* Like all new concepts and technological advances, data base concepts and technology need a public relations and marketing effort. It is not necessarily easy to displace current technology and applications based on it, even if the advantages of data base technology are evident and of several orders of magnitude. So the DBA function must devote efforts toward achieving some degree of acceptance and willingness by the organization to innovate, to modify systems and procedures, as long as cost-effectiveness considerations justify it, of course.

   The shortcomings of traditional data management technology and applications based on it were outlined in Chapter 3 as we introduced the following objectives of data base technology specifically aimed at alleviating such shortcomings: data independence, data shareability, nonredundancy of data stored, relatability, integrity, access flexibility, security, performance and efficiency, and administration and control. The meaning and achievement of these goals must be translated by the DBA into terms and cost/benefit achievements in the language of users.

   The introduction of data base technology in an organization for the first time may require a great deal of effort by the DBA. Very likely there will be an additional problem: there is no DBA function if data base technology has not been used in the organization. So it may fall upon the shoulders of the GDBMS vendor and/or an outside consultant to work with some data processing-oriented individual(s) in the organization and justify GDBMS. Once the first application(s) is up and running satisfactorily, introduction of data base technology to other application areas should be less difficult. The reluctant user with an attitude of "show me" may be more easily swayed to a favorable attitude after talking to another group "down the hall" about its experience with the innovative technology.

2. *Justify data base technology.* A major task of the DBA is to justify data base technology in cost/benefit terms. When should one stay with traditional technology? When should one upgrade to the data base realm? These are important questions. A data base approach might not be justified right away. For example, in many installations conventional file management technology is underutilized. Perhaps the next step is to introduce a generalized file management system. Or perhaps an administrative and organizational upgrading is what is more immediately needed before data base technology is introduced.

The elaboration of the method for arriving at the cost/benefit merit of a data base application must be accomplished with the participation of the DBA. The elaboration of the cost/benefit merit of a specific data base application versus other alternative approaches (e.g., using conventional technology) must be accomplished by an organization with the aid of the DBA.

3. *Assist in resolving incompatibilities and coordination and communication problems between groups sharing a data base.* The construction and use of a data base invariably involve resolving:

(a) *Incompatibilities of data form and meaning.* Data compatibility is the ability of data produced in one environment to be accepted and used in another environment. In many of today's large organizations data incompatibilites are widespread in naming conventions, form, and meaning, for example, different names and data formats for the same data object. Incompatibilities result from oversights, data redundancy, lack of standards or documentation, and coordination and communication problems between groups making use of what should really be the same data object. It is true that sometimes it is not feasible to standardize everybody; therefore, many GDBMS permit defining synonyms and several data mappings for a given object (e.g., DBTG systems). However, such data variations must be kept to a minimum; otherwise there will be a costly load on the DBA and the system. Data compatibility is necessary before integrating the data into the data base and sharing it among the users in an effective and economical manner.

A major task of the DBA is to establish standards, conventions, and documentation for the data resource. The data dictionary/directory (see Chapter 14) is practically an essential aid for the DBA to accomplish this task.

(b) *Coordination and communication problems between different groups.* The integration of data into a centralized or distributed data base is frequently not too difficult technically speaking. However, frequently it is *very* difficult as far as organizational or political aspects are concerned. For example, very often the problems that data base technology aims to help resolve arise not so much because of shortcomings of traditional technology, but primarily because of organizational and political problems. Widespread data redundancy and the existence of different data values for what is supposed to be the same data object may be due primarily to lack of coordination and communication between the groups carrying said data independently of each other.

The availability of a GDBMS will not solve organizational and coordination problems. The DBA must be aware of this and participate in bringing about the necessary organizational and political changes and environment to achieve the potential benefits of data base technology. In many cases organizational changes have had to be introduced in order to set up and obtain major benefits from information systems and associated data bases. People likely to be affected unfavorably will obviously react against any changes in the status quo. Problems of intergroup politics, communication, and coordination are said by many observers, including this author, to be the ones that cause more data base failures than any others. Yes, data base failures do occur!

A coordination problem might arise when a data base is formed. Not every user group may be able to obtain equally good performance from a centralized data base system. The hardware and software resources and the characteristics of the particular data base may be such that a given user group might not obtain as satisfactory a performance as others. Some groups may have to sacrifice some for the benefit of the whole user community. For example, an application system that accesses a very large portion of the data base may now be limited to certain hours for processing, and perhaps in fact pay more now (e.g., due to pointers that need to be used by other applications) than originally when it had its own stand-alone files and operation. Local optimization is not conducive to overall optimization. The DBA has to be a diplomat in coordinating usage by various users and in dealing with those that might not obtain the greatest benefit.

The previous realities lead to the need for the DBA to be at a sufficiently high organizational position, or at least work with some group at a sufficiently high position, e.g., a corporate information systems development group, with the ability to deal with or assist in dealing with intergroup issues. The DBA function must be mostly centralized (this is not saying that there should not be two or three DBA groups); it should not be diffused among the many related user groups.

4. *Participate as an integral part of the information system development cycle.* The establishment of a data base and its proper administration and control should not be an end goal in itself. The major goal is to support decision making and the myriad information systems necessary for the organization to achieve its goals. The DBA must participate with the information system development group(s) in developing a new data base, using a subset of an existing one or expanding an existing one for developing information systems or satisfying users' information needs. Very often the DBA, working closely of course with the users, spearheads the development of data base-oriented application systems.

5. *Carry out, manage, and control the data base design process.* A major function of the DBA is to carry out, manage, and control the data base design tasks summarized in Figure 13.1. Three phases are involved: logical data base design, physical data base design, and data base loading and operation. The data base design process has been presented with some detail phase by phase, step by step, in Section 13.2. Readers should examine carefully the many important decisions involved in this design process, a primary activity reserved for the DBA.

   As part of this design process, the DBA must also deal with the additional concerns reviewed below: performance, security, integrity, data sharing, and recovery.

6. *Achieve and maintain a satisfactory level of performance.* The DBA must achieve and maintain a satisfactory level of performance for every data base. No one user group should have a free hand in optimizing its own applications at the expense of the overall good. As mentioned earlier, some users may have to sacrifice some performance for the overall good. We have addressed performance issues of file and data base structures in detail throughout this text, particularly storage and processing time issues. Section 13.3 addresses the performance goal and gives an overview of quantitative performance aids and technology available to the DBA.

   A major criterion toward acceptance of data base technology is satisfactory performance. Performance includes not only machine resource utilization but also the various elements below (items 7−11) are well as other less technical aspects.

7. *Achieve and maintain a satisfactory level of security*. The DBA is responsible for assuring that satisfactory levels of security of data are achieved and maintained. The data base must be protected against unauthorized or illegal access, modification, or destruction. In some institutions security is of maximum importance. It may be one of the main performance criteria, for example, in military applications, criminology, financial applications, etc. The DBA is responsible for dealing with data base security as indicated in Section 13.4.

8. *Establish integrity constraints for preserving data correctness*. Integrity is concerned with protection against improper data base access and modification, whereas security is concerned with illegal data base accessing and modification (there may be a thin dividing line between improper and illegal). The category of integrity includes both the validity of data values and the consistency between different data objects. The DBA is responsible for establishing and maintaining a number of integrity constraints on the data base with the goal of preserving the correctness of the data resource. The DBA may establish constraints with facilities that may be provided with the data management system. Once the constraints are established, the system must monitor the usage of the data base under the direction of the DBA and make sure that the constraints are satisfied.

   The DBA must deal with the integrity concerns presented in Section 13.5, using a number of tools provided by the data management system and indicated therein.

9. *Coordinate data sharing and locking*. The DBA must be able to deal with a number of issues of coordination that may arise when data is shared by two or more users, each with transactions involving multiple operations on the data base. The DBA is expected to coordinate data sharing by proper use of concurrency mechanisms provided by the data management system, usually locking mechanisms, with the goal of ascertaining that at all times any one user sees the data base (his or her subschema) in a consistent state, and not in a possible temporarily inconsistent state that may be brought on by other concurrent processing not properly coordinated or locked. Section 13.6 addresses these issues and reviews the DBTG approach to them. Unfortunately, there is no industry-wide standard for data base concurrency mechanisms.

10. *Preserve the correctness of the data base and recover from any incorrect state incurred*. Each data item and each relationship in a data base must be cared for so that it is in a correct state at all times.

Security constraints, integrity constraints, and proper coordination of users via locking will be utilized to the fullest by the DBA so as to prevent the data base from falling into an incorrect state. However, not all sources of errors will be eliminated. The DBA may not have set up all the necessary constraints. Errors in the hardware, system and application software, data entry system, and way of using the data base do occur. Thus the DBA has the responsibility of performing a number of tasks toward maintaining the data base in a correct state: detect exactly the errors, take periodic snapshots of the correct data base, maintain proper audit trails, and then recover the correct state of the data base.

The types of errors that may occur and the means available to the DBA for recovering from them are presented in Section 13.7.

11. *Gather, prepare, and load the data base.* A not much publicized task of the DBA is to concentrate, prepare, and load the data base. This may be particularly time-consuming when a data base is set up for the first time. Different types of preparations of the data may be necessary before loading; for example, transform data from their source document format or type so as to meet loading requirements. In many organizations extensive efforts are being devoted to the data entry or preparation step.

12. *Keep abreast of data base technology.* Data base technology has developed rapidly and is advancing at a very fast pace; so are telecommunication, application development, and storage technologies. The DBA must devote time to keeping up with the technological advances and considering them for application to his or her organization. It is difficult to absorb a fast-evolving and improving technology.

The DBA in the Organizational Structure

The DBA functions and place in the organization have not been solidified or standardized. Thus differences exist in DBA practices from organization to organization. The DBA has a wide range of responsibilites, from the managerial realm to the highly technical realm. The major tasks of the DBA have been reviewed in the preceding list. Although not an exhaustive list of tasks, it does include the majority of the main ones.

The DBA has been given so many responsibilities that by now the reader may be convinced that one person cannot do it all alone in a large organization involving several large data bases, several large application systems, and dozens or hundreds of users. This is true. The DBA function will be staffed by a small group of individuals reporting to the chief DBA. Clearly there is the need for highly qualified technologists deeply familiar with the particular GDBMS, or in-house data management system, in use. There is also the need for highly qualified individuals with the diplomatic, organizational, and systems analysis finesse necessary to derive the potential benefits of data base technology. The head DBA has the responsibility of leading the DBA organizational unit and being a **diplomat**, **manager**, and **technologist**.

The DBA function must be centralized rather than diffused among the many related user groups for the various reasons already cited. This is not to say, however, that more than one DBA group should not exist. If may be justified to have some diffusion of the DBA function, perhaps one for accounting and financial systems and one for engineering systems, or due to geographic needs. Nevertheless, there should be one coordinating director in charge of it all.

The DBA function needs to be at sufficiently high organizational position, or at least work with some systems development group at such a level, for example, a corporate information systems group. The DBA must have the ability to deal with or assist in dealing with information systems crossing organizational units. It must not be subordinate to the EDP chief, unless the latter is at a sufficiently high level.

The role and organizational position of the DBA is evolving rapidly. Our perspectives in this section are highly representative of actual practice, but they should not be taken as a final word on such an important matter.

REFERENCES

1. Teorey, T. J., and J. P. Fry, "The Logical Record Access Approach to Database Design," *Computing Surveys*, Vol. 12, No. 2, June 1980, pp. 179–211.
2. Teorey, T. J. and J. P. Fry, *Data Base Design*, Prentice-Hall, Englewood Cliffs, N.J., 1982.
3. Yao, S. B. (ed.), *Principles of Data Base Design*, Prentice-Hall, Englewood Cliffs, N.J., 1984.
4. "Data Management Services Guide," IBM Reference Manual, Form GC26-3746.
5. "SCOPE Indexed Sequential Reference Manual," Control Data 6000 Computer Systems, For 60305400.
6. "Panda Disk File Usage Analysis System," Pansophic Systems, Inc., Oak Brook, Ill.
7. "SYSTEM 2000 Reference Manual," INTEL Systems Corp., Austin, Texas.
8. Lowenthal, E., "SYSTEM 2000 Performance Measurement and Data Base Evaluation," *Proceedings, 1975 ACM Conference*, Minneapolis, Minn., October 20–22, 1975, p. 50.
9. Major J., G. Galambos, and N. Dawalbi, "DBDCPERF Tool Documentation," IBM Canada, Eastern Region FSC.
10. Fernandez, S., R. Summers, and C. Wood, *Database Security and Integrity*, Addison-Wesley, Reading, Mass., 1981.

11. Griffiths, P. P., and B. W. Wade, "An Authorization Mechanism for a Relational Database System," *ACM Transactions on Database Sytems*, Vol. 1, No. 3, September 1976, pp. 242–255.

12. Everest, G. C., "Concurrent Update Control and Data Base Integrity," *Proceedings, IFIP TC-2 Conference on Data Base Management Systems*, April 1974, North Holland Publishing Co., Amsterdam, Holland.

13. Eswaran, K. P., J. N. Gray, R. A. Lorie, and I. L. Traiger, "The Notions of Consistency and Predicate Locks in a Data Base System," *Communications of the ACM*, Vol. 19, No. 11, November 1976, pp. 624–633.

14. Fossum, B., "Data Base Integrity as Provided by a Particular Data Base Management System," *Proceedings, IFIP TC-2 Conference on Data Base Management Systems*, April 1974, North Holland Publishing Co., Amsterdam, Holland.

15. Bernstein, P. A., D. W. Shipman, and E. Wong, "Formal Aspects of Serializability in Database Concurrency Control," *IEEE Transactions on Software Engineering*, SE-5, May 1979, pp. 203–216.

16. Gray, J. N., "Notes on Data Base Operating Systems," in *Operating Systems: An Advanced Course*, R. Bayer, R. M. Graham, and G. Seegmuller (eds.), Springer-Verlag, N.Y., 1979, pp. 393–481.

17. Kohler, W. H., "A Survey of Techniques for Synchronization and Recovery in Decentralized Computer Systems," *Computing Surveys*, Vol. 12, No. 2, June 1981, pp. 149–183.

18. Bjork, L. A., "Generalized Audit Trail Requirements and Concepts for Data Base Applications," *IBM Systems Journal*, Vol. 14, No. 3, 1975, pp. 229–245.

19. Gray, J., et al., "The Recovery Manager of the System R Database Manager," *ACM Computing Surveys*, Vol. 13, No. 2, June 1981, pp. 224–242.

20. Lohman, G., "Database Recovery," in *Principles of Data Base Design*, S. B. Yao (ed.), Prentice-Hall, Englewood Cliffs, N.J., 1984.

21. "CODASYL Data Base Administration Working Group, June 1975 Report," British Computer Society, London, England.

22. Weldon, J. L., *Data Base Administration*, Plenum, N.Y., 1981.

23. Martin, J., *Managing the Data-Base Environment*, Prentice-Hall, Englewood Cliffs, N.J., 1983.

24. Durell, W. R., *The Data Administrator's Handbook*, McGraw-Hill, New York, 1984.

EXERCISES

1. Consider a major objective of GDBMS: data independence.
   (a) Explain what data independence means.
   (b) Then provide a comparison of the relative degree of data independence possible in SYSTEM 2000 (or any inverted GDBMS), the hierarchic IMS, a DBTG system, and a relational model implementation. Provide

specific examples carefully selected to show the degree of data independence in these systems.

(c) What are the costs of data independence (do you achieve it for nothing)? Explain.

2. Suppose that a "data base expert" tells you that "DBTG systems provide a higher degree of data independence than IMS." Do you agree? Confirm or refute this statement convincingly. Justify your answer clearly by means of specific examples. Include at least five well-chosen examples using a sample data base that you are to diagram. Show your evidence with depth and clarity.

3. (a) Explain what "set membership" classes are in the DBTG data base architecture. Give an example of each.

(b) Consider now the relational data model. Are the problems addressed by the DBTG set membership eliminated by the relational model? Is the relational user shielded from them? Is the relational data base administrator shielded from them? Explain carefully.

4. In IMS, what is the purpose of "secondary data set groups"? Indicate the objectives. Are any of these objectives applicable in (a) the DBTG architecture? (b) the inverted-hierarchic architecture? (c) the relational architecture? Explain.

5. Suppose that an "expert consultant" tells you that an inverted network-oriented GDBMS is perhaps the closest relative of a relational GDBMS, closer than hierarchic and inverted hierarchic-oriented GDBMS. Do you agree or disagree? State your reasons.

6. Consider the logical and physical implementation aspects of relationships in relational and nonrelational GDBMS. Which of these two types of GDBMS consumes more storage space for implementing relationships? Explain.

7. Suppose that you are an expert consultant and someone tells you that "one of the great disadvantages of hierarchic GDBMS is that it is completely impossible (i.e., there is no way) to use them to handle a network data base" such as the following with the indicated record types:

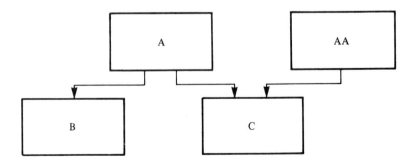

Do you agree with the statement for SYSTEM 2000? If not, refute the statement by showing how you can effectively do it. Explain and illustrate clearly for the above data base.

8. (a) Consider a "bill of materials" data base. What is it? Represent its logical structure in both IMS and a relational GDBMS. Strive for the best design.

    (b) Discuss the practical pros and cons of IMS versus a relational system for the bill of materials data base. Use a representative profile of data base accesses that may be posed. Which of the two systems performs better? Consider various aspects of "performance."

14
THE
DATA
DICTIONARY/
DIRECTORY

14.1 INTRODUCTION

A **data dictionary**, also called **data dictionary/directory** (and sometimes data catalog by some), is a centralized repository of data about data. It is a data base about the data bases and users of the data bases; this special data base is managed by the **data dictionary software system** or package and/or the GDBMS. We will use the terms data dictionary and data dictionary system interchangeably. Throughout this text we have dealt with directories that can also be considered dictionaries, for example, the ubiquitous directory of inverted fields in inverted systems. The latter, however, have been dictionaries used primarily by the software *internal* to the GDBMS. In contrast, the term data dictionary has evolved with data base development as a repository of *descriptive* data for direct use by the DBA and users, and, of course, by the GDBMS itself if it is used to manage and operate the data dictionaries as the DBA directs.

Data dictionaries have evolved and become popular rather recently as a result of the increasing size and complexity of data and information systems. In large organizations it is not uncommon to find application systems (e.g., an insurance policy-writing and inquiry system for several states) composed of several dozen programs totaling several hundred thousand lines of COBOL code; several hundred data field names arranged into several dozen record types; several dozen relationships between these record types; several data bases; several hundred reports being generated; dozens or hundreds of users; and dozens of computer professionals who maintain and expand the system.

When an organization starts using data base technology, the amount of data about data bases typically increases to such a degree and complexity that data dictionaries become a necessity. Even before evolving toward data base use, most organizations that have a significant data processing investment may realize that data dictionaries may already be a necessity. When evolving into data base utilization the need for data dictionaries becomes apparent. As a matter of fact, the data dictionary should be seriously considered the initial step toward properly designing and managing data bases and the associated applications.

There is no industry-wide data dictionary standard. In 1980 a CODASYL committee was formed to investigate the possibility and feasibility of a data dictionary standard. But by that time several dozen data dictionary products were already in use in hundreds of installations,[2] making the feasibility of an industry-wide standard difficult at best. Some vendors have developed data dictionaries to be essentially self-standing, that is, to be used by an organization without necessarily having to be used with a GDBMS. At the same time, such products have been provided with interfaces for use with the most popular GDBMS available. Popular data dictionaries of this kind are UCC-Ten by

University Computing Company, with interfaces for use with IMS data bases;[3] Datamanager by Management Systems and Programming Ltd. of London, capable of interfacing with a variety of systems;[4] and Data Catalog 2 by TSI International Corp., with interfaces to IMS, TOTAL, ADABAS, and DMS/1100.[5-7]

Data dictionaries should undoubtedly be a standard part of any GDBMS. Consequently, more and more GDBMS vendors are now marketing a data dictionary, with growing capabilities for use specifically with their GDBMS. So the choice to a user might be a data dictionary sold by the GDBMS vendor, or perhaps provided as part of the GDBMS, or a data dictionary by some competitor.

The availability, configuration, prices, and other general features of several major data dictionaries are summarized in Chapter 4.

A data dictionary package includes: a definition language for defining entries or entities to the dictionary; a manipulation language for inserting, modifying, and deleting entries; a means for validating the inputs to the dictionary; and a means to prepare the reports that are outlined later in this chapter.

14.2   STRUCTURE AND SCHEMA OF THE DATA DICTIONARY

Entities and Attributes

Since there is no standard, available data dictionaries exhibit differences. The differences are not only in the syntax and semantics of the data dictionary language and facilities but also in the types of entities and associated attributes that may be defined, that is, in the schema or data base structure of the data dictionary.

The most encompassing data dictionaries can contain information about and maintain relationships among entries in most of the following eleven categories:

1. Field or data item
2. File or record type
3. Data base schema
4. Subschema
5. Physical data base (e.g., IMS physical data base)
6. Transaction
7. Source document
8. Report
9. Program

10. System (e.g., insurance policy-writing system X)
11. User

Figure 14.1 shows major possible entries in a data dictionary.

Attributes may be defined as characteristics of each of the entities. For example, for the field or data item entity the following attributes may be included:

1. Name and synonyms
2. Authorization password(s) for retrieval, update, delete, etc.
3. Data type and format
4. Range of allowed values that may be stored
5. Units in which the entity is represented, e.g., feet, meters
6. Name of other entities that may initialize, update, or delete the data value
7. Programming language(s) for which it is written
8. Status, i.e., if the entity is in development, testing, damaged, or production status
9. Text (any text or comments may be written)

Some information that is defined as an attribute of an entity in some data dictionaries is defined as an entity in other data dictionaries. For example, the

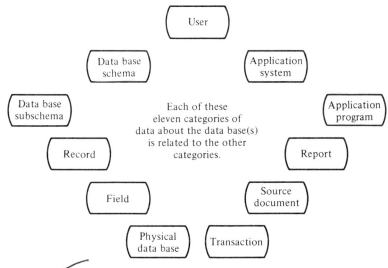

Figure 14.1. *Possible structure of an encompassing data dictionary: a data base of data bases*

"individual responsible" may be an attribute of entities, such as file, schema, and subschema in one case, or it may be an entity by itself but related to the other entities in another case.

A few data dictionaries allow definition of arbitrary entities, attributes, and relationships beyond those provided with specific names and meaning (e.g., those in Figure 14.1). As an example, a DBA may need to define the new entity "manual process" with the attributes name, description, department involved, frequency of performance, etc.

Relationships

Relationships may be envisioned among any or all of the entries that may be defined, as indicated in Figure 14.1. Any relationship could be 1 to N or M to N. For example, a user may use several subschemas and a subschema may have several users. Some data dictionary products allow definition of only certain relationships, namely, those most commonly used. The most general data dictionaries, such as those that use underneath a GDBMS, allow definition of any relationship between the defined entries.

Example 1: *Datamanager's Data Dictionary Structure and Relationships*

Figure 14.2 shows the data dictionary structure and direct (explicit) relationships that may be defined via Datamanager.[4] The segment entry is used in IMS and Mark IV environments. Some of the entries are considered "processes" and others "data." Available data dictionaries classify entities under various categories. In Datamanager any relationships may be established between entries, even recursively. In Figure 14.2 the recursive relationship denoted by straight-line segments indicates that a member may contain other members of the same type. The recursive relationship denoted by a circular line indicates that a member may *refer* to other members of the same type.

Example 2: *Global Description of an Organization's Information Systems*

Figure 14.3 shows an example of the data dictionary description of an organization's information systems. This pictorial and integrated description of the whole situation is much more convenient and visible than the equivalent description that is buried typically in several places: (1) the data descriptions in the schema and subschema data description language of the GDBMS and, if nondata base files are also used, in the programming language data descriptions, and (2) the application pro-

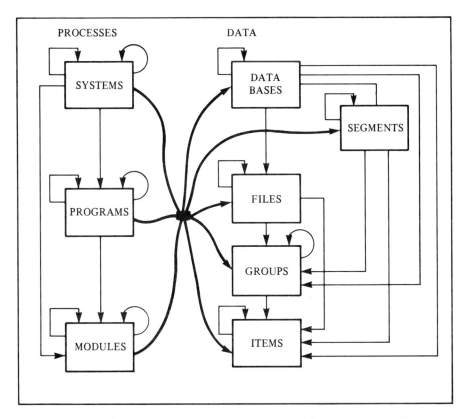

Figure 14.2.   *Direct relationships for process and data types that may be established in Datamanager (from Reference 4)*

gram description in possibly the text editor, librarian, or source code management system. The data dictionary provides a visible and centralized repository of all the entities, attributes, and relationships involved in an information systems architecture.

As an example of the data dictionary convenience, Figure 14.3 shows clearly that files F1 and F2 in data base schema SC1, and subschema SS1, are related to, i.e., include, data item I1. This is more readily visible than the equivalent indication buried in a schema description. See, for example, the CODASYL data base case in Section 5.3 where the schema program indicates that the data item EMPLOYEE NO (I1) is stored in the record type EMPLOYEE (F1) but appears also, as a virtual field, in CHILD (F2).

As another example, Figure 14.3 indicates that program P1, a part of system S1, makes use of the subschema SS1 and of the nondata base file FX. This would account for the System 2000 example COBOL application in Chapter 8.

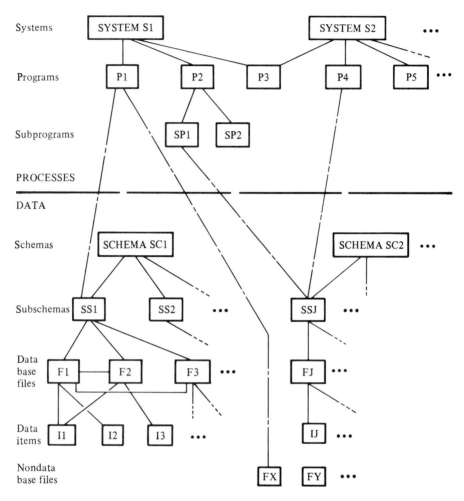

Figure 14.3.   *Data dictionary descriptions of an organization's information systems—an example*

Example 3: *Description of a System Including Manual Tasks*

Figure 14.4 defines and describes the types of entities and relationships in a given system. It is made up of several subsystems, each
of which is related to programs that perform the computerized tasks
and to the manual tasks that are needed to complete the subsystem function. The programs may point to component program modules or sub-

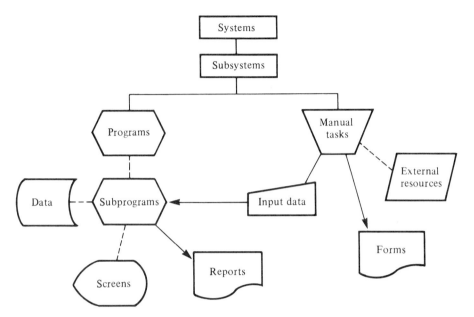

Figure 14.4. *Description of a system including manual tasks*

programs that are called and these may in turn point to the data bases or files that they access. The manual tasks may require access to data or to external resources (e.g., a government agency via telephone). The programs or the manual tasks may produce reports or require input transactions for their completion. Some subprograms may in fact be transaction processing modules operating on-line via certain preformatted screens.

Example 4: *Description Showing Relationships Between*
Data Base and Nondata Base Items

Figure 14.5 modifies the description of Figure 14.3 to include explicit relationships between data base and nondata base entries. Nondata base entries are those not under the control of the GDBMS. Program P1 uses item I1 via subschema SS1 and item X1, denoted by dashed lines. The relationship R1 could mean that data base item I1 affects, let us say, involves the use of item X1 when program P1 is processed; and R2 could mean that data base item I1 affects, let us say appears redundantly stored as Y1 (where Y1 is a field in the nondata base file FY).

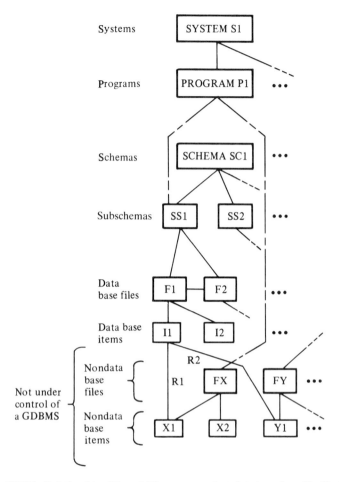

NOTE: Relationships R1 and R2 may mean that data base item I1 affects or involves the
use of items X1 and Y1 in files not under the control of a GDBMS. Program P1
uses I1, via subschema SS1, and FX, denoted by dashed lines.

Figure 14.5.   *Data dictionary description showing relationships between
data base and nondata base entries—an example*

14.3   USER OR SUB-DBA VIEWS OF THE DATA DICTIONARY

Analogous to the subschema facilities in a GDBMS, data dictionary
systems are evolving toward providing user or sub-DBA views of the data
dictionary. This is the result of the increasing number and complexity of the
data base/data communications-oriented information systems in organizations

and the consequent evolution of the DBA function to involve sub-DBAs or some users in acting as their own DBAs. Thus there is the need to limit and control the access to the descriptions of information systems and associated data base descriptions as well as the processing of these descriptions. Since there is no standard, the facilities and mechanisms toward this end vary a great deal from product to product.

14.4   QUERY LANGUAGE AND REPORT GENERATION

Most data dictionary systems provide user friendly, English-oriented, highly interactive languages for defining, updating, and manipulating the desired data dictionary structure. In the large majority of cases, particularly in those products provided by non-GDBMS vendors, the user or DBA dealing with the data dictionary does not have to deal with the data description, data manipulation, query language, and other facilities of a GDBMS. The interface between the data dictionary and GDBMS will be addressed in the following section.

The data dictionary package can produce reports on any or all of the entries in a category. The reports can show an entry's relationship with other entries within the same category, or with other entries in the other categories. The variety of reports that may be obtained are of direct help to the DBA, systems analysts, users, and programmers. The following are descriptions of some of the reports produced by typical data dictionaries. For example, all of these can be produced by Cincom's Data Dictionary[9] used in conjunction with the TOTAL GDBMS:

1. Listing of data base names and all file names or record names making up each data base.
2. Listing of file or record names and all data field names contained in each file.
3. Listing of field names and all attributes (e.g., data type, format) of each field.
4. Listing of field names and all alias names (synonyms) of each field.
5. Listing of fields and the editing assigned to them.
6. Listing of record names and the password assigned to each record.
7. Listing of field names and the password assigned to each field.
8. Listing of field names and the names of all application programs that use each field.
9. Listing of system names and all application programs that comprise each system.

10. Listing of application program names and all field names used in each program.

11. Listing of report names and all field names used in each report.

12. Listing of user names and all source document names controlled or received by each user.

13. Listing of user names and all report names controlled or received by each user.

The first seven reports may be obtained from any major GDBMS, although not necessarily via a high-level and interactive query language. The worth of the data dictionary becomes apparent through the usefulness of reports 8–13, which are not produced by the GDBMS. A GDBMS internal data dictionary deals only with the entities and attributes that may be defined via its schema and subschema DDL and device/media control language (or equivalent).

As an example of the reporting capabilities of robust data dictionaries, Figure 14.6 shows the query language definition in Data Catalog 2 for counting, listing the names, and showing the details of the qualifying entries indicated. The entries include entities for conventional file environments (i.e., nondata base environments using single files) and particularly UNIVAC DMS-1100 entities, i.e., CODASYL entities such as sets and areas. Let us look at some examples of interest to a DBA, auditor, system analyst, or user. Some of the following queries may be supported in various degrees by other robust data dictionary products:

1. Obtain a list of the names of all program modules that use the file SAVINGS-ACCT-FILE on a daily basis.

   LIST MODULES WITH SCYCLE = DAILY WHICH-USE SAVINGS-ACCT-FILE

   SCYCLE is an attribute of the module entity. This illustrates that searching may be on the basis of attribute values. Internally, many data dictionaries use inverted data base organizations to provide fast access by content.

2. List the entries used by the task called Verify-Order-Is-Valid. Here the task is a "manual process" entity type, Figure 14.4. It could be the

---

Figure 14.6.   *Definition of the count, list, and show query commands of Data Catalog 2, for DMS-1100, a CODASYL implementation (from Data Catalog 2, UNIVAC DMS-1100 Reference Manual, Courtesy of TSI International)*

The three commands COUNT, LIST, and SHOW can be used to display or print the number of qualifying entries, the names of the qualifying entries, and the details of the qualifying entries, respectively. Their use when applied to DMS-1100 entities is the same as for conventional file entries. Only the range has been changed: it is expanded. The expanded format is as follows:

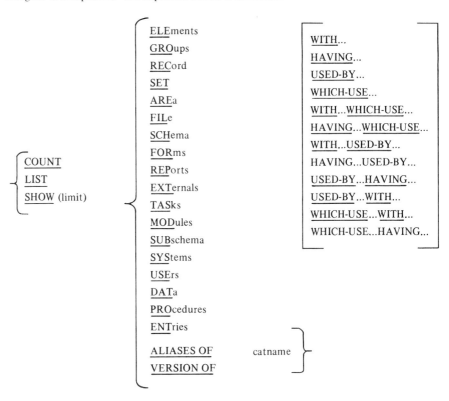

Where:

COUNT	indicates the response is to be a count of matched entries
LIST	requests a list of names of matched entries
SHOW	requests a detailed presentation of each matched entry
(limit)	is an optional output delimiting clause
ELEments through ENTries	is the range of entities that are to be scanned, including the DMS-1100 schema entities
ALIASES OF	requests the names of aliases
VERSION OF	requests the names of versions of
catname	a specific catalog name of an entry
WITH ... etc. ⟩ WHICH-USE...	a series of combinations of search arguments, all of which are fully explained in the Data Catalog Standard Facilities Manual

603

process of verifying the validity of an order via telephone or signed document.

> LIST ENT USED-BY VERIFY-ORDER-IS-VALID or
> LIST ENT USED-BY TASKS WITH NAME = VERIFY-
> ORDER-IS-VALID

3. Obtain a list of the modules written in COBOL that are involved in teleprocessing.

> LIST MODULES WITH LANGPRG = COBOL AND
> TYPE = TELEPROCESSED

LANGPRG and TYPE are attributes of the module entity that can take a number of alternative values.
4. Count the data fields or elements with length greater than 32.

> COUNT ELEMENT WITH LENGTH GT 32.

5. List and show the details (attributes) of any data fields or elements that have no connection with any other entries in the data dictionary.

> SHOW ELEMENTS HAVING NO REFERENCES

Any entry (report, subschema, etc.) can be similarly checked.
6. List the names of the entries in the data dictionary having no textual description.

> LIST ENT HAVING DESCRIPTION MISSING

7. List the names of the sets (CODASYL relationships) that are used by the subschema known as Market-Planning.

> LIST SETS USED-BY MARKET-PLANNING

8. List the name of the forms (form is an entity type) used by the system called Pollution-Distribution.

> LIST FORMS USED-BY SYSTEMS WITH NAME=
> POLLUTION-DISTRIBUTION

DBA Queries for Control of the Data Dictionary

Some specialized queries may be used by a DBA, especially when a number of other sub-DBAs or users may also be using the data dictionary directly. The two following examples illustrate these facilities specific to Data Catalog.

9. List the names of the entries that have been updated by the user AFC.

> LIST ENTRIES CHANGED BY AFC.

Data Catalog 2 can attach the updating individual's initial to all lines of data that the person changes.

10. Count the number of entries that were changed after 6/10/82 and also list the names of the subschemas that have been changed more than 50 times since they were added to the data dictionary.

> COUNT ENTRIES HAVING CHANGED AFTER 06-10-82
> LIST SUBSCHEMAS HAVING CHANGED MORE THAN
> 50 TIMES

Data Catalog keeps track of the last date on which an entry was updated and the number of times that it has been updated.

More complex reports

Many data dictionary requests may be of the on-line question-and-answer type, which are rather simple and suited for the data dictionary query languages, but other requests may be more complex or involve more information. Thus some data dictionary products also provide report-writing facilities to produce reports with more information and features such as formatting, column headings, etc. Some such reports may be a nicely formatted output of several pages for a final design document of an information system. For example, the output could be a report showing the hierarchical picture of the specific entities, their attributes and relationships involved for system S1 in Figure 14.3. Facilities are provided for limiting the types of entities that are to appear in an output.

In general, the data dictionary may list for each entry in each category a list of all the other entries in each category to which it is related. Thus the data dictionary package provides and manages a data base about data base and related categories (e.g., application programs). Since the data dictionary may be like any other application data base under the control of a GDBMS, one may perhaps use the GDBMS to generate reports tailored to unique information needs (e.g., list the field names and the users concerned with them for all fields that have alias names) not covered by the data dictionary.

Data Dictionary Audience

It is thus now clear that the data dictionary may serve different types of people in different ways: the DBA, users, auditors, systems analysts, and programmers. A data dictionary can tell managers and potential users what data might be used and who controls and uses it. It can tell programmers the precise formats of fields, records, subschemas, and schemas. The DBA can use it to spot data redundancies, inconsistencies, and unwarranted use of synonyms which surface as old systems are put in a data base environment or as new systems are being developed. Data fields that are essentially the same may have been used for years by various groups in slightly different ways, perhaps giving rise to different names and formats. Sometimes two separate objects (schemas, subschemas, records, fields, etc.) have been given by chance the same name or perhaps names which are too similar (e.g., AGE1 and AGE-1), thus causing confusion. These are just a few examples of real-life situations that may be brought into the open with the aid of a data dictionary as DBAs and application system specialists design, develop, or modify data bases and application systems. Comprehensive, standardized, up-to-date, centralized, and easy to use information and documentation on the data resource are essential to achieve good and cost-effective data base and information system design.

14.5 GENERATION OF DATA DEFINITIONS

A significant capability of data dictionary systems is the ability to generate automatically the data definitions for a GDBMS, a programming language, and perhaps a GFMS, through using the given entities, entity attributes, and relationships defined in the data dictionary. Schema and subschemas are generated for a given GDBMS. The file descriptions (FDs) and record structures for COBOL and the record declarations for PL/1 may be generated. The popular data dictionary available from a non-GDBMS vendor can generate definitions for several major GDBMS (but not all available ones), typically IMS, TOTAL, ADABAS, SYSTEM 2000, IDMS, and DMS-1100. Chapter 4 indicates the characteristics of major products from non-GDBMS vendors. GDBMS vendors provide some data dictionary products or aids that assist in generation of definitions only for their particular GDBMS.

Figure 14.7 outlines the process involved. First the DBA defines the desired entities, entity attributes, and relationships using the data dictionary language. Then the DBA requests the automatic generation of the corresponding data definitions for the particular GDBMS, programming language, or GFMS. Let us look at the attractiveness of this two-step process over the direct specification by the DBA of the definitions for the particular software package or compiler.

The definition of schemas and subschemas via the DDL in a particular GDBMS, and of file descriptions for a particular GFMS, may not be in a very attractive and user friendly manner. The same criticism can be made of conventional programming languages. Previous chapters have shown examples of schema and subschema definitions via the DDL of major representative GDBMS. Even if such definitions and changes to such definitions are done on-line, the syntax and semantics of the DDL may be rather tedious and procedural. The definition language of data dictionaries, however, is typically more user friendly, interactive, and nonprocedural. A data dictionary system provides an attractive alternative way of obtaining the required DDL specifications. The DBA can more easily define the entities, attributes, and relationships and then have the data dictionary generate the source code for the particular system taking care of the variety of uninteresting syntactic and formatting details. It is expected, of course, that all the major information of the schema or subschema declaration must be first defined via the data dictionary. For example, consider the CODASYL set membership clause Optional/Mandatory/Fixed. In UNIVAC's Data Dictionary System,[8] the DBA defines the desired membership as an attribute of the given set name; a set is an entity type that may be defined just like a schema, subschema, record, and so forth.

Looking at Figure 14.7, we see that it is possible for a less technically oriented DBA not to have to learn the uninteresting programming details and idiosyncracies of a particular DDL. Thus the DBA can concentrate more on "what" is being defined and less on the "how to define it."

In a typical organization, the growth of the data base usage is to such an extent that there may be several data bases, dozens of subschemas per data

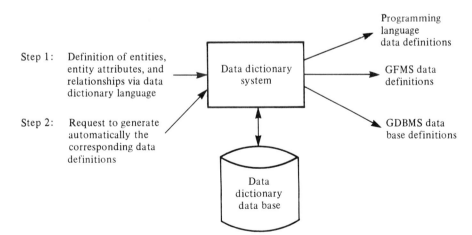

Figure 14.7.   *Generation of data definitions via a data dictionary system*

base, several hundred programs sharing the data bases, hundreds of users, and so on. In spite of all the data independence capabilities of GDBMS, there are some changes in the data descriptions that may require changes to many subschemas and corresponding application programs. For example, suppose that it is decided to change the name and particularly the format of a widely used field occurring in two data bases, e.g., increase the length of the field SN and name it Supplier-Name. A GDBMS, for example, a CODASYL system, would require the DBA to do the following:

1. Change the field description in the schema.
2. Find (typically manually) what subschemas must then be changed. Either the name, and perhaps also the format, of SN in the subschema is also changed, or else a clause is added to indicate that SN is the synonym of Supplier-Name to be used in the particular subschema.
3. Find (typically manually) what application programs use the data base field and see if there are field descriptions in the programming language data definitions that may necessitate changes. For example, there may be an image of the field description in the file descriptions in the GDBMS. The GDBMS does not manage such nondata base descriptions; it is up to the DBA to keep track of such connectivities.
4. Find out what reports generated are affected and take the appropriate measures.

These and perhaps other concerns will trouble and consume the time of any DBA. Task 1 is no problem. If a GDBMS does not provide a good library facility to be a repository for all GDBMS data definitions and is callable from any application program, then task 2 above will be tedious. Tasks 3 and 4 are not supported by a GDBMS. All of these tasks are easily done with the assistance of a data dictionary. For task 3, Figure 14.5 shows a sample data dictionary description including data base and nondata base entries that could be queried to indicate what nondata base items are affected by a change to the description of the given data base item; in this figure, say I1 denotes SN. With a data dictionary, (1) all data descriptions for both data base as well as nondata base processors are defined via one language and reside at one single place and (2) the data dictionary can generate the updated schema and subschema definitions for the particular GDBMS and the file declarations for the programming language and for the GFMS. Recall, however, that the generation supported by a data dictionary is at most for a few major GDMS (typically IMS, TOTAL, ADABAS, SYSTEM 2000, IDMS, and DMS-1100), for usually COBOL, PL/1, and BAL, and typically only for one GFMS, namely, Informatics' Mark IV.

14.6   IMPLEMENTATION OF DATA DICTIONARY SYSTEMS

The data dictionary system is a specialized data base management system. Entities and relationships can be defined; a data definition and high-level query language are provided; and so forth. The orientation of a data dictionary in terms of the data dictionary data base model and the type of data accessing or query language is often determined by the architecture of the GDBMS on which the data dictionary system may be built. Illustrative examples are IBM's data dictionary and UNIVAC's Data Dictionary System. IBM's data dictionary allows basically hierarchical-oriented data dictionary descriptions, as per IMS or DL/1, on which the data dictionary is implemented. A number of data dictionary systems, however, are not implemented on a given GDBMS. They embody tailormade data base management. Examples are Datamanager and Data Catalog 2. It may be observed in the marketplace that the flavor of a majority of the data dictionaries is that of a network and inverted-oriented specialized GDBMS.

It is obvious that any data dictionary description may be implemented on a GDBMS, as long as the description adheres to the data base model rules of the GDBMS. For example, any of the example descriptions in Figures 14.3, 14.4, and 14.5 may be implemented on a CODASYL GDBMS, but the convenience of the typically high-level, interactive, less procedural, and more user friendly data dictionary definition and query languages oriented toward data base administration will not be enjoyed.

In many GDBMS the essential descriptive information is buried in intricate syntax and idiosyncracies of the data definition languages; as an example, see the TOTAL data description in Chapter 6. Procedural data manipulation languages such as CODASYL's DML and IMS's DL/1 are not as convenient as the query languages typical of data dictionary systems to generate the kinds of data description reports needed. In addition, many specialized and useful features of data dictionaries are not present in GDBMS. Data dictionary systems have evolved to such a high degree in the 1980s that it is seldom cost-effective for an organization to build its own on its GDBMS to do the kinds of things typical of data dictionary practice.

It is a fact that in many large organizations there may be in use several programming languages, a GFMS such as Mark IV, and perhaps more than one GDBMS. This heterogeneity of software tools may be by design or, as is frequently the case, the result of lack of proper planning or control. In such a situation, it is practically a necessity to use data dictionaries that are independent of a particular GDBMS and capable of generating data descriptions for a variety of GDBMS and programming languages.

Curtice [11,12] and Lefkovitz[13] provide further details on a variety of data dictionary systems and practice.

14.7 SUMMARY

Data dictionary systems have evolved rather recently into an increasingly useful tool for DBAs, users, auditors, system analysts, and programmers. In cases where data bases and information systems achieve a high degree of evolution and sophistication, the data dictionary becomes a practical necessity. A data dictionary system is a specialized data base management system in which the data base is a repository of the *descriptive* information about the data in data bases or in traditional files, about the processing programs, and about other entities associated with information systems practice. The major types of entries or entities that may be defined in a data dictionary include: schema, subschema, record type, field, user, application system, program, subprogram, report, source document, and transaction. Other types of entities may be defined explicitly. In many cases, new entity types may be defined, for example, manual task. Each of these entities will have various attributes, such as name, textual description, status (e.g., test status, production status), author, date (e.g., date of approval, date of revision), and so forth. Relationships between these entities may be established.

There is no data dictionary standard. Thus existing data dictionaries exhibit differences with respect to (1) entities and particularly type of attributes and relationships that may be defined directly, (2) the facilities for defining these entries, (3) the query languages for obtaining needed information, (4) the variety of GDBMS for which data definitions may be automatically generated from the data dictionary descriptions, and (5) whether or not a GDBMS is used to implement the data dictionary (this remains somewhat transparent to the user, although not completely in all cases).

Data dictionaries continue evolving, some of them including functions performed by packages which other vendors consider separately. Most packages provide increasing facilities for generating the source language definition for data structures required by the programmers, conversion from file definitions to dictionary formats, generation of test data files for system testing, and so forth.

REFERENCES

1. Gradwell, D. S. L., "Data Dictionary—Why Data Dictionaries?" *Database*, Vol. 6, No. 2, March 1975, pp. 15–18.

2. Allen, F., Loomis, M. E., and M. V. Mannino, "The Integrated Dictionary/ Directory System," *ACM Computing Surveys*, Vol. 14, No. 2, June 1982, pp. 245–286.

3. "Data Dictionary and Manager—UCC Ten," Reference Manual, University Computing Company, Dallas, Texas.

4. "DATAMANAGER FACTBOOK," Management Systems and Programming Ltd., London, England, and Lexington, Mass.

5. "Data Catalog 2, System Overview," TSI International, San Jose, Calif.

6. "Data Catalog 2, Standard Facilities Manual," TSI International, San Jose, Calif.

7. "Data Catalog 2, Reference Manual, UNIVAC DMS-1100," Synergetics Corporation, Bedford, Mass.

8. "Data Dictionary System (DDS1100)," Sperry-Univac Computer Systems.

9. "TOTAL Data Dictionary System," Cincom Systems, Cincinnati, Ohio.

10. "Integrated Data Dictionary User's Guide," Cullinet Software, Westwood, Mass.

11. Curtice, R., and E. Dieckman, "A Survey of Data Dictionaries," *DATAMATION*, Vol. 27, No. 3, 1981, pp. 135–158.

12. Curtice, R., "Data Dictionaries: An Assessment of Current Practice and Problems," *Proceedings, 7th International Conference on Very Large Data Bases*, Cannes, France, 1981.

13. Lefkovitz, H. C., *Data Dictionary Systems*, Q.E.D. Information Sciences Inc., Wellesley, Mass., 1977.

EXERCISES

1. Suppose someone tells you that a data dictionary/directory system (DD/DS) is not really needed since with a GDBMS you can do anything that you can do with a DD/DS. What would be your pragmatic response to this?

2. Suppose your organization has ended up having several GDBMS: a CODASYL type, a relational type, and IMS. Since not all applications, data bases, and users are entirely insulated from each other, various problems have started to arise and users are getting upset about some of them.

   (a) What are some of the problems that you expect users are facing in this scenario?

   (b) Can data dictionary/directory systems help? How can they?

   (c) Is a GDBMS-independent data dictionary/directory the way to go in such a heterogeneous environment? Explain.

15
DATA BASE
MACHINES

15.1 INTRODUCTION

Several major trends can be cited for the emergence of data base machines not only as a subject of study but also as a new commercially available product line of the 1980s for data base management:

1. The evolution and growth of data base management needs. There has been a tremendous growth in terms of the following:
    (a) The number and size of data base;
    (b) The number and types of programmed applications;
    (c) The number and types of on-line users; and
    (d) The number of transactions per unit time on a data base.
    Current demands for acceptable data base performance are now being envisioned for environments that involve the following:
    (a) One or many data bases, some involving a small number of bytes and others exceeding the gigabyte range.
    (b) Many programmed applications involving not only the traditional business function applications to which most GDMS have been applied in many organizations but also new scientific and engineering applications, image and video applications, office automation applications, and so forth.
    (c) A growing number of on-line users through thousands of terminals, with a larger majority being end-users rather than professional programmers or analysts.
    (d) An explosive growth in the number of transactions, or data base accesses, growing in many organizations into thousands or tens of thousands transactions per minute.
2. The evolution and maturity of GDBMS. In the 1970s and early 1980s many of the earlier GDBMS matured in terms of:
    (a) The basic functional capabilities required by the marketplace and
    (b) An understanding of the internal GDBMS alternatives and performance trade-offs.
    Traditionally, all GDBMS introduced in previous chapters are implemented in software. Due to the maturity and consequent stability of GDBMS, it is now feasible to consider hardware-based implementation and tailoring of system software such as operating systems, etc. for data base management functions.
3. Advances in computer hardware architecture, especially VLSI and microprocessor technology, and in its price and performance. The

cost of memories, CPU processors, terminals, and communications devices has dropped and will continue to drop drastically, often accompanied by added functional capabilities. Thus designers have been able to implement functions in hardware that are traditionally carried in software.

4. Advances in data communications. Communications from computer to computer, via satellite links, via optical fiber technology, etc., have emerged; so have local networks linking dozens of computers and nonlocal networks linking many very large computer centers.

These pressures, advances, and opportunities led various researchers since the mid-1970s[1-12] to investigate the possibility and feasibility of allocating the functions now being executed by software on a general-purpose computer to special-purpose data management hardware. This data management hardware may offer orders of magnitude performance improvements over what is now achieved via software. These specialized functional units have generally become known as **data base machines**. A Data Base Machine (DBM) can be defined as any hardware, software, and firmware complex tailored to the performance of some or all of the data base management tasks of a computing system. A DBM can be anything from an intelligent terminal to a general-purpose computer dedicated to data base processing. We will see the range of DBM architectures in the next section.

A great deal of research and prototype development has been devoted to the configuration of DBM. Significant research and prototype projects can be cited, particularly DBC,[2,3] RAP,[6,7] CASSM,[8] DIRECT,[13,14] NDX-100.[3,4] These pioneering DBM designs and other efforts provided much of the base leading to significant advances in data base machinery commercially introduced in the 1980s.

In this chapter we will outline the following commercially available products: Britton-Lee's Intelligent Database Machine IDM,[15,16] Amperif's RDM-1100,[17] and Intel's SYSTEM 2000-FAST 3805 Data Base Assist Processor DBAP.[18,19] These initial and pioneering products are representative of the wide range of data base machinery. The Intel Data Processor iDBP[20] is another pioneering product along the lines of IDM and RDM-1100.

The textbook by Hsiao, the first text focusing exclusively on data base machines, provides further details beyond this chapter.[27]

15.2   LIMITATIONS OF CONVENTIONAL COMPUTERS FOR DATA BASE MANAGEMENT

The following are frequently cited as limitations of conventional computers for the purpose of GDBMS processing:

1. Mismatch of current (Von Neumann) computer architectures with data base needs.
2. Operating system/GDBMS conflicts.
3. Unintelligent I/O.
4. Software size and complexity.

Let us address each of these briefly.

Computer Architecture

The conventional general-purpose computer architecture is frequently not well-suited for major needs of data base applications because it focuses on numerical calculations. The numerical computations (add, subtract, multiply, etc.) differ from the basic operations required to better support data base applications (search, retrieve, update, etc.). The use of computers primarily oriented toward numerical calculations or number-crunching is a mismatch for many of the data base applications. Much overhead and complexity in software is involved in translating data base instructions and executing them using the base operations of the conventional computer.[12]

Operating System/GDBMS Conflicts

Conflicts frequently exist between the optimization goals of an operating system (OS) and a GDBMS. Operating systems have been designed to optimize the use of system resources for a certain mix of uses and users: batch and on-line applications, FORTRAN-like and Algol-like types of programs, array and matrix computations, file management or nondata base applications, and so on. The problem is that the typical OS design has not been biased sufficiently toward, or at least taken sufficiently into account, the data base client. Two examples can be cited: the efficient management of virtual memory (if it is a virtual memory machine) and the physical placement of data on external storage.

A conflict may arise when a well-designed GDBMS attempts to keep frequently used disk pages in main memory. The OS, in optimizing the use of the virtual memory by all its clients, may swap these pages out, thus creating more overall system work than if it listened to the desires or look-ahead know-how of the GDBMS.

Another conflict may arise over the control and optimization of placement of data on external storage. To optimize access to data, it is advantageous for the GDBMS to control the physical placement of data on external storage to a greater extent than is permitted or even possible in the operating system. An example is the convenience of placing certain different record types close together such as for the following type of query: provide all supplier and related part information for suppliers with characteristics a, b, ..., and with part characteristics x, y, ... Another example is the case for placing indexes [inverted indexes, B-trees, doubly-chained trees, and so forth (see Chapter 2)] near the data that they reference most frequently. An OS, on the other hand, will probably try to distribute stored data in order to utilize all resources as efficiently as possible. Other examples can be cited, particularly for less robust and flexible OS. The result is that most GDBMS software must be given special privileges by the OS and must play the role of its own operating system. This adds to the problems of size and complexity.

Unintelligent I/O

In data base applications very often the identification of data elements required for processing depends on the values of other elements. With the conventional Von Neumann architecture, all data processing is performed in the host computer and each data element must be processed sequentially, one at a time. If, for example, the query "list the total of salaries for employees earning more than $50,000 and in departments 10 and 11" aimed at the data base in Figure 11.8 is to be serviced, all the disk pages or blocks that contain the appropriate salary information for employees in those departments must be transferred to main memory. The host computer must then search each page to locate the specific records and compute the total of salaries. All of the pertinent data pages must be moved from external storage to main memory, thus impacting the I/O channels as well as the CPU.

It is often said that in conventional GDBMS on conventional computers usually 90 percent of the data bytes retrieved from external storage leads to no more than 10 percent of the data requested by a query or transaction.[3]

A DBM can reduce this channel I/O and much of the CPU processing by moving some of the GDBMS intelligent workload to external storage. Thus only those records that satisfy the where clause specification need to be sent to the host for processing. An even greater reduction could be achieved if some of the processing capability were off-loaded from the host processor so as to provide the host computer only with the requested information, in our example the total of salaries for employees earning more than $50,000 and in departments 10 and 11.

Software Size and Complexity

The growth in data base management capabilities and sophistication expected by users has brought on a growth in size and complexity of the internal GDBMS software required. Common user requirements that illustrate this are error detection and correction, backup and recovery, integrity controls, automatic data base restructuring and system tuning, automatic data migration through various types of storage (from archival storage to main memory), and so forth. All of this results in tremendous software size and complexity and its consequent reliability and overhead problems. Today's robust GDBMS are larger and more complex than the average operating system.

15.3   TAXONOMY AND RANGE OF DATA BASE MACHINE APPROACHES

Different taxonomies can be used to classify the variety of DBM hardware systems proposed.[3,11] Let us see the range of data base machinery and system configurations that may be envisioned to support data base management beyond the conventional general-purpose data base system shown in Figure 15.1.

1. *Back-end computer dedicated to data base management.* See Figure 15.2. All GDBMS tasks are off-loaded to the back-end and the host computer is freed to run application tasks rather than managing the data base and its storage devices. This back-end computer can be either (a) a standard general-purpose computer with a GDBMS or (b) a tailored computer with data base management, as shown in Figure 15.2. The tailored computer option could involve, for example, tailoring the operating system for data base interests and/or microcoding some of the GDBMS software.

2. *Intelligent I/O and controllers or associative processors.* See Figure 15.3. These processors provide several levels of data base searching and manipulation. Such devices may involve one or several microprocessors, parallel processing, and very large storage areas, as we shall describe. The **associative processor**; also called **content-addressable processor**, relieves the general-purpose host computer of logical to physical mapping. In this configuration the host computer serves as the GDBMS base in several levels.

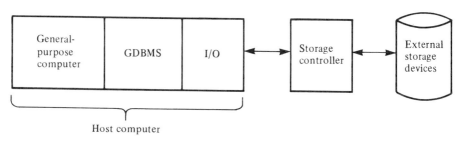

Figure 15.1. *Conventional general-purpose data base system*

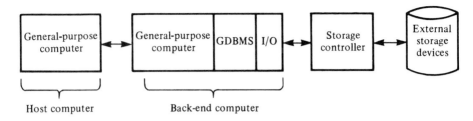

(a) With general-purpose back-end computer

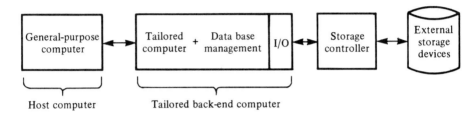

(b) With tailored back-end computer

Figure 15.2.   *Host computer with back-end computer*

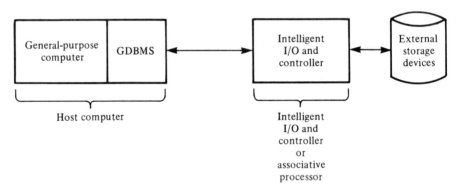

Figure 15.3.   *Host computer with intelligent I/O and controller or associative (content-addressable) processor*

3. *Back-end computer plus associative processor.* See Figure 15.4. The
    GDBMS tasks are off-loaded from the host computer. Here the
    back-end computer can be either (a) a standard general-purpose
    computer with a GDBMS or (b) a tailored computer with data base
    management, as shown in Figure 15.2.

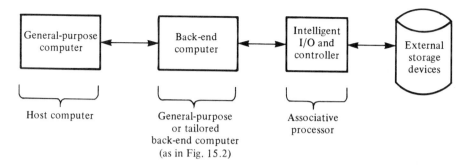

Figure 15.4. *Host computer with back-end computer and associative processor*

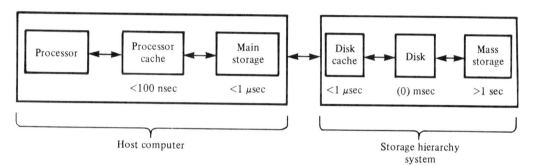

Figure 15.5. *Host computer with storage hierarchy*

4. *Storage hierarchies capable of easily migrating data along the hierarchy.* See Figure 15.5. The new memory technologies (bubble memory, CCD, etc.) which fill the cost-performance gap between and around the traditional main memory and external storage are used to implement a disk cache. This cache memory is slower, but cheaper, than main memory; and it is faster, but more costly, than external storage. The cache is managed so that disk pages most often used by the host (either a general-purpose computer or perhaps back-end computer) tend to remain in the cache and thus reduce page swapping. At the base of the storage hierarchy are Mass Storage Systems (MSS) which provide very large data base storage on the order of $> 10^{11}$ bytes with average access times on the order of a few seconds; MSS provide much larger storage but are slower than disk storage.

5. *Multiple-hosts with back-end DBM.* See Figure 15.6. In this computer network environment several hosts are served by a backend DBM which could involve any of the above four types of hardware. There could also be more than one back-end DBM serving the hosts. In this environment some host computers could have their own GDBMS and data bases in addition to relying on the back-end machine. Figure 15.6 also displays two popular environments: (a) "distributed processing" (several processors with data residing primarily in the back-end) and (b) "distributed data base processing" (several processors with data bases residing in several processors). We will address these two environments in Chapter 16 while in this chapter we will focus on DBM interests. Contrast Figure 15.6 with Figures 16.2, 16.3 and 16.4.

The major thrust of DBM is to increase the performance of installations with heavy data base requirements. A primary motivation for the DBM is that it may be an economic and attractive alternative to the consumption or upgrading of the host computer for data base management. In this light, let us pragmatically examine each of the above approaches and cite any commercial product support, if any. Lasting commercial product support is an indication of the feasibility and success of the approach.

The host computer with a general-purpose back-end computer configuration shown in Figure 15.2(a) was the first approach of early experiments[10] and of some initial commercial support.[21] The traditional primary selling point of this approach is that the attachment of a minicomputer dedicated to data base management to an existing mainframe computer is significantly cheaper than the consumption or upgrading of the larger mainframe for data base management. However, very little commercial support and production installations can be cited for a single-host with general-purpose back-end. Although the recent and strong commercial support for the so-called distributed data base or multiple systems coupling (MSC)[18] addressed in Chapter 16 includes solid support for the single-host with general-purpose back-end configuration, the interest and success of MSC are in distributed data and not in DBM. Thus, our focus in this chapter is not on general-purpose machines used exclusively for data base management but on machines *designed* or *tailored* for this task, or some portion of it.

The host computer with a tailored back-end computer configuration shown in Figure 15.2(b) became a commercial reality in the 1980s (although only for widely used host computers) with the introduction of the Britton-Lee IDM, the Amperif RDM-1100, and the Intel iDBP DBM. The RDM-1100 is basically the IDM with another shield. These two also utilize some disk cache elements (see Figure 15.5). These two products are presented in Section 15.4.

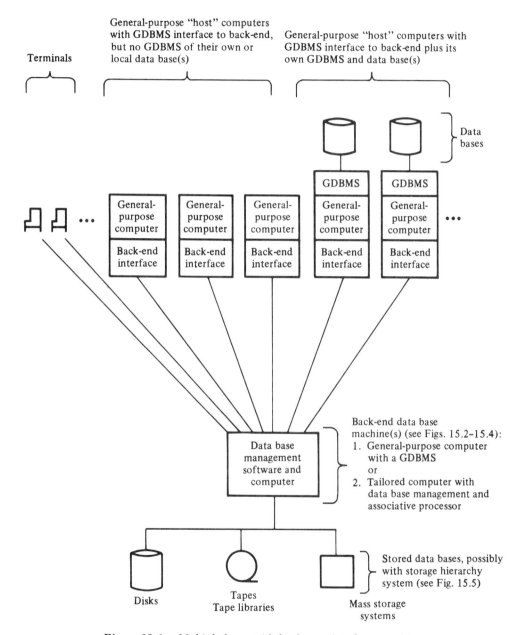

Figure 15.6. *Multiple-hosts with back-end data base machines*

The host computer with the intelligent I/O and controller configuration shown in Figure 15.3, or at least the beginning of it, became commercially available in the 1980s. The Intel SYSTEM 2000-FAST 3805 DBAP is an example of primarily this DBM approach complemented with semiconductor technology used as a disk cache.

The configuration shown in Figure 15.4 of a computer with tailored back-end computer and intelligent I/O and controller functions may become available commercially as the initial commercial offerings evolve and/or as the current research efforts become a commercial reality. It is expected that the demand for the high end of data base performance and throughput spectrum in large installations may result in commercial products along these lines and with more hardware intensity.

More hardware intensive implementations of the previous configurations, such as those proposed by research efforts largely conducted in universities,[2,3,6,8,13,23,27] are generally not yet commercially available. However, some initial commercial thrusts are expected in the near future. We will focus on these in Section 15.6.

15.4   THE INTELLIGENT DATABASE MACHINE IDM

Britton-Lee Inc. introduced the Intelligent Database Machine (IDM) in 1981.[15,16] It is an integrated hardware/software back-end computer dedicated to data base management. [See Figure 15.2(b).] The IDM is housed in a chassis measuring a mere 16 by 24 by 12 inches that is connected between front-end systems and conventional disks. Front-end systems can be intelligent (OEM programmable) terminals and/or host general-purpose computers. Hardware and programming language software interfaces are available for DEC PDP-11 and VAX computers with VMS and UNIX operating systems and for the IBM Personal Computer and the 3XXX and 43XX computers with the VM operating system.

The IDM was designed to be a low-cost, high-performance machine to support "mid-range" users:[15]

1. The price for end-users ranges from $35,000 to $150,000 and reflects the hardware and software options outlined below. The commonly installed configuration is in the upper price range. The price range is lower for OEM vendors who will embed the IDM in their systems.

2. The target data base accessing load is from 100 to 1,000 transactions per minute, where a transaction is a data base access rather than the execution of an application program which is done on a host computer.

3. The data base size can be up to several dozen gigabytes.

4. Standard moving head disks are used, although a disk cache feature is included.

The IDM is not intended for users who need extremely high transaction rates. Other more hardware intensive designs, such as those covered in Sections 15.6, are aimed at such users. If, however, the users deal with smaller data bases and lower transaction rates, then a host computer with its GDBMS might suffice.

The IDM contains a relational data base management system. From the logical point of view it is an outgrowth of the University of California, Berkeley, relational system INGRES which is very similar to SQL/DS presented in Chapter 10. IDM's Intelligent Database Language (IDL) is available for on-line data base creation, accessing, and modification. Interface software is available for data base management from application programs written in major programming languages (COBOL, FORTRAN, and C) executed in host computers. The IDM is not a general-purpose computer, does not have programming language compilers of its own, and hence does not execute application programs. Figure 15.7 briefly outlines the IDM software features.

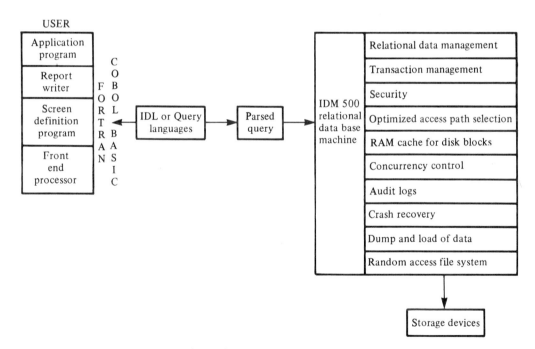

Figure 15.7.   Software features of the Intelligent Database Machine (IDM)

IDM includes robust capabilities for schema and subschema definition, data base retrieval and updating, security, concurrent accessing of a data base by multiple users, and large data bases (maximum of 32,000 tables per data base; 250 columns per table; 2 billion rows per table; row width of 2000 bytes).

Figure 15.8 shows the IDM hardware architecture. Each component shown is a simple board that plugs into the IDM bus. The following are the IDM highlights:

1. It is a dedicated data base computer whose operating system is specifically designed for such tasks.

2. It has several LSI microprocessors (data base processor, data base accelerator, and so forth), including Zilog Z-8000 microprocessor(s).

3. The data base processor is a general-purpose microprocessor that coordinates the overall IDM and executes most of the software.

4. The data base accelerator is a 10 MIPS pipeline microcomputer designed specifically to execute the most frequently used and time-critical data management functions. The DBMS code supporting such functions (e.g., memory transfer) totals under 4K and is micro-coded. Functions implemented in this microcode include: validating a query, searching tables for rows that qualify, deleting a row, locating a stored command, and sorting. The data base accelerator is an optional feature; in its absence the data base processor performs its functions. The data base accelerator board costs about twice as much as a microprocessor board but results in a 30 times increase in performance for the set of code it is designed to perform.[15] Such trade-offs are inherent in special-purpose architectures such as the DBM. There is no need for the accelerator for a small data base transaction rate. In most cases the accelerator can complete processing of a page by the time the page has been completely read in (the page size used is 2000 bytes).

5. Standard moving head disks are used (CDC SMD disks).

6. The indexing method used to optimize data base access time is the B-tree. Any or all of the columns of a table may be indexed. Up to 15 columns may be concatenated for an individual index. One of the indexes of each table may be clustered, that is, all rows of a table having the same value in the indexed column(s) are physically placed close together.

7. The random access memory (RAM) cache is used to speed up disk page referencing. Pages most frequently rereferenced are placed in the cache. Performance is improved if a disk page is referenced more than once in a reasonably short time. The RAM cache buffers disk pages and stores indexes, data dictionary information, programs and

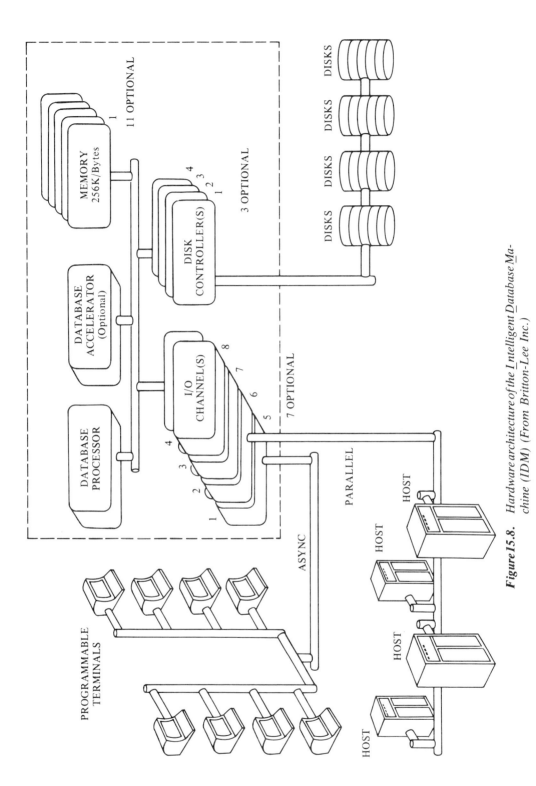

Figure 15.8. Hardware architecture of the Intelligent Database Machine (IDM) (From Britton-Lee Inc.)

627

data to process user commands, and locking information to support concurrent data base use.

Field comparisons of the performance of IDM versus all-software relational systems comparable to IDM, e.g., INGRES, show that for a variety of applications the IDM can provide orders of magnitude improvement in data base access time (in read and nonread operations); at the same time, the CPU utilization of the host by the all-software GDBMS is reduced by factors of 15 and more. Thus if the value of host CPU saved, the increase in data base throughput, and the cost of the host GDBMS itself added together are sufficiently larger than the cost of the IDM, then the IDM is an attractive alternative. This is the fundamental argument for a DBM. The IDM is not as attractive for relatively small data base processing loads or for a number of particular data base intensive applications with certain data base accessing features that may not be a good match to the IDM design.[22]

The RDM 1100

The RDM 1100[17] introduced by Amperif Corp. in 1982 for use with UNIVAC 1100 host computers and Amperif disk drives uses internally under its covers the Britton-Lee IDM. Figure 15.9 shows the RDM-1100 configura-

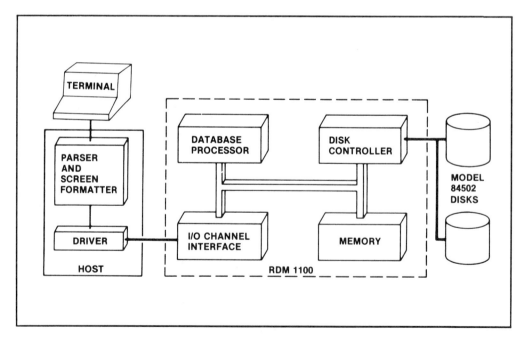

Figure 15.9.   *Configuration of the data base machine RDM 1100 (From Amperif Corp.)*

tion. Interface software for the host computer to utilize the RDM-1100 is available and requires no modification to the UNIVAC operating system. Callable interfaces from programming languages are available. A Relational Query Language provides a high-level, on-line interface to the RDM 1100. Underneath is the IDM with basically all the functional features covered above. Thus Amperif, as an OEM, takes the IDM and provides the necessary interface and appearance to its host computer(s), terminals, and disks. Translators provided by Amperif translate from RQL to the internal IDM query language. Such translation is of a primarily cosmetic and syntactic nature. Thus an OEM provides the desired "personality software" and interfaces.

Similar commercial introductions of DBM for other brands of host computers and peripherals are to be expected, using underneath the IDM, the Intel iDBP, and the likes available for OEM vendors to embed in their systems.

15.5 THE SYSTEM 2000-FAST 3805 DBAP

Intel Corp. introduced the SYSTEM 2000-FAST 3805 Data Base Assist Processor (DBAP) in the early 1980s.[19,20] It is intended to be used with a host computer and exemplifies the configuration in Figure 15.3, complemented with the use of a disk cache. The SYSTEM 2000 GDBMS covered in Chapter 8 resides in the host mainframe (IBM). The Intel FAST (Fast Access Semiconductor Technique) 3805 used is a semiconductor disk memory emulating standard large IBM disks, except that it provides faster access to data, on the order of .4 milleseconds versus more than a few milleseconds for standard disks, and faster transfer rates. The 3805 provides user storage capacity of up to 72 megabytes, and will undoubtedly provide much more in the future.

The primary memory device in the 3805 is a 16K-bit RAM. The RAM memory has been a primary component in the main memory of every major computer manufacturer. This MOS solid-state memory technology involves no electromechanical movement and provides higher reliability. For high reliability the 3805 incorporates one- and two-bit error correction; for further data integrity a 48-bit CRC code is appended to each record. In addition, an internal single-board computer performs preventive and corrective maintenance tasks such as relocation of data in case of significant failure.

Intel's DBAP option for the FAST 3805 works in concert with SYSTEM 2000 and improves the data base throughput rate and response time by several orders of magnitude. The use of the 3805 DBAP is transparent to users of a data base, except for increased performance. The 3805 option, as illustrated in Figure 15.10, represents an extension of SYSTEM 2000. SYSTEM 2000 has been enhanced to maintain strategic data base index and record location data on the 3805 and to allow user selected portions of files of one or more data bases to be staged from conventional disks to the 3805 DBAP. All user requests are processed via the 3805 prior to any access to the actual data base which is

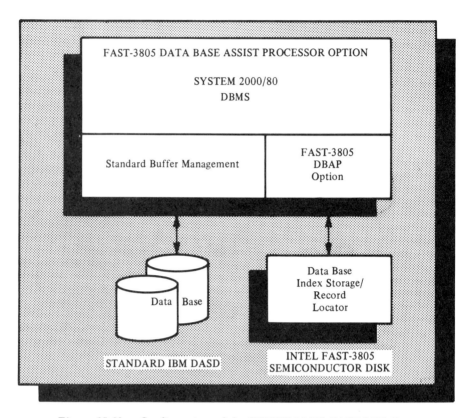

Figure 15.10. *Configuration of the SYSTEM 2000-FAST 3805 Data Base Assist Processor (DBAP) (From Intel Corp.)*

maintained on standard disks. When the SYSTEM 2000 buffer manager algorithm needs to read data into main memory, it will obtain it much faster if it resides in the 3805. For every data base update, the buffer manager will write the new buffer to both the conventional disk and the 3805 DBAP, overlapping the writes in order to minimize the impact of updates.

The data base designer controls the 3805 DBAP by specifying the files to the DBAP files. One or more inverted index files (SYSTEM 2000 uses the inverted approach as indicated in Chapters 2 and 8), and data base files from one or more data bases can be stored in the 3805 DBAP. Only the capacity of the 3805 (expected to grow into greater than hundreds of megabyte ranges) limits the amount of information stored there. Read/write activity of a data base varies according to the application. Applications that use complex where clauses extensively benefit when the inverted index files are in the 3805 DBAP. Applications that use extensive related record retrieves (that is, use extensively relationships defined between files in the schema) benefit when these files reside in the DBAP 3805. System performance is best when the files stored are read more than they are written.

15.6 PARALLEL CONTENT-ADDRESSABLE DATA BASE MACHINES

Higher performance DBM for higher data base transaction rates than those achieved by commercially available DBM presented in previous sections will require the use of very fast external storage (RAM, bubble memory, fixed-head disks, and so on) and/or mechanisms to search in parallel disk areas. The electromechanical nature of the traditional disks, pages, mass storage system, and so forth, binds data accessing to speeds that are orders of magnitude slower than an all-electronic external storage technology. The serial retrieval of disk pages to be subsequently searched and processed by usually single processors is certainly a frequent bottleneck. In this section we shall address more hardware intensive DBM referred to as **parallel content-addressable DBM** or **parallel content-addressable processors** whose architecture is designed to perform a number of data base operations in parallel on portions of the data base.

A major data base transaction is to search for records based on data contents, for example, "list the name, department, and salary of employees who owe more than $5,000 and who live in Beverly Hills." In commercial GDBMS and in the commercial data base machines IDM and SYSTEM 2000-DBAP this entails software programs using various techniques (e.g., inverted techniques, B-trees) to search, locate, and obtain the qualified data. Depending on how the schema is structured, the query might involve the use of the join operation. In the content-addressable processor approach this task would be done more directly with hardware search mechanisms, that is, the hardware would search for data based on its content. However, hardware support could go beyond the task of record searching by content and support, for example, the implementation of the relational join which is one of the most time-consuming data base operations.[3]

One of the important factors in the feasibility of parallel content-addressable DBM is the advance of microprocessor hardware and storage device technology to provide for less expensive processors and memory with faster data transfer rates. Although present technology may limit the use of such processors to relatively small data bases, i.e., hundreds to thousands of megabytes of shared data, the rapid technological advances are making it more feasible to manage larger data bases. These advances are expected to attain efficiency and economy by cost-effective use of very large-scale integration and related hardware technology. Microprocessor advances along the lines of Intel's 80XX, Zilog's Z-80, and Motorola's 68000 and further advances are enhancing hardware intensive DBM approaches, and so are computer memory chip advances such as 64K RAMs and more powerful future RAMs.

Figure 15.11 shows a model of the configuration of a parallel content-addressable data base processor. In this system, users may have access to the data base through a set of general-purpose host computers. The data base processor controls all the access to the data base and transfers the results of a query to the users through the set of general-purpose computers. The data base processor consists of a supervisor and a number of special-purpose area proces-

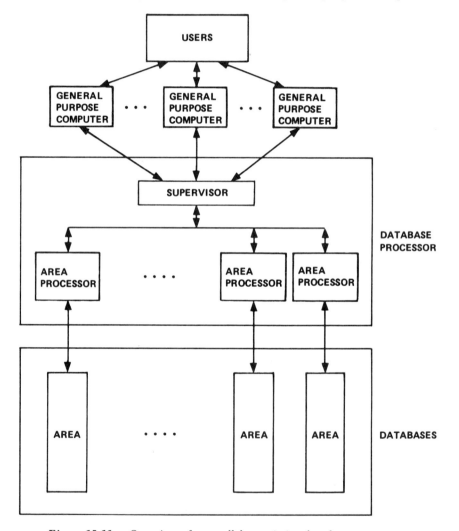

Figure 15.11.   *Overview of a parallel associative data base processor*

sors. The whole data base is divided into areas (e.g., disk track), and an area processor is assigned to each area. In general, the area processors are responsible for searching the areas; and the supervisor is in charge of the coordination between the area processors as well as the handling of the general-purpose computer interface and task scheduling. Various interface and task scheduling problems such as concurrency controls for updating shared data by multiple processors will have to be addressed by an implementation of this architecture.

Each processor executes the same basic data base retrieval and updating operations on an area or subset of the data base. The supervisor issues the commands to the area processors and assembles the individual responses into the result of the data base request for transmission to the host(s). All processors operate on the same data base request in parallel. The expectation is that the concurrent execution of the individual commands will result in an overall increase in throughput. Various studies show that the response time of a DBM is very dependent on the type of data base and data base request.[7,14,22,24] Beyond this, not all studies agree on the details. Some indicate that simple retrievals and updates are well-suited to simultaneous execution by multiple processors; however, an operation such as cross retrieval involving processing records (rows) sequentially may not be performed significantly better than in single processor configurations.[7] Other studies show that the use of different parallel content-addressable DBM features gives better performance for complex multifile (multitable) queries than for simple retrievals from a single file.[14] The actual commercial implementation and use of these designs will settle many of these issues.

Hardware intensive DBM approaches have been proposed and are being investigated, particularly DBC,[2,3] RAP,[6,7] CASSM,[8] DIRECT,[13,14] NDX-100,[23,24] and others being kept rather confidential in vendor environments and even in user environments. The architecture of the general model in Figure 15.11 represents "processor-per-track" machines described in the literature[6,8] and being investigated.[25] For example, in RAP[6] the memory part of a cell is the same as an area, and the processing part of a cell is the same as an area processor. The combination of the controller and the set function in RAP is represented by the supervisor in the general model. In CASSM[8] a segment and the combination of the processing logic and the read and write heads are represented by area and area processors in the general model, respectively. The user-CASSM interface computer is represented by the supervisor in the general model.

In the general model a number of mark bits are associated with each record. The purpose of these bits is to qualify a record if it satisfies a search criteria. Each area processor consists of a read mechanism, a write mechanism, a buffer, and a processing part. All area processors perform the same operation which is synchronized by the supervisor.

In each area the records are read into a buffer by the read mechanism and are written back on the area by the write mechanism. The revolution time of an area is the time taken by an area to have its entire content traversed by an area processor. For example, if an area consists of a disk track, the revolution time of an area is the time taken by the disk track to go around an area processor and return to its original position. Operations are performed on the records while they are in the buffer. If the records satisfy the search criteria, their mark bits are turned on. To retrieve the records during the first set of revolutions, the qualified records are marked; then, in the next set of revolutions, the records are actually retrieved. The number of revolutions depends on the number of mark bits, the sophistication of the area processors, and the complexity of the search criteria.

To delete the records, the qualified records are first marked and then flagged as deleted. The physical deletion of the records is performed by a garbage collector. To insert a new record, it must first be created in the buffer by the supervisor and then written in the appropriate area by the write mechanism.

The NDX-100 Machine

The NDX-100 "electronic filing machine"[23,24] is an initial prototype system of the hardware intensive class. Its architecture features a few or many microprocessors operating in parallel, concurrently, on a common data storage area in conventional random access devices. For the NDX-1100, Figure 15.11 applies when modified as follows: there is one storage area accessed by all the microprocessors concurrently, rather than separate areas each assigned to a given processor.

The NDX-1100 considers the inverted organization for a file, as per Chapter 2 and in particular as per Cardenas' model (Reference 25 in Chapter 2). When a query with any complexity as defined in Appendix B is to be processed, the NDX-1100 assigns to it a set of microprocessors available from a pool of microprocessors used to service queries. This pool contains dozens of microprocessors. Depending on the level of query complexity, different numbers of microprocessors are assigned to perform in parallel, where possible, the subtasks to answer the query that are otherwise performed sequentially in a single processor computer.

As an example, consider the sample query of complexity "query condition" in Appendix B and directed to a single file or table:

LIST . . . WHERE [(AGE>18) AND (SEX=FEMALE)] OR
[AGE>20) AND (SEX=MALE) AND (CLASS=SENIOR OR
CLASS=GRADUATE)]

This query may be serviced by several microprocessors, each executing in parallel different portions of this query. For example, one set of microprocessors may be working on the first part of the where clause [(AGE>18) AND (SEX=FEMALE)] and obtaining from external storage the data blocks that qualify; another set of microprocessors may be working in parallel, with respect to the previous set, on the rest of the query.

Orders of magnitude improvements are shown by the NDX-1100's highly concurrent and microprocessor intensive architecture over the sequential and single processor support with a conventional general-purpose computer.[26]

15.7   HARDWARE INTENSIVE GENERAL-PURPOSE PROCESSING SYSTEMS

Highly hardware intensive general-purpose computing systems have been recently introduced commercially to satisfy requirements for very high performance and reliability. An example is in banking applications where the data base may be millions of records of checking and savings accounts supporting thousands of distributed terminals and several computing centers. In a way, such computing systems may be viewed as multiprocessor DBM if we stretch the definition of a DBM. However, they are designed as general-purpose, multiprocessor, distributed computing systems that happen to satisfy some of the operating requirements that DBM happen to share in the high performance and reliable spectrum.

A pioneering product is the Tandem Non-Stop System introduced in the early 1980s.[26] The key thrust of this complete general-purpose processing system is high performance and reliability. Figure 15.12 shows its basic hardware structure and the duplication of components in the system. It consists of from 2 to 16 processor modules. Each module is a self-contained traditional mainframe with a CPU, main memory, and an I/O channel. The Inter-Processor Bus (IPB) interface provides communication between the processor and its peers in the system. The bus itself can be duplicated for fault tolerance. I/O device controllers can accept input from two different processors. Only one processor at a time has control of a controller, but if that processor fails, another processor, designated as the backup to it, takes over the on-going task with no need for a complete restart. This provides fault tolerance in the disk controllers. Fault tolerance at the disk level is also available by writing data in duplicate on two different disk drives to protect against head crash losses and interruption in service.

The Tandem System includes a relational GDBMS. An application program or terminal activity is considered a process. A process is always assigned to two processors, the primary processor and the backup processor. The

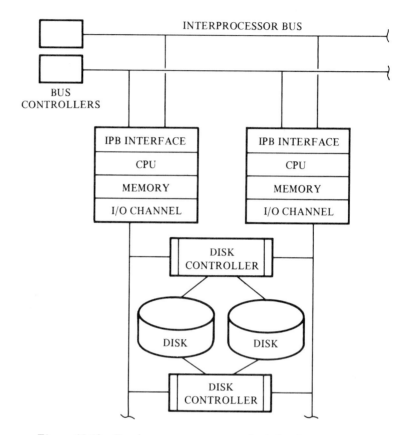

Figure 15.12   *Tandem computer system basic hardware structure*

primary processor does all the necessary work and provides frequent check-points. If the main processor fails, the backup processor detects it and takes over as the primary processor. When the failed processor is repaired, it becomes the backup.

This architecture provides intriguing possibilities for data base applications in two areas: high performance and reliability. It should be considered versus a data base machine and versus a GDBMS on a conventional computer. It is possible to establish a single controlling process that would allocate tasks (data base processes) to be executed concurrently on as many processors as necessary. This is very similar to the way the DIRECT DBM[13] is designed to operate.

REFERENCES

1. Parhami, B., "A Highly Parallel Computing System for Information Retrieval," *Fall Joint Computer Conference*, Vol. 41, December 1972, pp. 681−690.

2. Banerjee, J., D. K. Hsiao, and K. Kannan, "DBC—A Database Computer for Very Large Databases," *IEEE Transactions on Computers*, Vol. C-28, No. 6, June 1979, pp. 414−429.

3. Hsiao, D. K., "Database Computers," in *Advances in Computers*, Vol. 19, Academic Press, New York, 1980.

4. Yau, S. S., and H. S. Fung, "Associative Processor Architecture—a Survey," *ACM Computing Surveys*, Vol. 9, No. 1, March 1977, pp. 3−27.

5. Langdon, G., "A Note on Associative Processors for Data Management," *ACM Transactions on Database Systems*, June 1978, Vol. 3, No. 2, pp. 148−158.

6. Ozkarahan, E. A., S. A. Schuster, and K. C. Smith, "RAP—Associative Processor for Database Management," *Proceedings National Computer Conference*, 1975, Vol. 44, pp. 379−387.

7. Ozkarahan, E. A., et al., "Performance Evaluation of a Relational Associative Processor," *ACM Transactions on Database Systems*, Vol. 2, No.2, June 1977, pp. 175−195.

8. Su, S. Y., and G. J. Lipovski, "CASSM: A Cellular System for Very Large Databases," *Proceedings, International Conference on Very Large Data Bases*, September 1975, pp. 456−472.

9. Lin, S. C., D. C. Smith, and J. M. Smith, "The Design of a Rotating Associative Memory for Relational Database Applications," *ACM Transactions on Database Systems*, Vol. 1, No. 1, March 1976, pp. 53−75.

10. Maryanski, F. J., "Backend Database System," *ACM Computing Surveys*, Vol. 12, No. 1, March 1980, pp. 3−25.

11. Champine, G. H., "Backend Technology Trends," *IEEE Computer*, Vol. 13, No. 2, February 1980, pp. 50−58.

12. Su, S. Y. W., H. Chang, G. Copeland, P. Fisher, and S. Schuster, "Data Base Machines and Some Issues on Data Base Standards," *Proceedings, 1980 National Computer Conference*, Vol. 49, AFIPS Press, Arlington, Va., 1980, pp. 191−208.

13. Dewitt, D. J., "Direct-A Multiprocessor Organization for Supporting Relational Database Management Systems," *IEEE Transactions on Computers*, Vol. C-28, June 1979, pp. 395−406.

14. Hawthorn, P., and D. J. Dewitt, "Performance Analysis of Alternative Database Machine Architectures," *IEEE Transactions on Software Engineering*, Vol. SE-8, No. 1, January 1982, pp. 61−75.

15. Epstein, R., and P. Hawthorn, "Design Decisions for the Intelligent Database Machine," *Proceedings, 1980 National Computer Conference*, Vol. 49, AFIPS Press, Arlington, Va., 1980, pp. 237−241.

16. "IDM, Intelligent Data Base Machine Product Description," Britton-Lee, Inc., Los Gatos, Calif.

17. "The Relational Database Machine RDM-1100," Amperif Corp., Chatsworth, Calif.

18. "System Description, Intel's Information Resource Management Product Family," Intel-MRI Systems Corp., Austin, Texas.

19. "FAST-3805 Semiconductor Disk," Intel Corp., Phoenix, Ariz.

20. "Intel Database Processor (iDBP), System Summary," Intel Corp., Austin, Texas.

21. Cullinane, J., R. Goldman, T. Meurer, and R. Navarawa, "Commercial Data Management Processor Study," Cullinet Software, Westwood, Mass., December 1975.

22. Hawthorn, P., "The Effect of Target Applications on the Design of Database Machines," *Proceedings, ACM SIGMOD Conference*, Ann Arbor, Mich., April 29–May 1, 1981, pp. 188–197.

23. Slonim, J., L. J. McRae, N. Diamond, and W. E. Mennie, "NDX-100: An Electronic Filing Machine for the Office of the Future," *Computer*, Vol. 14, 1981, pp. 24–36.

24. Slonim, J., L. J. McRae, R. A. McBride, F. J. Maryanski, E. A. Unger, and P. S. Fisher, "A Throughput Model: Sequential vs. Concurrent Processing," *Information Systems*, Vol. 7, No. 1, Pergamon Press, New York, 1982, pp. 65–83.

25. Cardenas, A. F., F. Alavain, and A. Avizienis, "Performance of Recovery Architectures in Parallel Associative Database Processors," *ACM Transactions on Database Systems*, Vol. 8, No.3, September 1983, pp. 291–323.

26. "Tandem Non-Stop System Description Manual," Tandem Computers, Inc., Cupertino, Calif.

27. Hsiao, D., *Advanced Data Base Machine Architecture*, Prentice-Hall, Englewood Cliffs, N.J., 1983.

EXERCISES

1. You are called by a large company to consult on the following situation. The company has recently embarked on major new applications, many of which access new data bases being established. The existing computer capacity is no longer sufficient. The computer vendor says that an upgrade in CPU and external storage systems is needed, but several data base machine (DBM) vendors say that what is needed and is most cost-effective is to buy a data base machine to off-load the main CPU. What do you recommend needs to be examined and quantified, and what is your decision methodology, in order to arrive at the most cost-effective solution for the company?

2. Do you agree that the most fair and realistic experimental comparison of the performance merits of a data base machine (DBM), such as the Britton-Lee machine, and an all-software GDBMS, such as INGRES, on a general-purpose computer A is as follows:

   (a) Take a series of different data base queries.

(b) Measure the time taken by the GDBMS on a dedicated A to answer only the data base queries.

(c) Measure the time taken by the DBM connected to a dedicated A to answer the data base queries.

(d) Compare the corresponding access times. Assume that the same channels and disks are used in the DBM as in the dedicated A.

Explain. Is the above experiment the most favorable, or biased, toward (a) DBM or (b) the software GDBMS? Or (c) is it equally favorable (i.e., fair)? Justify your answer.

16

DISTRIBUTED DATA BASES AND PROCESSING

16.1 INTRODUCTION

Several major trends can be cited in the emergence and interest in distributed data bases and processing in the 1980s:

1. *Economies of scale.* Traditionally, computing facilities (CPU, main memory, external storage devices, and so forth) have tended to be centralized. Thus files and data bases have been largely centralized. A major reason has been economy of scale. Traditionally, more computational power and storage per dollar could be obtained in a larger computing facility employed in a centralized configuration than in smaller computing facilities used in a decentralized configuration. In the 1980s, however, the traditional economy of scale advantage has been increasingly diminished by significant technological and price/performance advances in minicomputers, microcomputers, and distributed systems technology. At the same time, economies of scale still tend to favor significant centralization of EDP talent and personnel and facilities management.

2. *Advances in data communications in the 1980s.* Communications from computer to computer, via satellite links, optical fiber technology, and so on, have emerged. This permits establishing:

   (a) Local networks linking a few or many computers; and

   (b) Nonlocal networks linking a few or many distant computer centers.

3. *Evolution and growth of data base needs.* Technological advances in GDBMS software have been accompanied by a tremendous growth in the following:

   (a) The number and size of data bases;

   (b) The number and type of programmed applications;

   (c) The number and different types of on-line users;

   (d) The number of transactions per unit time on a data base;

   (e) Demand for high reliability and availability of data;

   (f) Demand for incremental growth in computing and data resource capacity;

   (g) Demand for supporting data types not traditionally stored in a data base system (e.g., pictorial and voice data);

   (h) Demand for supporting a data base distributed over several heterogeneous GDBMS.

4. *Computerization of society in the 1980s.* A computer revolution is occurring in society, with the emergence of personal computers and

the increasing contact of all segments of society with computing facilities (video/home computers, banking terminals, point-of-sale terminals, ticket reservations terminals, and so on). This has contributed greatly to the growing interest of user groups in organizations, and sometimes of entrepreneurial politics, in decentralization of computer facilities and applications development and in a more "hands-on" and local autonomy environment.

These developments, opportunities, and pressures have led to the possibility and feasibility of distributing—to different degrees—processing functions, data resources, and computing facilities, which traditionally have been largely centralized. The terms **distributed processing** and **distributed data bases** are used with a wide variety of meanings. There is a wide range or spectrum of possible distributed processing and data base configurations. Section 16.2 presents this spectrum and focuses on the disposition of computer processors, GDBMS, and whole data bases. Section 16.3 addresses the distribution of both a data base schema and data base contents, including possible redundant storage of data. Section 16.4 addresses the distributed heterogeneous data base scenario, in which the distributed data may be managed by different GDBMS. The range of distributed data base management opportunities, challenges, and commercial support is highlighted in this chapter.

The different scenarios presented compose the spectrum of alternatives starting from a traditional centralized processing and data base approach toward a highly distributed processing and distributed data base approach. Each alternative has its advantages and disadvantages. The interests and goals of an organization, its users, and EDP professionals may dictate selecting different degrees of distribution at different times for different data bases and applications.

In a nutshell, the goal of a **distributed GDBMS** (D-GDBMS) is to support a network in which any user in any node can be given an integrated and tailored view or subschema; in reality, the data may reside in one single data base, in logically and physically separated data bases, or in a single logical data base but physically separated across the network, with perhaps some data redundantly stored. The D-GDBMS should provide this kind of **distribution and network transparency** such that the same data views and queries directed at a centralized data base can be directed at a distributed data base without burdening the user or application with having to know the details of physical data distribution or networking. Network and distribution transparency is desired for the same reasons that it is desired to relieve the user from having to know in what physical storage and via what channels and I/O controllers a given data element is available. The terms network transparency and distribution transparency imply each other. Data independence, a major objective of GDBMS, in its broadest sense, also includes network and distribution transparency. In a distributed heterogeneous data base environment, the transparency should also extend to permit accessing data as if it were managed by a single GDBMS, while in reality the data resource is managed by different GDBMS.

The differences between centralized and distributed approaches are not in function but in the economics of implementation, reliability, and the extent of local autonomy:

1. Communications costs and delays may be lower for distributed data bases, sometimes several orders of magnitude lower than for the centralized case. This is because, in the distributed approach, most communications between users and their data can be local if the data base is assigned to the proper network nodes. In contrast, in the centralized alternative most data communications are over expensive long-distance network links. However, advances in very large bandwidth communications (e.g., via satellite) and accompanying price/performance may offset the attractiveness of distribution.

2. The distributed approach offers potentially more reliability and resilience to failure than the centralized approach, because in the distributed case there is redundant equipment, communications, and perhaps even data; the loss of a single node does not bring down the network or the availability of all data.

3. The distributed approach can provide more local autonomy. The data bases can be loosely coupled and separately managed, and therefore organizational domains and interests may be preserved. In this mode, network sites may control and perform all operations on their own data and share different portions of this data to different degrees with other sites.

Since the late 1970s much effort has been devoted to considering and investigating the possibilities and feasibility of distributed data bases and processing.[1-14] In the late 1970s TANDEM computers introduced its highly distributed and pioneering hardware architecture with a distributed operating system including the beginnings of distributed data base management capabilities.[16] (See Section 15.7.) A number of efforts point the way toward commercial D-GDBMS in the near future to provide the higher degrees of distributed data base management now in research and development stages. These include initial commercial GDBMS support for some degree of distribution[15-20] and prototype GDBMS efforts for higher degrees of data base distribution.[4,6,8,9] Research and development efforts in the distributed heterogeneous GDBMS scenario[11-14,20] are also leading toward some initial degree of commercial support for it, providing transparency of GDBMS heterogeneity,[13,20] in addition to network and distribution transparency.

16.2 SPECTRUM OF DISTRIBUTED PROCESSING AND DATA BASE CONFIGURATIONS

In this section we focus on the disposition of processors, GDBMS, and whole data bases. The following scenarios of distributed processing and/or distributed data bases can be envisioned:

1. *Centralized processing and centralized data base, with no significant distribution of processing or data,* as shown in Figure 16.1. All application program execution and all data base management occur at the central processor. The GDBMS and the data base(s) reside in the central processor. Local terminals and remote terminals access the central data base in the central processor. If the terminals are "intelligent" terminals, they may perform some minimal processing (e.g., application program invocation and preanalysis, data entry functions) and hold some limited data (e.g., I/O data in buffers). This is the traditional scenario in which GDBMS technology has evolved, and which is well supported commercially.

2. *Distributed processing and centralized data base,* as shown in Figure 16.2. Multiple computers are now connected to the central computer. Application programs are executed at either the central computer or at another local or remote computer. These other computers are typically less powerful than the central one (but need not be), and thus the larger or more demanding applications will tend to be processed at the central computer. All data base management occurs at the central computer. The GDBMS and the data base(s) reside in the central processor only. However, either small or large volumes of non-

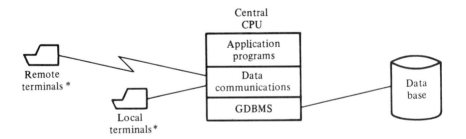

* "Intelligent" terminals may perform some minimal processing (e.g., application program invocation, data entry functions) and hold some limited data (I/O data buffers).

Figure 16.1.   *Centralized processing and data base environment with no significant distributed processing or distributed data*

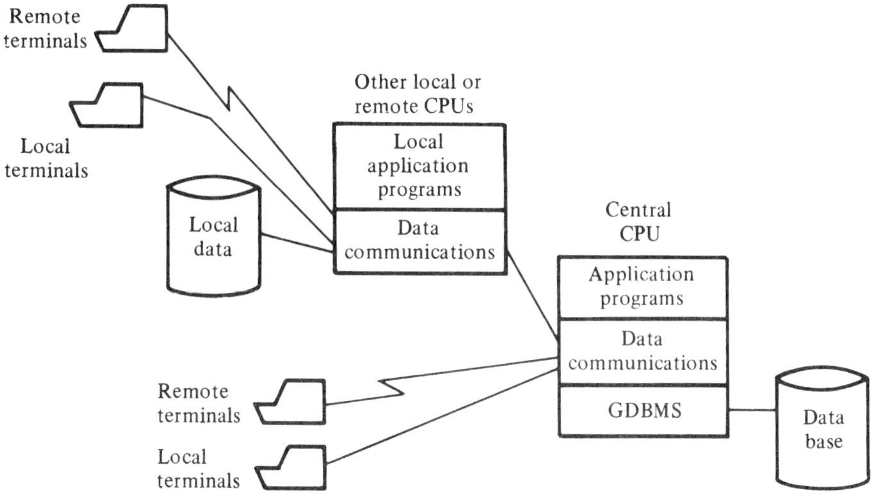

Figure 16.2.   *Distributed processing environment with data base(s) centralized at a single CPU*

GDBMS data may reside and be processed locally at each of the computers involved. Thus some authors may refer to this as a "distributed processing and distributed data or file" environment. However, it is not a distributed *data base* environment. This configuration is similar to the data base machine configuration, referred to as "host computer with general-purpose back-end computer" in Chapter 15. Initial commercial support for the configuration in Figure 16.2 became available in the 1980s[15-19] as part of the commercial support for the following scenario.

3. *Distributed processing network with data base(s) at a single CPU*, as shown in Figure 16.3. Multiple computers are interconnected in any arrangement, not just as in the previous scenario. In contrast, here there is little or no notion of which is the central computer. Application programs are executed at any of the participating computers. All data base management occurs at any of the network nodes selected to host the GDBMS and the data base(s). In addition, small or large volumes of non-GDBMS data may reside at, and be processed locally at, each of the computers involved. Some authors and vendors supporting this scenario refer to it as one of distributed processing and distributed data. Again, it is not a distributed *data base* environment.

   Each CPU wishing access to the data base(s) residing elsewhere, or wishing to permit other CPUs access to its local data base(s), hosts an interface software module called (initially by GDBMS vendors[15,17]) **Multiple Systems Coupling** (MSC). See Figure 16.3. The

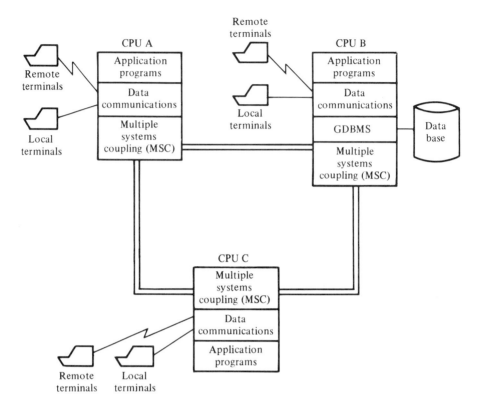

Note: Any number of CPUs can participate in the network; each CPU can be located at a remote site or several CPUs can be located at the same site.

Figure 16.3.   *Distributed processing network with data base(s) at a single CPU*

MSC is a generalized module that is usually developed by the GDBMS vendor and is architecturally a part of the GDBMS supporting this environment. The tasks of the MSC include the following:

(a) Holding data dictionary/directory information on where and what data is available to the computer hosting the MSC.

(b) Forwarding requests for remote data from a terminal or application program at its host computer to the computer where the data resides. The data base request may be sent directly to the data base, as from CPU A to CPU B in Figure 16.3; or it may be routed via other computers, as from CPU A to CPU B via CPU C.

(c) Serving as a router for data base requests that originate in other computers but are routed through the computer hosting the MSC, as mentioned in item b.

(d) Coordinating all data base communication with one or several computers.

(e) Maintaining network transparency, if desired, for a terminal user or application program such that the physical location of data or access paths to that data (via the network or internal to a data base) are hidden from the user or programs. Of course, performance penalties will be incurred in reaching data located in a distant computer as (but not in reaching data located in the host computer).

4. *Distributed processing and data base network with separate data bases at several CPUs*, as shown in Figure 16.4. As in the previous scenario, multiple computers are interconnected in any arrangement, there is little or no notion of a central computer, application programs are executed at any of the participating computers, and small or large volumes of non-GDBMS data may reside and be processed locally at each of the computers. In contrast to the previous scenario, here the GDBMS and data bases may reside in several or all the participating computers.

The tasks of the MSC cited for the previous scenario apply equally to this scenario. Now, however, an application program or terminal user could be requesting data residing in different data bases residing in different computers. In Figure 16.4 the following examples may be envisioned:

(a) A terminal user signs on CPU A and requests access to data via two subschemas, one on data base 1 and the other on data base 2. The MSC knows where these data bases reside, sends the request to the appropriate CPU, receives the response to the request from CPU B and CPU C, and presents the response to the user. The intent of network transparency is to hide all these access path or location concerns from the user.

(b) An application program executing in CPU A requests access to local non-GDBMS data and to data base data via two subschemas. These two subschemas could be defined on one of the data bases or on both.

(c) A terminal user invokes, say at CPU B, an application program residing in another CPU, say CPU C, and activates it to process at CPU C. This application program may request data via one or more subschemas, each of which may be at local or remote data

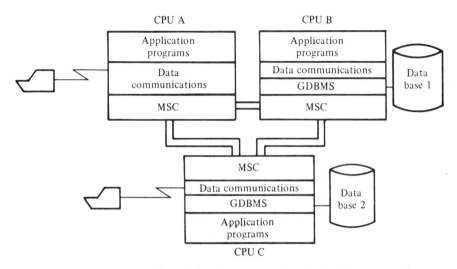

Figure 16.4. *Distributed data base network with data bases at multiple CPUs*

bases. Thus the following may occur in this sequence: request from B to C to start execution of an application at C, request from C to B to access data base 1, data response from B to C, request form C to K to access some other data base and its response to C, . . . , and finally response from C to B to the original invocation by the terminal user at B. Thus the user at B may not even be aware that the application program invoked made use of data base 1 at B or elsewhere.

In all of the above scenarios involving multiple computers, and in Section 16.3, each computer can be located physically at a remote site or several computers can be located at the same site. Any desired geographical distribution of the network nodes is envisioned in a distributed environment.

There may also be little distributed processing and much distributed data in the scenario in Figure 16.4. For example, although the data base contents might be spread evenly over all computers, most of the application load may be limited to processing on a few very large computers. This might be the case in some environments where the protection of data and resilience of data to failures, or to destruction of sites and communication lines, is a major objective.

16.3   LOGICALLY AND PHYSICALLY DISTRIBUTED DATA BASES

16.3.1   Framework

Section 16.2 portrays the distribution of data and processing macroscopically: the distribution of processors, GDBMS, and *whole* data bases. Let us now examine in detail the range of possible distribution of a data base schema and its contents, and the types of accessing that may be envisioned, in

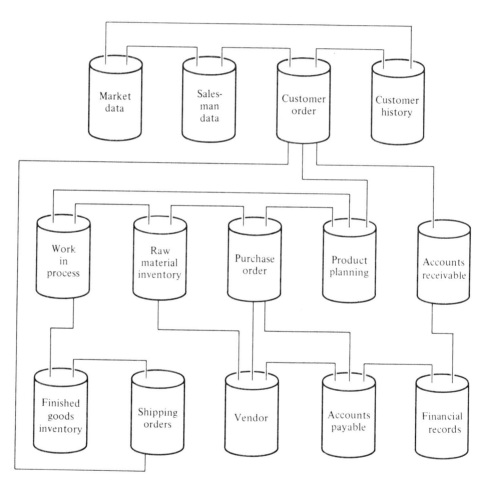

Figure 16.5. *A major data base*

the fourth scenario above. Much of the more advanced data base distribution and accessing presented in this section is not yet commercially available. Major problems and research challenges will be indicated.

We will use the major data base shown in Figure 16.5. This is the same as the one shown in Figure 2.15 and is reproduced here for convenience. Most of the entries shown are for a real-life data base at a major corporation. Figure 16.6 shows three sample subschemas or user views. Figure 16.7 shows a sample of data base contents viewed through subschema A. Figure 16.8 shows a sample of reasonable data base accessing and processing queries that may be directed at subschemas A and B. These examples and the foregoing discussion will not be bound to any specific GDBMS. It is applicable to any GDBMS environment. The queries will be expressed in plain English.

The scenario portrayed in Figures 16.5 through 16.8 is handled well by any major GDBMS when the data base and the GDBMS reside in the same

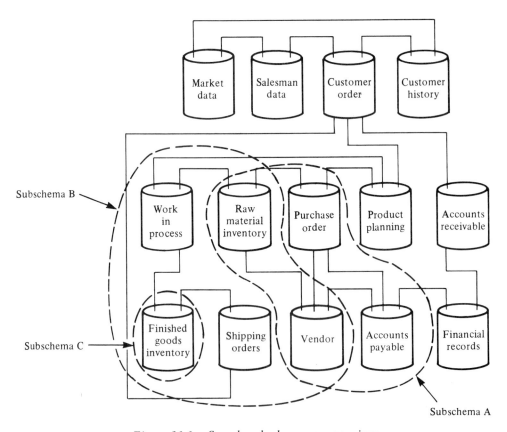

Figure 16.6. *Sample subschemas or user views*

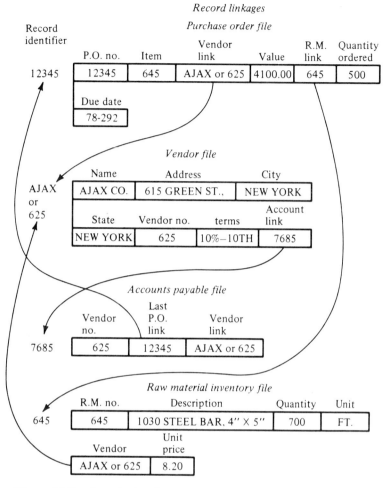

Figure 16.7.   *Sample data base contents viewed through subschema A in Figure 16.6*

computer. This data base/computer pair could be in any of the environments shown in Figures 16.1 and 16.2 or in the computer network environments shown in Figures 16.3 and 16.4. Let us now go beyond the distributed data base scenario in Figure 16.4.

It is practically attractive to consider the following types of distribution:

1. Distribution of the *contents* of the data base but with the same logical schema wherever such contents are distributed; call this type 1 distribution.

```
EXAMPLE DATA BASE USER REQUESTS


ON SUBSCHEMA A:


A1    LIST VENDOR DETAILS ASSOCIATED WITH PURCHASE
      ORDER # 12345

A2    LIST PURCHASE ORDER DETAILS ASSOCIATED WITH
      VENDOR WHOSE NAME IS AJAX CO.

A3    WHAT VENDOR(S) SUPPLY US WITH RAW MATERIAL #645?

A4    WHAT VENDOR(S) ARE IN NEW YORK STATE WHO
      SUPPLY 1030 STEEL BAR 4″ x 5″?

A5    LIST ALL VENDORS WITH PURCHASE ORDER VALUE
      GREATER THAN 4000 AND ITEM DESCRIPTION 1030 STEEL
      BAR   4″ x 5″.
```

Figure 16.8(a). *Sample data base requests on subschema A in Figures 16.6 and 16.7*

```
ON SUBSCHEMA B:


B1   WHAT MATERIALS ARE INVOLVED IN WHAT AMOUNTS (DATA IN
     THE WORK IN PROCESS FILE) IN PRODUCING ITEM Q REFERRED
     TO IN SHIPPING ORDER 10500?

B2   WHAT VENDORS (DATA IN THE VENDOR FILE) WERE RESPONSIBLE
     FOR SUPPLYING IN WHAT AMOUNTS (DATA IN THE PURCHASE ORDER
     FILE) 1031 STEEL BAR 4″ x 5″ OR A10 INSULATION PAD 4″ x 5″ (DATA
     IN THE RAW MATERIAL INVENTORY FILE) THAT WAS USED TO
     PRODUCE ITEM X80 LOT B (DATA IN FINISHED GOODS INVENTORY
     FILE)  REFERRED TO IN SHIPPING ORDER 10500 (DATA IN THE
     SHIPPING ORDER FILE)?
```

Figure 16.8(b). *Sample data base requests on subschema B in Figure 16.6*

654

2. Distribution of portions of the logical schema and the corresponding contents of each portion; call this type 2 distribution.

3. Distribution of types 1 and 2 combined.

4. Distribution of any of the above types but with some data redundantly stored.

Using as an example the data base in Figure 16.5 serving an international organization in the manufacturing industry, let us address each of these degrees of distribution.

16.3.2 Distribution of Data Base Contents with the Same Logical Schema—Type 1 Distribution

Suppose that the organization has major business and manufacturing operations and markets on the U.S. West Coast, on the U.S. East Coast, and in Canada. It may be reasonable to distribute part of the contents of the data base in Figure 16.5 as data base 1 for CPU B on the West Coast and the remainder as data base 2 for CPU C on the East Coast, as shown in Figure 16.4. The schema would be the same at the two sites. The Canadian part of the business would be served by CPU A but none of the data base would reside in Canada. Any user may then access any of the two data bases from any site. However, by judicious data base distribution and a priori guidelines set up to be followed by the distributed GDBMS, the majority of users would be serviced by the nearest CPU, which would also have the data base contents pertinent to such users. This strategy would reduce the delays and costs of communication, which is one of the major reasons for distributing data and processing.

The data base requests in Figure 16.8 could be received at any site, appropriately routed and coordinated by the MSC, and serviced by the particular site at which the desired data base contents reside. In order to avoid having to send the data base request to every site for service, a network-wide directory would have to know what data resides where.

This type of distribution of data may also be necessitated by throughput requirements, independent of any communications or geographical considerations. When computer throughput capability is exceeded by the demand of applications, the applications load may be split by partitioning or splitting the data base contents into two or more data bases, each serviced by a different CPU. This situation may be a good case for the multiple CPU approach of a Tandem-like configuration; see Section 15.7. It may also be a good case for a data base machine to relieve the mainframe computer of data base tasks, perhaps enough to avoid resorting to multiple host CPUs and having to split the data base (although, in a sense, a data base machine creates a multiple CPU configuration). These alternative approaches have to be considered carefully.

16.3.3 Distribution of Portions of the Logical Schema and Its Corresponding Contents—Type 2 Distribution

Suppose that the organization has its major manufacturing operations at geographical area or location A, its major client markets at location B, and its headquarters at location C. This is the real-life scenario for the organization served by our sample data base. The partitioning and distribution of the data base shown in Figure 16.9 would then coincide with the geographical reality of the everyday activities of the organization: data base parts A, B, and C stored in locations A, B, and C, respectively. The configuration of Figure 16.4 would support this scenario if the figure is modified to indicate that only a logical part of the overall data base and a copy of the GDBMS reside in each of the three CPUs.

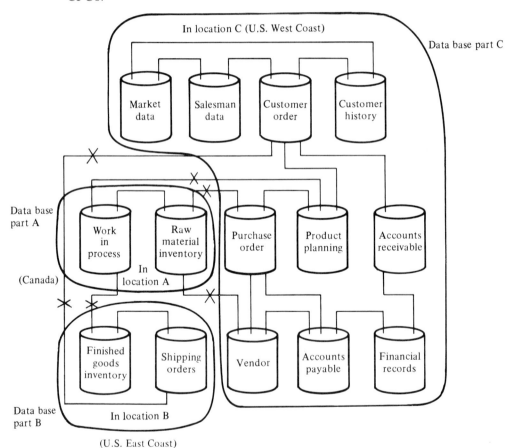

Figure 16.9. *Data base distributed logically in three parts, each part stored at a different location or site*

Under this planned distribution, the majority, although not all, of the data base requests would be serviced by the CPU and data base geographically nearest the requestor. However, there are some new challenges and difficulties in servicing requests that refer to entities in different locations. Figure 16.10 shows the subschemas (or user views) A and B of Figure 16.6 superimposed in dotted lines upon our geographically distributed data base. Let us consider servicing each of the A and B requests in Figure 16.8 directed at subschemas A and B.

Queries A.1 and A.2 present no problems, since they refer only to data in data base C. However, all other queries need to access data in different data bases or locations. Let us consider queries A.4 and B.2.

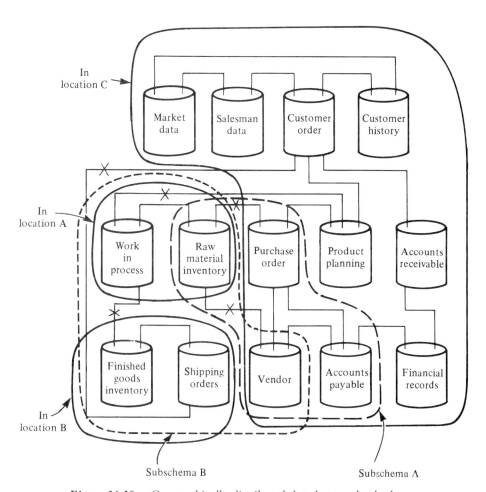

Figure 16.10. *Geographically distributed data base and subschemas*

Query A.4 necessitates accessing the data bases at locations A and C. You will see that in Figure 16.7 any of the three following strategies will answer the query:

1. Locate the raw material inventory entity instance with 1030 steel bar 4″ × 5″ and then follow the relationship(s) to find any corresponding vendor instances having an address in New York State.

2. Locate each vendor instance having an address in New York State and then follow the relationship to find any corresponding raw material inventory instances with the qualification 1030 steel bar 4″ × 5″.

3. If an intelligent directory with intelligent indexing set up by a DBA exists, such as similar to the inverted directory in Figure 2.19, then the query may be answered through the directory and accessing only one of the data bases rather than both (the reader should try this step by step and be assured that this is true).

Query B.2 necessitates accessing all three data bases. With an intelligent directory, perhaps accessing two of the data bases would be sufficient (try it as an exercise).

It is obvious that:

1. Consideration of possible alternative ways to answer the query is a complex task.

2. Following relationships from one data base to another is no longer going from a place in a disk to another disk but rather going from one geographical location to another via telecommunication lines.

3. The alternative ways to answer a query can have major differences in performance and can have impact on other concerns.

Thus it is a practical necessity that a distributed GDBMS provide the following:

1. Network and data distribution transparency such that the user sees the data base as if it were centralized at one location. Ideally, any program or query that was developed for the centralized data base in Figure 16.6 should work without any modification when the data base is distributed as in Figure 16.9, except for performance differences due to the distribution of data.

2. Intelligent query analysis, query decomposition, performance analyzers, MSC, integration of data base and data communications functions, and so forth, to make distributed data management possible.

The use of query languages in the distributed environment is generally favored over one-record-at-a-time or procedural data manipulation languages. A D-GDBMS has more flexibility in optimizing the servicing of a data base request that is expressed in a high-level query language than one that is expressed in a more step-by-step, procedural, or access path-oriented way. This is especially apparent in highly distributed data bases. This potential optimization and performance advantage of query languages is in addition to their attractiveness in allowing a user to express what is desired without having to express so much how it is to be done.

In the absence of commercial GDBMS support for the degree of distribution and transparency presented in the last scenario, some organizations have attempted to evolve toward such distribution by setting up separate data bases and accepting that the GDBMS cannot implement any of the relationships spanning from one data base to another. In other words, the data base is **physically distributed and logically unintegrated**. This may also be called a **decentralized data base**. Application programs and users can still access a data base and then use the information that was retrieved to formulate another request to access the other, separate data base. Thus the burden of relationships between each separate data base and the formulation of each request for each separate data base falls on the application or user, not on the GDBMS.

16.3.4   Distribution of Types 1 and 2 Combined

Suppose that the organization has decided the following:

1. To split its major manufacturing operations, originally centralized at location A in Figure 16.9, and to set up two new additional manufacturing centers closer to the client markets.
2. To distribute the finished goods inventory warehouses and shipping operations closer to the clusters of client markets by setting up four such centers, one at each of locations A, B, and C in Figure 16.9, plus another center. Figure 16.11 summarizes what portions of the logical schema are stored where. Note that at locations A and B schema parts A and B are integrated into one part and that at location C (the organization's headquarters) schema parts B and C are integrated into one part.

The same challenges and difficulties in servicing the queries in Figure 16.8, which were addressed in distribution scenario type 2, are also present here. However, some problems are magnified by the distribution of data base contents: the distributed GDBMS (D-GDBMS) will have to know the correspondence of data base contents to location, and not just where the logical parts are located, in order to appropriately route a query. If network directories containing such information are not set up, then each query will have to be broadcast to every pertinent location where the *types* of data involved in the query are known to be stored. The data base or the local directory at each of these locations will have to be searched to see if the desired contents reside there.

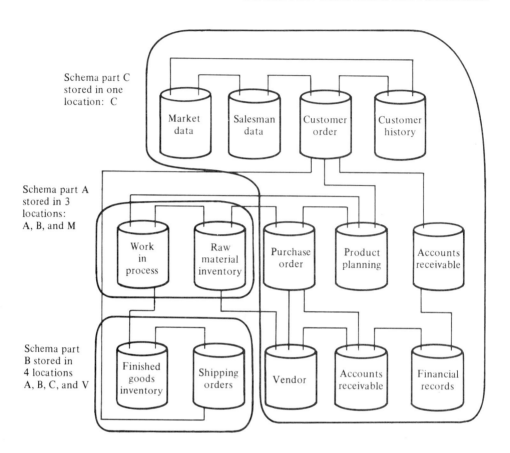

Schema part C
stored in one
location: C

Schema part A
stored in 3
locations:
A, B, and M

Schema part
B stored in
4 locations
A, B, C, and V

Note: At locations A and B schema parts A and B are integrated into one. At location C schema
        parts B and C are integrated into one.

Figure 16.11.   *Data base distributed logically into three parts, the contents of each part stored at one location or replicated
in several locations*

16.3.5   Distribution of Types 1 and 2 with Some Data Redundantly Stored (Replicated)

Suppose that the organization is concerned about (a) the reliability/
survival of the data base resource in case of malfunction or disaster and (b) the
performance aspects. It thus may be attractive and convenient to store the
contents of schema part C redundantly in locations C and B. Such redundancy
is often referred to as **data replication**. In general, different overlapping subsets
of a data base may be replicated in a network. Assuming that the scenario in

Figure 16.11 evolves into one including data redundancy, we can observe that at locations B and C (U.S. East Coast and U.S. West Coast, respectively, in our example) schema parts B and C are combined into one logical part with all of its contents stored redundantly.

The same challenges and difficulties in servicing the queries in Figure 16.8 that were addressed in the previous distribution scenario, Section 16.3.4, also apply here. However, some of the performance problems are relieved by the fact that for some queries the communication costs will be lower. Due to the redundant storage of part C of the data base, all of the data needed for some queries can be found in one location.

However, the challenges and problems in servicing data base updates in previous scenarios are magnified by data redundancy. A number of authors have proposed approaches to the variety of problems that arise, such as the problem of maintaining the consistency of redundantly stored and distributed data in a network environment.[21-24] Redundant copies of data may make distributed data base communication more costly when the ratio of update to read-only transactions is high as the result of increased communication of updates to remote data bases and the synchronization and concurrency control necessary to maintain the consistency of such replicated data. Thus a number of conflicting trade-offs must be considered in arriving at the best, or at least a reasonable, degree of distribution and replication.

As of the mid 1980s, there was no commercial GDBMS supporting this scenario. This is a very active area of research and prototype experimentation that should lead to some commercial D-GDBMS support in the near future. Prototype D-GDBMS efforts started in the early 1980s dealing with a high degree of data base distribution and involving redundantly stored data include in particular the University of California, Berkeley's distributed INGRES,[4] Computer Corporation of America's SDD-1[6] and its descendant DDM, INRIA's SIRIUS-DELTA in France,[8] and IBM Research's R*.[9] DDM and R* point toward possible commercial products in the near future.

16.4   DISTRIBUTED DATA BASES IN A HETEROGENEOUS ENVIRONMENT

Thus far in this chapter it has been assumed that the same GDBMS, or equivalent plug-compatible GDBMS, are used throughout the distributed environment. This does not necessarily mean that the hardware, operating system, or data communications environment has to be homogeneous. A number of GDBMS are available in a variety of hardware systems under several operating systems, as shown in Figure 4.1. Thus, for example, the ORACLE relational GDBMS could support data bases in a network tying together IBM, DEC, and perhaps other brands of computers. ORACLE would then make transparent any hardware and operating system differences to data base requests.

Recently, the heterogeneous distributed data base management system scenario has emerged. An example is shown in Figure 16.12. A variety of large and small computers and even microcomputers, most of them with their own and incompatible GDBMS, may be tied together in a network as shown. Satellite communication may be involved between distant nodes. Local networks of computers might be involved, such as at location X in Figure 16.12. Data base machines such as those described in Chapter 15 may be involved in managing the data base(s) either at a node or in a local network.

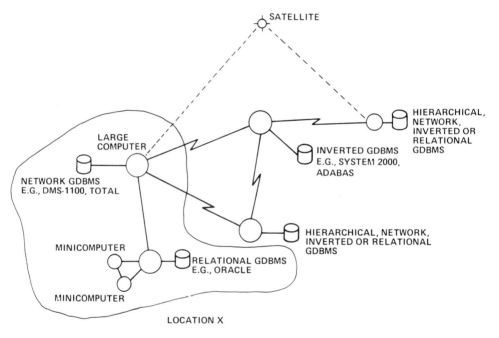

EMERGENCE OF SCENARIO DUE TO:

        PROLIFERATION OF DATA BASES

        PROLIFERATION OF DIFFERENT GDBMS (BOTH SYNTACTICALLY

        AND IN TERMS OF DATA BASE MODEL)

        EMERGENCE OF COMPUTER NETWORKS

        ADVANCES IN DATA COMMUNICATIONS

        LACK OF OVERALL (NOT JUST LOCAL) DATA BASE PLANNING

        DISTRIBUTED DATA BASES

Figure 16.12.   *Heterogeneous data base management system scenario*

The heterogeneous data base environment has emerged in large organizations, governmental environments, and computer networks due to the following:

1. The proliferation of data bases;
2. The proliferation of different GDBMS;
3. The proliferation of a variety of minicomputers and microcomputers;
4. The emergence of networks tying together heterogeneous hardware and software;
5. Advances in data communications;
6. Distributed data bases;
7. Lack of overall (not just local) data base planning and control.

This environment adds to all the challenges and problems outlined for the homogeneous distributed environment the problems of heterogeneity of GDBMS: different data models (network, hierarchical, relational), syntactically and semantically different GDBMS (e.g., even within the relational model family there are significant differences between SQL/DS and QBE), different types of controls in each GDBMS (e.g., back-up and recovery, locking and synchronization, etc.). It is desired that a future *heterogeneous distributed GDBMS* (**HD-GDBMS**) provide not only distribution transparency but also heterogeneity transparency.

As an example, consider Figure 16.13. Four data bases are to be involved: at location X there is a data base managed by a relational GDBMS and another managed by a network GDBMS (e.g., a CODASYL system) on another local computer, and at two other remote locations there are two separate data bases, each managed by a hierarchical GDBMS such as IMS. With current technology, every user accessing any data base is expected to use the facilities and abide by the syntactic and semantic regulations of the GDBMS which created each data base, unless some interface software is developed by the installation. Although some such interface software is, of necessity, being developed frequently by user installations, thus far it allows only cosmetic variations from the syntax and semantics of the GDBMS managing the particular data base.

What would be greatly desired to enhance the attractiveness and usefulness of sharing data resources in a heterogeneous network, as shown in Figure 16.13, is the ability for a user to access any data base as if it were managed under any one of the GDBMS at one central location. Thus a user could have access to any data base through a relational view at one of the minicomputers in the local network at location X, while another set of users, at nodes where IMS data bases reside, could have access to any data base as if it were managed by IMS. Ideally, a user anywhere could look at any data base through his or her favorite GDBMS, whether or not it was the preferred one at the site.

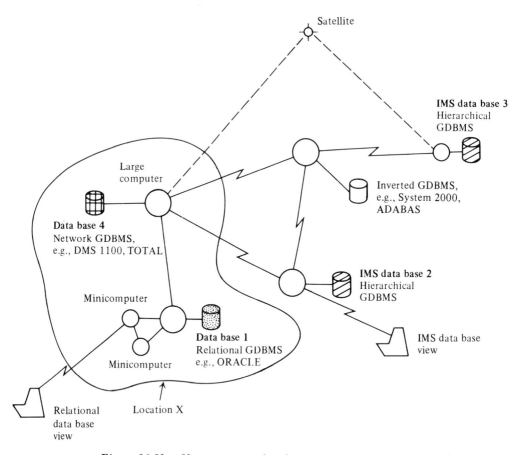

Figure 16.13. *Heterogeneous data base management system scenario*

In a nutshell, the ideal long-range goals would be for a HD-GDBMS to be able to support a network in which any user in any node can be given an integrated and tailored view or schema, while in reality the data may reside in one single data base or in physically separated data bases managed individually by the same type of GDBMS (by the only one the user understands) or by a different GDBMS. Figure 16.14 portrays a logically integrated but heterogeneous and distributed data base. No HD-GDBMS with such full capabilities is available today. There are many unsolved problems, and others remain to be uncovered. However, major research and development projects in this arena are leading toward some partial attainment of the previous long-range objectives. Major efforts include UCLA's HD-GDBMS project,[12] Computer Cor-

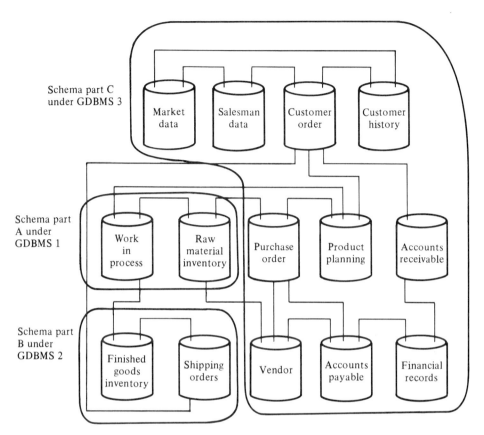

Figure 16.14.   *A heterogeneous distributed data base*

poration of America's MULTIBASE,[13] INRIA's heterogeneous SIRIUS-DELTA,[14] Informatics' DAG,[20] and others.[11]

The majority of the current research and development efforts and initial commercial support simplify the task by requiring every user to communicate using a common language and data model (MULTIBASE, DAG, SIRIUS-DELTA). A frequent choice is a relational model (SIRIUS-DELTA). MULTIBASE further simplifies the task for a more near-term achievable system by handling only read-type of data base requests. The complexity and restrictions of updating through user views were presented for relational GDBMS in Section 10.5.5. The initial commercial version of MULTIBASE may be available in the near future. It will provide distribution transparency and heterogeneity transparency for read-only queries using a common language and data model.[25]

DAG (Distributed Application Generator)[20] became commercially available recently. It is a generator of applications and also of the necessary GDBMS commands embedded in the application program to access data bases managed by IMS and/or SQL/DS. The data base view to the application is a logically integrated hierarchical IBM data base, although it may consist of portions residing in several separate IMS and/or SQL/DS data bases at different sites and under different IBM operating systems and data communications software (CICS, IMS/DC).

The HD-GDBMS project at UCLA strives to achieve the major long-range goals cited earlier, not constraining the user to a common arbitrary language or to read-only queries; however, it is a very long-range possibility, beyond the more achievable DAG, MULTIBASE, and SIRIUS-DELTA tasks, and such attractive goals may not be practically achievable.

16.5   RESEARCH AND DEVELOPMENT CHALLENGES

The extent to which high degrees of distributed data base management may be feasible depends very much on the success of research and development efforts, the technological and cost-effectiveness success of current prototype D-GDBMS, and eventual GDBMS vendor support. A number of specific challenges and problem areas in distributed data base management being addressed include the following:

1. Where and how to allocate files and data bases in a multiple computer system.[26,27] What data should be redundantly stored where and for what reliability and performance reasons?

2. How data bases should be designed and processed in a distributed environment.[7,28] What are the relevant administrative, political, and logical and physical data base organization issues?

3. How queries should be serviced in a distributed environment.[29-32] Issues include: how to minimize operating cost (processing cost and communication cost), which is a function of the selection of sites for processing query operations; sequence of operations or subqueries into which the user query may be decomposed; allocation of data base portions to the sites; selection from redundant data bases, distributed compilation, partitioning of records and/or tables, and so forth.

4. How to maintain the consistency and integrity of redundantly stored and distributed data in a network.[21-24] Concurrency control protocols, recovery mechanisms, and so on, in an updating environment are especially challenging.

5. How to manage and maintain network data dictionaries. Issues include: the extent to which the data dictionary should be centralized, distributed, or replicated; choice of user and object names; maintaining the consistency of directories; and so on.

6. How ease of use, network transparency, site autonomy, and reasonable performance can be achieved at the same time.[10] These objectives pose conflicting architectural demands on a D-GDBMS.

7. How closely coupled or loosely coupled data bases should be in a network for organizational, political, reliability, and performance reasons.[7]

8. How and to what extent transparency of GDBMS heterogeneity can be provided in a network sharing data bases.[11-14] How can data base models, user views or subschemas, queries, and so on, be translated from one GDBMS architecture to another?

9. To what extent can or should what type of distributed file management facilities at the operating system level[33] assist distributed data base management functions, as opposed to putting those functions in the GDBMS?

REFERENCES

1. Scherr, A. L., "Distributed Data Processing," *IBM Systems Journal*, Vol. 17, No. 4, 1978, pp. 324–343.

2. Rothnie, J. B., and N. Goodman, "A Survey of Research and Development in Distributed Database Management," *Proceedings, Third International Conference on Very Large Data Bases*, Tokyo, Japan, October 6–8, 1977, pp. 48–62.

3. Champine, G. A., *Distributed Computer Systems: Impact on Management, Design and Analysis*, AFIPS Press, Arlington, Va., 1980.

4. Stonebraker, M., and E. Neuhold, "A Distributed Database Version of INGRES," University of California, Berkeley, Research Report ERL-M612, September 11, 1976.

5. Rothnie, J. B., "Distributed DBMS No Longer Just a Concept," *Data Communications*, McGraw-Hill Inc., New York, January 1980.

6. Rothnie, J. B., et al., "Introduction to System for Distributed Databases (SDD-1)," *ACM Transactions on Database Systems*, Vol. 8, No. 1, March 1980.

7. McLeod, D., and D. Heimbigner, "A Federated Architecture for Database Systems," *Proceedings, 1980 National Computer Conference*, 1980, pp. 283–289.

8. Le Bihan, J., et al., "SIRIUS-DELTA Distributed Database System," *Proceedings, Fifth Berkeley Workshop on Distributed Data Management and Computer Networks*, Berkeley, Calif., February 3–5, 1981.

9. Williams, R., et al., "R*: An Overview of the Architecture," IBM Research Report RJ 3325, San Jose, Calif., December 1981.

10. Haas, L. M., et al., "R*: A Research Project on Distributed Relational DBMS," IBM Research Report RJ 3653, San Jose, Calif., October 21, 1982.

11. Adiba, M., and D. Portal, "A Cooperation System for Heterogeneous Database Management Systems," *Information Systems*, Vol. 3, No. 3, 1978, pp. 209–215.

12. Cardenas, A. F., and M. H. Pirahesh, "Data Base Communication in a Heterogeneous Data Base Management System Network," *Information Systems*, Vol. 5, 1980, pp. 55–79.

13. Smith, J. M., P. A. Bernstein, U. Dayal, N. Goodman, T. Landers, K. W. T. Lin, and E. Wong, "MULTIBASE—Integrating Heterogeneous Distributed Database Systems," *Proceedings 1981 National Computer Conference*, June 1981, pp. 487–499.

14. Ferrier, A., and C. Stangret, "Heterogeneity in the Distributed Database Management Systems SIRIUS-DELTA," *Proceedings, Eighth International Conference on Very Large Data Bases*, Mexico City, September 8–10, 1982, pp. 45–53.

15. "SYSTEM 2000/80 Distributed Data Base Environment, System Description," Intel's Information Resource Management Product Family, Intel-MRI Systems Corp., Austin, Texas.

16. "Tandem Non-Stop System Description Manual," Tandem Computers, Inc., Cupertino, Calif.

17. "IMS/VS Version 1, Release 3, System Administration Guide," IBM Reference Manual SH20-9178.

18. "IDMS Distributed Database System, Summary Description," Cullinet Software, Inc., Publication SDDB-110-20, Westwood, Mass.

19. "DATACOM/D-NET, Concepts and Facilities," Applied Data Research, Princeton, N.J.

20. "Distributed Application Generator, Technical System Description," Informatics, Inc., Canoga Park, Calif.

21. Stonebraker, M., "Concurrency Control and Consistency of Multiple Copies of Data in Distributed INGRES," *IEEE Transactions on Software Engineering*, SE-5, No. 3, May 1979, pp. 188–194.

22. Bernstein, P. A., and N. Goodman, "Concurrency Control in Distributed Database Systems," *Computing Surveys*, Vol. 13, No. 3, June 1981, pp. 185–221.

23. Bernstein, P. A., "A Sophisticate's Introduction to Distributed Database Concurrency Control," *Proceedings, Eighth International Conference on Very Large Data Bases*, Mexico City, September 8–10, 1982, pp. 62–76.

24. Chu, W. W., J. Hellerstein, and M. Lan, "The Exclusive-Writer Protocol: A Low Cost Approach for Updating Replicated Files in Distributed Real Time Systems," *Proceedings, Third International Conference on Distributed Computing Systems*, IEEE, 1982, pp. 269–277.

25. Shipman, D. W., "The Functional Data Model and the Data Language DAPLEX," *ACM Transactions on Database Systems*, Vol. 6, No. 1, March 1981.

26. Chu, W. W., "Optimal File Allocation in a Multiple Computer System," *IEEE Transactions on Computers*, Vol. C-18, No. 10, October 1969, pp. 885–889.

27. Chu, W. W., and P. Hurley, "Optimal Query Processing for Distributed Database Systems," *IEEE Transactions on Computers*, Vol. C-31, No. 9, September 1982, pp. 835–850.

28. Teorey, T., and J. P. Fry. *Design of Data Base Structures*, Prentice-Hall, Englewood Cliffs, N.J., 1982.

29. Wong, E., "Retrieving Dispersed Data from SDD-1: A System for Distributed Databases," *Proceedings, Second Berkeley Workshop on Distributed Data Management and Computer Networks*, May 1977, pp. 217–235.

30. Hevner, A. R., and S. B. Yao, "Query Processing in Distributed Database Systems," *IEEE Transactions on Software Engineering*, Vol. SE-5, No. 3, May 1979, pp. 179–187.

31. Selinger, P. G., and M. Adiba, "Access Path Selection in Distributed Database Systems," IBM Research Report RJ 2883, San Jose, Calif., August 1980.

32. Bernstein, P. A., et al., "Query Processing in a System for Distributed Databases (SDD-1)," *Transactions on Database Systems*, Vol. 6, No. 4, December 1981, pp. 602–625.

33. Popek, G., B. Walker, J. Chow, D. Edwards, C. Kline, G. Rudisin, and G. Thiel, "Locus: A Network Transparent, High Reliability Distributed System," *Proceedings of the Eighth Symposium on Operating Systems Principles*, Pacific Grove, Calif., December 1981.

EXERCISES

1. Consider the Type1 data distribution in which a data base is split or partitioned into two or more data bases, each with identical logical structure. Each partition will be serviced by a different CPU, since a single CPU cannot handle the transaction rate load. Suppose you are to do this with a GDBMS that has no distribution transparency facilities. What are some of the issues and specific problems you will have to either (a) handle with special software that you may have to build or (b) avoid altogether? For specific illustration, use the data base in Figure 7.2 and then expand it into a network by adding a relationship from CHILD to DOCTOR. Consider only the case in which no data is replicated.

2. Consider and answer Exercise 1 for the case in which data may be replicated. For example, EMPLOYEE instances may be replicated under two or more different DOCTOR instances. What are some of the pros and cons of this replication (recalling that you will have to provide all necessary facilities beyond those in your nondistributed GDBMS)? This is the task faced by systems architects given the mission of producing a distributed GDBMS!

3. To what extent are what problems alleviated by not permitting subschemas to span two or more partitions in a geographically distributed data base, Figure 16.10 in particular?

4. Your boss tells you that we have to use different GDBMS vendors to supply us with three different GDBMS to implement the partitioned data base in Figure 16.14. The reason is that "if any vendor's GDBMS fails us, or is retired, or we decide to abandon, we don't have to convert the whole data base and all the applications to another GDBMS." You have a choice of any major GDBMS in Figure 4.1. What/which would you recommend? Why? Consider the various challenges of the heterogeneous GDBMS environment.

Appendix A

EXTERNAL DATA STORAGE DEVICES AND SYSTEMS

672

A.1   INTRODUCTION

The computerized representation, storage, and management of information is molded by the computing devices involved. This appendix focuses on the external storage devices on which the masses of information are organized into the files and data bases central to information systems and other applications.

The ideal partner of a Central Processing Unit (CPU) would be a system providing unlimited storage, any part of which could be made available without delay to the program or user requesting it. Looking at today's technology, this ideal is approached most closely only by main memory, whose cost limits it to a finite size and requires a certain amount of time to access. The capabilities and limitations of the mass storage electromechanical devices that have been conceived shape the nature of the data management technology and facilities provided to users. An understanding of storage devices is essential toward understanding, appreciating, designing, and using data management systems.

Various types of data storage outside of main storage are provided by a number of so-called peripheral or input/output (I/O) devices in varying degrees. I/O devices include card reader/punchers, printers, typewriter-keyboard devices, magnetic tape units, direct access units, teleprocessing equipment, data entry units (e.g. key-to-disk units), microfilm storage systems, process control equipment, and so on. However, the bulk of data manipulated by application programs is based on two types of devices usually referred to as the **external storage devices**: magnetic tape units, and direct access storage devices. These are the focus of this appendix. They underlie the data management technology covered in this book. Note that external storage devices in their broadest sense definitely include systems that store any kind of information in computer readable form; for example, microfilm storage systems.[1]

Several attributes typify storage devices. These include data capacity, addressability or how data is located, access time to data, data transfer rate, physical advantages and limitations, and cost or economy. The devices are selected for use by evaluating these attributes against the requirements of the application or system. In the following section the attachment of devices to main processors is outlined; then the specifics of the main devices in use are examined: tapes, cassettes, disks, floppy disks, and mass storage systems. A view of the storage device marketplace and of what is expected in the next few years concludes this appendix.

A.2   THE STORAGE SUBSYSTEM—ATTACHING
DEVICES TO SYSTEMS

There are many different external storage devices with various characteristics offered by the dozens of commercial vendors. The lack of common architectures and of industry-wide standards has led to the situation in which different devices generally cannot be directly attached to a computer system (considered to be the mainframe and everything else but external storage devices) in the same manner. The **channel**, which is oriented to the central processing system and main storage, and the **control unit**, which is oriented to a particular device type, are functional units interfacing the storage devices to the system.

The control unit operates and controls an I/O device and adapts the characteristics of each I/O device to the standard form of control provided by the channel. The control unit may be housed separately or it may be physically and logically integrated with the I/O device. The channel governs the flow of information between I/O control units and main storage on a standard I/O interface to the control units. The channel may be housed separately or integrated under the covers of the CPU.

The circuitry necessary to manage a device is complex and is only required for a relatively small portion of the total device operation. Also, the normal use of the device itself may create long idle periods with busy intervals.

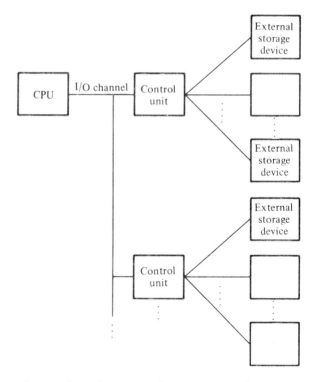

Figure A.1. *Block outline of a tape and/or external random access storage subsystem*

These factors and the need for economy have led to the frequent use of one control unit for several devices. Depending on the particular configuration, the control unit may permit many devices or only one device to be operated at a time. The channel is used for brief intervals by a device to read or write data or to control information in main storage. Thus in many cases a channel may have more than one control unit attached to it. Concurrent operation of control units may be provided depending on the particular channel. The machinery made up of a storage device or devices and the control unit is called a **storage subsystem**. Figure A.1 outlines in block diagram the usual configuration of storage devices, control unit(s), and channel. A storage subsystem (tape or disk) is often termed "storage system" depending on how much system hardware and software capability it includes. The two terms are actually used interchangeably in practice.

A plug-compatible peripheral device is one that can replace an existing one made by a mainframe manufacturer or by an independent maker. It is one that can be plugged into the main processor with little or no change to the existing systems or application software. Two classes of compatibility are visible. One can be called subsystem or system compatibility, and the other component compatibility. A subsystem is compatible if it will interface with the computer's I/O channel appropriately. A component is compatible if it interfaces correctly with the appropriate controller. Profit opportunities have led a number of peripherals vendors to market components and subsystems plug-compatible with mainframe vendors' equipment, particularly with IBM's computers (e.g., INTEL, Storage Technology, Telex).

A.3   MAGNETIC TAPES

Magnetic tapes are made of oxide-coated Mylar. The reels are about .5 inch wide. Data is recorded in binary bit form in a column across the width of the tape with the position of each bit along the width called a **track**. The unit of data usually recorded is the byte, which is made up of eight bits. Various methods have been used for recording binary digits on tapes and on disks. An additional parity bit track is used for checking errors. Various number of tracks and recording densities characterize products available. However, a large section of the market adheres to IBM established practices: 9 tracks at either 800, 1,600, or 6,250 bits per inch (bpi). Second-generation IBM machinery carried 7 tracks at 200, 550, or 800 bpi. The terms bytes per inch and bits per inch are used synonymously, the reason being that x bits per inch of a track is an equivalent term to x bytes per inch of the full width.

The unit of data physically transferred to and from tapes is called the **block**. The block consists of one or more bytes. Blocks written on a tape are separated by an **interblock gap**, which is a space about .6 inches for 9-track IBM tapes. For reasons of time and storage efficiency several logical records may be lumped into one block, giving rise to the term **blocking factor**, the number of logical records per block (physical record). The end of a data set or file made up of similar blocks is marked by perhaps a 3.5-inch gap followed by some special block of data written by the hardware and called a file or **tape mark**. Several files may be contained on a single reel of tape. A file may require several reels of tape. Reels of tape come in various lengths, a common one being 2,400 feet and 10.5 inches in diameter. A 2,400-foot tape may hold 480,000 80-column punched cards or equivalent with data in all 80 columns and blocked 4,800 bytes/block.

Data on tapes is read or written by moving the tape past **read/write heads**. The user's program can be notified if the file mark or end-of-tape marker is read. Tapes can be usually read backward by moving the tape in the opposite direction. When data is written on tape as it passes the write head, the data is immediately read back as it passes the read head to ensure that it is recorded correctly.

A reel of tape is physically attached to the tape mount of a **tape drive** unit for reading and writing. There is one mount per drive cabinet. Reels are of course mounted and dismounted manually. A tape drive is managed by the **tape controller** or tape control unit which in turn interfaces with the computer's I/O channel appropriately. A **tape subsystem** is made up of the controller and associated tape drives. The control unit interprets and executes the file commands obtained from the CPU via the channel. These commands control the operation of the devices. The control unit furnishes status information to the CPU (end of file reached, error detected, and so forth), provides a path for data transfer between the CPU and the devices, translates and interprets the data recording details between CPU and devices, and checks the validity of data encoded (such as parity bits). Within families of tape drives (e.g., the IBM 3420 family of several drives), different models can usually be intermixed on the same controller if appropriate density and formats are adjusted by special mechanisms.

A **two-channel switch** is an option that permits a tape subsystem to be switched under program control between two processors. Tape subsystems are expensive, and such sharing between two processors may be economical. **Track compatibility**, when present, permits mixing 7- and 9-track tape drives on the same controller. **Pooling** permits switching a group of drives among several controllers.

Tape speed (inches/second) and **transfer rate** (bytes/second) are self-explanatory. **Rewind time** is the time to rewind the tape to the beginning. The **tape transport** controls the movement speed of the tape. The **tape slack buffer** refers to the mechanism that controls the length of tape pulled off the tape reel ahead of reading or writing, in order to reduce the time necessary to speed up and stop the tape.

TABLE A.1 Representative Magnetic Tape Units and Characteristics (Courtesy of Datapro Research Corporation, Delran, N.J.)

Manufacturer and Model	IBM 3420 Model 4	IBM 3420 Model 8	Interscience 3650	Telex 8020-24
REPLACEMENT FOR:				
Tape drive vendor	—	—	Sperry Univac	IBM
Tape drive product and model numbers	—	—	Uniservo 34	3420-4
CONFIGURATION				
Attachment via mainframe controllers	IBM 3803-2	IBM 3803-2	No	No
Attachment via independent controllers	—	—	6804	See Comments
Tape drives per controller	1 to 8	1 to 8	1 to 8	2 to 4
Controller switch options	2/3/4 x 8/16	2/3/4 x 8/16	2 x 16	None
Channel switch options	Opt., 2 channels	Opt., 2 channels	2/3/4 channels	2 channels
RECORDING CHARACTERISTICS (Tape density)	9 track, 6250/1600 bpi	9 track, 6250/1600 bpi	9 track, 1600/6250 bpi	9 track, 1600/6250 bpi
FEATURES				
Simultaneous read/write	No	No	Std.	No
Read backwards	Yes	Yes	Std.	Yes
Mode compatibility	No	No	Std.	Opt.
PERFORMANCE				
Tape speed, inches/sec.	75	200	125	75
Transfer rate, Kbytes/sec.	470/120	1250/320	780	120/470
Rewind time, sec. (for 2400 feet)	60	45	55	60
Tape stack buffer	Vacuum column	Vacuum column	Vacuum column	Vacuum column
Tape transport	Single capstan	Single capstan	Vacuum capstan	Single capstan
PRICING AND MAINTENANCE (1982)				
Purchase price	$19,170 per drive; $34,430 per controller	$24,840 per drive; $34,430 per controller	$20,850 per drive; $52,500 per controller	$56,100 per subsystem; $17,325 per add-on drive
Monthly maintenance	$179 per drive; $165 per controller	$288 per drive; $165 per controller	$239 per drive; $400 per controller (prime shift)	$342 per subsystem; $92 per add-on drive ($24 hr./7 days)
Monthly lease charges (for a 2-year lease including maintenance)	$617 per drive; $1,117 per controller	$848 per drive; $1,117 per controller	$830 per drive; $1,710 per controller; $15 to $85 for options	Contact vendor
Overtime charges	10% on 30-day rental only	10% on 30-day rental only	5% to 160%	None
Maintenance included in basic 2-year lease plan	24 hrs./day, 7 days/week	24 hrs./day, 7 days/week	9 hrs./day, 5 days/week	9 hrs./day, 5 days/week
First delivery	10/73	10/73	10/78	March 1982
COMMENTS	Dual Density is optional; features are available with limited new production	Dual Density (6250/1600 bpi) is optional; limited new production	Compatible with Univac 418, 490, and 1100 Series	Basic subsystem includes Integrated controller and two tape drives

677

Table A.1 shows a representative sample of tape units and their respective costs and characteristics. The tape itself costs little, less than $10 for an 800-foot tape. A market survey in the early 1980s showed over fifty commercially available tapedrives as replacements for IBM units.[2] Not all manufacturers market their own controllers. The competition for the tape drive market has been intense for years. Needless to say, the offerings of tape units, the bread and butter storage of pre-data base EDP, are numerous.

Tapes are still widely used because tape is the most cost-effective storage for large, historical, and infrequently used data, for backup storage for large-capacity fixed-disk drives, and for applications with a very high hit ratio.

Cassette/Cartridge Tape Storage

Cassette/cartridge (cas/cart) magnetic tape storage subsystems have captured a substantial portion of the low-cost storage market. Maturing since the late 1960s when audio drives were modified for EDP applications, cas/cart units became available in strictly digital configurations to meet a wide spectrum of low-cost, low-volume storage needs.[3] The advent of minicomputers and intelligent terminals and then video games has been a major factor in the proliferation of many independent cas/cart vendors. Most makers of recorders and minicomputers generally do not manufacture their own cas/cart tape subsystems, but instead rely on the products of such independent vendors. Cas/cart tapes have been and are applied to a variety of applications. In data communications, cas/cart recorders have been used with keyboard teleprinter or CRT display terminals and in word processing typewriters to record, edit, store, and forward documents. However, one of the largest markets is the burgeoning video game market which uses cas/cart tapes to store programs/games.

Recording formats, the number of data channels, tape speeds, transport mechanisms, and most other hardware parameters vary among manufacturers. Many cas/cart systems use a Philips-type cassette, a reel-to-reel tape container holding up to 300 feet of .15-inch tape capable of storing from 80,000 to 150,000 words. Dimensionally, the cassette tape is similar to those used by audio recorders. An aperture in the container allows access to the read/write head, capstan, and tape sensors. Tape motion may be bidirectional between two accessible reels. Typical characteristics are an average access time of about 15 to 20 seconds for a 300-foot tape and a transfer rate of 333 words/second (dependent on format and read/write speed).

Another popular medium is the 3M-type cas/cart designed specifically for digital use. The 3M-type cartridge has up to 300 feet of .25-inch tape, is bidirectional, and can be formulated at densities up to 1,600 bpi for 1-, 2-, or 4-track phase encoded recording, each holding up to 360,000 words. Average access time at 90 inches per second (ips) is 20 seconds for a 300-foot tape and data transfer is 3,000 words/second per track. Other cas/cart storage systems besides the Philips and 3M types are offered by a number of manufacturers.[3]

A.4   RANDOM ACCESS STORAGE DEVICES

External storage random access devices are also called **direct access storage devices (DASD)**. They are generally rotating devices in which the surfaces on which data is stored are continuously in motion relative to the sensing mechanisms that read and write the data. These mechanisms are referred to as read/write heads. The basic unit of storage is a **track** which is a narrow circular strip on the recording surface. The number of **bytes per track** is an important characteristic. Tracks in the same plane parallel to the axis of rotation constitute a **cylinder**. A **disk pack** is a storage device or medium that contains one or more cylinders, each of which in turn contains one or more tracks.

The drum is another type of rotating random access device. Drums are generally faster but contain less data. They are used for small amounts of frequently used data. Other devices with more electromechanical moving parts have also been available in the past, for example, the IBM 2321 data cell drive. Disk devices predominate in number of installations over all other random access devices.

A **disk drive** is a device that has some type of access mechanism which transfers data to and from the disk pack that it houses. The mechanisms are different for each device. Each mechanism contains a number of read/write heads that transfer data as the recording surfaces rotate past them. One head at a time transfers data (either read or write). Figure A.2 shows the access

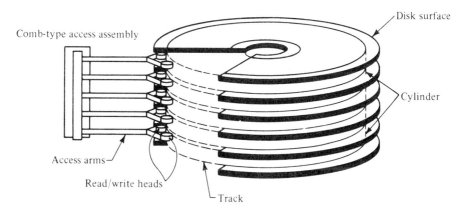

Figure A.2.   Comb-type access mechanism of the typical disk drive

mechanism of the typical disk drive. The access mechanism consists of a group of access "arms" that move together. In the IBM 3340 disk drive, this mechanism can move horizontally to 348 different cylinders including a few alternates. Each arm has two read/write heads. There are 12 heads in all, one for each of the 12 recording surfaces. An IBM 3340 cylinder has a maximum capacity of 100,416 data bytes (8,368 bytes per track, 12 tracks per cylinder). A pack has a maximum capacity of 34.9 million bytes.

Although most rotating devices have moving arm mechanisms, some have fixed heads, one for each track. Thus no moving arms are included and access time is improved. Such disk configurations are the drums essentially. In some recent devices both moving arms and fixed-head areas are available. For example, in the IBM 3340 disk drive and its associated 3348 "data module" (disk pack), fixed heads serve a half-million byte portion consisting of 5 cylinders of 12 tracks each.[5,6] This feature, although expensive, improves access time to frequently referenced data such as indexes. Figure A.3 shows the IBM 3340 disk storage facility with eight disk drives.

Disk drives contain a component called a **spindle** on which the disk pack is mounted. Some units incorporate two spindles in a single cabinet. Some drives carry only removable disk packs, and others only nonremovable packs. In some newer products, like the IBM 3340, the moving arm, the read/write heads, and some of the electronics involved are a part of the disk pack itself. The **controller** or control unit is a powerful device which interfaces the rotating drive with the main processor via an I/O channel. The controller in some cases is itself a modified and upgraded small computer, a special-purpose minicomputer. Various configurations of subsystems are available from more than a

Figure A.3.   The IBM 3340 direct access disk storage facility (Courtesy of IBM Corp.)

dozen vendors, with various numbers and types of storage devices (disks, drums) attached to a single controller. The control unit has been generally self-contained as a separate black box, although in recent IBM offerings it is a part of the disk drive enclosure.

Figure A.4 outlines the possible system attachments of the IBM 3340 direct access disk storage units to system 370 CPU models. The attachment is via the so-called "storage control." The storage control can be viewed as the

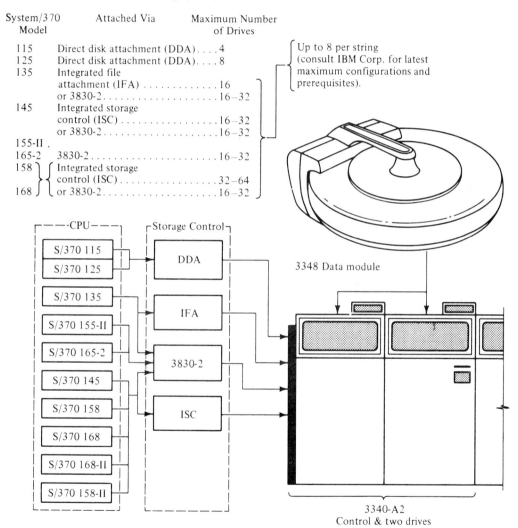

The 3340 is attached to the following System/370 models:

System/370 Model	Attached Via	Maximum Number of Drives
115	Direct disk attachment (DDA)	4
125	Direct disk attachment (DDA)	8
135	Integrated file attachment (IFA)	16
	or 3830-2	16–32
145	Integrated storage control (ISC)	16–32
	or 3830-2	16–32
155-II, 165-2	3830-2	16–32
158	Integrated storage control (ISC)	32–64
168	or 3830-2	16–32

Up to 8 per string (consult IBM Corp. for latest maximum configurations and prerequisites).

CPU

- S/370 115
- S/370 125
- S/370 135
- S/370 155-II
- S/370 165-2
- S/370 145
- S/370 158
- S/370 168
- S/370 168-II
- S/370 158-II

Storage Control

- DDA
- IFA
- 3830-2
- ISC

3348 Data module

3340-A2
Control & two drives

Figure A.4. *IBM System 370 (CPU) and 3340 direct access storage facility-system attachment (Courtesy of IBM Corp.)*

Basic:

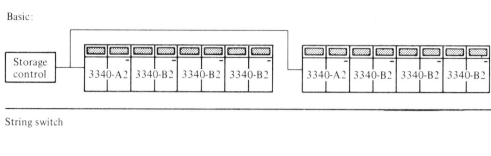

String switch

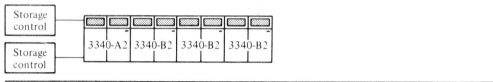

32 drive expansion

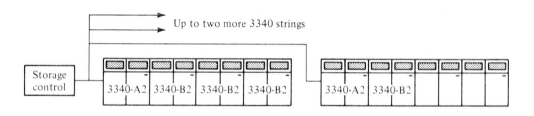

String switch, 32 drive expansion, and intermix:

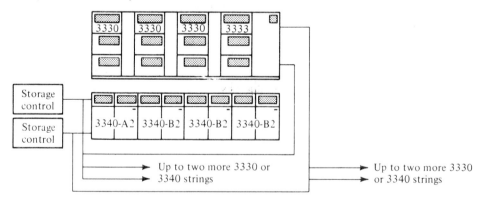

Note: The addressing options provided in string switch coupled with addressing options in the 32 drive expansion feature need special consideration. (Consult IBM Corp.)

Figure A.5. *IBM 3340 disk storage facility configurations (Courtesy of IBM Corp.)*

directorship of the control unit included in each string of IBM 3340 units. The control unit interprets and executes macro orders from the storage control. Figure A.5 outlines the variety of IBM 3340 disk storage subsystem attachment possibilities.[5]

Control Unit Tasks

The control unit has the following tasks:

1. Interpret and perform the file commands dictated by the CPU via the I/O channel (and storage control in the case of the IBM 3340 subsubsystem. Figures A.4, A.5); the file commands control the devices.
2. Send various status information to the CPU, such as end of file.
3. Provide the path and interface for data transfer between the CPU (where data may be parallel by byte) and the device (where data may be serial-by-bit).
4. Check the validity of data transfer.

The file commands interpreted by the control unit to carry out I/O operations fall into four categories: (1) control commands that position the access mechanism to the correct cylinder and/or select the specified read/write head; (2) search commands that cause a comparison between data from main storage and the specified data (identified by the access key); (3) read commands that cause the specified area to be transferred to main storage and checked; and (4) write commands that cause data to be transferred from main storage to the specified location in the device. High-level programming languages such as COBOL, PL/I, and RPG relieve the programmer of the need to know and program I/O operations at this command level.

The preceding paragraphs give a mere glimpse of the controller tasks and file commands at the operating system and controller levels. The details differ among computing systems offered by mainframe manufacturers.

Access and Transfer Time

The time required to access and transfer data is made up of four components:

1. *Access motion time.* This is the time required to position the access mechanism at the cylinder containing the record specified. If the mechanism is already at the correct cylinder, there is no need to move it; so access time is zero. Although the acceleration of the mechanism is a factor, the motion time is essentially a function of the number of cylinders moved. As an example, for the IBM 3340 the minimum time from one cylinder to another is 10 milliseconds (ms); the maxi-

mum from cylinder 1 to 348 is 50 ms; the average over the entire pack is 25 ms. The access motion time is nil in drum devices or in fixed-head (e.g., a portion of the IBM 3340 disk) since the access mechanism does not move.

2. *Head selection.* Electronic switching is required to select the correct read/write head of the mechanism. This time is negligible.

3. *Rotational delay.* This is the time required for the correct data to rotate to the read/write head which transfers data. Its range is from zero time to a full revolution. Half a revolution, the average rotational delay, is generally used for timing purposes. The IBM 3340 is characterized by a 20.2 ms full rotation, 10.1 ms average.

4. *Data transfer.* The time required to transfer data between the device and core storage depends on the rotation speed and the density at which the data is recorded. The IBM 3340 is characterized by a transfer rate of 885 kilobytes/second.

Quite often in practice, the total access time made up of the four constituents above is approximated by taking access motion time plus a full rotation as representative of both rotational delay and data transfer. The complete timing for a complete job must of course consider additional delays such as program processing time, access method processing time (e.g., indexed sequential organizations), and system control time. *Start-up* and *stop-time* are the times to take a pack from standstill to operating speed and to stop it, respectively.

The characteristics cited vary from device to device, and from vendor to vendor. Table A.2 shows the characteristics of a sample of available random access devices. More will be said on the plug-compatible device offerings.

Data Layout and Track Formats

The actual logical and physical layout of data on devices and the data management approaches vary from one mainframe vendor to another. But IBM's layout is widely followed by a large number of independent vendors of external storage devices supplying attractive replacements for IBM's large market of packs and subsystems. The layout and parameters involved are closely tied to the calculation of physical addresses within the disk subsystem; coding using these parameters is built into the operating system. Although in this and the following section, data layout and record formats applicable only to IBM are viewed, they will illuminate the main ingredients involved in other competitive offerings as well.

The general format and data layout are identical for all the IBM 360/370, 3XXX, and 4XXX devices. Data migration across systems would be more difficult if format and layout were not similar. Figure A.6 shows the track layout for IBM systems. Each track contains (1) overhead information, such as gaps, address of track, and so forth, and (2) the data stored. Note that each

TABLE A.2 Characteristics of a Sample of Available Random Access Devices (Courtesy of Datapro Research Corporation, Delran, N.J.)

Manufacturer and Model	IBM 2305 Model 1	IBM 3340	IBM 3380	Intel FAST-3805 Semiconductor Disk	STC 8380
REPLACEMENT FOR					
Disk vendor	—	—	—	IBM	IBM
Disk product and model numbers	—	—	—	2305, 3350, 3380	3380
Equivalent original vendor disk pack	Fixed-disk unit	3348-35/-70/-70F	Fixed-disk unit	Fixed-head disk	Fixed-disk
CONFIGURATION					
Spindles per cabinet	1	1 or 2	2	1 to 6 (pseudo)	2
Spindles per string	2	1 to 8	8	—	8
Strings per channel	1	1 to 4	—	—	—
String switch options	None	2 x 8	None	None	None
Channel switch options	2 channels	2/4 channels	1/2/4/8	2 channels	1/2/4/8
Attachment via integrated controllers	No	DDA/IFA/ISC	DASD adapter	Yes	No
Attachment via mainframe controllers	2835 Mod 2	3830 Model 2	3880	No	No
Attachment via independent controllers	—	No	—	No	STC 8880
Storage capacity, bytes per spindle	5.4M	34.9M/69.8M	1,260M	11.2M or 12M	1.26 gigabytes
PERFORMANCE					
Head movement time:					
1 track ms.	—	10	—	—	—
Average, ms.	—	25	16	—	16
All tracks, ms.	—	50	—	—	—
Rotational time, ms.	5.0	20.2	—	—	8.3
Average access time, ms.	2.5	35.1	24.3	0.4	16
Transfer rate, bytes per second	3,000,000	885,000	3,000,000	1.5M to 4.0M	3,000,000
Start-up time, seconds	—	20	—	—	—
Stop time, seconds	—	—	—	—	—
PRICING AND MAINTENANCE (1982)					
Purchase price	$92,120 per drive; $56,490 per controller	$24,570 (3340-A2); $13,510 (3340-B1); $17,200 (3340-B2); $42,200 (3830-2)	$116,050 (AA4); $101,550 (A4); $84,240 (B4)	Contact vendor	$99,515 (-A4); $114,025 (-AA4); $82,555 (-B4)
Maintenance price	$347 per drive; $208 per controller	$116 (3340-A2); $62 (3340-B1); $100 (3340-B2); $166 (3830-2)	$325 (AA4); $285 (-A4); $240 (B4)	Contact vendor	$285 (-A4); $325 (-AA4); $240 (-B4)
Monthly lease charges (for a 2-year lease including maintenance)	$6,395 per drive; $3,772 per controller	$1,290 (3340-A2); $724 (3340-B-1); $913 (3340-B2); $1,000 (3340-C2); $1.919 (3830-2);	$2,675 (AA4); $2,340 (A4); $1,940 (B4)	Contact vendor	$1,993 (-A4); $2,327 (-AA4); $1,652 (-B4)
Overtime charges	—	—	—	None	Contact vendor
Maintenance included in basic 2-year lease plan	24 hrs./day, 7 days/week	24 hrs./day, 7 days/week	24 hrs./day, 7 days/week	9 hrs./day, 5 days/week	9 hrs./5 days
First delivery	1971	11/73	1st qtr. 1981	5/80	2nd qtr. 1982
COMMENTS		3340-A2 includes first 2 drives; B1 includes 1 drive; B2 includes 2 drives; up to 3 -B1 or -B2 per 3340-A2; 3330 and 3340s can be intermixed.	Count-key-data format; dynamic path selection; thin-film head; four actuators dynamic reconnection with AA4.	A native mode (fixed block architecture) option increases paging performance.	Dual port option and media interchange switch available; four actuators

record entails a considerable amount of overhead space: an address marker; a gap whose size varies from device to device; and the "count" area which takes up 11 bytes. Figure A.6(b) indicates the makeup of the count area. Thus the smaller the record, the larger the percentage of the overall space in a storage device that is used as overhead information. For example, if the record length is only 11 bytes, more than half of the pack's space is used for overhead information! The difference between Figure A.6(a) and A.6(b) is the "key area" field. The key area, Figure A.6(b), contains the so-called key (employee number, part number, account number, and so on) that identifies the contiguous data area. Of course, in most cases records will be formatted with keys for quick random access.

Note that in Figure A.6 there are also for each track:

1. An index point indicating the beginning of each track.
2. A home address (7 bytes) defining the physical location (the track address) of the track and the condition of the track; the flag byte indicating the condition of the track (operative or defective) and the use of the track (primary or alternate).
3. The track descriptor record, RO, which stores various information about the track for use by the programming system.

The preceding control information is of course independent of the size of the record.

Record Formats

When IBM programming systems are used, records may be in one of five formats as shown in Figure A.7.[4] The formats shown are also permitted without key areas. These formats are predominantly available also in other non-IBM programming systems, although, again, the specifics may differ. The record formats in Figure A.7 are:

1. *Fixed, unblocked.* All records in the file have the same length. Each data area holds one logical record. The key is generally not repeated in the data areas.
2. *Fixed, blocked.* All records in the file have the same length. Each data area holds more than one logical record, e.g., logical records aaa, ccc, fff. All blocks are of the same length desired by the programmer. The key area usually contains the key of the highest record in the block. The key is also a field in each logical record so as to identify them during processing.
3. *Variable, unblocked.* The records in the file are of varying lengths. Each data area consists of: a logical record; a block length indicator,

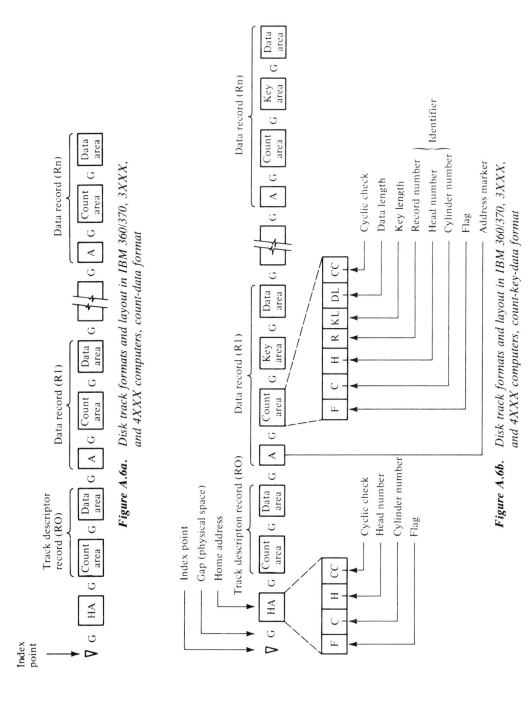

Figure A.6a. *Disk track formats and layout in IBM 360/370, 3XXX, and 4XXX computers, count-data format*

Figure A.6b. *Disk track formats and layout in IBM 360/370, 3XXX, and 4XXX computers, count-key-data format*

687

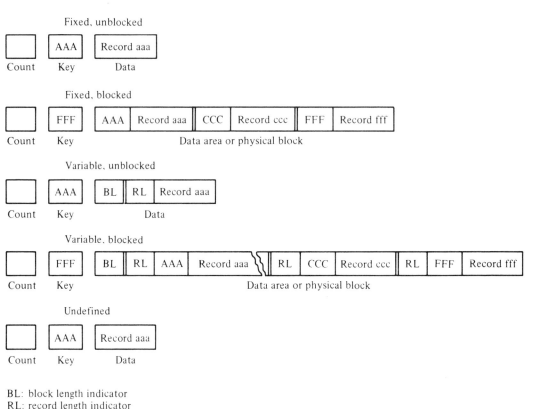

BL: block length indicator
RL: record length indicator

Figure A.7. *Record formats (IBM)*

BL, (four bytes) indicating the number of bytes in the block including itself; and a record length indicator, RL, (the first four bytes of the logical record) indicating the number of bytes in the record including itself.

4. *Variable, blocked.* The records in the file are of varying lengths and each data area consists of a block of logical records. BL and RL have the same function as for variable, unblocked.

5. *Undefined.* This is provided to permit the programmer to handle records that do not adhere to the other formats.

Variable Length Records

The main reason for worrying about variable length records and individual fields is due to storage and machine considerations. Variable length format is provided by many programming systems. Consider the typical length of a data item like last name. Some last names are short, others are long. If the fixed length format is used, then the longest last name before file loading dictates the length of that field for every record in the file, obviously wasting much unused space for short last names. Furthermore, should a longer last name appear after loading, it would be truncated.

Variable length facilities do take overhead control space. But in many applications, the savings obtained offset the overhead. It should be realized

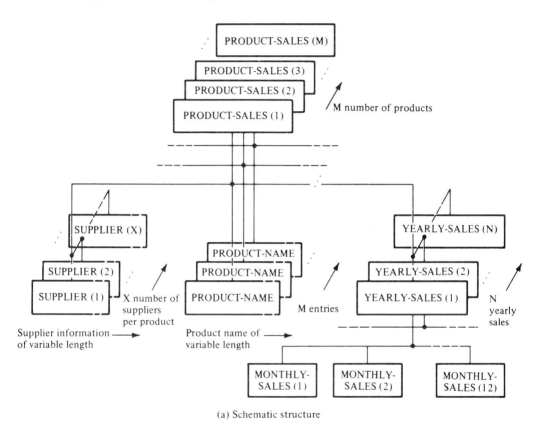

(a) Schematic structure

```
1 PRODUCT-SALES (M)          Total number of entries
  2 SUPPLIER (X)             in the record is
  2 PRODUCT-NAME             M (X + 1 + 12N)
  2 YEARLY-SALES (N)
    3 MONTHLY-SALES (12)
```

(b) Logical structure definition in a programming language

Figure A.8.   *Sample general record structure, a record of arrays, and the variable length possibilities*

that two types of length variability may be involved: one due to the variability in the length of a data item, the other due to the variability in the number of data items in a record. The latter arises of course in many practical applications since it is often necessary to add unforeseen data items to all records. Figure A.8 shows a sample general type of record structure, a record of arrays, exemplifying via arrows the places where expansion may be called for. Every data item or substructure is in fact a candidate for requiring additional members. Note that variability is three-dimensional.

Existing programming systems and associated disk data management provide various degrees of record variability, although many provide little or none, e.g., many minicomputer systems. Larger-scale programming systems will of course tend to support more variability than smaller ones. For example, IBM operating systems and PL/I file facilities include fixed, variable, and undefined record length facilities for sequential and random files. Various generalized data management systems go beyond these basic facilities and make it easier for the programmer to take advantage of various types of record and field length variability. If these generalized data management systems which we address in this text are not available, more programmer sophistication is required to take advantage of the basic variable length facilities. Thus the potential savings in storage and data transfer via these facilities must be carefully weighed against the high programming complexity involved in using them.

Note that the types of variability and the exact manner in which they are handled vary greatly from vendor to vendor. This is another source of factors which complicate the transferability of file structures.

Floppy Disks and Winchester Disks

Demands for lower-cost storage brought about the successful tape cassette storage. It has also brought another peripheral: the **floppy disk** drive. These so-called **floppies** or **diskettes** were first introduced by IBM buried in the 370 computer system announcements in 1970. They are used by IBM as microprogram loaders in the 3330 diskpack storage and as the storage media in the IBM 3740 key-to-disk data entry system. Falling between (1) the cassette and tape and (2) the larger disk storage in performance, the floppies are the equals of cassettes in price. Following IBM's floppy introduction, by 1977 more than 50 vendors offered such drives after shipping 103,000 units in 1976, in addition to the 45,000 drives built by IBM and other in-house system suppliers.[7] By the early 1980s millions of floppies were being sold annually. These minidisks predominate in personal computers/microcomputers and are very attractive in many minicomputer environments in which the otherwise relatively high cost of the peripherals is often reported to make up over 70 percent of total hardware expenditures related to nonmainframe equipment. However, the large disks are more commonly purchased for minicomputer configurations.

Floppy disk storage systems come in configurations of typically from one to eight disk drives with a drive controller, power supply, an interface to particular micro- or minicomputers, and diagnostic and I/O software. A disk operating system is often provided. The system allows the programmer to develop programs for the minicomputer and provides random access facilities for program and data storage and retrieval. A typical floppy system will have 131,000 (16-bit) words per disk capacity, 350 to 450 ms average access time, and 15,000 word/second data transfer rate. Capacity is usually under 2 megabytes. The floppy systems provide much less storage capacity and are physically much smaller than the larger disk systems (e.g., IBM 3330). The typical floppy disk controller board including teletypewriter and other communications interfaces is a mere 15-inch square or less.

The majority of floppy disk drives employ a cartridge similar or identical to the IBM 3740 floppy. Oxide-coated Mylar computer tape, cut into a one-ounce, 7/8-inch disk about the size of a small phonograph record, is the recording medium. The disk is packaged in an 8-inch square plastic envelope with aperture for drive hub mounting, index mark sense, and read/write head access. The disk cartridge is slid into the drive. The disk rotates while the envelope remains stationary. There are other non-IBM-type floppies whose cartridge and drive configurations are different. Diskette cartridge sizes are 8, 5¼, and 3½ inches. Like all other peripherals, floppies adhere to no universal standards on recording media or electromechanical design. Thus, data interchangeability problems are also continuing in this area. But many follow IBM, the initiator of floppies.

An intermediate disk is the so-called Winchester disk drive,[9] inspired by the IBM 3340. The disk, read/write heads, and head actuator are contained in a hermetically sealed head disk assembly. Most Winchester disk drives are fixed disk drives, i.e., the sealed head disk assembly cannot be removed from the disk unit. The disk platters are 14, 8, and 5¼ inches in diameter. Typical storage capacities are on the order of dozens of megabytes, with access speeds between those of floppies and the largest disks.

Floppies are midget images and Winchester disks are intermediate images of the larger disk systems. From the external information storage and retrieval points of view addressed in this text, logically and conceptually they look no different from mammoth disks. The difference is in storage capacity and access time, and, of course, in internal characteristics which in most cases remain transparent to data management principles and facilities addressed in this text.

A.5 MASS STORAGE SYSTEMS

The tremendous growth in the amount of data collected, stored, and retrieved, especially in large industrial and governmental organizations, led to the emergence of the **Mass Storage System (MSS)** starting in the mid-1970s. The MSS is an external storage device capable of storing on the order of 10^{11} to 10^{13} bytes, with record access speeds ranging from a few milliseconds to seconds. Figure A.9 shows the typical macroscopic configuration and data flow of an MSS. Conventional disk storage in the MSS provides the fastest access to a storage area of on the the order of 10^8 to 10^9 bytes, which is a small subset of the total MSS storage space. The bulk of the MSS storage resides in so-called **data cartridges** or **cells**.

A data cartridge is an evolutionary step from traditional tape technology, where data is recorded and accessed physically sequentially. Each cartridge holds typically on the order of 10^6 to 10^7 bytes. As an example, the IBM data cartridge is cylindrical and measures 4 inches in length by 2 inches in diameter, has 770 inches of recording tape, and stores 50.4 million bytes. The MSS may

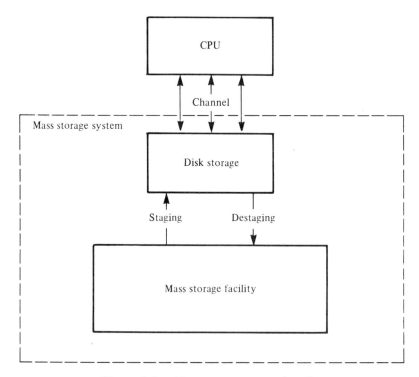

Figure A.9. *Mass storage system data flow*

have many thousands of such cartridges which are typically arranged in a honeycomb-like housing unit.

The process of taking data from cartridge storage to disk storage in the MSS is called **staging**. The reverse process is **destaging**. Once data is staged, it behaves like any other data on disk in terms of accessibility and organization. When data is no longer needed and the space it occupies on DASD is required for other data, the data in a few disk cylinders is destaged back onto a data cartridge where it is stored in DASD format images. The staging/destaging process takes on the order of seconds to many seconds. This time is due primarily to the following:

1. The cartridge is physically moved by a mechanical arm to/from the honeycomb housing.
2. The cartridge tape is read/written physically sequentially in a tape reading/writing unit.
3. The data is transferred between disk and cartridge.

Thus if a request is made to a record instance in a file stored in an MSS, the best performance will be as fast as its disks if the record is already staged. The worst performance will be when the record resides at the end of a tape in a cartridge which is the farthest from the current position of the mechanical arm(s) (which physically takes cartridges to/from the staging/destaging area); in this case, staging will take the longest.

An important storage hierarchy design issue is on what basis to decide what and when to stage/destage. A common strategy for selecting the cylinders to be destaged is the l̲east r̲ecently u̲sed (LRU) algorithm.

Major MSS vendors include IBM and Control Data. Typical prices for an MSS range from a few hundred thousand dollars to over one million dollars.

A.6   THE TAPE AND RANDOM ACCESS DEVICE MARKETPLACE

Practically every vendor of general-purpose digital computer mainframes (CPU and core) for end users, from minicomputers to large-scale computers, offers tape and disk devices. Industry sources estimated in 1974 that IBM had 150,000 disk spindles installed, and independent vendors of IBM plug-compatible disks had installed a total of about 25,000.[10] There are now more disk spindles installed than tape drives. A close look at the sources of external storage devices reveals a large number of independent vendors in addition to the mainframe manufacturers. Starting in the 1970s, and into the 1980s, a dozen manufacturers offer close to 40 disk subsystems as replacements for the IBM line and about 50 magnetic tape drives as replacements for the IBM line.[10] The market for plug-compatible replacements for disk and tape drives produced by mainframe manufacturers other than IBM is also opening as the competition for the IBM-compatible device stiffens. In addition to plug-compatible storage units for the end user, independents also produce a sizable number of units for the large OEM (original equipment manufacturer) market.

Technological and price improvements are constantly being announced. The variety of disk devices has mushroomed since the introduction of IBM-compatible storage devices in 1968 by independent vendors. The independents compete primarily for the large market created by IBM installations. It goes like this. IBM introduces an external storage device. A short time later, perhaps in a matter of a few months, the independents produce IBM-compatible equivalents at a lower cost and higher performance than that of IBM. IBM introduces newer models and/or lower prices. Independents cut their prices. IBM makes a move, and so on it goes. The net result is that the amount of storage capability per dollar keeps going down. Plug-compatible subsystems often carry better cost/performance tags than the subsystems that they replace, be they IBM's or somebody else's. If we consider that external storage devices and computer main memories represent close to half of a computer's hardware cost, then the competition and new announcements leading to more for a dollar are not surprising.

A.7   THE FUTURE

A look into the future reveals that magnetic tapes will continue to be an important external storage technology over at least the next ten years and, similarly, that moving-head disks and floppy disks will predominate. This is the forecast of several studies.[11] The forecast of such studies is based on anticipated advances in factors such as access speed, storage density, reliability, and power dissipation; and considering computer elements and techniques such as software, materials, logic design, and fabrication. Magnetic tape developments will continue giving an increase in bit storage densities and decreased cost per bit. Magnetic drums and fixed-head disks used in some commercial and rugged environments will likely be replaced by bubble memories,[12] charged coupled devices (CCD),[13] or other storage. The prediction is that the moving-head disk will definitely dominate on the basis of cost per bit in relation to access time. Mass storage systems will continue as the main storage devices for very large storage requirements, over 10^{12} bytes, in which slower average access times may be tolerated.

Swap memory, which is used on virtual machines, and calls for short access time, high transfer rate, and low cost, will be dominated by bubble technology, CCD and RAM memories due mainly to high access speed rather than to cost per bit. In the early to mid-1970s the cost-per-bit performance of core memory was surpassed by semiconductor memory, due to major advances and competition in the semiconductor market.

Figure A.10 estimates the average access time versus cost per bit through the next decade for the major technologies predicted to fare very well. Note the attractiveness of the movable-head disk system and the down trend in cost per bit for all technologies.

In spite of all the advances, the wide gap will continue between fast, expensive main memory devices and slow, relatively inexpensive secondary memory devices—although the gap is narrowing.[13] Associative memory and processor technology[14] and content-addressable logic processors may pick up major support in the near future. The rapid growth in data base use and

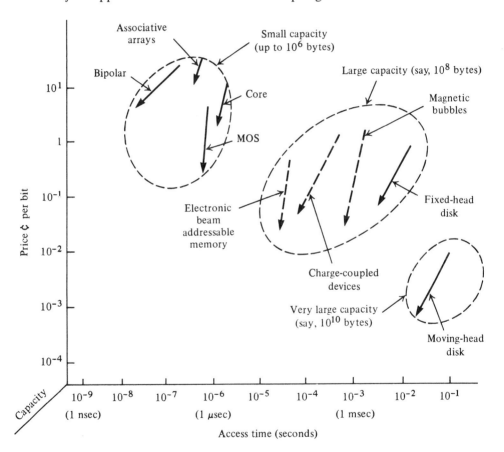

The arrows give the trend of values expected in the next decade

Figure A.10.   *Average access time and cost per bit expected in on-line data storage technology over the next decade (Courtesy of D. Hsiao, Reference 11)*

demands is pressuring for such more direct hardware support of data bases. The terms **associative memory** and **associative processor** are used interchangeably. Since the late 1960s a few small and experimental associative memories have been built and publicized. In the more advanced and recent **content-addressable storage** proposed, **hardware** logic searches data on the basis of given predicates which are logical combinations of the equality, greater than, and less than predicates. Predicates, defined in Appendix B, indicate the content of data, on the basis of which data is to be retrieved.

As a result of recent advances in VLSI technology, research in the design of associative and content-addressable processors has taken renewed interest aimed at constructing large-capacity associative processors, with millions of bytes of storage, large enough and cost-effective enough for current applications and eventually for very large data base applications. Thus such memories may start appearing in the 1980s as more than small and experimental memories.

After several years of experience with data base management systems and with the advent of very large and multi-user data bases, the idea of so-called **data base machines** or **data base processors** has evolved recently. This is the subject of Chapter 15. These are special processors specifically designed for enhancing the performance and capabilities of data base management systems. For example, index searching could be done perhaps by a dedicated microprocessor in parallel with other operations (e.g., translation of subsequent queries) performed by another processor. The make up of these data base machines and the related associative and content addressable processors is emerging.

The kind of hardware and storage available mold the underlying kind of data management software available for computer applications. The data management and information system architect must have a feeling for what kind of hardware and system software exists or is foreseen. The data base management technology embodied in this text reflects the fact that sequential tape devices and particularly random access disks will continue dominating at least through the foreseeable future.

REFERENCES

1. "All About Computer Output Microfilm (COM)," *Datapro 70*, Datapro Research Corporation, Report 70D7-010-80, September 1981.
2. "All About Plug-Compatible Tape Drives," *Datapro 70*, Datapro Research Corporation, Report 70D6-010-41, May 1982.
3. Murphy, J. A., "Cassette/Cartridge Tape Transports," *Modern Data*, May 1974, pp. 50–55.
4. IBM Reference Manual, "Introduction to IBM Direct Access Storage Devices and Organization Methods," Form GC20-1649.

5. "Reference Manual for IBM 3340 Disk Storage," *IBM Systems Reference Manual*, Form GA26-1619-3.

6. "IBM 3340 Disk Storage Fixed Head Feature, Users Guide," *IBM Systems Reference Manual*, Form GA26-1632.

7. Bowers, D., "Floppy Disk Drives and Systems—Part 1," *Mini-Micro Systems*, February 1977, pp. 36−51.

8. Porter, J. N., "Floppy-disk Drives—A Truly Flexible Industry Standard," *Mini-Micro Systems*, February 1982, pp. 165−172.

9. "All About Winchester Disk Drives," *Datapro 70*, Datapro Research Corporation, Report 70DG-010-50, June 1983.

10. "All About Plug-Compatible Disk Drives," *Datapro 70*, Datapro Research Corporation, Report 70D010-40, May 1976, and Report 70D6-010-40, July 1982.

11. Hsiao, D., ed., *Advanced Database Machine Architecture*, Prentice-Hall, Englewood Cliffs, N.J., 1983.

12. "The Outlook for Bubble Memory Devices," *Mini-Micro Systems*, February 1978, pp 32−33.

13. Theis, D. J., "An Overview of Memory Technologies," *DATAMATION*, January 1978, pp. 113−131.

14. Yau, S. S., and H. S. Fung, "Associative Processor Architecture—A Survey," *Computing Surveys*, Vol. 9, No. 1, March 1977, pp. 3−27.

Appendix B

CHARACTERIZATION OF QUERIES ACCORDING TO COMPLEXITY OF QUALIFICATION PART

Scheme used for classifying queries according to the complexity of the qualification part:

1. An *atomic condition*, A, will have the form

$$\text{NAME} \left\{ \begin{array}{c} \geq \\ \neq \\ \leq \end{array} \right\} \text{VALUE}$$

   where NAME is the item-name or field-name in the COBOL-record sense, or the domain in the tabular or relational sense.

2. An *item condition*, I, is a disjunction of atomic conditions, A_1 OR A_2 OR ... OR A_L, such that each A_i reflects the same item-name (field-name or domain). *ACI* is defined as the number of atomic conditions per item condition I. Example: AGE = 20 OR AGE = 21 where *ACI* = 2

3. A *record condition*, R, is a conjunction of item conditions I_1 AND I_2 AND ... AND I_M such that each I_j reflects a distinct item-name (field-name or domain). *ICR* is defined as the number of item conditions per record condition R. Example: (AGE > 20) AND (SEX = FEMALE)

$$\text{where } ICR = 2, (ACI_1 = ACI_2 = 1)$$

4. A *query condition*, Q is a disjunction of record conditions, R_1 OR R_2 OR ... OR R_N. *RCQ* is defined as the number of record conditions per query condition Q. Example: [(AGE > 18) AND (SEX = FEMALE)] OR [(AGE > 20) AND (SEX = MALE) AND (CLASS = SENIOR OR CLASS = GRADUATE)]

   where $RCQ = 2$;

$$ICR_1 = 2, (ACI_1 = ACI_2 = 1);$$

$$ICR_2 = 3, (ACI_1 = ACI_2 = 1, ACI_3 = 2)$$

A query or I/O transaction request is considered to have the form: ⟨operation part⟩ ⟨qualification part⟩. For example:

LIST NAME, DEPARTMENT AND SALARY

——————————————————————————

Operation part

WHERE BALANCE > 1000 AND INSURANCE_CO = XXX

——————————————————————————

Qualification part

GLOSSARY

Access Method— The technique or module that provides storage and retrieval of data in external storage and transfer of data between main memory and external storage.

Access Time— The time lapse between giving a command to access some data and the actual availability of the data for processing.

ADABAS— An inverted network-oriented GDBMS marketed by Software AG, West Germany; several hundred installations.

Area (in CODASYL DBTG)— A named portion of the total addressable physical space in which the data base is stored; the area may contain occurrences of records, sets, or parts of sets, as defined by the DBA.

ASI-ST— A GFMS marketed by Applications Software Incorporated, Torrance, California; several hundred installations.

Basic Access Method— A file management technique or module of the operating system providing users with a basic way of organizing, storing, and retrieving data in external files and transferring it between main memory and external storage; usually three methods provided: sequential, random, and indexed sequential.

BOMP (Bill of Materials Processor)— A specialized software package for defining, using, and administering BOM data bases, i.e., data bases in which a record instance is frequently both a child of an instance of a record of similar type and an owner of other record instances of similar type, for example, an assembly-subassembly data base, a course-prerequisite course data base; DBOMP is an IBM synonym for BOMP on a *d*isk operating system.

Bucket— An area of storage that contains data items or records and is easy or efficient to access or transfer to or from as a whole; the bucket might be a cylinder, a track, a block, etc; "page" is a synonym of bucket.

Cellular Multilist— A multilist organization in which pointers from one record in one bucket or cell (of physical storage) to records in other buckets are not allowed; these pointers reside instead in a directory (one directory pointer per bucket).

CODASYL— *Co*nference on *Da*ta *Sy*stems and *L*anguages, a small and autonomous group of experienced individuals from the vendor, user, and academic communities responsible for the COBOL and 1971 DBTG standards and the proposed 1978 CODASYL data base standards; the various committees now comprising CODASYL elaborate a number of proposals of interest to the whole field, with an eye toward standardization.

Collision— A situation in which two records with different values for a given field are hashed (field values are transformed via a hashing algorithm) to the same object field value or hashed address.

Concurrency Control— A control of the GDBMS to preserve the integrity of the data base when two or more transactions update the data base simultaneously.

Data Analyzer— A GFMS marketed by Program Products, Nanuet, N.Y.; several hundred installations.

Data Base— An integrated collection of occurrences of a number of record types, where the record types and their occurrences are interrelated by various specific *relationships*; synonyms also commonly used: data bank, integrated data base, integrated data bank. A data base with a single record type and no explicit relationships among record occurrences is the traditional file (in COBOL, PL/1, FORTRAN, RPG, etc.).

Data Base Administrator (DBA)— The individual(s) who will have to be responsible for defining schemas, subschemas, access rights, performance levels, integrity checks, etc.; in general, the DBA is in charge of the proper administration and control of the whole data base and its use.

Data Base Machine— A data base management system in which various functions (traditionally executed by software and general-purpose computer) are performed in special-purpose data management hardware.

Data Catalog— A major data dictionary/directory software system, marketed by TSI International for a variety of commercially available GDBMS.

Data Description Language (DDL)— A GDBMS language for defining the logical structure of data; there are three DDL languages: the schema DDL for the DBA, the subschema DDL for the DBA, and the subschema DDL for the user. The subschema DDLs of the DBA and of the user may be very similar.

Data Dictionary/Directory (DD/D) or Catalog— A centralized repository of descriptive information about data (data in files and/or data bases), applications using data, schemas, subschemas, and other types of information. The term DD/D also refers to the software data base system managing such repository.

Data Independence— A degree or independence of insulation of the correct functioning of an application program or query from a wide variety of *changes* in the logical organization, physical organization, access paths, and storage mapping of the data base.

Datamanager— A major data dictionary/directory software system, marketed by MSP Inc., for a variety of GDBMS, independent of any commercial GDBMS (implemented without using a commercial GDBMS).

Data Manipulation Language (DML)— The set of commands of a GDBMS for storing, retrieving, updating, adding, and deleting data from a data base; the DML includes all I/O commands and other data base navigation commands; DML commands are used in the Procedure Division of a COBOL program. The DML of a GFMS is essentially a query language designed for sorting and complex reports writing needs in single-file or nondatabase environments.

Data Replication— The redundant storage of data in different locations or distributed data base partitions for performance, reliability, and survival reasons.

dBase II— A relational micro-GDBMS marketed by Ashton-Tate, Inc.; over one hundred thousand sold in the vast micro and personal computer marketplace.

DBTG— *D*ata *B*ase *T*ask *G*roup, a special committee of CODASYL formed in the late 1960s to propose a standard for modern data base management systems.

Degree of Inversion— The extent to which fields are inverted in an inverted organization from zero degree of inversion in which no field is inverted to 100 percent inversion in which every field is inverted.

Device Media/Control Language (DM/CL)— The name coined by CODASYL for the physical data description language by which the DBA organizes the data base physically and maps it on storage devices; it includes means to define storage areas, devices to be used, access paths to be set up by the GDBMS, redundancies to be incurred, overflow areas, hashing techniques, etc. In practice, every GDBMS has its own particular mechanisms, usually in primitive form, for this task.

Dictionary— *See* directory.

Directory— A table containing information on records or other data items, often indicating their location; synonyms also used: dictionary, index.

Distributed Data Base— A data base in which either logical portions or certain instances of the data base are stored separately, frequently in different geographical locations.

Distributed GDBMS— A GDBMS with additional facilities to partition and distribute a data base, while providing distribution transparency and the necessary integrity controls (synchronization, etc.), some site autonomy, etc.

Distributed Processing— A processing scenario in which processing is done in two or more processors, but in which all or the large majority of stored (nonmain memory) data accessed resides in one processor. A typical scenario might involve one or more large processors to which smaller processors, such as personal computers, may be closely coupled/connected.

Distribution Transparency— The insulation between the user or application program view and any aspects of the distribution of the data base. This is a major goal of a distributed GDBMS.

DL/1 (Data Language/1)— IMS's data manipulation language; a version of the DL/1 package is also marketed by IBM as a self-standing package providing minimal data base capability, limited by the basic access methods of the operating system.

DMS-1100 (Data Management System-1100)— A DBTG GDBMS marketed by UNIVAC for its 1100 family of large computers; hundreds of installations.

File— A set of record occurrences of similar logical structure and data type.

Generalized Data Base/Data Communications System (DB/DC System)— A generalized package including the capabilities of both a GDBMS *and* a generalized DC system (also called a Teleprocessing Monitor) excelling in defining, servicing, and managing terminal users; a DC system provides a high degree of terminal independence, terminal message administration and control, terminal security, terminal integrity, etc.

Generalized Data Base Management System (GDBMS)— A widely applicable generalized software package permitting the definition, use, and management of a data base; a GDBMS provides a high degree of data independence, data shareability and nonredundancy of stored data, relatability between files, integrity, access flexibility, security, performance and efficiency, and data administration and control.

Generalized File Management System (GFMS)— A widely applicable generalized package integrating various I/O-oriented facilities of COBOL, report writers, report program generators, storage and retrieval systems, sort/merge packages and a variety of related facilities; a GFMS includes all the facilities of a report writer and goes beyond it; a GFMS uses the basic file management of the operating system underneath; a GFMS is not a GDBMS; a GFMS does replace a programming language in sort and report writing-oriented applications.

GIS (Generalized Information System)— An information storage and retrieval system with much of the ingredients of a modern GFMS; marketed by IBM Corporation.

Hashing— A direct addressing technique in which a nonnumeric key space or a coarsely populated numeric key space is converted to a densely populated numeric key space for more efficient use of available random access devices.

Heterogeneous Distributed Data Base— A distributed data base in which each partition may be stored and managed by a different GDBMS.

Hierarchic Data Base Model— A model or data structure for defining data bases in which a parent record type (or record instance) can have one or more child record types (or instances of these record types), but which does not allow (1) a child record type to have more than one parent record type or (2) an M:N relationship of instances between two record types. Tree data model is a synonym of hierarchic data model.

Higher Level File Organization— A powerful technique for organizing and accessing data efficiently while permitting complex multikey data content retrieval demands, rather than only the single-key or get-next accessing allowed by the basic access methods of the operating system. Other synonyms: secondary file organization, secondary index method.

Hit Ratio— The ratio of the number of records in the file or data base that satisfy a query to the total number of records in the file or data base.

Home Address— A storage location to which a data record is logically assigned for more efficient handling, as opposed to an overflow address involving less direct handling.

Host Language— The programming language (e.g., COBOL, Fortran, etc.) from which the GDBMS facilities may be invoked via the language interface provided by the GDBMS.

iDBP— *I*ntel's *D*ata *B*ase *P*rocessor; one of the first data base machines commercially available.

IDM— Britton-Lee's *I*ntelligent *D*atabase *M*achine; introduced in the early 1980s, the first commercially available data base machine.

IDMS (Integrated Data Management System)— A DBTG GDBMS marketed by Cullinet Software, Mass.; several hundred installations.

IDS (Integrated Data Store)— A network GDBMS marketed by Honeywell Information Systems; one of the pioneering GDBMS designed in the 1960s by General Electric; hundreds of installations.

IMS (Information Management System)— A hierarchic GDBMS marketed by IBM Corporation; over one thousand installations. The term IMS is also used by other vendors for lesser known products, such as Honeywell's *I*nventory *M*anagement *S*ystem.

Index— A table containing information on records or data items and their location.

INGRES— A major relational GDBMS developed by the University of California, Berkeley; a commercial version is marketed by Relational Technology, Inc.

Integrity— A very broad term in data base technology denoting the correct state of the data base.

Inverted File or Data Base— A file or data base in which a number of fields have been inverted; that is, all the values of a field are placed in an inverted directory along with a pointer to each record in the file or data base that has that particular field value; fast access is thus provided to the data on the basis of the inverted field contents.

Inverted Hierarchic Data Base Model— A fundamentally hierarchic data base model in which any fields of any file in a data base can be inverted to provide fast access to any portion on the basis of complex data base content qualification.

ISAM (Indexed Sequential Access Method)— A basic access method striving to provide the advantages of both the sequential access method (quick access only to the next physical record and no empty spaces in the file) and the random access method (quick access to any of the records and quick updating of the file); it may appear to the user externally as a sequential file, as a random file, or as both.

Key— A data item (data value or data name, field value or field name) used to locate a record effectively, e.g., the inverted key, the sort key, etc.

List Length— The number of records that are linked in a list.

List Organization— A data organization in which a series of records are linked into a chain via a pointer stored in each linked record.

Logical Data Base— The data base as perceived by users devoid of any aspects dealing with its physical organization. In IBM IMS terminology, it may refer to either a subschema or to a hierarchic collection of segments derived from one or more physical data bases by using pointer segments.

Mark IV— A GFMS marketed by Informatics, Canoga Park, California; over one thousand installations.

Multilist Organization— A data organization in which a set of records is linked by a variety of lists passing through the records.

NDX-100— An initial prototype parallel content-addressable data base machine.

Network Data Base Model— A model for defining data bases in which any record type can be related either as a child or as a parent record type to any number of other record types; for each parent record occurrence there may be one or many related child record occurrences.

Overflow Area— A physical area of external storage in which data not contained initially in the external prime data area is stored; there may be overflow areas for new record instances, new fields, extra long fields or records, etc.

Parallel Content-Addressable Data Base Machine—A data base machine which performs a number of data base operations in parallel on portions of the data base.

Partitioned Data Base— A distributed data base (see its definition).

PHOLAS— A DBTG GDBMS marketed by Philips, The Netherlands.

Pointer— An indicator that leads to a given data item or record from another point in the data space; a pointer may be a machine address, a relative record address, or a logical identifier of a record.

QBE— Query-by-Example, perhaps the first commercial GDBMS, marketed by IBM Corp. Several look-alikes and derivatives are marketed by other vendors.

Query Language— A high-level data manipulation language for interacting with the file or data base; the language is strongly nonprogrammer, nonprocedural, and natural-language oriented; the query language of a GDBMS is designed for quickly servicing ad hoc requests for accessing and storing low volumes of data based on complex data base content criteria. The DML of a GFMS is essentially a query language designed for sorting and report-writing needs, involving either high or low volumes of data, based on complex single-file content criteria.

Recovery— In a GDBMS, the process of recovering the correct state of the data base after an error has been introduced and detected; the error may be due to some fault in the hardware, system software, or application.

Relatability— The ability to define relationships between records in a data base management system.

Relation— A flat file or table; that is, a file whose records (called tuples) cannot have repeating groups. Each tuple must have a unique identifying field; the relation is made up of one or more domains or fields for each tuple. A relation is equivalent to a record type without repeating groups in a nonrelational GDBMS.

Relational Algebra— The language for manipulating relations composed of algebra operators including: projection, join, and division.

Relational Calculus— The nonprocedural-oriented language for manipulating relations; it is composed of relational calculus operators.

Relational Data Base Model— A data base model in which the data base is made up of a set of flat tables or relations, in which relationships are expressed by the fact that two relations have a field or domain in common and in which the relationships can be 1:N or M:N.

Report Writer— A program that provides various facilities for editing, tallying, formatting, and ordering data, and performing other related tasks for generating more complex reports; these facilities go beyond the primitive ones defined as part of the standard of programming languages.

Ring Organization— A list organization in which the last record in the list points to the first one of the list.

Rollback— In a GDBMS, the process of undoing or rolling back all updates, deletes, and insertions to the data base up to a correct state of the data base; after-images and before-images of affected data base areas and the corresponding transaction log are used for rolling back.

Rollforward— In a GDBMS, the process of redoing all updates, deletes, and insertions to the data base starting with a correct state of the data base; the transaction log is used for rolling forward.

Root— The head or main node of a tree structure.

Schema— The logical description of a data base, including the definition of the name and data type of each field making up each record and the definition of every relationship linking any two files; schema defined only by the data base administrator via a schema data description language.

Secondary File Organization— *See* Higher Level File Organization.

Set— In DBTG GDBMS, a structure composed of an owner record type instance and its chain of zero, one, or more member record type instances.

Set Type— A named relationship between one owner record type and one or more member record types.

SQL/DS (Structured Query Language/Data System)— A major relational GDBMS marketed by IBM Corporation. Several look-alikes are marketed by other vendors.

Sort— To order a set of records on the basis of the values of the field(s) chosen as the sort key.

Subschema— The logical description of a subset of the data base, including the fields, record types, and relationships of the data base assigned to a given user or application program; any number of subschemas may be defined over a schema; subschema defined via a subschema data definition language by a data base administrator (DBA) or by a user (to whom the subschema is his or her own schema) when describing the subschema already defined by the DBA.

SYSTEM 2000— An inverted-hierarchic GDBMS marketed by Intel Corp., Austin, Texas; several hundred installations.

Teleprocessing Monitor (TP)— A software package, also called a *data* communications system (DC system), for defining, servicing, and managing terminal users and associated data communication needs. A TP monitor does not include the functional capabilities of a GDBMS or of a GFMS.

TOTAL— A network GDBMS marketed by Cincom Systems Inc., Cincinnati, Ohio; available on a wide variety of computers; close to two thousand installations.

Transaction Log— A file in which a copy of each record updated is stored in order to allow for recovery. Usually both before- and after-images of the records updated are stored in the log along with the detail of the transaction causing each update. The log can be maintained on disk or tape. The GDBMS recovery manager uses the transaction log to restore the integrity of the data base after a failure.

Tree Structure— A hierarchic level-by-level data structure in which a parent data item (say a field or record) can have one or more child data items, but which does not allow a child data item to have more than one parent data item.

Tuple— A group of related field values in a relation, or row in a relation, i.e., a record occurrence with no repeating groups.

UCC-Ten— A major data dictionary/directory system for IBM's IMS, marketed by University Computing company, implemented using IMS.

View— A subschema, i.e., the logical description of a subset of the data base, including the fields, record types, and relationships of the data base assigned to a given user or application.

Virtual Field or Record— A field or record that appears to be but is not physically stored; rather, it is materialized when its value is requested by either (1) deriving it through a formula defined by the DBA or (2) locating its value actually physically stored in the place indicated by the pointer residing in the virtual field.

VSAM (Virtual Storage Access Method)— An IBM basic access method similar to ISAM externally but different internally with respect to physical organization and strategy for record updating, deletions, and additions. VSAM is an implementation of B-trees.

SOLUTIONS
TO
SELECTED
EXERCISES

CHAPTER 2

2.1. With respect to queries of type (a), there is no significant performance difference that can be cited in general between inverted and multilist organizations. However, with respect to queries of type (b), there is a significant performance advantage of the inverted strategy. The query can be answered by just examining the inverted directory without having to retrieve records from the data storage space, for any kind of query complexity. However, if the record field is not inverted and it is involved in the where clause of the query, then records will have to be retrieved to check for qualification on such noninverted field(s).

Let us see an example, Figure 2.6. To find out "how many employees there are in the business administration department and who have a Ph.D. degree," the following is done. The directory is searched, the two lists of pointers for BUS.AD and for PH.D. are retrieved from the directory and merged, and the number of pointers that match is computed to provide the answer to the query, namely, 1.

In the multilist organization, it will take more work to obtain the answer. As an exercise, indicate how the multilist organization can obtain the answer to the query.

2.3.

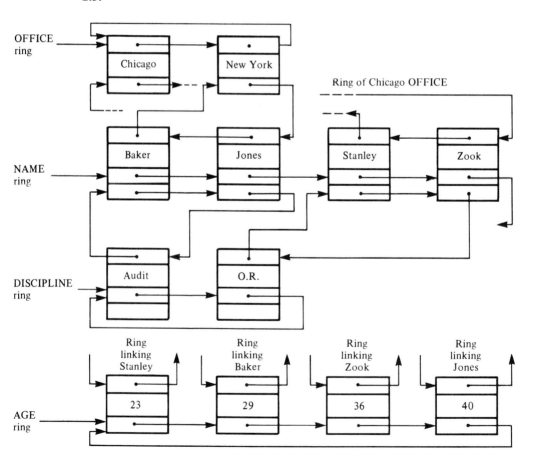

2.5. (a) Minimum storage space: fields with the larger number of unique field values should be placed at the bottom of the hierarchy, according to number of unique field values.

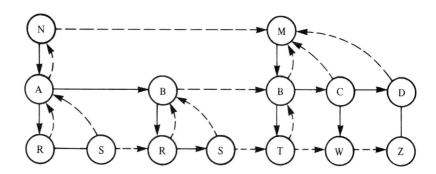

(b) Maximum storage space: fields with the larger number of unique field values should be placed at the top of the hierarchy, according to the number of unique field values.

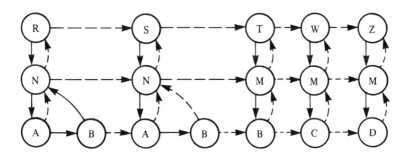

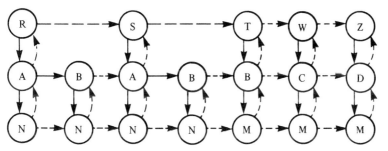

This is the maximum storage configuration.

2.7. In the doubly chained structure, queries referring to keys near the top of the index structure tend to take _less_ average access time, compared to those involving keys near the bottom. Update type of queries involving updating of keys near the top of the index structure tend to take _more_ average access time compared to those involving keys near the bottom.

In the inverted file structure, queries referring to subset X of the inverted keys result in _the same_ average access time compared to those referring to subset Y. (Keys X plus Y make up the whole index.) Assume the inverted structure discussed.

2.9. The cellular multilist organization provides the following:
(a) Less paging than with ring or multilist because, by definition, each list structure is constrained to one page and thus page retrieval and swapping are avoided or lessened. Performance should be better for cellular multilist than ring or multilist where complete lists spread over many pages must be accessed. In noncellular organizations, a page could be fetched more than once by a list touching a page X, then another page, and subsequently page X again.
(b) Higher performance through parallel processing. For example, with an OR condition, separate pages for records to be checked for satisfying each item condition can be brought into main memory for each separate CPU and checked. Access time will be saved. This does not hold for AND conditions or the condition in which just one record is needed. In these cases, multilist or ring structures _may_ perform equally well.
(c) Involves less indexing, i.e., fewer pointers in the index itself, than the inverted structure but more than the multilist organization. Also, it uses fewer all pointers than ring organizations such as the hierarchical or fully ringed organization. With the hierarchical organization, pointers are in record space; with the cellular multilist, only some pointers are in record space.
Multiple CPUs would help as follows in particular:
With cellular multilist on a single CPU, each page pointed at by each key value in the directory is brought into main memory at a time. With multiple CPUs and a query involving ORs between qualifications on keys, a page from one key (say key 1) could be brought into CPU1's main memory and checked while a page from another key (say key 2) is brought into CPU2's main memory. The result of an OR condition is the union of results from these CPUs. It is very efficient performance-wise for more than one page in memory to be simultaneously checked at a time. It is less efficient in a single CPU environment, even in a multiprogramming environment (if both pages were brought into main memory at the same time, chances are one would be swapped out before being completely checked and would have to be accessed again and brought back into main memory).

CHAPTER 3

3.1. No. However, in probably the majority of applications both a GFMS and a GDBMS should be used. Although functionally GFMS and GDBMS may overlap in some areas, they primarily complement each other and in the majority of applications their coverage is needed. In other cases, a GFMS alone is sufficient. In other cases, a GDBMS with some report writing facilities is sufficient, without the necessity of the very powerful report writing facilities of a GFMS.

GFMS excel in report writing, sorting/merging, editing for report writing, and related tasks. They are usually batch-oriented, sequential file-oriented processors. Significantly missing in GFMS are facilities to establish relationships among many files (which are absolutely needed in order to call a set of files a data base) and higher level organizations or secondary indexing facilities such as inversions, B-trees, etc. (which avoid expensive sequential scanning of files). Basic report writers are the less powerful relatives of GFMS. In the area of report writing, sorting/merging, etc., the spectrum goes from report writers providing elementary facilities to GFMS providing robust facilities.

GFMS are an attractive alternative to procedural programming languages for applications that are primarily report writing, sorting/merging, etc., in nature. GDBMS, on the other hand, are not, functionally speaking, an alternative to procedural languages or GFMS. GDBMS are a complement to procedural languages or GFMS.

In a number of applications with little or no report writing, sorting/merging, etc., tasks, a GDBMS is sufficient.

3.3. Yes, any relationship, such as a DBTG set, and any indexing, such as inversions and B-trees, can be represented in the DIAM string model as shown on page 714. This independence from any particular GDBMS is a major feature of the model. The E-strings RATING and CLAIM-CYCLE represent the corresponding inversions, or any type of indexing, in any GDBMS.

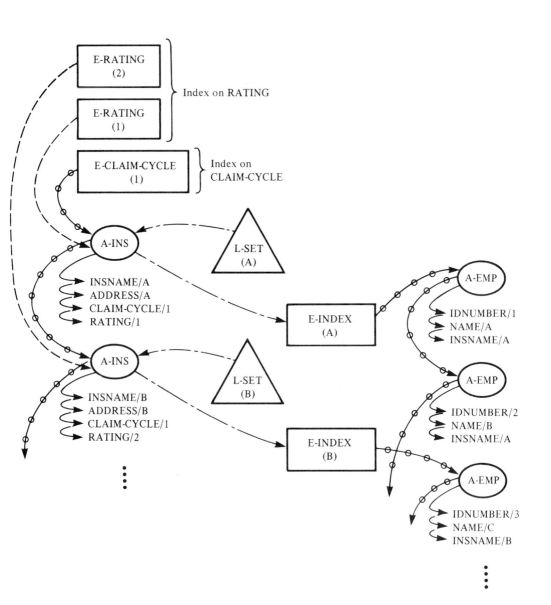

CHAPTER 5

5.1.   T   (a) A set type is a named relationship between record types.

    F   (b) A schema consists of only one set type.

    T   (c) For each record type the schema specifies the area or areas into which the occurrences of that record are to be placed when they are entered into the data base.

    F   (d) A set type within a schema may be unordered.

    T   (e) Any record type may be declared in the schema as a member of one or more set types.

    F   (f) The capability for a record type to participate as both owner and member in the same set type is not supported by the 1978 data description language.

    T   (g) A singular set consists of an owner record and at least one member record.

    F   (h) An M:N relationship can be represented with only one set type.

    T   (i) A set may have an arbitrary number of occurrences of the member record types declared for it in the schema.

    T   (j) Any record type may be declared in the schema as the owner of one or more set types.

5.3. (a) The following retrieval process using the DML obtains the answers to the requests. I do not provide the DML commands themselves; it is your turn to provide them now, since I already gave you several examples in this chapter!

1. The schema does not provide hashed direct access to CHILD. Thus, the way to get the answer is to retrieve each and every EMPLOYEE, scan its dependent CHILDren until one under X years old is found (there may or may not be one or several under X years old), and count the number of EMPLOYEEs that have CHILDren with such qualification. If a singular set is declared in the schema with 'SYSTEM' as owner and EMPLOYEE as child, then each EMPLOYEE can be retrieved without qualifying it or providing its hash key (we do not know and do not care what the key is of each EMPLOYEE that qualifies).

2. Another way of stating the question is this: provide the names of the clinics in which one or more doctors service two or more employees insured by the same insurance company. The *best* way to obtain the answer is as follows:

    (i) Retrieve the first DOCTOR; then retrieve its EMPLOYEE dependent, and then all its dependent INSURANCE-CO instances. Note that there is a schema integrity constraint that prohibits two or more INSURANCE CO records with the same INSUR-CO-NAME under the same EMPLOYEE. Repeat this for the next EMPLOYEE of the given DOCTOR. When two EMPLOYEEs are found insured by the same INSURANCE-CO, then present the CLINIC-NAME of the given DOCTOR.

(ii) Repeat the whole cycle A for the next DOCTOR instance.

Note that there may be a clinic qualified because a DOCTOR X services an EMPLOYEE A with INSUR-CO-NAME N and a DOC-TOR Y services an EMPLOYEE B with the same INSUR-CO-NAME N.

(b) I would define the following record types and relationships in the schema if maximum performance for these requests were a must. Now you define the schema additions using the DBTG DDL.

1. Establish a new record type X and a set, call it SET-X, from X to EMPLOYEE relating only EMPLOYEEs with CHILDren under X years old. Unfortunately, in DBTG a set is a static relationship predefined when the schema is generated; thus, a given X value will have to be defined when the schema is generated and a specific set of EMPLOYEEs will have to be chained at load time.

A more general approach would be to add the new record type X and several set types, each linking EMPLOYEEs with CHILDREN with a given age range, e.g., 10 to 15 years old. Then with the DML the proper set(s) would be searched.

The previous approaches, and any others that enhance read-only requests, will of course add processing time to updates which involve removing/adding EMPLOYEES to the new set(s).

2. A solution similar to the one above would work. Establish a new record type CLINIC and a set, call it SET-CO, from CLINIC to DOCTOR relating only DOCTORs in CLINICs that qualify. This set would be first established when the data is defined and loaded. If the INSUR-CO-NAME field content is changed as the data base is used, then the SET-CO may be affected: DOCTOR members may have to be added or deleted accordingly. To insure this, there should be a data base subroutine triggered whenever INSUR-CO-NAME changes, such that the proper updating of SET-CO takes place. This subroutine would actually be a search procedure with DML commands as in (a)2 above.

5.5. (a) In an assembly/manufacturing plant:

1. A SUPPLIER supplies zero, one, or many PARTs; at the same time, a PART may be supplied by zero, one, or more SUPPLIERS.

2. A PART is used in zero, one, or several PROJECTS, and a PROJECT may use zero, one, or several PARTs.

3. The 1:N relationship could represent the situation that a given PART may be used erroneously in zero, one, or more PROJECTS.

(b) The way that an M:N relationship is handled in DBTG is to transform it to two relationships and a new record type (intersection record type) as shown on page 717.

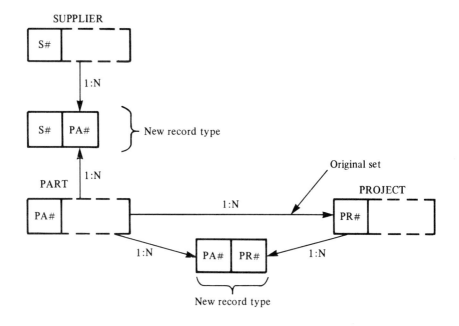

Now you define this schema in the DBTG DDL.
Below is a sample data base content.

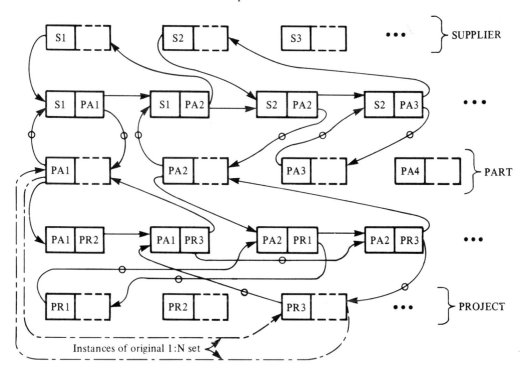

5.7. The various gains provided by this conditional mapping option of the DSDL are offset to various degrees when updating records already existing in the data base, not when adding or deleting records. The mapping option in question is shown in Figure 5.18. A specific example that illustrates the problem is the mapping described in Section 5.8 of the EMPLOYEE record type in Figure 5.6 to

(a) SINGLE_$OTD storage record if $OWED_TO_DOCTOR ≥ 10,000

(b) FIRST_$OTD linked to SECOND_$OTD storage records if $OWED_TO_DOCTOR ≥ 0 and < 10,000

(c) NEGATIVE_OTD storage record if $OWED_TO_DOCTOR < 0

Suppose that a specific EMPLOYEE has $OWED-TO-DOCTOR ≥ 10,000 and is stored in the data base. What happens if subsequently $OWED-TO-DOCTOR is updated to below 10,000? Is the GDBMS to automatically move and remap EMPLOYEE to the other storage record(s)? If this is done dynamically this may be expensive, and if done frequently it may offset the gains of the mapping for other types of data base accessing. On the other hand, if this remapping is not done when the updating takes place, then (a) the mapping declared in the DSDL is not being adhered to and (b) how does one subsequently know which of the storage record types has the updated EMPLOYEE? This question could be taken care of by some directory or indexing, but this is an extra cost that makes dynamic remapping perhaps preferable. Thus a difficult situation is posed when updating a schema record that is conditionally mapped to different DSDL storage record types, and there is no good solution.

CHAPTER 7

7.1. __T__ (a) An IMS PDBR contains a single type of root segment.

  __T__ (b) A root segment has an arbitrary number of child segment types.

  __T__ (c) No child segment occurrence can exist without its parent.

  __T__ (d) A sequence field is optional for all IMS segments except the root.

  __T__ (e) An M to N relationship can be represented only by using logical data base mechanisms (a LDB).

  __T__ (f) An IMS LDBR root must also be a PDBR root.

  __F__ (g) PROCOPTs may be defined for nonsequence fields of an IMS segment.

  __T__ (h) Initial loading of an IMS data base need not be performed in root occurrence sequence (ordered by its sequence field) for HDAM.

  __F__ (i) In HDAM the logical sequence of root segment occurrences is not lost.

___F___ (j) In HISAM only root segments may be placed in the ISAM data set (assuming no secondary data set groups).

___T___ (k) In HIDAM only the sequence field of root segments may be placed in the HISAM index data base (assuming no secondary data set groups).

___F___ (l) There is no restriction in HISAM and HDAM on the assignment of segment types to data set groups.

___F___ (m) Splitting an IMS data base into several data set groups increases the amount of storage fragmentation.

___T___ (n) In IMS, direct access to any segment type may be established via secondary data set groups, except for HISAM and HSAM.

___T___ (o) A child segment type can have a physical parent type which is also at the same time the logical parent type.

7.3. (a) 1. The retrieval process to answer this question is:

```
      X       = ......
      COUNT = 0
N     GU      DOCTOR
              EMPLOYEE
              CHILD (CHILD-AGE < X)
              Execute COUNT = COUNT + 1 if the previous
                 command finds such a CHILD, else stop and display
                 COUNT
      GO TO N
```

2. The same approach as for the DBTG in Exercise 5.3 should be followed. See the solution for that exercise. The only difference is that when the desired DOCTOR(s) are found, the CLINIC-NAME is retrieved from a dependent segment CLINIC rather than fields appearing in DOCTOR. Now you provide the corresponding DL/1 commands.

(b) The same answer as for the DBTG in Exercise 5.3 part (b) holds for IMS. You provide the corresponding DBD.

The previous relationships needed maintain the data base still in hierarchic form. Ha! I avoided having to answer for you again the problems and solutions of IMS dealing with nonhierarchic relationships (see the text!).

7.5. In the DBTG system there are four types of currency indicators: current of run unit, current of set type, current of record type, and current of area. In IMS there are equivalents to only some of these indicators, provided through the PCB parameters:

1. The "key feedback area," containing the hierarchically concatenated key which indicates the particular segment occurrence last retrieved and the particular ancestors (from the root to this segment occurrence). This is equivalent to the current of run unit and to much of the current of set type in DBTG.

2. The "segment name," indicating the last segment type retrieved, that appears to be but is not really exactly equivalent to the current of record type.

7.7. The resulting physical structure is as follows:

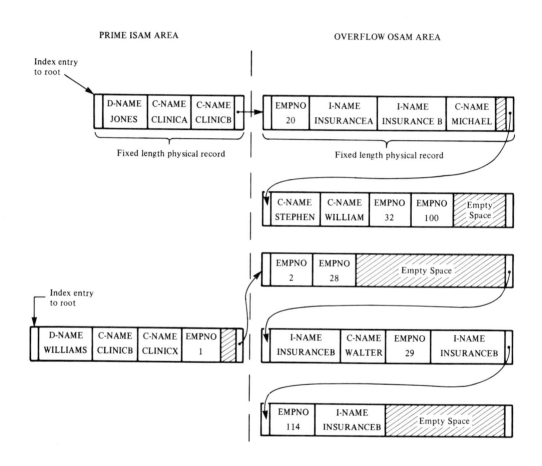

7.9. (a) The best solution is to redefine the schema by using IMS logical data base mechanisms: establish a pointer segment EI as a physical child of EMPLOYEE to point to INSUR-CO. This will avoid the storage redundancy problem of insurance information being stored for multiple employees, and at the same time it will provide the IMS logical data base view of Figure 7.2.

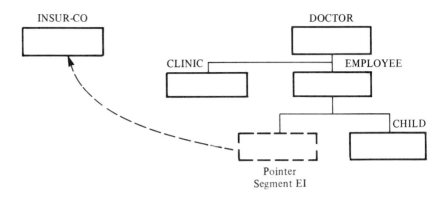

Pointer
Segment EI

(b) The best solution is to redefine the schema as before by using IMS logical data base mechanisms, but adding one other pointer segment IE as a physical child of INSUR-CO to point to EMPLOYEE.

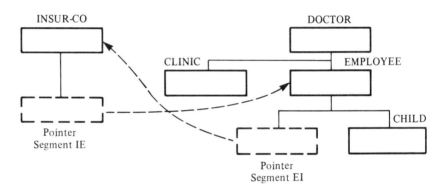

Now you do parts (c) and (d).

CHAPTER 8

8.1. Formatting and indexing clauses are not included below:

DEFINE:
NEW DATA BASE IS DOCTOR-CLINIC:
      1* D-NAME (KEY NAME...):
      2* SPECIALTY
      3* YRSEXPER
      4* CLINIC (REPEATING GROUP):

         5* C-NAME
         6* ADDRESS
         7* EMPLOYEE (REPEATING GROUP):
         8* EMPNO
         9* E-NAME
       10* ADDRESS
       11* AMT-OWED
       12* INSUR-CO (REPEATING GROUP IN 7):
       13* I-NAME
       14* ADDRESS
       15* CYCLE
       16* CHILD (REPEATING GROUP IN 7):
       17* C-NAME
       18* CHILD-AGE
       19* SCH-YEAR

8.3. (a) Retrieve all data files of EMPLOYEE 106 without concern for the particular DOCTOR involved.

    PRINT TREE EMPLOYEE WHERE EMPLOYEE EQ 106

(b) Retrieve all repeating groups in the data base.

        PRINT EMPLOYEE
        PRINT INSUR-CO
        PRINT CHILD
        PRINT CLINIC

(c) Retrieve all the CHILD information for each child whose age is > 14 and whose parent has AMT-OWED ≥ 600.

        PRINT CHILD WHERE AMT-OWED ≥ 600 AND CHILD-
        AGE > 14

(d) Retrieve the name and claim cycle of every insurance company of EMPLOYEE 106.

(e) For EMPLOYEE 106 change the address of his insurance company to DISAPPEARED and change the SPECIALTY of his DOCTOR to QUACK.

(f) Delete all fields of EMPLOYEE 106, all of the related CHILD information, and all information on the company that insures him.

(g) Retrieve the names of the insurance companies insuring employees with children older than 10.

CHAPTER 9

9.1. This is one possible answer; other answers are possible.

1. Project on PART by removing COLOR and WEIGHT:

		PART
N-PN	(NAME	NUMBER)
	Gear	78
	Wheel	125
	Chain	617

2. Join N-PN with SUPPLIES:

		PART		
N-PN-SUPPLIES	(NAME	NUMBER	QUANTITY	SUPPLIER#):
	Gear	78	33	4
	Chain	617	46	3
	Chain	617	51	2
	Wheel	125	4	1

3. Project the result above on NAME and SUPPLIER#:

NAME_SUPPLIER	(NAME	SUPPLIER#)
	Gear	4
	Chain	3
	Chain	2
	Wheel	1

4. Join the result in 3 with the SUPPLIERS relation:

RESULT	(NAME	SUPPLIER#	CITY	SUPPLIERNAME)
	Gear	4	Miami	Richards
	Chain	3	Houston	Johnson
	Chain	2	New York	Smith
	Wheel	1	Los Angeles	Jones

5. Project the result in 4 on NAME and CITY for the answer:

ANSWER	(NAME	CITY)
	Gear	Miami
	Chain	Houston
	Chain	New York
	Wheel	Los Angeles

CHAPTER 10

10.1. (a)

```
UPDATE       EMPLOYEE
SET          SALARY = 0.80 * SALARY
WHERE        DEPTNO =
             (SELECT DEPTNO
             FROM DEPARTMENT
             WHERE D-NAME = COMP-SCI OR
                   D-NAME = PLANNING)
```

(d) This cannot be done. No updates are allowed over view tables composed of columns from more than one base table. In this case, columns in the view table come from the two tables EMPLOYEES and DEPARTMENT joined together.

10.3. No, the function MAX can be applied only to a group of values; here it is requested that it be applied to a single value of SALARY of employee name. Actually, this exercise shows a potential contention. We could argue that this query should be valid and that its semantics are to retrieve the employee name and salary of the employee(s) with the maximum salary. Other implementations of SQL/DS could take this stand!

10.5.

        SELECT C-NAME, CHILD-AGE, SCH-YEAR
        FROM CHILD C, INSUR-CO I
        WHERE C.EMPNO = I.EMPNO
        AND I-NAME = 'PURITAN';

However, Examples 12 and 20 show cases where subqueries cannot be expressed as joins.

CHAPTER 11

11.1.

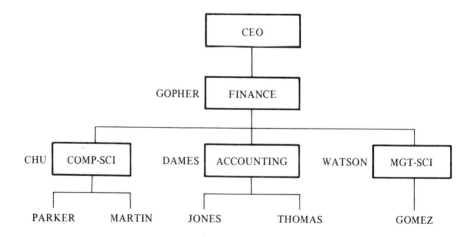

11.3.

EMPLOYEE	E-NAME	DEPTNO	MGRNO	SALARY
	P.			P.MAX.ALL

No, it is incorrect. The function MAXimum can be applied only to a group of values, but here it is requested to apply it and print its result for a single value of employee name.

CHAPTER 12

12.2. (a)

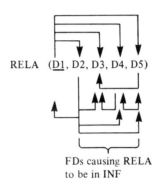

RELA (D1, D2, D3, D4, D5)

FDs causing RELA
to be in INF

D_1 and D_2 are candidate keys but D_1 is indicated in this exercise as the key. There are 12 FDs as shown by the arrows.

(b) Four equivalent models:

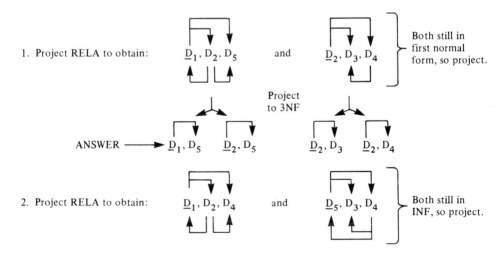

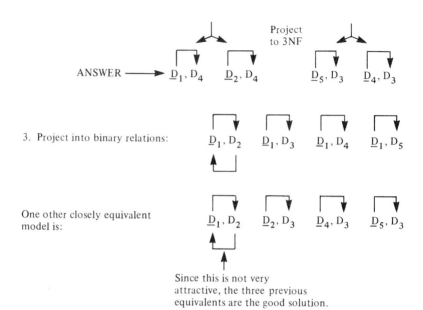

ANSWER ⟶ $\underline{D}_1, D_4$ $\underline{D}_2, D_4$ $\underline{D}_5, D_3$ $\underline{D}_4, D_3$

Project to 3NF

3. Project into binary relations: $\underline{D}_1, D_2$ $\underline{D}_1, D_3$ $\underline{D}_1, D_4$ $\underline{D}_1, D_5$

One other closely equivalent model is: $\underline{D}_1, D_2$ $\underline{D}_2, D_3$ $\underline{D}_4, D_3$ $\underline{D}_5, D_3$

Since this is not very attractive, the three previous equivalents are the good solution.

CHAPTER 13

13.1. (a) Data independence is defined as the transparency, insulation, or independence of the data view of an application program or user from certain changes in the logical or physical structure of the underlying files or data base(s). The intent is that any changes in the underlying structures be transparent to the application programs or users who are not concerned with such changes. There are many changes that may be contemplated, from logically oriented to physically oriented. There is no 100 percent data independence since there is no industry-wide agreement on what the list of changes should be. However, robust GDBMS generally provide data independence for at least a number of common changes; and beyond such changes, specific architectures and GDBMS will vary in the degree of data independence that they provide. Among the frequent changes for which data independence is provided are those listed in Section 3.3.

   (b) The relative ranking, from higher to lower degrees of data independence, is: relational systems, inverted-oriented systems, CODASYL DBTG Systems, and IMS. Relational systems are significantly superior in terms of data independence, as specifically indicated in Section 9.4. The ability to make up views composed of entities which in turn are composed of attributes from *any different* record types or relations (which translates into a high degree of data independence), is well supported by relational systems, is only somewhat supported by some inverted-oriented systems, and is not supported by CODASYL DBTG or IMS.

If a new record type PNEW is to be inserted between an existing parent record type P_1 and a child CH_1, (a) relational systems permit it while maintaining data independence, (b) inverted network systems and DBTG systems permit it with no problem by establishing a new relationship from P_1 to PNEW and from PNEW to CH_1 while maintaining the original relationship from P_1 to CH_1, and (c) IMS and inverted hierarchic systems such as System 2000 do not permit it effectively. IMS and System 2000 maintain data independence while adding new children at the bottom of the tree in a data base, but a new child cannot be inserted between existing records by adding a new relationship (in addition to the existing relationships) as in DBTG systems; IMS and System 2000 are hierarchic systems in terms of the relationships that may be established. However, in some hierarchic systems such as System 2000 the insertion of a new record type between two record types can to some extent remain transparent to a query language user, but not to the procedural data manipulation language user.

c) Data independence costs some storage and particularly CPU processing. The cost is due to the mappings, dictionary/directories, etc., that are usually involved in implementing data independence. The more the data independence provided and exercised, the more the cost in terms of developing it (from a vendor point of view) and in terms of processing costs for the applications involved. Thus, in general, the more complex the mapping between a user view and the actual physical data base, the costlier it is.

13.3. (a) Set membership classes are a characteristic of each set defined in the schema. They are defined to specify the type of relationship allowed between owner record and member records related via a set (relationship). There are two "insertion rules": automatic and manual. And there are three "retention rules" (which would be more appropriately called "integrity rules," which is what they really are): fixed, mandatory, and optional. These membership classes are defined in Section 5.2.

As an example, let us use the data base in Figure 5.9 to illustrate the definition of each membership class. For the set DOC_PAT, the membership classes and controls could mean the following:

1. AUTOMATIC: When an occurrence of EMPLOYEE is created or stored in the data base, it must become a member of an instance of the set DOC_PAT owned by the particular DOCTOR occurrence satisfying a selection criteria specified in an appropriate DML command.

2. MANUAL: When an occurrence of EMPLOYEE is created or stored in the data base, it does not have to be as a member of an instance of the set DOC_PAT.

3. FIXED: When an occurrence of EMPLOYEE is created or stored in the data base, it is constrained to a specific set occurrence of DOC_PAT (which is owned by a specific DOCTOR occurrence).

4. MANDATORY: When an occurrence of EMPLOYEE is stored in the data base and made a member of an occurrence of the set DOC_PAT, it cannot exist in the data base unless it is a member of some (possibly different) occurrence of this set type.

5. OPTIONAL: An occurrence of EMPLOYEE may exist in the data base either participating or not participating in an occurrence of the set DOC_PAT.

(b) The problems addressed by the DBTG set membership are not eliminated by the relational model. Relational data base administrators and users are not shielded from such aspects. The issues addressed are essentially integrity control issues. The relational data model originally presented by Codd and followed by various GDBMS does not include the variety of such integrity control mechanisms for dealing with essentially the same issues in the relational DOCTOR_EMPLOYEE data base equivalent, Figure 9.4. The relational situation is as follows. If an EMPLOYEE is to be inserted in the data base, then the doctor D_NAME must also be identified and inserted since it is a member of the key of EMPLOYEE. Thus a MANDATORY and AUTOMATIC situation exists between DOCTOR and EMPLOYEE. OPTIONAL, FIXED, and MANUAL are not available in the relational model.

13.5. I agree. A relational GDBMS can establish hierarchic or network relationships. Furthermore, the indexing allowed in relational GDBMS is internally an inverted strategy or a B-tree strategy or an equivalent one in terms of indexing robustness.

13.7. No, I do not agree with the statement. In a hierarchic GDBMS such as SYSTEM 2000; the solution will be to resort to two separate data bases headed by A and AA:

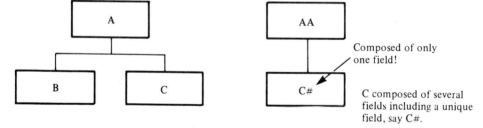

The idea is that under AA (or alternatively under A) a record child composed only of the identifier C# will be defined. Under A (or alternatively under AA) a record child composed of *all* the information fields of C, including C# also, will be defined. Thus only C# is redundantly stored. This is the best solution.

Another way of doing it, which is not acceptable, is to redundantly store all of C under both data bases:

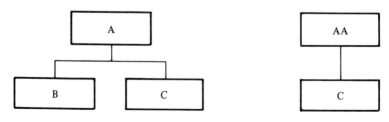

CHAPTER 14

14.1. It is true that you can do with a GDBMS much, but not all, of what you can do with a DD/DS, but not vice versa. However, the DD/DS is a specialized GDBMS with many facilities tailored for managing descriptions of entities such as those in Figure 14.1. These are major facilities, such as for writing extensive reports, that otherwise you, a a user of a GDBMS, may have to write. Furthermore, there are facilities in a DD/DS that have no equivalent in a GDBMS, particularly (a) facilities to scan source programs and automatically capture data declarations to store them in the DD/DS and (b) facilities to help generate from data descriptions the appropriate GDBMS data declarations, procedural language declarations, and declarations of some GFMS. Thus, pragmatically speaking, a DD/DS is a must for the typical installation. It is a must even for a personal computer GDBMS scenario. Even as a personal computer user, can you keep track of all the program versions you have written and what file versions each program is supposed to process? A DD/DS will help keep track of what entity is related to what entity. (Figure 14.1 as an example.)

CHAPTER 15

15.1. In summary, the acquisition of the DBM is the most cost-effective solution if the attachment of the DBM (dedicated to data base management) to the existing mainframe is significantly less expensive than the consumption or upgrading of the larger mainframe for data base management.

The extent to which the new applications involve a data base management load must be determined first. Then the following should be done at least:

(a) Determine how much of the mainframe is consumed when the data base applications are executed on top of the existing nondata base applications.

(b) Determine what the corresponding cost share, C-DB, is for data base applications.

(c) Connect the DBM to the mainframe, establish the data bases on the DBM, and run the data base applications on top of the nondata base applications on the mainframe.

(d) Determine what the extra cost, C-EXTRA, is on the mainframe.

(e) Compare (1) the cost of the DBM plus C-EXTRA versus (2) C-DB; if it is less than C-DB, then the DBM should be acquired. Otherwise the mainframe should be upgraded.

Of course, any conversion cost and delays in going the DBM route versus CPU upgrade must also be quantified and considered.

CHAPTER 16

16.1. Several issues and problems arise in partitioning:

1. Once the data base is partitioned, to which partition is a data base request to be sent for processing? Either the request has to be sent to each partition for searching (which is expensive) or else a directory/index will have to be built to determine in which partition the requested data reside. The request might be, for example, (a) "give me the DOCTOR names servicing the EMPLOYEEs Grafton, Cardenas, and Kleinrock or (b) "give me the EMPLOYEE names serviced by DOCTOR Jones".

2. Can the data base always be partitioned? How should it be partitioned? A hierarchic data base can always be partitioned, but a network data base cannot always be partitioned unless relationships between two partitions are tolerated:

   (a) *Hierarchic data base.* The easiest partitioning is one in which certain instances of the top entity are allocated to a given partition. All their dependents follow suit. However, partitioning on the basis of dependents introduces complexity. As an illustration, if in Figure 7.2 you wish to partition on the basis of EMPLOYEEs, for example, one partition to hold EMPLOYEEs owing more than X and another partition to hold EM-PLOYEES owing X or less, then a relationship between a given DOC-TOR and EMPLOYEE or between one EMPLOYEE and another may span from one partition to another. Now you will have to translate a given data base request into several subrequests, one for each cross-over from one partition to another. What you have to do is what a distributed GDBMS is expected to do automatically: generate the necessary subqueries for each partition and integrate the subanswers into one answer, while providing distribution transparency.

   (b) *Network data base.* Partitioning a network data base involving a cycle as in Figure 7.2 with a relationship added from CHILD to DOCTOR is not as straightforward as partitioning a hierarchic data base. If the grandparent DOCTOR instance of a CHILD instance is at the same time the dependent instance of CHILD, then partitioning on the basis of DOCTOR is straightforward; but if it is not at the same time the dependent instance of CHILD (and this is the usual case!), then partitioning is more intricate and problematic since there will be many relationships spanning from one partition to the other. In the latter situation, the request "give me the names of DOCTORs related to CHILDren whose 'ancestor' is DOCTOR Jones or Sheinbein or Lutsky" must be broken down into many subrequests, one for each of the relationship instances from partition to partition that qualify the request.

      Issues and problems in the nonreplicated data scenario are also present in the replicated data scenario. However, additional problems arise with data replication.

16.3. Various problems are significantly curtailed by limiting every subschema to a specific partition:

(a) Synchronizaton problems between a partition and others will be avoided. But if an application obtains a subschema A for a partition A and at the same time a subschema B for a partition B, then the synchronization problems will likely arise again, and the application ends up having to solve them.

(b) Relationships between different partitions are avoided. If no subschema needs such relationships, then why have them? Can you think of any reasons why they may be needed even if no subschema uses them? A relationship going from one partition to another involves perhaps covering a remote communication link, whereas a relationship within one partition is much simpler, since it involves going from one disk to another, or, more frequently, going from a point to another in the same disk.

INDEX